HANDBOOK of
EDUCATIONAL SUPERVISION

HANDBOOK of EDUCATIONAL SUPERVISION
A Guide for the Practitioner

James R. Marks

Professor, Behavioral Sciences Division, and
Supervising Director, Instructional Center
West Los Angeles College

Emery Stoops

Professor, Educational Administration and
Supervision
University of Southern California

Joyce King-Stoops

Assistant Professor of Education
University of Southern California

Allyn and Bacon, Inc.   Boston

Library of Congress Catalog Number: 72–
117630

Third printing . . . October, 1972

CONTENTS

Chapter

Chapter

Chapter

Chapter

Chapter

Quality of Office Management 638, How to Improve the Morale of Classified Personnel 640, How to Evaluate Classified Personnel Performance 642, How to Do It: Techniques Which Work 643, How to Plan for More Efficient Classified Personnel Performance 654, How to Get the Most Out of In-Service Education Programs for Classified Employees 655, Do 673, Don't 674, Supervisory Problems (In Basket) 674

How to Supervise Student Transportation 679, How to Improve Food Services 684, How to Evaluate the Program of School Food Services 684, How to Supervise Attendance and Welfare Services 684, How to Improve Health Services 689, How to Improve Library Services 691, How to Supervise Recreation Programs 704, Do 707, Don't 708, Supervisory Problem (In Basket) 708

Principles of Physical Facility Improvement 713, How to Supervise School Plant Improvement 720, How to Secure Optimum Utilization of Space and Content 727, How to Plan for Adequate Instructional Facilities 735, How to Improve Classroom Design 738, What the Supervisor Should Consider in a Physical Facilities Improvement Program 740, Do 741, Don't 742, Supervisory Problems (In Basket) 742

Definitions and Functions 748, Basic Principles 749, How the Staff Can Participate 754, How to Build a Community Relations Program 759, How to Evaluate the Community Relations Program 765, Do 773, Don't 774, Supervisory Problems (In Basket) 775

Chapter

Appendix

FOREWORD

In this handbook, and especially through its practical suggestions—the "how-to's"—James Robert Marks, Emery Stoops, and Joyce King-Stoops have insured higher quality education in depth for our children. The fundamental aim of the book is to improve instruction through the approach of assisting, supplementing, and encouraging the teacher—to inspire, not to impose; to strengthen, not to criticize harshly or destructively. The practical suggestions for action on the part of the educational supervisor are the result of more than twenty-five years of work and research.

The handbook deals with all elements of the learning situation; it dignifies the teacher as a cooperating member of the supervisory team.

I have personal knowledge of the competencies of the authors. Dr. Joyce King-Stoops, who provided needed technical services, has served as teacher, principal, and professor-in-charge of the Honors Intern Program, Teacher Education Department, University of Southern California.

Dr. Emery Stoops, who provided necessary resource material, has been teacher, counselor, supervisor, principal, and superintendent, and has filled administrative assignments in the Office of the Los Angeles County Superintendent of Schools. He has served as Professor of Education Administration and Supervision at the University of Southern California. During the past several years he has served as administrative consultant to the Riverside County Schools, and was named as a member of the survey team for the California State Department of Education.

As past international president of Phi Delta Kappa, professional education association and honor society for men, Dr. Stoops traveled and studied supervisory programs in all parts of the country. His numerous articles and textbooks reflect his unusual skill and deep understanding of the broad field of school supervision. His text, *Practices and Trends in School Administration*, has become a leader in its field.

Dr. James R. Marks, who did the lion's share of the writing, has been outstanding in general supervision, personnel and educational psychology, curriculum development, and administration. He currently is Professor in the Division of Behavioral Sciences and Supervising Director of the Instructional Center at West Los Angeles College. In the capacity of superintendent, he organized and administered a teacher education program for the Armed Forces. As Coordinator at the California State Polytechnic College's Kellogg

Campus, in addition to serving as Professor of Psychology and Education, he organized and supervised a teacher education and credentialing program. He has taught extensively through the graduate level. He has written and lectured widely in the areas of supervision, curriculum, educational and personnel psychology, administration, and in instructional technology and teaching techniques. His chief recognitions, however, point to proficiency in directing graduate level supervisory seminars and workshops in California, at Idaho State University, at the University of Hawaii, at the University of British Columbia, and in Puerto Rico.

Extensive experiences in educational therapy and in psychological services have enhanced his insight into educational supervision. His pioneering research in "Assignment Specifications" yielded perspective in the area of educational personnel psychology and in the selection, assignment, and supervision of certificated employees.

Dr. Marks is the recipient of numerous awards and honors, both from within and without his profession. His television program on supervision was selected by the American Broadcasting Company for replay as its *Scope* "Program of the Year."

The high quality material which comprises this handbook by Marks, Stoops, and King-Stoops will enable supervisors to help teachers do a better job more efficiently and with more facility. It emphasizes practical "how-to" suggestions for supervisory action. It suggests patterns of usable techniques which should prove invaluable to both the beginning and the more experienced supervisor.

> Maynard Bemis
> Executive Secretary
> Phi Delta Kappa

PREFACE

Today's supervisor faces a task—a challenge—that demands that he be both creative in his approach and competent in his knowledge of the skills and techniques employed by his successful colleagues in their practice of the art and science of supervision. While the authors have drawn the basic principles of supervision from the results of scientific research, it is from the caldron of experience in current practices and trends that the "how-to" sections of the work, which comprise the major portions of our recipes for the successful supervisor, have been elicited.

The purpose of this book is to provide specific, practical assistance to on-the-job supervisors in the successful realization of their main job: the improvement of instruction. John Dewey told us that theory must not be divorced from practice. While theory and research are present, they are included as the backdrop upon which the "Do-Don't" sections are projected.

In each task-area we have included patterns for supervision: definite procedures, techniques, and devices that have been proved in the fires of experience. Just as the housewife must alter and adapt a pattern she purchases at the department store to fit her needs, similarly the supervisor must adapt the patterns in supervision to the situation at hand: to himself, and to the individuals he supervises and to those with whom he works. The important point is that the patterns are here for him to sample. The pitfalls are noted; the musts are listed.

The graduate student of supervision will find in the book ideas which will help him solve many of the problems he will confront on the supervisory firing line. He will be aided by the practical *simulated "in-basket" supervisory problems,* by the clear statements of expert opinion and research findings which flavor each section of the book, and by the *questions and activities,* which include questions for analysis and discussion and suggested class activities.

In order to implement the important aspects of school supervision, the authors have identified certain unifying threads, such as human relations, effective communication, and team work. These, and the theory of supervision. To produce a well-balanced book readily adaptable to varied needs—that may be used with confidence by all who are engaged in school supervision. To produce a well-balanced book readily adaptable to varied needs—and in an attempt to make more concrete the principles discussed—numerous charts, tables, and figures have been included which qualify the techniques and procedures developed in the book. It is hoped that such a book will benefit the students of the schools and the democratic communities in which they live.

It would be impossible to list all of the individuals who contributed to this work. The authors do, however, wish to express their appreciation to several outstanding contributors.

Recognition goes to the supervising principals and other specialists in the field of educational supervision who participated; and to Jessie Levine, whose skill in manuscript production, typing, and editing is unsurpassed and whose patience must be the result of divine inspiration; to cartoonist Robert Whitehead; to Shirley Marks, Rose Rotter, and Beatrice Marks; and to Sol Rotter and Seymour I. Marks. A special thanks to Diana, Glenn, Bruce, and Gary Marks who were so patiently attentive while their father was in authorship.

James Robert Marks
Emery Stoops
Joyce King-Stoops

HANDBOOK of
EDUCATIONAL SUPERVISION

Background for
School Supervision

Mr. and Mrs. Supervisor, beware! The technological and sociological forces that are abroad in the land demand of you a continuous, powerful program of instructional improvement.

Before you may implement such a program, employing the tools and techniques that are presented in later chapters of this book, you must understand and appreciate the general nature of supervision. The following points are discussed in this chapter:

Need for the improvement of instruction
Definitions and principles
Emergence of democratic supervision
Do—don't
"In-Basket" supervisory problems
Chapter Supplement

Need For the Improvement of Instruction

Primitive societies generally are unconcerned with mass education; complex societies demand organized, formal school experiences. In a primitive society only the privileged few are selected to receive instruction; in a complex democracy it is hoped that all will be given an opportunity to progress in relation to their abilities. Equal opportunity, rather than identical experiences, is stressed.

In a democracy we have the freedom *to become*; we need not be content with the *status quo*. If the youth of today is to receive the best possible education, it is essential that teachers and supervisors keep pace with the tremendous advances made in institutions and in technology. Each society tends to measure the products of an educational system in terms of observable changes in behavior. Allport[1] noted that it is the maintaining, actualizing, and enhancing of the capacities of the individual organism that are the basic motives of life in the individual. We cannot deny that education at all levels is based upon behavioral anticipations.

Definitions and Principles

The value of supervision lies in the improvement of professional procedures and is reflected in the development of the student. Before listing the basic principles of supervision that will serve as a guide to the superstructure of this work, let us consider a few basic definitions.

Curriculum

The curriculum of the school is composed of all of the experiences that the individual receives under the guidance of the school. Our dynamic society requires that these experiences be organized and presented in the most efficient manner possible. If teachers are to keep pace with these changes and perform to the best of their abilities, the supervision of instruction, to be most effective, must be democratic in nature. Provisions for assisting the professional staff in the improvement of the curriculum must be made by the supervising principal.

The Supervising Principal and the Specialist-Consultant

The terms *principal, supervising principal,* and *specialist-consultant* appear throughout the text. As employed in this work, the terms *supervising principal* and *principal* are synonymous. Both refer to the executive leader at the individual school level.

The specialist-consultant serves in a staff capacity. He usually is as-

---

[1]Gordon W. Allport, *Becoming: Basic Considerations for a Psychology of Personality* (New Haven: Yale University Press, 1955), pp. 16–17.

signed at the school system offices and renders service at many different schools within the system.

The term *supervisor* refers to any individual rendering supervisory services, including the supervising principal, the assistant principal, the department head, the assistant dean, the dean, the specialist-consultant, and the assistant consultant or master teacher-consultant.

Principles of Supervision

Some basic principles of supervision which may serve as guideposts for further discussion follow:

1. Supervision, an integral part of an educational program, is a cooperative, team-type service.
2. All teachers need, and are entitled to, supervisory help. This service is the chief responsibility of the supervising principal.
3. Supervision should be adapted to meet the individual needs of school personnel.
4. Classified as well as certificated personnel need, and should benefit from, supervision.
5. Supervision should help clarify educational objectives and goals, and should illuminate the implications of these objectives and goals.
6. Supervision should help improve the attitudes and relationships of all members of the school staff, and should assist in the development of good rapport with the community.
7. Supervision should assist in the organization and proper administration of cocurricular activities for students.
8. The responsibility for the improvement of the program for school supervision rests with the teacher for his classroom. In a like manner, this responsibility rests with the principal for the school, and with the superintendent for the school system.
9. There should be adequate provision for supervision in the annual budget.
10. Both long- and short-term planning for supervision is essential. All affected, including certificated and classified personnel, professional associations, the school community, and the students should partici-

pate or be represented, in varying ways and degrees, in planning sessions and in the program for supervision.

11. The supervisory program, being serviced by administration and by staff personnel, should, at all levels below that of the community college, utilize consultant help from the intermediate unit superintendent's (county) office, the state department of education, colleges and universities, and other local, state, and national agencies.

12. Supervision should help to interpret and put into practice the latest findings of educational research.

13. The effectiveness of the program for supervision should be evaluated by both the participants and outside consultants.

Emergence of Democratic Supervision

European Backgrounds

R. F. Butts and L. A. Cremin[2] noted that when the colonists came to the New World in 1600, a study of literature and languages, especially Latin, Hebrew, and Greek, was well imbedded in the educational system, especially in secondary and higher education. The Protestant revolution produced scholars who found that they had to do holy battle with the learned Catholic philosophers and theologians. As a result they became as well grounded in the sacred and classical languages as were the Catholic philosophers.

Through the ages those who control education find that they must provide time for supervision. The need for supervision in the several ages is apparent as the student reviews some historical highlights beginning with the Homeric era.

EDUCATION IN EARLY GREECE. In the time of Homer there was no systematic education in Greece. It is suspected[3] that there might have been some private tutoring. Emphasis was placed upon physical education and training

[2]R. Freeman Butts and Lawrence A. Cremin, *A History of Education in American Culture* (New York: Henry Holt and Company, 1953), p. 75.
[3]S. E. Frost, *Essentials of History of Education* (New York: Barron's Educational Series Inc., 1947), p. 22.

for military service. The method used for instruction among the early Greeks was that of participation. After the ninth century B.C. there were, among the Aeolian Greeks, men who taught writing informally. With the cultural development of the Dorian Greeks, learning to write became a necessity, and it is suspected that schools for teaching writing were established prior to 500 B.C. The Greeks provided some public support for the education of poor children, but only boys were permitted to attend school. From 400 B.C. to 350 B.C. reading and writing were taught in most schools.

SPARTAN EDUCATION AND ITS SUPERVISION. S. E. Frost reported:

Near the eighth century B.C. a Dorian tribe of Greeks pushed into Laconia and conquered the original inhabitants of the area. They settled in a fertile plain, 5 by 18 miles, and isolated by high mountains. Here they established small villages which were little more than military barracks.[4]

A chief concern of the Spartan state was education for a purpose. The purpose of the education was to enhance, develop, maintain, and protect the Spartan state. The authority for education was placed in the hands of the chief rulers of the city who were called *Ephors.* Frost[5] noted that a *Paidonomous* was chosen for a period of one year from among the chief magistrates. It was the duty of the *Paidonomous* to supervise the training of the students. He was in absolute control and was assisted by whip bearers called *Bidioi.* There were no teachers or tutors. The student was given no freedom. Each citizen was responsible for the teaching of the young.

The elders selected those who were to live during the period of birth to seven years. The rest—the unfit—were exposed to the elements. Those who were to live were returned to their mothers, who functioned as state nurses. Education for the period of seven to eighteen years of age was, as noted earlier, in the hands of the *Paidonomous.* The boys lived in boarding schools operated by the state. The aim of the state boarding schools was to develop a feeling of equality, comraderie, and *esprit de corps.* The students were trained to endure hardships; food and clothing were scarce and hard to obtain. Gymnastic training, dance, choral work, and instrumental music were taught. There was neglect of intellectual training.

[4]Ibid.
[5]Ibid. p. 23.

Although the girls of the Spartan society lived at home, they received rigorous training which was quite similar to that received by the boys.

EDUCATION IN LATER GREECE. In later Athenian-led Greece the ideal of education was the development of the golden mean; professionalism and specialization were discouraged.

The curriculum consisted of gymnastics, music (which included all of the fine arts as well as handwriting), mathematics, reading, poetry, law, science, philosophy, and morals and manners. The first great teachers in Greece were not priests but poets. In the golden age of Greece, during the time that Pericles was sovereign (469–429 B.C.), art, literature, philosophy, and oratory, as well as science, were taught.

The famous teachers—Socrates, Plato, and Aristotle—were astounding all with their brilliant new ideas and concepts. Aristarchus founded a school of philology; Apollonius Dyscholus, who lived during the second century B.C., developed the science of grammar. It was during the same century that Eratosthenes did his great work in the science of geography.

EDUCATION IN ROME. When the Romans took over much of the Greek empire, they assimilated within themselves much of the Greek heritage of art, science, and education. In reality, however, the conquered captured the minds of the conquerors. We suspect that the Greeks had originally obtained much of their scientific, artistic, and educational ideals from the early travelers of the Aegean Sea who had settled in such places as Cnossus on the Island of Crete, and that possibly these early Aegean travelers had been highly influenced by the early Phoenicians and Hebrews. All this rich heritage they gave to the Romans.

When the liberal brothers Gracchus came into political power approximately 140 B.C., there arose schools of Latin grammar. Many books to be used in these schools appeared and research into the Latin language was increased. Since much Latin litererature was created, Latin grammar took form and substance. Suddenly there was a need for the improvement of instruction and curriculum in this subject! During the fourth and fifth centuries elementary and Latin grammar schools were to be seen everywhere throughout the empire. The subject matter, however, was classical and literary, and in most instances was not of social value.

EDUCATION AND ITS SUPERVISION IN THE MIDDLE AGES. The elementary "Reading and Writing Schools" of the Middle Ages that grew out of the Reformation were attended by both boys and girls. Instruction was in the vernacular language. Teachers were selected by the elders of the city and were paid out of the public treasury. There were many private schools.

During the time of the rebirth of learning, the *Renaissance,* Greek passages of Latin verse were added to the subjects already included in the school curriculum. The primary subjects were presented on a slightly more advanced level than they had been previously.

During the sixteenth century in England many patrons contributed money to grammar schools, and English catechisms and primers were given to the schools. All of the Song Schools were eliminated, and government supervision of both schools and teachers was begun. Many patrons provided additional funds to the English public schools in order to provide a free education for poor boys. These schools were "public" because they prepared students from many burgs and hamlets of England to become state officials.

Supervision rendered by the government appointee was, naturally, concerned that instruction be in line with the best interests of the state, and the supervising clergyman was interested in the religious and moral content of instruction. Little attention was paid to the quality of instruction, nor was a great deal of effort expended in attempting to improve educational conditions in general.

New World Precedents

The increasingly liberal ideas concerning religion and education for children in the Colonies of North America originated not only from within the newer religious sects, such as the Quakers and Anglicans, but also from within others of the more established or traditional sects. There was an increasing emphasis on gentle control rather than on harsh discipline in the Colonies. Many argued, even in those early days, that children varied in their individual aptitudes and interests. The spirit of Penn and Benezet was invading the community of fear established by Cotton Mather, Increase Mather, and Jonathan Edwards.

In 1647 the Massachusetts General Court passed what was perhaps one of the most important laws in the educational history of our country. It required towns containing fifty or more families to establish schools. A teacher of such a school was to give instruction in reading and writing, and his pay was to come from taxes, contributions from the parents, or fees levied on the parents. A Latin grammar school was to be established if there were 100 or more families in the town. The most important principle advanced here was that government had the right to require the establishment of schools and to control these schools.

During the Colonial period the elementary schools were designed mainly for the children of the lower classes, who were taught reading and writing, while the Latin grammar schools and colleges were designed strictly for the upper classes. There was instruction in religion in both types of schools. In the latter part of the eighteenth century the private "English schools" and then the academies were established.

The curriculum of the elementary school was well set during the early Colonial period. Those children who were planning to enter grammar schools were expected to have obtained the basic fundamentals of reading and writing by the age of eight. Apprentices were expected to learn from their masters, and the poorer children could attend publicly or privately endowed schools or religious schools.

Children of the upper classes might attend a private dame school. A woman would have many children come to her house and would instruct them, a few times a week, in reading and writing.

The Evolution of Supervision in the United States

In 1654 the General Court of the Massachusetts Bay Colonies passed a law that required the elders of a town, as well as the overseers of Harvard University, to insure that no teachers were hired who were "unsound in the faith or scandalous in their lives." Teachers were required to sign an oath of allegiance to the states when the War of Independence began, longbefore the advent of loyalty oaths during the so-called Cold War.

In 1709, Committees of Laymen had been appointed in Boston. These committees were to inspect and approve teachers, courses of study, and classroom instructional techniques. True supervisory authority of the superintendent of schools was acquired very slowly, since the committees were reluctant to give up their power in this area of educational concern.[6]

The supervisory authority of the principal also was acquired very slowly. In many instances the town committee was reluctant to surrender its authority in this area. Furthermore, the principal was looked upon as a super-teacher. He was not really viewed as one with sufficient skill and knowledge to act as a supervisor of instruction.

The superintendent, when he finally did gain power, was unwilling to delegate authority to the principal, and there was really no clear statement of who had the responsibility and authority for supervision in the new school organization. In many instances this confusion led to teacher resentment and to malpractice among those who struggled for control.

The improvement of instruction was not emphasized; rather, the discipline of the students was observed, the school plant was scrutinized, and the performance of the teacher received superficial attention and appraisal.

The growth of the nation during the *Nineteenth Century Period* demanded that the supervisory responsibilities be placed in the hands of professional school administrators. Laymen were, in general, unaware of—and perhaps therefore not generally averse to—this trend. They felt they were still in control through the local governing boards. The position of principal teacher (or principal) emerged during this period as an outcome of the discovery by the board members that they could no longer administer or "supervise" the rapidly growing school systems. Although the principalship was the first administrative position to emerge, it was the last to secure responsibility and authority for instructional improvement. The principal's duties were at first clerical, then disciplinary, then administrative, and—finally—supervisory. Even at this late date, "supervision" is taken by many to imply an emphasis upon inspection and control.

By the middle of the nineteenth century the position of chief state school officer ("state superintendent") was assuming a posture of importance and influence. The early state school chiefs, (including Horace Mann in Massachusetts and Calem Mills in Indiana, who led the fight for better schools)

[6]Butts and Cremin, *A History of Education in American Culture*, pp. 115–137.

worked without adequate personnel and financial support. The county or intermediate unit superintendent emerged as the chief state school officer's representative in local school matters, and was most influential in rural areas.

Although the emergence of the position of local superintendent of schools signified the true local characteristics of American education, recognition came slowly.

The *Early 1900's Period,* especially from the turn of the second decade of the century to approximately 1935, was marked by intensive interest in measurement, classroom management, and operation. The special supervisor or "helping teacher" appeared on the scene. There was little professional literature of note which championed the cause of the improvement of instruction through supervision. One work which was most influencial was H.W. Nutt's *The Supervision of Instruction* (Boston: Houghton Mifflin Co., 1920).

"Efficiency!"—the keynote of the time—resulted in the application of tremendous pressure to the "find something to improve" in each classroom visited. Out-of-class activities of students were tolerated but not encouraged; mental testing movements gained momentum; visitation became a mechanical process; elaborate rating systems were devised: with all this, there was an underlying laissez-faire attitude. There is considerable evidence that the super-saturation of classroom visitations and criticisms rarely served as a basis for improvement or even for guidance. Nonetheless, supervision of instruction was viewed as a worthy function, and expenditure of school funds for supervisory purposes was authorized; effort was sincere; techniques were developed which were to lead, eventually, toward the development of a program for the improvement of instruction.

The *Middle and Late 1900's* found supervision emerging as a democratic function, with supervisory assignments becoming broader in scope and purpose. The *human factor* was finally recognized as something to be considered while striving for efficient, productive instruction. The availability of federal grants forced supervisory personnel to conduct reasonably scientific research so as to find the best way to utilize the suddenly available funds in order to further existing programs and create new ones.

There was an increasing awareness of the need for positive, adequate programs of community relations in an attempt to reach the several publics involved with the school. It was finally recognized that the best program of

TABLE 1–1   Historical Periods in the Development of American School Supervision

Concepts of Supervision In American Education	Period of Influence	Parties Doing the Supervision	Nature of the Supervisory Program
1. Inspection of school and classroom	Colonial period through the Civil War	Laymen: clergy, school wardens, trustees, selectmen, citizens' committees.	Inspection for the sake of control. Emphasis upon observing rules and maintaining existing standards.
2. Inspection of school and classroom	Nineteenth century.	State, intermediate unit (county) local superintendents.	Inspection for the sake of control. Emphasis upon regulations, with some leadership for improvement.
3. Supervision of classroom instruction	1910–1935	Responsibility divided between principals and special supervisors or "helping teachers."	Improvement of instruction through direct classroom observation and demonstration with attention focused upon the teacher's weaknesses.
4. Cooperative educational leadership	1935–1963	Responsibility of principals and special supervisors, shared with co-ordinators, curriculum directors, consultants, and others.	Program centered in cooperative study enterprises, such as curriculum development, and in-service education courses, aiming toward improvement of instruction.
5. Supervision as cooperative effort, stimulated by democratic leadership and influenced by the availability of federal grants and interest of the community	1964 to Present	Responsibility of principals, and, in certain cases specialist consultants, special supervisors shared coordinators, curriculum directors, consultants, research personnel and public relations specialists.	Program still centered in cooperative study enterprises with the addition of community participation. Awareness of utilization of federal monies to best advantage.[a]

[a]Harold Spears, *Improving the Supervision of Instruction* (Englewood Cliffs, New Jersey: Prentice Hall, Inc., 1958) p. 38.

"public relations" is open, two-way communication, especially concerning evidence of the best possible instructional program. Table 1–1 shows the historical periods in the evolution of supervision.

The goals of supervision were, then, at first, administrative in character. Later, as we have seen, there appeared a shift toward the establishment of goals which were more truly supervisory in nature and which were concerned with the democratic improvement of instruction.[7]

The meaning of democracy as applied to educational supervision was well stated by the National Education Association Commission on the Reorganization of Secondary Education:

... Democracy sanctions neither the exploitation of the individual by society, nor the disregard of the interests of society by the individual ...

... This ideal demands that human activities be placed upon a high level of efficiency; that to this efficiency be added an appreciation of the significance of these activities. ... [8]

If we accept the idea that the goal of education is to develop in each student his highest potentialities, then we, as teachers and supervisors, must learn to produce such qualities within ourselves. These qualities must include independent thinking, initiative, self-reliance, democratic cooperation with others, and intellectual honesty. Boardman, Douglas, and Bent[9] noted that if the goal of supervision is the ideal of democracy, supervision must be democratic. The older supervisory techniques, which inhibited initiative, must be replaced by those techniques which encourage experimentation and creativity. If teachers are to develop the ability to adapt materials and procedures to the objectives of education, the supervising principal must use every means at his disposal in order to develop the *initiative, self-reliance, originality,* and *independence of thought* of the professional staff.

Traditional supervision centered on the teacher and the classroom situation and was based upon the misconception that teachers, being undertrained, needed constant direction and training. Modern supervision is per-

[7]Jack C. Goodwin, "Principles and Practices of Teacher Evaluation Programs in the Schools of the United States" (Doctoral dissertation, University of Southern California, 1956).

[8]R. Freeman Butts and Lawrence A. Cremin, *A History of Education in American Culture,* p. 131.

[9]Charles W. Boardman, Harl R. Douglas, and Rudyard K. Bent, *Democratic Supervision in Secondary Schools* (Boston: Houghton Mifflin Company, 1953).

ceived as a cooperative service. It is concerned, mainly, with the identification and solution of professional problems. Rather than focusing attention upon the teacher and the classroom situation, attention is focused upon the total learning-teaching situation. There is a trend away from supervision as superinspection and superrating, and toward the newer concepts of supervision as providing cooperative services, consultation, and in-service education.

Traditional and Modern Supervision Compared

Burton and Brueckner[10] summarized six major points in comparing traditional and modern practices in school supervision.

Traditional Supervision	Modern Supervision
1. Inspection	1. Pragmatic study and analysis
2. Teacher-focused	2. Goal, material, techniques, method, teacher, student, and environment-focused
3. Visitation and conference	3. Many diverse functions
4. Poorly planned or a meager formal plan	4. Definitely organized and planned
5. Imposed and authoritarian	5. Derived and cooperative
6. Usually by one person	6. By many persons

Traditional school supervision, then, consisted largely of inspection of the teacher, was poorly planned, and was authoritarian. Modern supervision, in sharp contrast, is based upon research and analysis of the total teaching-learning environment and its many functions by many individuals. Modern supervision is objective, systematic, democratic, creative, growth-centered and producing, and accentuates the spirit of inquiry by emphasizing experimentations and continuous evaluation. Democratic principles should control supervision and evaluation in the school.

[10]William H. Burton and Leo J. Brueckner, *Supervision, A Social Process* (New York: Appeton-Century-Crofts, Educational Division, Meredith Corp., 1955. Reprinted by permission of the publisher.

The success of supervision seems to depend more upon the element of good human relations than upon any other single factor. Keep in mind supervision is primarily the responsibility of the principal. Although teachers do have a part in the supervisory process, the extent of teacher participation in supervision, especially below the level of the community college, is still in question. Most school systems have some type of evaluation with the larger systems having the more formal type. There is a wide variety of practices in supervision and evaluation in the schools. Smaller school systems tend to avoid the more formalized programs of evaluation.

Supervision's Administrative Heritage

H. J. Otto[11] wrote that in the operation of schools it is difficult, if not impossible, to draw fine lines between the administrative, supervisory, and leadership functions. Many of the activities in which supervising principals ticipate do fall clearly in one or another of these three categories, but it seems that there is an endless number of activities which overlap the borders between these three functions.

Perhaps the best way of distinguishing between supervision and administration is to look at the purpose of the activity in question. If the purpose of the activity is to improve instruction, then the activity may be put in the supervisory column. If, on the other hand, the purpose of the activity is primarily concerned with areas other than the improvement of instruction, and if its influence on the improvement of instruction be only secondary, then the activity could well be termed administrative in character. For example, Shirley Rotter, principal of Pemberton High, visited Diana Bruce's classroom on Tuesday for the purpose of helping Diana to initiate a unit in geography.

Realizing that one goal of supervision is to help professionals grow and become independent, she brought many materials to Diana before the class session. She scheduled a follow-up conference after her visit so that she could discuss other resources, with an eye toward helping Diana become proficient in locating her own materials, and further to give her some specific ideas

[11]Henry J. Otto, *Elementary School Organization and Administration* (New York: Appleton-Century-Crofts, Inc., 1954), p. 296.

which would help her to make her instruction more effective and efficient.

The following day Mrs. Rotter visited the same teacher, but for a different purpose. It was May, and the class schedules for the following term were being prepared. She wished to determine the possibility of Mrs. Bruce's teaching a course on elementary Spanish to sixth-grade students.

The class assignment rating function was administrative in character, whereas the Tuesday unit initiation visit and follow-up conference were supervisory in nature.

For our purposes, then, let us consider any activity which is *primarily concerned with the improvement of instruction in the classroom* as an activity within the scope of supervision.

What Is the Role of Supervision Today?

The broad modern interpretation of the role of supervision would be action and experimentation aimed at the improvement of instruction and the instructional program. Using this definition, supervision would be the concern of superintendents, principals, specialists, directors, consultants, deans, coordinators, chairmen, and teachers. The following ways of improving the instructional program are utilized more frequently today:

1. Sharing ideas, procedures, and materials in order to evaluate and develop the curriculum;
2. Developing materials and procedures to implement the curriculum;
3. Planning for instructional improvement through in-service education, institutes, research, workshops, and projects;
4. Organizing a staff of professional specialist-consultants;
5. Directing teachers toward goals through democratic processes by supplying specific directions based upon a sound background in individual and group dynamics;
6. Allowing—indeed encouraging—teachers to participate in planning and organization;
7. Evaluating curriculum, materials, and procedures in the light of basic objectives and the findings of scientific research.

There is no place in modern supervision for the type of activity which we found occurring in one large city school system where the authoritarian type of school supervision is in operation (in spite of claims to the contrary by certain members of the staff). In the system investigated, coercion was a-chieved via ratings for probationary teachers, by the threat of poor ratings for promotion, by the threat of assignment to schools far from the indivi-dual's home, by withholding or the threat of withholding salary increases, and by the threat of disadvantageous class scheduling and assignment. Such authoritarianism leads to mediocre performance—performance just good enough to avoid reprisal. Democracy frees creativity.

Whose Job Is It?

The superintendent, staff members, specialists, principal, consultants, and department heads and teachers are all concerned with the improvement of the instructional program in the schools. However, this area is more the total responsibility of the principal and his staff.

It is the job of the principal to fulfill the objectives for his school's super-visory program. The ultimate responsibility for the program rests with the principal for his school, and with the superintendent for the school system.

Surely the hallmark for supervision today would include the factors of objectivity, systematic planning and procedures, a democratic approach, a creative atmosphere, pragmatic orientation, and a great deal of experimen-tation and evaluation. It should include a spirit of cooperative inquiry, empathy, service, creativity, openmindedness, appraisal, and skill in group processes. It is at once an expert, technical service concerned with studying and improving all conditions inherent in the teaching-learning process, and a supportive function, a service function, a human relations function.

BASIC CHANGES IN THE FUNCTIONS OF SCHOOL SUPERVISION IN THE LOCAL SCHOOL SYSTEM. The following list illustrates some of the more basic changes in school supervision which have occurred at the local level:

1. Supervision includes far more than it did in times past. This expansion is the result of continual critical thinking in connection with the nature of education and its relation to the individual and to society.

2. Supervision is increasingly objective and experimental in its methods. This change stems from the scientific movement in education.

3. Supervision is increasingly participatory and cooperative. Policies and plans are formulated through group discussion, with participation by all concerned. This alteration in approach and technique is the result of increasing insight into the nature of democracy and of democratic methods.

4. Supervisory activities and opportunities are distributed among an ever increasing number of persons as all come to contribute and to accept the challenge to exercise leadership.

5. Supervision is increasingly derived from the given situation, rather than imposed from above.

Everything in a school system is (or should be) designed for the ultimate purpose of stimulating learning and growth. Supervision deals with those items which primarily, and rather directly, condition learning and growth.

LOCAL SUPERVISION: A PROBLEM IN LEADERSHIP AND COOPERATION. Barr et al.[12] formulated the following outline of leadership functions for the school supervisor at the local level:

1. Evaluating the educational products in the light of accepted objectives of education.
   a) The cooperative determination and critical analysis of aims;
   b) The selection and application of the means of appraisal;
   c) The analysis of the data to discover strength and weakness in the product.

2. Studying the teaching-learning situation to determine the antecedents of satisfactory and unsatisfactory student growth and achievement.
   a) Studying the course of study and the curriculum-in-operation;
   b) Studying the materials of instruction, the equipment, and the socio-physical environment of learning and growth;
   c) Studying the factors related to instruction (the teacher's personality, academic and professional training, techniques);
   d) Studying the factors present in the learner (capacity, interest, work habits, intellectual development, and others).

[12]Barr et al., *Supervision*, pp. 9–11.

3. Improving the teaching-learning situation.
   a) Improving the course of study and the curriculum-in-operation;
   b) Improving the materials of instruction, the equipment, and the socio-physical environment of learning and growth;
   c) Improving the factors related directly to instruction;
   d) Improving factors present in the learner which affect his growth and achievement.
4. Evaluating the objectives, methods, and outcomes of supervision.
   a) Discovering and applying the techniques of evaluation;
   b) Evaluating the results of given supervisory programs, including factors which limit the success of these programs;
   c) Evaluating and improving the performance of the personnel of supervision.

The National Education Association[13] delineated the following functions of the school supervisor:

Per Cent	Functions
100	Attending meetings of professional associations
97	Discussing educational philosophy or objectives with teachers
96	Holding group conferences to discuss common problems
96	Making classroom visitations

In performing these functions the supervisor should call upon specialists from the intermediate and state units. Local system supervisors in a geographical area should cooperate in area meetings and in the sharing of materials.

THE IMPORTANCE OF SELF-SUPERVISION. The transition from imposed supervision, coupled with the desirable modern emphasis upon cooperative group endeavor, sometimes obscures one of the most important implications of modern philosophy and thinking in supervision; namely, the possibilities for

[13]Association for Supervision and Curriculum Development of the National Education Association, "Leadership through Supervision," *1946 Yearbook of the Association* (Washington, D.C.: The Association, 1946), pp. 37–38.

self-direction, self-guidance, and self-supervision. The mature individual will not only serve as a leader in group enterprise and make contributions to group discussions and decisions; he often will engage in a program for self-improvement.

Specialists engage in such a program when they work independently on a frontier problem. A member of the rank and file does this when he engages in a study of his own needs, or in tryouts of new methods in his classroom, or pursues a problem of his own through the available literature. Self-initiated attention to any problem usually grows out of group activities.[14]

The Principal as the Chief Supervisor in the Local School

The building principal must accept responsibility for all that transpires in the local school. This means that the principal is the chief supervisory officer. General, special, intermediate unit, and state supervisors must work always through, and in harmony with, the principal. Before visiting teachers individually or in groups, the staff supervisor (the specialist-consultant) should check with the principal's office. The functions of the supervisors at the state and intermediate unit levels are discussed in chapters 2 and 3.

DO

1. Combine efforts of teachers and supervisory personnel.
2. Offer and accept new ideas.
3. Work toward the optimum utilization of all instructional materials.
4. Respect staff opinions and suggestions.
5. Recognize that support and loyalty form a two-way street.
6. Have a sincere concern for staff members as professional individuals.
7. Praise and encourage good attitudes and procedures for specific accomplishments.
8. Use effective measures of evaluation.
9. Support the staff in relations with the community.
10. Accept the teacher as an equal, charged with specific responsibilities.

[14]Barr et al., *Supervision*, p. 13.

11. Enlist the cooperative efforts of the entire staff in the study of the educational problems of the school.
12. Provide opportunities from which teachers can develop potential leadership.
13. Accept deviations from the established order of doing things.
14. Conduct a continuous search for better and more effective ways of performing your duties.
15. Enlist the services of the specialist-consultants at the local, the intermediate, and the state levels.
16. Believe always that no best way has yet been found.

DON'T

1. Assume the role of a *superior*-visor.
2. Assume that the curriculum and the methods of implementing and teaching it are fixed.
3. Consider experimentation by teachers to be insubordination.
4. Make an official supervisory visit without making an appointment ahead of time.
5. Be afraid to make an informal, unscheduled visitation as needed.
6. Look upon yourself as a threat rather than as a helper.
7. Be afraid to call on neighboring principals, specialist-consultants, and teachers for additional help.

Supervisory Problems   In Basket

Throughout the text the reader will encounter "In-Basket (simulated) Supervisory Problems." These problems may be considered as representative of situations and problems a supervisor in the field may encounter as he goes about his everyday tasks. In establishing the ground rules for handling the problems, the seminar group may wish to indicate that the individuals assigned the task of providing a solution for the problem may assume any data they wish, when no information to the contrary is provided. Group leaders may wish to encourage the seminar members to bring in their own in-basket (simulated) supervisory problems. *If so, the* general *scope of the problem and a few basic references should be presented to the participants prior to the time of the problem presentation so as to permit adequate preparation for the seminar. The seminar leader (the student presenting the problem) should introduce the topic, set the environmental background, and summarize at the end of the session.*

The school district by which you are employed has a rather small but vociferous teacher's union local. Most of the teachers in the district belong to the District Teacher's Association and to the parent state and national associations. There has been some talk of establishing a professional relations committee, but no action has been taken.

Your superintendent has indicated that he believes that all probationary teachers should be rated once per month. As principal of Edward Elcott High, you have complied.

You have received a note in your in-basket that reads:

"Dear Snooper: Your supervisory techniques are deplorable: You must be living in the past! We want you to know that we can take just so much and no more! If you continue to visit the probationary teachers once per month and, therefore, fail to permit them to relax and teach, without worrying about putting on a show for you, we shall be forced to take this problem further."

What would you do?

(NOTE: *You may assume anything, but you may not change the facts, nor may you indicate that* in the past *you would have done something to avoid the problem. The question is, what will you do, given the facts as listed in the problem?*)

Selected Bibliography

Books

Allport, Gordon W. *Becoming: Basic Considerations for a Psychology of Personality*. New Haven: Yale University Press, 1955.

Barr, A. S., William H. Burton, and Leo J. Brueckner. *Supervision, Principles and Practices in the Improvement of Instruction*. New York: D. Appleton-Century Company, 1938.

Bartky, John A. *Supervision as Human Relations*. Boston: D. C. Heath and Company, 1953.

Boardman, Charles W., Harl R. Douglass, and Rudyard K. Bent. *Democratic Supervision in Secondary Schools*. Boston: Houghton Mifflin Company, 1953.

Burton, William H., and Leo J. Brueckner. *Supervision, A Social Process*. New York: Appleton-Century-Crofts, 1955.

Butts, R. Freeman, and Lawrence A. Cremin. *A History of Education in American Culture*. New York: Henry Holt and Company, 1953.

Cooper, Shirley, and Charles O. Fitzwater. *County School Administration*. New York: Harper and Brothers, 1954.

Gwynn, J. Minor. *Theory and Practice of Supervision*. New York: Dodd, Mead, & Company, 1961.

Lucio, William H., and John D. McNeil, *Supervision*. New York: McGraw-Hill Book Company, 1969.

McClure, William P. *The Intermediate School District in the United States*. Urbana: University of Illinois Press, 1956.

Morphet, Edgar L., Roe L. Johns, and Theodore L. Reller. *Educational Administration*. Englewood Cliffs, New Jersey: Prentice-Hall, Inc., 1959.

Otto, Henry J. *Elementary School Organization and Administration* (New York: Appleton-Century-Crofts, 1954.

Reavis, W. C., and C. H. Judd. *The Teacher and Educational Administration*. Boston: Houghton Mifflin Company, 1942.

Spears, Harold. *Improving the Supervision of Instruction*. Englewood Cliffs, New Jersey: Prentice-Hall, Inc., 1953.

Stoops, Emery, and M. L. Rafferty, Jr. *Practices and Trends in School Administration*. Boston: Ginn and Company, 1961.

Wiles, Kimball. *Supervision for Better Schools*. Englewood Cliffs, New Jersey: Prentice-Hall, Inc., 1950.

Periodicals

Bradfield, Luther E. "Basic Principles Underlying Techniques of Supervision." *American School Board Journal* CXXVIII (June 1954): 21–23.

Farley, Genevieve J., and John J. Santosuosso, "Techniques of Supervision." *Educational Administration and Supervision* XLIII (April 1957): 249–252.

Simpson, Roy E. "The Place of the State Superintendent in Public Education." *California Schools* XXI (September 1950): 307–312.

Other Sources

Alexander, William Marvin. "State Leadership in Improving Instruction." Unpublished Doctoral dissertation, Teachers College, Columbia University, 1940.

American Association of School Administrators. "Leadership at the State Level," Chapter XIII in *The American School Superintendent*. Thirtieth Yearbook of the Association. Washington, D.C.: The Association, 1952.

Association for Supervision and Curriculum Development of the National Education Association. "Leadership through Supervision," *1946 Yearbook of the Association*. Washington, D.C.: The Association, 1946.

Goodwin, Jack C. "Principles and Practices of Teacher Evaluation Programs in the Schools of the United States." Doctoral dissertation, University of Southern California, 1956.

Marks, James R. "An Analysis of Assignment Specifications for Certificated School Personnel in the United States." Doctoral dissertation, University of Southern California, 1962.

McGovern, Elcy. "A Critical Evaluation of California General Elementary County School Supervisors." Doctoral dissertation, University of Southern California, 1948.

National Education Association. *Rural Supervision at Work*. Edited by Marchia Everett. 1949 Yearbook. Washington, D.C.: National Education Association, 1949.

Trillingham, C. C. *The County Superintendent and County Service Foundation*. Second Report of Assembly Interim Committee on Public Education. Sacramento: Assembly of the State of California, 1949.

U.S. Department of Health, Education, and Welfare. *Curriculum Responsibilities of the States*. Washington, D.C.: Government Printing Office, 1968.

_____ . *Curriculum Responsibility of State Departments of Education*. Washington, D.C.: Government Printing Office, 1958.

A History of Educational Personnel Administration for the Supervisor

Public personnel supervision in the United States began "when the government became large enough to require a considerable number of employees."[1]

Employment practices appeared to form a pattern in the days of the craft guilds, but at this time the apprentice was selecting a trade or having it chosen for him by his family. Industry was not choosing the employee.[2] During the rapid national and economic growth of the country, labor was utilized indiscriminately. Nearly a century after public personnel administration was inaugurated in the United States, industry, spurred by the ever increasing stimulus of competition, initiated personnel administration as a definite function of management. By 1920 personnel administration was becoming a formidable complex. Powerful labor organizations forced industry to develop strong and adequate personnel departments emphasizing the human dynamics aspect of personnel management. According to J. M. Pfiffner, the "differences between private and public personnel practices are drawing closer together."[3]

Comparing the personnel function in industry with that in the public school, A. H. Simons wrote that "personnel administration in industry is years ahead of public school personnel administration."[4]

Early selection of teachers was accomplished by local lay boards of education. "The superintendent as a professional executive did not exist. The only specification for a teacher was that he would be considered competent 'if he could discipline.' "[5]

In New England, teachers were appointed at regular town meetings. Since the schools were so closely related to the church, the minister's approbation was essential. Selection was based on finding someone who was qualified and willing to teach, and who would accept the meager salary which had been voted for the purpose. Many teachers received payment "in kind," that is, in goods or services.[6]

[1]Marshall Edward Dimock and Gladys Ogden Dimock, *Public Administration* (New York: Rinehart Company, 1953), p. 146.
[2]Aubrey Hays Simons, "An Evaluation of Recruitment Methods in Medium-Sized School Districts in California" (Doctoral dissertation, University of Southern California, 1956), p. 18.
[3]John M. Pfiffner, *Public Administration* (New York: The Ronald Press Company, 1947.)
[4]Simons, p. 18.
[5]Ibid., p. 19.
[6]William A. Yeager, *Administration and the Teacher* (New York: Harper and Brothers, 1954), pp. 132–134.

The instructors were usually male school masters, since few women were employed. Since the demand exceeded the supply, a man had an excellent chance of being hired if he could "keep school." While his statement concerning his own ability normally was accepted, a letter of recommendation from a minister usually was sufficient to meet the qualifications for the office.

W. A. Yeager commented: "We cannot deny that favoritism, both political and social, had its place in the selection of teachers whose [other] qualifications were often quite lacking."[7] This condition led to E. H. Reisner's contention that teaching was the "last measure of professional and business incompetence . It was not even a well-defined trade with standards of preparation and fitness."[8]

Upgrading from these lowly origins has been a long and tedious process. Table Supp. 1–1 reflects developmental trends in education which have influenced the practice of educational personnel supervision. It was not until the selection process became a professional function that improvement in quality became noticeable. Three factors have influenced this movement: (1) the development of educational leaders, (2) the beginnings of the normal schools, and (3) the beginnings of local and later state controls over trainees both as to preparation and certification requirements.[9]

TABLE SUPP. 1–1   Developmental Trends Which Have Influenced Educational Personnel Supervision

The Past	The Present
Education for few	→ Education for all
Private, parochial, and pauper schools	→ Common schools for all, regardless of economic status or "social class"
Instruction in religion	→ Practical instruction for life in society
Education preserving class and social distinctions	→ Education aimed at equalization or harmonizing different social and economic groups; education as a social ladder

[7]Ibid., p. 67.
[8]Edward H. Reisner, *The Evaluation of the Common School* (New York: The Macmillan Company, 1930), p. 393.
[9]Yeager, p. 66.

2

Special Problems:
The Role of the Intermediate
Unit in Supervision

The intermediate unit has assumed a vital role in school supervision. The supervisor must be aware of the following major points, which are discussed in this chapter:

Intermediate unit variations, functions, and organizational status
The office of the intermediate unit superintendent of schools
Organizing the staff of the intermediate unit for the supervision of instruction
Supervisory services performed by the intermediate unit staff
Do—don't
"In Basket" supervisory problems

Intermediate Unit Variations,
Functions, and Organizational Status

Variations

Public education in this country has become more and more a local operation, a state responsibility, and a national concern.[1] Between the state department of education and the local systems lies the intermediate unit. There are several types of intermediate units, and there exists the distinct probability that no two are exactly alike. In the United States we have county units, parishes, townships, supervisory unions, and other political entities acting as intermediate units. These various administrative units, however, may be

[1] Emery Stoops and M. L. Rafferty, Jr., *Practices and Trends in School Administration* (Boston: Ginn and Company, 1961), p. 40.

classified into four general divisions: (1) state, (2) county unit, where the county unit is the local school district, (3) supervisory union or township, and (4) county intermediate unit.

The National Education Association has defined the intermediate unit:

[The intermediate unit is an] area comprising the territory of two or more basic administrative units and having a board, or officers, or both, responsible for performing stipulated services for the basic administrative units or for supervising their fiscal, administrative, or educational functions.[2]

This definition could be shortened to say that any agency that operates as a "middleman" between the local school district and the state department of education is an intermediate administrative school unit. The intermediate unit is an agent of the state for the purposes of enforcement of minimum standards. It is the agent between the local school system and the state department through which information and leadership are disseminated in the operation and improvement of local programs. No single definition can include all types.

THE STATE CENTRAL SYSTEM. The state central system exists only in Delaware, Alaska, and Hawaii. Delaware might truly be called the state department of education central system. Here the state directly administers most public schools as one district. Excluded from this system are the cities of Wilmington and Dover, and fifteen special districts.[3]

All school districts in Alaska are independent and report directly to the state department of education; however, the local school board is governed by state standards of operational procedure.

In Hawaii, education is controlled by the Hawaiian Department of Public Instruction in Honolulu, which has suboffices located in various sections of the state.[4]

---

[2]William P. McClure, *The Intermediate School District in the United States* (Urbana: University of Illinois Press, 1956), p. 1.
[3]Arthur B. Moehlman, *School Administration* (Boston: Houghton Mifflin Company, 1951), p. 123.
[4]Stoops and Rafferty, *Practices and Trends*, p. 41.

THE COUNTY UNIT SYSTEM. Twelve states are organized on the county unit system, with schools in these states operating under the control of an elected county board of education. The school systems follow the general boundaries of the county civil unit.[5]

In some of these states the larger cities are excluded from the county unit and operate as independent districts. The county unit is one of the most recent inventions in the field of local public school administration. Most county-unit systems were established during the last half of the nineteenth century.[6] States which are organized on this system are Alabama, Florida, Georgia, Kentucky, Louisiana, Maryland, New Mexico, North Carolina, Tennessee, Utah, Virginia, and West Virginia.

SUPERVISORY UNION OR TOWNSHIP. Township administrative units have been present since the beginning of public education in America.[7] Sometimes these units are referred to as supervisory unions. Essentially, these units are formed by the marriage of two or more towns in a single school unit for administrative purposes. These units are not necessarily coterminous with civil county boundaries. Generally, the supervisory union is found in the northeastern section of the nation. Michigan, however, is an exception to the rule. It provides for township districts on a permissive basis.[8] In addition to Michigan, other states allow high-school districts to be formed; and in some instances these districts include an entire county.

The states which generally are considered to be true supervisory unions are Connecticut, Maine, Massachusetts, New Hampshire, New York, Rhode Island, and Vermont. New York has 175 such systems. The unions are responsible to their state departments of education and are governed by state codes. As populations have increased, some of the large cities have formed their own independent supervisory unions.

[5]In only two states, Florida and West Virginia, the school systems and county unit boundaries are coterminous. In these states there are no independent school districts.
[6]Shirley Cooper and Charles O. Fitzwater, *County School Administration* (New York: Harper and Brothers, 1954), p. 173.
[7]Ibid.
[8]Moehlman, *School Administration*, p. 124.

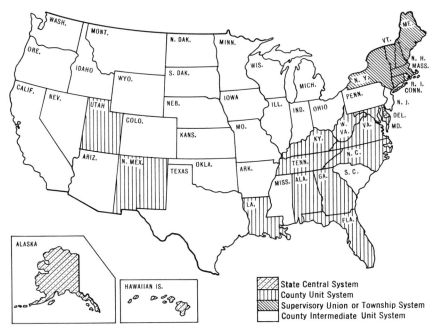

FIGURE 2–1   Forms of Intermediate Unit Organization in the United States.

COUNTY INTERMEDIATE UNIT. As may be seen by referring to the map appearing as Figure 2–1, more states use the county intermediate plan than any other type of unit. In all, twenty-eight states employ this system. A sample organization chart for this type of intermediate unit is included as Figure 2–2. All of these states are located in the West, Southwest, and Midwest. They are Arizona, Arkansas, California, Colorado, Idaho, Illinois, Indiana, Iowa, Kansas, Michigan, Minnesota, Mississippi, Missouri, Montana, Nebraska, Nevada, New Jersey, North Dakota, Ohio, Oklahoma, Oregon, Pennsylvania, South Carolina, South Dakota, Texas, Washington, Wisconsin, and Wyoming.

General Functions of the Intermediate Unit

An intermediate unit provides educational service in an area composed of two or more local school systems. The intermediate unit operates between the state and the local school system, and provides service for both the state

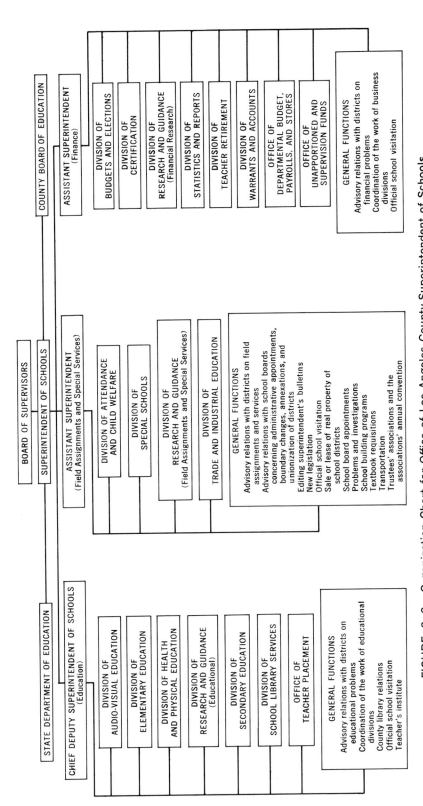

FIGURE 2–2   Organization Chart for Office of Los Angeles County Superintendent of Schools.

and the system. Regulations and standards governing these services are established in the state code. The intermediate unit provides professional services to the local system and serves as a supervisory standards agency for the state. Some researchers believe that the use of this type of organization renders possible the highest degree of autonomy for the local community while still providing an effective means of upholding state standards.

Limited Functions

The office of the intermediate unit superintendent has been limited in function; however, the office has been of vital importance in the improvement of local education, and has been of significant value to the rural school more than to urban areas. In a vast number of rural areas the intermediate unit superintendent is the educational leader of the community. He is called upon to advise and help coordinate many civic, cultural, and educational activities, including the juvenile court, health and welfare programs, and fund-raising drives.[9]

Organizational Status

The greatest number of school administrative units in this country are those located in unincorporated territories. Generally, these school systems do not include any civil metropolitan incorporated units of noteworthy size, such as a city or township, within the system boundaries. Many of these schools are one- or two-room buildings. Most enlightened citizens of the space age accept the concept that a modern learning environment cannot be developed in a one-room schoolhouse.

All American states except Alaska are divided into civil intermediate units for purposes of public adminstration. The smallest unit is Arlington County, Virginia, and the largest is San Bernardino County, California. Despite this wide range in size, almost half of the intermediate units in the nation are between 500 and 1,000 square miles in area.[10]

Differences in the density of population of the nation's intermediate units are even more striking than are differences in the area of these units. One

[9]Stoops and Rafferty, *Practices and Trends,* p. 39.
[10]Fred Engelhardt, *Public School Organization and Administration* (Boston: Ginn and Company, 1931), p. 12.

might compare, for example, the population of Hinsdale County, Colorado, with that of Los Angeles County, California.[11]

The intermediate unit has long been a local unit of government in this country, even since the nation's earliest beginnings. At the county seat will be found a large number of agencies and officials such as the sheriff, the courts, and the county recorder. These agencies and officials are actually state agencies and state officials, for they have been authorized by the state legislature to assist the state in carrying out state functions. It was decided, in the past, that the state was too far removed from the problems of the local areas, and that the intermediate unit could best operate as the agent of the state in a given geographic area.

In some of the northeastern states the only functions of the intermediate unit are in judicial, highway, and welfare matters. However, in some areas of the South, the intermediate unit is an active and highly important subdivision of the state. Between these extremes the intermediate units of the rest of the nation function at different levels of authority and importance.[12]

The Office of the Intermediate Unit Superintendent of Schools

Origins of the Intermediate Unit's Role in School Supervision

The intermediate superintendency began with the already established intermediate unit, and was well suited both geographically and legally for the general supervision and promotion of the public schools. The first office was established in Delaware in 1829. The legislature provided for an official whose duties would include supervision and visitation. This office later was abandoned and the schools were operated from the state office. By 1879 thirty-four of the existing states had established the office of intermediate unit superintendent of schools. Many states established the office only to discontinue it and reestablish it at another time.[13] Only six states have never had an intermediate unit superintendent of schools: Nevada, Alaska, Connecticut, Massachusetts, Hawaii, and Rhode Island.[14]

[11]It should be noted that New York City, which is divided into five boroughs, occupies parts of five different counties.
[12]Engelhardt, *Public School Organization*, p. 14.
[13]McClure, *The Intermediate School District*, p. 2.
[14]Stoops and Rafferty, *Practices and Trends*, p. 38.

The Purpose and Functions of the Office
of the Intermediate Unit Superintendent

At the time the office of the intermediate unit superintendent first was developing, school systems were small and communication was difficult. There was a critical need for an agency to establish services for both the schools and the state government. Since the intermediate units already had been established by the state as an intermediate civil agency, it seemed only proper and logical that an intermediate unit superintendent's office function in a similar manner to administer the schools in a given intermediate unit. The earliest demand seemed to be for an administrator to oversee the schools and to enforce state regulations, to collect and compile information for the state, to care for the distribution of state school monies within the intermediate unit, and to provide certain services for the school system.

Originally the intermediate unit superintendent was responsible for the schools of the entire intermediate unit. As time passed and the population of towns increased, his duties changed. Most cities developed organizations for separate local government and by-passed or ignored the intermediate unit except for limited services. State legislatures granted the cities independent status and separated them in varying degrees from the county government. In most states the county became an agency for limited control and service to rural areas.[15]

Under our democratic principle of equal opportunity it would seem proper that the youth of rural areas are entitled to standards of education which are equal to those established for city youth. The need for education in rural areas is just as great. Because of the difference in funds available, rural children generally would be denied the benefit of a standard of education on a par with their urban counterparts. Through the efforts of the intermediate unit superintendent's office it is possible to help provide the services that will insure a comparable minimum standard of education to both rural and urban youth.

Early Intermediate Unit Superintendents at Work

As was the case with early state superintendents, the early intermediate unit superintendents often were required to perform their duties on a part-time

[15]McClure, *The Intermediate School District*, p. 3.

basis while serving in another official capacity. Some of the other offices held were auditor, recorder, clerk, and assessor.

The first county superintendent's office was established in the State of Delaware in 1829. The legislature provided for an official whose duties would include supervision and visitation.

Some Functions of the Office

At the outset the intermediate unit superintendent performed three main functions: (1) he gathered records and prepared reports, (2) he performed professional services, and (3) he visited and inspected school facilities. Records and reports are needed in the daily business of budgets, accounting, comptrolling, attendance accounting, school boundary transactions, certification, and the enforcement of state school codes. These operations are chiefly routine and mechanical, but are as necessary as they would be in any efficient business organization. As time passes, the legislatures of the fifty states tend, generally, to increase the responsibilities of the intermediate unit superintendent.

Most intermediate units have established helpful services for their school systems. These services are chiefly to increase the effectiveness of instruction and, by nature, require the services of members of the professional staff. These services tend to strengthen the work of the individual school teachers, specialist-consultants, and principals.[16] Instructional plans, materials, techniques, and consultant help are provided:

> Ordinarily the intermediate unit does not organize or operate schools, but is ... [designed] to provide leadership and service ... This unit, among its other duties, also assists the state by compiling and transmitting reports.[17]

Under our nation's *Constitution* responsibility for the education of our youth was granted to the states. Due to the remoteness of the state department of education and its *modus operandi*, it is essential that the schools have some provision for leadership that is near to them physically. A principal duty of the intermediate unit superintendent is service as a professional

[16]Stoops and Rafferty, *Practices and Trends*, p. 46.
[17]Edgar L. Morphet, Roe L. Johns, and Theodore L. Reller, *Educational Administration* (Englewood Cliffs, New Jersey: Prentice-Hall, Inc., 1959), p. 15.

leader. He has, or should have, evolved from a bookkeeper to a professional leader who participates in the job of community coordination, supports worthwhile legislation, and provides expert service. He must be a competent instructional leader and a spokesman for the improvement of education.

The intermediate unit can strengthen the work of the state department of education. In order for a state department to be effective it must provide services and have lines of communication that reach every community. It is the function of the intermediate unit to assist in supplying these lines of communication and services. "Education can be more effective when intermediate channels carry on a continuous program of service, interpretation, and reports."[18]

Selection and Qualifications

Few decisions made in education have such importance to the school system as does the selection of an intermediate unit superintendent. No school system can move forward or achieve its goals without strong, capable leadership. In every system the effectiveness of the manner in which a competent superintendent is selected is of the greatest importance.[19] It has been said many times that no organization will rise above the competency of its leaders. Thus, the method used to select the intermediate unit superintendent will strongly affect the effectiveness of future leadership.

Forty-six states employ intermediate superintendents of some type. Twenty-four of the states appoint the superintendent, while twenty-two still elect him. The method of appointment is becoming more popular. County superintendents are appointed by widely varying methods. Some of the appointive bodies include:

1. The state department of education;
2. The state board of education;
3. Special supervisory districts which have no other duties than to select superintendents;

[18]Stoops and Rafferty, *Practices and Trends,* pp. 52–53.
[19]Cooper and Fitzwater, *County School Administration,* p. 142.

4. Conventions of trustees of school districts within the jurisdiction of the intermediate district;
5. Intermediate unit boards of education;
6. Special citizen's committees.

Sometimes different methods of selection exist from one intermediate unit to another within the same state. In some of the states employing the popular vote method of selection, strong efforts are made to keep the office from becoming partisan. Unfortunately the superintendent, in such instances, finds it difficult to be strong due to political pressures.

S. Cooper and C. O. Fitzwater described studies that tended to indicate that superintendents who were selected by appointment were generally superior to those selected by popular election. As evidence, Cooper and Fitzwater stated that appointed superintendents: (1) had more experience, (2) held their positions longer, (3) made more professional in-service improvements, and (4) provided higher quality leadership.[20]

Organizing the Staff of the Intermediate Unit for the Supervision of Instruction

The intermediate unit, a unique organization, has served as a right arm of the state department of education by functioning as a data processing and reporting agency. One of its responsibilities has been to gather information from the local school systems, compile the information, and pass it on to the state. Some outstanding intermediate offices have also helped the state department of education to develop realistic and effective policies for the operating procedures of the state codes.[21]

Some intermediate offices have developed from early times when they were staffed by one clerk. Today an intermediate superintendent must have a staff of up to 100 clerical and educational specialists. These specialists render service in many areas. All of these services are designed to improve instruction, although they are greatly varied and complex by nature. Cooper

[20]Ibid., p. 147.
[21]Stoops and Rafferty, *Practices and Trends*, p. 52.

and Fitzwater[22] have divided the services of the intermediate office into three broad areas including business services, special services, and curricular services.

Supervisory Services Performed by the Intermediate Unit Staff

Public Relations

The *special services division* of an intermediate unit generally is concerned with public relations. The task of this division is to communicate effectively with the citizens of the community. In so doing, all of the mass communications media available in the community, such as radio, television, public meetings, and the assistance of civic service organizations, are used.

Effective Communication

In striving to provide internal communication it is advantageous to publish newsletters, pamphlets, and reports to be distribtued to the staff of the schools within the area in the intermediate unit.

In conducting a truly effective two-way communications system with the public, the special services division should assist the electorate in expressing its needs and desires to the schools. The services of the division should be utilized to cordinate all lay groups in their efforts to work with the schools.

Teacher Personnel Placement

This division might also maintain a teacher personnel placement service and provide for credential registration and evaluation of training. In one large county in Southern California the Personnel Placement Office is involved in a majority of the selected interviews conducted by the several school districts in the county. An adequate file of assignment specifications is essential to the successful operation of such departments, as is an adequate,

[22]Cooper and Fitzwater, *County School Administration,* p. 272.

up-to-date, and readily accessible filing system. The use of the information retrieval capacities of a computer system, such as the IBM–360 series, is becoming more and more a need of the personnel placement office.

In a small intermediate unit, the responsibility of the special services division probably would be performed by the superintendent.

Curricular Services

The curricular services division is the largest and the one associated most closely with the classroom. In large- or medium-sized intermediate units the work of this division is divided into several general areas. Educational specialists direct the operations of each department. Some of the services offered by this division include instructional media, child study programs, research and guidance, attendance and counseling, and student transportation. An instructional materials laboratory should be maintained by the intermediate unit.

Special Assistance

Some intermediate units are able to offer the assistance of specialists in such areas as school nursing, audiometry and psychological testing, and dental hygiene. Sometimes intermediate units are able to offer assistance providing programs for exceptional children.

Supervision: the Final Goal

It would seem that the final outcome of all of the efforts of the intermediate unit staff is supervision in one form or another. This supervision takes the form of service to the school system. There are three factors necessary in order to carry out an effective program:

1. The superintendent
2. The staff
3. Supporting services of the intermediate unit

Trained specialists of the intermediate unit can do much to coordinate and improve instructional operations of local school systems. Cooper and Fitzwater[23] stated that the intermediate unit superintendent's most important task is to select a capable staff; and that wealth can never overcome a weakness in the professional staff. No service can exceed the importance of a qualified, capable staff.

Since one of the aspects of good supervision is leadership, it is essential that the intermediate unit superintendent and his staff (1) be educational leaders; (2) be resource persons who are informed on up-to-the minute developments in their fields and can make quick, sound decisions; (3) maintain an uninterrupted two-way communication system between their office and the people they serve; (4) command the respect and confidence of the people with whom they work; (5) be able to motivate the people with whom they work to achieve their fullest potential; (6) possess the skill and know-how to effectively carry on their professional specialties; (7) have personalities to fit into social and cultural life of the community in which they serve; and (8) have the courage to stand for their professional convictions and principles.[24]

In order to develop a successful intermediate unit staff and to provide effective service, the superintendent must instill a feeling of cooperation and teamwork. Teamwork becomes an unseen force as the staff members join together to accomplish the task of the intermediate unit.

It would be only sound reasoning to use accepted standards of appointment in securing these specialists. An application should show evidence of qualification and, if possible, appointments should be made from eligibility lists. Staff members should be selected on the basis of fitness rather than personal influence.

THE SPECIALIST-CONSULTANT AT THE INTERMEDIATE LEVEL WEARS MANY HATS. Supervision has many different meanings and reflections, depending upon individual backgrounds. To some it might mean only another unnecessary frill in the budget; to others it means an effective way of increasing the

---

[23]Shirley Cooper and Charles O. Fitzwater, *County School Administration* (New York: Harper and Brothers, 1954), p. 173.
[24]Ibid., p. 272.

effectiveness of instruction. The Department of Rural Education of the National Education Association stated:

> Supervision is not the sole responsibility of . . . one person. It is a function that is carried on by many people in many ways at many different times in many different places. There should be one or more persons whose primary responsibility is to make it possible for supervision to take place.[25]

One person, the supervisor, is essential to make this guidance and leadership become a reality. In many areas this person is known as a helping teacher, a coordinator, or a consultant.

Spears stated:

> Good supervision stimulates . . . personnel to the highest endeavor. It coordinates . . . efforts and facilitates . . . work. . . . It evaluates the whole undertaking.[26]

Often the specialist from the intermediate unit is able to help teachers and the school by providing the school board with timely and adequate information that they may need in formulating wise decisions. Such data may include statements concerning the achievements of the staff and children of the school and accounts of staff meetings, in-service education, committee work, and items of general interest.

CASE 1. Another role in which the supervisor may find himself is that of community helper. The Department of Rural Education of the National Education Association reported that an intermediate unit specialist-consultant helped a small isolated community in New Mexico to rehabilitate itself. This task was accomplished partly by bringing the community together, assisting in the problem of self-evaluation, helping to plan for reaching a solution, securing an expert to provide needed training, and coordinating the outside resources available.[27]

---

[25]National Education Association, *Rural Supervisor at Work,* edited by Marchia Everett, 1949 Yearbook (Washington, D.C.: National Education Association, 1949), p. 12.
[26]Harold Spears, *Improving the Supervision of Instruction* (Englewood Cliffs, New Jersey: Prentice-Hall, Inc., 1953), p. 236.
[27]Ibid., pp. 62–63.

CASE 2. This National Education Association department further reported that a specialist-consultant from a rural area in New Jersey was able to assist a county in establishing a visual aids library. This task was accomplished in spite of tremendous obstacles.

The work necessitated coordinating the resources of parents, teachers, school boards, other governmental agencies, and the citizens. This project required the services of all involved. As a result of the intermediate unit specialist-consultant's skill in coordination, the entire community was able to work together to provide a means of improving classroom education.[28]

PROBLEMS. The most logical step to be taken in providing good supervision, particularly in rural areas, is the furnishing of an adequate number of specialists. Since funds and personnel are limited, it is essential that both be used wisely. The provision for specialist-consultants at the intermediate unit level of supervision developed in the 1930's and 1940's. With increased competition for the tax dollar, the appropriation of significantly large additional funds for this field does not seem likely in the future. It will be necessary to use the existing supervisory services to the best possible advantage.

SERVICE. Supervision is not law enforcing but rather a program of leadership. By sharing a teacher's problem and offering technical advice, a supervisor may render service as effectively as in classroom visitation.

The supervisor at the intermediate unit level should be more than a classroom visitor. He should be a teacher's consultant. He should provide in-service education, help prepare courses of study, secure instructional aids, preview new educational films, and help teachers to keep abreast of research findings.

An intermediate unit consultant's task may be to bring teachers together to observe a fellow teacher who has developed an outstanding teaching technique. All of these activities are aimed at securing growth, competence, and independence to improve instruction. One of the greatest services that a specialist-consultant can provide is the operating of a curriculum laboratory

[28]Ibid., pp. 64–65.

center where teachers may conveniently gather to work and where they may discover new materials.

Many states have encouraged intermediate units to assume the supervisory service function needed to help make possible equality of education for the children of both rural and urban school systems. In all instances the emphasis is on service, not on control. C. C. Trillingham reported:

We try to lean over backwards to work, under the philosophy that the center of gravity of education is within the local district. It is not in the county office. We do not try to run the districts—we try to serve the districts.[29]

FURTHER PROBLEMS. E. McGovern[30] reported that teachers generally fear the intermediate unit specialist-consultant and do not understand his function. Teachers rated classroom activities of the intermediate unit supervisors very low, although the intermediate unit personnel expressed confidence in their program.

The author went on to note that teachers expressed a desire for concrete methods and techniques of instruction; that group discussion techniques were needed; that local school system superintendents gave low ratings to intermediate unit centered activities while the intermediate unit superintendents preferred activities that were centered in the intermediate unit offices. Educators in general desired more democratic leadership from the intermediate unit supervisors, and they stressed the importance of cooperation between the specialists at the intermediate unit office and the teacher-training institutions.

Summary of Services

The following outline summarizes the supervisory services rendered by the intermediate unit:

---

[29]C. C. Trillingham, *The County Superintendent and County Service Foundation.* Second Report of Assembly Interim Committee on Public Education (Sacramento: Assembly of the State of California, 1949), p. 113.
[30]Elcy McGovern, "A Critical Evaluation of California General County School Supervisors" (Doctoral dissertation, University of Southern California, 1948).

A. Services in the area of school supervision:
1. Curricular services
2. Communications
3. Operation of schools
4. Consultant services
5. Instructional technology (audio-visual) services and leadership
6. Library services
7. Guidance services
8. Special services
    a) Public relations
    b) Teacher personnel placement
    c) Others

B. Other services:
1. Business management
2. Auditing and accounting
3. School district reorganization
4. Purchasing

The changes that will affect the intermediate unit will be the result of new needs and problems. As school systems become larger, the services that they will be able to provide for themselves probably will alter the configuration of the intermediate unit. It seems possible that intermediate units could become higher echelon organizations coordinating and supplying complex research services. Perhaps these services will be in the areas of educational television and programmed learning, or in the research into special problems, such as methods of teaching brain-damaged children.

As a Supervisor at the Intermediate Level,

DO

1. Be an educational leader.
2. Be a resource person who is informed on up-to-the-minute developments in his field(s) and can make quick, sound decisions.

3. Maintain an uninterrupted two-way communication system between the office and those served.
4. Actively work to command the respect and confidence of the people with whom you work.
5. Learn to stimulate the people with whom you work to work up to their full potentials.
6. Have the courage to stand for your professional convictions and principles.
7. So as to develop a successful intermediate unit staff and to provide effective service, work to instill a feeling of cooperation and teamwork. This teamwork becomes an unseen force as the staff members join together to accomplish the task of the intermediate unit.
8. Continuously evaluate the level and effectiveness of the services of the intermediate unit office.
9. Work *with* the local districts and school systems to help them better serve their students. One of the major responsibilities of the intermediate unit is to help the local school system to help itself.

DON'T

1. Attempt, at the intermediate unit level, to help to strengthen education by exerting punitive regulations.
2. Approach the local school system and its personnel as an omnipotent oracle of the truth in education.
3. Forget that wealth can never overcome a weakness in the professional staff. No service can exceed the quantity, quality, and capacity of the staff.
4. Perform functions that readily could be performed on the local school system level.
5. Select staff members on a basis of personal influence. Use accepted standards of selection in securing these specialists. An applicant should show evidence of qualifications and, if possible, appointments should be made from eligibility lists. Staff members should be approved on a basis of fitness rather than personal influence.

Supervisory Problems

Problem 1

As specialist-consultant in the office of the intermediate unit superintendent of schools, you have been asked to help evaluate and develop instructional technology (audio-visual) and library collections services. The superintendent indicated to you that he and the assistant superintendent favor the development of a professional library collection as a part of the instructional media complex which will include the regular library collection and the now separate instructional technology collection.

How will you proceed?

What priorities will you establish?

What standards will you recommend?

Problem 2

The governing board of the Lourose School District has ordered the teaching of Spanish in grades three through six of the elementary school, in accordance with a recently enacted state law mandating such instruction. The district does not employ subject matter supervisors but rather is dependent upon the intermediate unit staff for its supervisory assistance. The superintendent of the Lourose District telephoned while you, the Assistant Superintendent for Instructional Services, were at a meeting of the County Board of Supervisors. Upon your return to the office you discovered a memorandum in your in-basket informing you of this message. The intermediate unit office does not presently employ a foreign language specialist.

What would you do? Assume that you must provide the assistance needed, and that adequate funds are available to carry our your plans.

How would you proceed, especially as concerns curriculum, staff, instructional materials, and in-service educational activities?

How would you evaluate the success of your activities?

Selected Bibliography

Books

Cooper, Shirley, and Charles O. Fitzwater. *County School Administration*. New York: Harper and Brothers, 1954.

Cubberley, Ellwood P. *Public Education in the United States*. Boston: Houghton Mifflin Company, 1934.

Dutton, Samuel T., and David Snedden. *The Administration of Public Education in the United States*. New York: The Macmillan Company, 1924.

Engelhardt, Fred. *Public School Organization and Administration*. Boston: Ginn and Company, 1931.

Jacobson, Paul B. *The American Secondary School*. Englewood Cliffs, New Jersey: Prentice-Hall, Inc., 1952.

McClure, William P. *The Intermediate School District in the United States*. Urbana: University of Illinois Press, 1956.

Moehlman, Arthur B. *School Administration*. Boston: Houghton Mifflin Company, 1951.

Monroe, Paul. *Founding of the American Public School System*. New York: The Macmillan Company, 1940.

Morphet, Edgar L., Roe L. Johns, and Theodore L. Reller. *Educational Administration*. Englewood Cliffs, New Jersey: Prentice-Hall, Inc., 1959.

Mort, Paul R., and Donald H. Ross. *Principles of School Administration*. 2d ed. New York: McGraw-Hill Book Company, 1957.

Reavis, W. C., and C. H. Judd. *The Teacher and Educational Administration*. Boston: Houghton Mifflin Company, 1942.

Sears, Harold. *Improving the Supervision of Instruction*. Englewood Cliffs, New Jersey: Prentice-Hall, Inc., 1953.

Stoops, Emery, and M.L. Rafferty, Jr. *Practices and Trends in School Administration*. Boston: Ginn and Company, 1961.

——————————, and Russell E. Johnson. *Elementary School Administration*. New York: McGraw-Hill Book Company, 1967.

Trillingham, C. C. *The County Superintendent and County Service Foundation*. Second Report of Assembly Interim Committee on Public Education. Sacramento: Assembly of the State of California, 1949.

Other Sources

Marks, James R. "An Analysis of Assignment Specifications for Certificated School Personnel in the United States." Doctoral dissertation, University of Southern California, 1962.

McGovern, Elcy. "A Critical Evaluation of California General Elementary County School Supervisors." Doctoral dissertation, University of Southern California, 1948.

National Education Association, *Rural Supervision at Work,* ed. Marchia Everett. 1949 Yearbook. Washington D.C.: National Education Association, 1949.

3

Special Problems:
The Role of the State
in School Supervision

Basic standards of organization, supervision administration, certification of teachers, curricula, and school plant layouts have been established either as suggested guides or as requirements by each of the fifty states. However, over the past several years the approach of the state in school supervision and administration has moved increasingly from an emphasis on inspection toward an emphasis on leadership. During this quarter century great forward strides have been made toward equalizing the quality and quantity of education available to our children.

A backward view at the accomplishments already effected in this monumental task of elevating and equalizing our school program tempts one to satisfaction; i.e., that the goal has been reached. However, as is true of all systems that are subject to sociological forces, our school system is characterized by dynamism and restiveness. Indeed, movement is inevitable. The continuing development and improvement of our educational program is the only alternative to social decadence. Merely to keep pace with technological and economic progress in this space age, the state must exert even greater energy in educational leadership.

In considering the state's role in supervision, it is assumed that the state will at all times work with and/or through the intermediate unit which, in most states, is the office of the intermediate unit superintendent of schools.

The topics discussed in this chapter are:

Historical development of the state departments of education
The position of chief state school officer
Functions of the state departments of education
Special problems: the state level

Do—don't
"In-Basket" supervisory problems
Chapter Supplement

Historical Development of the State Departments of Education

State Normal School Stimulates Development of the Position of Specialist-Consultant

J. M. Gwynn[1] reported that after 1870 the rapid expansion of the state normal school stimulated the development of the position of general supervisor in the public elementary schools. The most important task facing the normal school during the 1800's was that of improvement in the professional education curriculum for teachers. One of the ways in which the state normal schools planned to perform this function effectively was to provide for intensive supervision by the general supervisor of the elementary grade teacher training program at the normal schools.

State Departments of Education Develop

The state departments of education also influenced the direction taken by supervision, for early in the 1900's the state departments provided inspectional and supervisory services. These services were rendered primarily at the secondary school level.[2] After 1917 an increasing number of special subject supervisors was added to the professional staff.

The Position of Chief State School Officer

Historical Development

A LIMITING FACTOR: THE SEVERAL STATE CONSTITUTIONS. The state constitutions provide for the educational program in some manner in all fifty

---

[1] J. Minor Gwynn, *Theory and Practice of Supervision* (New York: Dodd, Mead, & Company, 1961), pp. 7–9.
[2] Ibid., p. 8.

states. Occasionally it is specified that education has first call on the funds of the states, and sometimes the teacher's minimum salary is indicated in the state constitution. The constitution can be changed by vote of the people only. The constitution; statutes, including the education code or school code of the state, the various other administrative codes of the state, the administrative code containing the rules of the state board of education; local board rules and regulations; and court decisions all act to determine the structure of education.

GROWTH OF THE POSITION OF CHIEF STATE SCHOOL OFFICER. The Tenth Amendment to the Constitution of the United States did, by virtue of the absence of a reference to education in the Federal Constitution, reserve the power for jurisdiction over education to the several states. By the early 1800's, most of the functions of education were being served by local school systems. Shortly thereafter there began a struggle wherein the states attempted to regain much of their lost power. New York was the first to develop a centralized school system with statutes restricting local districts.

R. F. Butts and L. A. Cremin emphasized the importance of a centralized state system for education in New York:

Moreover, New York was also the first state to create the office of superintendent of common schools. His duties, according to the Law of 1812, involved preparation of plans for improving the common school system, reporting and superintendence of school monies, and the providing of information concerning the schools to the legislature.[3]

A few states followed New York and created similar offices in the succeeding two decades, but it was not until 1850, when every northern state and some of the southern states created similar offices, that the position became firmly established. In reality, many of these early state superintendents of public instruction were really *ex officio* superintendents,[4] wherein an individual who was already an official of the state had certain limited school responsibilities added to his other duties. Other chief state school officers of the time were secretaries of the state boards of education. As the office grew

[3]R. Freeman Butts and Lawrence A. Cremin, *A History of Education in American Culture* (New York: Henry Holt and Company, Inc., 1953), pp. 225–256.
[4]Ibid.

in importance and stature, visitation and advisement functions in local school systems were added to the duties of the chief state school officers. One state's organization for education is represented graphically in Figure 3–1.

The Position Today

Excepting Hawaii, Delaware, and Alaska where the whole state is virtually one school system, and New York, where the chief state school officer is very powerful, the position of chief state school officer has been weakened by the elective nature of the office. Since there is little security in the position in most states because of the necessity of the chief state school officer's standing for election, it is difficult to obtain a top man for the position.

Functions of the State Departments of Education

Approval and Accreditation

HISTORICAL DEVELOPMENT. It is practically impossible to trace to a point of origin the accreditation of public schools by state departments of education. Accreditation, narrowly defined to include schools whose graduates were acceptable to a university without prior examination, can be traced to 1873 when the Indiana state board of education assumed this responsibility. Although accreditation applies mainly to the secondary school level, it has deep implications for the supervisor.

In 1837 it was the general practice for state universities rather than state boards of education to accredit schools, but around the turn of the century it was found to be more practical to have the state board take over this responsibility. The system spread rapidly. Its effect was a trend toward standardization of education within a given state, thus giving equal opportunities for college preparation.

APPROVAL PROGRAMS. Many approval programs of state departments of education stemmed from responsibilities delegated to them by the legislature in conjunction with allocation of state funds to aid education. For instance, in

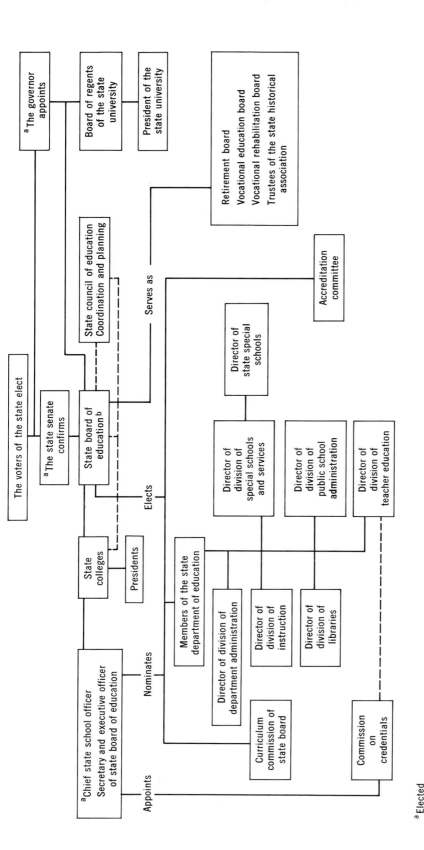

FIGURE 3–1   State Organization for Education.[c]

[a] Elected

[b] Perorms policy-making functions. The members are appointed by the governor.

[c] From Edward H. La Franchi, "School Organization and Administration" (Department of Administration and Supervision, School of Education, University of Southern California, Los Angeles, 1954), p. 14.

1878 the Minnesota State Legislature established a board whose responsibility it was to visit and inspect each school that was receiving $400 or more in state aid.

The objective in Minnesota was to provide better preparation for college. As state boards of education were charged with the dispersal of funds and accumulated responsibilities for the regulation of local schools, programs of approval or accreditation became necessary. Approval programs became the principal tool through which the state boards could exercise a regulatory function over management and operation on the local school level.

Approval programs differed widely. This disparity was a natural consequence of the variation in regulatory responsibilities as delegated by the state legislatures. In all cases, the state could exercise a regulatory function over management and operation at the local school level.

During the early part of the twentieth century a widespread method of exercising approval of schools was by inspection. The *school inspector,* in a unique position to observe a given number of schools at the "grass-roots" level, and to compare one with the other, saw the need for establishing standards. In all areas of programming, administration, and facilities the school inspector pioneered in the development of standards by which local schools could be rated, graded, or classified. A few states and the provinces of Canada still have standards or criteria that refer to the inspection of schools or to the school inspector. Accreditation and approval at the community college level has been a shared responsibility of the state and the several regional accrediting organizations which one encounters in higher education.

INCREASING FINANCIAL SUPPORT. Over the years, state legislatures have gradually increased their financial support of education. Deeper financial involvement has been paralleled by growing concern about the prudent expenditure of funds. This heightened concern served to spark the growth of statewide standards during the first half of this century. Although control of funds in many states have been effected through legislative statutes in areas quite separate from school approval programs, in some states control of funds is included within the approval program. This practice has serious overtones for the supervising principal. In the latter case the purpose appears to be to insure economy and efficiency in the operation of local schools. Formal standards for approval of schools were further encouraged by state requirements regarding the audit of school funds, insurance on school buildings, location and construction of school buildings, and provisions for economy and safety in the use and custody of school funds.

COMPULSORY ATTENDANCE LAWS. The institution of laws that made attendance compulsory focused attention on what was available to the children who were compelled to attend schools. Charged with carrying out compulsory attendance laws, the state boards of education necessarily became concerned with academic programs and what minimum standards would fulfill the intent of the compulsory attendance laws.

DEVELOPMENT AND IMPROVEMENT OF EDUCATIONAL PROGRAMS EMPHASIZED. As the stress on the inspection of schools changed to an emphasis on the development and improvement of educational programs in which state and local school officials were partners, local school authorities were more willing to conform to state minimum standards when they, the local officials, had a part in the development of these standards. Supervisors played a leading role in this development.

A UNIFIED APPROACH. The concept that one school, or one level of the school program, should not be improved at the expense of another has resulted in a trend to evaluate and improve the total school program throughout the school system. It especially was apparent in early accrediting programs that steps taken to enable high schools to achieve accredited status were often taken at the expense of the elementary schools. This factor, in many instances, encouraged the state education agency to develop approval or accreditation programs which include both elementary and secondary schools.

When accreditation standards were first developed they tended to emphasize physical facilities and the other facets of the school program which could be measured objectively, such as the number of students per teacher, the number of books in the library, the number of units offered in various subjects, and the number of classrooms. Modern accreditation processes include provisions for more subjective judgments emphasizing the quality of the school, its administration, its program, and its facilities.

APPROVAL VS. ACCREDITATION. The meaning and usage of the terms "approval" and "accreditation" vary considerably in different states. What is understood to be an accreditation program in one state may, in a neighboring state, be an approval program. Within a given state the state education agency may approve some schools while accrediting others. In another state some schools may be only approved, while others are both approved and accredited. Certain states with approval type programs refer to their schools as commissioned, classified, registered, recognized, chartered, or standardized.

Approval of a school may or may not be based on a judgment of the quality of the school on the part of the state department of education, while almost invariably *accreditation* of a school does require such judgment. The term "approval" may be used when the state education agency is administering a state statute that allows financial support if certain criteria are met, e.g., being open a specified number of days and employing only certified teachers. The department simply ascertains that the school has complied with the law and will approve the school for receipt of aid. In such a situation the department makes no attempt to inquire into or judge the quality of a school's program and facilities.

PROGRAM APPROVAL. A state department of education might approve only certain phases of a school's program, such as the course of study, textbooks, or buildings. The department might administer one or several such approval programs without, however, exercising a judgment on the quality of the total school and its instruction, administration, or facilities.

PROGRAMS FOR APPROVAL IN THE FIFTY STATES. The practices of state departments of education with respect to their approval or accreditation programs fall into three categories: (1) those which require *no state approval or accreditation* of public schools, (2) those which make approval or accreditation *voluntary* and extend it only on application by local public schools, and (3) those which *require* approval or accreditation.[5] As the

[5] See W. B. Rich, *Approval and Accreditation of Public Schools* (OE-20013) (Washington, D.C.: Government Printing Office, 1960); and H. H. Cummings and H. K. Mackintosh, *Curriculum Responsibilities of State Department of Education* (Washington, D.C.: Government Printing Office, 1958).

TABLE 3–1   State Requirements Concerning Approval
            (In percents)

	Nursery[a]	*Kindergarten*	*Elementary*	*High School*
No approval necessary	80	54	34	6
Approval voluntary; extended on application	8	14	28	42
Approval required	10	32	38	52
Total	98	100	100	100

[a]New Jersey has no public nursery schools.

academic ladder is ascended from nursery school to higher education, the trend throughout the country is to follow either plan (2) or (increasingly) plan (3). While 80 per cent of public nursery schools are without approval, only 6 per cent of high schools fall into this category. Unapproved elementary schools are found in 34 per cent of the states.

It also is apparent, from Table 3–1, that if approval or accreditation is considered at all there is a tendency to make it required rather than voluntary.

AUTHORITY TO APPROVE SCHOOLS AND SCHOOL PROGRAMS. State legislatures commit legal authority to accredit or approve schools to one of three agents: the state board of education, the chief state school officer, the state department of education or to a combination of these three. The exercise of this authority is carried on exclusively by the state board of education in twenty-six states, by the chief state school officer in seven states, and by the state department of education in three states. Sharing of authority by the state board of education and the chief state school officer occurs in eight states.

Combined authority is exercised by the state board of education and the state department of education in two states. Tripartite authority is delegated in four states to the state board, the state department, and the chief state school officer.

The wording of state statutes with regard to authority to approve schools is variable, but most direct that the schools shall be approved, accredited, commissioned, recognized, chartered, classified, graded, standardized, or rated. The states of California and Hawaii stand alone since they have no terms or categories that describe the type or level of approval.

PURPOSES OR OBJECTIVES OF APPROVAL PROGRAMS. Some clue as to the purposes of approval programs can be had from a perusal of state manuals or handbooks, and in legislative statutes themselves. Most are written in a style designed to be helpful and stimulating and do not make rigid, inflexible standards that must be met to the ultimate detail. In fact, mandatory standards occasionally are so closely interrelated with recommendations that exactness is sacrificed in attempting to achieve a salutary style. Nevertheless, it is generally clear to the most casual reader that the primary purpose of these publications is to assist local school officials with their administrative problems and to improve educational programs as a whole.

With regard to more specific purposes, eighteen out of the fifty states include as one purpose of the approval program the authorization of a school or school district to collect tuition from other districts for nonresident students.

Enforcing legal requirements or state board rules or regulations seems almost too obvious to mention, but only forty-three states outline this as a distinct responsibility. Coordination of the instructional programs throughout the state is set forth as a purpose of forty-one states. Forty-eight states encourage self-evaluation by local schools, although only rarely is this practice required. State financial aid is related directly to the approval program in thirty-three states.

SIGNIFICANCE OR EFFECT OF APPROVAL OR ACCREDITATION. As has been emphasized, the actual significance of approval is variable amongst the states, but all fifty are agreed that an approved school is one where minimum acceptable standards are met or exceeded. A few states do not base their approval on fulfilling a comprehensive set of standards or criteria. Throughout the country there are minimum state standards that schools are encouraged, but not necessarily required, to meet. Though an indication of the *extent* of the standards may be found in published form, it is difficult, if not impossible, to determine the *degree* to which minimum acceptable standards are either enforced or met. The degree to which they are met or exceeded is determined, in large part, by state supervisory policies and activities. The same applies to endorsement of the quality of a school's program. The *degree* to which endorsement is carried remains, in most cases, rather obscure. Exceptions are those states which categorize or classify schools, endorsing quality on two or more levels. At the college level, denial of accreditation or approval could mean that a student would not be able to transfer his credits to another institution, or that his degree would not be recognized.

PUBLISHED STANDARDS. The following outline gives some idea of the scope and areas upon which attention seems most frequently to be focused in these published standards:

	Number of States
1. Organization	
a) Grade organization	29
b) Length of school year	39
c) Length of school day	35
d) Length of class periods	35
e) Size of classes	27
f) Student-teacher ratio	28
g) Enrollment in school or ADA	18
2. Administration	
a) School board policies, meetings, and minutes	15
b) Self-evaluation	13
c) Financial records and reports	18
d) Internal accounting or auditing of activity funds	21
e) Student transportation	17
f) Records and reports required	34
g) Philosophy and/or objectives of school or system	14
h) School-community relations	9
i) Supervision	26
3. Personnel	
a) Minimum number of teachers	34

7. Other items
   a) Community use of school plant   7
   b) Space for special instruction such as music, art, and physical
      education   27
   c) Safety regulations   30
   d) Requirements for special schools and programs such as
      summer schools, night schools, veteran's programs   26
   e) Approval of vocational programs   27

Suggestions or recommendations have not been interpreted as require-ments, although in practice they often are fulfilled as if they were actual requirements. The absence of a written recommendation should not be construed to mean that a state does not have requirements covering the area.

TEACHER PREPARATION STANDARDS. The most frequently encountered item is that pertaining to the certification, qualifications, or preparation of teachers. All but one of the forty-four states that publish standards have requirements ranging from a simple statement that teachers must be certi-ficated to a detailed listing of the training required for teaching specific subjects. Requirements to be met by administrators are published by thirty-eight states. Specifications run the gamut from a statement requiring that the supervisor hold an administrative certificate, to descriptions of the amount of graduate work and experience a candidate must have completed or acquired. The situation is similar for superintendents of school districts.

STANDARDS FOR INSTRUCTIONAL SUPPLIES AND TEXTS. A frequently recur-ring item in these published school approval programs is standards pertaining to libraries. Forty-one states have standards for libraries, and of these about one-third are brief and general, stating that adequate library facilities will be provided and listing a few basic requirements. Another third go into moderate detail, listing requirements that cover up to a full printed page. The remaining third are extensively detailed, outlining specific requisites with regard to space, equipment, books, periodicals, cataloguing, records, expenditures, staff, and aids to be used by the librarian in the selection of library material.

EVALUATION OF STANDARDS OF THE STATE DEPARTMENTS OF EDUCATION. Review of standards or criteria for the approval of public schools occurs periodically, in accordance with established policies in thirty-seven out of the fifty states. A few of these policies specify the interval between reviews. For example, five states review their standards annually. In Florida, revisions are made approximately every three years, and in Wyoming about every five years. All of the states rely on the advice of local professional advisers to some extent before standards are revised. Seventeen states specifically mention accrediting committees, standards committees, or advisory commissions.

WORKSHOPS AND NEWSLETTERS. It is widespread practice for state departments of education to initiate consultation with local school supervisors and administrators aimed at the prevention or correction of violations of the standards or criteria for the approval or accreditation of the schools. Forty states sponsor periodic workshops or conferences to foster understanding of, to engender support for, and to improve more accurate compliance with state standards. Such services overlap the areas of service stressed in Figure 3–2.

These workshops are usually given as part of the state's supervisory or regulatory program. Activities such as these are supplemented by letters item-

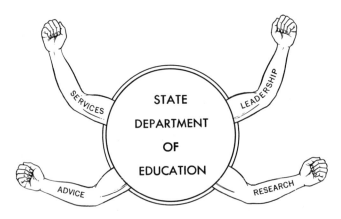

FIGURE 3–2   The Many Strong Arms of the State Department of Education Serve the Supervisor.

izing deficiencies and pointing out any violations which might exist. Some departments of education publish periodic newsletters or memorandums where problems in all spheres of education that relate to approval programs may be discussed. Local schools frequently are encouraged to request special consultative visits from the state's supervisory personnel for help in the prevention or correction of a transgression of the established standard. In at least one state a progress report citing steps taken to correct a standards violation is required from a school whose status is questionable.

FAILURE TO MEET STATE MINIMUM STANDARDS. Of twenty-five states in which approval has been discontinued or accreditation status lowered, nine withheld funds from schools for failure to meet the minimum standards. Funds were withheld from a kindergarten in one state, from elementary schools in four states, and from high schools in seven states. In any one state the total number of schools from which funds were withheld ranged from one to forty.

During a recent school year twelve states rejected or postponed applications for approval of schools. The number of schools applying in any one state ranged between one and 175.

These data lend support to the impression that the states move slowly in making changes in status in their schools. It also is apparent that even though the state boards of education of thirty-four states are empowered by the legislature to withhold funds where minimum standards are not met, it is rather unusual for them to do so.

STATE SUPERVISORY VISITS AND INSPECTION. Inspection and/or a visitation to the school as part of the approval procedure is required by thirty-nine states. In twenty-six states the evaluation is made by state professional personnel only. Eleven other states include local and state professional personnel in the evaluation. In rare instances community representatives participate with the state and local educators in the approval procedure. In all cases, state professional personnel participate in the required evaluation procedures.

The Texas Education Agency has adopted self-evaluation as part of its procedures for evaluation of accredited school systems:

Self-evaluation. Each local school system, through its own initiative, determines whether or not it wants to be accredited by the State Department of Education. When it decides to become accredited, it automatically accepts responsibility of meeting at least the minimum standards prescribed for accreditation. The initial responsibility, therefore, for meeting the standards for accreditation rests with the local school officials. Consequently, self-evaluation is the first step in the evaluative process. Each accredited school system shall establish and maintain in its own way a system of self-evaluation.[6]

There are various methods of notification of approval by the state authority. Official state bulletins listing approved or accredited schools are published by forty states. Notification by letter to the school occurs in forty states. About half the states send annual notices of approval; one state sends notices biannually. All states send out notifications regarding approval in some form or other.

Figure 3–3 indicates the organization of the major divisions of a state department of education. In general, then, the state departments of education perform the following tasks in the areas of approval and accreditation.

1. Standards are established;
2. These standards are evaluated and revised;
3. State personnel participate in visiting and evaluating schools;
4. Standard evaluations are corrected and a program for prevention and remediation of evaluations is approved;
5. Forms and reports are issued and processed.

Curriculum and Supervision Responsibilities of the State Department of Education

As state departments of education have moved from an inspection role to a leadership role, the curriculum guide has become much more than a course of study with a listing of subject matter which students are expected to learn. The increasing tendency to incorporate the term "guide" in the title indicates a growing acceptance of the idea that the instructional bulletin is suggestive and not prescribed.

[6]Texas Education Agency, *Principles and Standards for Accrediting Elementary and Secondary Schools*, Bulletin No. 560 (Austin: Texas Education Agency, July 1957).

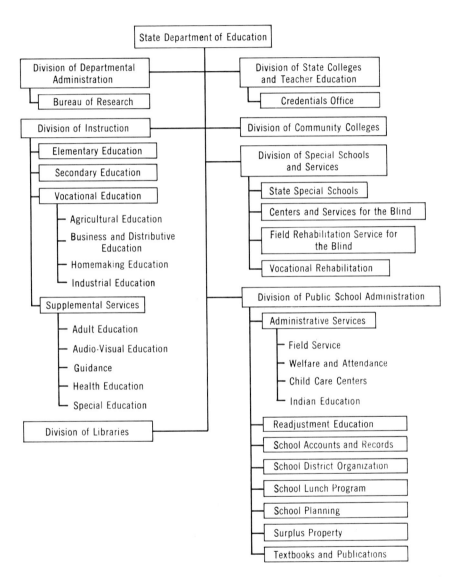

FIGURE 3–3   Organization of the Major Divisions of One State Department of Education.

Significant achievements in the field of curriculum development have been brought about by state departments of education as well as by local school systems.

STATE CURRICULUM WORKSHOP. The curriculum workshop is now the most important single method of developing curricula. Representatives of many groups come together to participate in workshops to produce a wide variety of material for the classroom teacher. Although the output of ideas in a workshop is important, the changes that take place in the members who participate may be even more important in influencing the successful implementation of the curriculum in the classroom. Constructing a curriculum is similar to making a prayer—it is most helpful to the person who makes it.

THE INSTRUCTIONAL PROGRAM AND THE STATE DEPARTMENT OF EDUCATION. State departments of education are almost uniformly responsible for maintaining an elementary school program that provides instruction in reading, literature, spelling, handwriting, oral and written expression, arithmetic, American history, geography, science, health, physical education, art, and music.[7] Such subjects usually are mandated by law but frequently are required by rulings of the state board or the state department of education and, with few exceptions, have been a part of the elementary school curriculum for many years. In general, the state laws are less specific for the programs in grades 9 to 12, and similar degrees of freedom are permitted in the selection of textbooks in the high schools. Community colleges enjoy even more autonomy.

TEXTBOOK SELECTION. The states handle the selection of textbooks in a number of different ways. Over the years there has been a trend away from the adoption of a single textbook in each subject and toward multiple adoptions on both state and local levels. Twenty-four states permit local school authorities to adopt textbooks without control from any state or intermediate

[7]U.S. Department of Health, Education, and Welfare, *Curriculum Responsibility of State Departments of Education* (Washington, D.C.: Government Printing Office, 1958). Data for this publication were gathered during 1955 and 1956, as well as during the five-year interval from 1950–1955. Included were forty-eight states, four territories (Alaska, Hawaii, Guam, and the Canal Zone), and the Commonwealth of Puerto Rico.

authority. Seven states place control in the hands of state textbook commissions or committees. Other states give control to the state board of education.

Eleven states present a list of textbooks to local authorities, who may choose one textbook for each subject. This list is compiled by the state board of education or the textbook commission. In addition, thirteen states permit multiple adoptions from such a list, and five permit multiple adoptions for certain subjects only.

ORGANIZATION FOR CURRICULUM DEVELOPMENT. Leadership in curriculum development programs usually comes from the state department of education. Involved are directors of curriculum; directors of elementary, secondary community college and vocational education; and supervisors in special subject fields.

Special Problems: The State Level

The state departments of education utilize several methods in achieving the involvement of as many individuals and groups as possible in curriculum development.[8] These methods include workshops, work conferences, meetings, and committee work. In some states these projects begin on a statewide level progressing to similar conferences and workshops on a local level at a later date. Other states begin projects on the local level and later work up to a large statewide meeting. Either route is effective, depending upon the nature of the curriculum problems at hand.

There are a number of state committees working in fields broader than any single subject at any one time. For example, early elementary education, adult education, and such topics as exceptional children, evaluation, and development of materials of instruction were being covered at the time of a survey in one large Midwestern state. Other statewide committees of rather

[8]The authors are grateful to the U.S. Department of Health, Education, and Welfare, *Curriculum Responsibilities of the States* (Washington, D.C.: Government Printing Office, 1968), for much of the data in this section.

common occurrence were those related to conservation, guidance, safety, instructional technology (audio-visual) programs, library service, supervision, and accreditation.

As far as the responsibilities of these committees go, they may be divided into three groups:

1. Those that advise the state department on supervisory problems;
2. Those that survey supervisory needs;
3. Those that help to provide supervisory publications and curriculum materials.

Individual teachers, administrators, and supervisors who have served on these committees have reported that they found them stimulating. The experiences in cooperative thinking and planning appear valuable. The pattern of development in committee work tends to follow a sequence.

1. Orientation
2. Study and research
3. Development of point of view
4. Listing basic assumptions
5. Determination of objectives
6. Development of a plan for the project
7. Production of a tentative manuscript.

The most common difficulties experienced by the state committees are usually related to three factors. (1) *Funds are short.* Committee work is costly. Providing travel funds for committee members, hiring substitute teachers while committee members are away, and printing of reports or syllabi are the major sources of expense. (2) *There is a shortage of personnel or time.* Busy teachers, supervisors, and administrators find it difficult to take part in long and exhaustive committee work projects. Research, a basic need of the committee, takes both time to assemble and training to interpret. People with such time and training are not available in sufficient numbers. (3) *There is difficulty in reaching a common working philosophy.* Harmonizing diverging points of view and reconciling different beliefs must occur before the committee may function productively.

Workshops and Work Conferences at the State Level

The workshop and work conference are widely used techniques for dealing with many different problems at the state level that range from the elementary school to the community college level. A *workshop* may be defined as a working situation in which the participants, with expert consultant help, attempt to solve their problems by means of a wide variety of activities. A workshop usually lasts for a week or more. A *work conference,* on the other hand, may be similar to a workshop in techniques used, but it is delimited in scope to a specific problem and reduced in time to a day or two. It is similar, then, to the institute, which will be discussed in a later chapter.

Expenses for workshops and work conferences usually come from state funds (seventeen states), from local school systems (in more than half of the states), and from the participants themselves (twenty-two states). Consultants to the workshop or conference are paid from state funds in thirty-six states, by organizations in twenty-eight states, or by other methods in the remaining states.

Statewide Conferences

The statewide conference, usually a more formally organized meeting, is a third method used in supervision at the state level. Methods used in conducting these meetings include speeches, committee reports, workshop activities, panel discussions, and contributions by consultants. Speeches usually occur at the beginning of the conference and serve the purpose of orientation. Panel discussions frequently are used in general meetings. Smaller groups analyze and discuss problems, and there is a closing general session or summary.

Some states have evaluating committees work while the conference is in progress and/or fulfilling follow-up functions in order to increase the effectiveness of statewide conferences. These evaluating committees have illuminated the factors important to the success of conferences. They have found that:

1. The specific purpose of the conference should be determined by representatives of the groups that attend.

2. Consultants should be selected for their experience and skill in working with groups.
3. Orientation programs should be provided for the conferees; a variety of meetings should be planned; everyone should be encouraged to participate actively and "get into the act."
4. Preplanning should be provided for the comfort of the conferees and for activities to develop fellowship.

Sectional Conferences

A fourth method for dealing with problems at the state level is the sectional conference. The pattern of organization is similar to that of the statewide conference except that participants are more likely to be drawn from special groups such as superintendents, principals, specialist-consultants, and teachers in special subject fields. Some sectional meetings include all teachers, supervisors, and administrators from an area in one meeting.

These smaller sectional conferences are particularly numerous in the larger and more popular states. California reported 477 sectional conferences during a recent five-year period. Fifteen states held fifty or more each during the same interval, and sixteen states held none.

The sectional conference has been quite successful in reaching large numbers of teachers and administrators. Purposes served include drawing ideas from as many educators as possible, discussing and refining ideas, and carrying them back to the classroom. Problems encountered are the common ones of time, funds, and personnel.

Specialist-Consultants Provide Assistance at the State Level

Specialist-consultants are drawn from various sources that more commonly include (1) educational institutions and (2) state departments of education either from within the state or from another state. Specialist-consultants also are called from industry, from the United States Office of Education, and from other federal sources as well as from the several national and state associations.

Services provided by specialist-consultants at the state level are wide and varied. In summary, they are called upon to:

1. Make presentations dealing with specific content, with trends, with the interpretation of research, with objectives, and with methods of teaching;
2. Discuss reasonable standards of achievement;
3. Lead discussion groups;
4. Advise on textbooks, present instructional technology materials, give demonstration lessons, demonstrate teaching techniques, and, in the case of the consultant from industry, demonstrate vocational skills;
5. Help in production of curriculum guides;
6. Edit material; and
7. Evaluate the activities involved in a conference.

Curricular Materials: Production, Distribution, and Application

State departments of education are unanimous in the opinion that production of curricular materials is an important function, if not a major responsibility, at the state level of supervision. Such materials usually are considered as guides to be used on a voluntary basis by the schools. These curricular materials are produced to define the requirements of law and the desires of the state department of education and to suggest content and methods which are considered as most appropriate and useful. As the established standards are met, most state departments permit considerable local variation in organizing and teaching courses; indeed, the trend is toward more and more local autonomy in this area.

The Supervisor at Work at the State Department of Education

There are three typical patterns of state-local cooperation:

1. Conferences or workshops with local teachers, followed by editorial work by a small committee;
2. Workshops of local teachers to consider tentative drafts of instructional materials and to follow up with a revision of the manuscripts;

3. A preliminary period of cooperative work between state and local people utilizing workshops and conferences prior to writing the final manuscripts.

The supervisor at the state level acts as leader, organizer, reporter, consultant, evaluator, and director. The material is then distributed to teachers, who apply the course of study for a year in the classroom. On the basis of criticisms received from the teachers, revisions are made by an editorial committee. Except in a very general way, most state department supervisors have not developed an effective follow-up procedure to determine the impact of new courses of study on the instructional program.

Most state departments of education employ one or more supervisors to maintain an instructional materials library. The supervisor so employed must:

1. Organize a distribution system for films, tapes, and other materials of instructional technology so that all schools receive these materials (without charge) at regular intervals.
2. Organize instructional centers (or libraries) of these materials.
3. Help teachers make wider and better selection and use of instructional media and materials in the classroom.
4. Cooperate in the production of films, filmstrips, tape recordings, programmed materials, and radio and television programs to meet needs peculiar to the state.

Research and Experimentation

Research and experimentation in supervision fall into two general categories at the state level: (1) research and fact-finding studies and (2) state-testing programs. Schools which are to participate in the study appear to be chosen with the subject to be studied in mind. Criteria upon which schools are selected involve geographic locations, size of the community, and the social and economic backgrounds of the students. When more than one school is used the point of view is expressed that a variety of situations is desirable. Interest in the project, plus facilities and personnel to carry on the work, seem to be essential.

E. L. Morphet and C. O. Ryan[9] described various programs of state leadership in improving instruction:

1. Attempts were made to coordinate the functions of the state departments only recently.
2. Staff positions in each state were usually filled by persons holding supervisory or administrative positions within the state.
3. Principals indicated less satisfaction with the program of supervision provided by the state than did supervisors and superintendents.
4. Cooperative, directive, and indirect programs were identified. In the cooperative program local participation and planning were secured, and no direct attempts to secure statewide participation were made.
5. The cooperative program, more than the directive, stressed the importance of stimulating local initiative.
6. The indirect programs made little provision for study, experimentation, and appraisal, whereas the directive program definitely provided for a study of instructional problems by local groups.
7. The clearinghouse aspect of state leadership was an essential phase of the cooperative program.

From the above findings the following recommendations may be derived:

1. Local workers should have ultimate responsibility for procedure in programs to improve instruction.
2. Each program should provide means for facilitating local study.
3. The improvement of instruction should be regarded as a common problem of local and state educators. State supervisors should coordinate the work of groups.
4. The type of service needed by the locality, and for modifying state activity accordingly, should be determined. The cooperative program should be employed; the direct program becomes authoritarian, and the indirect program is ineffective.

[9]See Edgar L. Morphet and Charles O. Ryan, *Designing Education for the Future,* No. 3: "Planning and Effecting Needed Changes in Education" (New York: Citation Press, 1967), and William Marvin Alexander, "State Leadership in Improving Instruction" (Doctoral dissertation, Teachers College, Columbia University, 1940).

From a practical point of view, the major responsibility of state departments of education is to assure the opportunity for all children to acquire a basic education. The fundamental program must be continually revised, augmented, and improved in order to keep abreast of changing times. The most successful approach to this goal has been to enlist the help of people with firsthand experience, and to bring them together in large numbers in workshops and conferences, with the state's responsibility being exercised in the role of leader and coordinator. Modern transportation, the high level of teacher education, and the growing number of people with supervisory training have been important factors in making such meetings productive and highly successful.

All efforts to improve education in general, by the very nature of the problems, must be experimental. Courses of study or curriculum guides should be revised at least every five years. These periodic revisions, together with the experimental method, make for a state of dynamic flux, ever striving toward improvement in our educational system.

One of the most important by-products that accrues in a democratic society is the progress made through maximal utilization of our human resources. Teamwork between the educational specialist and the classroom teacher, between state departments and private educational organizations, and between state and local administrators results in more effective education.

Problems in the State Program for Supervision

There are two persistent problems that burden and tend to decelerate the rate of progress in supervision at the state level. One is communication. Part of the problem exists between specialist-consultants and people who apply the suggested principles. Part of the difficulty is in effectively disseminating results of current research to teachers and to principals. Furthermore, there is a need for continuous evaluation of public opinion and its effects on the success or failure of a program. There is a great need not merely to keep the public informed, but to interest the general public in the welfare of the schools and to gain support for programs: *to communicate*. All means available are being put to use: the press, radio, television, recordings, private publications, and organizations.

Another persistent problem is the compelling need for repeated fact-finding studies and research geared to answer the following questions:

1. What is the nature of the school problems in this state?
2. What has research made available to help us solve these problems?
3. How can sufficiently trained and experienced people be made available to handle these studies?

In summary, effective communication, intensive and extensive research, and a continuously applied program of evaluation are essential to progress. The state department of education has a vital role in the area of educational legislation. It must perform the research needed to outline legislation, and must recommend such legislation to the elected representatives of the people.

Professional organizations concerned with school supervision should bring needed legislation to the attention of state departments of education. Through cooperation between all agencies seeking better education it is possible to secure needed legislation. In this way the state can exert leadership toward better instruction for children.

As a Supervisor at the State Level,

DO

1. Work to outline and obtain support for passing needed legislation.
2. Maintain an adequate curriculum materials and instructional media laboratory and information retrieval system.
3. Provide needed specialist-consultant services to the offices of the several intermediate unit superintendents and, if authorized, to the local school systems. Channel such services through the intermediate unit.
4. Provide for a liaison with university education departments.
5. Serve as a clearinghouse for instructional research and special programs throughout the state.
6. Provide essential liaison with the U.S. Office of Health, Education, and Welfare and with other federal agencies.

DON'T

1. Fail to provide for full-time staff personnel assignments to handle federally funded programs.
2. Fail to adequately assist local school systems and community colleges in becoming aware of keeping up-to-date concerning and applying for the several federal and state grants which may be available.
3. Bypass the intermediate unit by giving direct service to the local system, except in special authorized circumstances and with wholehearted support from the intermediate unit staff.
4. Be slow in responding to questions and requests from local school system and intermediate unit personnel.

Supervisory Problems

Problem 1

The Deputy Superintendent of Public Instruction has written you indicating his interest in the establishment of an adequate "really complete and functioning curriculum materials center" in the State Department of Education and asks that you accept the assignment. How would you go about your task, assuming that the State Board of Education has authorized released time for you and two assistants and has provided the necessary funding for the project?

> *Exactly what steps would you take?*
>
> *What materials and services would you recommend be available in such a curriculum center at the state level?*
>
> *How would you determine the adequacy of your suggestions?*
>
> *How would you provide for evaluation and feedback concerning these factors?*

Problem 2

The Educational Finance Committee of the State Legislature has asked you to appear as a resource person at its current budget hearings. You have one week to prepare for your appearance. You know that there is much sentiment on the committee to "economize," especially in what one assemblyman termed "the flowery frills of schooling nowadays." Further, you have heard that several committee members are dissatisfied with "those ethnic—so-called—studies programs," as a senior assemblyman put it. As curriculum specialist for the State Departemt of Education:

How would you prepare for your appearance before the legislative committee?

What areas would you anticipate as being most vulnerable to the economy thrust?

What points would you plan to emphasize during your appearance?

Selected Bibliography

Books

Butts, R. Freeman, and Lawrence A. Cremin. *A History of Education in American Culture.* New York: Henry Holt and Company, Inc., 1953.

DeYoung, Chris A. *Introduction to American Public Education.* New York: McGraw-Hill Book Company, Inc., 1950.

Frey, Sherman H., and Keith R. Getschman. *School Administration: Selected Readings.* New York: Thomas Y. Crowell Company, 1969.

Grieder, Calvin, and W. E. Rosenstengle. *Public School Administration.* New York: The Ronald Press Company, 1954.

Gwynn, J. Minor. *Theory and Practice of Supervision.* New York: Dodd, Mead, & Company, 1961.

Moehlman, Arthur B. *School Administration.* Rev. ed. Boston: Houghton Mifflin Company, 1951.

Reeder, Ward G. *The Fundamentals of Public School Administration.* New York: The Macmillan Company, 1951.

Periodicals

Atkinson, Byron H. "What Is a Modern State Board of Education?" *American School Board Journal* CXXVII (November 1953): 25–26.

Fuller, Edgar. "Public Schools and Separation of Church and State." *School Executive* LXVIII (February 1949): 11–18.

Simpson, Roy E. "The Place of the State Superintendent in Public Education." *California Schools* XXI (September 1950): 307–312.

Other Sources

Alexander, William Marvin. "State Leadership in Improving Instruction." Doctoral dissertation, Teachers College, Columbia University, 1940.

American Association of School Administrators. "Leadership at the State Level." Chapter XIII in *The American School Superintendent,* Thirtieth Yearbook of the Association. Washington, D.C.: The Association, 1952.

Council of State Governments. *The Forty-Eight State School Systems.* Chicago: The Council, 1949.

Cummings, H. H., and H. K. Mackintosh. *Curriculum Responsibilities of State Departments of Education.* Washington, D.C.: Government Printing Office, 1958.

LaFranchi, Edward H. "School Organization and Administration." Los Angeles: Department of Administration and Supervision, School of Education, University of Southern California, 1954. (Duplicated material copyrighted by the author.)

Rich W. B. *Approval and Accreditation of Public Schools.* Washington, D.C.: Government Printing Office, 1960.

Texas Education Agency, *Principles and Standards for Accrediting Elementary and Secondary Schools,* Bulletin No. 560. Austin: Texas Education Agency, July 1957.

U.S. Department of Health, Education, and Welfare, *Curriculum Responsibility of State Departments of Education.* Washington, D.C.: Government Printing Office, 1958.

The Role of the Federal Government in Supervision

Education, a function of the state and the responsibility of the local school system, is, without question, a national concern of great proportion. Yet as E. Benedetti emphasized, "It is incredible that a problem of such magnitude received no specific mention in the Federal Constitution."[1]

Surely any intention relating to supervision of instruction that the Federal Government entertained under the implied powers of the Constitution disappeared when the Tenth Amendment was adopted. This amendment confirmed that the powers not delegated by the Constitution of the United States, nor prohibited by it to the states, are reserved to the states, respectively, or to the people.

The Federal Government is endowed only with enumerative powers; since education is not specifically designated as a federal function, the Tenth Amendment has been interpreted as granting to the individual states plenary control over the administration of public education.[2]

The general welfare clause of the Federal Constitution, Article I, Section A, did render some federal participation in education possible, for it stipulated, "Congress shall have power to . . . provide for the common defense and general welfare . . . ." In 1962 the Supreme Court of the United States enjoined the schools of the State of New York from requiring pupils to participate in a morning prayer. This prayer had been prepared under the supervision of, and had been approved by, the New York State Board of Regents. The Federal Government, then, does have some role in education in general, and in school supervision in particular.

The American School System

American Education: A Most Complex Industry

AMERICAN EDUCATION BECOMES BIG BUSINESS. E. Stoops and M. L. Rafferty stressed the fact that more and more people go to school each year:

---

[1] Eugene Benedetti, "Legal Aspects of School Administration" (Duplicated material copyrighted by the author. Los Angeles: 1956), p. 2.
[2] Ibid.

From a meager beginning in the Colonies, with Dame Schools or Bible study for a negligible percentage of the population, school enrollments rose to about the 42 million mark in 1957–58, and were more than 45 million in 1960–61.[3]

Relationships between Federal, State, and Local Governments

THE AMERICAN SCHOOLS ARE A PRODUCT OF, ARE RESPONSIBLE TO, AND ARE OWNED BY THE PEOPLE. Stoops and Rafferty noted that the underlying principle of the American system of public education is its lack of system:

> It is at once the despair of the logical French, the scientific German, and the traditional English. In other lands the schools belong to the government and are administered by government bureaus and appointees. They are financed through national taxes and directed by a Secretary of Education. This enables the school systems in these countries to operate independently of local whims and upheavals and . . . insures a maximum of uniformity in school procedures. Indeed, some can state with confidence the subject, unit, and text chapter being studied in every classroom of the nation. Such uniformity . . . involves the granting of huge powers to the national government in the field of education, and a corresponding lessening of local control.[4]

Where other nations have proudly set up educational superstructures of gigantic proportions, the United States proudly points to a system of education in which the separate states of the union are completely independent; there is no national school system in the United States.

RELATIONS AND FUNCTIONS. One of the distinctive features of the American public schools is the relationship between the federal, state, and local levels of control. In Colonial times poor transportation made it difficult to supervise instruction in the schools located at opposite sides of the township. Thus, small separate districts and school systems developed.

State governments have responsibility for the educational systems, with certain powers delegated to local school districts. All of the states have established machinery for the administration and supervision of the school systems, and most states have state boards of education and a chief state school officer.

[3]Emery Stoops and M. L. Rafferty, Jr., *Practices and Trends in School Administration* (Boston: Ginn and Company, 1961), p. 15.
[4]Ibid.

More than half of the states have provided for a district system of local control of education, eight states have a township organization, twelve have an intermediate unit or county system, and two states, Hawaii and Delaware, have one massive school system for the entire state. Alaska follows closely.

Most of the states with a district system of control are located in the western part of the United States, while those with a township organization are located in the northeast. Most of these school systems operate under the county intermediate system. The parish system in Louisiana is included in this group.

IMPLICATIONS FOR THE SUPERVISION OF INSTRUCTION. The implications of the relationships between the federal, state, and local governments in the educational enterprise are many. The supervising principal must acquaint the professional staff with the obligations concerning mandatory, permitted, and prohibited instruction and classroom organization derived from laws, rules, regulations, and judicial decisions at the federal, state, and local levels.

For example, in the famous Oregon case the United States Supreme Court indicated that while the states could require school attendance, they could not require attendance in a public school. In the Everson case the court further declared that public funds could be used to provide free transportation for parochial school students under certain conditions. In the McCollum case it stated that released and dismissed time for religious education programs could not be conducted on public school property.

The Supreme Court had claimed jurisdiction in these cases by virtue of the First and Fourteenth Amendments to the Constitution. The First Amendment stated that "Congress shall make no law respecting an establishment of religion or prohibiting the free exercise thereof . . . or the right of people peaceably to assemble . . . ." The Fourteenth Amendment stipulated "nor shall any state deprive any person of life, liberty, or property without due process of law; nor deny to any person within its jurisdiction the equal protection of the laws."[5] The supervising principal must be aware of federal court decisions that have implications for the instructional program of the

[5]See Eugene Benedetti, "Federal Government Has a Bigger Stake in Schools," *Nation's Schools* LV (March 1955), 61; and Newton Edwards, *The Courts and the Public Schools* (Chicago: University of Chicago Press, 1955).

3
SUPPLEMENT

school, for the teacher, and for the student. Certainly he must keep abreast of laws that would authorize federal funding of programs aimed at the improvement of instruction.

History of Governmental Aid and Support for Supervision

The salary of a grammar school teacher in New England, in the Colonial period, probably ranged from twenty to sixty pounds a year, which would be roughly equivalent to $50 to $100. Meals and lodging were provided also. The higher paid teachers were in the middle socioeconomic class, while the more poorly paid teachers were in the lower class status and were comparable to tradesmen. "Salaries were often irregular in payment and often were paid in produce or livestock rather than in cash."[6]

In the Colonial period teachers did not think of themselves as part of a professional group. There were no professional organizations and fraternities, and no standards concerning preparation. By 1860 America's state school system had taken form. Twenty years prior to that time, it was the rule for New England children to have formal education.

R. F. Butts and L. A. Cremin noted that one of the most bitter struggles in securing public common schools was the struggle for public support. Certainly there were different rates of progress toward this goal in different states and sections of the country; there were many different kinds of public support for the schools including income from public lands, the Federal Government, fines and license fees, and public lotteries.

Finally the Land Ordinance of 1785 was passed by the Continental Congress. This ordinance provided that the sixteenth section of every township must be dedicated for the maintenance of public schools within the said township.

Two years later, in the Northwest Ordinance of 1787, Congress included Article III that stated "religion, morality, and knowledge being necessary to good government and the happiness of mankind, schools and the means of education shall forever be encouraged."

[6]R. Freeman Butts and Lawrence A. Cremin, *A History of Education in American Culture* (New York: Henry Holt and Company, 1953), p. 134.

SUPPLEMENT

3

In Massachusetts the legislature, following the arguments of James G. Carter, made compulsory the support of schools entirely by taxation in 1827. In 1834 a common school fund was established. In New England the principle of public support clearly had been accepted by the time of the Civil War.

Public Law 864, the National Defense Education Act of 1958, provided for loans to students and institutions of higher education; financial assistance for strengthening instruction in science, mathematics, and modern languages; national defense scholarships; funds for research and experimentation; more effective utilization of television, radio, and motion pictures for educational purposes; authorization for a national science foundation to establish a science information service and a science information council; and for the authorization of funds to improve the statistical services of state agencies.

General Federal Activities Affecting Supervision

The U.S. Office of Education

HISTORY OF THE OFFICE. The common school revival, as expounded by its champion Horace Mann in the Massachusetts of the 1840's, caused the people of the several states to think in terms of education and the improvement of the educational enterprise.

It was Henry Barnard who led the movement for a national education agency. C. A. DeYoung[7] noted that in 1866 a history-making proposal was presented to Congress by President James A. Garfield. This proposal was adopted by the National Association of State and City School Superintendents, which is now the American Association of School Administrators. It advocated the establishment of a federal bureau of education.

A public law authorizing the Department of Education was approved on the 2nd of March 1867. Originally adopted during the presidency of Andrew Johnson, it reads as follows:

Be it enacted *by the Senate and the House of Representatives of the United States of America, in Congress Assembled,* that there shall be established in the

[7]Chris A. DeYoung, *Introduction to American Public Education* 2d ed. (New York: McGraw-Hill Book Company, Inc., 1950), p. 23.

city of Washington, a department of education, for the purpose of collecting such statistics and facts as shall show the condition and progress of education in the several states and territories, and of diffusing such information respecting the organization and management of schools and school systems and methods of teaching as shall aid the people of the United States in the establishment and maintenance of efficient school systems, and otherwise PROMOTE THE CAUSE OF EDUCATION throughout the country.

39th Congress, 2nd Session
Approved by President Andrew Johnson
2 March 1867

In 1869, due to the opposition of several of the states, the department was made an office of education in the Department of the Interior. This title was changed in 1870 to the Bureau of Education, but was restored in 1929 as the Office of Education. In 1939, on the first of July, the Office of Education was transferred from the Department of the Interior to the Internal Security Agency, and in the 1950's was placed under the Department of Health, Education, and Welfare.

ACTIVITIES OF THE U.S. OFFICE OF EDUCATION IN THE FIELD OF SUPERVISION. The major duties that were enumerated in the basic law include the collection of statistics and facts promoting the cause of education in general, and the diffusion of information concerning the schools. Certainly the collecting, sifting, and organizing of statistics and facts in a country as far-flung and as full of school districts and systems as is the United States is a colossal task.[8]

The office diffuses information through its many conferences, exhibits, publications, letters, broadcasts, telecasts, and surplus property information center, and through the exchange of books, radio and television scripts, transcriptions, tape recordings, and motion picture material. The monthly periodical *School Life* as well as mimeographed circulars are printed by the Superintendent of Documents, Government Printing Office, Washington, D.C., 20025.

THE U.S. OFFICE AS A CLEARING HOUSE. From 1867 through 1906 a large amount of biographical historical research was published by the office. Since

---

[8]Ibid., p. 25.

the Indians of Alaska came under the jurisdiction of the office at this time, the education of Indian children was provided for by the office. Since 1917 the establishment of vocational education, under the Smith-Hughes Act, has added many responsibilities to the Office of Education.

Stoops and Rafferty emphasized:

It is in the field of services, however, that the office probably will play its most important role. A city . . . superintendent of schools today owes much of his success as an . . . [educator] to the research findings released at periodic intervals by the United States Office of Education. Statistics on almost every conceivable subject . . . related to education are painstakingly collected, correlated, and charted by the office personnel and made available, without cost, to educators . . . .[9]

Such services as these help to remove much of the guesswork from the field of school supervision and have made possible scientific planning on the part of the school supervisor. Included in the list of individuals and organizations who have made use of the United States Office of Education's services are (1) service clubs, (2) patriotic societies, (3) farmers' organizations and associations, (4) business and professional associations, (5) state school systems, (6) local school systems, (7) private schools, (8) colleges and universities, (9) public libraries, (10) foreign students and educators, (11) radio and television broadcasting stations and systems, (12) national, state, and local parent's associations, (13) educational associations, (14) labor groups, and (15) social-and service-civic organizations.

FURTHER ACTIVITIES OF THE U.S. OFFICE OF EDUCATION, AND IMPLICATIONS FOR SUPERVISION. The publication *Educational Teleguide,* issued by the U.S. Department of Health, Education and Welfare, is useful in the location of information concerning education on television. A. J. Burke and C. Alexander described the U.S. Office of Education publications as gold mines for both the practical school man and the research worker: "Sooner or later research in every phase of education is sure to be discussed and supplied with references in these publcations."[10]

---

[9]Stoops and Rafferty, *Practices and Trends,* pp. 22–23.
[10]Arvid J. Burke and Carter Alexander, *How to Locate Educational Information and Data* (New York: Bureau of Publications, Teachers College, Columbia University, 1958), p. 247.

In addition to the many bulletins, circulars, and pamphlets which are issued, the *Biennial Survey of Education,* including statistical and textual résumés of educational conditions in the United States, the *Education Directory,* the *Vocational Division Bulletins, Higher Education,* and *School Life* are published.

Many biographies have been issued that apply to the field of supervision, as have Guidance Leaflets, Higher Education Circulars, Home Economics Circulars, Industrial Circulars, International Education, Kindergarten Circulars, and posters, charts, and similar materials. A valuable series, published from 1926 to 1940, were the *Research Studies in Education.*

The supervising principal should write to the Librarian, U.S. Office of Education, Department of Health, Education, and Welfare, Washington, D.C., 20025, as well as to the Superintendent of Documents, Government Printing Office, Washington, D.C., 20025, for lists of publications referring to particular topics. Complete information, specifically delimiting the data needed, should be included in the request.

The Role of U.S. Commissioner of Education in Supervision

Many illustrious individuals have served as commissioner of the Office of Education. The first commissioner was Henry Barnard, who took office in 1838. The first three secretaries of the Department of Health, Education, and Welfare were Oveta Culp Hobby, Herbert Brownell, Jr., and Abraham A. Ribicoff.

Some educators who have been known for their critical thinking in the field of school administration and supervision have suggested that the Commissioner of Education become in effect a national superintendent of schools. The U.S. Office of Education would be established as a nonpartisan, independent agency, governed by a national board of education. This board would be composed of individuals assigned for overlapping terms by the president, with the consent of the Senate. The commissioner would serve as the executive officer and the secretary of the board.

The office would be responsible for the coordination of educational functions for the Federal Government, but with all federal participation and publications in education being transmitted through the departments of education of the several states.

Other individuals have gone so far as to suggest the need for a national curriculum, and for national control to the extent that the states now control education. The specifics of administration, curriculum, instruction, and student personnel services would remain with the individual school systems, as is now the case, within certain prescribed limits. The functions now served by the state legislatures would continue within prescribed limits established by Congress and the national board of education.

Still others in the areas of school supervision and administration have suggested that all federal support for education should be distributed directly to the state departments of education on the basis of need, combined with a basic aid formula.

Surprisingly, an overwhelming percentage of federal monies is expended for education through agencies other than the Office of Education. Such agencies govern the military academies and the Department of Defense; the Department of Justice and prison education; the school for postal inspectors in the Post Office Department; the Library of Congress; the Copyright Office; the Government Printing Office; the Pan-American Union; the Office of Indian Affairs; the Smithsonian Institute; the National Academy of Sciences; the Commission of Fine Arts; the American Printing House for the Blind in Louisville, Kentucky; and the Columbia Institute for the Deaf in Washington, D.C.

The Tennessee Valley Authority maintains public schools and educational facilities for children as well as for adults, and special schools have been established where there exists a large concentration of federal employees overseas.

Other U.S. Government Agencies Involved in Supervision

The Department of Agriculture has been very active in the areas of home economics, biology, and agriculture. The 4H Clubs have been sponsored by the department, with many new ideas being furnished through bulletins, films, books, pamphlets, and circulars.

The Department of Commerce includes the Bureau of the Census. Its reports regarding student age, sex, and geographical distribution are very valuable. Since the Coast and Geodetic Survey, Bureau of Standards, and Environmental Sciences Division (Weather Bureau) are also included in the Department of Commerce, it is obvious that this department and its agencies provide a wealth of material with which the elementary school principal should be familiar.

The Department of Labor provides a useful service to vocational counselors and teachers through long-range employment outlook in industry. One of its chief publications is the *Dictionary of Occupational Titles.*

Conclusions

The present system of American public education, decentralized as it is, does not and should not preclude an improved federal program of cooperation, leadership, and support. The Advisory Committee on Education stated:

> Education is, in a large sense, an individual matter, but individuals compose neighborhoods and communities, communities compose states, and in the United States the states compose the nation. As are the neighborhoods so will be the states and nation.
>
> Since the formation of the Union, Americans have been citizens both of the state and of the nation. Most Americans now feel that their federal government is their agent as much as is their state government.[11]

---

[11]Advisory Committee on Education, *Report of the Committee* (Washington, D.C.: Superintendent of Documents, Government Printing Office, 1938), p. 35.

4

Organizing the Supervisory Program

The organizational plan for supervision must provide a clear definition of the responsibilities, functions, and relationships of the professional staff. The following topics are treated in this chapter:

Basic principles of organization for the supervisor

Authority and organization: how to organize and implement a supervisory program

A shared responsibility

A new type of supervisor and a new type of supervision

How to provide for managerial coordination: The roles of the principal and the superintendent

How to plan your work as a supervisor

Do—don't

"In-Basket" supervisory problems

Chapter Supplement

Basic Principles of Organization for the Supervisor

In modern organization for school supervision the direction is toward the improvement of the total teaching-learning process, which subsumes the total setting, rather than toward the more delimited aim of improving teachers in service. Modern supervision directs attention toward the fundamentals of education and the improvement of learning. The focus of supervision is on the teaching-learning situation, with the groups and individuals involved in supervision working for the improvement of the total complex. The teacher in this type of supervision becomes a cooperating member of a group dedicated to the improvement of instruction. Before this dedication is to be translated into action leading to positive results, the prime requisite of *planning* must receive due consideration.

The Need for Coordination

The all-pervasive element in the process of both administration and supervision, and which is evident in the total management process, is coordination. Without coordination, planning cannot effectively reach fruition.

A POLICY SYSTEM APPROACH TO SUPERVISORY ORGANIZATION. Generally accepted policies, especially when those policies are in written form and have been adopted by the governing board, allow the supervisory system to function properly. They facilitate planning, encourage the delegation of authority and responsibility, and permit personnel to develop a clearer, more definite conception of their responsibilities and authority.

Policies may, of course, be general in nature, touching only on the broad outlines of the supervisory organization. They may be more detailed, taking the form of standard operating procedures, which may provide exact methods for accomplishing nearly every task. As policies are developed, the supervisor must take care to insure that there is provision for amendment so that the system does not stagnate. There must be room for individual initiative; administrative flexibility must not be denied.

A POLICY HANDBOOK. The development of a policy handbook, dealing with the system for supervision, should be initiated. Such a handbook exerts a stabilizing effect upon the organization, serves as a guide to performance, and provides a standard against which to measure accomplishment. It is at once the provider of goal and direction for the supervisory system.

PLANNING, COORDINATION, STIMULATION, AND GROWTH. In supervision there should be planning, coordination, stimulation, and growth of teachers. The student should be encouraged to exercise his talents toward a richer and more intelligent participation in the society and the world in which he lives.

Only when supervision is organized, both as a creative art and as a science, will instruction and instructional procedures be improved.

Educational supervision must be organized to:

1. Help the professional staff see more clearly the goals of education, and for those working in supervision at each of the three levels of education (elementary, secondary, and higher), to see the special role of the level in which the supervisor may find himself working in achieving these goals.
2. Help teachers see more clearly the problems and needs of children and youth.
3. Provide effective democratic leadership in promoting the professional improvement of the school and its activities in fostering harmonious and cooperative staff relations, in stimulating professional in-service education of teachers, and in enhancing school-community relations.
4. Construct strong group morale, and unify teachers into an effective team working to achieve the same general goals.
5. Determine the work for which each teacher is best suited, assign him to such work, and encourage him to develop his capabilities.
6. Assist the professional staff in the development of greater competence in teaching.
7. Assist teachers new to the school system.
8. Evaluate the results of each teacher's efforts in terms of student growth toward predetermined goals.
9. Aid teachers in the diagnosis and remediation of learning difficulties.
10. Interpret the instructional program to the community.
11. Protect the professional staff from unreasonable demands and from unwarranted, negative criticism.

The organizational format for the supervisory program must be clear as to what is to be achieved. The means which are to be employed must be chosen with a view toward appropriateness and toward the probability of their achieving the desired results. The program must have purpose and organization, related activities, and consistent objectives. Without these three the system breaks down.

A program of supervision must be a program of educational improvement.
Although many kinds of supervision are possible, supervisory activities may
be organized according to four general classifications: (1) creative, (2)
constructive, (3) preventative, and (4) corrective.[1]

The Systems Approach to Supervisory
Organization: Guidelines for Implementation

The following list of basic principles may be employed as a guide by the
professional staff in organizing for school supervision:

1. All major functions to be performed must be grouped with administrative or management positions to direct them. Such functions should be
   combined in closely related groups of similar functions to insure their
   coordination.

2. The number of persons directly responsible to a school system administrative officer should not exceed that which can be given reasonably
   adequate supervision. No position should be responsible to more than
   one higher position.

3. Titles should be used which indicate the level of control assigned to the
   several administrative positions. Titles used for school level positions
   should not be the same as for school system level positions. Similarly,
   titles used for the classified management positions should not be the
   same as those used for certificated positions. Such consistency can be
   of great help to school system personnel and the general public in understanding the staff organization.

4. School system level administrative and supervisory positions should be
   staffed on a full-time basis. This also applies to special service and special teaching positions although not quite to the same degree.

5. School system level administrative personnel should be employed on
   a twelve calendar month basis. Principals should be employed on a
   twelve school months basis. Other supervisory, special service, and
   special teaching positions typically should be staffed on the basis of
   eleven school months annually. Clerical positions generally should be

[1]See William H. Burton and Leo J. Brueckner, *Supervision,* 3d ed. (New York: Appleton-Century-Crofts, 1955), chapter V.

assigned on the same annual service basis as the management position to which they are attached.

6. All administrative and supervisory positions should be aided by an appropriate number of clerical employees. In no instance should well paid, highly trained personnel find it necessary to do a large part of their own clerical work.

7. An efficient organization must be planned to meet the needs of the school system, and personnel must be employed to fit the organization, rather than providing a plan around the personnel which a school system may happen to have in its employ at any given time.

8. An organizational pattern should be sufficiently flexible to allow the addition of staff members in existing types of positions and to permit the creation of new types of positions as required to care for school system growth, without altering the basic design of the organization. Patterns of organization should be designed to permit full compliance with this standard.

9. Good school system organization requires that there be a plan for the coordination of the administrative and supervisory functions, as well as of special service and special teaching functions. This normally is accomplished, in part, by a schedule of regular meetings between staff members.

10. Administrative-supervisory staff, special service personnel, and clerical assistants should have a place where they can work under conditions of comfort and efficiency. This means adequate office space with modern facilities and good conditions for effective and harmonious relationships. Lack of adequately planned and interrelated office spaces, adequate workrooms, and adequate lounge and restroom facilities for the school system level staff definitely reduces the efficiency of the staff. Similarly, inadequate provisions for maintenance and warehousing make these services less efficient.[2]

11. Authority should be delegated commensurate with the assignment of responsibility. High level supervisory and administrative positions should be free to provide a high level type of leadership, rather than to

[2]Irving R. Melbo et al., "Report of the Survey, Taft City School District" (Los Angeles: July 1960).

be occupied with details appropriate for delegation to lower level positions. Authority and responsibility should be delegated sufficiently to prevent the creation of the type of bottlenecks which occur when too great amounts of detail must cross the desk of top administrators.
12. Efficient functioning of school system organization depends, in large measure, upon effective channels of communication. Such channels should be clear-cut, two-way, short, and direct.

Coordination: a Universal Requirement

O. Tead[3] reported that a growing organization arises from a deliberate association of persons desiring to accomplish something together; to realize certain defined objectives which, as individuals, the persons either could not do for themselves or could not do so well. The customary outcome of intensive human relations is the development of a satisfying camaraderie. The task of keeping this sentiment flourishing is a challenge to supervisory skill.

Authority and Organization: How to Organize and Implement a Supervisory Program

General Principles of Organization

There are four basic general principles concerning organization with which the supervisory principal should be familiar:

1. The learning situation for students can be improved by the proper administrative organization of personnel engaged in supervisory services.
2. Organization for supervision should be based upon a generally accepted philosophy of education for the school system.
3. The governing board, as a policy-making body, has full authority over the supervisory program and should delegate responsibility and authority for administration of the program to the superintendent.

---

[3]Ordway Tead, *The Art of Administration* (New York: McGraw-Hill Book Company, Inc., 1951).

4. The school's organization for supervision should be appraised continuously and should be revised in the light of the appraisal.

Principles of External Organization

The generally accepted principles of *external* organization are essentially as follows:

1. Authority is centralized in the legally appointed person at the head.
   a) The superintendent of schools is, in the last analysis, responsible for the general instructional policy of the school system.
   b) The superintendent in a large school system should delegate the supervisory responsibility to a single assistant.
   c) The assistant superintendent in charge of instruction should serve in behalf of the superintendent in dealing with the supervising principal.
   d) The principal should be the administrative executive-in-charge of instruction within the school unit. He should be directly responsible to the superintendent or to the assistant superintendent.
   e) Supervisory staff members, including general supervisors, special subject supervisors, psychologists, research specialists, and others, should serve both teachers and the principal in an advisory relationship, and they should be responsible to the superintendent or the assistant superintendent.
2. The teacher should be responsible directly to the principal for the instructional program within the classroom.
3. The lines and channels through which delegated authority and responsibility flow should be defined sharply and unambiguously.
   a) The delegation of responsibility should follow clearly defined policies, and it should be set forth in writing.
   b) By means of periodic reports members of the supervisory staff should keep the superintendent informed concerning activities and achievements related to delegated responsibilities; the superintendent, likewise, should keep the staff informed concerning board policies related to supervision.
   c) Provisions must be made so that each individual or area in the

organization may be reached expeditiously from any higher administrative level.

d) Provision must be made for appeal from any individual or level to
higher administrative levels.

e) No individual should receive complete directions covering precisely
the same item from more than one person. (Assignments, notices,
and directions to teachers should originate with the principal.)

f) The performance of duties assigned to any level must be checked by
the next higher levels throughout the system.

4. Staff officers are instructional experts and consultants; they are thus differentiated from the line officers. Further, they have no executive power.

a) A principal is both an administrative and a supervisory officer.

b) The principal, in his supervisory capacity, may render his most effective service through direct assistance: visiting and conferring with
individual teachers; helping with individual students; making immediate suggestions; helping with lesson plans, devices, and units.

c) The general or special supervisors or "specialist-consultants" from
the central office may render their most effective services through
indirect and more remote assistance: making or taking leadership
in preparing courses of study, providing materials, interpreting standards, and helping principals and groups of teachers.

d) The bulk of everyday classroom visitation may be taken over by
the principal; the central office supervisor's visits usually occur upon
request.[4]

These principles are practically self-explanatory and will be familiar to
advanced students and workers in the field.

Principles of Internal Organization

The principles of *internal* organization are:

1. Facility for cooperation and coordination must be provided.

a) A common theory of education, a common technology, and common
goals must be established.

[4]Burton and Brueckner, *Supervision*, p. 103.

b) The work of the line officers and that of the staff officers must be coordinated by common planning under a deputy superintendent or some form of supervisory council.

c) Below the level of general coordination there should be many interlocking committees, conference groups, and small subcommittees.

d) Cases of conflict or disagreement between any officers or groups must be settled by the next higher administrative officer, and ultimately by the superintendent.

2. There must be flexibility of operation.

a) Adjustment of strictly logical lines and duties must be made when local circumstances demand it (type of community, size of system, traditions, previous policies, training, experience, and personalities.

b) Line officers, in some instances, perform duties which ordinarily are assigned to staff officers. The reverse is true only on special occasions.

c) A clear distinction should be made between authoritative (line) and advisory (staff) relationships.

d) *A linear responsibility chart,* which would go beyond the usual, simple display of lines of authority and communication should be developed. By using special symbols this chart should reveal job title–responsibility couplings such as: (1) advisory–consultive, (2) technical, (3) informational, (4) managerial, (5) operational, (6) supervisory, and (7) specialty.

VERTICAL AND HORIZONTAL ORGANIZATION. In vertical organization, supervisors are advisers concerning instructional conditions in a given subject or curriculum area throughout all grades. In horizontal organization, supervisors work only in given school divisions such as primary, upper elementary, secondary, or higher education.

Vertical supervision is strong in securing unity, coordination, integration, and articulation of materials and methods within each field. It is weak in that it tends to keep subjects or areas separate and provides less correlation between subjects or areas. It sometimes fails to secure integration of subjects or areas required by the objectives of the school.

Horizontal supervision is strong in securing unity and integration between subjects or areas within the delimitations of divisional levels. Its weaknesses lie in its possible failure to articulate between levels and in a possible lack of provision for expert specialist-consultant services in the individual subject matter fields.

Choice between the systems depends upon the training and attitudes of the given staff and upon local traditions. Staff specialist-consultants in conventional line-and-staff serve all principals and teachers.

A schematic representation of dualistic line organization for school supervision is included as Figure 4–1. In this type of organizational plan, both superintendent and business manager report directly to the governing board. The superintendent, then, who should be the champion of the instructional program, does not have the power of the purse (or the ear of the governing board concerning that power), whereas the individual who *does* have that power (or ear) may lack an instructional orientation. Problems in communications and in goal determination would most certainly reign in a school system where the dualistic plan was entertained.

A Shared Responsibility

Surely the program for school supervision is one in which the entire professional staff must assume certain duties and responsibilities.

As time goes on and organizations become growing concerns, with an established pattern of purposes and activities, a certain momentum usually is achieved; and supervisors often tend to assume that the agency will continue to function effectively. The supervisors may even assume further that all involved in the operation are anxious to seek the established goals. An immediate and continuing concern of the organization's leaders is for each new member to know what the organization seeks, and why, how, and where he shares its efforts and benefits.

The best type of school system organizational plan is the one which best supports the instructional program. Instruction is the only reason a school system has for existing. All other functions simply are supportive and facilitating in nature. They are not independent, nor are they justified in their own right. An organizational pattern which fulfills these requisites is represented in Figure 4–2. It recognizes the integral nature of all phases of the educational program. In this *unit plan*, the several supportive functions are coordinated under a central administration in such a way as to exert the efforts of many individuals toward a common goal: more effective instruction.

Figure 4–3 illustrates various relationships within the school system.

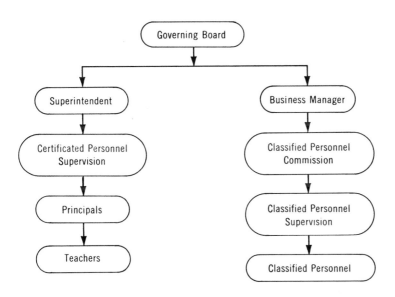

FIGURE 4–1   Dualistic Line Organization for Supervision—Not Recommended.

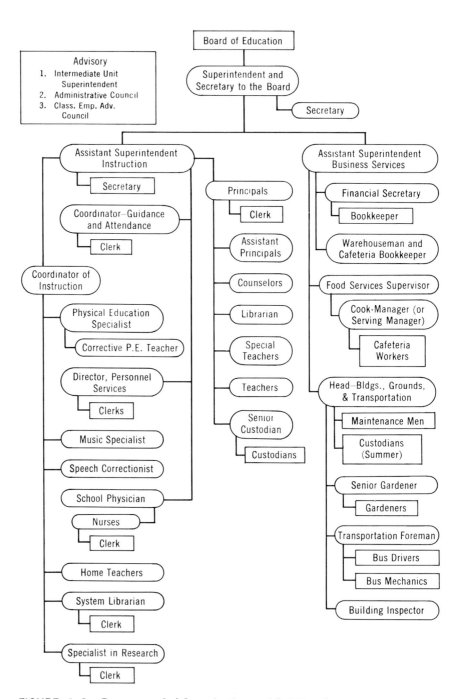

FIGURE 4–2 Recommended Organization and Relationships.

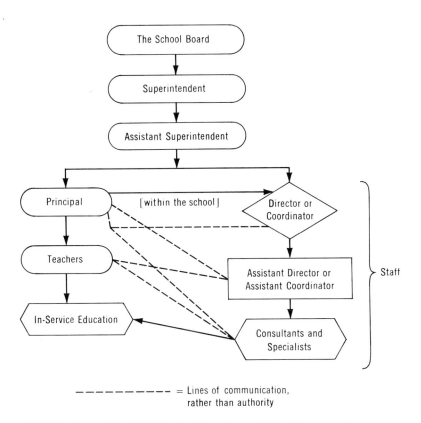

FIGURE 4–3   The Staff Works Together in School Supervision.

Legal Bases for Supervisory Organization

A public school teacher, supervising principal, specialist-consultant, or superintendent is subject to the authority of state codes and of the governing board. The legal responsibilities of certificated employees have been defined in general by the judiciary:

1. Public school teachers must be under the actual control and supervision of responsible school authorities,[5] and they must perform their labors

[5]New Mexico, Zellers v. Huff, 236 P. 2nd 949, 55 N. M. 501.

and duties under the control and direction of the school board in conformity to such lawful rules and regulations as the board may adopt or as may be imposed by statute.[6]

2. It has been held that the duties of school teachers are not defined or created by statute, but arise directly from the contract of hiring entered into by them with the school board,[7] and their power and duties are prescribed and limited thereby.[8]

3. It is the duty of a teacher to conduct himself in such a way as to command the respect and good will of the community, even though one result of the choice of a teacher's vocation may be to deprive him of the same freedom of action enjoyed by persons of other vocations.[9]

4. A supervising principal or a superintendent of a public school is subject at all times to the supervision and control of the school board or governing body of the school in all activities connected with the business of the school. The school specialist-consultant is, likewise, under the supervision and control of the governing board.[10]

5. A principal has the right to make and enforce proper and reasonable rules and regulations for teachers to follow,[11] but he cannot, in violation of statute, act as principal of any school other than the one for which he has been legally employed.[12]

6. The teacher is responsible, not to the public nor to the patrons of the school, but to the proper school officers, the trustees or board of education, the intermediate superintendent, and the state superintendent of public instruction.[13]

7. A superintendent has general supervision over the schools of the sys-

[6]New York, Parrish v. Moss, 106 N.Y.S. 2nd 5773, affirmed 107 N.Y.S. 2nd 580, 279 App. Div. 608.

[7]Pennsylvania, Malone v. Hayden, 197 A. 344, 329 Pa. 213.

[8]Iowa, Whitney v. Rural Independent School District No. 4 of Lafayette Township, 4 N.W. 2nd 394, 140 A.L.R. 1376.

[9]Donald Piety, "Legal Aspects of Recruitment, Selection, and Assignment of Certificated Personnel in Public Schools as Shown by Court Decisions, 1956" Doctoral dissertation, University of Southern California, 1956), p. 146.

[10]Massachusetts, Russell v. Gannon, 183 N.E. 736, 281 Mass. 398.

[11]Pennsylvania, Appeal of Cable, 61 Pa. Dist. and County 298.

[12]California, Cloverdale Union High School District v. Peters, 264 P. 273, 88 Cal. App. 731.

[13]Heath v. Johnson, 15 S.E. 980, 36 W. Va. 782.

tem.[14] In the same decision it was stated that the school system superintendent performs functions different from those of a teacher.

8. It is the duty of a teacher in the public schools to exercise proper supervision over students in his charge,[15] and to exercise reasonable care to prevent injury to them.[16] The school supervising principal must assist the teacher in complying with the meaning and intent of this decision.

9. It is the duty of the teacher to exercise care in the tasks assigned to students.[17] The relationship of a teacher to a student with respect to the law applicable to the duties of a teacher in the care and custody of the student is one of *in loco parentis*.[18] This relationship may be reflected in the assignment specifications developed for the position of school teacher. The teacher must exercise such care of his students as a parent of ordinary prudence would exercise under comparable circumstances.[19]

10. Where required by statute, it is the duty of teachers to observe the conduct of students to and from school, on the playground, and during any intermission.[20] The organization for school supervision must provide for assistance in this area.

11. Teachers may *not* be required to perform janitorial services, police service (traffic duty), nor school bus driving service.[21]

12. The term principal, or supervising principal, is commonly applied to the head of the school,[22] and it has been held to apply equally to elementary and high schools.[23]

13. A school principal, supervising principal, or specialist-consultant is the servant and agent of the school board.[24]

---

[14]Montana-State ex rel. Howard v. Irleland, 138 P. 2nd 569.
[15]New York, Miller v. Board of Education, Union School District No. 1, Town of Albion, 50 N.E. 2nd 529.
[16]New York, La Dalley v. Stamford, 272 App. Div. 183.
[17]New York, Gobel v. Board of Education of the City of Albany, 48 N.Y.S. 2nd 299, 267 App. Div. 621, affirmed 60 N.E. 2nd 133.
[18]Gaincott v. Davis, 275 N.W. 299.
[19]Ohman v. Board of Education of the City of New York, 90 N.E. 2nd 474. Reargument denied: 93 N.E. 2nd 927.
[20]Nevada, Nevada Industrial Commission v. Leonard, 68 P. 2nd 576.
[21]Parrish v. Moss. Reasonable hours for teachers are covered in 85 N.E. 2nd 792.
[22]A. S. Barr, William H. Burton, and Leo J. Brueckner, *Supervision* (New York: D. Appleton-Century Company, Inc., 1947), p. 11.
[23]Ibid., p. 12.
[24]Pennsylvania, Howell v. Kingston Township School District, 161 A. 559.

14. Although a superintendent has been held to be an executive officer and a public officer,[25] he also has been held to be an employee.[26]

Organizing the Work of the Supervisors of the School System

Knowledge of the teaching personnel is as necessary to the determination of policies as is a knowledge of the community. Democratic organization, moreover, demands that the teachers participate in establishing policies for the system as a whole, as well as for their individual schools. It is, therefore, highly important that provision be made for direct contact between the supervisory personnel and the teaching staff.

THE ASSISTANT SUPERINTENDENT IN CHARGE OF INSTRUCTION. Only a relatively small number of school systems employ assistant superintendents. The number is increasing, but it is evident that these officials are not always strictly instructional supervisors. The italicized words in the sample policy included as Figure 4–4 clearly show this, and this section is typical of most of the statements defining the duties of the assistant superintendent.

One item stands out clearly in the situation regarding the assistant superintendent: since the assistant is to act under the immediate direction of the

FIGURE 4–4   Sample Policy.

(School System), ARTICLE IV
Assistant Superintendent

SECTION 1. *Duties.* The duties of such assistant shall be those ordinarily incident to such position. He shall work and cooperate with the superintendent in all matters pertaining to school work and shall be under the direction of the superintendent in all such matters, and in the absence or disability of the superintendent, shall perform his duties.

SECTION 2. He shall, *in all matters pertaining to the financial and business interests of the schools, be under the general supervision of the superintendent alone, and shall make all reports directly to the superintendent.*

---

[25]Kansas-State ex rel. Hill v. Sinclair, 175 P. 41.
[26]Ibid.

superintendent, the superintendent may delegate to the assistant a major load of administrative duties and thus free himself to give more personal attention to instruction.[27]

FUNCTIONS OF THE ASSISTANT SUPERINTENDENT. In order to be of greatest assistance to the superintendent of schools and to be most effective in the improvement of instruction, the assistant superintendent should be assigned rather broad authority and responsibility in the area of instructional services. I. Melbo et al.[28] recommended the following functions:

1. Assist the superintendent in the program for community relations and in the development of educational policies and programs for the entire school system.
2. Assist the superintendent in the recruitment, selection, employment, induction, and assignment of certificated personnel (both regular and substitute) and in the maintenance of necessary school system personnel records for these employees.
3. Direct curriculum development, evaluation, textbooks and supplementary book adoptions, instructional procedures, and instructional material selection.
4. Direct the in-service education program.
5. Direct and coordinate the school system's program of health services and the program of education for physically handicapped children and for the home bound.
6. Supervise and coordinate the work of all personnel assigned to attached positions.

The reader may wish to compare the duties of the assistant superintendent and the superintendent as instructional leaders with the assistance of the thirty-fifth yearbook of the American Association of School Administrators.[29]

[27]Hubert Wilbur Nutt, *Current Problems in the Supervision of Instruction* (New York: Johnson Publishing Company, 1928), pp. 172–173.
[28]Melbo et al., "Report of the Survey," p. 50.
[29]American Association of School Administrators, *The Superintendent as an Instructional Leader,* Departmental Thirty-Fifth Yearbook (Washington, D.C.: The Association, 1957).

T. Freese[30] reported that the position of assistant superintendent in charge of instruction originally was established to aid the superintendent. Very little attention was given to the position until approximately 1945. Within a decade the position had become widespread in cities of over 25,000 census population, and was growing rapidly. The chief reasons for justifying the existence of the position have been the coordination and improvement of instruction and the relief given to the superintendent.

Freese recommended the creation of the position of assistant superintendent for instructional services in all school systems of over 20,000 population, and that curriculum development, supervision of instruction, and in-service education receive major emphasis.[31]

DIRECTOR OF RESEARCH. The director of research renders services such as the following:

1. Assisting the assistant superintendent in charge of instruction in the two broad areas of research and curriculum development.
2. Directing and coordinating various research projects including the retrieval, assembly, analysis, and dissemination of information, and the development of graphic and tabular representations of research results.
3. Directing and coordinating experiments in the improvement of instructional methods and materials.
4. Directing and coordinating the development of an instructional materials center.

[30]Theron Freese, "A Study of the Position of Assistant Superintendent in Charge of Instruction: Its History, Status, and Functions" (Doctoral dissertation, University of Southern California, 1955).

[31]The research of Freese may be compared with the findings of the research by Harold J. Smith, "Practices and Procedures in Recommending and Screening Candidates for the Position of Superintendent for Public School Districts in California" (Doctoral dissertation, University of Southern California, 1960), while administrative policies and practices, and their relation to teaching efficiency, are covered in a report of the research by Wilburn Smith, "Administrative Policies and Practices and Their Relation to Teaching Efficiency" (Doctoral dissertation, University of Southern California, 1954). General principles and practices in elementary supervision have been reported by Jack C. Goodwin, "Principles and Practices of Teacher Evaluation Programs in the Elementary Schools of the United States" (Doctoral dissertation, University of Southern California, 1960).

5. Directing and coordinating the utilization and evaluation of the materials of instructional technology, and of teaching laboratory programs.
6. Supervising attached personnel as required.

THE ASSISTANT PRINCIPAL. G. M. Weller[32] stated that 50 percent of a vice-principal's time was being spent in the general area of student direction and control. He suggested a more meaningful classification of duties, broken down into six primary areas: (1) student control, (2) student activity direction, (3) instructional supervision, (4) plant management, (5) community relations, and (6) miscellaneous administrative duties.

The assistant principal's responsibilities in the area of teacher evaluation were stressed by the authors in a symposium on evaluation and merit rating. The utilization of assignment specifications was implied, while the area of human dynamics was given prime focus:

> For a successful evaluation program, the administrator *must* accept the responsibility for acquainting the teacher with what is expected of [him] . . . , and what appraisal techniques are being used.
>
> . . . .
>
> In conclusion, evaluation cannot achieve its objective unless it is cooperatively approached by both teacher and administrator alike . . . supervision is a human relations study. . . . It seems . . . [the] main tasks, therefore, are determining ways of [stimulating] . . . teachers, attempting to fit method to teacher personality, and encouraging self-evaluation.[33]

ROLE OF THE SPECIALIST-CONSULTANT. In a larger school system the specialist-consultant carries as his greatest responsibilities those services which are arranged on a school system basis rather than those which are designed for a single school. Several schools may participate in the programs, and the specialist-consultant aids in the following ways:

1. Organizing and conducting workshops, institutes, and demonstrations.
2. Directing research in instruction.

[32]Gerald M. Weller, "The Role of the Boys' Vice-Principal," *Educational Administration and Supervision* XXIV (December 1938): 705–708.
[33]Emery Stoops and James R. Marks, "What About Teacher Evaluation?" *The School Executive* LXXVII (September 1957): 97.

3. Providing facilities for curriculum development.
4. Planning testing and evaluation programs.
5. Arranging for outside consultants and resource persons.
6. Informing school personnel about instructional trends and developments.

. . . .

8. Making recommendations as to instructional policy.
9. Assisting with planning school buildings and facilities.

. . . .

11. Working with colleges to plan courses for teachers and to co-ordinate practice teaching.[34]

The relationship of the specialist-consultant to the classroom teacher appears to be changing. Because of the steady growth in student enrollment, more effective ways need to be sought. The whole idea of supervision seems to be assuming broader dimensions. With this change in theory and practice comes a new emphasis:

1. The human relationship aspect of professional guidance and leadership as well as leadership in interpreting content and method.
2. The use of the team approach with the principal, teacher, and specialist-consultant working cooperatively in small group conferences, workshops, and in-service education classes for the improvement of classroom instruction.
3. The maintenance of a resource team for the coordination of central office services with the staff of the school to improve and maintain quality education.

THE SPECIALIST-CONSULTANT AND THE SUPERVISORY ORGANIZATION. The specialist-consultant usually is attached to the office of the assistant superintendent, but when he enters a school he automatically assumes the role of a staff member assisting the principal of that school. There are three cate-

[34]Clarence Fielstra, "Student Reviews of Selected Literature in the Field of Instructional Supervision," Mimeographed Monograph. (University of California at Los Angeles, 1961), p. 37.

gories of specialist-consultants: (1) specialists in specific subjects, (2) general consultants, and (3) curriculum directors or coordinators. In some school systems experienced master teacher-consultants are employed. The work of the curriculum specialist is discussed in chapter twelve.

If a school system wishes to give particular emphasis to the improvement of teaching in a specific subject, one way in which to proceed is to appoint a specialist-consultant for that subject. It is practically impossible, and perhaps this is as it should be, to make specialist-consultants understand that there are subjects other than theirs that are at least significant to the curriculum.

The general consultant is specialized more by grade level than by subject. Thus we find primary or lower grade consultants, middle grade consultants, and upper grade consultants.

THE ROLE OF THE MASTER TEACHER-CONSULTANT. The master teacher, helping teacher, or teacher-consultant, under the direction of the principal, assists the individual classroom teacher in the improvement of his instructional program. This function is, perhaps, most effectively accomplished by providing for direct and practical help in the classroom.

The master teacher-consultant, by assisting the teacher in the area of lesson planning and evaluation, becomes more aware of the teacher's immediate needs. The consultant quickly can learn the classroom needs and can help to develop the immediate strengths of the teacher. By assisting in the teaching-learning program the consultant becomes more a partner than an observer.

The teacher-consultant helps the teacher by assisting in the selection and use of teaching materials and equipment. For example, by setting up a multi-media listening center in a classroom, both the children and the teacher may be introduced to a new concept. The sharing of the new idea often results in the continuance of the teaching technique. Many new and creative ideas are gained and shared by an interested and enthusiastic teacher.

By demonstrating specific techniques and procedures, new methods of instruction are encountered by the teacher. Valuable teacher time is saved, and the result is that the children's learning experience shows growth.

Very often the beginning teacher will ask a question more readily when he feels he is working with someone who will in no way participate in his evaluation.

The master teacher-consultant aids the supervisory program by working with groups of teachers in orientation and grade-level meetings and workshops. The acceptance of these meetings is shown by the requests of the teachers for more meetings on specific subjects. The master teacher-consultant shares in planning, presenting, and evaluating these meetings.

ORGANIZATION FOR SCHOOL SUPERVISION THROUGH THE PARTICIPATION OF THE ENTIRE PROFESSIONAL STAFF. The supervisory organization should be formulated cooperatively as an expression of the combined thinking of the superintendent, principals, supervisors, teachers, and lay members of the community. A planned, effective system of communication including adequate records, information retrieval, and policy systems, through which all members may be kept informed, should be provided for in the organization. Assignment specifications should be a vital part of the organization for supervision. These specifications permit balancing work load of the professional staff both with respect to time allotted and in the number of relationships or span of control designated to each supervisor and administrator. The administrator of the future will have fewer individuals directly responsible to him. Supervisory organization in the future thus will be permanent and consistent, but will be sufficiently flexible to permit revision to meet changing needs. Information retrieval systems, coupled with advanced business data processing techniques, will be commonplace in the school system.

A New Type of Supervisor and a New Type of Supervision

The creative supervisor will continuously foster creative activity and self-leadership within his staff, helping the teachers to become less dependent upon outside direction and more reliant upon their own resources. The supervisor should feel free to advise, criticize, and make suggestions, but by directing his help toward growth in personal and professional stature he will promote and enrich the understanding and the program of his school.

W. S. Elsbree and H. J. McNally, in discussing the use of staff members in a supervisory program, stated:

The process of discovering and utilizing the talents of staff members is the function of the principal and poses a more challenging problem than giving direct counsel to teachers on how to improve their instructional methods. [35]

G. C. Kyte[36] noted that the principal's organizational activities should be governed by certain principles. An efficient principal:

1. Formulates a definite, well-organized plan of activities.
2. Provides for a democratic, cooperative program of working relations.
3. Provides for the necessary authority and definite responsibility which will insure educational leadership and professional organization.
4. Utilizes scientific knowledge, skill, and attitudes.
5. Is kind and understanding.

A second list of guides to action for the supervisor was proposed by W. G. Reeder.[37] The supervisor should:

1. Keep an open mind.
2. Employ methods which are impersonal and free from bias.
3. Realize that there are few procedures in education about which he can be sure, and nothing about which he can be dogmatic.
4. Remember that the science of education is only at its beginning.
5. Go about his work in a spirit of inquiry and humility.
6. Remember that his methods should seldom, if ever, be THE methods.
7. Make the teacher feel that he is his friend and is there to help him and his students.
8. Exemplify the spirit and the methods of democracy.

[35]Willard S. Elsbree and Harold J. McNally, *Elementary School Administration and Supervision* (New York: American Book Company, 1959), p. 59.
[36]George C. Kyte, *The Principal at Work* (rev. ed.; Boston: Ginn and Company, 1952), p. 9.
[37]Ward G. Reeder, *The Fundamentals of Public School Administration* (New York: The Macmillan Company, 1951.

Organization for supervision should direct the systematic and continuous effort to encourage a teacher to become increasingly more effective in contributing to the achievement of recognized educational objectives. T. H. Briggs and J. Justman[38] offered lists of both negative and positive principles which should influence the principal's organization for supervision.

The negative principles included the following points:

1. Supervision should seldom, if ever, be arbitrary or authoritative. It should not be based on personal power.
2. Supervision should never be divorced from a constant recognition of the goals of education.
3. Supervision should not be largely concerned with trivia, nor should it be concerned only with the immediate.
4. Supervision should never be nagging or impatient.

The positive principles in the organization of supervision included:

1. Supervision should be constructive, creative, and democratic.
2. Supervision should rely upon the collective resources of the group rather than upon the efforts of the supervisor alone, and should be based upon professional rather than personal relationships.
3. Supervision should seek to promote the growth of teachers by developing their special strengths.
4. Supervision should be concerned with the personal welfare of teachers and with good intrastaff relations.
5. Supervision should begin with conditions and practices as they are, and should be gradually but persistently progressive.
6. Supervision should be adapted within proper delimitations to the capacities, attitudes, and even the prejudices of the professional staff.
7. Supervision should be characterized by simplicity and informality, and should be cumulative in its results.
8. Supervision must be objective and rigorous in self-evaluation.

[38]Thomas H. Briggs and Joseph Justman, *Improving Instruction through Supervision* (New York: The Macmillan Company, 1952).

How to Plan Your Work as a Supervisor

Basic Aspects of Supervisory Planning

The great French industrialist and pioneer student of organization and management, Henri Fayol, reported that "if foresight is not the whole of management, at least it is an essential part of it. To foresee, in this context, means both to assess the future and make provision for it; that is, forecasting is itself action already."[39] Planning involves, then:

1. The process of fact interpretation.
2. The determination of a line of action to be taken in the light of all the data available and of the objectives sought.
3. The detailing of the steps to be taken in keeping with the action determined.
4. The making of provisions to carry through the plan to a successful conclusion.
5. The establishment and maintenance of a system of evaluation to see how close performance comes to plans.

Planning requires, then, a good deal of supervisory foresight, and requires a high degree of constructive analysis. Certainly, ability and willingness to plan is one of the essentials of supervisory leadership. If a supervisor is not willing to plan ahead to facilitate and improve instruction, he does not deserve the confidence of the educators with whom he works.

One way in which the supervisor can plan ahead is to handle routine administrative matters by bulletin or note, saving the staff meetings and conference sessions before and after school for discussion of instructional matters. If he is a teaching principal he may wish to arrange for a substitute teacher on a regular basis to permit time for classroom visitations, conferences, meetings, and other supervisory activities. It is recommended that a substitute teacher handle the principal's class at least two days per week.

The teaching principal may find that it is possible to employ older students on a part-time basis, using school district funds and/or the funds provided

[39]Henri Fayol, *General and Industrial Management* (New York: Pitman Publishing Corporation, 1949), p. 43.

by special federal programs for payroll demands of individuals so employed. These students could then handle many of the more routine responsibilities in office, supply room, and cafeteria, and could relieve the office clerk from telephone answering duties.

It is recommended that the principal plan his time by scheduling his supervisory visits and conferences through the use of a weekly schedule chart such as is found in Figure 4–5.

A school is organized that it may be administered; it is administered that instruction may take place. The major responsibility of the supervisor is to lead teachers to the steady, continuous, and progressive improvement of the curriculum, of instructional media, and of the techniques of teaching

FIGURE 4–5   Program Schedule for Planning Supervisory
Visits and Conferences

Week of School Month	School Month				
	Day				
	M	T	W	T	F
First					
	(A.M. P.M.)	(A.M. P.M.)	(A.M. P.M.)	(A.M. P.M.)	(A.M. P.M.)
Second					
	(A.M. P.M.)	(A.M. P.M.)	(A.M. P.M.)	(A.M. P.M.)	(A.M. P.M.)
Third					
	(A.M. P.M.)	(A.M. P.M.)	(A.M. P.M.)	(A.M. P.M.)	(A.M. P.M.)
Fourth					
	(A.M. P.M.)	(A.M. P.M.)	(A.M. P.M.)	(A.M. P.M.)	(A.M. P.M.)

KEY: V = Visit[a]   A = Other Appointment
       C = Conference   PR = Probationary Rating
       R = Request   T = Teaching Assignment for Principal

[a]School principals usually find it difficult to schedule more than one supervisory visit per day. The principal should attempt to visit for an entire lesson.

that enable children most assuredly and most economically to profit from it. Leadership must be democratic, constructive and creative, and professionally informed.

How to Organize

A principal will need to ask himself many questions before deciding to organize a supervisory program. He will need to decide what should and can be done to improve education. He will need to question the extent that his efforts and those of his colleagues can contribute to the improvement of supervision.

T. H. Briggs and J. Justman[40] have outlined certain steps which may be used in organizing a program of supervision, recognizing that each situation and each program must be approached in a unique manner:

1. Estimate the situation.
2. Plan the way.
3. Prepare the way.
4. Share the responsibility.
5. Get under way.
6. Guide the development.
7. Relate the program to the community.
8. Measure and evaluate progress.
9. Provide for educational continuity.

Others have listed these steps as:

1. Surveying
2. Planning
3. Organizing
4. Staffing
5. Directing
6. Coordinating, evaluating, and planning for further action
7. Reporting
8. Budgeting

[40]Briggs and Justman, *Improving Instruction through Supervision.*

In order to estimate the situation it is necessary to know facts regarding the school and its program, the students, the teaching personnel, and the community. A supervisor must know the interests, needs, attitudes, problems, accomplishments, and characteristics of various groups. Plans must fit situations and must be suited to the school. In order to insure a sound program, program planning should be a cooperative enterprise.

Abilities Prerequisite to Effective Planning

Many supervisors make the mistake of too much personal operation and too little constructive planning. If the supervisor is going to do the job he was hired to do, then a great deal of planning will be required. Since planning requires prediction, or looking ahead in terms of present and anticipated facts, it seems evident that planning requires analysis—an ability to project activities which are yet to take place.

The prerequisites to effective planning include:

1. The ability to see the entire situation—the *gestalt.*
2. The ability to analyze a problem—to break it down into its simplest elements.
3. Resourcefulness, a constructive imagination, and versatility, combined with the willingness to convert old methods into new, if warranted.
4. An analytical approach which is impersonal in nature and is not dominated by either the idols of the cave or the idols of the marketplace.
5. The willingness and ability to evaluate the effectiveness of a given plan or procedure.
6. Fortitude, personality, and capacity which permits one to avoid becoming so entangled in the details of the daily operation of the educational enterprise that there is no time left for planning.

How to Provide for Managerial Coordination: the Roles of the Principal and the Superintendent

The Principal as Instructional Leader

If we accept the premise that the prime purpose of the school is the establishment of a creative environment wherein the learning process can most effectively be achieved, then we must conclude that the principal's chief role lies in his being able to effect such an environment through dynamic leadership.

Principals place high priority on their role in the improvement of instruction. Although the increasing demands upon the principal's time tend to erode his role as an instructional leader, research[41] has indicated this area as the one of greatest concern to principals. It is the one to which principals state they most would like to devote themselves.

B. C. Browning and H. J. Otto[42] reported that superintendents view the principal as the key person in the improvement of instruction. Lack of time, involvement in a myriad of other duties, and a feeling of personal inadequacy have hampered the achievement of this goal. There remains, nevertheless, a chief goal toward which most principals are striving—the development of their professional capacities as dynamic, creative, and effective instructional leaders.

The supervising principal as an instructional leader must clear avenues for growth and improvement, identify talents and abilities in others, and release the potential within all persons concerned.

If we accept the concept of leadership in the improvement of the instructional program for the supervising principal, then the definition of responsibility becomes more meaningful and far less overpowering. The principal then becomes the coordinator of knowledge and abilities, and he strives for the development and improvement of the total instructional program.

The general structure of the instructional program is a major concern of the principal, and it requires that he assume certain vital responsibilities. Primarily, the principal must have a broad understanding of the basic purpose of education in our democratic society.

THE PRINCIPAL AND THE TEACHERS. If a principal is to practice a democratic form of leadership, there are certain attitudes which must precede practice:

[41]National Education Association, "The Principal and Supervision," *The National Elementary Principal,* Thirty-Seventh Yearbook (Washington, D.C.: National Education Research Division, 1958).
[42]Bruce C. Browning and Henry J. Otto, *Organization for Instructional Supervision in Elementary Schools,* A Monogram (Austin: University of Texas, 1957).

1. He must look upon himself as a member of the group; a colleague and co-worker working along with other members of the staff. They are in the process of learning; he must also put himself in a position of learning. He should approach any problem-solving situation as a co-learner, working together with the group to achieve a satisfactory solution.

2. He must be sensitive to the feelings and needs of others. Those most frequently chosen for leadership in supervision have insight into the needs of co-workers. The principal who is attempting to develop sensitivity to the feelings of others must first develop his skill as a listener.

3. The principal must make a consistent effort to listen to his fellow staff members. He should be available to hear the complaints and the praises of the people with whom he works. He also should become an inquisitive observer. People reveal their feelings through their physical behavior and by their casual conversation in informal as well as formal situations. The principal should make a continuous observation of conditions and attitudes in the classroom, the staffroom, and at faculty meetings.

4. He must recognize that he is not the only person attempting to improve instruction, although he does have the primary responsibility for such improvement. No leader can be successful if he operates under the preconceived idea that improvement will come only when *he* initiates programs, practices, and techniques.

5. He should exhibit a basic respect for, and faith in, other members of the staff. He should recognize their professional integrity and their basic desire to improve themselves and the profession.

6. The principal must recognize and understand that teachers are individuals, as are children. Educators have talked long about meeting the individual needs of children, but little attention has been paid to the importance of meeting the individual needs of teachers. The principal cannot deal with each teacher similarly—his approach to the improvement of an individual teacher's instructional program must take into account the teacher's own interests, needs, and abilities.

THE PRINCIPAL CREATES A CLIMATE CONDUCIVE TO PRODUCTIVITY. The principal must help create a psychologically healthful organizational climate[43]

[43]See Andrew W. Halpin, *Theory and Research in Administration* (New York: The Macmillan Company, 1966), chapter 4, for a discussion of research and theory concerned with the organizational climate of schools.

that is free from fear, threats, and coercion. He can do this, first of all, by accepting the premise that diverse opinions are an asset rather than detriment. If people are to feel free to express their opinions, they must also feel that these opinions will be heard and that they will not be penalized, however diverse these opinions may be from the "norm" of the group. Effective solutions to simple and complex problems come out of the true dialectic of free discussion.

When the principal does give problems to the faculty for discussion of possible solutions, he must never overrule these decisions by the sheer weight of his status authority. This action will immediately result in a cessation of communication. Further, it will cause members of the group to revert to the position of attempting to please the status leader. Ideas which might have benefited education go unvoiced. The principal continuously must foster creative action and experimentation by members of the staff. They should feel free to try out new ideas, methods, and techniques.

Ten commandments for the humane administrator were listed by D. E. Lawson:[44]

1. Do not rebuke or correct any teacher in the presence of students or any other persons.
2. Praise teachers, and in the fields of their special preparation walk humbly.
3. Deal not lightly with any person's problem, but treat it as if it were your own.
4. Forget not the days of your youth. Keep a sense of humor.
5. Honor your custodians and your teachers, that your days may be long in the job that the governing board has given you.
6. Let no child be judged by his behavior alone, but seek the causes of such behavior that they may be corrected.
7. Strive to see each child through the eyes of his parents, and treat that child with love as if it were your own.
8. When you have a teacher who is old in the service so that he no longer teaches well, deal with him tenderly and understandingly. (Teachers do grow older—and they don't just fade away.)

[44]Douglas E. Lawson, an Address at Southern Illinois University, Carbondale, Illinois, 1955.

9. Be sensitive to the needs of your whole community and faith in its people, for in that faith you will find your strength.
10. Have vision as well as devotion, that you might use all your talents for the benefit of all humanity.

Unfortunately, more frequently than not, it is the first of these commandments that is broken. When a teacher is rebuked or corrected by the principal in the presence of students or adults, the principal is guilty of a gross breach of professional ethics.

By appreciating the teachers' strengths and recognizing their needs, the principal builds rapport. Many teachers consistently do an outstanding job, and they need recognition for such work. It is upon this strength that the principal builds.

It is assumed that the teacher is the most important single factor in the educative process. The kind of behavior that he exhibits in the classroom determines the kind of learning that will take place. The teacher must be actively involved in pursuing personal improvement of his professional competencies. It is further assumed, in the consideration of change, that only the teacher can alter himself; no one else can make the change for him. In other words, the principal can help best by setting up situations whereby the teacher can be stimulated, see the need for innovation and, as a result, experiment with new ideas and techniques, internalizing them, in the end, as his own, and not as techniques that have been superimposed on him by the principal.

The principal must exhibit an implicit belief in his professional staff, at the same time stressing that there is no field of human endeavor in which there cannot be improvement.

CHANGE: A SLOW PROCESS. Any modification of practice, any improvement in techniques, will be a slow process. Change takes time, if it is to be change in the true sense of the word. If change takes place, it must come from the teacher's desire for change. When contemplating new techniques, the teacher judges them in the light of experience. What has worked? What will work best for students? The teacher must have faith in new techniques before he honestly can accept them.

The principal must not assume that teachers will modify their behavior simply as a result of a logical presentation. Neither will they change when ideas are imposed upon them, or by subtly manipulating them into positions that denote change.

Teacher Individuality

There is no one style of teaching, no one pattern of classroom organization, no special technique of teaching that should be universally adopted by all. One of the principal's major functions is to help teachers reach agreement on problems of instruction, and then to provide these same teachers with an opportunity to work cooperatively together. He must keep in mind that teachers are busy individuals, and if there is to be any improvement of instruction it will result from a supervisory program which is an integral part of the regular school program.

THE PRINCIPAL COORDINATES WITH OTHERS IN THE IMPROVEMENT OF INSTRUCTION. The people who contribute to the instructional program are perhaps the most important resource for continued improvement. Consequently, the principal must possess skill in human relations so that he may secure the maximum contributions from each individual.

It is extremely important that he know these persons well. What things does each do well? What special talents do different individuals possess? What special abilities do they have? Do they have skill in organizing, skill in writing, skill in speaking, skill in dramatics, skill in working with others? What are the personality qualities of each one? Such information will go a long way toward insuring the utmost benefits from personnel.

Kyte[45] maintained that all supervisory officers, other than the superintendent of schools, the assistant superintendent in charge of instruction, and the principal, are technical advisers to the superintendent, the assistant superintendent in charge of instruction, the principal, and the teacher.

The specialist-consultant is responsible for aiding teachers within the specialty, and performs under the direction of the principal. It is always the principal who maintains the responsibility and authority for school supervision.

[45]Kyte, *The Principal at Work*.

TRENDS IN THE EVOLVING ROLE OF THE PRINCIPAL AS AN INSTRUCTIONAL LEADER. Although there is a trend toward the acceptance of the principal as a supervisor of instruction as well as the administrative leader in the school, his role in supervision appears to be in jeopardy. As school systems grow in size there is increased erosion of the role of the principal as the supervisor of instruction. Further clerical assistance must be provided so that many routine duties, formerly performed by principals, may be handled by school clerks. This practice would provide more time for the supervision of instruction. The "specialist-consultant" or "coordinator" or "director," working out of the central office of the school system, is being called upon as a resource person to assist the principal; he should not replace the principal in the area of supervision.

Perhaps the principal of the future will be recognized as a *chief-of-staff* officer—an instructional leader—a plan termed *the academic equivalent*. Most of the purely administrative and pseudoadministrative functions presently performed by many principals would be put in the hands of assistants and classified employees under this plan.

PREPARATION FOR THE PRINCIPAL. The principal of the future will be highly trained in the formation of small study groups and curriculum committees; in how to orient substitute teachers and teachers new to the school; in how to keep the staff informed concerning new materials, methods, techniques, and ideas; in curriculum construction; in instructional techniques; and in methods of coordinating the efforts of resource people and specialists. Further, the principal will be expected to be generally conversant in broad cultural areas including the natural sciences, the fine arts, the social sciences, foreign languages, and the humanities. No one individual can be expert in several areas, but the principal is expected, increasingly, to be broadly educated as well as to be a specialist in *how* to educate.

EXPERIENCE AND EDUCATION FOR THE SUPERVISING PRINCIPAL. An increasing number of principals will go on toward an advanced two-year degree in education, or for the Doctoral degree. An increasing number of preparing universities are offering advanced programs leading to the advanced degree of Master of Education in school supervision. This degree requires one to two years of preparation in addition to that required for the basic Master of Science or Master of Arts degree.

The potential principal's background should include not less than five years of successful classroom experience at the level he expects to supervise. In addition to the increase in the amount of education, there will be an increase in the amount of teaching experience required by the local school systems for the position of supervising principal.

DELEGATION OF DUTIES BY THE SUPERVISING PRINCIPAL. There appears to have been a change during the past twenty years concerning the adequacy of the duties generally recommended for the principalship. There has been an increased delegation of duties by the principal to members of the professional staff qualified to administer them. The main functions retained by principals should be policy-making and supervision. Routine administrative and supervisory functions, such as those included in the following listing, should be delegated to the assistant principal as readily as he becomes successful in administering them:

1. Assistance in planning with individual teachers and in observing classroom teaching;
2. Orienting and guiding new teachers;
3. Working with small groups of teachers and with grade level or department group on instructional problems;
4. Helping teachers provide for individual differences;
5. Conducting faculty meetings;
6. Assisting in selection of equipment and supplies;
7. Initiating and coordinating research programs.

Principals tend to delegate supervisory tasks such as the following to the assistant principal:

1. Directing and coordinating the school program for guidance and psychological services;
2. Developing and maintaining student personnel records;
3. Directing student welfare work and attendance accounting;

4. Directing the program of student co-curricular activities;
5. Directing and coordinating the program for school health and safety;
6. Coordinating student transportation at the school level;
7. Coordinating the school program of food services.

The Superintendent as Instructional Leader

Local public school system superintendencies came into existence in Buffalo, New York and Louisville, Kentucky in 1837. As a position, the school superintendency is relatively young. It began chiefly as a business operation, but was compelled to assume responsibility for instructional leadership along with personnel management and community relations. Many developments are still to come. Recent developments focus attention upon the improvement of the instructional program as the appropriate role of the modern school superintendent. The superintendent needs to be aware of current curriculum problems, research results, and practices and trends in modern education.

LEADERSHIP IN THE IMPROVEMENT OF INSTRUCTION. The following list of duties shows the general conception held by school boards as to the activities of the superintendent that are important, in rank order:

1. Visiting schools as often as practicable;
2. Holding teachers' meetings to discuss methods;
3. Carefully noting methods of instruction of each teacher;
4. Advising teachers on methods of instruction;
5. Noting qualities of teachers;
6. Suggesting improvements in teaching;
7. Controlling methods of instruction;
8. Using teachers' meetings for demonstration lessons;
9. Noting methods of instruction of supervisors.

The principal duty of the superintendent in the area of in-service education is that of leadership. The American Association of School Administrators[46] selected for emphasis the following responsibilities and activities:

1. The superintendent or his representative should visit teacher-training institutions.
2. He should strive to improve the salary schedule.
3. He systematically should attempt to increase the participation of teachers in the in-service education program.
4. He must maintain a systematic record system.
5. He must see to it that functions and responsibilities are clarified.
6. He must initiate and direct study of the work loads of employee personnel.
7. He must select and orient new personnel.
8. He must maintain an *esprit de corps.*
9. He should obtain adequate financial support.
10. He must insure the topics covered in in-service education programs are fundamental and are not composed of trivia.
11. He should provide workshops, curriculum laboratories, materials, and texts.
12. He should obtain the assistance of specialist-consultants.
13. He should keep the governing board informed concerning the program for in-service education, and must have the program included in the official minutes of the governing board.
14. He must organize committees of teachers to study and report on the curriculum, and must initiate in-service study programs related to child growth and development and provide for cooperative study of the total program.
15. He should provide leadership, analysis, and coordination of a comprehensive program for the improvement of curriculum and instruction:
    a) Assisting in the establishment of group purpose;
    b) Coordinating efforts;
    c) Providing resource specialists;
    d) Stimulating creative leadership;
    e) Arranging prime working conditions and relationships;

[46]American Association of School Administrators, *The American School Superintendency,* Departmental Thirtieth Yearbook. Washington, D.C.: The Association, 1952.

f) Establishing curriculum committees;

g) Putting a recommended, tentative plan into action;

h) Evaluating the outcome and plan for further study.

Individual teachers should be encouraged to identify problems, should seek help, and should try out solutions. The superintendent should create an atmosphere whereby he helps others to see problems, to get started, to make decisions, to put plans into action, to evaluate, and to improve both group and individual performance. Experimentation is good.

THE SUPERINTENDENT ORGANIZES TO IMPROVE INSTRUCTION. The superintendent must develop a framework for a cooperative approach to effective communication. Time and materials must be provided, staff relationships taken into account, and a flexible organization provided which will develop staff potential through shared responsibility. The superintendent should try to improve the instructional program so that:

1. Each individual teacher should be given broad authority for adapting content, method, and organization of learning experiences to student needs.
2. Each school should be given wide authority and responsibility for improving instruction through community relations.
3. The school system can establish general policies as *guideposts* to each school in exercising the autonomy granted to it.

The superintendent should encourage the formulation and adoption of written policies as guides to action when any problem concerning the instructional program is recurrent or when it involves more than one individual, so that:

1. The delegation of responsibility and authority is facilitated;
2. Favoritism tends to be avoided;
3. Responsibilities tend to be fixed;
4. The authority of the governing board is utilized constructively.

OPERATION OF THE PLAN FOR INSTRUCTIONAL IMPROVEMENT. After a plan to improve instruction has been established and all involved are cognizant of it, the situation as it stands must be appraised. The staff must then recognize what the situation should be and what should be projected for five to ten years.

THE SUPERINTENDENT PLANS FOR BETTER PHYSICAL FACILITIES. The educational program, the selection of an architect, and temporal limitations should be considered in the financial planning for the program of schoolhouse construction. Preservation, maintenance, and modernization of existing buildings are responsibilities of the governing board and of the superintendent. Physical facilities are important to instruction. It should be remembered, however, that they are a means to an end. That end is the best instructional program that the school system can provide.

Auxiliary Services

Auxiliary services should be provided based upon the needs of the students and the interest and ability of the community. Broadly defined, such services include responsibilities in the areas of health, transportation, guidance, psychology, child welfare and attendance, food services, library, and recreation programs. An adequate staff is essential. The hiring of the staff should be the responsibility of the superintendent, with the governing board completing the legal contract.

Staff Relations and Quality of Instruction

The school system is no better than the classroom teachers it employs, and the teachers employed are no better than the quality of staff relations maintained by the school system. The superintendent must be aware of forces that motivate human behavior, factors affecting group work, procedures for working together for individual growth, working conditions and staff relations, economic and community status of staff members, and ways in which the professional staff may work together for good school-community relations.

The effects of good staff relations are constructive modification of the curriculum, improved instruction, better staff morale, individual growth of staff members, and improved school-community relations.

The superintendent must eliminate the following roadblocks to the improvement of staff relations: (1) long hours, (2) extra assignments, (3) nonteaching duties, (4) large classes, (5) inadequate facilities, (6) poor salary plans, and (7) lack of fringe benefits and satisfactions.

The administration, teacher, and staff must work together with the governing board and the community in order to correct conditions which act as roadblocks to the improvement of staff relations. One of the first places to start would be the long after-school faculty meeting, especially if it is devoted to the reading of announcements.

DO

1. As superintendent, see that the principal is delegated sufficient authority, that he has the necessary time for supervision, and that he is given adequate stimulation, direction, support, and help.
2. As superintendent, work cooperatively with school principals in effecting educational improvement—stimulating, encouraging, and guiding rather than ordering and criticizing.
3. As supervisor, maintain a relationship with your fellow educators (superintendent, principals, and teachers) which is based upon mutual respect, trust, and recognition of responsibilities.
4. Clarify beliefs and goals, and reflect continuously on how they may be applied.
5. Develop the will to grow.
6. Analyze assignments and determine which can be done best.
7. Write articles for publication in professional journals. The superintendent and principal also should read the professional literature.
8. Learn from public administration and from industry.
9. Discuss problems with others and participate actively in small discussion groups.

DON'T

1. As supervising principal, tell anyone, nor imply by deed or tone of voice, that you fail to support the instructional policies of the superintendent.

Policies which you believe to be in error can be revised, but until such time as they are altered they deserve your support.

2. Omit your own supervisory practices from reflection.
3. Fail to enroll for courses in higher institutions of learning on a regular basis.
4. As supervisor, avoid rating yourself occasionally. You may wish to invite teachers to evaluate your performance.

Supervisory Problems

Problem 1

Assume that you are the supervising principal of a large junior high school in a district which includes three other junior high schools and two high schools. You have been asked by the district superintendent to organize and coordinate the supervisory efforts of the district in solving the following problem:

Twelve members of the liberal arts faculties in the district were participants in a summer workshop devoted to a study of the development of an "English and Literature Guide" to accompany the newly adopted textbooks to be used for the coming school year. The district paid the summer workshop registration fees for the participants.

These guides were developed for each grade, seven through twelve, on three levels of difficulty. A copy of the appropriate guide was presented to each English and literature teacher at the start of the fall term.

Supervising principals were requested by the superintendent to inform the teachers involved that these guides would be collected at the end of the school term along with their corrections, recommendations, suggestions, and evaluation of each unit of work included therein.

How would you, as the supervisory concerned, follow through on the request of the superintendent and organize the supervisory forces of the district to obtain full participation and cooperation on a professional basis when:

1. Many members of each faculty did not approve of the adopted text;
2. Some schools did not have representation at the summer workshop;

3. There was a great deal of resistance on the part of the faculty—
"what was good enough was good enough!"

Problem 2

The Arrowhead Valley Unified School District is situated in a peaceful
recreational center in the foothills of the Sierra Nevada. The average daily
attendance for the district is 2,800. Superintendent Lawrence Alan Douglas,
who majored in psychology and education at Rochelle State Teachers, prides
himself on the "relaxed, friendly, informal administrative atmosphere" of
the district.

The Board of Education of the Arrowhead Valley Unified School District,
on motion of Mr. Ross, its president, asked Superintendent Douglas for a
summary of the organization for the improvement of instruction through
supervision for the district.

At the weekly meeting of the administrative council, the superintendent
asked those present to select from the topics listed below:

1. The advantages of centralized vs. decentralized supervisory programs
   in the district.
2. The advantages of horizontal vs. vertical supervision as pertains to the
   district.
3. Agencies and levels of education other than the local district which provide supervisory service to the district.
4. The organization of the staff of the assistant superintendent for instruction for the district, and recommendations for reorganization.
5. The schedule and program for the supervision of probationary teachers
   in the district.
6. Provisions for research and experimentation in the district.

Each individual was asked to prepare a short survey of the situation for that
topic as it existed at that time in the district, and to propose a program of
improvement for that aspect of the organization for supervision.

The superintendent also requested that each supervising principal be
prepared to present his recommendations, along with the values and pit-

falls, concerning the extent to which teachers should participate in planning for supervision.

As supervising principal:
1. *Which topic would you select?*
2. *How would you proceed in organizing to prepare your response? What would you do?*
3. *What would be contained in your response?*
4. *How would you respond to the superintendent's query concerning teacher participation in planning for the organization of supervisory services?*

Selected Bibliography

Books

Barr, A. S., William H. Burton, and Leo J. Brueckner. *Supervision.* New York: D. Appleton-Century Company, Inc., 1947.

Bolton, F. E., T. R. Cole, and J. H. Jessup. *The Beginning Superintendent.* New York: The Macmillan Company, 1937.

Briggs, Thomas H., and Joseph Justman. *Improving Instruction through Supervision.* New York: The Macmillan Company, 1952.

Browning, Bruce C., and Henry J. Otto. *Organization for Instructional Supervision in Elementary Schools.* A Monogram. Austin: University of Texas, 1957.

Burton, William H., and Leo J. Brueckner. *Supervision, A Social Process.* 3rd edition. New York: Appleton-Century-Crofts, Inc., 1955.

Cleland, David I., and William R. King. *Systems Analysis and Project Management.* New York: McGraw-Hill Book Company, 1968.

Crosby, Muriel. *Supervision as Co-operative Action.* New York: Appleton-Century Crofts, Inc., 1957.

Elsbree, Willard S., and Harold J. McNally. *Elementary School Administration and Supervision.* New York: American Book Company, 1959.

Fayol, Henri. *General and Industrial Management.* New York: Pitman Publishing Corporation, 1949.

Frey, Sherman H., and Keith R. Getschman, *School Administration: Selected Readings.* New York: Thomas Y. Crowell Company, 1969.

Kyte, George C. *The Principal at Work.* Rev. ed. Boston: Ginn and Company, 1952.

Nutt, Hubert Wilbur. *Current Problems in the Supervision of Instruction.* New York: Johnson Publishing Company, 1928.

Owens, Robert G. *Organizational Behavior in Schools.* Englewood Cliffs, New Jersey: Prentice-Hall, Inc., 1970.

Reeder, Ward G. *The Fundamentals of Public School Administration.* New York: The Macmillan Company, 1951.

Tead, Ordway. *The Art of Administration.* New York: McGraw-Hill Book Company, Inc., 1951.

Periodicals

Adelsbach, Cleo G. "Small Districts Offer a Better Way of Life." *California Teachers Association Journal* LVII (March 1961): 8.

Carpenter, C. C. "Large Districts Offer Professional Growth." *California Teachers Association Journal* LVII (March 1961): 9.

Stoops, Emery, and James R. Marks, "What About Teacher Evaluation?" *The School Executive* LXXVII (September 1957): 97.

Warmke, Roman F. "A Concept of Supervision." *National Business Education Quarterly* XXIX (May 1961): 3.

Weller, Gerald M. "The Role of the Boys' Vice-Principal." *Educational Administration and Supervision* XXIV (December 1938): 705–708.

Other Sources

American Association of School Administrators. *The American School Superintendency*. Departmental Thirtieth Yearbook. Washington, D.C.: The Association, 1952.

_____ . *Staff Relations in School Administration*. Departmental Thirty-Third Yearbook. Washington, D.C.: The Association, 1955.

_____ . *The Superintendent as an Instructional Leader*. Departmental Thirty-Fifth Yearbook. Washington, D.C.: The Association, 1957.

California, Cloverdale Union High School District v. Peters, 264 P. 273, 88 Cal. App. 731.

Fielstra, Clarence. "Student Reviews of Selected Literature in the Field of Instructional Supervision." Mimeographed Monograph. Los Angeles: University of California at Los Angeles, 1961.

Freese, Theron. "A Study of the Position of Assistant Superintendent in Charge of Instruction: Its History, Status, and Functions." Doctoral dissertation, University of Southern California, 1955.

Gaincott v. Davis, 275 N.W. 299.

Heath v. Johnson, 15 S.E. 980, 36 W. Va. 782.

Iowa, Whitney v. Rural Independent School District No. 4 of Lafayette Township, 4 N.W. 2nd 394, 140 A.L.R. 1376.

Kansas-State ex rel. Hill v. Sinclair, 175 P. 41.

Lawson, Douglas E. An Address at Southern Illinois University, Carbondale, Illinois, 1955.

Massachusetts, Russell v. Gannon, 183 N.E. 736, 281 Mass. 398.

Melbo, Irving R. et al. "Report of the Survey, Taft City School District." Duplicated material copyrighted by the author. Los Angeles: July 1960.

Montana-State ex rel. Howard v. Irleand, 138 P. 2nd 569.

National Education Association. "The Principal and Supervision," *The National*

Elementary Principal. Thirty-Seventh Yearbook. Washington, D.C.: National Education Research Division, 1958.

Nevada, Nevada Industrial Commission v. Leonard, 68 P. 2nd 576.

New Mexico, Zellers v. Huff, 236 P. 2nd 949, 55 N.M. 501.

New York, Gobel v. Board of Education of the City of Albany, 48 N.Y.S. 2nd 299, 267 App. Div. 621, affirmed 60 N.E. 2nd 133.

New York, La Dalley v. Stamford, 272 App. Div. 183.

New York, Miller v. Board of Education, Union School District No. 1, Town of Albion, 50 N.E. 2nd 529.

New York, Parrish v. Moss, 106 N.Y.S. 2nd 5773, affirmed 107 N.Y.S. 2nd 580, 279 App. Div. 608.

Oakes, Keith Ronald. "Statutory Responsibilities of District Superintendents in the United States." Doctoral dissertation, University of Southern California, 1954.

Ohman v. Board of Education of the City of New York, 90 N.E. 2nd 474. Reargument denied: 93 N.E. 2nd 927.

Parrish v. Moss, 85 N.E. 2nd 792.

Pennsylvania, Appeal of Cable, 61 Pa. Dist. and County 298.

Pennsylvania, Howell v. Kingston Township School District, 161 A. 559.

Pennsylvania, Malone v. Hayden, 197 A. 344, 329 Pa. 213.

Piety, Donald. "Legal Aspects of Recruitment, Selection, and Assignment of Certificated Personnel in Public Schools as Shown by Court Decisions, 1956." Doctoral dissertation, University of Southern California, 1956.

Smith, Harold J. "Practices and Procedures in Recommending and Screening Candidates for the Position of Superintendent for Public School Districts in California." Doctoral dissertation, University of Southern California, 1960.

Smith, Wilburn. "Administrative Policies and Practices and Their Relation to Teaching Efficiency." Doctoral dissertation, University of Southern California, 1954.

Conflicting Organizational Demands

Job Demands[1]

The many bases upon which he is evaluated make it easy for the typical supervisor to find himself facing conflicts in demands for his time, conflicts of interests among those with whom he must work, and conflicts between his own needs and the requirements of his job. He sees serious discrepancies between how his boss treats him and how he is supposed to treat his workers. He complains that management fails to make its policies clear about supervisor-subordinate relations:

Personal dependence upon the judgments and decisions of his superiors so characteristic of the subordinate-superior relation in modern industry makes the . . . situation basically insecure. . . . In some cases this preoccupation with what the boss thinks becomes so acute that it accounts for everything [said or done] . . .[2]

Men-in-the-middle in industry suffer anxiety from the ambiguities of their roles for it is seldom clear to them how they can satisfy both their bosses and their subordinates at the same time. The foreman, in particular, may see himself in an impossible situation, especially where workers are unionized and top management deals directly with union officials to settle important matters. The least power in such circumstances often is with the marginal man between workers and upper management.

Time Demands

How much time executives say they spend in supervision correlates negatively with the amount of authority they say they have. However, reported supervisory time does not correlate with how much responsibility they feel they have nor with how often and to what extent they delegate

[1]The authors are grateful to Bernard M. Bass for his reflections on supervisory behavior in industry [Bernard M. Bass, *Organizational Psychology* (Boston: Allyn and Bacon, Inc., 1965] and for much of the material in this section.
[2]F. J. Roethlesberger, "The Foreman: Master and Victim of Double Talk," *Harvard Business Review* XXIII (1945): 285–295.

authority. Perhaps because they feel production problems take precedence, they actually overestimate how much time they spend on production and underestimate the amount of time they devote to personnel matters. Higher level executives seem to be able to spend more time in innovation, in attending to personnel relations, and in coordination, according to a survey of 96 management personnel. The first-line foreman, however, usually must devote more of his attention to quantity of production if he is to be evaluated highly, particularly by his superiors. Yet, while subordinates give greater weight in their evaluations to personal leadership, only about 7 percent of the time of a large sample of blue-collar supervisors seems to be spent on personal matters.

Some supervisors bury themselves or are buried in paperwork and have little time left for such important functions as stimulating subordinates. In banks, in particular, executives may be kept busy with customers with consequent neglect of many supervisory activities.

An unpublished study of the contact patterns of 80 members of management indicated that the executive heading a productive department was never at either extreme in how he distributed his time. He avoided being tied up all day in meetings but spent more time in meetings than a supervisor of an unproductive department. Compared to ineffective supervisors the effective manager did not spend more time with one subordinate than another or with his superiors rather than his subordinates.

Conflicting Loyalties

While his superiors are likely to want him to demonstrate more initiative in organization, a supervisor's subordinates evaluate him more highly when he exhibits more consideration. The effective supervisor must be able to resolve the incompatibility of supervisor's and subordinates' interests. As a man-in-the-middle he must initiate an organizational structure which requires more energy expenditure by his subordinates while at the same time it offers more reward potential for his superiors if he succeeds. At the same time, he must be seen as considerate by his subordinates.

Some men-in-the-middle employ a variety of power tactics which they at least believe may do more good for themselves than for their organization. They avoid seeking advice when they actually need it. They form cliques to obtain support on issues rather than allowing the issues to be settled rationally. They never completely commit themselves to ideas, arguments, individuals, or groups. They withhold information and use it to serve their own purposes when useful to them. They compromise superficially without really accepting other points of view. When they find orders objectionable they do not attempt to have the orders rescinded but are slow to execute them. They exude confidence even when they make decisions in the face of considerable uncertainty. They always are the "boss" to their subordinates. All of this requires artful acting and a willingness to lead a Machiavellian (and possibly ulcer-ridden) existence in situations which may be a heavy price to pay for success. This is particularly so where the same person might be even more successful if he could achieve a more rational solution, merging his self-interests with organizational objectives so that he could be "open," frank, and free to "level" with others.

The man-in-the-middle who succeeds in solving the dilemma receives the accolade of both his superiors and subordinates. Of those supervisors who were judged immediately promotable by their bosses, 75 percent were seen as "pulling for the company and the men" by their subordinates. On the other hand, among those supervisors judged questionable or unsatisfactory by their superiors, only 40 percent were seen by their subordinates as pulling both for the company and the men.

Conflicting Channels of Communication

Thirty-two executives indicated to what extent they consulted with their boss, peers, subordinates, outsiders, rulebooks, or only themselves when faced with various kinds of problems such as whether to participate, how to plan something, or how to assign rewards. No matter what the problem, some executives attended strongly to the rule books; others did not. Consistent differences also existed among these executives in how often they consulted with their boss, peers, subordinates, and themselves, but not persons outside their organization. On the other hand, the nature of the problem led to no consistent response differences.

In a laboratory simulation of the pressures confronting the man-in-the-middle, this differential attention was a function of the general orientation of subjects. When the boss threatened and subordinates were dissatisfied, *self-oriented* and *interaction-oriented* supervisors increased their communications to the boss. *Task-oriented* supervisors increased their communications to their presumed subordinates.

The supervisor is a member of a formal organization—almost a society—based on the patterns of formal relations between job occupants above and below him. He is also in an informal organization based on relations between persons regardless of the jobs they occupy. The informal organization is likely to diverge from the formal, particularly when formal upward channels of communication are "noisy" or blocked. The man-in-the-middle is a central relay station, and the development of conflicting informal patterns may depend to a considerable degree on his performance. He must learn to accommodate and to use the informal organization, if a strong one be present. What he receives from superiors, subordinates, peers, and others will depend on how much attention he pays to each source of communication.

Who Evaluates?

But "if you try to please everybody, you may not please anybody," for there appears to be no correlation between the evaluations supervisors receive from their subordinates and from their superiors, although two superiors' evaluations tend to agree, and—to a lesser extent—the evaluations of two of the supervisor's peers show some agreement with each other and with superiors' evaluations.

Above and beyond these considerations is the almost complete lack of agreement between what the supervisor thinks he does and what his subordinates say he does. Table Supp. 4–1 shows this glaring discrepancy by comparing supervisors' descriptions of their own behavior with the experience reported by workers in the same utility company. For example, while 52 percent of the supervisors said that they give privileges very often, only 14 percent of the workers said they received such privileges.

TABLE SUPP. 4–1   Comparison of Supervisors' Description of Their Behavior With Employees' Description of Their Experience[a]

Asked of Supervisors: "How do you give recognition for good work done by employes in your work group?"		Asked of Employes: "How does your supervisor give recognition for good work done by the employes in your work group?"
Percentage of supervisors who said "very often":		Percentage of employees who said "very often":
Gives privileges	52	14
Gives more responsibility	48	10
Gives a pat on the back	82	13
Gives sincere and thorough praise	80	14
Trains for better jobs	65	9
Gives more interesting work	51	5

[a]After Likert, 1961, p. 91.

Importance of Immediacy

Most complicating of all is the probability that the evaluations to which a supervisor gears his own actions direct how he spends his time; and how he concentrates his efforts will depend on relatively immediate evaluations. Yet ten years after a supervisor is discharged from his job, his associates may reflect that he was the best executive they ever had on that job.

5

How to Be a Successful Supervisor Through Leadership and Human Dynamics

Have you ever been criticized by *your* supervisor in front of those with whom you work?

Have *you* ever received a supervisory bulletin you just did not understand?

Have *you* ever suggested a changed and met with a brick wall of opposition?

Have *you* ever worked in a situation where morale seemed to be low and dropping fast—where *loyalty* seemed to be nonexistent?

One result of common intention is common effort. If common intention is to operate, certain commonly accepted and acceptable goals are required. These goals are, in turn, the result of needs, desires, and satisfactions that are shaped by the professional or occupational staff. Ordway Tead, in his book *The Art of Administration*,[1] commented that the degree of individual commitment to common effort varies according to the degree of satisfaction experienced on the job.

The main responsibility for supervision in an industrial enterprise may rest with the department manager; in a governmental service agency it may rest with a division supervisor; in a hospital it may rest with a chief of staff for medical personnel and with a supervising nurse; in a school it rests with the principal. Whatever his title may be, the supervisor, along with those specialists working as consultants in staff positions, must realize that *loyalty is a two-way street.*

[1]Ordway Tead, *The Art of Administration* (New York: McGraw-Hill Book Company, Inc., 1951).

If the school or company or service agency or hospital administration expects loyalty and support from the staff employees, it must produce evidence of being loyal to the staff. There must be genuine solicitude shown for the interests, aims, and satisfactions of the staff. Opportunity must be provided for individual creativity and development. There must be sufficient freedom to allow for personal initiative.

We are obliged, then, to understand human nature. Only with this knowledge will men's activities fall into a meaningful pattern. The supervising principal should be among the first to make use of the results of the findings

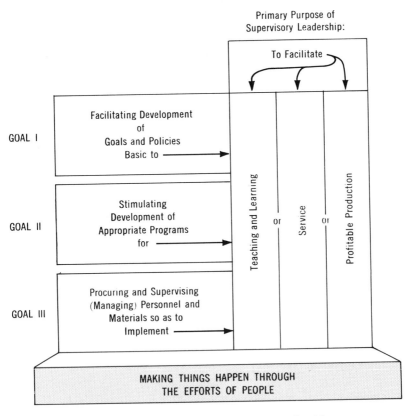

FIGURE 5–1   Primary Purposes of Supervisory Leadership.

of specialists in such allied fields as psychology and sociology in the areas of leadership and human dynamics, since his goal is to make things happen through the efforts of people. As may be seen in Figure 5-1, this ultimate goal of making things happen through the efforts of people is operational whether the goal of the organization be in the area of service, profitable production (as in private industry), or teaching and learning.

If the supervisor is to operate as an effective leader, he must understand his own place and function in the organization and the requisites for strong, resourceful leadership.

This chapter includes a discussion of the following topics:

How leaders succeed
How to criticize: leadership, criticism, and human nature
How to obtain support for a change
How to communicate effectively
How to be a success as a leader in a social setting
Keys to leadership for the supervisor
Do—don't
"In-Basket" supervisory problems

How Leaders Succeed

Leadership is necessary for a local school system to carry on a successful educational program. It is this leadership that is a corequisite of effective supervision.

Educational leadership has been defined as "that action or behavior among individuals and groups which causes both the individual and the group to move toward educational goals that are increasingly acceptable to them."[2]

[2]Association for Supervision and Curriculum Development, *Leadership for Improving Instruction* (Washington, D.C.: National Education Association, 1960).

With this concept of educational leadership, it is the responsibility of the local school system to perform various leadership tasks:

1. The superintendent and the supervising principal must inform the community as to the needs and purposes of the school.
2. The community needs help in defining its educational goals. This help should come from the supervising principal.
3. The role of educational leadership is to facilitate instruction so that teaching and learning become more effective and efficient.
4. Leadership, if it is truly democratic, helps to create growth and to stimulate the development of new leadership.

The supervisor is a part of a team. As such he should be interested in the characteristics possessed by successful enterprises. The basic factors or characteristics of an organization which are essential if it is to function efficiently are:

1. Strong, resourceful leadership;
2. Clearly defined responsibilities;
3. A staff which has been carefully selected, educated, trained, and assigned;
4. Methods which have been standardized to reduce redundancy;
5. An accurate, adequate, and reliable record-keeping system;
6. An efficient information retrieval system coupled with two-way open channels of effective communication;
7. An atmosphere of high morale and its concomitant, cooperation.

As a strong, resourceful leader the supervisor must possess the ability to recognize and anticipate problems. He must have the capacity to develop sound solutions to these problems, and the ability and willingness to take decisive action so as to put the solution into effect. The supervisor must possess confidence in his own ability, tact, and self-control if he is to win the confidence of his fellow educators. He must have the ability to develop the staff into a hard-hitting, well-coordinated unit. The patrons of the schools demand this degree of efficiency in their educational enterprise. Leadership is essential in the largest organization and in the smallest department in the school, if the goals are to be met successfully.

A majority of the most effective men who have climbed the executive ladder to success have possessed personal characteristics such as the following:

1. Technical competence for the job to be done;
2. Social competence—being able to work well and competitively with others;
3. A knowledge of to whom to go so as to get things done;
4. Both the ability and willingness to delegate responsibilities and commensurate authority;
5. A strong sense of and skill in organization, so that tasks may be completed and goals realized;
6. Skill in designating objectives and the ability to plan so as to achieve these objectives;
7. A sound, working knowledge of leadership dynamics.[3]
8. A strong drive for achievement and job competence and a desire for recognition;
9. The distinct ability to make many sound, rapid fire decisions among several alternative courses, and to translate these decisions into action;
10. Strong motivation and strong orientation to what is real, practical, and useful, and an aggressive, active desire to participate in the struggle for status and prestige—to be a part of the authority system, and even to dominate it;
11. A strong respect for, but not dependence on, his own considered judgment; and decisive and self-directional orientation within the frameworks of school system policy and organization[4]

---

[3]See William R. Spriegel, Edward Schulz, and William B. Spriegel, *Elements of Supervision* (New York: John Wiley & Sons, Inc., 1966), especially pp. 19–22.
[4]See especially Russell H. Ewing, *The Leadership Functions of Executives and Managers: An Evaluation of Current Leadership Theory and Practice* (Beverly Hills, California: National Institute of Leadership, 1962), pp. 10–11.

How To Be a Successful Leader

Being a leader requires one to be true to one's own ideals but, at the same time, to be sufficiently flexible so as to be able to perform the many specialized duties and functions for a group or organization in a continuously changing environment. Leadership is the performance, in various and variable situations, of the functions of a leader, while at the same time meeting the expectations, aspirations, needs, and demands of the group. The successful leader is one who is:

1. Sensitive to the feelings of others while being at once considerate, helpful, responsive, and friendly;
2. Loyal to one's ideas and ideals and respectful of the beliefs, rights, and dignity of others;
3. Strong in his feeling of self-confidence and the ability to identify easily with co-workers, including those who supervise him and those whom he supervises;
4. Consistent, generous, humble, modest, fair and honest in dealing with others;
5. Enthusiastic in informing others about the policies and regulations of the school system;
6. Interested in the improvement of the group while at the same time possessing the ability to get the job done quickly and in the most economical, efficient, and correct manner;
7. Aware of the need to avoid envy, jealousy, and indulging in personalities while at the same time being willing to take the blame for one's own mistakes;
8. Certain to give his co-workers the benefit of the doubt and the advantage whenever possible;
9. Firm but not stubborn in his own judgments and decisions;
10. Apparently sincere, straightforward, approachable, easy to talk to, alert to getting the best out of people without aggressive shouting, open to suggestion, encouraging, enthusiastic, stimulating, inspiring, relaxed, and, finally, an interested dynamic leader who has maintained his sense of humor.[5]

[5] Ibid.

Delegation

Many supervisors are unwilling or reluctant to deputize or delegate. Others will willingly delegate *responsibilities*, but fail to give the necessary *authority* to get results. Still others will delegate authority and responsibility and then attempt to abdicate their own ultimate responsibility for what happens. No supervisor can say, "the responsibility is yours," and then forget it. The amount of follow-up is a function of the amount and type of work and of the individual to whom the responsibility has been delegated. Bruce, who joined the faculty two days ago, will require more follow-up, than will Gary, who has been with the school for twenty years.

Recall, the supervisor is primarily responsible for making things happen through the efforts of people. Only when he perceives this facet of his position will he be successful in improving instruction. Supervising calls for:

1. Building morale and cooperation;
2. Using sound techniques of supervision;
3. Basing decisions on a sound knowledge of human nature;
4. Developing the ability and willingness to delegate.

The supervisor must possess the ability and willingness to delegate if he is to be successful in improving instruction. Recall the story of the school superintendent of a relatively wealthy school system in Orange County in California. Superintendent Raboy followed the old axiom, "If you want it done right, do it yourself." Superintendent Raboy did almost everything himself, then he had a heart attack himself, and the only thing he could not do himself was to read his own eulogy. Some of the responsibilities which can be delegated, some which cannot, and some which should be shared are listed in Table 5–1.

One of the more reliable measures of a supervisor's leadership ability is the manner in which he delegates. A successful leader has the courage to delegate to others and the organizational ability to institute controls (checks) to see that delegated responsibilities are accomplished according to plan. Supervisors who are weak in the skill of delegation are usually weak in organization. They do not realize that proper organization provides natural channels for delegating and fixing responsibilities.

TABLE 5–1   Supervisory Delegation

Do Delegate	*Do Not Delegate*
1. Accident prevention SHARE	1. The responsibility for delegating
2. Maintaining quality, quantity of production; cost control SHARE	2. Maintaining appropriate relationships with other departments; ultimate responsibility for quality and quantity control
3. Proper use and control of materials; training beginning employees SHARE	3. Personnel procurement and *planning* for the in-service education and training of new personnel
4. Maintenance of proper *records* upon which reports are based	4. Reports to *your* supervisor(s)
5. Inspection and care of materials, equipment, tools	5. Settlement of basic disagreements between subordinates
6. Encouraging cooperation and teamwork SHARE	6. Discharges; final responsibility for promotion
7. Recording employees' working time	7. Consideration of absences, tardinesses, discipline (control)
8. Health, sanitation factors: inspection and planning	8. Final responsibility for maintaining a safe environment[a]

[a]William R. Spriegel, Edward Schulz, and William B. Spriegel, *Elements of Supervision* (New York: John Wiley and Sons, Inc., 1966).

The supervising principal must keep in mind that although he may deputize someone to perform a continuing task, the supervisor himself, is, in the last analysis, responsible for seeing that the task is accomplished—for getting it done.

How to Criticize: Leadership, Criticism, and Human Nature

Leadership is necessary if an enterprise is to carry on its function successfully. It is this leadership that is a corequisite of successful supervision.

Supervisory leadership we have defined as that action or behavior among individuals and groups which causes both the individual and the group to move toward goals that are increasingly acceptable to them. Moreover, democratic leaders help to create growth and to stimulate new leadership; they do not *stifle,* inhibit, and slash or control others through destructive criticism. In their book, *The Human Side,* J. Beckley and R. Baldwin[6] emphasized that it is easy to criticize, but it is not easy to criticize skillfully. Offering corrective criticism without arousing resentment is a fine art in human relations. Few supervisors master this art.

The problem is that all psychologically normal human beings have an intense desire to protect the ego, or self. In all of us there is a certain amount of vanity. Beckley and Baldwin reported:

> The trouble is that most of us ... —whether we admit it or not—are born with a fat streak of vanity. We like to criticize—it takes the other fellow down a peg and makes us feel superior, but when the shoe is on the other foot, that's a different story.[7]

Destructive Criticism

An unfortunate error made by many supervising principals is the use of severe criticism. Such criticism is of a destructive nature and does not usually get results.

Criticism is most effective when it is done in a relaxed manner. Experienced supervisors have found this to be one of the most important keys to leadership. *It is not necessary to criticize severely in order to obtain results.* Such criticism does more harm than good.

Planning for Constructive Criticism

When it is necessary to criticize, one should not do so without careful prior planning. Beckley and Baldwin[8] reported that when the supervisor is about to criticize, he must take the time to appreciate the fact that he is about to

[6]J. Beckley and R. Baldwin, *The Human Side—A Fine Art,* Bulletin No. 229 (New London, Conn.: National Foremen's Institute, 1960).
[7]Ibid., p. 2; see also Harry Mier and Joan Mier, *If the Shoe Fits* (Beverly Hills, California: Merit Publishers, 1967).
[8]Ibid., p. 5.

tackle one of the most ticklish tasks in the field of personnel mangement. Many supervisors bungle it badly. The supervising principal must remember this: the purpose of criticism is neither to show anger, nor to punish, nor to create unhappiness. The purpose is to help the individual to understand what can be improved and to make him anxious to do better.

PROTECTING THE TEACHER'S EGO. Criticism, to be effective, although it be constructive, should be softened with praise. *This praise must,* of course, *be deserved. . . .* What a marvelous lesson! And you obviously have such a fine relationship with the students! Glenn really understood the meaning of . . . ! Perhaps your lesson would be even more effective if you would try . . . . I know it would be easier and take you less time to prepare for the lesson demonstration if you would . . . . . . great work! Let me know if I can help in any way or get you some of those . . .

Before anyone is criticized, time must be taken to appreciate positive aspects of the individual's performance. Criticism is much easier to take when there is a good deal of praise mixed into the recipe.

OPPORTUNITY FOR SELF-CRITIQUE. Before offering suggestions for the solution of a professional problem, the teacher should be given a chance to criticize himself. The subject should probably be brought up in an incidental manner. Remember—and react to—a good technique is to bring up the subject and see what the employee thinks about it. If the individual is aware of the need for improvement he may prefer to admit his shortcomings, at least to himself, rather than have the supervisor point them out.

When offering constructive criticism the supervising principal must use due caution. He must not seem to act superior nor appear insincere. All human beings make mistakes. Administrative performance is somewhat short of perfect. Supervisors can set an example by recognizing their own mistakes—and tactical errors—and correcting them as promptly as possible.

When discussing a particular point with a teacher, the supervisor could recall having made a similar error himself. One cannot turn a poor worker into a good one by whipping him with words. Criticism must aim at the duo-goals of good will and improved performance. It is used to assist the professional staff, not to punish it.

How to Obtain Support for a Change

As human beings we have a strong instinct for self-preservation and for security. Most human beings are conservative, security-seeking creatures and resist change almost instinctively. Beckley and Baldwin[9] stated that regardless of the rut we are in, it is a familiar rut, and we are adjusted to it. There are no unknown or unexpected angles.

Don't Try to Change the World in a School Year

A child can change the shape of an inflatable, plastic globe by opening a valve and squeezing, but the supervising principal must not attempt to change the world in a work week nor in a school year. If the reader is, or is going to be, a beginning supervisor or a supervisor new to the scene, he must realize that the mere fact that he has arrived is enough to cause feelings of insecurity and anxiety on the part of the staff. The proposal to alter things that are familiar will (not may, *will*) immediately arouse fear of the unknown. Many good ideas, which should have worked, have failed miserably because they were put into effect too quickly.

A Case in Point

Let us consider a case from the field of industrial supervision. The principles are the same; only the setting has changed. Lewis Rose was appointed to the position of supervisor three days ago. Today, at his first formal meeting with his staff, disaster struck. He had suggested a few changes, such as introducing a team quota system for increasing production through incentives which was to be preceded by a time-motion study and followed by a statistical, cost control analysis. He announced that he planned to delegate many of his responsibilities to the production team leaders. These modifications would necessitate half the employees changing production assignments, specific duties, and/or shifts.

The employees were not receptive. As Lew's system went into operation, it readily became apparent that some of his ideas had value. But the employees were not cooperating. A grievance committee was formed. Many resignations were submitted.

[9]J. Beckley and R. Baldwin, *The Human Side—Step by Step*, Bulletin No. 302 (New London, Conn.: National Foremen's Institute, 1960).

Proceed Slowly, and With Caution

The same plan or at least portions of it, introduced more gradually, with time to adjust the thinking of the professional individuals involved, might have been a success.

When the supervisor is thinking of changing any of the standard operating procedures of the school, such changes should be made gradually, step by step. The staff must be prepared, carefully and expertly, for that which is to follow. They should have time to develop *enthusiasm* for the change.

Steps in Obtaining Support for a Change

When the supervisor intends to try something new he must not announce it abruptly, without warning. Rather, he should:

1. Discuss the problem several times, with several individuals, and get a commitment from indigenous group leaders;
2. Attempt to stimulate the staff to a realization that *some* sort of change may be desirable. Aim for a consensus, rather than for majority approval;
3. Attempt to draw the suggestions from the staff. A suggestion from the staff will be easier to put across than would a proclamation from above;
4. Avoid presenting the new idea as an accomplished fact. The idea should be presented as a suggestion—as something for the staff to consider and to discuss, whenever possible;
5. Take his time, even if he plans to proceed in spite of objections raised by the staff. People must become accustomed to the idea and have an opportunity to overcome some of their impulsive resistance to change. This concept is illustrated graphically in Figure 5–2.

How to Use the Staff's Brainpower

The procedure of making changes gradually instead of abruptly helps to lessen opposition and often results in a better solution to the problem at hand. Even the most appealing plan probably has some limitations in design or concept that have not occurred to the originator of the idea. We know that group effort has a good chance of being superior to individual endeavor.

FIGURE 5–2   "I Understand Your Point, Mr. Horn, and Perhaps We Should Evaluate that Portion of the Plan Again After We've Had a Chance to See How It Works, But I Really Don't Think You Have Anything To Worry About."

The brainpower of the professional staff should be tapped so as to accrue the greatest benefit to the students of the school.

Even when we are convinced that our ideas will work as we have planned, we must not rush headlong into such changes. These changes must be made slowly. Any plan has a better chance for success (and survival) if the professional staff has had a chance to adjust its thinking and to cooperate in its production.

All of this is not to imply that the supervisor should avoid taking a stand. He is responsible for all that transpires within the scope of his assignment; he must be forthright. Rather, it is the *manner* in which his ideas are put into action that is important. If a group of employees proposes an idea that the supervisor is convinced will not work, or that is against the policy of the organization (i.e., the governing board) or state law or regulation, he must say so. He must have the capacity to "stick to his guns" while still maintaining an open mind. If the idea has merit, policy can be changed. In supervision, we strive toward strong, democratic leadership, not toward anarchy or tyranny. The principal should use caution in rejecting an idea. He must *never* imply that the superintendent does not like the idea, but that he, as supervisor, approves of it. He must support the superintendent if he expects to receive support in kind. The teachers soon lose faith in him if he implies that he does not support the superintendent or the governing board.

How to Work with the Group and with the Individual

Tead, in *The Art of Administration,*[10] reported that there is a common factor running through the activities of all organizations: the close association of individuals, under direction, to accomplish certain stipulated tasks —to realize certain goals. But the relationships involved in these organized activities do not necessarily produce harmonious, productive results.

The problem is, people do not work together naturally and eagerly. There is friction, misunderstanding, indifferences, and conflict between individuals and between groups. "Illogical" employee reactions may sometimes be understood if the possible cause of the illogical reaction, be it environmental or as stated by the individual, is analyzed with an eye to the personal preferences, sentiments, desires, and group pressures which may account for the behavior which may not seem logical in terms of the possible cause as related by the individual. Both the social past and the social present must be considered, as may be seen in Figure 5–3.

In addition to the required personal adjustments, divergent or conflicting group relations may arise. High morale is not universal; eager and informed cooperation is atypical. Loyalty and partnership receive a great deal of lip service, but are seldom in operation. When indifference and conflict between individuals and between groups do exist there is cooperation of sorts, as may be seen in Figure 5–4, or no productive outcomes would result. Unfortunately, this cooperation often could be described as passive acquiescence, or as antagonistic submission.

Supervision at its best exhibits a finite fragment of human creativity, while at its worst supervision can be a serious social liability. Or, as Tead[11]

[10]Tead, *The Art of Administration,* pp. ix, 223.
[11]Ibid., chapter XIII.

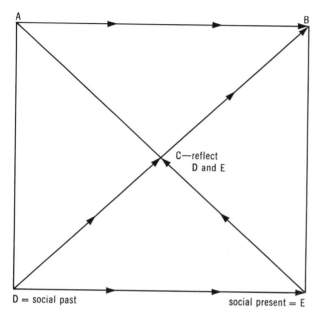

A = Possible cause, environmental or as
    stated by individual.

B = Behavior; may not seem logical in
    terms of A.

C = Personal preference, sentiments,
    desires, which account for action B.

FIGURE 5–3   Understanding "Illogical" Employee Reactions.

noted, it can be boring, impersonal, and domineering. As such it could be
stifling and could operate in opposition to the best interests of society.
Supervision is, then, both an art and a science. It operates (1) through organizations, (2) through human beings, (3) through groups, and (4) within
the democratic political-social-economic society.

Human Dynamics: A Social Product

A great deal depends upon how we appeal to others. Human dynamics is
largely a social product. This means it is malleable to a degree, variable in
its responses, and often predictable.

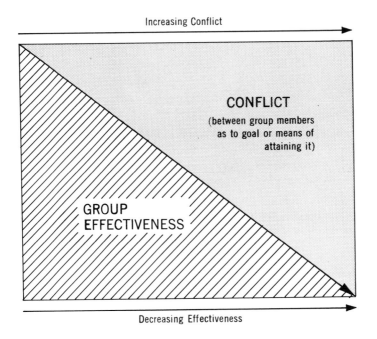

FIGURE 5–4   Conflict vs. Effectiveness.

How to Understand Individual Differences

Each person is seeking to become established as a self, and thus continuously is shaped by the standards, values, expectations, and restrictions which he confronts in home, school, community, nation, and professional societies.

EGO DEFENSE. We all have a two-way interest in the maintenance of our psychological integrities. The desire for a sense of personal worth is tremendously strong. People want to be identified and acknowledged as individuals with meritorious qualities.

Constructing an Image of the Self

When an individual's interests, associations, and creative participations extend into social channels with distinctive, productive social results, the quality of the ego is manifestly enhanced. Sincere, friendly attitudes tend to beget friendship and cooperation. The more inclusive the fronts on which the person registers and finds worthwhile expressions, the better adjusted, more productive, and more mature he may be.

If a member of the staff discovers that his job relations are stultifying and he finds little satisfying expression in the course of his employment, he will invest as little energy as possible in the job or will invest it in a destructive manner. A dangerous situation would be one in which a supervisor was thwarted and stifled at home. He might attempt to compensate for his frustrations at home by being unduly harsh, aggressive, and domineering with the staff.

The supervisor must be alert to the following criteria in detecting individual differences:

1. No supervisor should rely entirely upon his personal ability to judge personnel by interviewing or talking with them;
2. Actual, on-the-job performance is probably the best method for measuring individual differences, but only for the specific task at hand;
3. The same teacher changes from year to year and from day to day in performance and interests, both in degree and kind;
4. If we grant equal ability (and skill), different kinds of work are best performed by individuals who are particularly interested in them;
5. Changes in the environment (both physical and social) and in the complex of factors which govern individual reactions, as are indicated in Figure 5–5, can exert a decided influence upon individual reactions and, therefore, upon human relations;
6. The supervisor must recognize the emotional, mental, and physical differences between individuals as to nature, extent, and influence, and must appreciate the influence that the attitudinal complex and morale of the group have upon individual staff members;
7. In general, a group tends to change more slowly than does the individual, the group possessing more stability than the individual staff member;
8. Power reclines in the fads and fancies that appear to be harmonious with the group's sentiments, with irrational emotions tending to influence the group's actions along lines manifested by its sentiments, with individuals responding to slogans which may tend to unite the sentiments of the staff

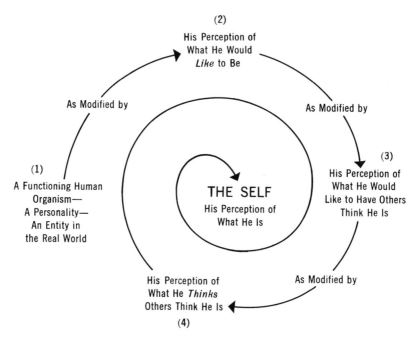

FIGURE 5–5   Four Factors Governing Individual Reactions.

members and to direct group effort toward objectives associated with the slogans and sentiment;

9. Individuals tend to respond positively when they have the whole story, which tends to displace the individual's irrational reactions to rumor.

How to Be Alert to Potential Trouble: Symptoms of Problems to Come

J. Minor Gwynn[12] listed several symptoms which may indicate that a teacher has a developing personal problem. These typical warning signs include:

1. When a teacher cannot sit down and talk quietly and at length, but has to stand up, and perhaps walks about while talking with the principal or another colleague.

[12]Reprinted by permission of Dodd, Mead & Company, Inc., from *Theory and Practice of Supervision* by J. Minor Gwynn. Copyright © 1961 by Dodd, Mead & Company, Inc.

2. When a teacher who has normally been rather talkative becomes suddenly and unexplainably more silent than talkative; and the reverse of this, when a teacher who is normally prone to be rather silent changes radically into a very talkative person.
3. When a teacher's classes have a much larger number of "personality conflicts" than usual between teacher and students.
4. When a teacher who has been consistently pleasant and mild in attitude becomes "snappy" and fault-finding with his students.
5. When a teacher who has a record of promptness gets into the habit of not being able to complete tasks or responsibilities on time.
6. When a teacher suddenly develops a tic or nervous mannerism which he did not have before.
7. When little things or irrelevant matters irritate a teacher easily and assume an importance that is not warranted.
8. When a teacher begins to tell the same story, the same episode over and over again to the same person with the same details, not realizing that he is doing it.
9. When a teacher who is normally rather calm and of moderate voice changes and starts each day on a higher key, with his voice getting louder, until the children are keyed up and talking excitedly too.
10. When a teacher begins to lose or gain weight steadily and noticeably when not on a diet under a physician's care.
11. When a teacher consistently cannot wait for someone to finish before he interrupts.
12. When a teacher begins to blame someone or some thing else for his own failure to perform a task well or to carry out a responsibility.
13. When a teacher who is well known for his liking and love for children changes his attitude to one of constant criticism of students.
14. When a teacher who is a temperate person begins to drink more or less steadily.
15. When a teacher who likes social life and contacts begins to withdraw more and more into privacy and solitude.
16. When a teacher who formerly seemed to love and enjoy his work dreads going to school in the morning, no longer finds joy or satisfaction in his work, and thinks only of dismissal on Friday.

You Too Have Needs, Mr. Supervisor

It is important for all supervisors to remember thay have a personal life. How much one involves, shares, and communicates school concerns with one's spouse should be a function of the couple's relationship and is a very personal matter.

The supervisor needs to maintain a balance in his life by having variety, relaxation, and adventure. By so doing he is more effective and productive. How hard one works, as evidenced in apparent effort, and the amount of time one stays on the job (how late in the day he leaves) are not factors that determine a supervisor's success. Supervisors' needs have been summarized as including a feeling of accomplishment, security, friendship, and service. Table 5–2 presents a summary of these needs.

TABLE 5–2   Needs of Supervisors

Personal *Off-the Job Needs*	*On-the-Job Needs*	
	EGOISTIC	SOCIAL
Good standard of living	Accomplishment	Friendship
Family	Feeling important	Identification
Social life	Feeling for whole	Team work
Recreation	Skill	Helping others
Sexual fulfillment	Program	Being helped
Financial security	Completion	Fair treatment
Community recognition	Autonomy	Praise
Reputation	Knowledge	Acceptance
	Security	Attention
	Job advancement	*Knowledge of where one stands*

How to Communicate Effectively

Have you ever thought to yourself:

1. "All of my good ideas stick in my throat whenever I get up at a meeting. I sit down feeling like a fool." OR

2. "On my way home from the faculty meeting I think of all the things I should have said." OR
3. "I often think how much more effective I could be as a supervisor if I could just communicate!"

Recall Aristotle's maxim, "It is not enough to know what to say; it is necessary also to know how to say it." Leadership is practically impossible for a person who lacks the ability to express his ideas.

Effective Communication for the Supervisor

Putting even the few hints listed below into practice right now can help you become a more effective communicator of ideas and, therefore, a more successful school supervisor:

1. Speak wisely and well—the following anonymous lines offer a bit of good advice:
   "If wisdom's ways you wisely seek,
   Five things you will observe with care;
   Of whom you speak, to whom you speak;
   And how and when and where."
2. Develop a liking for people—whether you speak to one person or a thousand, they can tell in a split second whether or not you are eager to share good ideas with them or if your words come only from your lips, not from your heart.
3. Keep informed—this task is not easy and often means sacrificing leisure time. But you will be a much more effective supervisory leader if you keep abreast of what is going on in education in general and in supervision in particular; in the social and professional organizations to which you belong; and on the local, national, and international scenes.
4. Go and keep going—if you belong to an organization or group, be informed and play an active role in its meetings and programs. Above all else, make your voice heard. Remember that *unexpressed ideas are of no more value than the kernels in a nut before it is cracked.*
5. Think before you speak—take a few seconds to organize your thoughts, rather than blurting out a gush of words that do not know where they

are going. Clear thinking must precede clear speaking. *A moment's thinking is worth an hour in words.*

6. Keep the other fellow in mind—
   - Try to understand the other person's point of view;
   - Avoid sarcasm, barbed remarks, and personal insults, for the use of these weapons is an indication of weakness, not of strength;
   - Display a calm manner and clear, sound thinking in the midst of heated discussion.

   Let these qualities be manifest:
   - In your tone of voice;
   - In your facial expression and your posture;
   - In the volume and rate at which you speak.

7. Concentrate on your message, not on yourself—focus attention on what you have to say and you automatically will forget yourself. Fear of being misunderstood, taken with a grain of salt, or even laughed at, will be put in the background once you realize you are an instrument for serving children by bringing helpful ideas to others.

8. Collect material for your discussions—look for facts and "slices of life" that can be used in your talks. Tear out items in newspapers and magazines and underscore passages in books; collect materials that teachers may wish to see, rather than hear about, which pertain to your topic. Jot down your ideas on index cards or keep a small notebook with you.

9. Be brief and precise—
   - Do not bite off more than you can chew or more than your listeners can digest;
   - Omit long and unnecessary explanations;
   - Select your point and get to it;
   - Use short sentences. Be economical in your use of words, never using three or four where one would do.

10. Make nervousness work for you—most people are a bit frightened when speaking before a group. The beginning supervisor especially may be fearful when addressing his first faculty meeting or parent association get together. But a little fear can be an asset. It can sharpen your talks

and make them sparkle. Before you begin, consciously relax your muscles and quietly look around at your audience for ten or fifteen seconds.

11. Be enthusiastic. Recall that the word "enthusiasm" comes from two Greek words, *en* and *theos,* meaning "in God." So let the divine spark show through when you want to communicate constructive ideas; but do not confuse enthusiasm with bombast, wild gestures, or emotional display. You can be enthusiastic in a whisper or without moving so much as a finger.

12. Let gestures help you—they can be an outward expression of inner convictions and add dimension to your words. A wave of the arm, a raising of the eyebrow, shrugging the shoulders, nodding the head, are types of gestures.

13. Communicate with your eyes. "Eye communication" means more than "eye contact." It implies looking directly at your listeners and actually talking with your eyes. Sweep the audience gently with a warm, friendly gaze, allowing your glance to rest here and there for a brief second or two. It is far easier to know whether you are making your point if you look at your listeners, rather than at the floor or ceiling.

14. Keep trying—the type of leadership we stress offers little in the way of ease, honor, or personal gain. In fact, it usually involves hardship, misunderstanding, personal risk, and sometimes personal loss.

15. Be a good listener. Learn from the thoughts and ideas of others. Recall from Epictetus: "Nature has given to man one tongue, but two ears, that we may hear from others twice as much as we speak."

16. Know when to stop—as this verse puts it:
    "I love a finished speaker;
    Oh yes indeed I do.
    I don't mean one who's polished,
    I just mean one who's through."

Specialists in the language arts, in psychology, in supervision, and in communication theory have presented several listings of the principles of effective communication. R. C. Borden's[13] four major principles which are

[13]Richard C. Borden, *Public Speaking as Listeners Like It!* (New York: Harper and Row, Publishers, 1935).

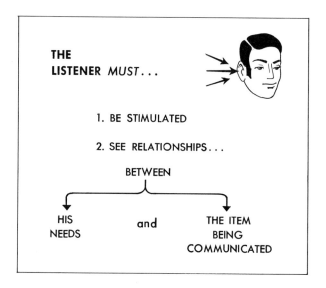

FIGURE 5–6   The Successful Listener's Requirements.

prerequisite to making communication effective toward improving human relations are illustrated in Figures 5–6 and 5–7.

Those who are receiving the communication, be they listeners or readers, appreciate:

1. Specific examples included in the communication:
   a) Examples which involve either familiar individuals or the recipients of the communication;
   b) Examples which make more concrete the ideas which the communicator is attempting to present;
   c) Colorful analogies;
   d) Important satistical material, well dramatized or illustrated;
   e) Examples presented through the use of the materials of instructional technology.

2. Terminology which is free from superlatives, trite expressions, groping

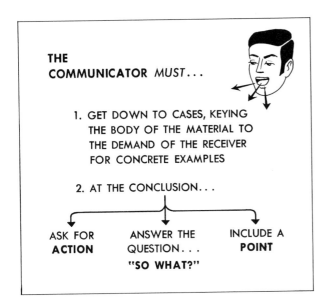

FIGURE 5–7   The Successful Communicator's Requirements.

expressions, repetitive expressions, and the words "et cetera" or "and so forth."

Listeners dislike statements such as, "Of course, it's only my opinion, . . ." Naturally it is your opinion, that is why you are expressing it. Naturally "it seems to you," or you would not be saying it. They also dislike punch-pulling phrases such as "more or less," or, "to a greater or lesser degree."

Recipients of communication appreciate phraseology that is grammatically sure-footed and easily understood. Sentences should not exceed twenty words in length in the usual communication. Periods should be inserted when a sentence begins to crumble under its own weight, or when a dependent clause starts to miss on one grammatical cylinder. Listeners appreciate phraseology that is:

- Conversational
- Specific

- Picturesque
- Clear
- To the point

Written Personnel Policies Are Vital to Effective Communication

Without clear information employees are likely to be confused, do not know what is expected of them, and are apt to believe that favoritism or pull is the major factor in assignment in obtaining instructional materials, and even in selection and rating. Such beliefs are devastating to good human relations and morale. It is here that heated disputes are most likely to develop within the school organization and between school and community.

The school system is charged with the task of setting forth such personnel policies in writing so that they may be *adhered to carefully* to enhance effective communication and serve as a means of eliminating favoritism, poor morale, and much ill will. Governing boards must not bow to the pressures of militant, aggressive groups within the community to avoid the establishment of a written personnel policy system nor should governing boards yield to pressures to violate their own policies.

The supervising principal should take the lead in developing a teacher's handbook containing major policies. Such handbooks help human relations and should be available to all teachers in the school system. Such a handbook should include sections concerning:

1. School system organization and point of view
2. Assignment specifications
3. Auxiliary services
4. Specialized instructional services
5. Student management
6. Management of forms, supplies, and equipment
7. Certificated personnel policies
8. Special services
9. Professional responsibilities and ethics

In order to acquire free expression and maximum cooperation, the staff must work together in an atmosphere of freedom. A system of instructional policies should be cooperatively formulated and assignment specifications should be officially adopted by the governing boards. Morale will be elevated in many ways including the use of teacher committees, cooperatively planned policies, effective two-way communication, timely information, and due consideration to personal problems.

B. O. Smith, W. O. Stanley, and J. H. Shores[14] reported that good communication must be regarded not from a standpoint of the dissemination of information, but rather as a means of developing perspective. If that perspective is distorted, the information will be interpreted incorrectly. If instruction is to be improved, the channels of communication must work more effectively than they do today.

How to Be a Success as a Leader in a Social Setting

If a supervisor is to be effective in improving instruction, he must show initiative in drawing out the creative abilities of the staff. He realizes that groups have both status leaders and emergent leaders in a democracy. L. Calvert and M. S. Olson[15] reported that the status leader occupies his position because of his professional assignment, such as superintendent of schools or supervising principal, while emergent or shared leadership provides an opportunity for each member of the group to occupy the leadership position temporarily because he can make a contribution. It is essential that the status leader, especially, operate in a democratic, permissive atmosphere within established policies, and that he:

1. Attempt to improve human relations within the professional staff;
2. Encourage free discussion;
3. Assist in the development of cooperative techniques for getting the job(s) done and the goal(s) met;
4. Assist in the development of future leaders;

---

[14]B. Othanel Smith, William O. Stanley, and J. Harlan Shores, *Fundamentals of Curriculum Development* (New York: The World Book Company, 1960).
[15]Leonard Calvert and Myron S. Olson, *Secondary Education: A Resource Syllabus* (Los Angeles: University of Southern California, 1965).

5. Coordinate functions of the staff;
6. Provide advice as needed.

How to Recognize Types of Leadership and Identify Pleasing and Displeasing Leadership Behavior

Specialists in the field have traditionally identified four major types of leaders. These are *laissez faire* leaders, democratic leaders, and two types of autocratic leaders—hard-boiled autocrats and benevolent autocrats. The democratic leaders, who could be represented graphically as occupying the central position in the leadership continuum as may be seen in Figure 5–8, provide the best possible type of leadership.[16] Others have differentiated between the charismatic, symbolic, head man, expert, theorist, agitator, authoritarian, and groupocratic types of leadership behavior, as outlined in Table 5–3.

Types of Leaders

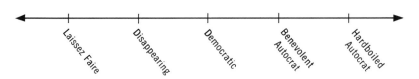

FIGURE 5–8   Types of Leaders.

Concerning the type of leadership behavior which is indicated as Group VIII in Table 5–3, and which is the absence of leadership, the reader should recall that the people will support the tyrant rather than live in a state of anarchy.

Perhaps of more vital concern to the supervisor were the findings of research concerning pleasing and displeasing leader behavior.

[16]See Kenneth D. Benne, et al., *Role-Playing and Discussion Method* (Washington, D.C.: National Education Association, 1950).

Pleasing Leadership Behavior

Clifford Campbell[17] reported the types of pleasing supervising principal behavior, as viewed by his staff and by parents' association presidents, in order, as indicated below:

1. Shows an interest in work and offers assistance
2. Possesses pleasing personality traits, such as courtesy, firmness, high integrity
3. Praises personnel and passes on compliments
4. Supports actions and decisions of personnel
5. Is a good organizer
6. Assumes authority and stands by convictions
7. Allows self-direction in work and shows confidence in ability
8. Makes wishes clearly known
9. Allows participation in decision making
10. Is firm with school standards and student discipline, and considerate of employees' work load

Displeasing Leadership Behavior

The types of supervising principal leadership behavior which were classified by Campbell[18] as displeasing included, in rank order:

1. Possesses poor personality traits, such as rudeness, unfairness, low integrity, and moral offensiveness
2. Is a "fence-sitter" and seems afraid to assume authority rightfully his
3. Is a poor disciplinarian
4. Is not a good organizer
5. Does not allow participation in decision making
6. Is not considerate of the work load of personnel
7. Does not support personnel in decisions or actions

---

[17]Clifford W. Campbell, "The Elementary School Principal as Viewed by His Staff and Parent-Teacher Association Presidents," Doctoral dissertation (University of Southern California, 1964), pp. 223–227.
[18]Ibid.

8. Does not make wishes clearly known
9. Does not show an interest in, or offer assistance with work
10. Does not allow self-direction in work or show confidence in ability
11. Allows too much parental influence
12. Is hypercritical, too demanding about details
13. Shows inadequate job knowledge and does not praise personnel

The Importance of a Sense of Humor in Leadership Behavior

A sense of humor can help in keeping a good leader from taking himself too seriously.[19] It can make his efforts in dealing with others much less tense and more amiable: it helps people to retain a sense of proportion between activity and effort. As an aspect of leadership behavior, it is invaluable, for it often can lessen tensions as no other remedy can. Abraham Lincoln was a master at this technique of leadership.

TABLE 5–3   Types of Leadership Behavior[a]

Group	Character	Comments and Behavioral Characteristics	Examples
I	Charismatic	Introduced by the German sociologist Max Weber, denotes leadership based on supposedly divine or supernatural powers	Jesus, Mohammed, Joan of Arc, the Pope, Father Divine
II	Symbolic	A leader with prestige but little power, symbolizing a nation or an institution which has symbolic value	The remaining European Kings and Queens
III	Head man	An institutional leader who fills a traditional position and whose authority is derived from custom and tradition	The chancellor of a university is often the head man type of leader

[19]Emery Stoops and Russell E. Johnson, *Elementary School Administration* (New York: McGraw-Hill Book Company, 1967), pp. 38–40.

TABLE 5-3   (Continued)

Group	Character	Comments and Behavioral Characteristics	Examples
IV	Expert	Based solely on achieved eminence in a certain field	Darwin, Einstein, Beethoven
V	Administrative leader or Theorist	This kind of leader is found in all societies and functions chiefly in business, politics, and government	Bismarck, Lincoln, Franklin D. Roosevelt
VI	Agitator or Reformer	Rests on persuasive and propagandastic ability rather than on executive or administrative skill, although these two factors may be present	Thomas Paine, William Jennings Bryan, Hitler, Norman Thomas
VII	Authoritarian	Individuals who have conscious or unconscious drives toward dogmatism, absolutism, and an inflexible exercise of power	Hitler, Stalin
VIII	Groupocratic	An offbeat system of leadership which some students of the subject label "anarchy." Has been called upside down leadership or management in which the subordinate may dictate to his supervisor. Although these theories are shrouded in the cloak of democracy, many specialists[a] indicate that this character of leadership could result in anarchy or chaos if practiced in any wide scale in government, business, industry, education, or military organizations.	Sensitivity trainers, group dynamics theorists, unstructured training theorists

[a]Russell H. Ewing, *The Leadership Functions of Executives and Managers* (Beverly Hills, California: National Institute of Leadership, 1962), p. 7.

The following films may prove helpful:

1. "Democracy"—Encyclopedia Britannica Films (ten minutes)
2. "Despotism"—Encyclopedia Britannica Films (ten minutes)
3. "Role-Playing in Human Relations"—Department of Adult Education, National Education Association, Washington, D. C. (twenty-five minutes)
4. "We Plan Together"—Teachers College, Columbia University (twenty minutes)

How the Power of the Supervisor Is Secured

Personal power over others may be acquired in three ways: (1) by *inheritance,* (2) by *seizure,* and (3) by demonstrated expertise or other influence leading to *appointment or election.* The effectiveness of the supervisor apparently depends more upon how well he deals with people than on how he obtained his position. Supervisors may demonstrate their power by being ruthless, domineering, and autocratic in command, or they may gain cooperation by their expertise and by their friendly, helpful, persuasive leadership. The effects of democratic and authoritarian atmospheres are compared in Table 5–4.

TABLE 5–4   Comparison Between Effects of
Democratic and Authoritarian Atmospheres[a]

Effects of Democratic Atmosphere	*Effects of Authoritarian Atmosphere*
1. More "we-feeling; more frequent use of "we" and "our."	1. More "I-feeling; more frequent use of "my" and "I."
2. Group-minded suggestions; relatively few demands for individual focus of attention.	2. Suggestions more designed to focus attention from leader on self.
3. Positive identification with whole group, including leaders and non-leaders.	3. No group identification; leader identification rather than group identification.

TABLE 5–4 (Continued)

Effects of Democratic Atmosphere	Effects of Authoritarian Atmosphere
4. Positive group identification and unity.	4. Relatively less group unity, members may temporarily unite to defy leader, but this does not necessarily indicate existence of genuine group identification.
5. Activity and productivity begins before leader arrives and continues during his absence.	5. Activity and productivity decreases with absence of leader and increases during his presence.
6. Greater job satisfaction and morale with few or no rumors.	6. Less job satisfaction and morale, with relatively more anxiety about the present and future, leading to formation and spreading of rumors.
7. Relatively little aggression toward leader and other group members; generally more friendly behavior when frustrated, aggression is directed toward real source of aggression.	7. Considerable aggression toward other members. Tendency to displace aggression to scapegoats, outsiders, "beginners"; when frustration is very great, apathy and inwardly directed aggression are evident.
8. Fewer "gripe sessions."	8. More "gripe sessions."
9. Relatively less obvious dependence on leader, who is admired.	9. Overdependence on and submission to leader, who is less liked; in extreme situations there may be regression toward childlike dependence.
10. Relatively broader perspective of problems and their possible solutions.	10. Piecemeal perception of problems.
11. More variability and flexibility of behavior.	11. More stereotyped, inflexible behavior.

aFrom pp. 107–108 in *Practical Applications of Democratic Administration* by Clyde M. Campbell. Copyright 1952 by Harper and Row, Publishers, Inc. Reprinted by permission of the publisher.

Leadership which is ruthless, domineering, and autocratic may be reflected in indifference and in passive, reluctant obedience.

Security, confidence in one's own competence, job satisfaction, and absence of frustrations in the home are essential conditions in the lives of those who are to wield their personal power over others in wholesome and productive ways.

The supervisor exercises power with integrity when he is solicitous of the welfare of the staff. The response of the staff to *sincere* and competent effort is confidence in judgment, admiration and respect for technical resourcefulness, and pride in his profession. In a democratic atmosphere, then, the leader operates within established policies, attempts to improve human relations within the staff, encourages free discussion, assists in the development of future leaders, coordinates functions and activities, provides advice, and assists in the development of cooperative techniques for problem-solving.

Supervisory Leadership in the Good Old Days

We have come a long way. The following list of rules for teachers was posted by a New York City principal in 1872:

1. Teachers each day will fill lamps, clean chimneys, and trim wicks.
2. Each teacher will bring a bucket of water and a scuttle of coal for the day's session.
3. Make your pens carefully; you may whittle nibs to the individual tastes of the children.
4. Men teachers may take one evening each week for courting purposes, or two evenings a week if they go to church regularly.
5. After ten hours in school, the teachers should spend the remaining time reading the Bible or other good books.
6. Women teachers who marry or engage in *other unseemly conduct* will be dismissed.
7. Every teacher should lay aside from each pay a good sum of his earnings for his benefit during his declining years so that he will not become a burden on society.

8. Any teacher who smokes, uses liquor in any form, frequents pool or public halls, or gets shaved in a barber shop, will give good reason to suspect his worth, intentions, integrity, and honesty.
9. The teacher who performs his labors faithfully and without fault for five years will be given an increase of twenty-five cents per week in his pay providing the board of education approves.

Of course trimming wicks or carrying coal has not been a part of the education profession for some time, but many teachers remember vividly the role that was expected of them:

1. The educator was a purveyor of learning, or more directly, a person who distributed knowledge. Of course, this knowledge must not have been in opposition to the accepted community mores. He was not to be controversial nor an "all round" human being. He was not permitted to expound new social theories.
2. He had to be active in community affairs, that is, in youth groups, church activities, community welfare drives, and the like. He was expected to be a "do-gooder." He must not, under any condition, have been a competitor for top community honors; he could not run for office. He was expected to operate actively at the "second level" in the social life of the community.
3. The teacher's personal life was under constant community scrutiny. If he was male, he was expected to be married to a girl who did not work. A female teacher was expected to be single, dress very conservatively, and wear little or no make-up. One superintendent insisted that any teacher who wanted to leave town for the weekend get special permission from him.

Keys to Leadership for the Supervisor

If a supervisor is to be effective in our democratic society, he must show initiative in drawing out the abilities of his staff. We know that individuals are more productive and perform most effectively when they are operating within a familiar framework, using familiar techniques and methods, and proceeding toward a readily obtainable goal.

The production of the staff is enhanced both qualitatively and quantitatively when the individuals involved have had an opportunity to assist in the establishment of goals.

The leader must be concerned, then, not only with the profitable and efficient attainment of desired objectives, but also with the *methods employed* and with the *individuals participating.*

Thus is loyalty won. Thus is the educational or institutional or industrial product advanced, enhanced, and elevated.

The complexity of leadership is like a safety deposit box at the bank—it requires not one but many keys to open. The potential for leadership is inherent, and all persons have a degree of that potential. Some have more than others to begin with—just as some men are taller than others. As a matter of fact, height does have a positive correlation with leadership ability. Of course, many "small" men have overcompensated for their lack of height, e.g., Napoleon and Caesar. But we are chiefly concerned with leadership characteristics that are learned. These we can improve. Here are some of the keys which improve leadership performance.

DO

1. Work beyond requirements—and do not call upon subordinates for tasks that you are unwilling to undertake yourself;
2. Report to work on time, regularly, and without obvious effort or complaint;
3. Keep your mind focused upon work to be done instead of watching the clock. You should excuse a subordinate for a dental appointment sooner than you would take the privilege for yourself;
4. Supervise by policy, and remember that you are subject to the policy which you yourself helped to create;
5. Appreciate difficulties involved in puzzling assignments and offer praise when a colleague solves the problem;
6. Express concern through action, not mere verbalization, for the welfare of the staff, as a means of maintaining high morale;

7. Maintain faith in the staff (if you doubt them, they will doubt you);
8. Involve others in policy decisions. Wait out the slowness of group problem solving, for if you pressure too hard the slower members of the group will lose interest;
9. Improve programs by starting with worker dissatisfactions and help find an answer, as opposed to belittling their dissatisfactions or giving them ready-made solutions;
10. Keep all members of the staff fully informed and look upon some internal disagreement as the doorway to further growth.
11. Solve a problem rather than sell a solution;
12. Stress what is right rather than who is right;
13. Allow time for consensus rather than ramming through a majority vote;
14. Accept responsibility for the outcomes of the group's decisions;
15. Agree with Walter Lippman that "the final test of a leader is that he leaves behind him in other men the conviction and the will to carry on";
16. Delegate authority, responsibility, and function. *The leader is effective only as he works through people.*

The leader must avoid certain behaviors if he is to maintain the "leader goose" position at the head of his flock.

DON'T

1. Show favoritism, but do recognize individual differences in the group and capitalize upon them. Where is the fine line between recognizing ability and showing favoritism? The leader must find and follow it.
2. Tend toward intimacy. When students call a teacher by his first name, or nickname, respect and leadership qualities tend to evaporate. The oriental philosopher, Laotzu, has said, "A leader is best when people hardly know he exists."
3. Take criticisms personally. Keep calm and weigh all criticisms objectively.
4. Expect social concourse; accept loneliness. The crowd has company, but the leader stands by himself.
5. Be tempted by power. The strong, effective leader must beware of the temptation to exert power. Paraphrasing Lord Action, "power tends to corrupt; absolute power corrupts absolutely." Plato saw this danger when

he said in *The Republic*, "people always have some champion whom they set over them and nurse into greatness. . . this and no other is the root from which the tyrant springs; when first he appears he is a protector . . . In the early days of his power, he is full of smiles, and he salutes everyone whom he meets." Beware the temptation to exert power.

6. Fail to avoid the temptation to feel tall by cutting down enemies, much less fellow workers, and much, much less a subordinate staff member. This kind of person can hold power only through status positions, or the methods of coercion, and not through the loyalty and respect of devoted staff.

Leadership, then, is not moral; neither is it immoral. It is amoral. Leaders can be good or bad. It is the direction and results of leadership that count. Genghis Khan, Alexander, Napoleon, Tojo, and Hitler were leaders, but to destruction. Moses, Socrates, Jesus, Mohammed, Gandhi, Horace Mann, and Florence Nightingale were leaders, but to a better life.

Supervisory Problems
In Basket

Problem 1

In a large elementary school there are four first grade teachers. Each has her own individual problems:

Mrs. Horn is quiet and keeps very much to herself, and rarely shares ideas with other teachers. Her classroom door is always closed. She is, nevertheless, very efficient and handles her students well. She always complies with the principal's requests and her reports always are turned in on time.

Mrs. Brown is a widow. Her personality has changed since the death of her husband, and with the absence of her only child—a daughter. At school she tends to mother Mrs. Douglas, a young first-grade teacher. Her reports are accurate and on time. She thinks mainly of her class and her students. However, she is willing to share ideas and materials.

Mrs. Green is the oldest of the four first-grade teachers. According to others she offers too much advice and much of it has little meaning. She would be willing to share materials, but has trouble finding them in the chaotic conditions which usually exist in her room. Her reports usually are late and at times incorrect.

Mrs. Douglas is a young teacher who wants to do a good job. She turned to Mrs. Brown for help. This caused hard feelings between Mrs. Brown and Mrs. Green, who had been co-workers for many years.

At last the problem boiled over. On the afternoon of March 6 seven teachers were gathered in the faculty room having soft drinks during recess. Mrs. Brown and Mrs. Douglas were seated together talking about the approaching First Grade Spring Music Festival. Mrs. Green entered the teacher's room and went directly to the vending machine and got a soft drink. She added a comment to the conversation. Mrs. Douglas turned to Mrs. Brown and made a remark. Mrs. Green did not hear the remark, and she assumed it was about her. Becoming enraged at the two, she threw her coke bottle on the floor, breaking it. Mrs. Douglas' foot was cut, and the relationships of the teachers were shattered.

How would you, as the supervising principal, work to re-establish a positive relationship between the four first grade teachers?

Problem 2

Miss Ross has been teaching for ten years in several different schools. This year she is teaching in a school whose faculty is made up of 50 per cent "freshmen" teachers. She has a very dominating personality, she loves to talk and complain, and is unhappy when she does not get things done her way. Whenever any new ideas are brought up for discussion, this teacher immediately gives her views on why the idea is without merit. This causes an uneasy feeling among the teachers. The younger teachers are afraid to speak up. Because of this type behavior on the part of Miss Ross, communications between teachers and between faculty and administration are somewhat strained.

As the supervising principal, what would you do to help ease this situation?

Selected Bibliography

Books

Bartky, John A. *Supervision as Human Relations*. Boston: D. C. Heath and Company, 1953.

Baxter, Bernice, and Rosalind Cassidy. *Group Experience—The Democratic Way*. New York: Harper and Brothers, 1943.

Benne, Kenneth, and Bozidar Muntyan. *Human Relations in Curriculum Change*. New York: The Dryden Press, 1951.

Berne, Eric. *The Structure and Dynamics of Organizations and Groups*. Philadelphia: J. B. Lippincott Company, 1963.

Boardman, Charles W., Harl R. Douglass, and Rudyard K. Bent. *Democratic Supervision in Secondary Schools*. Boston: Houghton Mifflin Company, 1953.

Bonner, Hubert. *Group Dynamics: Principles and Practices*. New York: The Ronald Press Company, 1959.

Borden, Richard D. *Public Speaking as Listeners Like It!* New York: Harper and Brothers, 1935.

Bradfield, Luther E. *Supervision for Modern Elementary Schools*. Columbus, Ohio: Charles E. Merrill Books, Inc., 1964.

Cartwright, Dorwin, and Alvin Zander, *Group Dynamics: Research and Theory*. White Plains, New York: Row, Peterson and Company, 1953.

Chase, Stuart. *Roads to Agreement*. New York: Harper and Brothers, 1951.

Clement, J. A., and J. H. Clement. *Cooperative Supervision in Grades Seven to Twelve*. New York: The Century Company, 1930.

Collins, Barry E., and Harold Guetzkaw. *A Social Psychology of Group Processes for Decision Making*. New York: John Wiley & Sons, Inc., 1964.

Corbally, J. E., T. J. Jenson, and F. W. Staub. *Educational Administration: The Secondary School*. Boston: Allyn and Bacon, Inc., 1961.

DeHuszar, George G. *Practical Applications of Democracy*. New York: Harper and Brothers, 1945.

Ewing, Russell H. *The Leadership Functions of Executives and Managers: An Evaluation of Current Leadership Theory and Practice*. Beverly Hills, California: National Institute of Leadership, 1962.

Frey, Sherman H., and Keith R. Getschman, *School Administration: Selected Readings*. New York: Thomas Y. Crowell Company, 1969.

Gordon, Thomas. *Group Centered Leadership*. Boston: Houghton Mifflin Company, 1955.

Gwynn, J. Minor. *Theory and Practice of Supervision*. New York: Dodd, Mead & Company, 1961.

Mackenzie, G. N., and S. M. Corey, *Instructional Leadership*. New York: Bureau of Publications, Teachers College, Columbia University, 1954.

Mier, Harry, and Joan Mier. *If the Shoe Fits*. Beverly Hills, California: Merit Publishers, 1967.

Riesman, David. *The Lonely Crowd*. New Haven: Yale University Press, 1950.

Spriegel, William R., Edward Shulz, and William B. Spriegel. *Elements of Supervision*. New York: John Wiley & Sons, Inc., 1966.

Stoops, Emery, and Russell E. Johnson. *Elementary School Administration*. New York: McGraw-Hill Book Company, 1967.

Tead, Ordway. *The Art of Administration*. New York: McGraw-Hill Book Company, Inc., 1951.

Utterback, William E. *Group Thinking and Conference Leadership*. New York: Rinehart, 1950.

Wiles, Kimball. *Supervision for Better Schools*. Englewood Cliffs, New Jersey: Prentice-Hall, Inc., 1950.

Periodicals

Philippi, Harlan A., and Jack R. Childress. "The School Administrator and Organizational Groupings." *The Clearing House* XLII (September 1967): 54–56.

Sargent, Edward H., Jr. "Ground Rules for Group Process." *Adult Leadership* XV (October 1966): 122, 145.

Singer, Laura J. "The Development and Use of Teaching Materials for the Training of Discussion Leaders." *The Family Coordinator* XVIII (October 1969): 318–321.

Other Sources

Association for Supervision and Curriculum Development. *Group Planning in Education*. Washington, D.C.: The Association, 1945.

_____. *Group Processes and Supervision*. Washington, D.C.: The Association, 1948.

_____. *Leadership for Improving Instruction*. Washington, D.C.: National Education Association, 1960.

Beckley, J., and R. Baldwin. *The Human Side—A Fine Art*. Bulletin No. 229. New London, Conn.: National Foremen's Institute, 1960.

_____. *The Human Side—Step by Step*. Bulletin No. 302. New London, Conn.: National Foremen's Institute, 1960.

Benne, Kenneth D. et al. *Role-Playing and Discussion Method*. Washington, D.C.: National Education Association, 1950.

Grambs, Jean D. *Group Processes in Intergroup Education*. New York: National Conference of Christians and Jews, [n.d.].

Jennings, Helen H. *Sociometry in Group Relations*. Washington, D.C.: American Council on Education, 1948.

Marks, James R. "An Analysis of Assignment Specifications for Certificated School Personnel in the United States." Doctoral dissertation, University of Southern California, 1962.

Taba, Hilda, and Deborah Elkins. *With Focus on Human Relations*. Washington, D.C.: American Council on Education, 1950.

The Department of Superintendence. *The Superintendent Surveys Supervision*. Eighth Yearbook of the Department. Washington, D.C.: National Education Association, 1930.

Psychological Implications of Supervisory Behavior

Democratic Leadership Implies General Rather Than Close Supervision

By avoiding supervising too closely, the democratic leader maintains feelings of freedom among his subordinates. And in turn these feelings, translated into behavior, affect how he feels toward his subordinates.[1]

Close Supervision and Mistrust

In a laboratory experiment, two "subordinates" were monitored by a subject who served as the laboratory "supervisor." High output was required on a dull task. One of the subordinates was monitored closely; the other was checked very little. Both subordinates performed equally well, but the attitude of the supervisor towards the two subordinates was quite different as a consequence of how he had to supervise them. The supervisor following orders to monitor a subordinate closely felt the subordinate was less trustworthy, was less dependable, and was complying with the supervisor's request because he was being watched. On the other hand, the supervisor felt that the subordinate he had been asked to check very little was complying because "he was a nice guy" or he "wanted to."

Mistrust feeds on itself. If a supervisor feels compelled to supervise a subordinate closely, he increases his belief in the need for close supervision of that same subordinate. At the same time, if conditions are democratic and the subordinate does his work equally well, then the supervisor increases his belief in the trustworthiness of the subordinate, and presumably he is able to become even more permissive in his dealings with the subordinate.

Close Supervision and Productivity

According to a similar laboratory experiment, tension is lower in workers and productivity higher under general rather than close supervision.

A real premium from general rather than close supervision is the extent to which *partial reinforcement* effects can keep workers at their task in the absence of the supervisor. Experiments suggest that the learner who is

---

[1] The authors are grateful to Bernard M. Bass, *Organizational Psychology* (Boston: Allyn and Bacon, Inc., 1965), for much of the material in this section.

checked as correct or incorrect after each trial in the learning process will extinguish or forget more quickly what he has learned, if the correction suddenly ceases, than will the learner who has been corrected intermittently. Some schedule of partial reinforcement is most efficacious. This fits with the observation that the permissive, general, supervisor can be absent from his work group with less deleterious effects on the productivity of the group than the close supervisor. When the close supervisor leaves, one is likely to see an increase in time wasting, wandering off the job, and "horseplay" among the workers.

Democratic Leadership Promotes Productivity

In addition to fostering acceptance, agreement, change, satisfaction, and trust, in many circumstances democratic supervision seems to contribute to the quality and quantity of output by subordinates. Work groups were more productive among those first-line supervisors in an insurance company who encouraged their workers to participate in decisions, were more democratic in their dealings with them, and supervised them less closely. Again, 975 delivery men at 27 parcel delivery stations throughout the United States rated the extent to which their opinions were requested by their supervisor and the ease they felt in getting their ideas across to the supervisor. The ease and freedom they felt in communicating with their superiors at a station correlated between .39 and .48 with the average deliveries the men completed daily relative to the standard time allotted for completion. Employees also felt more influential and more likely to be supported by their supervisor at the more productive stations. Workers permitted to set goals, whether in office or factory operations, significantly raised their productivity although mere opportunity to discuss work had less effect on performance.

Democracy, Not License!

Critics confuse democratic leadership with lax, uncontrolled, unrestrained supervision. In this case, the supervisor avoids attempting to influence his subordinates and shirks his supervisor duties:

... [and] has no confidence in his ability to supervise and consequently buries himself in paper work or stays away from employes. He may also be the one who believes that to be a "good fellow" means licence. He leaves too much responsibility with the employees; sets no clear goals toward which they may work; is incapable of making decisions or helping the group arrive at decision; and tends to let things drift . . .[2]

Such *laissez-faire* leadership should not be confused with the activities of the democratic supervisor who:

... whenever possible, . . . shares with his group the decision-making about work planning, assignment, and scheduling. Where a decision must be made by him, he helps the group to understand clearly the basis for his decision. He is careful to develop as much participation, opinion-giving . . . and a feeling of responsibility for the success of the work on the part of everyone. He is concerned that each employee clearly understand his work and have opportunities for success in it . . . He encourages worthwhile suggestions and the development of new procedures . . ."[3]

Democratic Participation Does Not Necessarily Lower Decision Quality

Critics also argue that if a supervisor permits his subordinates to participate in the decision-making process, the group product will be inferior. The supervisor, with his special knowledge and training, is in the best position to evaluate the situation and can make the best decision. The compromises resulting from group discussions are regarded by critics as likely to reduce the quality of solutions. But the evidence runs counter to the criticism. Experiments generally show that group decisions are superior to decisions reached by the average member of that group, although it is also true that the group decision may not be as good as that of the best member in the group. But how often is the supervisor the best? If excellence could be guaranteed, then decision quality might be better when decisions were made by the supervisor alone. When 66 air force officers wrote decisions prior to discussion and then met as an *ad hoc* staff to write the decisions, the decisions

[2]L. P. Bradford and R. Lippitt, "Building a Democratic Work Group," *Personnel* XXII (1945): 142–148.
[3]Ibid.

written by the staff were superior to the average quality of decisions written by individuals without discussion. At the same time, the quality was the same after discussion whether the decision was written by the staff or by the commander who had listened to the staff discussion. Group discussions contributed to better decision-making, whether or not the final decision was written by the group or by the person leading the group.

Some Negative Consequences of Permissiveness

While the usual concerns that democratic leadership will promote licentiousness, lowered standards, anarchy, and less control are unfounded, there are some potential negative consequences. The person who shares in the decision-making process not only derives greater self-satisfaction from his job; he also develops greater frustration with it, according to nationwide American mental health survey:

[Having] a personal stake in the outcomes of decisions taken . . . can be a satisfying, even an exhilarating experience, but it can also lead to sleepless nights.

This mixed blessing which power sometimes represents is illustrated by the experiment in a large clerical organization . . . in which about 200 clerks were given greater responsibility to make decisions about some of the things that affected their work groups. In general, morale increased in these divisions as a result of the change in control. Clerks felt more satisfied with the company, with supervision, with their work in general. They were, in large measure, favorable toward the increased control which they were able to exercise. However, despite the general increase in satisfaction, the clerks felt less of a sense of accomplishment at the end of the work day. They were also less satisfied with their present level in the organization. . . . In acquiring an increased feeling of responsibility for the work through the added control which they were able to exercise, the clerks no doubt developed standards of achievement which are harder to satisfy.[4]

When Permissiveness Is Contraindicated

Permissive, and to some extent, persuasive supervision appear, in general, most effective in promoting satisfaction and productivity among employees.

[4]A. S. Tannenbaum, "Control in Organizations: Individual Adjustment and Organizational Performance," *Seminar on Basic Research in Management Controls* (Palo Alto: Stanford University, 1963), p. 184.

Nonetheless, numerous circumstances require more authoritative action by the supervisor, more direct application of his power to reward or punish, and more decisions by him without consulting his subordinates.

When Interaction Is Restricted

When contact between superior and subordinate is restricted because of the size of the group, infrequent meetings between superior and subordinate, or poor communications, the supervisor must be ready to direct and to structure the situation—to give orders and see that they are obeyed. In small, intimate groups, where interaction between supervisor and all members is quick and easy, the supervisor can remain permissive. In the small, intimate, communicative group many more attempted leadership acts can occur in a given amount of time than in the large, distant group. Conversely, it is more important that each attempted leadership act be successful and effective in the large, distant group, if it is to reach the same degree of effectiveness as the small, intimate, communicative one in the same amount of time with the same expenditure of energy. Each leadership attempt must "count more" in the large group since relatively fewer are possible. As groups become larger than 30, the demands from subordinates for strong, central leadership become stronger. There is more reliance placed on whoever is appointed leader, regardless of who he is personally. There is more tolerance of leader-centered direction in larger groups.

Figure Supp. 5–1 shows how the productivity of scientists in a medical research laboratory is greatest when they have daily contact with their group chief, but only if they are treated democratically and allowed to share in decision-making or given the freedom to make most of their own decisions. This approach works best when meetings are frequent. But when contact between chief and subordinates is only a few times a week or less, productivity falls off with this same permissiveness by the chief. Permissiveness is thus contraindicated when interaction is low between leader and led.

The Nature of the Task

The nature of the task may mitigate against permissive approaches, particularly if it restricts interaction. A person who is at the center of a network of communications from four peripheral locations will promote the fastest, clearest, most accurate communication system if he accepts the responsibility for making the decisions for the network. Although those in the periphery may be unsatisfied with this arrangement, the system works most effectively if the central person is authoritative. On the other hand, if all locations are interconnected, more equalitarian decision-making becomes possible.

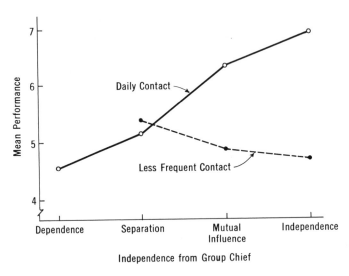

FIGURE SUPP. 5–1. The Relationship of Scientific Performance to Independence from Group Chief and Contact with Chief.[5]

Whether the task is simple or complex may make a difference. If the task is easy and uncomplicated for the worker, close supervision of what he is doing is likely to be detrimental, since he already knows what to do and how to do it. On the other hand, if the task is complex or the worker has little understanding of how to tackle the task with which he must cope, permissiveness may be contraindicated. The worker may prefer a great deal of guidance and attention from his supervisor until he has mastered the job, particularly if it does not involve much creativity from the worker but only attention to routine details which he must learn.

[5]Bernard M. Bass, *Organizational Psychology*, p. 184.

Higher Authority

If rules and regulations set by higher authority restrict subordinates' decisions, then supervisors dominate the group, make the decisions, and structure the situation. They also are less likely to be informal and to mix with their men, according to a survey of 100 groups. Higher authority indirectly can prevent participation in decisions by subordinates by demanding immediate answers from supervisors with no opportunity allowed for workers to be consulted.

Both in a progressive petrochemical refinery and in a national food processing firm, the extent to which a supervisor felt he should be considerate was positively correlated with how highly he was rated by his superiors. Yet in other companies no such correlation has been found, and one can easily imagine settings where considerate, permissive superiors would be severely downgraded by *their* supervisors. A real conflict is likely if top management insists on sacrificing all else in the interests of maximizing productivity and has the power to coerce workers to that end.

Maximum Productivity Demanded

Since workers and managers tend to seek *satisfactory* not maximum levels of goal attainment, permissive techniques may serve to reduce tensions, hostility, and frustration at the expense of failing to yield maximum output, particularly when such output is to some extent irrelevant to the income or other satisfactions of the work group. If maximum effort is demanded, promises of reward or punishment may be more effective in the short run than are discussions about the matter.

Expectations of Subordinates

If custom restricts what the worker is permitted to decide, the supervisor will define and structure the work. Thus, whether Norwegian factory employees would participate in decisions depended on whether they deemed that the activity was legitimate for them. Similarly, Israeli sailors who had expectations that their commander would be authoritarian were as satisfied with him as they were with a permissive commander.

Studies in other more traditional cultures such as Japan and Great Britain generally support the utility of permissive techniques, but more analyses repeating American experiments need to be done abroad.

Military field studies indicate that more important to the effectiveness of the team is whether the leader conforms to the role expected of him by his subordinates, not whether he is permissive or coercive.

Personality and Ability of Subordinates

Supervisors will have difficulty in promoting participation in decisions among their subordinates if the subordinates lack the capacity to express themselves or the interest and ability to become involved or to appreciate what they could contribute. Subordinates may personally dislike making decisions. They may dislike (1) living without immediate decisions from supervisors and (2) remaining in ambiguous, unstructured circumstances. Such intolerance for ambiguity is one of the characteristics associated with authoritarian attitudes. Individuals with *authoritarian* rather than *equalitarian* attitudes are likely to reject permissive leadership. A survey of Philadelphia residents disclosed that highly authoritarian personalities wanted powerful, prestigeful leaders who would direct them strongly. They emphasized material support, wanting the leader to serve their special interests. On the other hand, equalitarian persons preferred leaders who could help them solve the problems with which they had to cope. They wanted warmth and consideration in their leaders. In a study of 108 supervisors in a retail parcel delivery service, productivity was found correlated with felt influence on decisions much more among equalitarians than among authoritarians.

Personality and Expectations of Would-Be Permissive Leaders

An authoritarian manager who cannot tolerate uncertainty, who has strong power needs, and who finds himself unable to accept equalitarian attitudes toward his fellow men may be more effective if he does not try to disguise his true feelings by a superficial display of permissive practices. If he maintains a consistent authoritative position, his subordinates at least may be able to develop a consistent, reasonably tolerable way of getting along with him. They know what to expect and, although they may react to coercion in the ways described earlier in this chapter supplement, they will react possibly even more strongly to the executive who forcefully declares, "We'll be democratic around here, or else . . . ."

What we are saying is that it pays to be democratically permissive, but some supervisors may simply be unable to bring themselves around to a way of thinking and behaving that is required for a true sharing of leadership between supervisor and subordinate. In such cases, they may be better off maintaining practices with which they, at least, will be more comfortable. Otherwise, their own conflicts in what they prefer to do and what they actually do may generate even more difficulties with subordinates. For example, the professor who lectures for the full 50 minutes to his classes and refuses to allow time for discussion because he simply cannot tolerate or deal with questioning or skeptical students may be more effective in refusing to open discussions with students than he would be if he allowed time for interaction which was likely to arouse hostility, anxiety, and conflict in himself and, in turn, his students. He might effectively solve his dilemma by informal discussions with individual students outside of class. Naturally, it might be even better for all concerned if he were not teaching at all or if his personality were different or could be changed; but given his current state, his inability to deal with uncertainty or rejection suggests he is wise to avoid the possibility.

A cross-cultural survey of approximately 2,800 managers at training centers in 14 different countries noted a surprising degree of uniformity in to what extent these managers say they accept such permissive practices as participative management, sharing objectives, self-control by subordinates through commitment and understanding rather than control by coercion. Yet, except for the U.S. sample, there was little comparable acceptance in any of the other countries of the underlying beliefs on which permissive leadership is based. For example, the idea that individuals—employees as well as supervisors—all have the potential to exhibit initiative, share leadership, and contribute to the problem-solving process in organizations was unacceptable. Fostering permissive supervisory practices in such countries as Spain, France, Italy, Belgium, Denmark, Norway, Germany, and Sweden (interestingly the lowest in mean acceptance of individual employee leadership potential) may be a little like building the techniques and practices of a Jeffersonian democracy on a basic belief in the divine right of kings. However these societies all are changing, partly influencing the extent management practices can become more progressive and partly being influenced by more progressive practices in government and industrial supervision.

Emergencies

Subordinates want to be told what to do, and in a hurry, when danger threatens. Time does not always permit a democratic discussion of alternatives. Rapid, decisive leadership may be demanded. From one-half to two-thirds of 181 airmen asked their opinions concerning missile teams, rescue teams, scientific teams or other small crews facing emergencies, strongly agreed that they should respond to the orders of the commander with less question than they usually do. In an emergency the commander was expected to "check more closely to see that everyone is carrying out his responsibility." Half to three-fourths felt that "the commander should not be 'just one of the boys.' "

Analyses of the survival experiences of 200 crews which required them to fight hunger, cold, fatigue, and the enemy suggests that the effective leader in such stressful circumstances differs from the ineffective leader in the extent to which he exercises power, maintains communications in the group, rapidly restructures the situation, and maintains the group's goal orientation so that panic will be avoided. Panic occurs when members suddenly seek individual goals—the everyone for himself syndrome. Although the best decisions occur when the leader accepts information, ideas, and opinions of members for evaluation, still he must express his own opinions, assume responsibility for making decisions, and, when required, make decisions without consulting the group.

Summary

The impact of the supervisor on the staff is such that we often can describe his behavior just by observing his subordinates and their productivity, grievances, absenteeism, and tardiness, and by noting how apathetic or energetic they are about departmental matters.

Supervisors vary from each other in many ways. Most significant in effects on their organization are the extent to which they initiate structure, show consideration for their subordinates, and balance their objectives and loyalties. They differ in the manner in which they make use of their abilities to persuade subordinates, yet often this is an effective style of leadership. They can use their power to coerce subordinates with promises and threats, but this practice has open and hidden costs. With power and ability they can treat subordinates democratically: setting the constraints liberally within which their subordinates can pursue objectives, sharing in decisions with subordinates, and discussing with them matters which affect all concerned. However, such permissiveness is less effective when groups are large, when time is limited, and in a variety of other circumstances limiting interaction possibilities between the supervisor and his subordinates. Yet, in the aggregate, where it is feasible, democratic permissiveness (*not* anarchy) pays off, particularly in the small, face-to-face working situation.[5]

---

[5]Science Research Associates have published a paperback which has significance for the psychology of supervisory behavior. (Elwood N. Chapman, *Supervisor's Survival Kit* [Chicago: Science Research Associates, 1970].)

6

Professional Responsibilities of the Supervisor

An educator needs to develop technical skills, but his concern must go far beyond the scope of those skills. He cannot delimit his activities and perform only as a technician.

The motivations that form the basic foundations of education do not operate on an eight-hour day—they are a constant part of daily life. In a sense, the educator has no choice of whether or not he is in a profession or a trade. The vital function of education in all areas of national concern has established the status of education.

The discussion of professional responsibilities calls attention to the need for identifying current practices and for defining the term "professional." Theology, law, and medicine long have been considered the learned professions, and in themselves involve many educational activities. During the Renaissance doctoral degrees were earned in these three areas. To these areas have been added professional degrees in engineering, in the sciences, in pharmacy, and in education.

A true profession involves a desire to serve mankind through the skills and knowledge accumulated within itself. A profession has a well-defined body of established factual material that can be verified by research. A scholarly concern for truth and continual dedicated search for new material and applications is in evidence. It involves both the present and the future —the long-range goals and hopes as well as daily practice.

The points discussed in this chapter include:

Requirements for professional status
Qualities of a profession
The graduate program of professional studies
The educator's responsibilities

Requirements for Professional Status

Each profession, old or new, undergoes misuse of position, forays into the mystical, and unfounded and untrue claims and practices. However, a true profession can meet the tests of truth: serious research and scholarly study.

Education is approaching the definitive criteria of a profession. During the last century the world has seen the rise of active study and research in education and of the establishment of the sociological, psychological, and philosophical foundations of education. Knowledge of the field of educational statistics is growing. Educators have become increasingly articulate in writing material for publication.

Many universities have established professional schools of education devoted to the training of educators and to the furtherance of the profession. Professional degree programs have been established at the Master's and Doctor's levels, aimed at training highly qualified individuals for work in professional education.

A professional worker originally was one who professed or had committed himself to a recognized system of values and standards. This original meaning still is implicit in the broader usage in which the term ordinarily is employed.

A physician professes—i.e., publicly commits himself—to the codes and standards of his group. So does the lawyer and the clergyman. Each of these individuals *follows a calling* rather than holds a job.

The professional worker who follows a calling has engaged in a rigorous program of preparation. Presently, this means preparation well beyond the requirements of the first academic degree. After he has met the minimum standards for admission to the parctice of his profession, he continues to study. He engages in research, attends meetings and conventions where his colleagues present the findings of their research, and by other means increases his grasp of the subject matter of his calling and enhances the quality of his practice.

The professional keeps abreast of developments in his field. The physician, the attorney, or the engineer who does not subscribe to and read professional journals, who fails to study important new books written by his colleagues, soon falls so far behind that he loses his effectiveness, and his patients or his clients.

Because the professional writer has equipped himself to exercise independent judgment, and because the work he does can be performed adequately only by the exercise of independent judgment, he decides what procedures and what materials are called for in any given case.

Of course he confers and seeks advice, but the course of action he adopts—the medication he prescribes, the dimensions of the structural beams in the building he plans, the precedent he cites when he argues a case in court—these are the individual, informed, and responsible decisions of the professional.

Working within the framework the professional man has no choice but to accept responsibility for his decisions. He does not expect, however, to perform without error. The physician is permitted rediagnosis; in each civil suit one qualified attorney is successful, one is not. When the professional man makes a mistake, he is responsible for it. Although an error carries no negative connotation, a mistake is unnecessary and should be avoided.

Perhaps most significant of all, if the professional man violates the ethical code of his calling he is subject to disciplinary action or even expulsion— by the action of his peers in the profession.

It is by these criteria that education must be judged. The professional educator should be prepared to work independently and should be able to decide for himself, *on the basis of sound knowledge and informed judgment.* how best to proceed in the always complex and constantly changing situations in the classroom.

Education will not be recognized as a *mature* profession as long as many educators hold jobs rather than follow a calling, or as long as there are large numbers of educators who fail to keep abreast of developments in their field. When educators themselves set the standards for admission to their ranks, and when they make the decision about who may be retained and who is to be expelled from these ranks, then the profession will have come of age.

In the light of what has been said, it may be seen that any means by which the educator can more effectively follow his calling, any *ethical* means by which he can better perform the work to which he has dedicated himself, is by definition appropriate for a person who operates on a professional level.

A major portion of costs for the services provided by the other professionals cited usually are *paid for by the individual,* except for the Public Defender and a few others. Hence, the cost actually is *less* to the public, on an individual basis, for this most important of professions. How would the doctor, or the lawyer, or the engineer, or even the clergyman achieve the occupational goals without the educator?

Qualities of a Profession

The following may be considered as a set of criteria for determining whether or not professional status has been earned, based upon present-day qualities of professionals. A profession possesses:

1. A craft which is comparatively conservative in practice;
2. Requirements for extensive and intensive training;
3. The maintenance of high standards for admission to the craft—an exclusiveness in selection;
4. A strict code of ethics;
5. A high level of social status accompanied by a high rate of remuneration;
6. An intellectual aura;
7. A program of research on both an organized and an individual level;
8. The practical application of research within the craft;
9. Techniques which can be taught, but only with difficulty;
10. A brotherhood—almost a caste;
11. Responsiveness and service to the public;

12. Foresight regarding theory concerning the nature of elements relevant to the profession;
13. Advanced training and certification.

Generally, people in a profession cannot agree as to what constitutes a profession. Everyone stresses service to the public. This denotes an intense desire to serve and to participate in the profession. When young people choose service as a way of life, they are ready to become professional educators.

The Graduate Program of Professional Studies

A supervising principal begins his formal training during his undergraduate years by acquiring basic knowledge and skills in some subject matter area. The graduate program:

1. Serves the need for acquiring a thorough grounding in educational philosophy, psychology, sociology, organization, and administration;
2. Introduces the techniques of research;
3. Instructs in curriculum, methods, techniques, and subject matter;
4. Provides instruction and practice in supervision.

Advanced research techniques and research design are covered at the doctoral level.

Special training in supervision usually is gained in this period of formal graduate work. Those educators who wish added competence in educational leadership, or who desire to teach at the college level, will continue to study in order to obtain a doctoral degree. Significant evidence of the growth of education as a profession is the creation of professional degrees in education on both the Master's and Doctor's levels, as listed below:

Master of Arts in Education
Master of Science in Education
Master of Education (Advanced Master's degree)
Doctor of Philosophy in Education
Doctor of Education

Further Graduate Studies

Intelligent selection of colleges and studies should be made in the light of the educator's professional interests. Evidence substantiates the fact that, in many instances, certain courses taken after an individual has begun his professional career have more meaning and significance than do similar courses taken prior to employment. Problems encountered in actual on-the-job situations can be correlated more directly to the content of the course. This correlation allows an educator to bring new ideas back to his local situation and to take advantage of the new methods presented in the course.

The educator thus has the responsibility for keeping abreast of the broad educational scene. Additionally, he must develop broad interests in other fields. He must possess an interest in the arts, sciences, and humanities and in local, state, national, and international affairs. In short, he must be an informed person. Awareness and sensitivity that can be gained only through involvement in these extra-professional concerns give the educator insights that may be applied to everyday educational pursuits.

It may seem at this point that an educator must be all things to all men if he is to meet the criteria mentioned in the preceding pages. This has not been the intent. This is not solely a quantitative issue; rather, it is both quantitative and qualitative, with emphasis on the latter. Also, it is not de-limited in time—it is a temporal continuum.

General Reading

When an educator begins his career he must expand and maintain his knowledge and understanding of the world. He should learn to assimilate, interpret, and evaluate what he reads on current problems and affairs. A sound reading program should be established if he wishes to enrich his experiences. A suggested reading program follows:

1. Read regularly at least one daily newspaper that has accurate state, national, and international news coverage, even if it arrives a day late from a city some distance away.
2. Read a community newspaper.
3. Read at least one weekly news periodical.
4. Read at least ten books each year on problems outside the profession.

Professional Reading

The greatest opportunity for in-service education is a well-balanced program of reading that includes a few of the best professional publications. Current books and journals often suggest methods for improving instruction. A good program of professional reading should include the following elements:

1. Significant developments and trends in public education;
2. New ideas in the areas of educational statistics, philosophy, psychology, and sociology;
3. Practices in curriculum organization and instructional procedures;
4. Developments and trends in the educator's major area of concern;
5. Developments in educational materials and environmental control.

The schools have not exploited the possibilities of a professional library for teachers within each school, although individual schools are the best units through which professional library materials may be made available. If school sytem budgets do not include the annual purchase of professional books, the educators in each school might consider contributing a used book apiece for this purpose. Within a few years such a plan would build up a very respectable professional collection for the faculty.

Professional Writing

Professional writing brings recognition to the individual and contributes to the profession. The firsthand experience serves as a practical basis for insights and understandings for professional writing, and professional writing helps the supervisor to clarify his thoughts and ideas.

Travel

Reality of places and individuals can be substantiated greatly by seeing them in their natural surroundings. Many governing boards have recognized the importance of travel and have allowed sabbatical leaves for educational travel.

Professional Activities for the Supervisor

Supervisory personnel should exhibit:

1. An active interest and noticeable pride in being a member of the profession.
2. A positive approach toward the status of the profession and the gains made toward professional status.
3. A willingness to do the "extra" expected of the strongly stimulated individual.
4. Interest in working with fellow educators and citizens to solve educational problems and to plan for improvement and evaluation.
5. Academic advancement in general degree work and also within the particular field, or fields, of the educator's responsibilities.
6. Willingness to endure temporary setbacks while working toward long-range improvements.
7. An insistence (when deserved) upon recognition as a professional in matters of student-teacher, supervisor-teacher, citizen-educator, and other personal relationships.
8. Courage to speak out when a situation demands attention.
9. A dissatisfaction with the unprofessional and unethical activities and conduct of other educators, such as exhibiting a manifest lack of interest in in-service education, pettiness in attempting to gain favor by reporting trivial mistakes of a fellow educator to the administrator, attempting to obtain a position already held by a professional educator, or undermining efforts of groups endeavoring to advance the effectiveness of education.
10. An awareness of the deep responsibility those in education bear to the nation's needs as well as to the needs of each student.
11. An image of the profession to the lay public as well as to other professions as one of purpose, quality, and high standards.
12. An insistence upon progress toward financial support for educators which will permit their elevation from mere subsistence levels of living.
13. A development of mutual respect for other professional members in education, going beyond employee-employer relationships found in other vocations.

14. A desire to clean his own linen when the situation warrants corrective action. The creation of a labor versus management situation, which may tend to degrade one segment of the educational team, should be avoided.

15. A realization that moderation in most instances is a virtue, and that patience must be a constant companion in progress toward professional goals. Students have been taught, and will continue to be taught, under the direction of many who never have attained professional status, just as some persons have been helped by other than fully licensed practitioners for hundreds of years.

The Educator's Responsibilities

Responsibility 1—To Himself

Only when one has learned to respect himself can he gain the respect of others. Certain attitudes of the educator toward himself and his work have considerable bearing on his total professional efficiency. He must respect himself and his own ideas without becoming dogmatic or intolerant of the ideas of others. He also should be able to view matters according to their relative importance because he otherwise might be in danger of devoting all of his time and energy to items that are considered trivial or routine.

The personal life of the educator also needs to be considered. He should attempt to lead a life as normal and as rich as possible. If he delimits his energy and interests to his job he is selling himself short; a well-rounded personal life will make him a more effective leader.

Responsibility 2—To Students

Children constitute an educator's most important professional responsibilities, taking up a good share of his thinking and effort throughout his tenure. An educator has the responsibility for knowing the entire program of public education, not merely at his own level — be it elementary, secondary, or higher — but at all levels. Many difficulties have resulted from a lack of articulation.

The educator should employ all available resources to the task of providing leadership in the development of the instructional program. Merely having a dedicated attitude toward children is insufficient. This attitude must be reflected by actual practice, and frequently this is not an easy task.

In order to provide the most profitable experiences to students, the educator will have to set up machinery to study their needs. The present *and future* needs of the students always should be in the foreground, and the educator should use these needs as the bases for all educational planning.

Responsibility 3—To the Patrons of the School

The effective educator recognizes his responsibility to the community. If he is thought of as a competent individual in whom the citizenry can put its trust, his success and the smooth operation of the school will be enhanced.

The educator's relationship with the general public, with the students, and with the parents must be characterized by honesty, sincerity, and integrity.

Responsibility 4—To the Members of the Staff

The supervising principal who believes and practices the basic democratic tenets in his relations with teachers in the school finds it much easier to stimulate similar practices and attitudes on the part of teachers in the classrooms.

Supervisory leaders occasionally find it necessary, in order to protect the rights of individuals or groups, to uphold principles which may be unpopular in the community. Although he will exercise the greatest tact in such situations, the leader of stature will not shrink from the role of advocate of a just cause.

Responsibility 5—To the Superintendent and the Governing Board

The principal has certain responsibilities to those who appoint him. These responsibilities encompass loyalty to the general purposes and welfare of the school system as a whole:

[Problems should be] dealt with impersonally, in a friendly but forthright manner, and through the proper channels. The effective principal is both honest and cooperative in his relations with those who select him.[1]

Any person who assumes the great responsibility of becoming a supervisor always should be acutely aware of his professional responsibilities to the superintendent of the school system in which he performs. He can be outstanding in all other areas, but if he falters in this association he may be doomed to certain failure.

Professional Organizations

The principal of a school is an important member of a great profession. This membership carries with it the obligation to carry out responsibilities in such a manner as to reflect credit upon the entire profession.[2]

Membership in Professional Organizations

One basis of in-service growth that the educator can promote is membership in professional organizations. These professional organizations and their publications have proven to be a major source of growth and intellectual stimulatin during the preparatory years and throughout the professional career of the supervisor. Virtually every facet of education has a professional organization and a periodical through which the educator can keep abreast of current developments in his field, and publish his contributions and critical reactions.

The educator of today usually obtains membership in more than one association, each organization serving a particular need. For example, national issues and coverages are found within the National Education Association; research and creative writings in education are emphasized in organizations such as Phi Delta Kappa. However, he cannot effectively be active in more than a few organizations even if one of the organizations, in reality, be a local edition of a second organization.

[1]Henry J. Otto, *Elementary School Organization and Administration* (New York: Appleton-Century-Crofts, Inc., 1954), p. 20.
[2]Ibid., p. 24.

Some representative organizations for education and educational supervision are:

Various state elementary, secondary, and community college school administrators' associations
The National Education Association
American Association of School Administrators
Department of Elementary School Principals
Department of Secondary School Principals
Association for Supervision and Curriculum Development
Various state teachers' associations
National Society for the Study of Education
Phi Delta Kappa
Pi Lambda Theta
Association for Childhood Education International
Many content and special interest associations

The supervising principal who never attends the local, regional, state, or national meetings of his professional organizations will suffer from the lack of opportunity to mingle and to exchange ideas with others. There are many branches of the national association in which an educator may enroll, according to his interests.

Membership in the Most Powerful Associations

All supervisors should be members of the strongest professional organizations available. Supervisors should realize that education association or teacher-union membership per se, is neither professional nor unprofessional, It is possible for any local organization to come under the domination of malcontents who become obsessed with shortsighted goals and who conceive their ends selfishly and apart from the ultimate considerations of the educational welfare of students.

A number of arguments, pro and con, concerning teacher unions are listed for the edification of the supervising principal:

Pro—people say:
1. Academic freedom is stressed.

2. Tenure provisions are strengthened.
3. Pay increases, as do fringe benefits.
4. Administrators and teachers should not be in the same organization under present conditions. Administrators and quasi-administrators are responsible to the governing board as employees and will take over the organization. (This often does happen, and is natural, for administrators usually are known to more people.)
5. Prestige increases for large organizations.
6. Other professional organizations are encouraged to take stronger stands. For example, the teachers of one midwestern state take a much stronger stand concerning academic freedom than they did in the past.
7. Associations are as militant as are unions, and therefore the more vigorous posture is already assumed by the association, rendering the union unneeded.

Con—people say:
1. Teachers teach children from homes of *both* labor and management.
2. Unions lower prestige and status, and are unprofessional.
3. The teacher becomes a civil servant.
4. Fringe benefits are degrading.
5. The tone of union arguments often is abusive.
6. Union methods are overly aggressive and are degrading.
7. The union implies that teachers and administrators are *not* all educators working on a professional level.

Questionable arguments include number (4) in the "pro" grouping and numbers (2), (4), and (6) in the "con" section. The merger of the local association and union in Los Angeles in 1970 was a most interesting development. If education is to be considered as a true profession, then the supervising principal and the teacher must think of themselves as fellow *educators,* rather than as manager and employee.

Broad Interests

A profession, we have seen, requires a high regard for the codes of professional conduct. This regard for the codes of professional conduct should be demonstrated by the supervising principal in his relationship with his fellow principals, as well as in the performance of his duties. The supervising principal can contribute to his profession by *actively supporting* professional organizations.

Moving Toward Professional Status

The demands of supervision are so varied that versatility is one of the basic requisites for proficiency on the part of the principal.

Roles in a Profession

The job of a supervisor is such that he must be able to assume many roles with ease. He must be:

1. An executive officer
2. A stimulator
3. An expert
4. An adviser
5. A coordinator
6. A mediator
7. An interpreter
8. An evaluator
9. An educational prophet

There is an ever-growing group of educators who have reached professional levels. As the ranks swell, the acceptance and desire for professional status grow also. Those professional educators sincerely working toward improving their profession, and thus the effectiveness of their efforts to educate, have definite responsibilities for leadership and for encouraging others within the vocation.

The listings included in the do—don't sections below may be considered as sets of criteria which, when met, may assist in gaining recognition of the educational endeavor as a true profession.

DO

1. Everything possible to combat anti-intellectualism.
2. Everything possible in the area of basic research.

3. Remember that there is nothing wrong with being concerned with remuneration. The way the concern is carried into action is important. Students are entitled to be taught by the most capable teachers possible. If they are to be taught by these capable individuals, there must be concern with pay and fringe benefits.
4. Everything in your power to increase standards of professional training.
5. Be active in a few professional organizations, but strongly resist efforts to require membership in many professional organizations.
6. Participate actively in the internship program. Encourage professional training in conjunction with practice teaching and internship.
7. Work to produce and elevate a professional code of ethics.
8. Use your best judgment in making recommendations.

DON'T

1. Apologize for the profession.
2. Run down theory except if the theory is completely cut off from practice and is proven inaccurate. (Remember: teaching is an art with a scientific basis.)
3. Be tempted into the sin of pettiness; it can be stifling. (Show that you respect your colleagues!)
4. Gossip; it endangers privileged communication.
5. Make remarks concerning students in public.

When the lay person thinks of a medical doctor or of a lawyer, he assumes a rigorous professional preparation and also a dedication of purpose beyond mere earnings. This type of thinking can and needs to be encouraged in the field of education.

Supervisory Problems

Problem 1

A teacher in the school to which you are assigned reports to you that a co-worker has made an error in judgment.

How would you handle the situation?

Problem 2

You have been asked by the superintendent to indicate how policies could be developed and submitted to the governing board which would indicate to the professional staff and to the lay public that the superintendent and the governing board consider the professional staff to be true professionals.

How would you proceed?

What policies would you recommend?

Problem 3

You have been asked by the state professional association to prepare a suggested bill for submission to the legislature which would establish procedures under which professional educators would select those to be admitted to the profession, and by which the professional educators would pass judgment on those who may have to be asked to retire from the profession.

How would you proceed?

What policies would you recommend?

Problem 4

You find a memorandum in your in-basket. In the memorandum a member of your staff indicates that he is applying for a position that is already held by a co-worker.

How would you handle the matter?

Selected Bibliography

Books

Frazen, C. G. *Foundations of Secondary Education.* New York: Harper and Brothers, 1955.

Frey, Sherman H. and Keith R. Getschman. *School Administration: Selected Readings.* New York: Thomas Y. Crowell Company, 1969.

Grinnell, J. E., and R. J. Young. *The School and the Community.* New York: The Ronald Press Company, 1955.

Hicks, Hanne J. *Administrative Leadership in the Elementary School.* New York: The Ronald Press Company, 1956.

Jacobson, Paul B., and William C. Reavis. *Duties of School Principals.* Englewood Cliffs, New Jersey: Prentice-Hall, Inc., 1941.

Jordan, William C. *Elementary School Leadership.* New York: McGraw-Hill Book Company, Inc., 1959.

Kyte, George C. *The Principal at Work.* Boston: Ginn and Company, 1952.

Marchus, Sando. *Mr. Principal, How Do You Do?* Martinez, California: Sandemark Enterprises, 1956.

Miller, V., and W. B. Spaulding. *The Public Administration of American Schools.* Yonkers, New York: World Book Company, 1952.

Mort, Paul R. *Principles of School Administration.* New York: McGraw-Hill Book Company, Inc., 1946.

Otto, Henry J. *Elementary School Organization and Administration.* New York: Appleton-Century-Crofts, Inc., 1954.

Pierce, T. M. et al. *Community Leadership for Public Education.* Englewood Cliffs, New Jersey: Prentice-Hall, Inc., 1955.

Reavis, W. C. et al. *Administering the Elementary School.* Englewood Cliffs, New Jersey: Prentice-Hall, Inc., 1953.

Reeder, Ward G. *Public School Administration.* New York: The Macmillan Company, Inc., 1949.

Sears, Jesse B. *Public School Administration.* New York: The Ronald Press Company, 1947.

Stoops, Emery, and Russell E. Johnson. *Elementary School Administration.* New York: McGraw-Hill Book Co., 1967.

Periodicals

Armstrong, G. O. "His Teacher Must Advance His Profession." *Minnesota Journal of Education* XLI (April 1961): 15–17.

Kinnaird, Virginia. "Privileges Entail Obligations." *National Education Association Journal* XLIII (April 1954): 245.

Robinson, T. E. "The Ten Best Public Relation Devices." *The School Executive* LXVIII (August 1949): 36–38.

The Editor. "News and Trends." *National Education Association Journal* LI (January 1962): 4.

Wardner, Philip. "They Teach Themselves." *National Education Association Journal* XXXIX (December 1950): 675–676.

Yeager, H. V. "Profession Anyone?" *Journal of Teacher Education* XI (December 1960): 460–463.

Other Sources

American Association of School Administrator. *Staff Relations in School Administration*. Washington, D.C.: National Education Association, 1955.

Hall, Roy M. *Achievements and Changes in Educational Administration*. Austin: The Southwest School Administration Center, University of Texas, 1956.

Haring, Roy J. *The Role of the Superintendent in the Interrelationship of School and Community*. New York: Columbia University, published for the Pennsylvania Association of District Superintendents, 1953.

Midcentury White House Counference on Children and Youth. *Platform Recommendations, and Pledge to Children*. Washington, D.C.: Government Printing Office, 1950.

National School Public Relations Association. *Eighty-Eight Techniques in School Public Relations for Teachers and Administrators*. Washington, D.C.: National Education Association, 1951.

The Conference. *Education for Professional Responsibility. A Report of the Proceedings of the Inter-Professions Conference on Education for Professional Responsibility*. Pittsburgh: Carnegie Press, 1948.

Ethics for the Supervisor in Handling Personnel Matters[1]

To fulfill his special responsibilities to students, parents, the community, and the profession as an executor of board policies, as adviser to the board on policies and procedures, and as a professional leader in the school district, the educator employed in a supervisory position recognizes and adheres to these standards of personnel administration:

In the selection and employment of new personnel, he:

1. Spares no effort to maintain and increase professional standards, utilizing professional placement agencies to obtain properly qualified teachers and administrators before employing provisionally credentialed personnel.
2. Provides opportunities to employees to make known their desires for transfer or advancement and gives consideration to their wishes.
3. Considers no position vacant and seeks no applicants for it before the present employee has resigned or has been notified that he will not be re-employed.
4. Adheres strictly to adopted salary schedules in employing new personnel.
5. Describes as accurately as possible the employment policies and educational philosophy of the district, the salary schedule and the grade level, subject areas, or other assignment for which the candidate is being considered.
6. Informs out-of-state candidates clearly about the loss of service credits toward retirement that they may incur by changing states and advises them to consider this factor in arriving at their decision.
7. Makes no offer of employment for a period of time concurrent to that covered by a contract to another district unless that district has first notified him of its willingness to release the employee.

---

[1]The statement on ethics in personnel matters was developed by a special committee composed of representatives of the California Association of School Administrators, California Association of Secondary School Administrators, California Elementary School Administrators Association, and the California Teachers Association Personnel Standards Commission. This definition is aimed primarily to serve as a guide to supervisors to aid them in avoiding unethical personnel practices. It also may serve as a basis for interpretation of specific acts when malpractice is charged.

In the supervision and leadership of his staff, he:

1. Assumes responsibility for promoting the success of all employees, realizing that the difference between the success and failure of an employee may be dependent on his efforts in selection, in supervision, and in assignment.
2. Makes sure that as soon as significant weaknesses are observed they are called to the attention of the employee and that assistance toward their correction is extended.
3. Makes no formal criticism of any employee to his superiors or the board without having first discussed this criticism with the employee involved.
4. Informs superiors and the board about the good performance and contributions of employees.
5. Is alert to opportunities to further the advancement of each qualified employee and is willing to assist him in his efforts in improving his personal and professional status.
6. Values the professional suggestions and criticisms of staff members, according to each the recognition to which he is entitled as a fellow professional in the field of education.
7. Provides opportunity for employees to discuss their problems or complaints freely with him and assists in the cooperative development of systematic channels for reporting and discussing employee problems and suggestions.

In recommending re-employment or dismissal of employees, he:

1. Establishes a systematic procedure for periodic written evaluation of probationary teachers. Teachers are kept informed of their employment status as it will effect re-employment, tenure, or dismissal.
2. Recommends that an employee be rehired unless the employee has been notified regarding his weaknesses and has been given time for and assistance toward their correction.
3. Does not jeopardize the educational welfare of students in order to avoid an unpleasant dismissal relationship.

In respect to recommendations for former employees, he:

1. Realizes that an honest appraisal is necessary to do justice to the teacher, the profession, and to the students in any district contemplating employing this teacher.
2. Does not suggest to an employee by implication or direct statement that a letter of recommendation will be affected by submission of a resignation or failure to resign.
3. Records no negative criticism in a letter of reference or in direct conversation with potential employers except those which have been called to the employee's attention during appraisal conferences.
4. Complies with the request to supply a letter of recommendation within a reasonable time.
5. Keeps confidential the content of confidential professional papers.

To meet his responsibility to the profession, he:

1. Endorses the principle that the profession must accept responsibility for the conduct of its members and understands that his own conduct will be regarded as a sample of the quality of the profession.
2. Makes his professional life one of continuous growth.
3. Maintains an attitude that strengthens public respect for the teaching profession and for the school system of which he is a part.
4. Maintains active membership in professional organizations and works through them to attain the objectives that will advance the status of the profession.
5. Exercises his right to participate in the democratic processes which determine school policy.
6. Follows ethical business procedures. He:
   a) Patronizes reputable employment agencies.
   b) Requests honest recommendations for himself; gives honest recommendations for others.
   c) Does not underbid for a position or apply for a specific position until he knows it is vacant.

    d) Works for the appointment and advancement of those who are best qualified by ability and experience.

    e) Conducts school affairs through the established channels of the school system.

7. Acts with consideration in his contacts with fellow teachers. He:

    a) Is kind, tolerant, and loyal, and avoids pettiness, jealousy, and rancor.

    b) Takes pride in their achievements, is grateful for their assistance.

    c) Respects their confidence.

    d) Criticizes with discretion, knowing that only that criticism is valid that stems from a desire to improve the educational process and that is directed at issues rather than personalities.

7

Supervisory Techniques
and How to Apply Them

The rapidly changing scene in the instructional program is a challenge to instructional leadership in our school systems. It must be met with increased skills and understandings through professional growth.

The competency with which the principal, through skill in leadership, inspires teachers to participate in group and individual programs for professional growth will be reflected in the operational efficiency success of the instructional program.

This chapter includes a discussion of the following topics:

Principles of the program for in-service education
Individual endeavors for in-service education
How to help the beginning teacher
How to improve orientation meetings
How to help the superior teacher
How to help the senior teacher
How to work with the dissenting teacher
How to work with the "undemocratic" staff member
How to improve workshops and institutes
How to use group problem-solving techniques in supervision
Do—don't
"In Basket" supervisory problems
Chapter Supplements

Principles of the Program for In-Service Education

In-service education includes all activities of school personnel which contribute to their continued professional growth and competence. The following may be considered as a set of basic principles:

1. The in-service education program emerges from recognized needs of the school and community.
2. All school personnel need in-service education.
3. Proper supervision is an effective means of accelerating the in-service professional growth of personnel.
4. Improving the quality of instruction is the immediate and long-range objective of in-service education.
5. In-service education leads to a continuous process of reexamination and revision of the educational program. Additionally, it encourages participants to attain self-realization through competence, accomplishment, and security.
6. In-service education has become an increasing concern of state agencies, colleges and universities, school boards, school administrators, and teachers.
7. Supervisors should create an atmosphere that will stimulate a desire on the part of teachers for in-service growth.
8. The in-service program should provide for keeping personnel abreast with research and advances in education.
9. An in-service education program is most effective when cooperatively initiated and planned.

The in-service program is one in which both supervisors and teachers grow in improving the learning situation of children. According to H. Spears,[1] there are certain principles of the in-service program which have become apparent:

1. The professional education of the teacher does not cease as he leaves college.
2. Professional development cannot be adequately served by teaching experience alone.
3. Although it is reasonable to expect a teacher to guide his own future development, it is the obligation of the school system to stimulate advancement by providing opportunities for in-service growth. These op-

[1]Harold Spears, *Curriculum Planning through In-Service Programs* (Englewood Cliffs, New Jersey: Prentice-Hall, Inc., 1957), p. 315.

portunities, properly planned and coordinated, constitute the in-service education program of the school system.

4. The provision of staff leadership for this program is a legitimate school expenditure.
5. The test of the in-service program lies in its consequences in instruction and student development.
6. The program for in-service education can be separated from neither curriculum planning, nor supervision. The three represent overlapping functions of the program for instructional improvement.

There are many clues which may help one to ascertain what type of in-service education is needed. One such clue might come from the evaluation of the staff by the supervising principal; another clue might come from apparent faculty competence in curriculum changes; and still another might come from community needs changes that require understanding of the problems contained therein.[2]

OBJECTIVES. In the report of the Teacher Education Workshop, conducted at George Peabody College for Teachers, the following principles were presented:

1. Ultimately . . . [in-service education] must contribute to the growth and development of . . . [children] and to the quality of living in the community.
2. It emerges from the needs of the total school.
3. It is based on long term plans with broadly defined goals.
4. It is a democratic enterprise.
5. It is realistic and practical.
6. It maintains balance.
7. It contributes to a well rounded scholarship, to professional competence, and to the social understanding of all teachers in service.
8. It develops in teachers an awareness of the values in resources and their own obligation with respect to resource education.

[2]Kimball Wiles, *Supervision for Better Schools* (Englewood Cliffs, New Jersey: Prentice-Hall, Inc., 1951), p. 223.

9. It coordinates the efforts of many individuals and agencies.
10. It discovers and develops leaders.
11. It discovers, develops, and uses teachers with special talents.
12. It promotes professional advancement.
13. It works toward the security of teachers.
14. It is continuous and provides for continuous evaluation in the light of
    its purposes.[3]

With reference to teacher growth, A. S. Barr, W. H. Burton, and L. J.
Brueckner suggested the deletion of a phrase which was popular in the
past. They stated:

The expression "training of teachers in service" is no longer in good repute:
at least, its standing is not so clear as it was some time back. The expression as
used by many is undoubtedly very closely associated with the teacher-centered
concept of supervision which we hope now may be supplanted by a goal-cen-
tered, cooperative type of group activity in which teachers, pupils, supervisors,
administrators, and all others concerned work and grow together.[4]

There are many changes in the role of the supervisor which increasingly
are becoming apparent in theory and practice. The new concept emphasizes the use of the approach of the principal, teacher, and specialist-
consultant working together as a team for the improvement of classroom
instruction.

With many schools of thought centered on the role of supervision, the
basic function can be interpreted as the improvement of instruction and of
the instructional program, with the supervising principal helping the
teacher to do a better job. The means utilized to realize this goal constitute
a program of in-service education.

How to Plan for Supervision

Planning appears to be the most essential factor for effective leadership in a
supervisory program. Planning for supervision must provide: (1) for ade-

[3]Teacher Education Workshop, "Report of the Teacher Education Workshop," duplicated material. (Nashville: The George Peabody College for Teachers, 1945), pp.
24–25.
[4]A. S. Barr, William H. Burton, and Leo J. Brueckner, *Supervision, Democratic Leadership in the Improvement of Learning* (New York: D. Appleton-Century Company,
1947), p. 565.

quate budgeting of the supervising principal's day so that he may spend the major portion of his time on supervision, (2) for the determination of the methods and techniques which will insure the effective use of available time, and (3) for the construction of adequate schedules and definite plans so that available time may be utilized efficiently.

Care and skill in continuous, comprehensive, flexible, and cooperative planning are the keys to effective instructional improvement. Without planning, a constructive and comprehensive program cannot be developed.

While all plans must be considered as tentative, both long- and short-term planning are required. Short-term plans emphasize but one or two major goals. Planning must be creative, for each school system, school, classroom, teacher, and class offers unique circumstances, capabilities, and personalities. Applying the techniques of supervision, then, is not merely a mechanical procedure.

Most Beneficial Techniques

According to the *Twelfth Yearbook* of the Department of Supervisors and Directors of Instruction,[5] supervision is planning for all-around improvement of those school factors that seem to affect seriously the teacher-learning process, especially the school building and its equipment, the materials of instruction, the organization and management of the school, the curriculum, the methods of teaching, and the personality of the teacher. The Department reported the most beneficitl techniques for supervision to include:

1. *Faculty meetings.* These faculty meetings include curriculum meetings, institutes, workshops, study groups and clubs, excursions, travel, seminars, committee work, curriculum revision, experimentation, and research.

   A faculty meeting offers many opportunities in a program of in-service education because usually it is the major means of communication within a school. Despite its many advantages, evidence indicates that these meetings usually are not popular with the teachers. If properly planned and executed, staff meetings can create an atmosphere of working relationships and improve the quality of education within the school.

[5]Department of Supervisors and Directors of Instruction, *Newer Instructional Practices of Promise,* Twelfth Yearbook (Washington, D.C.: National Education Association, 1940), pp. 328–349.

2. *Supervisory visits.* Visits generally should be followed by conferences. The supervisor should study the total learning situation, giving attention to all the factors which affect student growth.

3. *Professional bulletins.* Unfortunately, a majority of professional bulletins are prepared by those engaged in supervision. If they were teacher prepared, perhaps they would have more meaning. These bulletins constitute effective communication media, and may include announcements, summaries of research, analyses of presentations at professional association meetings, acknowledgments, and developments in the various subject matter fields.

4. *Professional libraries.* A convenient source of information is the school professional library. Teacher contributions could become a part of this repository of information. The professional library provides not only a source of information, but is also an incentive for personal satisfaction. Books on the professional point of view, plays, newer supplementary readers, and many professional periodicals should be available to all teachers.

5. *Materials center or curriculum laboratories.* Curriculum laboratories supply instructional guides, sample materials of instructional technology, and textbooks.

Additional methods used in supervision include:

1. *Teacher assignment.* For optimum success the assignment of a particular teacher to a certain class, grade level, and subject should be determined on the basis of staff needs, training, experience, personality, and the desire of the teacher. Anything the principal does to make the teacher more secure will improve the teacher's results with his students.

2. *Demonstration teaching.* Demonstration teaching is a valuable technique. Prepared plans, printed in advance, emphasizing important points or the value of certain teaching techniques, are helpful. A conference following the demonstration may clarify many points. An analysis of the observation is necessary.

3. *Curriculum development.* Curriculum planning offers an excellent opportunity for staff participation. It is up to the principal to create the interest and desire for this important and continuous work.

4. *Development of instructional guides.* This enterprise explores and lists suggestions aimed at assisting the teacher in instructional planning. Unfortunately, in many schools teachers are given very little opportunity for assisting in the determination of the objectives of instruction, the subject matter content, or in the selection of instructional materials, including textbooks. Since the democratic movement, more teachers are encouraged to participate in cooperative curriculum development.
5. *Excursions.* Trips to the community and local industries are excellent methods of education, especially in the teacher-student relationship.
6. *Workshops and institutes.* Workshops provide for group cooperation, for the pooling of ideas, for discussion on mutual or specific problems, and for personal and professional growth in the various subject matter areas. Specific suggestions concerning workshops and institutes appear later in this chapter.
7. *Intervisitation of classes.* Studies reveal that intervisitation is quite popular and effective. These visits usually are planned upon the teacher's request. This technique is much more effective if a careful analysis follows each observation.
8. *Professional reading.* Professional reading is widely encouraged by specialists. Teachers should be urged to read on various topics, by many authors, and not restrict themselves to a particular author.
9. *School-community survey.* A comprehensive study of the community will help the teacher and the supervising principal understand more clearly the type of program which will meet the needs and interests of the students.

There is no single method. The first problem is to determine needs. Then the problem is to determine ways in which the teachers can be helped. There are many techniques, and those selected should contribute in a marked degree to a particular aim or objective.

Barr, Barton, and Brueckner referred to all methods of supervision as "subsidiary techniques in improvement programs."[6] This appears to be an appropriate phrase, since any method used to promote teacher growth is

[6]A. S. Barr, W. S. Burton, and L. J. Brueckner, *Supervision* (New York: Appleton-Century-Crofts, 1938), chapters I and IV.

subsidiary to the basic objective—that of student growth and development. They have listed, under separate classifications, some of the devices for personnel growth and improvement in the educational program, as follows:

I. *Group Devices*
  A. *Doing Techniques*
    1. Workshops
    2. Committees
  B. *Verbal Techniques*
    1. Staff Meetings
    2. Group Counseling
    3. Course Work
    4. Documentary Aids
    5. Directed Reading
  C. *Observational Techniques*
    1. Directed Observation
    2. Field Trips
    3. Travel Seminars
    4. Audio-Visual Aids

II. *Individual Devices*
  A. *Active Techniques*
    1. Participation in the total teaching act
    2. Individual problem-solving
  B. *Verbal Techniques*
    1. Individual conferences
    2. Adjustment counseling
  C. *Observational Techniques*
    1. Directed observation
    2. Intervisitation[7]

Other useful techniques also are effective, including experimental studies, study of tests and measurements, research, and use of the professional library and learning or instructional center.

[7]Ibid., p. 465.

The Specialists Agree

Specialists are in general agreement that staff relations based on democratic leadership provide the key to successful attainment of supervisory objectives. There is some general agreement on many techniques and methods utilized in instructional improvement, but many leading specialists do not agree on the degree of effectiveness of certain techniques.

Planning appears to be the most essential factor for effective leadership in a supervisory program. It is agreed that planning must have these three factors present:

1. It cannot be standardized.
2. It must be comprehensive.
3. It must be flexible.

Specialists tend to agree that an effective program needs the full cooperation of staff, teachers, and resource persons, and that selection of method depends upon many variables, and is a function of need.

Individual Endeavors for In-Service Education

One objective of supervision is to achieve self-directed growth. C. T. McNerney[8] said that teacher improvement can be achieved only through teacher effort.

There are many ways in which the individual teacher initiates growth in professional competency. The principal can help by securing annotated bibliographies to facilitate professional and general reading. Some teachers, under pressure of time from different sources, would rather investigate at their convenience those areas in which a need is felt. Periodicals, particularly, help the supervisor and the teacher to keep abreast of immediate thinking in curriculum improvement, pointing out changing ideas and giving food for thought.

The supervising principal can suggest further graduate courses. Here he

[8]Chester T. McNerney, *Educational Supervision* (New York: McGraw-Hill Book Company, Inc., 1951), p. 297.

would endeavor to stimulate the teacher by noting that the product of additional learning would benefit the entire school. Recent research and theory, brought out in the university class, could be reported to the faculty.

Conference Attendance and Experimental Research Programs

Principals should encourage teachers to attend conferences on trends in education, curriculum development, subject matter, or any number of programs that may help the teacher to grow in service. Some teachers work in experimental programs, discovering new ideas or exploring the possibilities of untried projects.

Educational Travel

Travel is still another way for the classroom teacher to broaden his horizons. Accumulating other points of view, learning to understand other cultures, and the experience of travel add to the teacher's personal development.

Expanding his cultural background provides the teacher with an assurance in further studies and a firsthand knowledge for his class. Sabbatical leaves, as well as grants, fellowships, and scholarships, often bring travel within the financial reach of the educator.

Membership in Professional Organizations

Membership in professional organizations permits the educator to come into contact with other interested members. Expounding new trends and providing constructive criticism concerning current problems enables the members to exchange ideas in a democratic situation. The supervising principal should encourage teachers to join those organizations from which they will benefit. Coercion, however, must not be used. The principal also should inform the new teacher of the kinds of local, state, and national educational associations available to him, and the type of services each renders.

Professional Writing

Professional writing is another way in which the individual may share valuable experiences or new ideas with other teachers. Since each person contributes to the growth of the profession and to his personal development in a unique manner, writing creates an outlet for his talents which may stimulate other educators to respond. The supervising principal must encourage and assist the writer in any manner possible.

How to Help the Beginning Teacher

The teachers most in need of help, and the ones who should profit most by the help given, are the beginning teachers.

The Beginning Teacher

A principal often fails to appreciate the difficulties that a beginning teacher has to encounter. For what could be a multitude of reasons, the beginning teacher sometimes experiences difficulties before the principal realizes.

Naturally a beginning teacher, with little experience in the teaching profession, may be depressed, since he finds that adjustment to the school society, administration, and supervision is not an easy task. The orientation of the beginning teacher, if it is thorough and constructive, constitutes the initial steps in his adjustment. At the start a new teacher should not be given extra responsibilities, such as work on curriculum revision committees.

Greeting the Beginning Teacher

A hearty welcome to the beginning teacher by the principal, and encouraging words by the "old timers" on the staff, may alleviate the pain of his integrating into the faculty.

The beginning teacher will continue to feel insecure when the students are not cooperative and lessons do not run smoothly. In such a situation teachers' suggestions often are more effective and acceptable to the beginning teacher than is the principal's help, for the teacher may feel too uncomfortable about difficulties to be frank with the principal. When the beginning teacher feels more at home in the new environment he should be encouraged to visit, voluntarily, an experienced teacher's room for observation purposes.

Many new teachers are employed each year in the school systems of the

United States. The successful assimilation of these new teachers into the system is a major concern of the principal and of the teachers of the school to which the beginners are assigned.

Specialists agree that no matter how well trained the new teachers are, there is still a need for supervision and in-service edutcation. E. H. Reeder explained:

> The problem of harmonizing theory and practice in a highly complicated and createive activity like teaching is a confusing and difficult one, not likely to be solved by individuals working alone.[9]

Growth in teaching ability is not assured merely by obtaining experience. There must be evaluation and in-service education. Barr and Burton expressed the following opinion:

> There is no teacher at present, nor is there likely to be for a long time any teacher who is so expert and so well trained that . . . [he] cannot profit by some of the improvement devices.[10]

Supervision has a responsibility toward helping the new teacher, who is entitled to all the help necessary to do a good job. This help should be given as the teacher's needs arise, and in a way that will benefit him most.

ACQUAINTING THE BEGINNING TEACHER WITH AVAILABLE SERVICES. The new teacher needs to be acquainted with the supervisory services available. H. Spears[11] defined the limits of supervisory service as (1) curriculum development, (2) the selection of instructional materials, (3) in-service education, and (4) direct supervisory services to the teacher, including supervisory visits and conferences.

Community Relations for the Beginning Teacher

The beginning teacher should understand the basic factors of the parent-teacher relationship:[12]

---

[9]Edwin H. Reeder, *Supervision in the Elementary School* (Boston: Houghton Mifflin Company, 1953), p. 270.
[10]A. S. Barr et al., *Supervision, Democratic Leadership in the Improvement of Learning* (New York: D. Appleton-Century Company, 1947), p. 415.
[11]Harold Spears, *Improving the Supervision of Instruction* (Englewood Cliffs, New Jersey: Prentice-Hall, Inc., 1953).
[12]See Wilber A. Yauch, *Improving Human Relations in School Administration* (New York: Harper and Brothers, 1949), pp. 216–217.

1. Parents often look upon the teachers as being rather different from normal human beings.
2. Teachers frequently feel that parents exercise undue and unnecessary control over school activities.
3. Unmarried teachers may not understand the perspective with which most parents view their own children.
4. Parents measure the value of their child's school program against the one they followed.
5. Teachers may possess an understanding of the principles of child growth and development not possessed by the parents.
6. Success in parent-teacher relations is based upon empathy, understanding, and acceptance. Differences should be welded into an approach which is based upon the student's welfare. There seldom is any conflict caused by one side being interested in the student and the other being indifferent. Problems arise from disagreement concerning what is the best approach to aiding the student, rather than over the extent of interest the teacher or parent has in the student's welfare.

The principal should encourage the beginning teacher to observe the following points in conducting parent-teacher conferences:

1. Be a good listener.
2. Remember empathy. Say, "I certainly can understand why you would be upset."
3. Be sincere. Do not use vocabulary with which the parent is unfamiliar.
4. Be honest, yet be diplomatic.
5. Do not discuss other teachers, departments, or students.
6. Let the solution to a problem be "our" solution.

A teacher should not encourage a parent to question him regarding specific techniques of teaching. He should be welcomed as an observer. Neither a teacher nor a supervising principal should attempt to teach a parent in a fifteen-minute conference what it took him five or more years of higher education plus experience to learn. Suggest that the parent may visit the classroom. Such observations probably should be delimited to a maximum of twenty minutes.

A more complete discussion of parent-teacher conferences is included as the supplement to chapter 18.

The Beginning Teacher and Student Relations

The beginning teacher may profit from the following students' comments, gathered by E. Stoops and A. R. Evans,[13] if he wishes to gain and maintain student respect:

1. The teacher should keep the class in a studious attitude.
2. The teacher should be someone who has his heart in the work. He should not be someone who is doing it just to have some income.
3. Beginning teachers should joke—not all the time, but once or twice in the lesson. They should look happy and smile.
4. Teachers should be neat and clean.
5. Someone who keeps order, so as to have the attention of the whole class when he wants it, and who is consistent, will be respected.
6. The teacher should make the subject interesting.
7. The students want a teacher to say frankly, "I don't know, but I'll find out."

How to Use the Group Conference to Help Beginning Teachers

SUGGESTED TOPICS FOR DISCUSSION IN THE GROUP CONFERENCE. The following topics are recommended for discussion in the weekly conference:

1. Becoming acquainted with the background of the children.
2. Becoming acquainted with the school and classroom routines.
3. Learning to plan (see Figure 7–1), including long-range plans for a semester and planning for shorter periods. Semester plans, weekly plans, and daily plans should be discussed.
4. *Suggestions for self-evaluation,* such as those included in Table 7–1.
5. Becoming acquainted with teaching aids, including the materials of in-

---

[13]Emery Stoops and Albert R. Evans, "Helping the Beginning Teacher," *The Nation's Schools* LVII (April 1956): 74.

Periods or Times		Name _____ Dates _____				
		Grade _____ Received _____				
		(List Objectives, Pages, Assignments, Special Materials)				
	Subjects	Monday	Tuesday	Wednesday	Thursday	Friday
I						
II						
VI						
VII						
VIII						

FIGURE 7-1   Sample Weekly Plan Block Form.

structional technology (such as computer-assisted learning, instructional modules including tape recordings, graphic materials, single-concept 8mm film loops, and slides), teaching machines, and programmed instruction.

6. Helping teachers to understand children.
7. Learning about the use of time in the daily program, including legal requirements.
8. Learning about reports to parents.
9. Learning about attendance accounting.
10. Learning to conduct a parent-teacher conference.
11. Learning about the ethics of the profession.

12. Discussing matters of personal effectiveness.
13. Learning about the school health program.
14. Learning about the safety program.
15. Planning to help the child who is below grade level in accomplishments, and how to plan corrective, remedial, and developmental activities.
16. Developing class organization and environment.

TABLE 7–1   Points in Self-evaluation for the Beginning Teacher

Item	*Comments*
1. Were the preparation and organization of subject matter adequate?	
2. Were goals (objectives) clearly stated in operational terms?	
3. Was the presentation satisfactory?	
4. Were the social controls of the class satisfactory?	
5. Were the students interested? If so, how was the interest secured and maintained?	
6. Was there a maximum of participation on the part of the students?	
7. Were there valuable contributions from the class? If so, were they capitalized on? How?	
8. Were new situations utilized to the best advantage?	
9. Was student growth apparent? If so, along what lines was this growth? Was it in: Development of skills and abilities? Gain in knowledge of subject matter? Development of wholesome attitudes? Development of independent thinking?	
10. Was there student growth in terms of the teacher's objectives? To what extent?	
11. Was there self-improvement on the part of the teacher? What further needs are evident?	

How to Help the Beginning Teacher Work
with the Disturbed Child in the Classroom

The beginning teacher needs specific assistance in meeting the needs of the disturbed child and in protecting the other students from aggressive acts or other actions which may be taken by an emotionally disturbed individual. At all times the rights of the group must be preserved. One child must not be permitted to keep thirty or thirty-five other children from learning effectively and efficiently. A supervising principal suggested the following three methods:

1. Releasing tension
2. Giving recognition
3. Building interest

A possible pattern for working with the emotionally disturbed child in the classroom follows:
1. Have individual talks with the student before problems arise;
2. Speak directly to the child;
3. Isolate him from the group if necessary; always give opportunity for him to come back when he is ready;
4. Bring him close to the teacher;
5. Differentiate between disapproval of activity and disapproval of the child;
6. Do not become so upset that you punish the whole group;
7. Avoid too much talking and watch the pitch of your voice, raising it only when needed;
8. Prevent problems by proper timing and rapid movement from one activity to another;
9. Have private conferences with offenders;
10. Use praise where deserved;
11. Speak with firmness to insure attention but do not shock; obtain the student's undivided attention so far as possible;
12. Remember: causes of poor self-control should be analyzed.

Suggestions for classroom control which the supervising principal may wish to communicate to the beginning teacher are included in the chapter supplement.

How to Help the Beginning Teacher Prepare for the Beginning of the School Term

Probably the time of decision in the professional life of an educator occurs during the first two months of teaching. Serious problems should be solved by the end of this time.

The beginning teacher requires specific assistance in preparing for the initial days of this vital period — the beginning of the school term. One large city school system offered suggestions covering the following topics:

1. Before school begins:
    a) Find the answers to vital questions.
    b) Make a lesson plan for the entire day.
    c) Have instructional materials ready.
2. The first day:
    a) With the children
    b) With the parents
    c) Room organization
    d) Work habits
    e) Control
3. The first week:
    a) Find the answers to vital questions.
    b) Make a general plan for the first two weeks.

How to Improve Orientation Meetings

There are several categories of beginning teachers who come into a school system every year: the teacher fresh from teacher training who has never taught before, the experienced teacher from another state or system, and the teacher within the school system who is changing grade levels. All of these teachers will require some degree of help from the supervising principal to acquaint them with local policies and procedures, as well as help in planning for instruction.

Orientation programs are designed to welcome beginning teachers to the school and community, to assist them in developing professional confidence, and to help them in solving both personal and professional problems. The terms "orientation" and "induction" are used synonymously.

One aim of an orientation program is to provide specific information to the beginning teacher regarding his teaching assignment. Teachers should be shown around the school plant and should be given full information to acquaint them with the services that will be available to them. Help in ordering appropriate equipment, materials, and supplies also is needed. A study completed by the American Association of School Administrators[14] warned against distributing an excessive quantity of professional publications.

K. Wiles[15] cited as good practice the scheduling of orientation or induction programs for a period of one week before school begins. The new teachers meet with their principals, discuss the educational goals of the system, and make plans. Summer workshops also help the teacher prepare for a successful start. Salary should be paid for the week's course. Conducting in-service education classes on the employee's own time following the end of a work day is at best a questionable practice.

Most specialists who have worked with beginning teachers agree that these teachers need help in relating theories learned in teacher-training institutions to their own situations. They must learn content, methods, and procedures, and classroom routines and control. Inexperienced teachers are not always certain as to what constitutes acceptable standards of work and behavior in the various learning situations.

While he observed that in a broad sense all supervision is in-service education, J. A. Bartky[16] narrowed his definition of the latter to be teacher education that is accomplished in small groups under the direction of the supervisor, possibly with specialist-consultant help. It is coordinated with the overall supervision program.

[14]American Association of School Administrators, *Off to a Good Start* (Washington, D.C.: The Association, 1956).

[15]Wiles, *Supervision for Better Schools,* p. 225.

[16]John A. Bartky, *Supervision as Human Relations* (Boston: D. C. Heath and Company, 1953), p. 28.

Initial orientation meetings, which should include small group meetings of the various grade levels, are vital to success. Here teachers will learn what is expected of them and will become acquainted with the people in the field who can give them assistance and an interpretation of the instructional program.

Different programs, materials, and goals are found at each grade level. The overall philosophy of the school system, however, will remain the same. Induction meetings are held for various subject areas, thus acquainting the faculty with a background of knowledge for preparation for the first day of school.

Wiles reported:

An explanation to new teachers of the way the program has developed enables them to understand the things that have already been attempted, the types of difficulties that have been encountered, and the compromises that have been made.[17]

Instilling confidence and courage within the new teacher at the orientation meetings paves the way for greater receptivity later on. The principal helps the new teacher not only to appreciate his own capabilities, but also to realize his valued contribution to the community. He strengthens the new teacher's long-range objectives, gives him an insight into the standards and ethics of the profession, and makes him feel proud to be a member of the team.

In one school system the preschool orientation meetings are the first of the services provided for beginning teachers. Their purpose is to orient new teachers to the school system and to assist them in initial planning for their teaching assignments. Several members of the professional staff help with the planning and preparation of these meetings, which are scheduled for three days during the week prior to the opening of school.

The teachers are welcomed by the superintendent who gives a brief description of professional responsibilities and opportunities for advancement. He then introduces the specialist-consultants. During the remainder of the induction period an opportunity is provided for the teachers to meet by grade level with their principal and with specialist-consultants.

[17]Wiles, *Supervision for Better Schools,* p. 221.

The content of the group meetings is designed to give practical, specific help in the areas most needed by the new teacher. The following is a list of the activities frequently included in these meetings:

1. Suggestions for the first day of school;
2. Suggestions for the first two weeks of school;
3. Instructions for ordering supplementary books;
4. Instructions for ordering audio-visual material;
5. Suggestions for organizing classroom materials;
6. An overview of the content in the various subject fields;
7. Tours to see arranged classroom environments in the school adjoining the system office;
8. Distribution of supervisory bulletins and curriculum publications (caution!);
9. Seeing video tape recordings and filmstrips of teaching techniques in various subject fields;
10. Suggestions for initiating units of work.

In another school system, orientation classes are scheduled approximately two weeks after the beginning of every school term for the inexperienced teachers in the school system. The classes are organized by master teachers under the direction of the specialist-consultant of the appropriate grade level. The classes are intended to provide information about materials, techniques, methods, and content in the subject fields. Classroom routines, control techniques, and individual problems are also within the scope of the classes. Meeting after school, each class consists of eight two-hour sessions, and the participants receive two points of credit applicable to advancement on the salary schedule.

Various group activities are used in the meetings: lectures relating theory and practice, discussions, workshops, role-playing, and demonstrations. The assignments for outside preparation extend the ideas gained in class for use in the classroom. Suggested techniques are tried, and materials are made and used to supplement the lessons.

During orientation new teachers should be encouraged to request the services of the specialist-consultant, whose first duty is to the inexperienced teacher. The type of help provided depends upon the individual and the situation. The specialist-consultant may be help through:

1. Consultation
2. Observation and conference
3. Demonstration
4. Coteaching with the teacher
5. Workshops
6. Grade-level meetings
7. Providing materials

The following recommendations for improvement of the program of supervision for inexperienced employees require the cooperation of the entire professional staff:

1. Positive attitudes should be developed toward supervisory assistance. Seeking such assistance indicates strength rather than weakness.
2. The principal should plan for an initial conference between the specialist-consultant and the beginning teacher during the first two weeks of the term. The first conference helps build rapport and provides the basis for future planning and cooperative action.
3. The goals of induction meetings should be delimited to meeting the immediate needs of beginning teachers. Attention to teaching procedures in each of the subject fields is more meaningful after the teacher has met his class and discovered needs for more specific techniques.
4. Well-constructed, brief questionnaires could be used to evaluate orientation meetings.
5. Specialist help should be provided in art and in music, as well as in physical education and in the academic subjects.
6. Demonstrations should be planned in connection with the orientation classes, and principals should be encouraged to release their beginning teachers in order to observe these demonstrations.
7. Teacher participation in the orientation classes should be encouraged. Cooperative group techniques should be developed to meet specifically the needs and interests of the teachers.

8. Provision should be made for the development of the leadership potentials of all members of the professional staff. Beginning teachers who show promise of becoming outstanding educators should be encouraged to continue to work with the supervisor after the semester of orientation. They should be included in leadership classes after the completion of their first year of teaching.

In conclusion, many people in a school system are responsible for the organization of supervisory services to teachers. The entire professional staff is concerned with helping teachers work more effectively in the classroom. Each of these individuals plays a different role, but all are striving for the fundamental goal of a better system of education through enlightened supervision.

How to Help the Superior Teacher

While giving due attention to the beginning teachers and/or to the weak teachers, the supervising principal may tend to forget to give encouragement and help to the superior teachers. Perhaps as a consequence of their apparent competency in teaching or supervising other school activities, the principal may consider that their abilities need no further growth. Such an idea, or unconscious negligence, may result in complacency which could result in the creation of a static condition that would be injurious to a member of any profession.

Teaching is an on-going business and not a job to be learned once and for always.[18] Whenever new research discoveries are made and ideas are developed, a short refresher course should be given to the superior teachers along with the rest of the staff.

The experienced teacher should be used as a supervising master teacher. He should assist the less experienced or the beginning teacher through demonstration teaching, through supervisory conferences, and—perhaps more importantly—through friendship, and through examples at informal get-togethers.

[18]Harold Spears, *The Teacher and Curriculum Planning* (Englewood Cliffs, New Jersey: Prentice-Hall, Inc., 1951), p. 83.

How to Help the Senior Teacher

Teachers do grow older—and they don't just fade away. Some of our best teachers are older teachers. The supervisor may feel that some of them are seeking the easiest way to complete their final years in service, or even that they may wish to prevent change through dictation on the basis of their seniority.

The supervising principal must realize that one of his most important functions is to recognize and utilize the worth of each teacher, including the older teacher. It is the supervisor's responsibility to insure that the older teacher does not lose his sense of leadership and importance.

The supervising principal can help teachers who are older in service by:

1. Recalling that older teachers have information about the school that is not possessed by the beginning staff member, and such information should be put to use in the solution of professional problems;
2. Securing the advice of the older teacher, demonstrating that the teacher is respected, but not asking for suggestions in such a manner that the supervisor or staff is placed in the position of being forced to follow the advice;
3. Encouraging beginning teachers to seek the advice of the more experienced teachers on the staff;
4. Considering the teacher older in service as one who can provide a feeling of continuity and tradition to the institution and to its staff;
5. Giving due consideration to any problems of a physical nature in programming and scheduling.

How to Work with the Dissenting Teacher

In any school situation there will be staff members who are not in total agreement with the supervising principal; indeed, recent thinking has focused on the necessity of divergent and conflicting (but logically derived and not ritualistic) opinions for professional growth. Such disagreement may be quite obviously on the surface or, more seriously, it may be of a repressed, sullen nature. A supervising principal in Montana reported that he had used the following techniques successfully in working with the "dissenting" teacher:

1. He was concerned with teacher growth rather than with winning his own way;
2. He was not concerned that he would "lose" an argument, since the emphasis was upon development of teachers;
3. At times he would suspend judgment on the point in question;
4. He made it a practice never to lose his dignity in an attempt to "battle it out" with a dissenting staff member;
5. He refused to permit a situation to develop to the point where winning an argument or—more specifically—winning the other person over to his point of view—became the primary goal;
6. He recognized that disagreement must not be considered as a personal affront, and worked as closely with those who disagreed with his point of view as those who were most enthusiastically "with him";
7. He recognized that the teacher might be correct in his point of view, and that dissension could be healthy, since without it little fruitful discussion would take place, and problems would be handled conveniently rather than solved after adequate investigation and consideration.[19]

How to Work with the "Undemocratic" Staff Member

If the supervising principal believes that a teacher is not operating in a "democratic" manner in the classroom, or that the teacher may wish to force his own ideas upon the faculty through undemocratic procedures, he should look at:

1. The in-service education program, determining whether or not he has brought to the staff teachers or specialist-consultants who stress democracy in their presentations;

[19]See Wiles, *Supervision for Better Schools*, pp. 118–120; and Ross L. Neagley and N. Dean Evans, *Handbook for Effective Supervision of Instruction* (Englewood Cliffs, New Jersey: Prentice-Hall, Inc., 1951), pp. 154–159.

2. Faculty-planning sessions and discussions to determine whether or not democratic values have received sufficient attention;
3. The procedures he has established for the staff meetings;
4. The professional library, determining whether it contains professional journals and texts which contain subject matter related to democratic faculty and classroom procedures;
5. Administrative and supervisory procedures which might violate democratic principles, and therefore provide ammunition to those who have become bitter and resentful;
6. His relationship with the faculty association, insuring that he is not in reality attempting to manipulate the faculty through control of the association;
7. His own supervisory practices—and whether he insists that the staff operate in a democratic manner, "or else!"[20]

How to Improve Workshops and Institutes

How to Conduct Workshops

Workshops constitute one means of stimulating professional growth. These meetings generally are called as a result of teachers' requests for assistance. T. H. Briggs and J. Justman[21] believed workshops possessed certain advantages over conventional faculty meetings.

WORKSHOP CHARACTERISTICS. Workshops tend to have rather clearly defined and recognized purposes. These purposes usually are related directly to problems and needs emerging out of the teachers' daily work. Workshops are planned, organized, and conducted by teachers and principals.

A broadly representative membership is attracted to workshops. They are not delimited to the faculty of one school, or even of one school system. The exchange of new ideas is, therefore, facilitated.

Workshops attract people who have a special interest in the subject matter, a special contribution to make, or a special problem with which they need assistance. The success of the workshop depends upon the quality

[20]Wiles, *Supervision for Better Schools,* pp. 118–120.
[21]Thomas H. Briggs, and Joseph Justman, *Improving Instruction through Supervision* (New York: The Macmillan Company, 1952), p. 452.
of the collective effort of the group. Workshops usually are conducted with

greater informality and with stronger emphasis on promoting good human relations than are formal faculty meetings.

Workshops tend to be fairly brief, lasting six to eight weeks in one-hour or two-hour sessions. Materials often are supplied at the workshop, although at times the teachers bring their own supplies from their individual schools. Outside preparation, which is shared with the participating members, often is required.

TYPES OF WORKSHOPS. There are many different kinds of workshops. In an art workshop, probably most of the time would be spent in actual participation, learning the skills and techniques of art activities.

In a mathematics workshop, more emphasis would be placed on analyzing and selecting appropriate learning experiences, devising instructional technology materials and methods of content presentation, and evaluating current and new programs.

The launching of the first Sputnik caused many teachers to realize that there were gaps in their knowledge of their subject areas. Workshops may supplement the backgrounds of teachers and bring the educator up-to-date with respect to advances in research in subject matter and in instructional techniques.

The needs of all teachers are not indentical. Many phases of in-service education are needed in order to facilitate teacher growth. These needs are of a finite nature. Some teachers need assistance in enhancing classroom contributions in measurement and evaluation, others in content, and still others in the methods and techniques of instruction and in instructional technology.

The supervisor must make provisions for the wide variance in teachers' interests, needs, and capacities when planning the workshop. He should fuse personal qualities for the teacher, as a person, into the subject matter of the workshop. Even though workshops are made available through teachers' requests, it is up to the supervisor to stimulate interest in the interchange of new ideas, mutual problems, and competent solutions.

LIMITATIONS OF WORKSHOPS. Based on his investigation of workshops, J. R. Mitchell reported the following dangers and limitations to workshop procedure:

1. Too little preparation for the job at hand, little understanding of the meaning of group interaction, and inadequate skill in group techniques;
2. A tendency to underestimate the potentials of the group, individually and collectively—a lack of faith in the group's ability;
3. Inability to stimulate and challenge participants to critical thinking;
4. Lack of personal qualities which would attract and hold the confidence of associates; lack of tact and patience in dealing with participants;
5. Waste of participants' time by engaging in trivia; too much floundering;
6. Promotion of social at the expense of intellectual activities; too much informality;
7. Lack of flexibility; too much domination, too much lecturing . . . ; inability to get away from the classroom atmosphere;
8. Insufficient sensitivity to individual needs; lack of concern for setting up and maintaining a congenial climate, emotional, physical, and intellectual for the group;
9. Contempt of inadequate attempts made by members to solve problems;
10. Lack of foresight, intuition, and planning;
11. Fear of giving leadership and guidance (some leaders, failing to see their specific role as leaders, bend over backwards to keep from giving directions);
12. Failure to plan for getting the workshop under way expeditiously;
13. Reliance on the totally indefensible notion that democratic procedure means that the leader should not lead—that situations should remain almost completely unstructured;
14. Inability to control aggressive participants.[22]

How to Conduct Institutes

Institutes in various subject areas are another way in which the supervisor aids the teacher in doing a better job. Institutes are organized in different ways in different school systems.

Institutes differ from workshops in that less group participation and discussion occur at the former. Salary schedule credits often may be gained

[22]James Russell Mitchell, "The Workshop as an In-Service Education Procedure" (Doctoral dissertation, Indiana University, 1954), pp. 67–68.

from workshop attendance. Workshops usually are scheduled approximately for eight to sixteen meetings. The institutes, while coordinated, generally are completed in one to three meetings.

Since teachers have a genuine interest in bettering themselves, the trend appears to be toward fewer *required* institutes. Attaching vacation pay to required institute attendance is a highly questionable practice.

PLANNING THE INSTITUTE. Supervising principals should plan, organize, and produce institutes. However, in the planning stage, advisement and cooperation with other interested parties are essential. Early meetings are scheduled to work out a calendar. Next, meetings are held with specialist-consultants in order to decide which areas will be stressed. The specialists in the fields to be covered then meet to ascertain specific needs and to discuss new techniques in their particular areas. A preview in the form of a written synopsis of each institute should be given to all concerned.

MATERIAL FOR INSTITUTES. Institutes provide an opportunity for teachers to see the latest textbooks. New library books are exhibited for examination. Other exhibits enable teachers to become acquainted with the latest types of equipment and supplies, and with advances and current practices in such areas as audio-assisted learning, computer supported instruction, computer-assisted learning, and computer-managed instruction.

Leadership opportunities should be offered by the supervising principal for teachers to work with and become a part of the institute proceedings through their participation. Teachers should be asked to bring their special skills and knowledge to the attention of others who might benefit from them. Recognition is a fine morale builder, and the realization that the contribution of work well done is appreciated generally stimulates confidence for continuing success.

How to Use Group Problem-Solving Techniques in Supervision

Whether it be at the conference workshop, institute, staff conference, or in the area of general research, the supervising principal should insure that a system analysis approach to problem-solving is employed. The steps to be followed in supervisory problem-solving are indicated in Figure 7–2.

FIGURE 7–2   Steps in Solving Supervisory Problems

1. Problems are selected, defined, and delimited. Objectives are stated clearly and operationally.

2. A survey is conducted of the situation as it presently exists.

3. Related research findings are reported to the group.

4. The problem is stated clearly, and hypotheses are formulated and tested. The barriers which are a function of the use of each suggested procedure are listed.

5. Accurate records are kept of the proceedings.

6. A critical appraisal of each proposal is accomplished.

7. The most powerful techniques available are used to analyze the data and the limitations inherent in the research design reported.

8. A summary in written form is formulated listing the findings, the conclusions, and recommendations for action.

9. The findings and recommendations are put to work.

10. The results of the research are evaluated and recommendations made for further investigation.

Recycle as Necessary

Case Study

Stone W. Jackson, principal of school No. 1 of the Sierra Way Union School District, was cautious in the manner in which he led the faculty in attacking a problem which had arisen at the previous staff meeting through group discussion. Being well versed in the area of group processes, Jackson initiated the following procedures:

1. The problem was defined;
2. The implications, possibilities, and hazards implicit in each of the suggested possible solutions were considered by the group;

3. Knowledge and experience from outside specialists, as well as from literature, interviews, and other sources, were utilized;
4. The information bearing on the problem was brought together, and tentative and final conclusions were developed;
5. A report of the proceedings was carefully prepared.

Jackson guided the members of his faculty through the following techniques:

1. He helped individual members of the group to establish their places within the group.
2. He saw to it that information concerning each member was exchanged, that strong leadership was available, and that cohesiveness was developed between group members.
3. Finally, he was able to stimulate the group due to the real problem they were attacking. The result was an increase in responsibility in each individual.

Finally, Jackson evaluated his own performance as a group leader by using a technique similar to that which appears in Figure 7–3. He kept his study groups to a reasonable size. D. Cartwright and A. Zander[23] reported a study which seemed to indicate that the optimum size of a group for the study of a problem is approximately five, with the upper limit approximately twelve. Jackson was aware of the major functions that must be accomplished if any group is to meet with success. These functions are illustrated in Figure 7–4.

Guidelines for Evaluating Group Action

Every group needs guidelines if its deliberations are to be successful. Good human relations in group processes are as dependent upon rules as is a baseball game. The leader or chairman must referee the conference with specific rules in mind. The rules of fair play and full participation must be

[23]Dorwin Cartwright and Alvin Zander, *Group Dynamics:* Research and Theory (New York: Harper and Row, Publishers, 1953).

FIGURE 7–3   Checklist for Group Leaders

Preparation

1. Were members notified about meeting time, place, and topic? _____

2. Were the physical arrangements right for good discussion? _____

3. Did I prepare an outline for the discussion?   _____

4. Did I provide sufficient background and factual material?   _____

5. Were the visual or other aids in place and ready for use?   _____

6. Was a friendly, personal atmosphere developed before the
   discussion started?   _____

Leading the Discussion

7. Did my introduction state the topic?   _____
   Define the areas of discussion?   _____
   Relate them to the interest of the group?   _____

8. Was it too long?   _____

9. Did it insure that the group had enough information on which
   to base the discussion?   _____

10. Did the group come right into the discussion after the intro-
    duction?   _____

11. How did I "toss the ball" to the group?   _____

12. Did I keep the discussion moving by frequent transitional
    summaries?_____Checking repetitions?_____Calling
    attention to digressions and irrelevancies?_____Point-
    ing up differences of opinion?_____Clarifying the dis-
    cussion?_____Allowing sufficient time for each major
    area of the topic?   _____

13. Were the questions and other methods I used to guide the
    discussion:
    Aimed at bringing out reasons, opinions, causes?   _____
    Designed to bring out all shades of opinion?   _____
    Presented objectively (not slanted or argumentative)?   _____
    Worded briefly and clearly?   _____
    Thought-provoking (not rhetorical or "yes-no" in form)?   _____
    Fairly and tactfully distributed among all members?   _____

14. Did I encourage participation by:
    Keeping any one member from "hogging the show"?   _____
    Drawing out the reticent members?   _____

Expressing appreciation of individual contributions?
Re-directing questions to other members? _____
Maintaining good humor and fair play? _____

15. Did I bring the discussion to a clear and definite conclusion? _____

16. Did my final summary fairly review all points of view expressed?
State the agreements reached? _____
And the points of disagreement? _____
Call attention to sources of information? _____
Announce the next meeting? _____

Results

17. Were there any indications of satisfaction from members of the group? _____
Any indications of dissatisfaction from members of the group? _____

18. Were there any unusual problems?
Did I handle them properly? _____

19. How many members did not participate at all? _____

20. Was the topic suitable for discussion? _____

21. Were any important aspects of the question omitted? _____

22. Was there a clearer understanding of the subject after the discussion? _____

23. What conclusions did the group reach?

_____

24. What could I have done better?

_____

FIGURE 7—4   Four Major Functions

_____

THE GROUP AT WORK

(1) Leader ⟶ Guides
               Directs

(2) Recorder ⟶ Keeps account of group decisions

(3) Observer ⟶ Evaluates efficiency, quality of group functions

(4) Consultant- ⟶ Provides technical information;
    Specialist ⟶ Helps the group

understood and accepted by the group lest the process end in conflict and futility. The following guidelines furnish more than adequate bases for the formulation of criteria which may be employed in the evaluation of group endeavors in problem-solving:

1. Was the meeting attended by all representatives concerned?
2. Did the participants stick to the point in question?
3. Were preliminary plans formulated, and was a tentative outline of procedure followed?
4. Did the individuals work as a group?
5. Was democratic cooperation with truly strong leadership present?
6. Were suggestions of previous groups followed or noted?
7. Did the individuals arrive on time for the meeting?
8. Did any one individual spend more time working at attacking the problem than did the other participants?
9. Did any one individual not perform to the best of his ability?
10. Were individual tasks accomplished?
11. Was the problem attacked with an open mind?
12. Were possible solutions checked?
13. Was each member made to feel that he was needed and wanted as a member of the group?
14. Were the rules, mechanisms, procedures, and policies determined by the group or were they imposed from above the group?[24]
15. Was there a stimulating environment, rich in experiences and materials, designed to facilitate maximum interaction?
16. Were conditions arranged which afforded opportunities for individuals to make special contributions through their particular interest and talents, and were these contributions utilized in group deliberations?
17. Did the members have an opportunity to evaluate the outcomes of their planning, and was their evaluation continuous?
18. Was the contribution of each member recognized and evaluated?
19. Were the contributions of the members relevant to the problem solution?

[24]Charles A. Stone, "The Teachers' Institute in American Education" (Doctoral dissertation, Stanford University, 1950).

20. Were the conflicts in points of view resolved into common understanding?
21. Were the worth and dignity of each member of the group fully recognized?
22. Did all share the responsibility of leadership and duties?
23. Did all the members of the group participate, and was the fullest participation from all concerned secured?
24. Were cooperative attacks made on the problem and did the group reach a decision as a result of group planning, discussion, action, and evaluation?
25. Were good human relations and satisfactory personal interactions developed within the group so that a cooperative, permissive atmosphere was characterized in its functioning?
26. Did the group aim at achieving unity in general purpose, and diversity in ways of achieving that purpose?
27. Did the group have sufficient interest and/or adequate knowledge to pursue and expedite their attainment?
28. Was the problem worthy of individual and group consideration?

Many supervising principals have found an end-of-the-conference "suggestion slip" invaluable. An example of such a slip is included as Figure 7–5. The Supplement B to this chapter should prove helpful.

The following list of techniques may prove useful in planning for in-service education:

DO

1. Hold conferences prior to the opening of school in the fall. These meetings will serve the purpose of orienting new staff members, and act as a reorientation for returning members of the faculty.
2. Open the way for faculty meetings concerned with educational problems which have been planned by teacher-principal committees to enhance in-service growth.
3. Encourage visitation within the system or with neighboring school systems.
4. Stress the better understanding of educational problems and improved

FIGURE 7–5   End-of-the Conference Suggestion Slip

What did you think of this meeting? Please be frank. Your comments can contribute a great deal to the success of our meetings.

1. How did you feel about this meeting?

	(Check)	Without value	( )
		Poor	( )
		Mediocre	( )
		Good	( )
		Excellent	( )

2. What were the weaknesses?

_____

3. What were the strong points?

_____

4. What improvements would you suggest?

_____

articulation between grades which should result from subject matter area meetings which include teachers from all levels of education.

5. Assign staff members to conduct a survey of various educational problems of the school and to report their findings to the faculty.

6. Help the school staff to interpret effectively the school program to the public through articles, talks, student presentations, open house activities, and demonstration teaching.

7. Encourage attendance at graduate school and professional conventions in order that school personnel may continue their professional growth and keep abreast of educational progress.

8. Conduct teacher-principal rating conferences, by utilizing a form designed by teachers that indicates strengths and areas of needed improvement in each teacher's training.

9. Make available professional literature which is pertinent to the interests and needs of teachers, supervisors, and administrators.

10. Make all personnel aware of school handbooks, monographs, manuals, and guides on policies and procedures.
11. Make provision in the budget which could encourage in-service education of teachers. Remuneration should be provided for summer school, educational travel, consultant services, professional meetings, sabbatical leave, workshops, and institutes.

DON'T

1. Rebuke or correct any teacher in the presence of students or other staff members.
2. Tread heavily in the field of teacher's specialty.
3. Deal lightly with any person's problems, but treat them as if they were your own.
4. Forget the days of your youth—keep a sense of humor.
5. Deal harshly with a teacher who is old in the service—deal with him kindly and with understanding.
6. Set a time limit when working with a new teacher. Give him all the help he needs now over a period of time; even if he requires a major portion of the supervisor's time for three days, three weeks, or three months. Recall that, after all, the teacher was hired on the basis of his capabilities and potentialities, his qualifications and promise. Do not let him fail.[25]

Supervisory Problems

In Basket

Problem 1

Mr. Angel is a dynamic young man in his first year of teaching. He is a Phi Delta Kappan and graduated from his state university with honors. He is a person with a "strong ego." He tends to dominate almost all discussion, and although he produces many good ideas he quickly has become obnoxious to the staff. He has not yet learned to listen. He is apparently having problems in orienting himself to his role as a member of a professional staff.

[25]See J. Minor Gwynn, *Theory and Practice of Supervision* (New York: Dodd, Mead, 1965), pp. 215–218.

How should the supervising principal handle Mr. Angel in order to utilize his strength and to minimize his weakness?

Problem 2

Mr. Raboy has returned to the teaching profession after an absence of twenty years. He was a very successful teacher in his early professional career and was active in both his state and local professional organizations. During his absence he has had little or no contact with his profession and has done little professional reading nor returned to the university for study. His activities during his absence have been in vastly different areas. He is certain that the innovations that he finds in the school, such as team teaching and the individualization of instruction and the use of the materials of instructional technology including computer-supported instruction and programmed instructional aids, are but "fads" and transitory and a "waste of the taxpayers' money." He is critical of his fellow teachers and often is arrogant. He uses the methods he was trained to use well in his classroom. Both students and teachers are cowed by his temper.

How can the supervising principal help Mr. Raboy to grow and at the same time protect his psychological integrity?

Selected Bibliography

Books

Adams, Harold P., and Frank Dickey. *Basic Principles of Supervision.* New York: American Book Company, 1953.

Barr, A. S., William H. Burton, and Leo J. Brueckner. *Supervision, Democratic Leadership in the Improvement of Learning.* New York: D. Appleton-Century Company, Inc., 1947.

Bartky, John A. *Supervision as Human Relations.* Boston: D. C. Heath and Company, 1953.

Briggs, Thomas H., and Joseph Justman. *Improving Instruction through Supervision.* New York: The Macmillan Company, 1952.

Burton, William H., and Leo J. Brueckner. *Supervision, A Social Process.* New York: Appleton-Century-Crafts, Educational Division, Meredith Corp., 1955.

Campbell, Clyde M. *Practical Application of Democratic Administration.* New York: Harper and Brothers, 1952.

Cartwright, Dorwin, and Alvin Zander. *Group Dynamics: Research and Theory.* New York: Harper and Row, Publishers, 1953.

Dale, Edgar. *Audio-Visual Methods in Teaching.* New York: Dryden Press, 1954.

Elsbree, Willard S., and Harold J. McNally. *Elementary School Administration and Supervision.* New York: American Book Company, 1959.

Frey, Sherman H., and Keith R. Getschman. *School Administration: Selected Readings.* New York: Thomas Y. Crowell Company, 1969.

Gwynn, J. Minor. *Theory and Practice of Supervision.* New York: Dodd, Mead, 1965.

Kelley, Earl C. *The Workshop Way of Learning.* New York: Harper and Brothers, 1951.

McNerney, Chester T. *Educational Supervision.* New York: McGraw-Hill Book Company, Inc., 1951.

Miles, M. B. *Learning to Work in Groups.* New York: Columbia University, Teacher's College Press, 1969.

Neagley, Ross L., and N. Dean Evans. *Handbook for Effective Supervision of Instruction.* Englewood Cliffs, New Jersey: Prentice-Hall, Inc.

Reeder, Edwin H. *Supervision in the Elementary School.* Boston: Houghton Mifflin Company, 1953.

Spears, Harold. *The Teacher and Curriculum Planning.* Englewood Cliffs, New Jersey: Prentice-Hall, Inc., 1951.

_____ . *Improving the Supervision of Instruction.* Englewood Cliffs, New Jersey: Prentice-Hall, Inc., 1953.

_____. *Curriculum Planning through In-Service Programs.* Englewood Cliffs, New Jersey: Prentice-Hall, Inc., 1957.

Stoops, Emery, and John Dunworth. *Classroom Disciplines.* Montclair, New Jersey: The Economics Press, 1958.

Wiles, Kimball. *Supervision for Better Schools,* Englewood Cliffs, New Jersey: Prentice-Hall, Inc., 1951.

Yauch, Wilber A. *Improving Human Relations in School Administration.* New York: Harper and Brothers, 1949.

Periodicals

Abrahamson, S. "Toward Better In-Service Education." *Educational Leadership* XI (November 1953): 82–85.

Anderson, George F. "Evaluating Teacher Education." *American Association Health, Physical Education, and Recreation Journal* XXIV (February 1953): 11.

Baker, T. P. "What Is an Effective In-Service Education Program?" *National Association of Secondary School Principals* XXXV (March 1951): 46–48.

Cory, N. Durward. "Incentives Used in Motivating Professional Growth of Teachers." *North Central Association Quarterly* XXVII (April 1953): 385–409.

Harnly, P. W. "In-Service Education of Teachers." *North Central Association Quarterly* XXIII (January 1949): 273–275.

Hightower, H. W. "In-Service Education." *Educational Administration and Supervision* XXXVIII (April 1952): 243–246.

Mackenzie, G. N. "In-Service Teacher Education: A Challenge to College and Schools." *Educational Outlook* XXIV (March 1950): 144–150.

Mallison, Jacqueline V. "The Current Status of Science Education in the Elementary Schools." *School Science and Mathematics* LXI (April 1961): 252–270.

Moffitt, J. C. "Administration of In-Service Education." *Educational Administration and Supervision* XXXVII (October 1951): 355–361.

Murphy, Rose M. "Troy Plans for In-Service Training." *The American School Board Journal* CXXII (June 1951): 26.

Stoops, Emery, and Albert R. Evans. "Helping the Beginning Teacher." *The Nation's Schools* LVII (April 1956): 74.

Weber, C. A. "Reactions of Teachers to In-Service Education in Their Schools." *School Review* LI (1943): 234–240.

Wood, Hugh B. "In-Service Education of Teachers." *Journal of Teacher Education* II (December 1951): 243–247.

Other Sources

American Association of School Administrators. *Off to a Good Start*. Washington, D.C.: The Association, 1956.

Council of Directors and Supervisors. "Supervision, Los Angeles City Schools." Duplicated material. Los Angeles: Operating Division, Division of Elementary Education, 1953.

Denver Public Schools. *Denver Serves Its Children*. Denver: Board of Education, 1948.

Mitchell, James Russell. "The Workshop as an In-Service Education Procedure." Doctoral dissertation, Indiana University, 1954.

Stone, Charles A. "The Teachers' Institute in American Education." Doctoral dissertation, Stanford University, 1950.

Teacher Education Workshop. "Report of the Teacher Education Workshop." Duplicated material. Nashville: The George Peabody College for Teachers, 1945.

The beginning teacher usually encounters his first trouble with classroom control or "discipline." The principal's job is not to do the disciplining, but rather to analyze the difficulty and to tell the teacher why the methods and techniques he uses fail. He should point out better methods and bolster the teacher's courage by showing confidence in his ability to ultimately pull through.

Helpful forms, such as the one included as Figure Supp. 7–1, should be made available to the beginning teacher.

The following is a list of points influencing classroom control which should be stressed by the supervising principal in a conference with the beginning teacher:

1. Know each individual student through the cumulative card and health card. Have him sit where he can see and hear. Determine the general socio-economic background by taking a drive around the community. Study the general characteristics of the community and of the age group.
2. Maintain a neat room environment. Provide furniture of the right height, proper ventilation and lighting, and attempt to arrange the room so students can move around without disturbing one another. Bulletin boards should be on the eye level of students, properly grouped, with natural colors for the background. A smooth organization of routines should be planned and agreed upon by teachers and students. See Figure Supp. 7–2 for a sample homework assignment plan. In the elementary school it is helpful to have a pencil monitor sharpen pencils in the morning. One then should allow no sharpening during the day unless it is an emergency. Supplies and equipment should be arranged conveniently. Even the simplest organization of routine activities pays off.
3. Plan for the group, but consider the individual. Keep the lesson length within the attention span of the group, and provide maximum opportunity for student participation. The lesson should be interesting, varied, challenging, and presented with confidence.
4. Be prepared by having all necessary materials on hand. Anticipate routine needs, including passing and collecting materials. Anticipate clean up.
5. When teaching a lesson stimulate, provide variety, use different methods of presentation, be sure each student knows what to do, allow time for

SUPPLEMENT A

7

FIGURE SUPP. 7–1   Form to Inform Parents of Student's Unsatisfactory Work

_____

Name of School and Address

Date _____

Dear _____

    I wish to inform you that up to this time_____'s accomplishment in_____ has not been up to the average standard expected at this grade level.

    I shall be happy to discuss his/her work with you and to plan for its improvement.

_____ A personal conference is desirable, but is not essential at this time.

_____ An appointment has been made for our conference at_____ on _____

If this appointment is not convenient, please so indicate below, noting a more preferable time.

    Thank you for your kind attention to this matter. Please sign below and return this correspondence to school.

Cordially,

_____
Teacher

_____
Principal

Please sign and return

_____

Parent's Signature

FIGURE SUPP. 7–2 Sample Elementary School Homework Assignment Schedule

Monday: History / geography / science
Tuesday and *Thursday:* Reading and spelling
Monday and *Wednesday:* Language and mathematics

asking and answering questions, and provide for slow learners and gifted children. Do not ask questions which could result in a chorus answer. Instead of "Did we do that?" say "Did we do that, Bill?"

6. When the need arises, students evaluate behavior and build standards through teacher guidance. It is the teacher's responsibility to see that each student adheres to the group's standards. One standard could be chosen for emphasis at the beginning of a lesson. The class could evaluate how well they did with reference to the standard at the end of the lesson. A sample procedure for building room standards is included as Figure Supp. 7–3.

7. Obtain attention through a signal which says, "May I have your attention, please?" *Obtain undivided attention.* Establish the fact that the signal is given *once. Never* teach to inattention. Compliment those who are ready—who are really helping the group. Remember to speak definitely, firmly, with confidence and authority, yet softly. Give one direction at a time, clearly, using a minimum of words. Give students an opportunity to ask legitimate questions. *Expect the best!*

A principal of a high school that incorporates grades 7 and 8 prepared the following classroom control techniques:

1. Get a good start. Be in your room early and make preparations to start class activities as soon as the bell rings. Do not permit any student to monopolize your time at the very beginning of a class. Establish a routine for roll taking and getting into the activities of the day. If you know what you are going to do, and the students know what you are going to do and what is expected of them, the battle is half won.

2. Teach on your feet as much as possible. Not only are you in a position

FIGURE SUPP. 7–3   Building Room Standards

SAMPLE PROCEDURE

Step 1: Discuss the idea that the more people there are living together in one place, the more problems. What are some of the problems?

	Number of Rooms in Home	People (Living There)
Leo	5	3
Billy	5	2
Rose	3	4
Our room	1	31

Step 2: Through discussion and questions, have students state their contributions regarding room standards.
Write them on chalkboard.
Transfer to chart at a later date.

Step 3: "So many people living in one room leads to problems, therefore room standards are *important.*"
(Compare chart of standards from last term. Check off those no longer applicable.)

Step 4: Teacher reminds class of standard to walk quietly before dismissing.

OUR STANDARDS

(Sample Standards Chart)

1. Work harder
2. Be quieter walking in halls
3. Keep pencils where they belong
4. Take turns talking
5. Listen to the speaker
6. Be polite
7. Do not be a waster of time or supplies

to see and hear what goes on, but students can see and hear you better. A student who can only half hear what you say and who is unable to see you is not likely to be very attentive.

3. Change your pace. It is overly optimistic to expect a group of students to give complete attention to a given line of work for an hour. Plan changes in pace and different methods of attacking the problem at hand. A change is almost as good as a rest. Alternate quiet study periods with periods of class activity.

4. Be fair. Students are particularly sensitive to any injustice, real or imagined. Do not have obvious pets. Give each student a chance to gain some recognition. Marks are the paycheck which these students receive from you for their work. Be sure the grades are fair. When a question concerning the fairness or accuracy of a grade arises, nothing can be lost by discussing the matter with the student. If there is any doubt in your mind after the discussion, no harm can come in giving the student the benefit of the doubt.

5. Do not harangue an entire class. It usually is fruitless. If an entire class seems to be in error, the trouble may be at least partly your own doing. If a disciplinary matter arises in which several students are involved, you probably will be more successful in handling them one at a time. Pick the most flagrant offender first, and ignore the others until you have finished with him. This procedure may take a little longer, but in the long run it will be worth it.

6. Reprimand in private. Do not call down a student for a monor infraction in front of the class. Accord him the courtesy of a private dressing down.

7. Learn the names of your students as quickly as possible, and permit them to see that you have a sincere interest in their work and that you respect them as individuals even as you demand respect from them. A seating chart is indispensable.

8. Comraderie vs. familiarity. Be consistent. There is a fine distinction between comradeship with your students which breeds familiarity and that which commands respect. There is no known formula which can be given which will help you to attain the latter, but by all means avoid the former.

9. Do not threaten any action which you might not be able to carry out. It is better not to threaten at all. Act! Act with consistency. A particular type of behavior always brings the same result. Save the talk. Students understand *fair, consistent,* and *certain* action better.

10. Work for *esprit de corps*. When the class participates as a group, try to have each student feel his responsibility for the conduct of the group.

Behavioral Guidelines for Working in Groups

Much of the behavior of the individual can be understood only in the context of the small group in which he works. Commitment to goals, acceptance of leadership, satisfaction with work, and effectiveness of performance all tend to depend on the relations of the individual with his immediate face-to-face co-workers.[1]

Any group, whether participating in a supervisory conference or in another group activity, reaches maturity when members have learned to accept and trust each other; when they can communicate openly and share in decisions about the group; when they can identify their individual goals with the group's objectives; and when the governance of their behavior is based on mutual support and restraint.

Groups can be too large or too small depending on the task. The task determines whether it will be efficacious to assemble employees into groups according to their similarities or differences in ability and attitude.

Decisions are reached in groups in many ways, but it is profitable to strive for genuine consensus rather than settle for majority vote or decision by a single person. A group will also be more effective to the extent that (1) expectations of the members' roles are clear, (2) the members are cooperative rather than competitive, (3) the members are tolerant of each other, and (4) the members provide mutual feedback as a self-corrective mechanism for learning. Consider the following case taken from Bass:

The mechanization of English coal mines destroyed the traditional face-to-face teams of two to four miners. As a supposed move toward greater efficiency, the new "longwall" method broke the operation in a series of steps—cutting, ripping, and filling—to be completed during three shifts by about 40 men. But the expected increases in productivity failed to materialize. Instead there were increases in absenteeism, turnover, sickness, and the incidence of psychosomatic disorders. Remedial action was taken. Small, stable, responsible teams were reestablished with some opportunity to set their own pace. Following this social modification there was as much as a 30 percent increase in output.[2]

This case illustrates how the primary work group often determines what its members will do. Management may set quotas, but the primary work

---

[1]The authors are grateful to Bernard M. Bass, *Organizational Psychology* (Boston: Allyn and Bacon, Inc., 1965), especially Chapter VI, for much of the data in this section.

[2]B. M. Bass, "Feelings of Pleasantness and Work Group Efficiency," *Personnel Psychology* VII (1954): 81–91.

group of peers may decide whether or not its members will meet those or some other standards established by the group, with or without management's blessing. The extent to which the group can set and maintain standards for its members depends on its cohesiveness. The cohesion of members in a work group strongly influences how hard they will work and how they feel about their jobs.

Group Character and Member Performance

The character, composition, and history of a work group will strongly affect the performance and attitudes of its members. Consistently observed differences in the character of 300 groups in 30 plants made it possible to distinguish four types: apathetic, erratic, strategic, and conservative. In each category, the members revealed distinct patterns of behavior which differed from the behavior of members in other type groups. *Apathetic* groups had few grievances. Low in prestige, they took little concerted action against management. Neither were they a bother to the union. *Erratic* groups, high in prestige, ranged from near apathy to explosive activity. They started "wildcat" strikes over minor issues. Also high in prestige were *strategic* groups, holding important assignments with the firm. These groups exerted strong and continuous pressure on management, helped by their own cohesion. *Conservative* groups were composed of highly skilled workers who obtained what they wanted without pressure. Subsequent analyses suggest that strategic and conservative groups are more likely to win grievance disputes than apathetic or erratic ones.

Importance of Group Effort

"A camel is a horse designed by a committee." So quip critics of group effort. But work in groups both by management and workers, is as commonplace in industry as it is in education. Why? A primary reason is that modern technology usually makes it difficult for one man to assemble, organize, and digest the facts necessary to make an appropriate decision or complete an operation. An individual very often finds himself, as in the case of steel fabrication, forced to depend on his peers, and they find they must depend on him in order to complete their mutual tasks successfully. An operator of a new catalytic cracking unit in an oil refinery may be puzzled about the unusual behavior of an instrument metering the input of feedstock. He may need to consult with an instrument maintenance man, a chemical engineer from the design department, the operator on the night shift, his own foreman, the shift foreman, and possibly also his old buddy who works on the unit next to his. A meeting of design, maintenance, and operating people may be called to discuss the problem. No man has the knowledge or capability to deal with the problem alone. Thus it is not a question of whether groups are better than individuals in problem solving and in quality of performance than individuals working alone. Rather, there are numerous working situations in which it is impossible or most inefficient for an individual to attempt to handle the problems involved alone: repairing heavy equipment, piloting a large boat, monitoring the output of a utility plant, manufacturing shoes, or designing merchandising displays. Supervision, at all levels, is a group effort.

Working Together or Alone

Actually, research which has been accumulating since the turn of the century on whether the group or its individual member turns out the superior product indicates that the group does a better job than its *average* member. (Otherwise, teachers might not need to proctor examinations.) Yet group products or solutions to problems are often not as good as the output of the *best* member of the group when he works alone. There are some circumstances where even the average member proportionately does better alone than the group does as a whole. For example, the sum and overall quality of ideas generated in response to a problem by individuals, each working alone and then added together, is considerably greater than in the case where the same individuals who have not worked much together in the past meet as a group to try to "brainstorm" the same variety of ideas. But, again, often we must work in groups. Rather than argue whether it would be better to work alone, we wish to explore in this chapter supplement ways to maximize the effectiveness and satisfaction of the group when work *must* be done by a group, as for example in industries with continuously flowing production.

For instance, in the petrochemical industry, management decisions are usually made by committee because no one man normally has the variety of technical and business acumen to decide by himself.

Group Development

As individuals learn, so groups learn. The eventual performance of a group depends both on the individual learning of its members and how well the members learn to work with each other, how well they capitalize on the talents of their fellow group members, and how well they coordinate their efforts. Performance of a group will be impaired if members are too hasty and superficial in their agreement, substituting their initial unanimity for a rational analysis of the problem they face. Performance also will be impaired if decisions are compromises to resolve conflicts to "save face," rather than if the decisions are based on a careful deliberation of the problem and a thorough exploration and evaluation of all other alternatives. Taking a quick vote before any really serious discussion has been completed often "short-circuits" the formulation of a high-quality solution to a problem by a group which has the resources to come to such a solution. Groups can and must learn how to use the resources their members bring to the group. Four stages have been described in the learning process for committees, discussion groups, and many kinds of work groups.

Stages in Group Development

A four-stage learning process describes the development and maintenance of typical management committees or conference groups responsible for innovation, planning, operating decisions, sharing information, or evaluating. First, members must learn to accept each other and develop mutual confidence and trust. Only after this has occurred can they proceed to communicate openly and freely and to act and react with their full resources to set and achieve desired goals at a high rate of productivity. After such productivity has been demonstrated, the immature, formal controls based on power can be modified so the group operates with more spontaneous informality. The members move from concern about trusting each other to concern about how to communicate effectively. From there they proceed to concern about what goals to set and finally to concern about how controls shall be maintained.

FIRST STAGE: DEVELOPING MUTUAL ACCEPTANCE AND MEMBERSHIP. Members initially are hampered by their mistrust of each other (which they are often quick to deny). They respect the motives of others, but they fear their own inadequacies as well as those of other members. Protection is sought in cliques and mutual admiration pairings. They resist initiation of new ways of operating through legalism and quibbling. Remaining defensive, they restrict the range of permitted behavior through conformity and ritual.

When members learn to accept each other and themselves, they more easily can express their feelings and conflicting attitudes. Norms are established about how they will proceed, but individual differences are tolerated. Legitimate influence is accepted, and members develop a liking for each other.

SECOND STAGE: MOTIVATION AND DECISION-MAKING. During this phase, what first were ambiguous expressions are clarified in meaning. Strategy, gimmicks, and tricks are replaced by problem-solving behavior. Caution, pretense, and protective phraseology give way to open communications and reactions. Sufficient time is spent in reaching decisions.

THIRD STAGE: MOTIVATION AND PRODUCTIVITY. The group has reached maturity in resolving problems of its members' motivation when creativity is observed in sustained work, when members are involved in the work, when extrinsic or irrelevant rewards are not needed to maintain a high level of productivity, and when members are cooperative rather than competitive.

FOURTH STAGE: CONTROL AND ORGANIZATION. A group has succeeded in organizing effectively when work is allocated according to abilities and by agreements among those involved. Members are interdependent, but the organization remains flexible and ready to change in the face of new challenges. Informality and spontaneity are stressed with little expression of concern about the form of the organization.

The Mature Group

Eventually, the mature, effective group that emerges has the characteristics enumerated by 250 respondents who were each asked to make use of a checklist instrument to describe an efficient and an inefficient work group to which they had belonged. They described clerical, sales, manufacturing, business, maintenance, and military work groups. The five clusters of statements which best discriminated the effective from the ineffective work groups were (in order of importance):

1. The members functioned as a unit. The group worked as a team. The members did not disturb each other . . .
2. The members participated fully in group effort. They worked hard when there was something to do. Members did not loaf if they got the opportunity . . .
3. The members were oriented toward a single goal. They worked for common purposes . . .
4. The members had the equipment, tools, and skills necessary to attain the group's goals. The group members were taught various parts of their jobs by experts. The group was not shorthanded . . .
5. Members asked and received suggestions, opinions, and information from each other. If a member was uncertain about something, he stopped working and obtained more information. The members talked to each other frequently. . . .

Thus the effective work group is one in which the individual members are highly interdependent, coordinated, and cooperative in their efforts. They are capable and highly motivated as individuals, and information flows freely among them.

We shall now look at conditions conducive to the creation and maintenance of an effective work group. Two basic questions confront us: how large should a group be, and who should be grouped with whom.

How Groups Should Be Composed:
The Case for Homogeneity

Suppose we have decided to form six-man teams from an available pool of 72 men. If we assemble in teams those men who are most alike in interests, abilities, and personality, we shall promote interaction within each team. Members will be able to communicate more easily with each other. There will be less conflict and fewer differences in opinions, standards, and ways of doing things.

Homogeneity and Influence

Members who are alike can influence each other more easily. There is less resistance to influence where members are similar rather than different. This axiom was illustrated by an experiment where it was found that the experimenter could more successfully condition his subject verbally if the experimenter and his subject agreed on what were proper ways to interact. That is, the experiment could more successfully make the subject respond each time in the same way upon hearing a particular verbal cue in order to obtain a reward or avoid a punishment. In addition, if experimenter and subject were compatible, conditioned responses took longer to relinquish when they no longer were reinforced by the experimenter.

Homogeneity and Mutual Acceptance

We tend to like those similar to us and to reject those whom we think are unlike us. Members who are alike or who think they are alike will be more satisfied with the group, as well as with each other, than members who see differences between themselves and others in the group.

Differing Tasks

If the task facing a team is a simple one, such as folding and packing equipment into containers where a variety of resources are not needed to complete the task, but merely six pairs of hands instead of one pair, then a *homogeneous* team is likely to be highly productive. *If productivity depends on easy, smooth, cooperative, conflict-free, coordinated efforts* among the members, all of whom have been highly trained to interact routinely and automatically, then again a homogeneous membership, a membership where men are alike, should prove more productive.

Where a chain of reactions is required of a group, the total chain may depend upon the adequacy of each and every link. Again homogeneity is favored, for the group is no better than its poorest member. The failure of one link will destroy the entire chain. On some tasks the group can proceed no faster than its slowest member. In some groups one member can veto the decisions of the entire group or be so deviant in opinion as to block a group which cannot convert him, compromise with him, or expel him from the group. Under such conditions, such as when subjects had to coordinate completely an interlocking system of levers to turn on lights of a group maze, the typical group did worse than its average member working alone. Presumably, the more varied are the abilities of the members in such circumstances, the greater is the chance that the group will contain an extremely poor member who would drag the performance of the group down to his level.

How Groups Should Be Composed: The Case for Heterogeneity

Where rapid, smooth interactions are less important than a creative solution to a complex problem, a *heterogeneous* group—a group where members differ in abilities or opinions—may be more desirable than a group in which members are alike.

If the Task Is Complex

The main reason for grouping often is that no single individual has the varied resources to deal with complex problems. If we wish to ensure that each of the 12 teams drawn from a pool of 72 employees will have the varied resources for handling a complex problem, say, designing various components for a missile system, then heterogeneous assemblies of employees may prove more productive.

If Speed Is Deleterious

The very speed with which a homogeneous group can reach decisions may prove a handicap. When members have already reached the same opinion even before they have discussed an issue, they are less likely to make as good a decision as a group as when they are in disagreement when they begin deliberations. Groups homogeneous in opinion may close debate too quickly with a decisive vote.

A fictional illustration of this factor was the motion picture *Twelve Angry Men*. Eleven jurors were ready to convict an innocent boy on superficial evidence without any discussion. They were saved from a quick and erroneous decision by the skillful interposition of one juror who had some doubts and insisted on a delay in the final vote to permit discussion of the evidence. As the discussion proceeded, one by one the jurors drew forth from their own memories information that was obscured during the trial but which when put together pointed to the innocence rather than the guilt of the defendant.

If Creativity Is Required

While employees who are alike may do a better job facing assignments requiring routine, coordinated, or linked efforts, employees who are different are likely to be more creative as a group, although they may experience more difficulties as they attempt to interact.

Sixty-four groups of two, three, or four had to compose captions for a *Saturday Evening Post* cartoon. The captions were evaluated for fluency and originality. Where a group added, removed, or replaced members during its efforts, fluency and originality were higher than when it retained the same membership.

More conflict and difference of opinion will be observed in heterogeneous groups; but assuming these groups learn how to tolerate and use conflict, they can make better decisions (although they are likely to have more difficulties interacting and to take longer to reach these decisions).

In a related experiment, groups were formed on the basis of the Guilford-Zimmerman Temperament Survey scores of individual members. The Survey permits the respondent to indicate to what extent he sees himself as energetic, moody, ascendant, sociable, emotionally stable, objective, friendly, thoughtful, cooperative, and masculine. Groups with members who were similar in personality profiles had less difficulty in regulating their internal relations but more difficulty in creative problem-solving than groups of heterogeneous membership. Where members differed in personality, they more often rejected an easy choice of two superficial alternatives to a problem offered to them. These members developed, on their own, a third, more creative, integrated solution.

Optimum Mix

As there is an optimum size for groups depending on the task, so there is also an optimum mix of men for a given group task. If men are too different they have so much trouble interacting that they cannot begin to bring to bear on the complex problem they face the varied resources they have. If men are too similar, they reach agreement too easily and too often on the same wrong answers. They are more likely to fail to consider various alternatives and to explore the problem as widely. For simple, routine assignments, the optimum mix is composed of fairly similar types of men. For complex tasks with creative demands, the optimum becomes a more diversified assemblage. For assignments requiring easy, cooperative interaction, the optimum again is of similar men. But when such cooperation is less important, the men can differ more.

How Else to Compose Groups to Promote Interaction?

In addition to considering the number and homogeneity of employees to assign to a group, we may foster interaction and the ease with which individuals can work together by grouping together members who are already familiar with each other, who already are attracted to each other, who esteem each other, who are geographically and socially close to each other, and who can communicate fluently, accurately, and rapidly with each other.

Familiarity Breeds Interaction

If we are intimate, familiar, or experienced with other persons, we feel more comfortable about initiating and maintaining interaction with them. Our familiarity makes it possible to predict with less risk of error, their likely reactions to us. We feel more secure about interacting with them. In turn, continued interaction breeds familiarity, so we are more likely to interact with those we have interacted with before. At a gathering we usually approach friends before strangers.

Since they interact more readily, friends can work together faster than strangers. Thus an experiment disclosed that pairs of close friends could solve codes, puzzles, and arithmetic problems more quickly than could pairs of strangers.

Mutual Esteem, Attractiveness, Interaction, and Productivity

Cohesive groups (groups in which members are attracted to each other, and choose each other as work partners, or in which members value each other's potential contributions) may be highly productive or highly unproductive, depending on whether the members share management's goals for high productivity. These groups could just as readily set goals of low productivity as a means of maintaining job security or as a hostile reaction to management. Members of cohesive groups will confirm more closely to whatever standards—high or low—are set by their group.

Consensus: False, Forced, and True

Full participation of all concerned, resulting in complete agreement as to a decision, is the ideal toward which an effective group strives.

False consensus may be mistaken for true agreement. For example, silence does not mean consent. When relatively few members speak out on issues, it is just as reasonable to assume that they are against a proposition as it is to assume that they are for it. Each member must express his view (if he has any) if the group is to achieve true consensus, or he must indicate that he does not care which way a matter is decided. At the same time, it is the responsibility of the group or its chairman to see that everyone has an opportunity to speak before a decision is made.

Consensus cannot be forced. If members are silent, it is unwise for a chairman or a self-appointed leader to point his finger at each member in turn to ask them how they stand on a matter. It is equally unsound for the group to agree, "Let's go around the table to see what each person thinks we ought to do." A member may have to render an opinion when he does not really have one, or he may have to offer an evaluation before he has had an opportunity to hear what some of his more knowledgeable co-workers have to say. His best potential contributions may be inspired after his turn to speak has passed, and he may now hesitate to interrupt "going around the table" since he feels he has been given his chance—although he has not used it fully.

True consensus only comes when members feel free to express their opinions and are willing to keep working together to develop a decision which satisfies the desires of the group as a whole. True consensus occurs when members may use fully whatever resources they can bring to bear on the group's problems. Mechanical procedures such as voting or taking turns to force contributions are avoided, but everyone who has something to contribute has a chance to do so and a chance to see his contribution considered and if possible worked into the final decision.

Analyses of over 100 conference groups in business and public administration revealed that true consensus was likely to be achieved in a group focused on one issue at a time: in a group which followed orderly, understandable, problem-solving procedures rather than formal parliamentary methods. True consensus was more likely if members recognized a need for unified action, not when they felt a sense of urgency to reach a decision quickly. A friendly atmosphere also helped.

Groups that strive for true consensus must be ready to settle for less than complete agreement on all matters. Thus if conflicts in the conference groups were emotional, only simple issues could be resolved, while complex questions had to be postponed. In fact, a majority of conflicts did not end in complete agreement. Yet a group is more likely to operate effectively if it knows where its members stand in disagreement than if it obscures the situation with majority decisions or forced or false consensus. Then, if agreement is impossible, the members at least feel that the matter has been fully examined; and they may be more willing to commit themselves to an alternative solution. When consensus cannot be obtained, at least everyone should be aware of the fact and should not be seduced into believing that complete commitment has been obtained, as might be the case if a decision were based on a majority vote.

While consensus may not produce the best possible solution to a problem, neither will a majority vote. Yet a consensual decision is likely to be a satisfactory one and one which is more likely to be executed more efficiently than a decision based on a majority vote. Where opportunities to work for consensus are provided, members exhibit more cooperation with each other and more satisfaction with activities than do members who do not have the opportunity to interact as much or to move in the direction of consensus. Consensus-directed discussions by school administrators at first produced much defensive behavior. But with continued meetings the consensual discussions yielded increased warmth, friendly attitudes of members toward each other, and better overall performance. Similar results were obtained with aircrews and research engineers.

The chairman of a committee or the supervisor heading a department can serve an important function by using his power to move his group to a state of maturity where all members will share in the group's leadership, where all will share in stating issues, in summarizing, in testing for consensus, in making proposals, in giving support and encouragement to others, and in influencing the course of group action.

The chairman or executive, the man with more power than any other person in the group, can help the group to achieve decision-making consensus in many ways. He can prevent self-authorized agendas from developing. He can block members who seem to be monopolizing the group's activities or trying to dominate the group. By using suitable questions he can challenge a member who continually argues and opposes without logical consistency. He may bring into the discussion members who seem to be uninterested by asking them for their advice and opinion. The powerful executive may do nothing more than show his willingness to share his power to provide the arena in which the group, including himself, can explore together the basis for obtaining group agreements. He may provide the kinds of information to the group not formerly available to it which will serve to set the boundaries of the group's responsibilities and authority.

Further Impediments to Effective Utilization of Group Resources

In addition to the inadequate decision-making processes and interaction difficulties mentioned earlier, such as those caused by enlarging a group, a variety of other causes of group ineffectiveness have been demonstrated. Removing these impediments should result in improving a group's performance.

Unclear Role Expectations

Trouble arises when members are unclear about what others expect of them. Moreover, they become defensive if they are unable to forecast what other members are likely to do. Thus, when "stooges" of an experimenter remained silent, the groups of which they were supposedly members remained less productive, more dissatisfied, and defensive. When these silent plants clarified the reasons for their silence and their behavior became predictable and understandable, their groups improved in effectiveness and satisfaction.

Competitiveness

If members see each other as competing for the supervisor's favor, or as competing for promotion, recognition, or pay raises, self-interest will conflict with the need to cooperate with other members to work toward group goals. When such self-oriented needs become dominant, consensus becomes most difficult to obtain. Competitors see each other as less similar in personality than those who can achieve mutual rewards through cooperation. Therefore, competition among members increases perceived differences in a group and consequently reduces the potential to interact and the likely effectiveness of the members as a group.

In comparison to groups in which members must cooperate with each other to achieve personal rewards, members who must compete for rewards are less coordinated and vary more in what they contribute. Their activities are less likely to be subdivided, and they are less attentive to each other. There are more misunderstood and differently evaluated communications. They are more disorderly, less productive in quantity and quality, less friendly, and less favorable to the group, its products, and its functioning.

Unstable, Ambiguous Environment

A group is likely to standardize the behavior of its members to a degree, making it inflexible in the face of new demands on it, particularly if the new demands are ambiguous. Groups ritualize ways of handling problems which were once successful and which are now outmoded. In an experimental comparison, groups were more likely to maintain obsolete, irrelevant procedures rather than create new methods when the new conditions which they had to learn were unclear. On the other hand, when the new signals were distinct in meaning, there was more innovation and less ritualism in the group.

Intolerance

When one member in a group takes an unpopular position, different and opposed to that maintained by all the others, the dominant majority first tries to convert the deviant; then, if he will not convert, they psychologically eject him from the group. They act as if he did not exist, paying little or no attention to him thereafter. The rejection is even more severe if the group —except for the deviant—is highly cohesive. Yet the deviant may be the one member in his group with the right idea, the pioneering attitude, the most original outlook on the problem, who—if listened to—might shake the group out of its comfortable but pedestrian approach to work and attain a more creative solution to the problem faced by the group. As mentioned earlier, hasty decisions are pushed in groups in which most members are alike. Such groups are most intolerant of deviants. On the other hand, recent research suggested that where members are highly task-oriented, deviant opinion is more likely to be tolerated.

Absence of Specialized Resources or Activities

Ordinarily, effective groups may suffer lowered productivity and dissatisfaction owing to the failure of any of the members to accept a particular responsibility or to take a particular role when needed by the group. The problem-solving process will be disrupted, for example, if no one offers the group an evaluation of alternatives. In the same way, a weak or missing link in the chain severely reduces group effectiveness. For instance, inadequate secretarial service was a strong factor in retarding the effectiveness of 72 observed conferences.

Absence of Positive Feedback

Groups are less likely to solve problems effectively, and members are likely to be more dissatisfied with their work, if feedback is not provided indicating the success with which the group is carrying out its assignments. Knowledge of results is as important in group work as it is in individual endeavors. But merely learning about the group's success only contributes slightly to team performance. On the other hand, the performance of individuals working as a group improves the most when they receive constructive information concerning their individual efforts as well as about the group's success as a whole, particularly if the tasks are complex and the goals difficult to achieve. Equally useful is personal feedback from one member to another in improving the problem-solving efficiency of all. Yet merely emphasizing what is wrong with an individual member's performance serves only to increase his defensiveness in the group, particularly if remarks are personal.

Summary

The key to effective supervision and satisfied employees lies in forming and maintaining attractive and effective work groups. If one enters an educational organization in which the groups are already committed to processes that are inadequate or to goals that are in conflict with the aims of the organization as a whole, one may be able to bring about desired changes in the individual employee only after his group has first examined and accepted the possibilities of changing procedures and directions.

Understanding group life is essential in the promotion of effective supervision, for modern supervision is seen as a cooperative team effort aimed at the improvement of instruction and it must take place in groups.

8

How to Improve Supervisory Visits

The supervising principal must give considerable thought to classroom visitation for supervisory purposes. This chapter analyzes this important function of the supervisor and proposes a model for the supervisory visit that will aid the supervising principal in conducting the visit in a manner that will be in keeping with the encompassing goal of any modern supervisory program, i.e.: the improvement of instruction. The natural companion of the supervisory visit—the follow-up conference—is studied in chapter 9.

This chapter includes a discussion of the following topics:

Principles and purposes of supervisory visits
How to plan for classroom visitation
Mechanics of observation
Techniques in visitation
Do—don't
"In-Basket" supervisory problem
Chapter Supplement

Principles and Purposes of Supervisory Visits

While the emphasis placed on the supervisory visit may not be as great as that which was exhibited from the 1930's through the 1960's, it still is considered as very much a part of the program of supervision. Classroom visitation successfully fulfills a variety of needs when performed by someone who is aware of his responsibilities.

In terms of general values, consider first the theory that teaching is not a stagnated, routine function, but rather that it is both a science and creative skill, ever growing, ever capable of improvement. As the creative teacher seeks to improve his skills it becomes obvious to him that one cannot examine, in a truly objective fashion, his own performance as well as can another individual who has been trained for this function on a professional level.

The need for having a competent instructional leader constructively evaluate—but not inspect—the performance of the teacher is recognized as
essential to the acceptance of the supervisory visit and its corollary — the
follow-up conference.

Basic Principles and Purposes

Teachers want supervision that is well planned, constructive, and democratically applied. If these expectations are to be realized, the following
criteria should be met:

1. Supervisory visits should be focused upon all elements of the teaching-
   learning situation, not merely upon the teacher.
2. The chief purpose of supervisory visits should be the improvement of
   learning; they should be inspirational and instructive rather than inspectional and repressive.
3. Supervisory visits should afford each teacher a definite and concrete
   basis for improvement.
4. The principal, not the staff specialist-consultant, should be responsible
   for the rating of teachers. The principal is responsible for what transpires
   in the classroom. He is responsible for the improvement of instruction in
   all areas, at all levels.
5. The principal's first concern should be for the safety, welfare, and
   development of the students; and then for the safety, welfare, and
   development of the staff.
6. The principal should help the teachers to use various measures of self-
   evaluation.
7. Teachers should feel free to discuss their problems and to make suggestions. The principal must respect the opinions and points of view of the
   professional staff.

A Democratic Approach to Classroom Observation

When the head master contemplated visiting a classroom in colonial days,
the visit under consideration was in the nature of an inspectional tour, and

the conference following the visit was fraught with negative, destructive connotations. Since that time there have been numerous modifications with regard to the supervisory visit and follow-up conference.

Today, the acknowledged purpose of these visits and conferences is the improvement of the instructional program. Despite this shift from focus on the teacher toward an emphasis on the total teaching-learning situation, a problem still exists. Many teachers fear a visit by the principal, often with good reason. They dislike having to defend methods and techniques which they have found successful. They object to being told what to do. They are in fear of being rated by someone who too frequently drifts into and out of the classroom on an unannounced, unplanned visit.

A number of the shortcomings in the program for classroom visitation have been emphasized by M. S. Norton,[1] who stressed such items as perfunctory visits, failure to establish rapport, poor conference techniques, lack of worthwhile assistance with classroom problems, and insufficient planning. Any one of the reasons listed could cause deep dissatisfaction with the program. The problem facing the supervisor is not a question of the need for supervisory visits and conferences, but rather one of how to improve the practice in order to increase its effectiveness. Perhaps the increasing tendency of various professional associations to be concerned with the improvement of instruction utilizing the techniques described in this chapter bodes well for the future of the supervisory evaluation of instruction.

How to Plan for Classroom Visitation

The improvement of instruction is the primary duty of a supervising principal. If he is to perform this function effectively he must become proficient in the use of modern techniques for supervisory visits and conferences.[2] Careful planning by the supervisor should precede his visit to the classroom.

[1]Monte S. Norton, "Are Classroom Visits Worthwhile?" *The Clearing House* XXV (September 1960): 41.
[2]See Edwin H. Reeder, *Supervision in the Elementary School* (Boston: Houghton Mifflin Company, 1953), pp. 197–199; and Reba M. Burnham and Martha L. King, *Supervision in Action* (Washington, D.C.: Association for Supervision and Curriculum Development, National Education Association, 1961), p. 56.

He might select those activities from the following list which are applicable to a specific visit:

1. The supervisor will be clear as to the purpose of the visit and he will insure that the teacher has a clear understanding of his purpose.
2. The supervisor will know as much as possible about the teaching-learning situation prior to his visit.
3. The supervisor will discuss with the teacher the area of the instructional program with which the teacher has requested help prior to the visit.
4. The supervisor will review all available pertinent materials, including records of previous visits and follow-up conferences which might pertain to the proposed visit.
5. The supervisor will refer to any pertinent professional material.
6. Prior to the time of the supervisory visit, the supervisor will plan with the teacher for a follow-up conference.
7. The supervisor will complete a monthly schedule of supervisory visits and conferences, such as that which was included in Chapter 4 and which is reported here as Figure 8–1, so that he will know when and for how long he will be in the classroom. Another form which may prove helpful in programming classroom visits and follow-up conferences is included as Figure 8–2.

Mechanics of Observation

Duration and Frequency

The duration of the supervisory visit will be determined both by the type of teaching-learning situation being observed and by the type of visit—whether it is of the standard or survey variety and whether or not it is scheduled. Establishing the purpose for the visit in advance will enable the principal to gauge the length of his visit accordingly. If the teaching-learning situation happens to be a lesson in political science, the principal may well plan to be in the classroom for a full hour. A music lesson in an elementary school probably would consume less than half that time.

FIGURE 8–1   Sample Planning Schedule for Supervisory Visits and Conferences

SUPERVISORY VISITS* AND CONFERENCES

SCHEDULE

_____ School Month

Week of School Month	M	T	W	T	F
First	___ (A.M. P.M.) ___	___ (A.M. P.M.) ___	___ (A.M. P.M.) ___	___ (A.M. P.M.) ___	___ (A.M. P.M.)
Second	___ (A.M. P.M.) ___	___ (A.M. P.M.) ___	___ (A.M. P.M.) ___	___ (A.M. P.M.) ___	___ (A.M. P.M.)
Third	___ (A.M. P.M.) ___	___ (A.M. P.M.) ___	___ (A.M. P.M.) ___	___ (A.M. P.M.) ___	___ (A.M. P.M.)
Fourth	___ (A.M. P.M.) ___	___ (A.M. P.M.) ___	___ (A.M. P.M.) ___	___ (A.M. P.M.) ___	___ (A.M. P.M.)

Day

KEY: V = Visit   A = Other Appointment
KEY: C = Conference   PR = Probationary Rating
KEY: R = Request   T = Teaching Assignment for Principal

*Elementary school principals usually find it difficult to schedule more than one supervisory visit per day. The principal should attempt to visit for an entire lesson. An average visit may be thirty minutes in length.

FIGURE 8–2   Supervisory Visit and Follow-Up Conference Programming Form

1. Preparation for the visit:
   a) Obtain information, check previous notes_____
   _____
   b) Preconference and results_____
   _____
   c) Contact_____

2. The classroom visit:
   a) Time allotment_____
      (Check teacher's daily program)
   b) Method_____
   c) Planned objective_____
   d) Other_____

3. Analysis of the observed performance:
   _____
   _____
   _____

4. The follow-up conference:
   a) Preceding activities
   b) When_____
   c) Where_____
   d) What discussed_____
   e) Written report_____
   f) Plans/materials to bring_____
   _____
   g) Teacher's reactions_____
   h) Closing_____
   _____

If the teacher took the initiative by inviting the principal to visit, or if the principal had informed the teacher of his intention to visit, he will be expected to remain until the lesson is completed. In the preplanning session with the teacher, the duration of the principal's visit should be discussed. Certainly the principal will be in a better position to discuss the lesson intelligently in the follow-up conference if he has observed the total lesson.

The frequency of supervisory visits will depend on (1) the purpose of the visit, and (2) who initiates the visit. If the supervising principal is observing a teacher who has requested help with a specific area of the instructional program, he may want to contemplate a return visit within a very short time following the initial observation, so that he may gather more data or so that he may demonstrate a teaching technique. His function will be to provide as much help as is needed at the time it is needed.

If the principal initiates the supervisory visit, it is possible that he will plan to visit the teacher a minimum of once per month; whereas if the teacher initiates the visit, visits could occur either more or less frequently, depending upon the function of the visitation. The frequency of supervisory visits should be a function if an effective program. H. Spears[3] stated clearly the need for a regular program of visitation, commenting that perhaps fear of supervision results from the fact that visits are infrequent as well as from the fact that they are handled improperly.

Types of Visits

Both scheduled and unscheduled visits need to be made by the supervising principal to beginning teachers. The supervising principal should concentrate on establishing rapport with the teacher to be visited. For this reason alone, it might be best to *schedule* at least the initial visits, so that the teachers involved may prepare carefully. They will appreciate the principal's thoughtfulness. Standard scheduled visits are in order for both experienced and beginning teachers.

The beginning teacher realizes that he will be rated by the principal. The principal's dropping in unexpectedly will only add to his feelings of insecurity. Once rapport has been established, the teacher will accept the supervising principal's visit as a matter of course.

If the principal wishes to learn more about a particular phase of the instructional program through observation, then he will want to plan especially carefully for the visit. M. S. Norton wrote:

. . . [the supervisor] must arrange for visitations at times when he can best analyze the learning situation and obtain the best cross-section of a particular unit of study.[4]

[3]Harold Spears, *Improving the Supervision of Instruction* (Englewood Cliffs, New Jersey: Prentice-Hall, Inc., 1953), p. 62.
[4]Norton, "Are Classroom Visits Worthwhile?" p. 41.

This principle should be applied to visits to experienced teachers as well

Not all scheduled visits are proposed by the principal. Rather, as E. H. Reeder suggested, "some of the principal's visits will be the result of invitations from the new teachers, if the right supervisory relationships have been established."[5]

Once rapport has been established, the principal should feel free to make an unscheduled visit. If he has demonstrated a sincere interest in what happens within the classroom, the teacher will welcome his presence and look forward to a conference later in the day. The unscheduled visit can serve to reinforce any conclusions the principal may have formulated concerning the instructional program. Conversely, it may result in a change of opinion. Whatever the result, if the supervisor has responded negatively to that which he has observed in the classroom, he should reserve final judgment until he has discussed the lesson with the teacher.

Helping the Experienced Teacher through Visitation

Standard *unscheduled* visits to competent, experienced teachers with tenure have been termed a questionable practice by specialists in this area. The principal should plan for standard *scheduled* visits and for scheduled and unscheduled *survey type* visits to the classrooms of experienced teachers. The supervising principal must remember that it is he who has the responsibility for accounting for all that transpires within the school. If a situation involving an experienced teacher arises which the supervising principal cannot ignore, quite properly he might have to handle it in a different manner and through established channels. The supervising principal must always keep uppermost in his thinking the safety, welfare, and development of students and staff. Improvement in the instructional program is a means of reaching the goals concomitant to these functions of the principalship.

Scheduled and Unscheduled Survey Visits to the Experienced Teacher

At times a teacher will request that the principal make a complete survey of his instructional techniques. It is then that the principal will want to schedule

[5]Reeder, *Supervision in the Elementary School*, p. 197.

and provide for a scheduled survey visit to the classroom. The *scheduled* survey type visit should be made to the experienced teacher *only* upon the invitation of the teacher.[6] These visits will be planned:

1. When the teacher is conducting one phase of study of a problem that was established by group decision, and he is seeking judgment concerning the effectiveness of certain aspects of his program of action research;
2. When an experienced teacher asks for help with a specific area of the instructional program.

It appears to be fairly general practice for supervising principals to complete what is termed an unscheduled survey visit to all classrooms approximately four times each school year. The purpose of the unscheduled survey visit is to provide the principal with a general overview of the general status of the school and of its instructional program. It is not the purpose of the unscheduled survey visit to focus attention on individual teachers and/ or problems. Unscheduled survey visits are too short in duration for the principal to formulate judgments based upon individual situations.

Unscheduled survey visits should be planned by the principal. They are made without the invitation of the teachers, whereas the scheduled survey visit is made on invitation *only*. Good human relations require that the supervising principal usually prepare the faculty to expect a visit within a designated period, and to offer an explanation of the purpose for the visit. In summation, the supervising principal plans both scheduled and unscheduled survey type visits to the experienced teacher. The scheduled survey visit involves an *exhaustive* analysis of teaching techniques in instructional programs, and occurs only upon invitation. The *unscheduled* survey visit does not involve a critique of progress of the individual teacher, but it is designed to present an overall picture of the general status of the entire school with regard to one or more variables.

In the case of the beginning teacher, the principal probably will wish periodically to apply both types of survey visits. He also will employ the standard supervisory visit both of the scheduled and unscheduled variety.

[6]Ibid., p. 199.

Standard visits, especially those which are unscheduled, are designed to aid teachers who have not as yet reached as high a degree of instructional proficiency as have the experienced, permanent professional educators. See Table 8–1 for a representation of these relationships.

Techniques in Visitation

Responsibilities of the Visitor

Discussion of how the supervising principal conducts himself in the classroom is important only insofar as the teacher and the class are affected by what he does.

In conducting the visit, the supervising principal should:

1. Have arranged the time of the visit with the teacher during the previsit conference;
2. Enter the classroom quietly and avoid drawing unnecessary attention to himself (in a secondary school the interval between classes would be a good time);

TABLE 8–1   Interrelationships Between the Various
Major Types of Supervisory Visits

	To Experienced Teachers	To Beginning Teachers	May Be "On Call"	Usually Only upon Request	Observation Time Determined by Length of Lesson	Shortest Observation Time	Longest Observation Time	Critique of Individual Performance
Unscheduled Survey Visits	X	X					X	
Scheduled Survey Visits	X	X	X	X			X	X
Standard Unscheduled Visits		X			X			X
Standard Scheduled Visits	X	X	X		X			X

3. Smile, so as to let the teacher and the class know that he is glad to be there;
4. Try to become a temporary part of the class.

Some points to consider concerning the management of the observation phase include:

1. The supervisor should gauge his mobility by the activity taking place in the class. If the class is engaged in the stimulation and planning phase of a creative writing lesson, the supervising principal will wish to observe at close hand.
2. The supervising principal will make his observation practice known to teacher in the previsit planning conference.
3. *Notes should not be made in the classroom* but should be recorded directly after the visit, in private. If the scheduled survey type of visit is being made and notes are taken by agreement in the previsit conference, the teacher should be shown the notes in the follow-up conference.
4. The supervising principal must keep an accurate and detailed record of the strengths and weaknesses of the lesson for follow-up conferences.
5. Emphasis should be placed on the teaching-learning situation and not on the teacher, and should gather data for the follow-up conference evaluation.

FIGURE 8–3   Too Many Visits May Spoil the Supervisory Broth.

What to Look for During the Visit

The supervising principal should prepare in advance for the observation by completing a listing of points to be observed. The following outline was prepared by one supervising principal and may prove helpful:

1. Do the students participate in the selection and/or formulation of classroom standards of conduct? Is self-control encouraged?
2. Do students recognize the reasons for their being corrected? Are the observable or predictable consequences of an action stressed? Is disciplinary action considered a form of constructive criticism?
3. What is the teacher trying to accomplish? Is there a definite objective? Does the teacher seem to be guided by it?
4. Is the teacher's attitude friendly and accepting? Does the teacher ridicule or threaten? Is he overly familiar?
5. Is his voice well modulated and of sufficient volume?
6. Does the teacher have leadership qualities? Is he confident, positive, and consistent?
7. Does the teacher know the subject matter? Is the teacher well prepared? Does he have adequate lesson plans? Does he plan for varied activities? Does he have materials and instructional technology aids readily available? Is the teacher well organized? Does he post an agenda for the period? Does he have a seating plan? Does he have an efficient way to handle routines? Does he have a definite place to write assignments? Are assignments clear, reasonable, pertinent, and varied? Do they meet individual and group needs?
8. What teaching method or combination of methods and techniques are observed? Is the method used skillfully?
   What is the reaction of the class? Is there much participation? Caution —participation (or the lack of it) does not necessarily make a lesson. How much disturbance is there? How much enthusiasm?
10. Does the lesson come to a useful conclusion? Does the teacher provide for enrichment activities for fast workers? Does he show how the lesson relates to the present and/or future psychosociological world of the student?

Interaction Matrices and the Use of Video Tape Recordings in Instructional Supervision

INTERACTION MATRICES: THE FLANDERS SYSTEM. One concrete device which could be used by the supervisor during visitation to help the teacher increase his effectiveness is the employment of different interaction matrices, such as that developed by Flanders and by Medley, by Withall, and by Perkins.[7] Interaction analysis schemes attempt to quantify and categorize the spoken-verbal communications during a lesson, and to record and chart the results of the analysis. The categories generally differentiate between teacher-originated and student-originated vocal communication. The categories and three forms used in recording and charging the results of the application of this technique are included as Appendix B.

The supervisor must beware the temptation to apply the interaction matrice technique without due consideration of its limitations. There is a tendency to fail to differentiate between an analysis or how much "teacher-talk" is occurring in a classroom and the prescription of how much *should* be in evidence: "Perhaps the . . . percentage of teacher questioning and confirming should be increased—at least in some learning situations," as noted by Lucio and McNeil.[8] Furthermore, the supervisor must keep in mind that this technique does not analyze all teacher effectiveness, but only an aspect of student-teacher verbal behavior.

USE OF VIDEO-TAPE RECORDINGS AND MICRO-TEACHING TECHNIQUES IN SUPERVISION. A video-tape recording can work wonders in the area of supervision. The technique of recording a lesson on a video-tape recorder can, if handled properly, permit the teacher to visit his own classroom at his leisure. The video-tape recorder not only provides direct aid to the student, as in micro-teaching, but also permits instructors to appraise the quality and ef-

[7]Ned Flanders, "Intent, Action, Feedback: A Preparation for Teaching," *Journal of Teacher Education* XIV (September 1963), no. 3; Donald M. Medley, "Experience with the OSCAR Technique," and John Withall, "Mental Health: Teacher Education Report," both in *Journal of Teacher Education* XIV (September 1963) no. 3; and Hugh Perkins, "A Procedure for Assessing the Classroom Behavior of Students and Teachers," *American Educational Research Journal* (November 1964).
[8]William H. Lucio and John D. McNeil, *Supervision* (New York: McGraw-Hill Book Company, 1969), p. 314.

fectiveness of their presentations to their classes, and to analyze their lessons at a higher level than the traditional visit and "hearsay" follow-up conference.

The video-tape recorder should be set up in the classroom several days prior to the visit (or to its intended use as described above) so as to permit the teacher to become acquainted with the equipment and its operation, and to minimize the "on-stage" syndrome. The supervisor should emphasize that the tape will be available for the use of the teacher ONLY, that the supervising principal will view the results ONLY if requested to do so by the teacher, and that the tape becomes the property of the teacher and is in his custody immediately upon recording. The authors recommend that the supervisor encourage the purchase of color video-recording equipment. The small price differential is more than compensated for by the added dimension and impact of the color programming.

Checklist for Recording Data about Observed Instruction

The supervising principal may wish to involve the staff in the preparation of a checklist instrument for recording data obtained during observation. One such visitation record is included as Figure 8–4.

Shorter Continuous Records Observed Instruction:

The three observation report forms that have been helpful are illustrated in Figures 8–5, 8–6, 8–7.

If, by district policy, the supervising principal must complete a teacher evaluation sheet that will be considered as pertinent in determining whether or not the teacher is to be rehired, forms such as the three that are included as Figures 8–8, 8–9, and 8–10 might be used.

Use of Rating Instruments

The several evaluation forms available, then, differ in detail, but essentially focus upon performance in the eight areas listed on page 307.

FIGURE 8–4   Sample Visitation Record

VISITATION RECORD

Name of staff member
making visit: _____ Date _____

Name of teacher visited: _____

School where teacher employed: _____

Grade and/or subjects being taught: _____

Previsitation interview: _____

Postvisitation conference: _____

Observation Criteria	Superior	Good	Average	Needs Impr.
General appearance and poise				
Room appearance and physical condition				
Teaching materials and procedures				
Student-teacher relationship				
Interest and activity of students				
Classroom management				
Attitude toward teaching				
Command of language: effective communication				
Chalkboard ability				

Comments and suggestions resulting from visit:

FIGURE 8–5   Sample Observation Report Form

OBSERVATION REPORT

School _____

Teacher_____Grade _____Date_____

Subject observed_____Time_____

1. STUDENTS:
   - a) Attitude_____
   - b) Attention_____
   - c) Discipline_____

   - d) Effort_____
   - e) Seating_____
   - f) Number in room_____

2. TEACHER:
   - a) Preparation_____
   - b) Following plan _____
   - c) Response of students_____
   - d) Skill_____

   - e) Speech_____
   - f) Voice quality_____
   - g) Appearance_____

3. LESSON:
   - a) Topic _____
   - b) Technique_____

   - c) Student participa-
        tion_____
   - d) Use of Instruc-
        tion aids_____

4. ROOM:
   - a) Bulletin boards /
        displays_____
   - b) Writing aids posted _____
   - c) Environment_____

   - d) Ventilation_____
   - e) Lighting_____
   - f) General appear-
        ance_____

5. OVERALL EVALUATION:
   - a) Strong points_____
   - c) Additional suggestions_____

   - b) Weak points_____

Follow-up conference held:

No_____Yes _____ Date_____Observer's signature

FIGURE 8–6   Sample Observation Report

JOINT SCHOOL DISTRICT NO. 407
St. Marcus, Idaho
OBSERVATION REPORT

School _____ Instructor _____

Date _____ No. of Students _____ Subject or Grade _____

Lesson Title _____ Observer _____

NOTES: _____

1. Room appearance

2. Personal appearance

3. Emotional climate of room

4. General classroom management

5. Presentation of material

6. Lesson preparation

7. Assignments

8. Student-teacher relations

9. Punctuality

10. Supervisory work

11. Administration-teacher relations

12. Lesson Plan Book

13. Grade Book

14. Comments

Signed: _____

Teacher   Date   Principal

FIGURE 8–7   Sample Report of Principal's Classroom Visit

REPORT OF PRINCIPAL'S CLASSROOM VISIT

Teacher _____ Class _____ Hour _____Date _____

I. *Physical Characteristics of Classroom:*

   1. Ventilation _____

   2. Lighting_____

   3. Temperature _____

   4. Seating arrangements _____

   5. Decorations _____

   6. Displays _____

   7. Orderliness _____

II. *Teaching:*

   1. Are classroom activities in line with stated objectives:

_____

_____

   2. Student reactions:

_____

_____

   3. Work in progress:

_____

_____

   4. Evaluation:

_____

_____

_____

_____

Principal

FIGURE 8–8   Teacher Evaluation Sheet for Instructional Improvement

---

Name and Place of School System

Teacher's name _____ Grade _____

School _____ Date _____

Subject being taught during observation
   or evaluation _____

Conditions: 1. Excellent   3. Weak, needs improvement
              2. Satisfactory   4. Unsatisfactory, needs improvement

FACTORS OF EVALUATION

    1 2 3 4   A. *Objectives*

1.   . . . . Objectives clearly defined (long-term and immediate)?
2.   . . . . Instruction guided by objectives?

B. *Planning*

3.   . . . . Evidence of careful and definite planning?
4.   . . . . Evidence of following plan?

C. *General Room Atmosphere*

5.   . . . . Does the room atmosphere encourage intellectual activity?
6.   . . . . Does the arrangement of furniture give unity in the room?
7.   . . . . Are there present pictures, flowers or other conditions
           which tend to make the classroom pleasant?

D. *General Room Appearance*

8.   . . . . Clean?
9.   . . . . Well ventilated?
10. . . . . Students' desks and room clean and tidy?
11. . . . . No evidence of willful destruction of desks or other school
           property?

E. *Personal Characteristics*

12. . . . . Dressed appropriately and well groomed?
13. . . . . Speaks clearly and uses good English?

FIGURE 8–8   (Continued)

---

1 2 3 4

14.   . . . .   Is physically able to perform duties?
                  Is not handicapped by too frequent absence or illness?
15.   . . . .   Maintains sound emotional adjustment; has good self-control?
16.   . . . .   Has a sense of humor?
17.   . . . .   Is a resourceful person?
18.   . . . .   Can accept deserved criticism and praise with poise?
19.   . . . .   Shows understanding and concern for individual students?
20.   . . . .   Punctual to work and with reports and assignments?
21.   . . . .   Attempts to correct personal habits and mannerisms that de-
                  tract from effective teaching?
22.   . . . .   Displays knowledge of subject being taught?

F. Classroom Control: Teaching

Methods and Tools

23.   . . . .   Handles behavior problems individually as far as possible?
24.   . . . .   Is consistently fair and firm in dealing with classroom be-
                  havior problems?
25.   . . . .   Is respected by students and secures voluntary cooperation?
26.   . . . .   Adapts to the teaching-learning situation?
                  (Underline method used: Lecture, Recitation, Drill, Story-Tell-
                  ing, Project or Laboratory, Audio-Visual, Dramatic or Role
                  Playing, Group Discussion, Manual.)
27.   . . . .   Skillful and timely use of teaching aids?
28.   . . . .   Avoids scolding, nagging, shouting, or loud talking?
29.   . . . .   Belives in, maintains, or helps maintain good order in the
                  classroom, halls, and all parts of the building?

G. Instructional and Guidance Skills

30.   . . . .   Provides for individual differences?
31.   . . . .   Provides for effective class and group work?
32.   . . . .   Encourages good work and study habits?
33.   . . . .   Insists on thorough and neat work; done on time?
34.   . . . .   Evidence of students mastering skills being taught?
35.   . . . .   Students are being taught self-direction and democratic prin-
                  ciples?
36.   . . . .   Provides opportunities for working effectively in groups or as
                  individuals?

FIGURE 8–8   (Continued)

	1	2	3	4

37. . . . . Inspires eager responses from students; many participating?
38. . . . . Exercises care, supervision, and provides special instruction in health, safety, moral, and spiritual values?
39. . . . . Respects students' suggestions and opinions?
40. . . . . No favoritism; no pets?
41. . . . . Praise and criticism based on fact; no hasty conclusions?
42. . . . . Students devoid of tensions and free to speak, express opinions?

H. Assignments

43. . . . . Assignments definite and clear, reasonable in length and difficulty?
44. . . . . Establishes a link between the new lesson and the past lesson?
45. . . . . Explains and motivates for assignments, rather than mere page and chapter assignments?

I. Professional and Staff Characteristics

46. . . . . Conducts relations with students and teachers on a high plane?
47. . . . . Aids in developing and maintaining faculty and student morale?
48. . . . . Actively supports local, state, and national professional organizations in accordance with district policies and directions of superiors?
49. . . . . Does not talk unethically about other teachers, administrators, parents, or students?

J. Classroom Mechanics

50. . . . . Follows school policies in marking roll books?
51. . . . . Proper and timely assignment and correction of written assignments (including work books)?
52. . . . . Proper and timely follow-up of written work?
53. . . . . Accuracy in accomplishing routine details and assignments?

Remarks: (Feel free to make remarks on any factor above. When so doing, list letter and number.)

FIGURE 8–9   Sample Teacher Evaluation Form

EVALUATION FOR PROFESSIONAL GROWTH

This form will be used as a guide for teacher eveluation. It should prove helpful both for self-evaluation and for evaluation by the principal or superintendent or both. Summaries are to be mutually agreed upon and will be recorded as an indication of progress. These summaries should indicate teacher strengths and points of improvement. The intent is not negative but to give a positive approach to mutual growth. All interviews will be held in strict confidence.

This form is to be used as often as necessary but at least one interview is required each year for all teaching staff members. One copy completed is retained by the principal and one copy is retained by the superintendent.

The five areas listed below form the basis for the improvement and evaluation of professional services

TEACHER EVALUATION FORM

	Superior	Good	Satis-factory	Needs Im-provement
I. Personal Characteristics				
Statement: A superior teacher has a wholesome personality, a sound character, and enjoys good physical, mental, and emotional health.				
a. Personal appearance				
b. Emotional stability (self-control)				
c. High ethical and moral standards				
d. Punctuality				
e. Dependability				
f. Poise				
g. Tact				

FIGURE 8–9   (Continued)

	Superior	Good	Satis- factory	Needs Im- provement
h. Voice				
i. Health				
j. Fulfills obligations				
II. Instruction Skills Statement: A superior teacher controls all classroom activities to assure that work of individuals and groups is orderly and effective; that each student contributes according to his ability; and that each one gains a sense of worth through achievement. a. Classroom control (discipline)				
b. Knowledge of subject matter				
c. Preparation				
d. Leadership				
e. Ability to stimulate student				
III. Teacher–Staff Relationships Statement: A superior teacher is a good team worker who is conscious that his attitudes affect all others on the school staff. He is loyal to the school's program and its policies.				

FIGURE 8–9   (Continued)

	Superior	Good	Satis-factory	Needs Im-provement
a. Cooperation with staff administration				
b. Adheres to school regulations				
c. Loyalty				
d. Serves willingly				
IV. Self-Improvement Statement: A superior teacher takes responsibility for, and participates in, various types of student and faculty activities; takes responsibility for formal and informal guidance beyond regular classroom contacts; appears always as an important and valuable member of the professional "team" operating the school. a. Cultural interests				
b. Evidences of professional growth				
c. Participation in professional and/or subject area organizations				
V. Social and Community Participation Statement: A superior teacher will utilize community resources and take part in community activities.				

FIGURE 8–9 (Continued)

	Superior	Good	Satis-factory	Needs Im-provement
a. Professional relationship with students				
b. Participation in activities, community affairs				
c. Relationships with parents				

General comments:

Teacher's Signature _____ Signature of Evaluator _____

Date of Evaluation _____

1. Classroom management and disciplinary control;
2. Knowledge of subject matter;
3. Teaching techniques and instructional skills;
4. Dependability and record keeping;
5. Personal characteristics such as appearance, punctuality, tact, voice, cooperation, sense of humor, initiative, enthusiasm, poise, and good grooming;
6. Personal fitness for the job;
7. Human relationships with students, parents, other staff members, and the community;
8. Professional conduct, ethics, and evidence of professional growth.

Limitations

The practitioner in supervision should keep in mind the many limitations of such checklists and rating scales. No method of evaluation has yet been (nor shall be) developed which is foolproof. Too many variables and judgment decisions are involved.

There is a lack of hard research data concerning what really constitutes good teaching performance. Two observers of the same classroom lesson will not agree upon its effectiveness in every detail. One may look for

FIGURE 8–10 Teacher Observation Record Sheet

Name of School System

Name of Teacher _____ Status _____ File or Employee Number _____

School _____ Principal _____

Subject/Grade Taught _____ Date _____ Time _____

Directions: Please indicate by a check in the appropriate parentheses the description which fits best.

	Unsatis-factory	Weak	Satis-factory	Strong	Out-standing	No Oppor-tunity to Observe
Personal Qualities:						
1. Appearance, manner, and bearing	( )	( )	( )	( )	( )	( )
2. Mental alertness	( )	( )	( )	( )	( )	( )
3. Effectiveness of voice and speech	( )	( )	( )	( )	( )	( )
4. Oral and written expression	( )	( )	( )	( )	( )	( )
5. Emotional poise	( )	( )	( )	( )	( )	( )
6. Health and physical condition	( )	( )	( )	( )	( )	( )
Professional Competence:						
1. Knowledge of subject matter	( )	( )	( )	( )	( )	( )
2. Knowledge and use of basic skills (reading, spelling, language usage, arithmetic)	( )	( )	( )	( )	( )	( )
3. Development of classroom control (discipline) and morale	( )	( )	( )	( )	( )	( )
4. Leadership qualities	( )	( )	( )	( )	( )	( )
5. Success in planning for instruction	( )	( )	( )	( )	( )	( )
6. Effectiveness of teaching procedures	( )	( )	( )	( )	( )	( )
7. Management of classroom environment and routine	( )	( )	( )	( )	( )	( )

	Unsatis-factory	Weak	Satis-factory	Strong	Out-standing	No Oppor-tunity to Observe
8. Assumption of share or responsibility for school activities	( )	( )	( )	( )	( )	( )
9. Ability to work with others (members of school staff, parents, community leaders)	( )	( )	( )	( )	( )	( )
10. Reaction to constructive criticism of a professional nature	( )	( )	( )	( )	( )	( )

Comments: Be Objective:

1. Attitude _____
2. Relations with people/ability to adjust _____
3. Professionalism: ethics and acts _____
4. Poise/appearance _____
5. Organization _____
6. Sense of humor/manner with children _____
7. Discipline (control) _____
8. Understanding of principles of educational psychology and guidance _____
9. Honesty and consistency _____
10. Cocurricular activities _____
11. Community relations _____
12. Further comments _____

*Conferences held on _____ Recommend continued employment _____
(dates)

Special recommendations _____ Recommend dismissal _____

to teacher: _____ Recommend transfer _____

Overall Rating: Unsatisfactory ( )   Weak ( )   Date _____ Signed _____

            Satisfactory ( )   Strong ( )

            Outstanding ( )   (optional)   (Principal)

* The remainder of the form usually would be completed only after numerous administrative (not supervisory) visits and follow-up conferences, aimed primarily at rating and at determining the teacher's qualifications for reemployment purposes, had been held.

quiet, controlled participation of students, while another may look for dynamic, challenging discussion with many students trying to present their ideas—often at the same time. Would either technique indicate best teaching in all classrooms at all times for all teachers and students? Certainly not!

No form has yet been developed which is acceptable to all supervisors. Rating scales inherently include errors and, if used without awareness of their many limitations, can rate a teacher unfairly. Unreliable evaluation is worse than no evaluation.

Trends

Several trends are becoming apparent in teacher evaluation. Rating devices are becoming less rigid and more constructive. Cooperatively developed rating instruments are coming into more common use. There will be more coevaluation by teachers and supervisors. The principle of multiple evaluation will be used more extensively, with professional associations joining in the evaluation process.

DO

1. Evaluate the job (performance)—not the person.
2. Base evaluations on *firsthand* observations.
3. Use a positive approach; consider what will help to improve the teacher's effectiveness.
4. Combine the measurement of personality traits, student progress, and teacher performance in your program of teacher evaluation.
5. Keep the evaluation program flexible enough to meet changing conditions.
6. Consider evaluation as an important means toward achieving goals—not an end in itself.
7. Be thoroughly familiar with the teacher's abilities and background, as well as those of the students in the class to be observed.
8. Record observations immediately and arrange a conference with the teacher to cooperatively analyze findings.
9. Smile; maintain a cheerful and sincere attitude.
10. Plan your work—work your plan—and evaluate.
11. Discuss what appear to be the strong and weak aspects of the teacher's performance, and make definite plans for correction and improvement.

12. Encourage an experimental environment where teachers and supervisors feel free to explore, to experiment, and to test methods, processes, and materials used in teaching.

DON'T

1. View the visit as an inspection tour.
2. Direct criticism at the individual.
3. Make a visit without first establishing good rapport.
4. Criticize a teacher's work in front of others.
5. Discuss a teacher's problems with other teachers.

Supervisory Problem

In Basket

The problem develops in a fourth-grade classroom in an elementary school of about 600 students. The teacher involved (Miss Galzin) had one year of experience prior to her assignment to this school. She seems to do an excellent job. The students like her and work hard for her. She plans her work well and is an enthusiastic teacher. She is not unattractive, but is slightly "dowdy" in her appearance.

It is the policy of the principal (her immediate supervisor) to visit the classrooms of all teachers at least twice during the school year. The first visit is always a standard scheduled visit, while the second visit usually is of the unscheduled standard variety.

When the supervising principal entered Miss Galzin's classroom for the first time he noticed that she was, apparently, quite disturbed by his presence. She rapidly became more flustered until she finally embarrassed herself and the principal before he could leave the room. She was extremely upset when the principal tried to hold a conference with her. He learned later that she was upset whenever *any* adult entered her room, and was especially distraught if that adult was another educator.

How can the supervising principal develop the kind of rapport with the teacher that will allow him to visit her classroom in his capacity as a supervisor?

[9]Emery Stoops and Russell E. Johnson, *Elementary School Supervision* (New York: McGraw-Hill Book Company, 1967), p. 288.

Selected Bibliography

Books

Adams, H. P. et al. *Basic Principles of Supervision.* New York: American Book Company, 1953.

Anderson, Richard C. et al. *Current Research on Instruction.* Englewood Cliffs, New Jersey: Prentice-Hall, Inc., 1969.

Ayer, Fred C. *Fundamentals of Instructional Supervision.* New York: Harper and Row, Publishers, 1954.

Bartky, John A. *Supervision as Human Relations.* Boston: D. C. Heath and Company, 1953.

Douglas, H. R. et al. *Democratic Supervision in Secondary Schools.* Cambridge: The Riverside Press, 1961.

Faunce, Roland C. *Secondary School Administration.* New York: Harper and Brothers, 1955.

Hicks, Hanne J. *Educational Supervision in Principle and Practice.* New York: The Ronald Press Company, 1960.

Kyte, George C. *The Principle at Work.* Boston: Ginn and Company, 1952.

Lucio, William H. et al. *Supervision: A Synthesis of Thought and Action.* New York: McGraw-Hill Book Company, 1962.

Neagley, Ross L., and N. Dean Evans. *Handbook for Effective Supervision of Instruction.* Englewood Cliffs, New Jersey: Prentice-Hall, Inc., 1965.

Reeder, Edwin H. *Supervision in the Elementary School.* Boston: Houghton Mifflin Company, 1953.

Spears, Harold. *Improving the Supervision of Instruction.* Englewood Cliffs, New Jersey: Prentice-Hall, Inc., 1953.

Torrance, E. Paul. *Guiding Creative Talent.* Englewood Cliffs, New Jersey: Prentice-Hall, Inc., 1962. Especially chapter X.

Periodicals

Gross, R. S. "Teachers Want Supervision." *School Executive* LXXII (August 1953): 52–53.

Harman, A. C. "Classroom Visitation as a Phase of Supervision." *American School Board Journal* CXVIII (June 1949): 39–40.

Norton, Monte S. "Are Classroom Visits Worthwhile?" *The Clearing House* XXV (September 1960): 41.

Other Sources

Association for Supervision and Curriculum Development. *Leadership for Improving Instruction*. 1960 Yearbook. Washington, D.C.: National Education Association, 1960.

Burnham, Reba M., and Martha L. King. *Supervision in Action*. Washington, D.C.: Association for Supervision and Curriculum Development, National Education Association, 1961.

Southwest Cooperative Program in Educational Administration. *The Role of the Administrator in the Analysis and Improvement of Instruction*. Austin: University of Texas Press, 1954.

Steel, Sanger. *Improving Instruction*. New York: Metropolitan School Study Council, 1954.

An improved program of supervisory visits include individual and group visitation opportunities for teachers and principals. If carefully planned and managed, it is one of the best ways to present the use of desirable methods and techniques. Principals and teachers alike can benefit by this type of experience.

Teachers who are new to a school system and who need an opportunity to learn about a particular phase of the program should find demonstration lessons helpful. However, this is an excellent way to familiarize all staff members with a new way of working. They may adapt it to their own needs, or reject it, once they have seen it in action.

The supervising principal can be of help in providing demonstration lessons for group observation purposes, and he can direct an individual to a master teacher for observation of a particular lesson.

Individual Visits

When a need arises, if there is no one in the principal's school to whom he can send the teacher to observe, he can turn to the principal of a neighboring school for assistance. A principal may be able to suggest two or three teachers who would be willing and able to present the kind of lesson desired.

Final arrangements for the visit of a teacher to another school should be made by the principal. These arrangements should include contacting the principal of the other school and receiving his approval of the proposed visit. He, in turn, can discuss the visit with the host teacher. Usually the demonstration teacher's regular schedule would be observed in planning a time for the visit.

If at all possible, it is suggested that the supervising principal accompany the observing teacher on the day of the visit. The observing teacher should take notes to help him remember successful techniques, and a conference should follow the observation. Asking the demonstration teacher to participate in the discussion is a desirable practice.

When it is necessary for the teacher to visit without the principal, it is still desirable to have the visiting teacher and his principal discuss the lesson upon the teacher's return to his school. The teacher should decide upon a course of action that will result from his observation experience.

Group Visitation

One of the most noteworthy aspects of the group visitation program is the amount of learning that results on the part of all who participate. Teachers, principals, and specialist-consultants alike benefit by the experience.

Group visitations involve more extensive planning on the part of the principal than is involved in scheduling individual visitations. The planning includes (1) determining the type of lesson to be presented, (2) selecting the demonstration teacher, (3) scheduling the visit, (4) preparing the class for the visit, (5) selecting the observation techniques to be used, and (6) scheduling the preplanning and evaluation conferences for the observers.

In making a decision as to the type of lesson to be presented, the most common determining factor is a general need for improvement in a particular area of the instructional program. An awareness of this need can come about as a result of conferences such as the grade-level meeting, or through supervisory visits.

The following suggestions may be given to the group prior to the visit:

1. Be aware of class differences, especially where there is homogeneous grouping and type class.
2. Become acquainted with the demonstration teacher before the visit.
3. Create as little disturbance as possible in entering and leaving the classroom. The observers should be present at the beginning of the class period and remain in the room until the period is over.
4. Observe the reactions of the pupils.
5. Observe the use of the materials of instructional technology and the techniques of programmed learning.
6. Note all steps in the lesson and the amount of time spent on each step. Observe how the teacher stimulates the students.
7. Remember to appear happy, relaxed, and free from strain or uneasiness before, during, and after the visit.

Preparing for the Visit

When arrangements have been made for a group to observe a demonstration lesson, the observation period always should be preceded by a preplanning conference with the observers. In this conference period the purpose of the demonstration is established, pertinent background information is provided concerning the children to be observed, and group activities that have led up to the lesson to be presented are listed.

SOME HELPFUL DEVICES. A valuable preplanning technique involves the use of a carefully prepared observation sheet on which the observers may make notes as the lesson is developed. Questions on the observation sheet will add to the observer's awareness of techniques employed by the demonstration teacher and will help to make the teaching-learning situation more meaningful.

The principal should be familiar with the various types of fact-gathering techniques that can be employed during observations. He also should be aware of their limitations. He must be skillful in choosing techniques to apply in a given situation.

SETTING THE DATE AND TIME. Once the school and the teacher have been selected, a date for the visitation is arrived at cooperatively by the principals and the teachers involved. Usually the host principal suggests one or two dates that will not be in conflict with the master calendar. Then the visiting principal and the teachers will select one of the dates suggested. An effort is made to plan the visit at a time when teachers will not have to be away from their classroom for a prolonged period.

The visit may be planned for the first instructional period of either the morning or afternoon session in order that the planning conference can be held during the half hour before school begins, thus not cutting into the instructional time. Or it may be held the last period of the morning or of the afternoon, allowing for the evaluation conference after the children have been excused.

PREPARING THE HOST CLASS. To prepare the class for the visit, the principal must work closely with the teacher and the class in developing readiness for the teaching-learning situation to be demonstrated. This preparation may involve several supervisory visits to the classroom, followed by conferences.

If the purpose of such visits is to help the visiting teachers in their use of new techniques and to help the class learn how to handle new ways of working, the teacher and the class should have a sufficient amount of time to adjust to the changes.

A class should not practice or rehearse the lesson that will be presented during the demonstration. It must in no way be an artificial situation. However, the host principal may want to review the teacher's final plans with him and assist him in every way possible to prepare for the lesson.

It is suggested that the host principal select those observation techniques that will guide the observers toward the intended goal—namely, that of discovering ways to utilize in their own classrooms the techniques that are to be demonstrated.

Plan to Schedule a Pre-Visit Conference

In scheduling the group visitation, adequate time should be provided for discussing the lesson with the master teacher. A visitation without these conferences would have little value.

An important part of preparing for a group visitation is making certain that all individuals included or affected by the visit are properly notified. Usually a supervisory memorandum is prepared that includes all essential information.

The memorandum should contain a brief description of the type of lesson to be presented, information as to the grade level for which it is planned, and the place and time of visitation. The principal should make sure that his teachers receive the information and should expedite plans for their attendance.

The Visitors Arrive

Common courtesies need to be observed by the visiting principal, the host principal, and the teachers during a group interschool supervisory visit. A courteous principal does much toward making his visit a welcome event; and a courteous host principal and teaching staff, in turn, make their school a pleasant place to visit.

The dictates of good supervisory practices demand that the visiting principal announce his arrival at the host school both as a matter of courtesy and to keep his whereabouts known in case an emergency should arise. He should introduce himself to the school clerk, who should be expecting him. The host principal should be present to greet the group and to accompany the guests throughout the visit.

In either conference situation the principals will need to remember that the purposes of the conference are to discuss good ways of working with children and to encourage teachers to experiment with different techniques, to keep abreast in subject matter, and to adapt what is observed to their particular situations.

Plan for a Post-Visit Conference

When the visit draws to a close, the principals may wish to hold a short conference to review the day's work. Any discussion of individual situations remains on a highly professional level and must not become a supervisory rating session. If good planning preceded the visit, and good practices were followed during the visit, much should have been accomplished.

9

How to Improve Supervisory Conferences

Most specialists in supervision suggest that the principal make some kind of follow-up conference shortly following classroom visitation. It is the purpose of this chapter to present specific suggestions as to how the supervising principal may improve the supervisory conference. The following topics will be discussed:

Principles and purposes of supervisory conferences
How to conduct a successful conference
How to interview
Do—don't
"In-Basket" supervisory problem

Principles and Purposes of Supervisory Conferences

Objectives of Follow-Up Conferences

Five criteria to be followed by the supervising principal in the formal follow-up conference:

1. He should, first of all, establish rapport with the teacher at the beginning of the conference.
2. He should include a general commendation of the lesson as a whole, and specific approval of a specific aspect of the lesson.
3. He should commend the teacher on his skill.
4. He should help further the teacher's confidence in himself and his work.
5. He should include constructive suggestions whereby the teacher's good work may be further improved.

A follow-up conference between a supervisor and a teacher has as its goal the production of cooperative planning, not the imposition of a plan on the teacher. A conference is an attempt to reach a union of minds and purposes.[1]

The individual conference is probably the most important supervisory technique for use in the specific improvement of instruction. If correctly employed, it gives each teacher the special help he needs to become proficient in self-analysis, self-appraisal, and self-improvement. Being a form of personal interview, the individual conference provides an excellent opportunity for the two participants to define the subject to be discussed, to agree on the educational point of view, to recognize the need for improvement, and to solve the problem cooperatively.

The supervisory conference is a difficult activity because of the personal element involved. Misgivings are faced by both the principal and the teacher, regardless of the amount of experience each has had. The principal wonders if the teacher will understand the professional purposes, and if his assistance will be thorough and clear.

New and experienced teachers alike panic at the thought of an individual conference. They will wonder what is wrong with their work. Was the lesson really all right? If not, will they be given a chance to improve?

The Nature of the Conference

No set plan for holding conferences can be outlined. However, there are some factors which will determine the need for scheduling a conference. The need exists:

1. When the principal has visited a classroom.
2. When a teacher has requested an individual conference.
3. When participants in a group project need to meet. Such a conference can be scheduled several weeks in advance or on a regular basis.
4. When a beginning teacher is employed.
5. When the principal wishes to discuss a problem with an individual staff member or with a group.

[1]See George C. Kyte, *The Principal at Work,* rev. ed. (Boston: Ginn and Company, 1952). Chapters XIV and XV are especially helpful.

How to Conduct a Successful Conference

Preparing for the Conference

Preparing for the supervisory conference is every bit as important as preparing for a supervisory visit. Great knowledge, skill, and understanding are required to carry on a successful conference. It will be to the advantage of the principal to have every available resource within reach.

Some of the following suggested activities may apply more to one specific type of conference than to another. The principal should select those that will help him in a particular situation.

1. Recall the purpose of the conference.
2. Review all records pertinent to this conference.
3. Develop tentative hypotheses by anticipating probable conclusions and recommendations.
4. Note possible courses of action.
5. Review and assemble additional professional materials that will be of assistance to the teacher.
6. Assemble instructional materials which the teacher may use and evaluate.
7. Check with the custodian to learn if the room is ready.
8. Remind all participants of the conference time and place.
9. Plan to provide simple refreshments.

Teacher committees might assist with some of the preparations, particularly refreshments, if this is a group conference. For an individual conference, a teacher will appreciate the principal's thoughtfulness if some refreshment is planned. It creates a more relaxed, informal atmosphere which is conducive to the sharing of ideas.

Scheduling a Time and a Place for the Conference

More importance seems to be attached to the time for which the principal sets the conference than to the place where it will be held. Both decisions can be arrived at cooperatively by the principal and by the teachers involved.

OPTIMUM CONFERENCE TIME. When the conference concerns a visit to a classroom it is wise to arrange for the conference to be held as soon as possible following the visit. The discussion will have more meaning if the details of the teaching-learning situation are not allowed to fade because too much time has elapsed. However, it is important to schedule the conference at an hour when enough time can be allotted in order to allow for a discussion that is satisfying to all participants. Many times a conference before school or after school will be best for this reason. In the event that a teacher has a free work period, a conference could be scheduled at that particular time.

Conferences that are most likely to be held after school would include the group conference (with the exception of the group visitation conference, which will be discussed later) and the individual conference that is not related to a recent visitation. The individual conference easily might be held before school, if time permits.

CONFERENCE LOCATION. As to the place in which the conference is held, the size of the group that will meet with the principal is a determining factor. Obviously, an individual conference can be held in a place that is not at all suitable for a group conference.

Individual conferences following visitations frequently are held in the classroom. It often is easier to visualize the total situation when discussing the lesson within the same environmental setting.

Although the teacher should have a choice as to the meeting place, usually *he will feel more secure within his own classroom* than in the principal's office. Other individual conferences most likely will be held in the office unless the principal asks to come to the classroom. He may wish to talk about the use of new materials and will feel that the place in which they will be put to use is the best place to hold the conference.

Group conferences often are held in the faculty conference room or workroom. However, if the group plans to work with the various materials of instructional technology, such as a motion picture projector, the choice might be either the audio-visual room or the auditorium. Some classrooms used by older children serve the purpose very well.

The important points with which the principal needs to be concerned are: (1) insuring privacy, (2) being careful to protect the ego of all, and (3) making certain that every teacher involved is informed of the time and the place for the conference. The information could be posted or could be included in a weekly bulletin.

The Principal's Actions and Reactions During a Conference

The principal is responsible for the success of the conference. As the instructional leader of his school he should typify certain personal qualities and professional abilities if he is to establish rapport with his staff members and if he is to maintain a superior instructional program within the school. Professional conduct begets professional conduct.

The following are suggestions for working with teachers in a conference situation. If conscientiously followed, they should result in a fruitful conference period. It is suggested that the principal should:

1. Be friendly.
2. Listen carefully.
3. Invite participation from all present.
4. Share the responsibility of analyzing techniques and prescribing a subsequent course of action.
5. Offer suggestions.
6. Keep adequate records of plans and suggestions.
7. Make certain that some course of action has been decided upon.
8. Summarize findings, conclusions, and decisions.
9. Provide for adequate evaluation.

Following a classroom visit from the principal, the teacher will expect an evaluation of the lesson observed during the supervisory visit because he desires to improve his skills as a teacher. An awareness of the fact that professional associates care about his service and wish to assist him may determine the difference between a mediocre teacher and a skilled educator.

The importance of including the teacher in the process of analyzing and prescribing must be emphasized. If the teacher and the supervising principal are to perform as a professional team, it is important that they share a common professional orientation. Additionally, the teacher and the supervising principal must jointly accept effective methods and techniques of objective analysis. Only then can the factors observed during the course of the supervisory visit be treated adequately; only then may the teacher and the supervisor be capable of professional consultation which may determine a program leading to improvement of instruction.

Deciding upon a program of action does not imply necessarily that a final decision has been reached. It might mean that the conference group plans to engage in further exploration along the lines already agreed upon before finding a solution. An individual staff member might decide to try out a suggestion that is mutually acceptable. In this instance the principal must make the teacher's problems his own. He should plan a follow-up visit on the day the suggestion is tried by the teacher.

The principal who displays a sincere interest in improving the program of supervisory conferences within the school will be rewarded by increased cooperation and enthusiasm on the part of the members of the staff. Educators naturally respond to recognition of their worth as contributing members of the profession.

It is hoped that in the process of helping to evaluate a teaching-learning situation supervising principals will grow in their ability to apply objective criteria of self-evaluation. As supervising principals visit the classroom and have the opportunity to compare the learning situation that exists in one class with that which exists in others, and their skills in handling various problems with the skills of others, they can make a better use of criteria of self-evaluation.

The following are some points to consider while holding a follow-up conference:

1. Remember to be understanding. Try not to upset the teacher. Use the Golden Rule. The principal should ask himself, "How would I feel if I

were the teacher?" Empathy should be emphasized. Show interest in the teacher as an individual.

2. Be sincere and friendly. Approach the teacher as a peer and as a qualified member of the profession.

3. Use all of the time necessary; do not appear to be rushed.

4. Start the conference with a positive approach. *Something* must be all right!

5. If criticisms are necessary, criticize methods and techniques rather than the teacher. The individual's psychological integrity must be protected and preserved. Proper rapport places the teacher at ease.

6. Help the teacher by leading the way. "How do you feel about teaching now?" "What has been the easiest?" "Where and when do you find it least easy?"

7. Accept and start with the teacher's problems as he sees them. Analyze difficulties together.

8. Discuss possible solutions, such as:
   a) Constructing lesson plans together.
   b) Discussing ways to stimulate students.
   c) Suggesting various types of assignments and the appropriateness of each
   d) Discussing how to help students to participate.
   e) Reviewing steps in a lesson.
   f) Suggesting ways to check and evaluate.

9. Consider the possibility of this being an "off" day. Try a new approach.

10. Do not be afraid to suggest. The teacher would rather have an idea expressed than to wonder what you are thinking.

11. Do not bluff. If you do not know something, say so! The teacher may learn later that you really did not know.

12. Summarize together the ideas brought out during the conference.

13. Close the conference on a friendly note with praise or commendation. *Be encouraging.* Leave the teacher with something to grow on, something to go on, and something to glow on.

FIGURE 9–1   Sample Conference Report Form

CONFERENCE REPORT FORM

Date _____

Name of Teacher _____

Grade _____

Subject _____

Time: From _____ to _____

Good points of the lesson: _____

_____

Physical and learning environment: _____

_____

Detailed, specific suggestions for improvement: _____

_____

Questions: _____

_____

Statements: _____

_____

Recording the Conference Results

It is important that an adequate record of the supervisory conference be
maintained for further reference to serve as a vehicle for planning future
supervisory visits and follow-up conferences. Two convenient conference
report forms which the supervising principal may find useful are included
as Figures 9-1 and 9-2.

FIGURE 9–2   Record of Supervisory Follow-Up Conference

NAME _____DATE _____

SUBJECT _____DATE OF OBSERVATION _____

TIME OF CONFERENCE _____

Notes Preceding Conference: (See record of classroom visit)

Topics Discussed:

Direction and Suggestions:

Teacher's Reactions in Conference:

Follow-Up:

How to Interview

The Supervisor and the Orientation Interview

In some large school systems it is possible that the employment and assignment phases of the personnel process are completed without the partici-

pation of the supervising principal. Such an unenlightened personnel practice places the principal in the position of having to discover the new employee's interests, experiences, educational and other personal data through an exploratory interview. It is important that the supervising principal remember that this first interview with the beginning teacher establishes a pattern for future relations.

At the time of the initial interview the new employee should be told about the important phases of his work, what his specific assignment will be, the location of various offices and facilities in the school, and anything else that a new employee should know (see chapter 7 for a more complete description of the orientation process). If the supervising principal is pressed for time and cannot give the new teacher the attention he deserves, he should tell him that he will talk with him later but that for the present time he will have to place him in the hands of the assistant principal, a department head, or another teacher. In this event, the supervising principal should make a point of visiting the new employee as soon as possible. At that time he must indicate his sincere interest in the new employee and his desire to be of assistance. There is no substitute for the supervising principal's personal attention. Recall W. V. Bingham's enduring axiom, "the functions of the ... interview are: to get information, to give information, and to make a friend."[2]

Closed, Patterned, and Open Interviews

The function of the *closed* interview is the gaining or imparting of information. The supervising principal may wish to make a preliminary listing of questions, or he may formulate his questions as the interview progresses, but always with the same purpose in mind.

The *patterned interview* is one wherein a series of questions is memorized or listed. The patterned interview's advantage lies in the certainty that desired questions will be asked. This technique is helpful if the supervising

[2]W. V. Bingham, "The Three Functions of the Interview in Employment," *The Management Review* XV (26 January 1926): 36.

principal has not had much skill in interviewing. As the supervisor gains skill in interviewing, the patterned interview may be utilized without its appearing formal.

The *open interview* usually is not designed to obtain answers to specific questions, but rather to permit the supervisor to set an atmosphere wherein the employee may discuss interests. This type of interview is especially helpful in permitting an employee to discuss his complaints and grievances.[3]

The evolution of the open interview technique is described in *Management and the Worker*.[4] In utilizing the open interview technique:

1. Put the teacher (or other employee) at ease by careful control of the environment and of the attitude you present to him.
2. When conditions warrant, guarantee the teacher strict confidence with reference to anything he may say.
3. Encourage the teacher to talk freely. Give him the feeling that there is no rush; he has all the time needed to discuss his problem.
4. Be a good listener. Never interrupt the interviewee.
5. In the open interview, the supervising principal never disputes a point nor gives advice. Rather, he strives to discover how the teacher thinks, what his feelings are, and seeks information as to why he believes as he does.
6. The supervising principal's attitude must be one of interest and sympathetic curiosity if this technique is to work.
7. The supervising principal must exhibit as much interest in interviewing satisfied teachers as he does in interviewing those who are dissatisfied.
8. The teacher takes the necessary steps to remedy a situation or solve a problem when his thinking has been clarified by discussing his difficulty in detail with the supervising principal. He then initiates his own action, and assumes the responsibility for his acts.

[3]See W. R. Spriegel, Edward Schulz, and W. B. Spriegel, *Elements of Supervision* (New York: John Wiley & Sons, Inc., 1957) especially pages 62–63.
[4]F. J. Roethlisberger, William J. Dickson, and Harold A. Wright, *Management and the Worker* (Cambridge: Harvard University Press, 1939).

The Control Interview

While a serious offense by teacher or other staff member will usually be met by the supervising principal with dispatch, the control interview concerning a less serious offense—one that in itself is not serious and just gets by "under the wire" so far as compliance with the school's policies are concerned—is the type of interview which is most often avoided by the supervising principal.

No matter what the nature of the topic of the control interview:

1. The interview must be planned carefully. In an emergency it may not be possible to plan in detail, but operating on the basis of policy considerations will sustain the supervising principal and may help to prevent his being impetuous.
2. The nature of the control interview must be impersonal. It must arise out of the needs of the situation, with vindictiveness and personal anger being prohibited.
3. The interview must be constructive rather than punitive in nature. The purpose of the interview is to correct a situation, to help to insure that the situation will not arise again, and to serve the best interests of the school, its students, and its classified and certificated personnel, as well as the best interests of the superintendent, the governing board, and the patrons of the school.
4. Hope must be provided for the disciplined. For as long as an employee maintains his psychological integrity, his self-respect, and hope for the future, there is a chance for improvement.
5. The employee who has been disciplined must depart with a feeling that he has paid whatever penalties required; that the supervising principal is not one who holds a "grudge"; and that he now has an opportunity to go ahead with a clean slate.

In evaluating the control interview, the supervisor should ask himself the following questions:

1. *Prior to the control review*. Did I survey the problem effectively? Did I obtain all needed data so that I would have an adequate background

for the interview? Did I consider the background data from a viewpoint of empathy? Did I wait to begin the interview until tempers had been soothed and I was in the proper frame of mind? Was I sure that I was concentrating on the problem at hand rather than on the personalities (including my own) involved? Then, was I prepared to listen?

2. *During the control interview.* Did I watch the volume and intonation of my voice? Did I praise the employee for some recently completed task well done? Was I careful to protect the employee's psychological integrity, to make him feel that he is a person of worth to the school, and to give him an out by which to "save face"? Did I call attention to errors and improper approaches or attitudes, wherever possible, indirectly and with empathy? Did I show an interest in and sympathy for his needs and wants, and for his suggestions for solving the problem? Did I avoid arguing over unimportant factors? Did I build specifics into a logical construct, rather than challenging statements directly, so that the employee would have an opportunity to see his own mistakes without my having to defend and attack in a "nit-picking" fashion?

If I was wrong, did I say so? Did I challenge him to demonstrate improvement? Did I review the interview and our plans for the future with the employee? Did I close the interview on a friendly note?[5]

After completing the interview the supervisor should carefully complete an interview memorandum for his files. He should remember to notice and praise improvement and should keep his relationship with the employee on a professionally friendly basis.

The supervisor should consider the following points in evaluating the effectiveness of the interview. Was my approach during the interview one of control or correction, rather than one of punishment or revenge? Was I fair but firm; gentle but forthright in stating needs and/or requirements; kind and concerned with the employee and his viewpoint but clear and pre-

[5]After W. S. Ferguson, "Handling Personnel Problems (a Checklist)," *Factory Management and Maintenance,* CIX (June 1951): 109; and W. R. Spriegel, Edward Schulz, and W. B. Spriegel, op. cit, pp. 292–294.

cise in reviewing the problem and the probable consequences of the proposed plans for solving it? Was my voice control adequate?

Remember, it is not necessary to be abusive or to shout in order to attain correction and control. Beware of overkill, Mr. Supervisor!

Outline for a Successful Interview

The supervising principal may wish to have the following outline duplicated for facility in planning for successful interviewing:

I. *The Problem*
   A. Purpose of the interview
   B. Positive points
   C. Weaknesses (note *facts*)
II. *Employee's Reactions Obtained*
   A. Ask, "Are these facts correct?" "Is this the way it is?" (Note teacher's answer here:)
   B. If the teacher presents new facts or offers a valid explanation, the supervising principal may wish to close the interview for the present and investigate the matter further.
      1. Note reasons here:
      2. Future appointment? When?
   C. If the teacher has no valid explanation, presents no new facts, and disagrees, note statement of the teacher here:
   D. If the supervising principal disagrees with the teacher he should say, "Sorry, but that is not the solution"; or he could say, "Even if you don't agree, I feel we should take some action."
III. *Action Consideration*
   A. Solicit the teacher's ideas concerning the problem solution. Ask, "What suggestions have you?" or "What do you think we can do?" (Note his suggestions here:)
      1. The supervising principal should indicate that he sincerely wants the teacher to solve the problem, and he should state that he will help the teacher in any way he can.
      2. If suggestion requires study, or if new data is presented, close

the interview, set a date for another meeting, and investigate the matter further.

B. If the supervising principal disagrees with the suggestion he should say, "I'm sorry, but I do not believe that plan would work," or "I don't think that would do."

IV. *The Plan*

A. It is recommended that the supervising principal have a plan worked out in advance of the interview. If the teacher's plan does not seem feasible, or if he has no plan, say, "Let us try this . . ." (Plan of action.) (It is sometimes helpful to establish a time limit for the proposal after which an evaluation interview will be held.)

B. If the teacher objects without validity (if he objects to the plan but the objection is not based upon valid data), the supervising principal should say, "I'm sorry, but this is a real problem and I will have to ask you to do this . . ." (If the teacher has strong objections to the plan which is proposed, perhaps a modification of the plan made in section IV-A is called for.) (Note modifications here:)

V. *Terminate the Interview on a Cordial Note.*

A. Insure that the teacher knows exactly what has been suggested and what is expected of him. The supervising principal should say, "Have I been clear?"

1. Note date for the follow-up interview.
2. Restate the plan. Say, "This is what we are going to do."
3. Leave the teacher with a definite feeling that you are really interested in being of assistance to him.

VI. *The Follow-Up Interview*

A. Date of the interview

B. Has the teacher's performance improved? Yes ( ) No ( ) Further investigation required ( ) The supervising principal should tell the teacher he has improved, if such is the case.[6]

C. Interview summary:

---

[6]John J. Grela, "Work Sheet Helps Supervisors Talk Constructively with Employees," *Personnel Journal* (April 1955); and W. R. Spriegel, Edward Schulz, and W. B. Spriegel, op. cit., pp. 70–71.

DO

1. Remember that a follow-up conference is obligatory if visitation and observation is for the purpose of improving instruction and learning; for helping teachers grow in methods and techniques of instruction and in subject matter content; or for general professional development.

2. Systematically plan, appraise, and evaluate teacher growth. Have specific objectives for a follow-up conference.

3. Conduct many conferences during the year. Proper scheduling is important. Usually the follow-up conference should follow the supervisory visit within thirty-six hours. The conference should be held while the specifics of the lesson are clearly in mind.

4. Base the conference on the written analysis of the specific venture. The successful supervising principal tries to arouse the teacher's interest and to challenge his professional curiosity.

5. Include both strong points and weaknesses in the same conference. Supervisory conferences based upon weak points alone are rare and should be used only as a last resort with exceptional teachers who fail to respond to any other methods and resist improvement. Human beings respond well to praise, praise which is honestly deserved and honestly given.

6. Consider conferences as essential, *cooperative* endeavors.

7. Provide a quiet, uninterrupted atmosphere.

8. Recall that if a teacher needs to discuss a problem, he needs to do so soon.

9. Allow approximately thirty minutes for the conference.

10. Sense how much to say, and *know when to stop*.

11. Provide for a "cooling off period" if circumstances warrant.

12. Remember that frequent visits and conferences are better than one that is drawn out.

13. Remember to be a good listener.

14. Determine a pivotal question.

15. Announce the purpose of the meeting, so as not to keep the teacher in the dark as to what to expect.

16. Strive for rapport.
17. Remember—the goal of the principal's participation in supervisory conferences is to help teachers.

DON'T

1. Cover more than two or three points at one interview. When too much is planned for one interview, the entire conference suffers because of the lack of time. This crowded agenda renders the conference ineffective.
2. Use the same set pattern for all conferences.
3. Use the conference to force the teacher to accept your plan.
4. Overplan for the impending conference.
5. Read directly from notes for the classroom visitation; do refer to them occasionally.
6. Schedule the conference without having a definite purpose in mind.
7. Hold the conference in a noisy place with the possibility of interruptions.
8. Keep the desk between yourself and the teacher.
9. Use formal titles; maintain a friendly, informal air throughout the conference. Use first names.
10. Be overly verbose. Don't select vocabulary which does not communicate effectively. A begining teacher especially may be hesitant to pry into meanings of terminology which the supervising principal may have acquired at regional, state, and national conferences, lest he expose either an ignorance of or reluctance to accept the practice that seems to be preferred. Do not swamp the teacher in an excess of unmeaningful verbalism. (The principal must say exactly what he means—effectively, succinctly, and clearly.)

Supervisory Problem

In Basket

The problem develops in a public junior high school with an enrollment of 750 students in grades seven, eight, and nine. Mrs. Doe, who is thirty-five years old and has eight years' teaching experience, is the teacher of girls' physical education and health. All seventh and eighth grade girls are required to take physical education. Ninth grade girls may select one class as an elective. Average enrollment in Mrs. Doe's P. E. classes is thirty-six girls. The standard uniform required is a white blouse, blue shorts, and gym shoes. These items are stocked at a local department store.

Mrs. Doe conducts an outstanding, well-rounded program for the girls that includes physical fitness and the development of poise and grace. She is well suited for this program because of her own physical appearance and abilities in dance and acrobatics.

Mrs. Doe is very severe with the girls. She tends to be sarcastic and demands immediate and unquestioning reaction to her requests. Many of the girls appear to be frightened of her. The supervising principal occasionally receives calls from concerned parents who question her teaching procedures. Usually an explanation is made and the parent is satisfied. Today, however, an irate parent called and announced he was coming "to have it out with Mrs. Doe." The principal determined that he must prepare her for the ordeal. He is very happy with the *results* of her program, but he feels she must modify her domineering attitude. If she is offended, he may lose her. Since her husband has an excellent position and they have no children, Mrs. Debbie Doe does not depend on her paycheck.

How can the supervising principal approach this problem? How should he plan for the supervisory conference with Mrs. Doe?

Selected Bibliography

Books

Bradfield, Luther E. *Supervision for Modern Elementary Schools.* Columbus, Ohio: Charles E. Merrill Books, Inc., 1964.

Brighten, Stayner F. *Increasing Your Accuracy in Teacher Evaluation.* Englewood Cliffs, New Jersey: Prentice Hall, Inc., 1965.

Douglas, Karl R., Rudyard K. Bent, and Charles W. Boardman. *Democratic Supervision in the Secondary Schools.* Boston: Houghton Mifflin Company, 1961.

Gwynn, J. Minor. *Theory and Practice in Supervision.* New York: Dodd, Mead, & Company, 1961.

Kyte, George C. *The Principal at Work.* Boston: Ginn and Company, 1952.

Lucio, William H., and John D. McNeil. *Supervision: A Synthesis of Thought and Action.* New York: McGraw-Hill Company, 1962.

Roethlisberger, F. J., William J. Dickson, and Harold A. Wright. *Management and the Worker.* Cambridge: Harvard University Press, 1939.

Stoops, Emery, and James R. Marks. *Elementary School Supervision.* Boston: Allyn and Bacon, Inc., 1965.

Wiles, Kimball. *Supervision for Better Schools.* Englewood Cliffs, New Jersey: Prentice Hall, Inc., 1956.

Periodicals

Aubrey, Roger F. "What Is the Role of the Elementary School Teacher?" *The Elementary School Journal* LXVIII (March 1968): 36.

Bingham, W. V. "The Three Functions of the Interview in Employment." *The Management Review* XV (26 January 1926): 36.

Imin, David. "The Changing Role of the Urban Principal." *The Elementary School Journal* LXVIII (April 1968): 329–333.

Nelson, W. Donald. "Supervision or Snoopervision." *The Balance Sheet* XXVII (December 1961): 158–159.

Pray, Walter J. "The Climate for Supervision." *American School Board Journal* CXXIX (November 1963): 12–13.

10

How to Provide Successful
Faculty Meetings and Group Conferences

Staff meetings play a crucial role in the success of a supervisory program by furnishing the means for communicating common understanding, workable techniques, and uniform purposes.

Staff meetings should help in the upgrading of the instructional program and in solving school problems. Typically, the supervising principal serves as an interpreter, director, and coordinator for staff meetings.

Teachers and principles do not always agree on the types of activities which are the most valuable for improving instruction. Differences in points of view concerning what services are needed and how they can be provided suggest that open discussions are needed. Trends in educational thinking and practice should be discussed at faculty meetings and interpreted as they affect the school or the community. Skill must be exercised in organizing and conducting faculty meetings to enhance cooperative thinking and professional growth. Before these discussions can be fruitful, a *mutual, sincere feeling of trust* must be generated. Indeed, trust is a prerequisite to all effective communication and certainly to working with people toward instructional improvement.

This chapter includes a discussion of the following topics:

Principles and practices
How to conduct the meeting
Do—don't
"In-Basket" supervisory problem

Principles and Practices

If staff meetings and group conferences are to be interesting and valuable to teachers, they must be planned with teachers and concentrate on the problems of teachers. A planning committee, chosen by the staff, may aid in meeting this goal.

The teacher is a professional worker, as is the supervising principal. With this fact in mind, there should be mutual respect for, and evaluation of, suggestions. Since there are many types of teachers, necessity demands that human relations play an important part in stimulating individual responses toward growth.

There are great differences in the preparation and experience of teachers. States differ as to requirements, and various colleges and universities emphasize different aspects of the teacher-education program. Nevertheless, there are certain basic principles concerning the improvement of faculty meetings and group conferences that have been defined.

1. Groups are composed of two or more individuals who come together to solve some problem which is common to all and which cannot be solved by the individuals alone.
2. Group successes are due chiefly to individual cooperation and understanding, and to supervisory leadership.
3. The total-faculty meeting has long been used as one of the devices for securing improvements in instruction, as contrasted to administrative purposes.
4. Groups must meet frequently to make progress. Reports, questionnaires, checklists, and bulletins cannot take the place of group interaction.
5. Cooperation with the group provides the supervisor with an opportunity for leadership.
6. The supervisor who brings about group action may be the supervising principal or another worker from within the school, or he may be a specialist-consultant from without.
7. The supervisor should see that no individual or faction dominates the meeting and speaks for the entire group.
8. Developing good leadership within the group is a function of supervision.
9. The supervisor needs to exercise patience while elevating the group to a higher level of understanding.
10. A resourceful supervisor will substitute emergent leadership from the group for his own directorship. This emerging leadership may revolve among various subgroups and individuals within the groups.
11. Grade level and small group meetings may have more uniformity of purpose and be more efficient than large staff meetings.

How to Improve Staff Meetings

The following techniques may be employed by the supervisor in improving the supervisory meeting:

1. The problems to be discussed should be important to the entire staff and should be chosen by the group, with leadership from the principal.
2. The meeting should contribute directly to the professional needs of teachers and administrators.
3. Throughout the meeting teacher participation and activity should predominate.
4. The experience and knowledge of the teachers, pertinent to the discussion, should be utilized fully by a supervisory leader.
5. In very large schools, the staff should be broken into smaller groups. The large meeting should be reserved for staff decisions, personnel problems or benefits, and for all-school planning.
6. The meeting place should be as pleasant, comfortable, and informal as possible.
7. The frequency of staff meetings should be decided upon by the staff itself.
8. The group should decide upon the time and place of meetings, and should decide on a definite adjournment time. Meetings should be kept as brief as possible.
9. Members of the meeting should work toward a consensus.
10. Some agenda items should be merely for *information,* others should require *action.* Action should never be called for until full information has been provided.
11. A permanent record should summarize the results of each meeting. If the meeting is worth calling, something should result.
12. Each meeting should lead to improved competency and morale.

Purposes of Staff Meetings

The prime purpose of staff meetings is to improve the quality of personnel and of the school program. These meetings should provide opportunities for cooperative thinking, for staff planning, for presentation of stimulating talks by resourceful people, and for becoming acquainted with the total educational environment. In the staff meeting of today this opportunity for full teacher participation has not as yet been given.

Unfortunately, most teachers apparently feel that staff meetings deserve a very low rating in providing specific help in improving the technique of instruction and in presenting new research data and subject matter findings.

The development of a staff into a working group is a long-term project. One means of achieving this goal is through effective staff meetings. It is in these meetings that the important business of the school is handled, to wit: planning for the educational experiences of students.

The old-fashioned faculty meeting at which the principal made announcements and gave directions regarding administrative routines will no longer suffice. These meetings were characterized by the issuing of orders; interpretations of orders previously given, perhaps even given in writing; or a discussion of ways in which teachers could help to lessen the noise near the principal's office. Drives and collections, and the preparation of various programs, also were discussed. The use of staff meetings for such activities is not only ineffectual but also deplorably damaging to the very purposes for which they are held.

The premise that all who are involved with a policy, rule, or technique should have a part in planning it is basic to effective staff meetings. This democratic approach still reserves the right of decision-making for the principal. The principal not only directs and coordinates his staff; he is a member of it. It would be expected, therefore, that staff intelligence in operation, orchestrated through principal leadership, should result in a harmonious and successful working group.

A staff meeting should be concerned only with items that are of importance to those individuals present. A cooperative solution of common problems is not only good in theory; it is the most practical and successful method known.

Meetings should inspire and stimulate a teacher's educational thinking; they should clarify or be of practical assistance in classroom, schoolwide, or school system-wide situations; and they should help the teacher to develop and to maintain a consistent pattern of growth.

How to Plan Staff Meetings

The conduct and planning of staff meetings should be shifted from administrators and supervisors to teacher councils or to a planning committee chosen by the faculty. A series of meetings then are planned in accord with the supervisory plan for the school. The wishes of the staff should govern the decisions made.

During the early stages the principal should assume considerable responsibility for the conduct of the meeting, but later these major responsibilities should be shifted to the staff. The principal's role primarily should be that of a consultant or adviser. He is to guide without manipulating, and to provide leadership without dominating.

FREQUENCY AND SCHEDULING. Need determines the frequency and length of scheduled meetings. Experienced principals recognize that meetings that are held too frequently or that are too lengthy are as detrimental and ineffectual as are meetings that are held too infrequently or that do not allow sufficient time for the business to be covered.

Faculties often discover that a minimum of general meetings of the entire staff plus a few short meetings of grade levels will satisfy their needs. Staff members will be more eager to attend if they know from past experience that the meetings regularly draw to a close at the pre-determined time.

It is helpful for all concerned to reserve a specific, consistent day and hour of the week for the entire school system. Such planning would permit scheduling a meeting if desired. School-system policy should not require supervising principals to hold meetings at each scheduled date.

Fridays are very bad days for general meetings. Other than the usual emotional and physical condition of the staff on Fridays, it would be well to remember that the two-day interim definitely affects desired carry-over. Tuesday is apparently a preferred day for staff meetings.

Members of the staff should determine whether they prefer before-or after-school meetings. Most teachers apparently prefer short before-school meetings. Generally, if teachers are required to stay one-half hour after the close of school on the day of a faculty meeting they should be permitted to leave promptly after class dismissal on the following day. *The trend is to hold faculty meetings as a part of the normal working day,* early in the day, rather than to require members of the staff to work an additional number of hours because of necessary staff meetings.

Class schedules, individual duties, and programming will affect the availability of many faculty members. Brief grade level or departmental meetings work well before school or during common conference periods. Sufficient time should be allowed for teachers to arrive and to relax, so that their powers of concentration may be more effective.

ENVIRONMENT. The room in which the staff meeting is held should be restful in appearance and conducive to good thinking. It should be conveniently located, be permanent, and afford privacy. The faculty deserves at least one well-designed, functional, and comfortably furnished room in which to hold meetings. The room should contain a chalkboard.

REFRESHMENTS. Refreshments are always a hospitable and welcome sight to a weary, dusty traveler—especially if he is a teacher attending an after-school staff meeting. Refreshments are not only good morale builders but also, as the term suggests, refreshing and physically stimulating. Usually teachers, via grade levels or other organized cooperative means, are more than happy to assist in preparation.

THE AGENDA. Preplanned agendas are a must. Without such organization routine matters can become lost in the last minute rush, the meeting may lapse into overtime, one may tend to digress from essential subjects, and items may be neglected or overemphasized. It is most helpful, and also a matter of courtesy, for staff members to be given a copy of the agenda in advance of the meeting.

How to Encourage Teacher Involvement

Teachers should be involved in the planning of a meeting as well as in the meeting itself. Idea memorandum sheets, distributed a week in advance to all teachers and returned to the meeting chairman after they have been filled in, have proven to be helpful. See Figure 10–2 for a sample of such a memorandum sheet.

In schools with large faculties, teacher planning committees, composed of grade level representatives, may meet briefly with the principal to assist in planning the agenda.

FIGURE 10–1   Staff Meetings Should Be Conducted in a Restful Environment. Refreshments Should Be Served.

Meetings in which teachers take an active part are more beneficial and interesting for all concerned. Demonstrations, explanations, committee reports, study-group information, and resource presentations are examples of the individual methods by which teachers might take a meaningful, stimulating, and satisfying part in staff meetings. This participation should help to create staff meetings that reflect the efforts of a dynamic, harmonious working group. True discussions, where the opinions of the members of the staff are as respected as are those of the principal, add a feeling of purpose, mutual respect, participation, and accomplishment for all involved.

Timing of Materials and Ideas

The timing of ideas or materials being presented can create or destroy a meeting. A highly controversial statement or question entertained at the beginning of a meeting may destroy an agenda. It could waste the time of

FIGURE 10–2   Memorandum Sheet

STAFF MEETING IDEA MEMORANDUM SHEET

Date _____

Topic _____

Problem _____

Idea _____

_____

_____

_____

What will be accomplished _____

_____

_____

                                        _____
                                              Name (optional)

all involved and demolish the program if much of the meeting time were devoted to arguing the point in question. If this same highly controversial statement had occurred near or at the end of the agenda, preferably at the end, brief discussion may have caused the participants to leave the meeting thinking and talking about the particular point. This practice would have enabled them to arrive at a more rational conclusion. Time and timing are basic and sensitive ingredients of decision-making and require great thought and care.

How to Conduct the Meeting

Attitudes and Skills Needed in Conducting Staff Meetings

New concepts and procedures in supervision demand a variety of new skills for the principal. These might be grouped under five categories: (1) skills in leadership, (2) skills in human relations, (3) skills in group processes, (4) skills in personnel administration, and (5) skills in evaluation.[1]

[1]Kimball Wiles, *Supervision for Better Schools* (Englewood Cliffs, New Jersey: Prentice-Hall, Inc., 1955).

Experience and research have provided some clues for improving group action.

1. The size of the group can be a barrier to effectiveness. As a group grows beyond thirty members, effective group action becomes increasingly difficult. A desirable size cannot be reached by arbitrarily setting up one figure, for function and make-up condition the most desirable size.
2. Physical settings must be conducive to group processes. The size and type of a room as well as physical arrangement within the room are important. For effective participation the group members must be able to hear and see each other; the seating arrangement must facilitate good human relations.
3. The plan of action that emerges should be appraised to the end that individuals in the group receive their share of work to be done. In the final analysis, a group can act efficiently only through individuals. Responsibility for action should be delegated in terms of individual interests and abilities. A division of labor is not disruptive of cooperation.
4. Sufficient time must be allowed to insure a successful attack upon a problem and the development of action suggestions.
5. Consideration of group metabolism increases effectiveness. Fatigue, tension, tempo, pace, atmosphere affect group action. Within the process, provision for brief recesses and for adjusting the length of the meetings will result in more efficiency.
6. Within the process itself the most difficult step is moving from the problem inventory and identification . . . [to *how* and *who*]. What the problem is is not usually difficult. Effective group action depends upon the how and who.[2]

In order that a faculty may function successfully within the group process (thinking, discussing, planning, deciding, acting, and evaluating), the leader and the group might best be alerted to the hazards involved. The supervising principal must learn to avoid: (1) group pressures, (2) domination by a few individuals, (3) implied threats to job security, (4) the

[2]Association for Supervision and Curriculum Development, *Group Process in Supervision* (Washington, D. C.: National Education Association, 1948), p. 49.

sense of extreme newness or difference, and (5) the threat of the administrative role.

Realistic leadership recognizes that all people have certain common needs. Imaginative leadership goes one step further and builds a program accordingly, with respect and appreciation toward the individuals' common needs. The principal who demonstrates a genuine respect for the professional integrity and worth of his staff will be at the helm of a dynamic and productive program designed to offer the best education possible to the students.

In order to be an effective group leader, one must help set the emotional tone in the group. The effective leader understands and appreciates people and, what is most important, has respect for the unique contributions that each group member can make.

STAFF MEETING EVALUATION. The basic concept underlying the improvement of meetings is that staff meeting evaluation must be a part of the planning. Evaluation is fundamental in achieving the purposes of a faculty and in revising purposes and procedures. The suggestion box idea has merit.

BASIC FUNCTIONS OF THE SUPERVISOR. Cooperative action is basic to group process. The skilled supervisor can help others to learn to think, discuss, plan, decide, act, and evaluate together. A leader should be skilled in the techniques of group discussion and action. His prime responsibility is to help the group function efficiently.

Coordinating the efforts of others is basic to effective working within the group. To be an effective coordinator the supervising principal starts where the group is. A true leader must be accepted as a member of the group, for leader and followers are interdependent. Each needs the other for successful accomplishment of group goals.[3]

The role of the democratic supervising principal is to carry out the policies that are the result of cooperative action. The faculty must be willing to abide by the majority's decisions, although a consensus rather than a majority vote should be sought.

[3]Ibid., pp. 59–61.

Basically, teacher participation is an attitude of mind more than it is the completion of a specific task.[4] It is based on the idea that collective thinking is superior to individual thought. The principal must, of course, reserve the ultimate responsibility for a major program to himself, since he is the responsible supervisory leader in the school.

Following the Agenda

Meetings should begin promptly, and the agenda should be followed. Emergencies and changing conditions, however, require flexibility. Attempt to hold to the schedule, but strive to reduce tension and promote informality. Insure that participants understand the reason for their attendance and attempt to obtain a commitment for positive action from them. Leaders should be very conscious of group processes and should attempt to employ proper techniques of group action.[5]

A record should be made that summarizes the discussion, conclusions, and plans for each participant. A meeting should not just end. The supervisor should attempt always to provide a plan for action which includes follow-up and evaluation.[6]

The leader should involve the entire staff and avoid domination. The leader has the responsibility for keeping order and should observe all members of the group.[7] Feelings that are expressed, verbally or nonverbally, are elements which the leader will have to understand and use in effective problem-solving.[8]

Each participant may have a contribution to problem-solving. Ideally, all should feel a responsibility for the success of the meeting and for imple-

---

[4]Willard D. Elsbree and Harold J. McNally, *Elementary School Administration and Supervision* (New York: American Book Company, 1959), p. 414.
[5]J. Minor Gwynn, *Theory and Practice of Supervision* (New York: Dodd, Mead & Company, 1961), p. 356.
[6]Harold P. Adams and Frank G. Dickey, *Basic Principles of Supervision* (New York: American Book Company, 1953), pp. 163–165.
[7]Wiles, *Supervision for Better Schools*, pp. 189–191.
[8]Daniel W. Fullmer and Harold W. Bernard, *Counseling: Content and Process* (Chicago: Science Research Associates, Inc., 1964), pp. 131, 210.

menting a plan for action. This will necessitate involvement, thinking, listening, and assisting the leader.

Some groups are unusually productive, whereas others consistently perform at a low level. If the leader wants to understand the individual, he must know the dynamics of individual roles in groups as well as the effect the groups have on the individual.

The roles typically played by participants may be classified in three categories. (1) *Roles which facilitate and coordinate group activities* include: initiator, contributor, information seeker, opinion seeker, information giver, opinion giver, elaborator, coordinator, orienter, evaluator-critic, energizer, procedural technician, and recorder. (2) *Roles that build up group attitudes and encourage group morale* include: encourager, harmonizer, compromiser, expediter, standard setter, commentator, and follower. (3) *Roles which indicate individuals are trying to satisfy their own needs* often by ill-advised methods include: aggressor, blocker, recognition seeker, self-confessor, playboy, dominator, help-seeker, special interest pleader.[9]

K. O. Benne and P. Sheats[10] delineated a three-fold classification of member roles:

1. Roles which are focused upon the *group-task;*
2. Roles which are focused upon *group maintenance;* and
3. Roles which are focused upon the needs of the individuals in the group.

For the discussion group, they suggested as group-task roles: (a) the initiator, (b) information seeker, (c) opinion seeker, (d) information giver, (e) opinion giver, (f) elaborator, (g) coordinator, (h) orienter, (i) evaluator-critic, (j) energizer, (k) procedural technician, and (l) the recorder.

Identification of the contributions to the group process that each role plays will enable the leader to more effectively understand what is happening. Through this understanding he will be able to provide for agenda which will lead to improved problem-solving and professional growth for more of the participants.

[9]Ibid, pp. 38–40.
[10]K. D. Benne and P. Sheats, "Functional Roles of Group Members," *Journal of Social Issues* XXIV (1948): 41–49.

The Role of the Agenda

WHY HAVE AN AGENDA? An agenda helps to determine short- and long-range objectives. It assists in controlling effectively the use of time in the meeting. The agenda is helpful also in securing the cooperative participation of the entire group by clarifying assignments and responsibilities through confining attention and time to important items.

HOW TO BUILD AN AGENDA. The steps listed below should prove helpful in building an agenda:

1. Decide how far in advance of your meeting your agenda should be complete.
    a) Begin immediately following the close of previous meeting.
    b) Recheck several times.
    c) Change and alter if emergencies arise and as conditions are modified.
2. Provide for items of regular procedure. The use of a form helps.
    a) Welcome; rapport building.
    b) Introductions of new members or visitors.
    c) Minutes of last meeting.
    d) Unfinished business and new business.
    e) Announcement of items not otherwise covered.
    f) Announcements of appreciation and recognition.
3. List specific matters that may be considered at the meeting.
4. Rate each item on the basis of relative importance.
5. Allocate proper time to be devoted to each item.
6. Eliminate the least important items if time restrictions demand.
7. Plan for the most effective techniques and methods for presentation and participation.
    a) Make advance assignments.
    b) Employ the techniques of the symposium, panel, demonstration, and other methods.
    c) Make specific plans concerning instructional technology aids.
8. Distribute copies of the agenda in advance of the meeting to all who will or are invited to attend.

Flexibility of the Agenda

R. H. Lane[11] said that an agenda should be flexible enough to allow for change in the order in which items are to be discussed.

The planning committee, in addition to determining the agenda, may have the responsibility for the other items needed to make a faculty meeting a success, such as establishing the meeting time, selecting the meeting place, arranging the furniture, making provisions for refreshments, and securing special consultants.

The questions of how often to have faculty meetings and when they should be held present an issue that will have to be solved by the whole faculty. Ways should be devised to hold faculty meetings on regular school time, thus attempting to eliminate the feeling that faculty meetings are something beyond the regular job. If necessary, shorter meetings could be called to cover matters of an emergency nature.

Further Techniques for the Supervisor

In organizing the faculty the supervising principal usually will act as the chairman. The discussion leader sets the mood of the meeting, and his skill as an umpire determines the flow of the discussion. He has many responsibilities. If the staff lacks skill in leading discussions, the official leader has an obligation to help members in developing the skill.

According to Wiles,[12] the principal:

1. Creates an atmosphere that is informal, yet businesslike.
2. Guides the flow of discussion by keeping in mind the main purpose of the discussion. He is then able to provide the transition from one question to another.
3. Clarifies questions. There are two ways in which this can be done:
   a) By asking the questioner to define certain words, or to state the question so that it will be more clearly understood by all.

[11]Robert Hill Lane, *The Principal in the Modern Elementary School* (Boston: Houghton Mifflin Company, 1938), pp. 185–188.
[12]Wiles, *Supervision for Better Schools*, p. 214.

b) By restating the question in a brief, direct form. If this be done, the restatement should be accepted by the questioner.
4. Keeps the group on the subject and does not lead away from it.

The principal will have to make judgments at times concerning the degree of deviation from the issue that will be allowed. He must be tactful in bringing the discussion back to the subject. He should not offend the person who is leading the discussion in the wrong direction.

Wiles concluded that summarization of the discussion is one of the most valuable functions the chairman can perform. Through this process he gives order to the discussion.

Staff Meeting Records

P. E. Jacobson[13] pointed out vital facts concerning records of the faculty meeting. A person should be selected by the group to record, on the chalkboard, issues being discussed, the points made, and the agreements reached. In addition, there should be a permanent record kept by the faculty recorder. This record should include:

1. Date
2. Meeting place
3. Members present
4. Members absent
5. Problems discussed
6. Suggestions made
7. Problems referred
8. Decisions reached
9. Responsibilities accepted or assigned
10. Plans for next meeting

A copy of this record should be made and given to each member of the faculty. This would keep all informed as to what has taken place, and would

[13]P. E. Jacobson, *Duties of School Principals* (Englewood Cliffs, New Jersey: Prentice-Hall, Inc., 1941), pp. 197–199.

give a sense of direction and achievement. It would be most helpful in evaluation of the effectiveness of their work.

Survey of Teachers' Reactions to Meetings

In personal interviews with six teachers, opinions were obtained relating to attitudes toward meetings.

Teachers A and B were first-year teachers just out of the preparing university. Teachers C and D had taught for approximately fifteen years. Teachers E and F possessed administrative credentials. Teacher E had been teaching for five years, three in another school system. Teacher F had three years of experience. Teachers A and C were female.

PROBLEM 1. The teachers were asked what the qualities of a good faculty meeting are. This question took into consideration time, place, role of the principal, and material to be covered in the meeting.

Teacher A responded, "Faculty meetings should be held after school, once a week, and should not last more than one hour. They should cover the problems of the school and the individual problems of the teachers. They should also be used to explain district policy as well as that of the plant itself. A great deal of time should be allowed for question and answer periods, and discussion of problems which have arisen during the week. The principal should preside over the meeting and lead the discussions, but not dominate them with his opinions. This is very important, as sometimes the opinions and experiences of other teachers are far more valuable than the opinion of a man who has been out of the classroom for a period of time."

Teacher B responded, "Faculty meetings should be used to help strengthen the school curriculum. The principal should provide materials showing district policy regarding the teaching of certain subjects. What teachers learn in college and the policy of the school system are often two different things. Too much time is wasted on points that are not of interest to the entire faculty.

"The principal should not only lead the meeting but should make himself responsible for keeping it moving. His agenda should be well planned, and he should stick to it as best he can. Meetings should be held in the faculty room once a week either before or after the school day, but should not last more than one hour.

"If the principal conducts the meeting in an orderly fashion and does not allow the discussion to wander away from the main points at hand, one hour should be sufficient time. It is his responsibility to see that the meeting keeps progressing to the best interests of all attending."

Teacher C replied, "The faculty meeting should be a time of cooperation and sharing. The place is not important as long as it is one of comfort and pleasantness. Meetings should be held whenever necessary, usually once a week.

"These meetings primarily should be to help teachers who need it. Teachers should submit problems during the week so that the principal can add them to his agenda for discussion by the group. These problems should be ones of general interest and concern, and not those of individual children. Such problems as are not of general interest should be taken up with the principal privately.

"Meetings also should be a time to share good ideas and creativity. This gives the industrious teacher recognition and a better feeling of accomplishment, besides motivating the other members of the staff. This sharing of ideas should be in the form of workshops as well as informal discussions. The principal should have some control over the meeting, but should allow one of the teachers to preside and lead discussions whenever possible."

Teacher D responded, "The faculty meeting should be held one-half hour before school as this is the time of day most teachers are the most alert and will display the most willingness to cooperate. The material covered should be presented by the principal in outline form. There is a great deal of time wasted in discussions, so they should be held to a minimum by the principal. The main purpose of a faculty meeting is to inform the teachers of events, procedure, and policy. The group meeting is no place for airing individual grievances and such discussions should be avoided. Problems such as these should be discussed privately. Some faculty meetings may be skipped in preference to a printed bulletin."

Teachers E and F agreed with Teacher D. They believed teachers' meetings should be structured around general problems which concern the whole group. There should be group discussions on these problems, and provisions should be made for workshops conducted by various members of the staff. The meeting should be led by the principal in a businesslike manner, and should include information about coming events and occasional reminders of school system policy. Any questions concerning this policy can be taken up, but opinions should be avoided since the faculty meeting is not the proper place for teachers to try changing this policy.

The meeting should not last more than an hour. Personal problems could be taken up after the meeting, either with the principal or with other teachers. Lengthy discussions which may lead to arguments and discontent should be avoided. When such a situation arises the principal should appoint a committee consisting of interested members. This committee can then discuss the problem and submit their ideas at the next meeting. This procedure will help to reduce animosities among the staff members.

PROBLEM 2. The teachers were asked to what degree they believed the school can and should be run democratically. Opinions on this topic ranged greatly between democracy and complete dictatorship, with the majority for democracy.

Teacher C noted, "The teachers should have total say over the way the school is run. They should elect a leader from their group and this person should preside over all meetings. The principal should have a certain period of every meeting to pass on what he has learned from the higher administration. This should be in the form of a report and be only a small part of the meeting, not the central theme of it.

"The remainder of the meeting should be devoted to discussing the running of the school and any problems that have arisen. In this portion the supervising principal should have equal rights as the rest of the staff, and should not be allowed to dominate the discussion."

It was interesting to note that Teachers A, B, E, and F agreed. This group included the two first-year teachers and the two holding administrative credentials. They seemed to feel that the democratic approach was far superior, but that the principal figured largely in this type of meeting. Since it is the responsibility of the principal to see that the school is running smoothly and he has to answer for whatever goes on, they felt he should have a great deal to say about how the school is run.

According to these four teachers, the principal should preside over the meetings and allow the teachers to express their opinions at all times. He also should allow the group to make the decisions, but should always reserve the right of veto. He should not lose his identity or his authority. If a decision of the group does not meet with his approval he should explain why, and try to work out something that would satisfy all concerned. However, as the man in charge, he should not be entirely bound by the teachers' decisions. By the use of common sense and good judgment, the principal can run the school in a democratic way without letting the system run him.

Teacher D's response was slightly different. This teacher went to the opposite extreme. He felt the principal should preside as absolute ruler. Because the responsibility of efficient running of the plant rests with him, he should make all decisions as to how it should be run.

"He should be able to present his decisions as rules to be followed and not to be questioned. Any problems the teachers have should be discussed with the principal. He can help the teacher, or direct him to a teacher who can help.

"The teacher's primary function is to teach, not to run the school. Any time and energy spent on the latter can only take away from the former."

PROBLEM 3. The teachers were asked what some common mistakes were that many principals make in the running of faculty meetings. The following is a collective list of the mistakes named by all six teachers interviewed. Most of the items listed were named by at least half of the group.

1. There is too much time wasted on discussion of individual problems which do not interest the group as a whole.
2. The meetings sometime run too long due to poor leadership by the principal.
3. Discussions often get sidetracked and are apt to go on for a great deal of time without reaching any conclusion about the problem at hand.
4. The principal tries to influence the thinking of the members too much instead of letting them express their own opinions.
5. Most principals do not hand out or post a copy of the agenda in advance so that the members can come to the meeting prepared for discussion.

PROBLEM 4. The last question asked was, "If you were a principal, what one thing would you change in the way staff meetings are run?"

Teachers A and B responded, "I would set aside a definite time in each meeting for the discussion of school problems, instead of just using whatever time is left over."

Teacher C said, "I would select, or have the group select, a teacher to preside over the meetings."

Teacher D noted, "I would write up the meeting and run it off to be distributed to the teachers in addition to the agenda for the following week's meeting."

Teachers E and F responded (in chorus), "We would have more workshops."

Evaluation Needed

As is true with all other supervisory procedures, the staff meeting is in need of continuous, formal evaluation. One supervising principal recommended: (1) the formulation of a faculty study group to which would be delegated the responsibility for staff meeting evaluation; (2) the development of rating instruments designed and built according to the needs and wishes of the faculty, which would be basic in evaluation; and (3) the analysis of group processes with assistance from the publications and institutes of such resources as the National Training Laboratories and the National Institute of Leadership, cited in Appendix A and in Chapter 5.

DO

1. Organize faculty meetings around teachers' problems in general, but not around individual difficulties. There must be a definite plan for the faculty meeting. The agenda should be developed by a planning committee selected by members of the staff. The meeting should be presided over by the principal, but should not be dominated by him.
2. Set aside a definite time for the faculty meeting. Every effort should be made to stick to that time.
3. Make provisions for social activities that will provide opportunities for

the staff to get to know each other better. Refreshments help to set the correct social atmosphere that could improve the meeting.

4. Get the faculty organized so that the principal acts as the chairman until other leadership is evident, then the chairmanship should be given to another. The democratic leader will be looking to see what leadership his staff contains, and encourage the development of this leadership.

5. Give the faculty partial responsibility for determining the place, agenda, and length of a faculty meeting.

6. Hold the faculty meeting during regular school hours or as close thereto as possible, thus eliminating the feeling that faculty meetings are an added burden.

7. Set aside a definite time for discussion of general teaching problems, with individual problems being solved in committees or in conferences with the supervisor.

8. Give the meeting purpose and direction, and assist the staff to accomplish the desired objectives.

9. State the purpose of the meeting from the beginning.

10. Allow all members of the staff to state their positions briefly with regard to the topic under discussion.

11. Emphasize a variety of opinions so that the teachers may see alternate courses for action.

12. Adopt reasonable rules of order.

13. Summarize important points to show how much progress was made in that session.

14. Avoid lecturing.

15. Recognize pertinent contributions of other staff members and maintain an air of impartiality.

16. Seek to obtain a consensus.

17. Help the staff to recognize that final decisions are not always possible or desirable.

18. Complete the checklist for group leaders included as Figure 10-3.

19. Use care in ascribing statements to individuals.

20. Insure that while some agenda items are included for informational purposes, others are calls for action.

FIGURE 10–3   Checklist for Group Leaders

PREPARATION

1. Were members notified about meeting time, place, and topic? ....

2. Were the physical arrangements right for good discussion? ....

3. Did I prepare an outline for the discussion? ....

4. Did I provide sufficient background and factual material? ....

5. Were the visual or other aids in place and ready for use? ....

6. Was a friendly, personal atmosphere developed before the discussions started? ....

LEADING THE DISCUSSION

7. Did my introduction state the topic?_____Define the areas for
discussion?_____Relate them to the interests of the group?..............

8. Was it too long? ....

9. Did it insure that the group had enough information on which to base the discussion? ......

10. Did the group come right into the discussion after the introduction? ....

11. How did I "toss the ball" to the group? ....

12. Did I keep the discussion moving by:
Frequent transitional summaries?_____Checking repetitions? ....
Calling attention to digressions and irrelevancies? ....
Pointing up differences of opinion?_____Clarifying the discussion? ....
Allowing sufficient time for each major area of the topic? ....

13. Were the questions and other methods I used to guide the discussion:
Aimed at bringing out reasons, opinions, causes? ....
Designed to bring out all shades of opinion? ....
Presented objectively (not slanted or argumentative)? ....

FIGURE 10-3

Worded briefly and clearly? . . . .
Thought-provoking (not rhetorical or "yes—no" in form)? . . . .
Fairly and tactfully distributed among all members? . . . . . .

14. Did I encourage participation by:
    Keeping any one member from "hogging the show"? . . . .
    Drawing out the reticent members? . . . .
    Expressing appreciation of individual contributions? . . . .
    Re-directing questions to other members? . . . .
    Maintaining good humor and fair play? . . . .

15. Did I bring the discussion to a clear and definite conclusion? . . . . .
16. Did my final summary fairly review all points of view expressed? . . . .
    State the agreements reached?____And the points of disagreement?
    Call attention to sources of information? . . . .
    Announce the next meeting? . . . .

RESULTS

17. Were there any indications of satisfaction from members of the group? . . . . .
    Any indications of dissatisfaction from members of the group? . . . . .
18. Were there any unusual problems?____Did I handle them properly? . . . . .
19. How many members did not participate at all? . . . .
20. Was the topic suitable for discussion? . . . .
21. Were any important aspects of the question omitted? . . . .
22. Was there a clearer understanding of the subject after the discussion? . . . . .
23. What conclusions did the group reach?____

24. What could I have done better?____

DON'T

1. Allow the group to stray from issues presented.
2. As leader, fail to give direction to the discussion.
3. Permit a statement of a derogatory nature concerning a fellow staff member to be made at a staff meeting.

Staff meetings can be interesting. By following a few proven techniques that have been used by many, they may lose their low popularity rating.

If staff meetings are to contribute to the growth of the professional staff they require careful, cooperative planning, judicious leadership, continuous evaluation, and prompt adjournment.

Supervisory Problem

In Basket

Mrs. G. and Mr. M. were standing in front of the bulletin board when the following dialogue was spoken:

Mrs. G. : Another of Mr. B's monologue sessions.

Mr. M. : I'm glad the only time I could make an appointment with my doctor is for 4:30 tomorrow. These notices usually mean extra long sessions.

Mrs. G. : Then you'll have an excuse for leaving the meeting. You can feel for me. I'll be sitting at one of those terrible lunch-table benches. I really need a crane to get into one of them. You can't hear anything in the lunchroom, and Mr. B. insists on standing at the head of the table to pronounce his dictums. The last meeting he called I sat at the far end of the table and couldn't hear much that he said. Mrs. P. sat across the table from me and corrected test papers.

Mr. M. : Did you understand what the principal meant in the last item of that handout he gave us at the last meeting?

Mrs. G. : No, and I couldn't hear what time he told us to put on the paper because of all of the noise the paper made as it was passed down the line.

Mr. M. : What did you think of the data he gave us comparing our students' basic skills levels with those of the other schools in the school system?

Mrs. G. : He erased his figures and replaced them with another set so fast that I couldn't keep up with him. What was he driving at?

Mr. M. : I'm not certain. I wish he had had time to answer a few questions. By the time he had finished his lecture, it was too late to do anything but go home.

Mrs. G. : I wonder if he'll have time for me to report about the activities of our last association council meeting?

Mr. M. : You'll be lucky if you get to do it, because he didn't allow me time for my science committee report at the meeting last week.

What can be done to change the environment of the staff meeting? How can the teachers' attitudes be changed favorably toward staff meetings?

Selected Bibliography

Books

Adams, Harold P., and Frank G. Dickey. *Basic Principles of Supervision.* New York: American Book Company, 1953.

Ayars, Albert L. *Administering the People's Schools.* New York: McGraw-Hill Book Company, Inc., 1957.

Barr, A. S., William H. Burton, and Leo J. Brueckner. *Supervision: Democratic Leadership in the Improvement of Learning.* New York: D. Appleton-Century Company, Inc., 1947.

Burton, William H. and Leo J. Brueckner. *Supervision: A Social Process.* New York: Appleton-Century-Crofts, 1955.

Campbell, Clyde. *Practical Applications of Democratic Administration.* New York: Harper and Brothers, 1952.

Crosby, Muriel. *Supervision as Cooperative Action.* New York: Appleton-Century-Crofts, 1957.

Elsbree, Willard D., and Harold J. McNally. *Elementary School Administration and Supervision.* New York: American Book Company, 1959.

Fullmer, Daniel W., and Harold W. Bernard. *Counseling: Content and Process.* Chicago: Science Research Associates, Inc., 1964.

Gwynn, J. Minor. *Theory and Practice of Supervision.* New York: Dodd, Mead & Company, 1961.

Hamachek, Don E. *Human Dynamics in Psychology and Education.* Boston: Allyn & Bacon, Inc., 1968.

Jacobson, P. E. *Duties of School Principals.* Englewood Cliffs, New Jersey: Prentice-Hall, Inc., 1941.

Kyte, George C. *The Principal at Work.* Boston: Ginn and Company, 1941.

Lane, Robert Hill. *The Principal in the Modern Elementary School.* Boston: Houghton Mifflin Company, 1948.

Stoops, Emery, and James R. Marks. *Elementary School Supervision—Practices and Trends.* Boston: Allyn and Bacon, Inc., 1965.

Wiles, Kimball. *Supervision for Better Schools.* Englewood Cliffs, New Jersey: Prentice-Hall, Inc., 1955.

Periodicals

Bickford, Jean F. "Weekly Team Conference." *The National Elementary Principal* XLV (January 1966): 44–45.

Foss, P. R. "Faculty Meetings and How to Make the Most of Them." *Michigan Education Journal* XLIII (Fall 1966): 31.

Hunt, Douglas. "Teacher Induction—A Key to Excellence." *The Bulletin of the National Association of Secondary School Principals* CCCXX (May 1960): 60–70.

McGrew, John F. "Improving Staff Communications." *The Clearing House* XL (April 1966): 475–477.

Ross, F. W., A. D. Erb, and F. M. Saunders. "Principals' Forum." *The Instructor* LXXV (May 1966): 25.

Winters, Kay. "Perk Up Your Faculty Meeting." *NEA Journal* LV (October 1966): 30–31.

Other Sources

Association for Supervision and Curriculum Development. *Group Process in Supervision*. Washington, D.C.: National Education Association, 1948.

How to Help the Staff
Understand and Guide Children

The teacher who does not understand the behavior of children may well find himself in an awkward situation. The supervisor who does not effectively help the staff to develop a better understanding of the nature of children will find himself in the position of correcting a problem that should not have raised its head—a problem that could prove to be embarrassing to the teacher, to the supervising principal, and to the specialist-consultant. Such a problem can leave all concerned defeated and discouraged.

The supervisor who can effectively help his staff to develop a better understanding of children will find that fewer problems arise, leaving the entire instructional staff freer to devote more of their time and energies to teaching. Helping the staff to bridge the gap from the exasperated to the satisfied should be one of the chief roles of the supervisor. His attitude is all-important since it sets the pace and can spell success or failure. A positive approach will encourage the staff, while a negative approach may well stifle initiative and creativity.

It is the purpose of this chapter to illustrate various methods and techniques whereby the supervisor can help the staff to understand children better. A better understanding rests upon general principles. Staff members, as well as children, are individuals and react as such, each with his own personality.

Topics covered in this chapter include:

Need for the improvement of the staff's understanding of children
How to help the staff understand children through the in-service education
program
Interplay of sociological factors
How to help the staff understand children through health records, observation, anecdotal records, and related techniques

How to help the staff understand students through intervisitation

How to help the staff understand students through the use of sociometric techniques

How to help the staff understand students through the interstaff conference

How to help teachers understand students through cumulative records

Case studies

How to supervise the assignment of a student to a classroom

Do — don't

"In-Basket" supervisory problems

Chapter Supplements

Need for the Improvement of the Staff's Understanding of Children

The modern school is more than a place where children are taught subjects and skills. One of the primary objectives of education today is to assist the individual to live a happier, more productive, and more satisfying life. The school, therefore, must recognize and provide for the individual differences which are manifest in the school's population. All children have the right to come to school, and it is the obligation of the supervising principal to assist the staff in understanding these children.

A Cultural Dichotomy

Certain dichotomies exist in our society and are reinforced in the schools. Aggression is a very necessary ingredient in this highly competitive world, but it is viewed with much concern if employed by the developing student in the school situation. Yet the student must compete for marks and for status among his peers. To reason and judge what is the right way to handle his behavior in any given situation presents a confusing problem to the adult directing the student, and, indeed, to the student himself.

The implications are that the teacher should be many things, but this is impractical. The role of the teacher should be restricted for if his role is not clarified, frustration is inevitable.

There is the need for school personnel to cultivate the habit of seeing behavior of students as the most important clue to understanding children, and also to understanding themselves. Adults often forget the many years of observation, imitation, and experience that were needed to give them their present background of behavior, and it is hard for them to go back to the world as seen by children. There is the need to be an effective listener and also to understand the language of children.

The social needs of children and of all human beings are deep-seated and powerful motivators to behavior. Security in social relationships is a need that influences all that people are and all that they do. Interpersonal relationships with children are a definite therapeutic tool that have a real effect on the course of total learning. Certainly there is a positive relationship between the teacher's understanding of children and the classroom environment.

Some Controversies

The most dramatic examples of the importance of understanding children are seen in situations that involve individual and group behavior and discipline. Some educators believe that teacher-training programs have not given enough attention to preparing teachers to meet these situations. Clichés which insist that the well-managed classroom does not present discipline problems have forced many a worried teacher to try to conceal his problems, instead of bringing them out in the open for diagnosis and help. He may feel that failure to solve problems of discipline is an indication of professional weakness. Nor is this feeling of inadequacy restricted to the beginning teacher. The number of years a teacher has taught proves very little. In fact, a teacher may adhere to the same old ways for so long that they come to seem like the only ways. The person does not exist who is so skilled or experienced that he cannot increase his understanding. The entire staff will benefit from a school atmosphere which fosters mutual growth and understanding. In such an environment occasional mistakes will be seen as the inevitable by-products of any genuine effort to try out new and better approaches to working with students.

Attempts to separate academic training from teaching the "whole child" are unrealistic. It cannot be done. Surely, any *good* teacher must work with the entire child and understand and respect him as an individual.

However, this is not to state that the schools should accept the total responsibility for the total child. The child is in the classroom, at the maximum, slightly less than one-fourth of the day and slightly less than three-sixteenths of the year. The teacher is not expected to perform as a psychiatrist, as a psychologist, or as an educational therapist; nor do the patrons of the schools expect such performance, although implications of early statements of members of the child-centered wing of the Progressive Education Association seem to point to the contrary. This does not mean, however, that the teacher is working with part of a child. Rather, it is to emphasize that those problems of the individual which are adversely influencing his ability to learn and to profit from classroom instruction are legitimately a part of the teacher's professional concern. Yet he must not be expected to provide psychiatric care, nor must an entire class suffer in various manners because one individual apparently has "emotional difficulties." This is correct as far as it goes, but it is incomplete.

It has been said that we teach children, not subjects. This statement is not precise. We teach children *mathematics*. We teach children *reading*. We do NOT teach children methodology; we do NOT teach children guidance and counseling. Rather, we utilize methodology as a vehicle for efficient and profitable instruction; and we employ the techniques of guidance and counseling to assist the individual in the task of learning, and to encourage him to learn to the best of his ability. To this extent the school is guidance-centered.

It is sometimes assumed that teachers are selected on the basis of (1) their interest in and love for children, and (2) their college training. Some believe it naturally follows that teachers will be able to teach and that they will have an adequate understanding of children. Unfortunately, interest in children is not necessarily synonymous with understanding. Nor is it synonymous with ability to teach. And college courses are only the starting point. Real understanding is a dynamic force that will demand unending effort on the part of the teacher as each year brings new children—each child an individual and different from all of the others.

General Principles

Helping teachers to understand children is not a topic that may be treated in isolation. It involves all means that are at the disposal of the schools. It is hoped, but never assured, that this will produce insight, understanding, adjustment, and intellectual comprehension of the child by the teacher. It is further hoped that this comprehension will lead to more effective student learning.

The following general principles are intended to serve as guildeposts to action:

1. Stimulation of student growth by the teacher is dependent upon a better understanding of student needs, interests, and abilities.
2. Channels of communication must be established between parents, principals, teachers, and classified personnel for the better understanding of each child.
3. Supervisory help should assist teachers in providing an adequate program of testing, measurement, and evaluation for each child.
4. An effective supervisory program will provide the teacher with readily accessible records concerning each child. These records should be comprehensive and cumulative.
5. A sound program of supervision makes readily accessible to the teacher all information which has been gathered from school, home, and community sources.
6. Although general growth sequences may be roughly predicted, children have individual and unique patterns of growth and development.
7. Principals must help eliminate arbitrary and unrealistic marking standards. They must encourage teachers to work with children as individuals with varying interests, abilities, experiences, and achievements.
8. A sound supervisory program may effectively provide child study groups for teachers.
9. A supervisory program designed to help teachers understand children will establish adequate referral methods when assistance outside the province of the school is required. Adequate policies concerning follow-

up for cases referred to child welfare agencies must be developed and be continuously evaluated.

10. The administration may help teachers to understand children by providing sufficient facilities, funds, and staff time for adequate research, study, and conferences.

How to Help the Staff Understand Children through the In-Service Education Program

The in-service education program offers an excellent opportunity for the supervisor to work with the staff in the evaluation of policies and practices, to discuss new methods and techniques, to review past experiences, and to coordinate future programs. A few of the more useful approaches to understanding children through the in-service education program are discussed here briefly.

Preschool Meetings

Many school systems now utilize the week before classes commence for staff meetings and conferences. For beginning teachers it is "orientation" week. During this week the teacher has time not only to meet with other staff members, but also to prepare his own room environment for the opening of school. Meeting with the supervising principal and with other faculty members, he is introduced to the school plant, other teacher and classified personnel, the size and characteristics of his classes, the cumulative record system, and school policies.

During the year follow-up conferences should be scheduled, especially with beginning teachers, to discuss the validity of assignments and policies. At the end of the year a formal evaluation should be made in writing, indicating the successes, failures, and needs and making recommendations for the following year. If feasible, especially in the elementary school, the students' present teacher should confer with the teacher of the next grade in order to facilitate the students' transition. There is, perhaps, no better way to pass on information about children than by personal contact.

Specialists

Another aspect of the in-service education program is to bring to the school system speakers representing specialized fields. This may be done on a district level two or three times a year. Such meetings unify the staff. Specialist-consultants may be secured for a grade level or subject matter area meeting whenever a definite need arises.

System-Wide Programs

Some examples of school system-wide in-service training programs that could help the teacher to understand children would be: (1) how to recognize and help the exceptional child, and (2) the selection and use of curriculum materials. Careful organization of the curriculum and selection of materials can help to solve classroom problems.

Demonstration Teaching Within the School

Demonstrations within the school are helpful. A teacher could show his fellow educators how a certain problem arose in the classroom, the analysis of the problem, the method of solving the problem, and the results obtained.

The use of both teachers and children as active participants in the in-service training program carries the greatest amount of learning with it, for both bring into play the people who are involved in similar situations.

Exchanging Ideas

Another valuable aspect of the in-service education program that the supervisor should not neglect is the exchange of ideas on different grade levels. This practice is especially helpful between the elementary and secondary teachers. The staff of one grade level often is ignorant of the learning that takes place at other levels. They know, of course, that reading, writing, and mathematics were taught, but they are not sure of what children really learned. Consequently, the junior high-school teacher may mutter to himself, "Jimmy didn't learn how to spell in the lower grades"; the sixth-grade teacher may wonder about how much her students learned in the fifth; and so on. If each teacher were aware of the complaints of other teachers, if effective communication were in operation, it would aid each teacher in evaluating his own program. A meeting between different grade levels enhances understanding and teaching.

Coordination and articulation between grade levels should bring about a greater understanding and unity among the staff members, a greater appreciation for the work performed by others, and a strengthening of the instructional program in general.

Collaboration between the several teachers sharing the problems of similar classes offers such obvious advantages that it may mistakenly be assumed that this will happen automatically. Every effort should be made to develop a cooperative feeling between teachers, rather than the competitive one which sometimes prevails.

Within the group setting there are a variety of ways in which the supervisor can direct the learning that occurs. Some of the most casual and informal ways are also the most effective. For instance, he might relate his personal impressions of appropriate articles or books that he is reading and stimulate staff members to read them also. The crucial factor here is that the supervisor is not telling his staff what to do; he is doing it himself and enjoying it. Having led teachers to such outstanding material, the principal will find that most of them will become so interested in the practical nature of the content that they will not require additional outside stimulation.

Another technique is giving recognition to someone taking one of the graduate courses related to child guidance or in educational psychology. Here is a golden opportunity to draw on the opinions and experiences of specialists and experts; it is also an opportunity to give status to the teacher who is attending the class. Teachers who are taking graduate courses should receive all possible encouragement.

Use of Instructional Technology Materials

There are now many fine films on child development, fear, rejection, shyness, anger, discipline, learning, and individual differences that can be obtained directly from the companies producing them, from city libraries, or from the county or school district audio-visual departments. One of the best services for schools is "Discipline," furnished by The Economics Press, Montclair, New Jersey. This publisher also provides "Classroom Discipline."

In the larger city school system the supervisor would logically start with materials available within the system audio-visual department. But, these materials should not set a limit to what he uses, and his very interest and suggestions will encourage efforts on the part of the audio-visual department to get the kind of films he finds most useful. Some very large systems have produced their own films. "You and Your Classroom," produced by the Los Angeles City Schools, is an example. Although this film does not go into detailed student study, it does present a series of classroom incidents and asks the teacher, "What would you do?"

Such films provide a springboard for discussion of ways of working with students. The teacher need not feel threatened, as he might were he discussing how he actually handled students in a given situation in his own room. He could talk more objectively and freely; he could also be more open to suggestion and criticism on his approach to a problem.

Child-Study Groups

Child-study groups have been established in schools in cooperation with universities which offer college credit for such participation. In other schools they have been initiated by the school system or the principal. In either case, there are a number of advantages to be gained from a systematic program of child study.

The supervisor who plans to organize a child-study group within the school may wish to obtain the assistance of outside consultants. The supervisor whose district has set up such a program will want to encourage teacher participation in every way possible.

Interplay of Sociological Factors

There is one common avenue children must take in our society — they must attend school. Here all children come together and compete for status in the democratic educational system of our country. Conflicts in the total school situation may be seen between the working-class children and the middle-class criteria upon which the school operates.

Techniques suitable for the middle-class student may be relatively ineffective for the lower-class student. These children are likely to be found wanting in the school because of their lack of interest in intellectual achievement and the apparent lack of reinforcement by the home of the requirements of the school. Indeed, some educators appear to feel that in certain cases students have been encouraged to "cause problems" through their apparent lack of effort and through their disruptive behavior.

Similar conflicts may be seen between middle-class values of the school staff and lower-class values of many of the children who attend the public schools. It is an important implication that commonly held values form the basis of strong group cohesion in any situation. Teachers, supervisors, and administrators must be recruited from all segments of the population to enhance effective communication and make identification more probable.

SOCIAL CLASS: As citizens in a democracy, Americans do not like to think of their society as being characterized by social class. Unfortunately, there is present in America not only social class, but also caste distinctions as well, although the latter does not have the deep connotation it has in India.

Social class has been defined in a number of ways, although most of the definitions involve such variables as occupation of the head of household, source of income, housing, and education of the father. One of the most widely used definitions of social class is that provided by A. Hollingshead and F. Redlick.[1] Their "Index of Social Position" is premised upon three assumptions: (1) that social stratification exists in the community, (2) that status positions are determined mainly by a few commonly accepted cultural characteristics, and (3) that items symbolic of status may be scaled and combined by the use of statistical procedures.

The most common division of social class by sociologists, as well as educators and psychologists, is into (1) upper class (relatively aristocratic, well-established people); (2) middle class (the great body of professional and

[1]August Hollingshead and Frederick Redlick, *Social Class and Mental Illness* (New York: John Wiley & Sons, Inc., 1958), especially chapter III.

white collar workers); and (3) lower class, the upper-lower class being made up of skilled workers and the lower-lower class being made up of unskilled workers.

There are social class differences in tastes concerning food, clothing, social cliques, values, religion, intellectual interests, and social beliefs. Middle-class people in general espouse hard work, thrift, ambition, cleanliness, self-control, restraint of sexual and aggressive impulses, honesty and correctness in speech and action, and learning for learning's sake. The school's enrollment form may provide some clues to social class status. Such a form is included as Figure 11–1.

SUPERVISORY IMPLICATIONS OF SOCIAL CLASS STRUCTURE. Most educators are members of the middle class, and school policy is set by middle-class people. However, their students come from a variety of homes. The gap in values between middle-class teachers and lower-lower class children is enormous. This implication is equally relevant for other groups, such as public health personnel, speech therapists, recreation specialists, probation officers, and social workers. The identification of persons with other persons who share similar cultural values, attitudes, beliefs, and customs produces group solidarity as well as group differences.

Problems in Effective Communication

Differences in social structure obstruct barriers or tend to break down interclass communications. When there is deficiency in communication, there is little understanding, and when there is little understanding, suspicion and hostility are likely to develop. Hostility, in turn, breeds hostility.

These problems in communication and conflict of interest are particularly severe in public education. Teachers, who are almost without exception middle-class people, must try to communicate clearly and effectively with children of all social classes. Problems of communication also exist between different ethnic and national groups. The integration of minority groups into the general population is complicated by their social class position. This position is lower, on the average, than is the position of the so-called core culture. Educators, therefore, always are laboring under the heavy burden of attempting to solve the professional problem of how to

FIGURE 11–1 Enrollment Form Completed When the Student Enters School

KENTON CITY SCHOOLS

School

ENROLLMENT FORM

Child's Name_____Male_____Female_____

        Last   First   Middle

Address_____Phone_____

Birth: Month_____Day _____Year_____City_____State_____

Father's Name_____Birthplace_____

        Last   First

Father's Occupation_____ Employer _____

Father's Business Address_____Phone_____

Mother's Name _____

        Last   First   Maiden Name

Birthplace_____

Mother's Occupation_____Employer_____

Mother's Business Address_____Phone_____

Name of Guardian or Relation_____

(If Child Is Not Living with Mother or Father)

Guardian's Occupation _____

Guardian's Business Address_____Phone_____

Person Authorized to Care for Child in Emergency if Mother and Father Cannot Be Reached

    Name_____

    Address_____Phone_____

Family Physician_____

    Address_____Phone_____

Is Child Living with (1) Both Parents?_____

              (2) Mother Only?_____

    (3) Father Only?_____(4) Guardian?_____

    (5) Other?_____

Language Spoken in Home_____

Brothers		Sisters	
Older	Younger	Older	Younger
_____	_____	_____	_____
_____	_____	_____	_____
_____	_____	_____	_____

School last Attended: Name _____

City_____State_____Date Left_____

Kenton School Attended Previously_____

balance these sociological forces so that *learning* (we would have said "optimum learning" a few years ago) may take place in the school.

Implications for the Staff

Specifically, supervisors must try to help teachers to know these families better and to develop a more realistic understanding of the needs of the children and their parents. The staff must examine, justify, and perhaps modify its own system of values in order to develop attitudes of objectivity and acceptance. After investigating these social and psychological problems, L. E. Harper concluded: "If the teacher makes an attempt to understand the possible cultural differences behind behavior, he may even conclude that a different way of looking at such things is as defensible as his own."[2] The supplement to Chapter 18 should prove helpful in assisting teachers in planning for more effective conferences with parents.

How to Help the Staff Understand Children through Health Records, Observation, Anecdotal Records, and Related Techniques

Health Records

One source of information which is so obvious that it often is overlooked is the health record. A parent often assumes that because the kindergarten teacher knew Diana had a hearing loss, this information will automatically be communicated to subsequent teachers. If the next teacher fails to talk to the nurse or to read the health card, and if this information is not in the cumulative folder, he may interpret the hearing loss as dullness and inattentiveness. If success is especially important to Diana, she may learn to camouflage her handicap by copying her neighbors' work. One second-grade girl even managed to conceal her deafness from the audiometrist the first time she was tested.

[2]Louis E. Harper and Benjamin Wright, "Dealing with Emotional Problems in the Classroom," *Elementary School Journal* LXIII (March 1958): 316–325.

CUMULATIVE FOLDERS CONTAIN HEALTH INFORMATION. Cumulative folders, which may include psychological and health records, are excellent sources of information. A conscientious teacher should be encouraged to avail himself of this kind of information before the semester has even begun.

ADJUNCT HEALTH INFORMATION. Information concerning the health reasons for which children may be excluded from school, general information concerning communicable diseases, and other health data which are of concern to teachers and parents should be made available by the supervising principal. These topics are treated briefly in Appendix C.

Observation and Listening

Observation and listening are basic ingredients in all techniques which develop teacher understanding of children. Supervisors can help teachers to improve their observation techniques. G. P. Driscoll suggested that teachers watch for children whose responses to situations are inappropriate, and, believing that every response must have a cause, seek out that cause. She listed four directives based on observation as the principal method in the study of children's behavior:

1. Use school situations to observe behavior.
2. Learn to describe behavior objectively.
3. Study cumulative descriptions of behavior; don't spend too much time directing behavior—study it.
4. Study the child from the standpoint of his developmental age, i.e., his physical, intellectual, and social development.[3]

School situations provide a wide variety of opportunities for the observation of the students. For example, the teacher can discover a great deal about a student by developing an awareness of the messages conveyed through his creative products.

[3]Reprinted with permission of the publisher from Gertrude P. Driscoll, *Child Guidance in the Classroom* (New York: Bureau of Publications, Teachers College, Columbia University, 1955), p. 27.

The observation of children at play generally provides valuable insights into the behavior of children and is used widely in child guidance clinics. Much of the same insight can be derived by the teacher from study of the particular item which the student draws, writes, models, or represents dramatically.

The teacher is not a therapist and should not try to go beyond his own role as a teacher in analyzing what he finds in a student's products, but the supervising principal should encourage the teacher to watch for extremes which indicate the possible need for psychological study. The teacher may be the first person to note an extreme individual difference in a student which would pass unnoticed in the student's home setting.

Take, for example, the case of twelve-year-old Joseph, who loved jig-saw puzzles but could not assemble them without extreme rigidity and tremor of the hand. His handwriting invariably was traced and retraced, until the page was smudgy and torn. In other respects he was a tidy, well-mannered youngster whose oral responses were well above average. A perceptive teacher would question the reasons for the disparity between written and oral work and look for some answers.

Learning to describe behavior objectively sharpens the teacher's awareness of how subjective we really are in our daily conversation and thinking. As he becomes aware of this the teacher will discover that it is possible to accept and understand a student without judging him.

The importance of objective description will be most obvious in analysis and maintenance of student personnel records. Some teachers say they do not care to read cumulative records since they fear they will be prejudiced by the impressions of previous teachers. While the concern for impartiality is commendable, it would be more constructive if they would learn to distinguish between subjective and objective description. A discerning observer will do this and will try to base his opinions on facts and on factual, objective accounts, rather than on another person's opinion.

C. E. Moustakas[4] urged teachers to listen to students as they express themselves, without trying to press their own thinking and feelings upon them. The teacher who spends too much time talking will have little time

[4]Clark E. Moustakas, *The Teacher and the Child: Personal Interaction in the Classroom* (New York: McGraw-Hill Book Company, Inc., 1956), p. 42.

to study behavior. Being a good listener is one of the best ways to maintain clear channels of communication. Teachers sometimes feel that they must have an immediate answer for everything. Perhaps many of the unprecedented demands being made by the more militant students would be forestalled or automatically met if teachers, and supervisors, and administrators were more skilled in the art of listening.

Anecdotal Records

Anecdotal records offer the advantage of being written. Time has a way of clouding and confusing the true picture even when seen by the most skilled listener and observer who, after all, may infect his own biases in his observations and recordings.

The anecdotal record is a study device for improving professional insights which may be sparse but should eventually develop into a rather free-flowing, selective, many-sided collection of vivid and detailed information about a student. It is important that the teacher feel free to give a picture of the student as he appears to him in order to facilitate recording.

It is unfortunate that some school systems are so fearful of lawsuits and/or parental criticism that incomplete, inaccurate, or even dishonest written comments by teachers are encouraged to avoid rocking the educational ship of state. These systems would do better by emphasizing objective record-keeping free from malice.

The value of anecdotal records in helping one understand the role he plays in the school situation becomes more apparent in their use in the study group. Here the group can help one another with short cuts and suggestions about techniques and meanings. A kind of "co-responsibility for professional understanding of teachers' difficulties, as well as those of the child, develops."[5]

How to Help the Teacher Record and Interpret Anecdotal Records

SUGGESTIONS FOR RECORDING. The following suggestions may be useful in helping the teacher record and interpret anecdotal records.

[5]California School Board Association of the California Teachers Association, *Sample Personnel Policies,* Third Progress Report, Joint Committee on Personnel (San Francisco: The Association, October 1954), p. 200.

1. The form used for recording anecdotes should be short and informal, including the name of the student, date, situation or setting, description of behavior, and observer's name (see Figure 11–2).

FIGURE 11–2   Anecdotal Record Card

Name of Student_____
Date_____
Setting_____
Anecdote_____
_____
_____
Teacher_____

2. Brief sentences are advisable, with a minimum of adverbs and adjectives.
3. Anecdotal records should contain objective statements such as, "Glenn offered to show Bruce a new game," rather than, "Glenn is a helpful student."
4. Both strengths and weaknesses should be reported.
5. Anecdotes do not suggest meaning or ideas not supported by facts. The following statement, "Bill poked Gary during reading class," is better than, "Bill poked Gary as soon as I was busy helping Esther." The latter implies deceit.
6. The facts should be presented without interpretation. "Darlene is lazy" is neither objective nor descriptive of an incident.
7. Because behavior is conditioned by the situation or environment in which it occurs, it is advisable to record the setting.
8. Record the anecdote as soon as possible after the incident.

USES AND LIMITATIONS OF THE ANECDOTAL RECORD. A survey revealed the following uses:

1. Anecdotal records facilitate the understanding of personality and increase teacher ability to interpret behavior.
2. They provide a picture of the pattern of the student's behavior.

3. They assist in evaluating materials for sections of the cumulative record card.
4. They serve as a basis for student and parent conferences. Dated written descriptions of specific behavior are more satisfactory than vague recollections.

Teachers and supervisors have noted the following limitations with the greatest frequency:

1. Possible subjectivity of anecdotal records may lead to inaccurate or faulty interpretation.
2. The observer's personal reaction to certain types of behavior may color his description or influence his selection of incidents.
3. There may be a tendency toward regarding only negative behavior. Positive factors should be recorded in order to give a complete picture of the student's behavior.
4. Lack of setting or background can limit the interpretation of data.
5. Quiet, submissive behavior may be more significant than the aggressive, overt type, but may be more difficult to detect and record.
6. Interpretations from anecdotal records do not form conclusive evidence but are considered in the light of other findings.

Anecdotal records, then, are records of facts as objective as we can make them; they are *not* interpretations. They contain details regarding specific situations. The date, the situation, a brief description of behavior, possible explanation, and the recorder's signature constitute one entry. This record often is kept for some time in order to better establish patterns of behavior.

These records may be used as an aid in gaining insight into a student's development — a comparison between present behavior and that previously recorded — to determine consistent characteristics as opposed to new growth. The records may sometimes be used as a basis for a cooperative conference with parents, teacher, nurse, supervising principal, and psychologist.

The importance of anecdotal records as documentation for a principal who is considering some special action cannot be overlooked. An accurate anecdotal record often indicates the best possible solution for the student and the school.

Checklists and Rating Scales

Checklists and rating scales are used for summarizing observations of student behavior and abilities. These forms are employed widely as economical methods of categorizing information about groups as well as about individuals.

Checklists can be used to indicate teacher judgment relative to whether certain behavior traits, social attributes, abilities, interests, and personality characteristics are present. Figure 11–3 is an example of a checklist concerning student responsibility.

FIGURE 11–3   Responsibility Checklist

Names	Usually Does His Best	Good Leader	Good Follower	Continues at Task Until Finished	Cooperates with Fellow Students	Depend-able	Follows Direc-tions

Rating scales may list the same type of traits and characteristics as checklists. However, in rating scales the items are worked on gradual value scales. Rating scales also are used for the evaluation of students in relation to objectives of the instructional program. A rating scale in the area of work habits is shown as Figure 11–4.

FIGURE 11–4   Rating Scale

	Consistently	Most of the Time	Some of the Time	Seldom	Never
Follows directions					
Works independently					
Shows initiative					
Completes work					
Enjoys work					

USES OF CHECKLISTS AND RATING SCALES. The following is a list of uses of checklists and rating scales which could be suggested by the supervisor:

1. Checklists and rating scales provide a specific situation for observation.
2. They provide an evaluation of a student's emotional and social adjustment, interests, and values.
3. They provide for observation of behavior in relation to established objectives.

LIMITATIONS OF CHECKLISTS AND RATING SCALES. The supervisor should bring the following limitations of these instruments to the attention of the teacher:

1. Observation is limited to items on the list.
2. Data are relatively subjective in that judgments of the observer are recorded.
3. Lack of common agreement concerning the meaning of behavior traits may influence the use of these data.
4. Reliability of these forms varies with the trait observed.

The Autobiography

The autobiography is a valuable technique for obtaining information about students. Teachers need supervisorial help in interpretation. A student's version of his life story will give clues as to his regard for himself, his interests, problems, friends, and past experiences.

Autobiographies may be written either in narrative or story form, or the form may be construed to provide information in particular areas. The following outline may suggest topics for the autobiography:

1. My life before I went to school
   a) My birthplace
   b) Places I have lived
   c) My family
   d) My best friends
   e) Activities I enjoy
2. My life since I've come to school
   a) My best friends
   b) My favorite games, work, and hobbies
   c) My happiest time at school
   d) My happiest time at home
   e) My favorite subject in school
   f) My least favorite subject in school
   g) Plans for work after I complete my schooling

USES OF AUTOBIOGRAPHIES. The uses of the autobiography include the following:

1. The autobiography is useful as a supplementary procedure for collecting information about all students, and will be particularly useful in obtaining information about students new to the school.
2. It may be used to appraise changes in student adjustment.
3. Student attitudes toward school, health, teachers, parents, associates, and self are sometimes revealed through these written accounts of personal experiences.

LIMITATIONS OF AUTOBIOGRAPHIES. The supervisor should note the following limitations:

1. Data must be interpreted in light of their subjectivity.
2. Lapse of time between the occurrence of the event and the recording may affect recall.

3. Students may incorrectly interpret events in order to rationalize or excuse problems. This possibility presents limitations in accepting all information at face value, but can be of aid in seeing the situation as the student perceives it.

Unfinished Stories and Sentences

Teachers may obtain information about students' ideas and attitudes from their written and oral compositions. Sometimes unfinished sentences and stories, designed to reveal students' attitudes about specific situations and problems, are particularly useful for this purpose. The teacher may provide pupils with a short story or a list of sentences without endings and encourage the students to complete them. The unfinished story below has been used by a supervising principal in an elementary school.

One day Leo and Sol were walking along the street near the school. As they walked, they noticed a wallet which had evidently been dropped from a passing car. The boys hurried to pick up the wallet and examine it. They found two five dollar bills. Leo suggested that they _____

_____

_____

_____

_____

How to Help the Staff Understand Students through Intervisitation

Supervisory observation takes two main forms: (1) observation by the supervising principal, specialist-consultant, or counselor for supervisory or administrative purposes; and (2) observations by the teacher of techniques used by another instructor. The latter is termed "intervisitation."

The school system should have a policy of allowing teachers to observe other teachers at least once or twice a year. These observations should be arranged beforehand, with a definite purpose in mind. For example, a teacher in the fifth grade may observe the techniques employed by another in teaching social studies as he presents a certain concept about the "westward movement" or as he initiates work on a mural about this segment of American history. While this intervisitation could quite easily be accommodated within the teacher's own school, it is often advisable to visit another school or one that is outside the district in order to see different viewpoints and methods in teaching the subjects, as well as for morale reasons.

The school system should provide a substitute for the teacher while he observes in another room. It is advisable for the principal or staff specialist-consultant to accompany the teacher. Preparation should always precede the observation. For a description of how the supervisor can prepare for and handle intervisitation, see the supplement to Chapter 8.

How to Help the Staff Understand Students through the Use of Sociometric Techniques

Aspects of Group Structure and Function

It is a general notion that people are basically gregarious; i.e., are group creatures, and are never free from group situations and group interactions. Students work, function, and live in groups. The satisfaction the student gets out of living depends on his group. It is important that staff members realize that behavior varies and even changes in group situations.

Understanding a student requires that the teacher also understand his role in the group. A student in a solitary situation is quite different from what he is in the classroom or on the playground.

The use of sociometry can be extremely helpful to the staff in learning to understand students. It provides a rather systematic approach whereby the teachers can make spot checks on the students in many areas. For example, a student's acceptance or rejection of other students may be revealed by answers to questions such as, "Whom would you take to a movie? Whom would you choose to play on your team? With whom would you want to work on a science project? Whom would you invite to a party?"

This questionnaire method of obtaining information can be supplemented by the teacher's observations of the students during the nutrition, recess, lunch, before and after school, physical education activities periods, and in other areas where the children come into contact with one another. The teacher should note the individual choices of the children. Sociometry can help him bring the "inside" of the student "outside."

The main functions of sociometry help the teacher identify social isolates and stars; select students for study groups, teams, or special activities; analyze the makeup of cliques; get ideas for working with shy students, bullies, and discipline problems; and evaluate the progress of social patterns within a classroom.

The supervisor should help the teacher use sociometric techniques effectively in order to give him one more effective tool for analyzing and understanding students.

Two useful techniques which the teacher seeking an understanding of the role of the student within the group may use are the sociogram and the sociodrama. The teacher about to embark on either technique will want to do some careful studying and planning and consult with specialists on the subject. It is not the purpose of this chapter to provide a complete description of these techniques, but rather to present certain key points which the supervisor should remember as he guides and supports the teacher in his efforts.

The Sociodrama

The supervisor should suggest two principles with respect to the sociodrama:

1. The situation must be representative of the problems of the group members.
2. The majority of the group members, as well as the teacher, must want to explore the situation.

It should be added that many teachers, particularly less experienced ones, may feel somewhat threatened when first attempting to employ the technique of the sociodrama. Initial efforts in which the teacher discovers all the pitfalls of the sociodrama may be disheartening. The least he will need to know is that the principal is fully supportive and will not interpret a free situation as indicating a deficiency in the area of classroom control.

Sociometrics and the Sociogram

The main criterion concerning the use of sociometrics is that the test is not considered as an end in itself, and in which there is an immediacy to the choosing.[6] It has been described as a "charting of the dynamic interrelationships expressed by the members of a group at a given time in a given context.[7] It does not reveal why relationships are the way they are; only *what* they are. Techniques vary and are sometimes very complicated. Again, the teacher will need to prepare with a review of material in the field before he attempts sociometrics.

Sociometric Interest Inventories

For some purposes, not necessarily concerned with group interaction, the interest inventory may be more appropriate. Sociometrics may evolve from some kinds of interest inventories in which the questions concerning social preferences are interwoven with others dealing with personal and vocational likes or dislikes. The major difference is that there is no charting of the outcomes in the interest inventory, and that the interest inventory more probably concerns the individual alone. This is only one more way of getting information about a child. How valuable it is will depend upon how skillful the teacher is in using this additional information in his work with the student.

The sociometric test includes three main steps: (1) obtaining information from students through a questionnaire, (2) tabulating and charting the data in the form of a sociogram, and (3) using the data to improve relationships in the group.

The wording of the questionnaire determines the usefulness of the data and explains the use of the results in relation to classwork. Emphasis is placed on the free choice of any student, so that the students understand in advance that any direction of choice is approved. The teacher records oral choices. His manner in presenting the questionnaire should be direct, interested, and matter-of-fact, as in the following example:

We shall need committees to work on our science project. Each of you know with whom you particularly enjoy working. Write your name in the upper left-hand corner of the paper. Number 1, 2, and 3 on the lines below. Opposite

[6]Henry J. Otto, *Elementary School Organization and Administration* (New York: Appleton-Century-Crofts 1964), p. 204.
[7]Ibid.

"1" write the name of the boy or girl with whom you would most like to work on the committee; after "2" write your second choice; and after "3" place your third choice. You may choose a boy or girl who is absent.

Some teachers work from five by seven inch tabulation cards in tabulating choices and making the sociogram. Others use a tabulation form as a basis for constructing the sociogram. Principals should be able to suggest workable alternatives.

In the tabulation form illustrated as Figure 11–5, the names of the chosen students are written across the top, and the names of the students making the selection are placed along the left side. All class names appear in both places, and numbers representing first and second choices are recorded.

In constructing the sociogram it is suggested that symbols for the most chosen girls be placed first, mutually chosen girls next, and the girls chosen

Chosen / Chooser	Gary Douglas	Mary Smith	Shirley Brown	Beatrice Scher	Glenn Rochelle	Bruce Marks	Marvin Conn	Billy Batson	Richard Muriel	Neila Stanley		
Gary Douglas	■											
Mary Smith		■										
Shirley Brown			■									
Beatrice Scher				■								
Glenn Rochelle					■							
Bruce Marks						■						
Marvin Conn							■					
Billy Batson								■				
Richard Muriel									■			
Neila Stanley										■		
											■	
												■

FIGURE 11–5   Sample Tabulation Form Showing a Part of a Class.

least on the outside. The same procedure would apply to the boys' half of the sociogram.

In reading a sociogram, it is suggested that teachers begin by following the lines leading to and from one person, as shown in Figure 11–6.

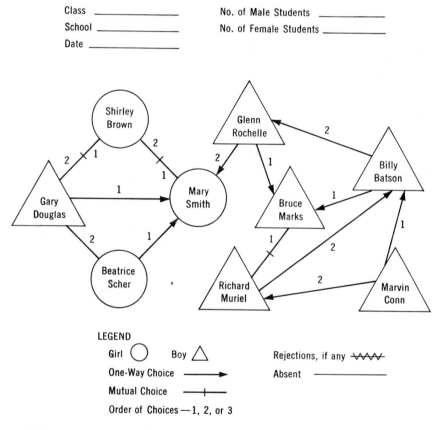

FIGURE 11–6   Sample Sociogram Charting the First and Second Choices of Part of a Class.

Identification of the following is possible:

1. Isolates—students who are not chosen;
2. Fringers—seldom chosen;

3. Stars—most frequently chosen;
4. Rejectees—only when negative questions are used;
5. Mutual choices—students who choose one another;
6. Chains—one person chooses another who, in turn, chooses another.

The longer the chain, the better the chance of communication.

Small, tightly knit groups within the class are noted so that provision may be made for wider communication. Class leaders are identified, as well as indications of students' values with reference to peer leaders. The effects of using sociometric data are determined by the use of a series of sociometric tests. Indications of cultural values which affect group structure should be noted.

CAUTIONS AND LIMITATIONS. Rapport with the class should be established before using sociometric tests. Since relationships in classes change, sociometric choices will change and subsequent sociograms will be needed. Students should not see the original slips on which their choices were made. The term "sociometric testing" is not used with students.

Supervisors and teachers should study and use sociograms with the following cautions in mind:

1. The teacher's attitude toward the stars, fringers, and isolates should be examined for possible influences upon students' choices.
2. Sociograms point to opportunities for further study, but do not supply causes for existing relationships.
3. A looseness and lack of direction in the sociometric structure may prevent successful organization of groups within the class.

"Guess Who" Technique

The "guess who" technique has been employed by teachers to gain insight into students' opinions of their classmates. Written descriptions of individuals are given to students, who are asked to write which of their classmates fit the descriptions. The following descriptions illustrate the type of statements which might be used:

This person is very careful about following directions. He listens and works carefully. His work is complete and is done correctly. Write his name.

_____

This person is a very good sport; he is fair and cooperative with other boys and girls. Write his name. _____

USES OF "GUESS WHO" TECHNIQUE. Principals may point out the following uses for this technique:

1. The teacher gains information about peer opinion.
2. Student values, insights, and attitudes toward cooperation, responsibility, and social concern are revealed.
3. The value of the technique is greater with older students.

CAUTIONS AND LIMITATIONS. Four precautions that the supervising principal should emphasize are:

1. To avoid harm to an individual it is advisable to include only descriptions of positive, acceptable types of behavior.
2. Remember that personal standards influence choices.
3. Data gathered are subjective, and this must be considered when interpretation is made.
4. Student judgment may be influenced by recent associations with classmates. A temporary "falling out" with a friend would temper his choice.

How to Help the Staff Understand Students through the Interstaff Conference

Interstaff Conferences

Conferences with other staff members are extremely helpful in supplementing the teacher's understanding of children, and they are a good way to delve professionally into a student's problems. The most important type of conference is one with representatives from the classroom, health office, guidance, supervision, and administration. The participation in the conference would be a function of the nature of the problem. The results of the conference should be summarized and entered in the student's cumulative record.

A schedule of action for interstaff conferences in an Illinois school district follows:

- *Meeting 1*—Describe the plan for the series of meetings. Discuss the problem areas found in the school. Each participant should keep a written record of his findings. Each group or member of a group selects a student for study.
- *Meeting 2*—Discuss the problems chosen for study. State tentative hypotheses. Agree on initial data needed for studies. Bring any sample data that may prove useful.
- *Meeting 3*—Share initial data related to original plans, and agree on further data to be gathered.
- *Meeting 4*—Meeting 4 is initially the same as Meeting 3, in that data are shared and an agreement is reached as to what further data are needed. Share any individual problems that have arisen. The group may try to suggest helpful answers.
- *Meetings 5, 6, 7*—Share further data and suggest remedies for student adjustment. Include the action in written records being kept. Agree on further data needed concerning the student.
- *Meetings 8, 9, 10*—Use additional data to test remedial action. Agree on further data needed. Share any progress or setbacks in individual behavior with the group.
- *Meetings 11, 12, 13*—Report on some conclusions reached—the applications, implications, and suggestions from studies which the group has carried on.
- *Meeting 14*—Provide for continuous evaluation and plan for future action.

Roles in Interstaff Teamwork

By observing students at work and play, other members of the school staff may better understand them. Classified personnel also need to understand students' feelings, but they are seldom trained in this field. They must work with students in the office and on the grounds, and often they must work with a wider age span than does the teacher. Custodians, secretaries, and cafeteria workers often need help in understanding and working with students.

A friendly and interested feeling between adult and student benefits both. The supervisor may point out that the adult who is objective and sympathetic, and who shows sincere interest, can command a student's respect from the beginning; but preaching and moralizing will lose a student's attention almost immediately.

Tone of voice and facial expression may frighten a student before there has been any effective communication. A smile and quiet voice with secure sounding overtones help give a student a feeling of security and confidence.

Playground directors may sometimes watch student activities looking only for signs of trouble, instead of looking for positive behavior. Much real insight into the behavior of students is gained by watching them objectively at play while they are absorbed and unaware of the observation. Posture, activity, laughter, tears, and voice pitch are just a few factors that may indicate health problems or emotional strain that need further investigation. When a supervisor is aware of these factors he can enlist the aid of the teacher and playground director for some really purposeful observation.

THE SUPERVISING PRINCIPAL. The principal has overall responsibility for the guidance program within the school. Success of the program depends upon his leadership in determining the needs, as well as initiating means of meeting the needs. There is no phase of the guidance program with which he is not directly concerned. The principal functions as leader of the guidance staff in organizing, supervising, coordinating, and administering the program. A few of the individuals whose efforts he coordinates are caricatured in Figure 11–7.

FIGURE 11–7   Many Individuals May Contribute Valuable Information Based on Observation of the Student at Work and at Play.

The principal provides the leadership for the teachers in increasing their understanding of, and their capacity for, molding student behavior. He accomplishes this by setting a good example, by coordinating in-service educational activities, by suggestion, and by furnishing or recommending materials for individual student study. The principal also arranges placement in special classes or schools, helps improve school and parent relationships, and maintains contact with all referral agencies.

WHAT THE SUPERVISING PRINCIPAL CAN DO: FURTHER TECHNIQUES. Is it true, as some believe, that the greatest weakness of supervisors, as well as administrators, is their poor relationships with teachers? The best possible place to start in building an understanding of children is the development of the best possible relationships between the supervisor and the rest of the instructional staff:

1. *Teachers want supervisory leaders who create an informal atmosphere and who appreciate effective group participation.* This appreciation helps teachers place more emphasis on the cooperative clinical team approach to the diagnosis of student difficulties as a requisite for dealing with individual needs. Teachers sense the need for more assistance with

problems related to diagnosis, remediation, and evaluation in working with students. The supervisor's understanding helps.

2. *Often teachers are not sufficiently informed of effective ways and means of working with children.* Desirable supervisory assistance is democratic, provides suggestions, yet permits freedom of initiative, choice, and independence in carrying out suggestions. The supervisor who strives to understand teachers will use every contact, whether a casual comment in the hallway or a private supervisory conference, to build teacher confidence.

3. *The next step is to help the teacher understand himself and his roles as a teacher.* The supervisor is in a unique position to help the teacher adjust to the welter of expectations and demands which his teaching roles make of him. No one teacher can be expert and comfortable in every role that parents, students, the community, and the administration may expect of him; but, with help and support to ease tensions, he can discover where his real strengths lie. Having learned to understand his own experiences, he will then be better able to help students understand their reactions to the environment in which they live.

THE SUPERVISOR OF GUIDANCE. In school systems employing a supervisor of guidance, he is responsible for improving the operation of the individual and group guidance programs in each school. His duties are as follows:

1. He plans and supervises programs of help for individual students by:
   a) Cooperating with the staff in gathering information about students;
   b) Aiding in counseling;
   c) Conferring with school personnel on strengths and weaknesses of individual students and recommending adjustment in student placement where indicated;
   d) Helping with follow-up devices.
2. He plans and supervises the group guidance program by:
   a) Conferring with principals on learning trends as implied from performance on standardized tests;
   b) Conferring with teachers on strengths and weaknesses revealed through test results;

  c) Assisting principals and teachers regarding student placement, acceleration, retardation, and changes in grouping;

  d) Providing for individual needs through organization of special classes, and making recommendations for placement of students in these classes.

3. He assists in the construction, revision, and interpretation of:
  a) Report card forms;
  b) Cumulative record cards;
  c) Remedial reading record forms;
  d) Welfare cards;
  e) Authorization cards to administer group intelligence tests;
  f) Interschool transfer data cards.

4. He assists in research projects regarding:
  a) New tests and other techniques;
  b) Articulation between schools;
  c) Selection and appraisal of rapid learners;
  d) Study of potential "dropouts";
  e) Reporting to parents.

5. He plans and conducts in-service education, which includes:
  a) Training teachers to administer and interpret group tests;
  b) Orientation meetings of beginning teachers;
  c) Institutes in guidance and counseling;
  d) Guidance workshops;
  e) Faculty meetings.

THE SCHOOL COUNSELOR. The school counselor makes individual psychological studies of students who have special needs, for the purpose of helping these students to make a more satisfactory adjustment in school. The duties and responsibilities of the school counselor fall into two broad categories:

1. Direct service to students, teachers, principals, and parents by:
  a) Making psychological studies of students who are presenting problems of school achievement and personal adjustment;

    b) Administering individual psychological examinations to these students and assembling all data necessary to an understanding of their needs;

    c) Securing the necessary assistance from other resources of the school system and community agencies in making such studies;

    d) Interpreting the findings of these studies to principals, teachers, parents, and others directly concerned with the welfare of the individual student;

    e) Recommending a program for the adjustment of students as determined by studies;

    f) Continuing follow-up studies of students needing such help;

    g) Providing consultant service to principals, teachers, and parents concerning the needs of students.

2. Staff duties and responsibilities consist of:

    a) Assisting in integrating counseling activities with the activities of other staff members within the division to promote a coordinated educational program;

    b) Assisting in advancing the understanding of school personnel in the principles and recent research in the fields of mental hygiene and child growth and development;

    c) Assisting with organization and leadership of teacher in-service training activities in the area of individual study of children;

    d) Serving as speaker for school and community groups.

Increasingly, schools are obtaining specialists to help teachers understand and plan for students more adequately. These specialists, through diagnostic and therapeutic procedures, aid in student adjustment and educational planning. Maximum aid is given to teachers and students when efforts of the various specialists are coordinated within the school—when each special resource person is able to work as a member of a team.

FACULTY GUIDANCE COMMITTEE. Principals may profit from the help of a guidance advisory committee. This committee serves a dual purpose. First, the committee makes recommendations regarding the improvement of the guidance and counseling program. Second, questions may be referred to the guidance committee for reactions and recommendations. The chairman of the guidance committee can do much to support the principal and improve guidance services in the school.

THE CLINICAL TEAM. The clinical team approach is vital in obtaining adequate information about a student with special needs, in interpreting the findings, and in planning a course of action aimed at correcting deficiencies and building upon strengths.

THE SCHOOL NURSE AND PHYSICIAN. The student's health should be considered first. As guidance and counseling personnel study the student's personality development, his mental growth, and his attainments in basic learnings, cooperative planning with the school nurse and physician is imperative.

Through the school physician, nurse, and other related personnel, each school is given the medical service necessary to identify any defects which might impede the student's maximum development. Health personnel also are vitally interested in helping students to establish proper health habits. They work in this area not only through direct contact with students, but also through faculty discussions and through preparation of materials for teachers to use in the health education program.

EVALUATION AND RESEARCH. Guidance and counseling personnel work closely with those responsible for evaluation and research. In small school systems the counselors have the responsibility for planning the various evaluation programs in schools and for interpreting results to the administration, to the board of education, and to the general public. In larger systems a special evaluation and research section, which conducts research in various guidance areas including vocational guidance, is becoming more prevalent.

CHILD WELFARE AND ATTENDANCE PERSONNEL. Guidance workers work closely with child welfare attendance personnel. Welfare and attendance personnel are concerned with adjustment difficulties of students as manifested by irregular school attendance. Welfare and attendance personnel work usually with problems that may be manifested in school, but which are chiefly home- or community-centered, and they provide for referral to community agencies.

A WEAK LINK IN THE COUNSELING CHAIN. Follow-up after initial study and evaluation is often the weakest link in the counseling program. Programs are sometimes planned to help a student, but due to an overloaded staff the programs are not evaluated and replanned throughout the school career of the student involved. In some instances the student may no longer need any special guidance, but this information may not be recorded for future reference. Two forms utilized by one school system for referrals and reports in this area are included as Figures 11–8 and 11–9.

Since not all schools have the advantage of a full-time nurse and psychologist, the principal must be able to aid the classroom teacher toward the best possible working relationships with parents and students.

The principal, as the leader in the school, can help all persons involved realize that improvement takes time and patience, as well as effort.

Success, the Teacher, and the Guidance Program

The success of the individual teacher depends largely upon assistance given him by others in the school, especially the technical assistance of the supervisor and the administrative assistance of the principal.

Certainly, the principal has overall responsibility for the guidance program within his school. Success of the guidance program depends upon the leadership of the principal in determining needs as well as in initiating means of meeting the needs. There is no phase of the guidance program with which the principal is not directly concerned. The supervising principal functions as leader of the guidance staff in organizing, supervising, coordinating, and administering the program. It is, however, a teacher sensitive to the needs of the students who is the foundation upon which any good guidance program is built. The teacher at all levels should:

1. Understand and carry out the guidance policies and procedures within the facilities of the school.

FIGURE 11–8   Request for Study

(Name of School District)

Date _____

1. Identifying information:
    (to be obtained by school employee)

    Name _____

    Age _____ Birthdate _____ Grade _____

    Address _____ Phone _____
                 Street   City   Zone

    School _____ Phone _____

    Father _____ Age _____
                       Name

    Mother _____ Age _____
                       Name

    Other Children: _____   _____

    _____   _____

2. Problem for which you wish child examined: _____

3. Description of school behavior: _____
    (Teachers, principals, counselors, etc.)

4. Record of scholastic capacity and educational achievement:
    (Copy latest test data from cumulative card)

    Date _____ Grade _____ Test_____

    Ch. Age _____ Ment. Age_____ Index_____

    XA—GP _____ Reading GP—Voc. _____

                              —Comp. _____

                         Arith. GP—Reas. _____

                         Fund._____

    Lang. GP_____ Spell. GP_____

5a. Any health data you have: _____

  b. Please list other clinics, hospitals, agencies, doctors, etc. to whom child
     and family are known: _____

6. Any social or family data you may already have: _____
    (Home calls and social history not essential.)

7. Signature of Principal_____

    Name of person who
    conferred with parent
    about referral_____

    Name of others concerned with child's problem:

    _____   _____

FIGURE 11–9   Consent Slip

Date _____

This consent will authorize the School Guidance Center to carry out such physical, psychological, psychiatric, laboratory, and other examinations and treatments for my_____ , _____
                                          Relation   Name of Child

as may be deemed advisable by the School Guidance Center.

_____
                                                                      Parent or Legal Guardian

---

2. Provide classroom atmosphere which is conducive to guidance.
3. Help each student develop a sense of belonging.
4. Know each student's strengths and weaknesses and accept him as a person.
5. Perceive significant attitudes, abilities, behavior, and health of students; and in light of these findings provide for individual needs.
6. Provide group and individual guidance opportunities in the classroom.
7. Guide each student in developing good study habits.
8. Provide opportunities for continuous evaluation and appraisal of student growth and achievement in skills and attitudes.
9. Assist students to understand and accept attitudes and habits of good citizenship.
10. Teach basic concepts of moral and spiritual values.
11. Obtain pertinent information and records that have permanent value.
12. Select carefully, from available sources, that information which can be used for effective guidance.
13. Adapt instruction to the range of individual differences.
14. Attempt to work out problems of student adjustment from the point of view that guidance is based upon friendliness, mutual respect, and understanding.
15. Encourage a balance of varied experiences in curricular and extracurricular fields.
16. Make suitable referrals of individuals who need additional help or study, and contribute pertinent information.
17. Participate in case studies and conferences concerning students.

18. Follow up recommendations for improving student adjustment.
19. Participate in evaluation of school and district guidance programs.
20. Accept responsibility for professional growth.

Particularly at the *elementary school* level, the teacher should:

1. Assist students in coping with the transition from home to school.
2. Know the students' parents and maintain a close relationship with them.
3. Adapt instruction to the range of individual differences through grouping and adjustment of method and curriculum within the class.
4. Notify and confer periodically with parents on student achievement and social growth.
5. Prepare students for transfer to the secondary school.

Criteria for the Study of an Individual Student by the Teacher

The supervising principal should help teachers understand the characteristics of the age groups with which they are to work. Helping teachers to realize the importance of listing to students and watching them purposefully is another important responsibility of the supervisor.

The supervising principal should provide data and assistance so that a teacher may study and weigh carefully the many factors involved before planning a program of adjustment for the student. The effectiveness of a teacher in classroom situations often is determined by his acquaintance with the developmental history of each student.

Perhaps the principal's most important role in this area is to insure that each staff member is familiar with the many criteria for the individual study of a student. The supervisor should stress the following:

1. *Observation.* The teacher watches for activities where the student shows the most interest and response, has the most success, or shows the most fatigue or boredom.
2. *Health.* Cumulative health records that have been kept up-to-date are valuable. Responses to food, amount of activity shown in the classroom and on the playground, nail-biting, and frequent tardiness are other signs for the teacher to note.

3. *Social Relationship*. The careful use of a sociogram may show situations where a student lacks confidence or security.
4. *Time-sampling observation*. The teacher may observe a certain student for a week at preplanned intervals in the school day and record his observations. A period of five minutes at nine o'clock, another five minutes at ten-thirty, and another five minutes after lunch may give a broad and realistic picture of a student's normal behavior.
5. *Particular situation observation*. The teacher may observe and record the different responses of several students in a special situation. This method helps the teacher plan for individual and group needs.
6. *Interests*. A questionnaire concerning daily activities, hobbies, family relationships, or any number of other things may help the teacher plan his program. In one situation the students kept a diary, noting daily activities, books they had read, satisfactory situations and experiences, and their successes or failures. The teacher involved gained valuable information about each student's daily thinking through this method of observation.
7. *Achievement*. Test achievement does not always give a clear picture of a student's ability or daily achievement. Samples of the student's work in handwriting, arithmetic, art, and all other areas, taken at regular intervals, show any weaknesses as well as growth and improvement. The testing program per se is considered in a later section of this chapter.

OBSERVATION BY THE PARENT. For additional data to add to the teacher's methods of observation, the health record, the cumulative record, and an observation form for parents may be employed. Parents who are eager to help their children often welcome this personal participation. A copy of a parent observation form used in a midwest school system is included as Figure 11–10.

CLASSROOM COUNSELOR. It is important that the teacher know how to use himself in the role of classroom counselor in order to earn the student's respect and to facilitate his adjustment to the classroom environment. The principal should discuss this role at staff meetings. Guidance personnel and specialist-consultants from the nearby university can be called in for further

FIGURE 11–10   Parent Observation Form

Student's Name_____

PARENT'S OBSERVATIONS

1. Are there any health problems that may be related to the child's behavior?

2. How does he get along with his brothers and sisters? With children in the neighborhood?

3. What are the child's interests and abilities?

4. What forms of discipline have been used?
   How does he respond?

5. For what is he usually punished?
   For what is he praised?

6. What have you found to be the most satisfactory ways of helping your child with his problems?

7. How does he act when he succeeds?

8. How does he act when he fails?

9. What does he like to do in his spare time?

10. Do you approve of his friends?

11. Does he like school?

12. What jobs does the child have around the home?
    What does he do best?
    What is the most difficult for him?

13. What do you consider to be the child's chief problem, and what do you believe is the cause?

Signature _____

Date _____

assistance. Extension or university classes should be taken to enrich the teacher's background.

How to Help Teachers Understand Students Through Cumulative Records

Cumulative records may be defined as permanent records of pupil progress and adjustment in school. A cumulative record may contain the following information:

1. Identification and personal data
2. School history
3. Family and home data
4. Educational and mental development
5. Emotional development and attitudes
6. Social adjustment and attitudes
7. Health and physical development
8. School experiences and plans
9. Special activities and interests
10. References to other sources of information

Cumulative records: (1) serve as a basic student guidance tool for teachers, counselors, specialist-consultants, and administrators; (2) provide assistance in planning school policy and curriculum; (3) furnish a basis for planning student programs; and (4) serve as a means for identifying student differences and group tendencies.

Suggestions for Cumulative Records

Comments should assist a teacher in understanding the student and his needs. They should convey usable, accurate information. They should not be a record of the teacher's emotional reactions.

Comments should be as objective and specific as possible. Instead of using comments such as "improving" or "good worker," the subjects or character traits in which the student shows or needs improvement should be indicated.

Criteria for determining location of files which the supervising principal should consider are:

1. Safety and security of the records;
2. Accessibility of records to all staff members;
3. Convenience of location to those persons using them frequently;
4. Available facilities.

CUMULATIVE RECORDS MAY BE TRANSFERRED AND MAY BE DUPLICATED. Cumulative records generally may be transferred to another public school, public agency, private school, or private agency when a student transfers to such agency. A record of the pupil enrollment and scholarship should be retained by the school system from which he has transferred. The following information should be kept:

1. Name of student
2. Date of birth, if student is a minor
3. Method of verification of date of birth of student being admitted to kindergarten or first grade
4. Place of birth
5. Name and address of parents or guardian, if student is a minor
6. Entering and leaving date for each school year, and for any summer or other extra session

CUMULATIVE RECORDS ARE CONFIDENTIAL DATA IN MOST STATES. Giving out any personal information concerning students in grade twelve or below, except to designated persons, is prohibited in most states, for such records constitute privileged communications. Persons to whom personal information *may be given*:

1. Parent or guardian of student, or person designated by parent or guardian in writing;
2. Officer or employee of a public, private, or parochial school where student attends, has attended, or intends to enroll;
3. Governmental officer or employee seeking information in the course of his duties;

4. Guidance or welfare agency officer or employee to whom student is going for assistance;
5. Employer or potential employer of student.

CHARACTERISTICS OF AN EFFECTIVE CUMULATIVE RECORD SYSTEM. An effective cumulative record system:

1. Reflects objectives of educational program.
2. Shows trends in student's development.
3. Contains information meaningful to teachers in understandable form.
4. Furnishes data for all students, not for problem cases only.
5. Consists of items significant in all-around development of the student.
6. Presents information from year to year in consistent and comparable form.
7. Involves simple standardized method of recording.
8. Is readily filed and used—a folder is recommended.
9. Lends itself to accurate and easy reproduction for teacher use and for other schools.

Case Studies

How to Help the Teacher Construct and Interpret the Case Study

A case study of a student is designed to give a rather complete cross-section of his development at a given time, and should be used in conjunction with other types of information available. It might result from the coordinated needs and efforts of a number of staff members, such as the nurse, the psychologist, the teacher, and the principal.

One variation on the case study, which may be available in some situations, is the school-community conference which involves more than school personnel. For instance, Detroit evolved a "school-community behavior project" in which a school action team consisting of a principal, one or more teachers, a visiting teacher, an attendance officer, and a nurse worked cooperatively with consultants from a wide range of community agencies,

both public and private. The team attacked the problem of the early identification and treatment of delinquent or pre-delinquent behavior.[8]

Less ambitious approaches are available in other communities where a
relatively spontaneous conference of the members of agencies working with
a child can achieve greater understanding and work together to produce
results more rewarding to all concerned.

Types of Case Studies

There are, generally speaking, two kinds of case studies. One is the concentrated study of an individual student about whom more information is
needed before a plan attempting to solve a particular problem regarding
that student can be put into effect. The other is a less concentrated study of
a student, usually within the so-called normal ranges, for the purpose of
learning more about children and their psychological structuring in general,
so that the teacher may make practical application of the basic principles
gleaned from the study.

The first study, the type most commonly encountered, begins when a
teacher feels inadequate in dealing with a student. Aware that all is not
well with this student, the teacher records incidents of his behavior, checks
the cumulative records, obtains family data, and then presents his case to
the principal or counselor for guidance and opinion. Upon approval the case
is referred to the school psychologist, who should be trained in handling the
more extreme cases. The school nurse is asked to conduct a health check to
see if there are any outstanding physical factors involved in the case. The
school psychometrist tests the student and also may interview the student's
parents, teachers, and other school personnel.

It may be best to recommend halting the study at this point, with suggestions for the teacher, or to continue the study by calling for a case conference. This conference would involve the principal, the counselor, the

[8]Detroit Commission on Children and Youth, "Handbook for Use in the Detroit School-
Community Behavior Project," Prepared cooperatively by the Detroit Board of Education and the Detroit Commission on Children and Youth, revised September, 1969,
p. 2. Mimeographed. R. L. Thisdell, Principal Administrative Assistant, Management
Services Division, Los Angeles Police Department, stated, "It is my personal opinion
that such early identification and treament is extremely important." (Los Angeles,
California, September 21, 1970.)

psychologist, the student's teacher, and others as needed (i.e., the parents, assistant principal, nurse, and physician).

Upon completion of the case conference the recommendation may be given that the need has been satisfied and the study may be terminated, or, that it is necessary to continue with further studying, testing, and conferring. The conferees will suggest actions to pursue in the classroom with this particular student. A follow-up conference always should be set to evaluate the results.

The case study may be brief or it may span several years, even to the extent of lasting for the student's entire school life. Symptoms which may indicate that a case study is necessary are:

1. Marked contrasts and inconsistencies in the student's total life pattern;
2. Sudden changes, shifts, and reversals in his established patterns of behavior;
3. Evidence of undeveloped or wasted resources;
4. Continued evidence of dissatisfaction with the student's adjustment in school, either on the part of the student or of his parents.

Types of problems calling for a referral or further testing are:

1. Group test scores and other data which indicate the possibility of mental retardation;
2. Social immaturity and a lack of readiness for the academic learning in kindergarten and the primary grades;
3. Referral for remedial reading;
4. Evaluation as a gifted child;
5. Level of achievement inconsistent with scores on mental development tests;
6. Factors indicating the child may benefit by retention in his grade;
7. Information needed to determine the proper grade placement of the student;
8. Situations calling for a more extensive study of the student's intellectual functioning.

The second type of case study is not the study of one particular student for his benefit as much as it is for the benefit of the class as a whole through the study of one student. This plan is best initiated with a group of teachers who will follow the study for one or two years.

By meeting as a child-study group from time to time they can compare notes and ideas, make suggestions, and contribute to each other's work. This plan calls for the selection of a student to be used as the subject of the study. Usually a student classified as being within the normal regions is selected, so that the learning gleaned from studying him may be applied to as many children as possible. Data regarding this student are collected and organized. Many sources of information are tapped; observations are made in the room, on the playground, and at lunch; excerpts of his products, such as stories and paintings, are studied; visits are made to the home; and conferences are held with his former teachers and the custodians. These data are organized into behavioral patterns. The teachers base some of their actions upon this information and evaluate the results.

At the end of a certain period of time the study is summarized and evaluated. By conscientiously following this study plan the teachers should become aware of the general behavioral patterns in students and be better able to understand and cope with the individual student, setting the classroom environment to more fully meet student needs. An example of a psychological referral is included as Figure 11–11. Information which should be covered by case studies is included as Supplement B to this chapter. Information pertaining to specifics on how to help the teacher in testing, test interpretation, statistical concepts and assigning marks is included as Supplement A to this chapter.[9]

Follow-Up Parent Conference

No case study would be complete without a parent conference. This might well be the parent conference which is held as a part of reporting to parents on student progress in many school systems, but it would more likely be an additional conference. It could occur at school; it would afford even greater insight if it could be held in the home. Although some protest that teachers who visit the homes of the less economically privileged make the parents

[9]The authors are indebted to Shirley R. Marks for her contribution to this and other chapters.

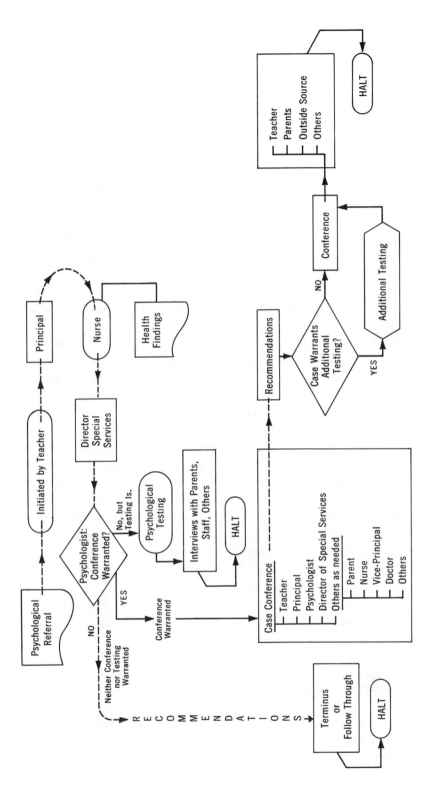

FIGURE 11–11 An Example of a Psychological Referral.

feel self-conscious and ill at ease, many parents have real difficulty feeling comfortable at school.

Apart from the parents' feelings, a visit to the home deepens the teacher's understanding of a given child in many ways—some of them subliminal, some rather obvious. The teacher may find that he is less impatient and more sympathetic when the child forgets his lunch or misses the bus, knowing that there may not have been enough food in the house for a packed lunch or that the child had to help his ailing mother get smaller children ready for school.

The teacher may be able to see a relationship between the relative position the student holds in the family constellation and the kind of role he plays at school. For some children, especially those showing signs of "educaphobia," the visit to the home may have the immediate value of bridging the gap between home and school.

If a teacher is expected to make a home visit, the time for this visit should come out of the assigned school day. Ways to permit teachers to be off campus during the school day are numerous, two of the most common and successful being the employment of a substitute teacher or the utilization of the vice-principal to cover the teacher's classes. Such home visits must, of necessity, be few and far between, and utilized *only* in special cases in conjunction with intensive case studies. The more routine type of home visit should be handled by the counselor, nurse, or administrator.

The supervising principal should help the staff to become aware of the potential of case studies—their purposes, procedures to follow in utilizing them, and what to expect in the way of results. The staff that is well acquainted with the case study program will profit accordingly.

How to Supervise the Assignment of a Student to a Classroom

The assignment of a student to a classroom can best be determined by the principal and teacher(s), working together in harmony and considering all factors involved for the benefit of the student. Correct placement can result in better adjustment.

Although the initial placement of the student is the responsibility of the principal, he should consult with the teacher. The specialist-consultant should aid in the evaluation of the placement from a staff standpoint *only*. Once the student has been placed, the specialist-consultant may render additional help. He can answer such questions as where the student should sit, and in which reading group he should be placed.

The students are grouped within the class at various times for instruction in reading, mathematics, singing activities, English, spelling, physical education, and committee and group work. With careful thought, the teacher places the student in order to overcome shyness, to improve his study habits and skills, to develop self-confidence, to dissolve friction between classmates, to bring the isolate into the group, to remove a negative influence from a follower, to achieve maximum growth in the subject matter area. The teacher whom the supervising principal helps to see the value of correct placement will find himself in a more enjoyable teaching situation than his counterpart who, from apathy or lack of knowledge, does not give it much thought.

Although most placements are the result of the teacher's work once the student has been admitted to the classroom, changes in school-system policy can effect a change from without. Recently the board of education in one school system decided to accelerate the mathematics instructional program. This policy necessitated the creation of an accelerated group starting with the third and fourth grades. Placing the student in this group was accomplished through the coordination of the director of special services, the principal, the specialist-consultant, and the teacher.

There should be a systematic follow-up of all placement to determine:

1. If the educational program is meeting the needs of individual students;
2. If the students are achieving at an optimum rate;
3. If there is adequate articulation so the students are oriented for new situations and for the next grade level.

Conclusions

It might be concluded that there are implications for supervisory leadership in encouraging teachers to make every effort to try to do the best they know how, whether or not it is identical with approaches ordinarily used by the principal. The enlightened principal will want each teacher to use his imagination and resourcefulness in working with students; he will not want to bind him to his own way of thinking. If he is to work with a staff which continuously strives to understand students, he will have to set the example by using every opportunity to develop his own understandings, as well as those of the teachers.

The teacher's understanding of students will be enhanced in an atmosphere of professional democracy. It will be stifled in a situation bordering upon an empire, where administrative comfort is the fountainhead of educational dynamics.

The supervising principal can help the staff to better understand students by setting the pace with his own attitude and activities. The studies he encourages, the training he approves, the creative ideas to which he is receptive, can mean the difference between personnel that merely exist and personnel that work with that extra spark because they know their work is meaningful, is functional, and is appreciated.

The teacher who gives himself a chance, and makes that extra effort to do a little better and to know a little more, and the supervisor who encourages and helps him, both by word and example, will make a teaching team that will be hard to beat.

DO

1. See to it that teachers are provided with accessible files of pertinent, objective information about students.
2. Encourage satisfactory home-teacher relations as a means of teachers understanding students.
3. Provide opportunities for teachers to observe students in the cafeteria, in assemblies, on the playground, and in cocurricular activities.
4. Encourage teachers to become better acquainted with parents and to take an active interest in association and community activities.
5. Encourage teachers to participate in local service organizations and community clubs in order to help teachers understand the demands being placed upon students by the local community.
6. Plan meetings which are designed to stimulate teacher growth in de-

veloping aims, plans, methods, and procedures for learning about student needs, interests, and abilities.

7. Help teachers consider the many patterns of student growth in the formulation of promotional policies.

8. Discuss with teachers the common problems of group standards, conduct, and discipline as they relate to the developing nature of the student.

9. Set up panels of students for service clubs, parent associations, and others to discuss problems requiring understanding from both parents and teachers.

10. Resolve problems, needs, and frustrations by encouraging teacher-supervisor cooperation in a case study which leads to conferences with both parents and students.

11. Encourage teachers to determine personality and character traits of students by means of observation, autobiographies, diaries, and interviews with previous teachers.

12. Encourage the librarian to assemble professional reading matter on child growth and development.

13. Encourage the school nurse to report to the teacher findings from home visits and examinations, and to provide the teacher with literature pertinent to the development of a sound health program for students.

14. Work with the psychologist or specialist-consultant in planning meetings for teachers in order to assist them in observing students and in writing objective anecdotal records.

15. Request the instructional technology and programmed materials supervisor to obtain films on student behavior, and use his services in discussions with teachers.

16. Meet with each teacher to emphasize the need for planning and organizing materials; one must attempt to keep a problem from developing by using a preventive method.

17. Set up a classroom observation appointment; see the problem in action.

18. Make a conference appointment with the teacher, at his convenience.

19. During the conference help the teacher to see, if he has a classroom control problem, that his problem of classroom control is not unique—that most teachers share in it in varying degrees.

20. Ask the teacher how he feels about his plans and organization, whether he feels they are adequate, and what suggestions he might have for improvement.
21. Point out the need for a variety of methods (unit teaching, inquiry approach, in-depth studies).
22. Make available media materials, including records, video and audio tapes, overhead projectors, opaque projectors, models, exhibits, programmed material, picture cards, microfilm, motion pictures, and so forth.
23. Recommend involvement of students in planning and evaluation.
24. Suggest books and articles which may give further guidance in planning and organizing material.
25. Suggest appropriate in-service education.

DON'T

1. *Require* teachers to employ such techniques as sociograms and sociodrama.
2. Monopolize any conferences with the teacher.
3. Point out a teacher in the same building as an ideal to follow.
4. Remind the teacher that educational institutions are like industry and must be run by those in control.

Supervisory Problems   In Basket

Problem 1

The problem develops in a public grade-school classroom. The school district is located in a rural, middle-middle class socioeconomic area. The teachers in this school are traditional in their approach to classroom control. The teacher involved in this problem, Miss Smith, is a new teacher with no teaching experience. She is burdened with an exceptionally large third-grade class of thirty-three students. Miss Smith's first month of teaching has been quite successful with the exception of one student, George, who has created continuous disturbances.

Miss Smith has tried a number of approaches in attempting to cope with George's disturbing influence upon the class. She first tried to control George by verbally reprimanding him for his objectionable behavior, but this seemed to have no effect on him. Next she attempted to embarrass George by having the class stare at him whenever he said something undesirable, but still met with no success. Miss Smith asked the other teachers in the building for suggestions. They suggested that Miss Smith require George to stay in after school, and also that she could contact George's parents concerning this problem. Still no solution was achieved.

Miss Smith finally turned to her supervising principal for help. She explained the approaches that had been tried in attempting to cope with George's obnoxious behavior and requested the principal's assistance. What suggestions might the principal give Miss Smith?

Problem 2

The problem develops in a junior high-school which has an enrollment of 300, with approximately 25 percent of these students being Spanish-American. Several black students also are enrolled.

Mary has had the reputation of being a "problem" since her grade-school days. When she entered junior high-school her attitude was extremely negative and she was sent to the principal's office consistently for disciplinary reasons. Mary usually responded by saying that she was being "picked on" because she was of Spanish-American descent.

This student was below average in ability. Her parents were fairly interested in helping her become a better citizen of the school. The father was very strict and often used physical force while disciplining her. What corrective procedures might a supervisor suggest? What should he do?

Selected Bibliography

Books

Brim, Orville G., Jr. *Education for Child Rearing.* New York: Russell Sage Foundation, 1959.

Corcoran, Sister Mary Jerome. *The Catholic Elementary School Principal.* Milwaukee: The Bruce Publishing Company, 1961.

Cunningham, Ruth. *Understanding Group Behavior of Boys and Girls.* New York: Columbia University Press, 1951.

Cutt, N. E., and Nicholas Moseley. *Teaching the Disorderly Pupil.* New York: Longmans, Green and Company, Inc., 1957.

Driscoll, Gertrude P. *Child Guidance in the Classroom.* New York: Bureau of Publications, Teachers College, Columbia University, 1955.

Elkin, Frederick. *The Child and Society: The Process of Socialization.* New York: Random House, Inc., 1960.

Elsbree, Willard S., and Harold J. McNally. *Elementary School Administration and Supervision.* New York: American Book Company, 1951.

Fenlason, Anne. *Essentials in Interviewing.* New York: Harper and Brothers, 1952.

Frank, Mary and Lawrence K. *Your Adolescent at Home and in School.* New York: The Viking Press, Inc., 1956.

Garrett, Henry E. *Statistics in Psychology and Education.* 5th ed. London: Longmans, Green and Company, 1958.

Grieder, Calvin, and William E. Rosenstengel. *Public School Administration.* New York: The Ronald Press Company, 1954.

Gruenberg, Sidonie M., and the Staff of the Child Study Association of America. *Our Children Today.* New York: The Viking Press, Inc., 1952.

Guilford, J. P. *Fundamental Statistics in Psychology and Education.* New York: McGraw-Hill Book Company, Inc., 1956.

———, and William B. Michael. *Intermediate Statistical Exercises.* New York: McGraw-Hill Book Company, Inc., 1957.

Hatch, Raymond H. *Guidance Service.* Dubuque, Iowa: William C. Brown Company, 1951.

Hicks, Hanne J. *Administrative Leadership in the Elementary School.* New York: The Ronald Press Company, 1956.

Hollingshead, August, and Frederick Redlick. *Social Class and Mental Illness.* New York: John Wiley & Sons, Inc., 1958.

Jacobson, Paul B., William C. Reavis, and James D. Logsdon. *The Effective School Principal.* Englewood Cliffs, New Jersey: Prentice-Hall, Inc., 1954.

Jersild, Arthur T. *When Teachers Face Themselves*. New York: Bureau of Publications, Teachers College, Columbia University, 1955.

Kyte, George C. The Principal at Work. Rev. ed. Boston: Ginn and Company, 1953.

McCandless, Boyd R. *Children and Adolescents*. New York: Holt, Rinehart, Winston, Publishers, 1961.

McDonald, Blanche. *Successful Classroom Control*. Boston: D. C. Heath and Company, 1963.

Menninger, William C. *Self-Understanding: A First Step to Understanding Children*. Chicago: Science Research Associates, Inc., 1952.

Moustakas, Clark E. *The Teacher and the Child: Personal Interaction in the Classroom*. New York: McGraw-Hill Book Company, 1956.

Neisser, Edith G., and the Staff of the Association for Family Living. *How to Live with Children*. Chicago: Science Research Associates, Inc., 1950.

Otto, Henry J. *Elementary School Organization and Administration*. New York: Appleton-Century-Crofts, 1964.

Pearman, Jean, and Albert Burrows. *Social Services in the Schools*. Washington, D.C.: Public Affairs Press, 1965.

Prescott, Daniel A. *The Child in the Educative Process*. New York: McGraw-Hill Book Company, 1957.

Rasey, Marie, and J. W. Menge. *What We Learn from Children*. New York: Harper and Brothers, 1956.

Reavis, William C. *Administering the Elementary School*. Englewood Cliffs, New Jersey: Prentice-Hall, Inc., 1953.

Reinoehl, Charles Myron, and Frey Ayer. *Classroom Administration and Pupil Adjustment*. New York: Appleton-Century-Crofts, 1940.

Ruch, Floyd L. *Elementary Statistics in Psychology and Education*. Columbia, Missouri: Lucas Brothers, 1957.

Selye, Hans. *The Stress of Life*. New York: McGraw-Hill Book Company, 1956.

Slavson, S. R. *An Introduction to Group Therapy*. New York: International Universities Press, Inc., 1943.

Smith, Henry P., and Emerald V. Dechant. *Psychology in Teaching Reading*. Englewood Cliffs, New Jersey: Prentice-Hall, Inc., 1961.

Stoops, Emery (ed.). *Guidance Services: Organization and Administration*. New York: McGraw-Hill Book Company, 1959.

Sullivan, H. S. *The Interpersonal Theory of Psychiatry*. New York: W. W. Norton & Company, Inc., 1953.

Sylvester, Robert. *Common Sense in Classroom Relations*. West Nyack, New York: Parker Publishing Company, 1968.

Thorpe, Louis P., and Allen M. Schmuller. *Contemporary Theories of Learning*. New York: The Ronald Press Company, 1954.

White, Verna. *Studying the Individual Pupil*. New York: Harper and Brothers, 1958.

Periodicals

Adams, John C. "Teaching the Problem Child in Your Class." *Education* LXXXI (September 1961): 46–49.

Adlerblum, Evelyn D. "Social Differences among Children." *Childhood Education* XXXII (January 1956): 214–218.

Baxter, Lindley C. "What Made Johnny Run?" *The Journal of Education* CXXXIII (January 1950): 19–21.

Bradfield, Luther F. "Elementary School Teachers: Their Problems and Supervisory Assistance." *Educational Administration and Supervision* XLV (March 1959): 102–106.

Dobbs, Harrison. "Working Together for Troubled Children and Youth." *Peabody Journal of Education* (September 1958): 73–83.

Harper, Louise E., and Benjamin Wright. "Dealing with Emotional Problems in the Classroom." *Elementary School Journal LXIII* (March 1958): 316–325.

Leton, D. A. "A New Frontier in Special Education." *Education* LXXX (February 1960): 349–353.

Mathias, David. "Parent-Teacher Conferences: There *Is* a Better Way." *The Grade Teacher* LXXXV (October 1967): 55–57.

Michael-Smith, Harold. "It Takes Self-Understanding." *National Education Association Journal* XLIX (April 1960): 37–40.

Prescott, D. A. "Role of Supervisor in Reducing Tensions." *California Journal of Elementary Education* XX (November 1951): 87–97.

Smitter, Faith. "Teachers' Beliefs Regarding Control of Behavior." *California Journal of Elementary Education* XXVII (August 1958): 11–15.

Vincent, Nicholas M. P., and Helen L. Merrill. "Effective Classroom Motivation." *Peabody Journal of Education* XXXVIII (July 1960): 10–13.

West, James T. "We Found a Better Way to Have Parent-Teacher Conferences." *The Instructor* LXXVI (October 1966): 43–45.

Williams, Lois, and Sybil Richardson. "Methods of Control Teachers Find Most Effective." *California Journal of Elementary Education* XXVII (August 1958): 12–16.

Other Sources

Association for Supervision and Curriculum Development. *Growing Up in an Anxious Age*. Washington, D.C.: National Education Association, 1952.

————. *Forces Affecting American Education.* Washington, D.C.: National Education Association, 1953.

Bieker, Helen. "Using Anecdotal Records to Know the Child," *Fostering Mental Health in Our Schools.* 1950 Yearbook, Association for Supervision and Curriculum Development. Washington, D.C.: National Education Association, 1950.

California School Board Association of the California Teachers Association. *Sample Personnel Policies.* Third Progress Report, Joint Committee on Personnel. San Francisco: The Association, October 1954.

Detroit Commission on Children and Youth. "Handbook for Use in the Detroit School-Community Behavior Project." Prepared cooperatively by the Detroit Board of Education and the Detroit Commission on Children and Youth. Revised September, 1969. Mimeographed.

Driscoll, Gertrude P. *How to Study the Behavior of Children.* Edited by Hollis L. Caswell. No. 2 of "Practical Suggestions for Teaching." New York: Bureau of Publications, Teachers College, Columbia University, 1951.

Henry, William E. "The Child Tells about Himself through His Creative Products." *Fostering Mental Health in Our Schools.* 1950 Yearbook, Association for Supervision and Curriculum Development. Washington, D.C.: National Education Association, 1950.

Jennings, Helen Hall. "Sociodrama as Educative Process." *Fostering Mental Health in Our Schools.* 1950 Yearbook, Association for Supervision and Curriculum Development. Washington, D.C.: National Education Association, 1950.

————. "Sociometric Grouping in Relation to Child Development." *Fostering Mental Health in Our Schools.* 1950 Yearbook, Association for Supervision and Curriculum Development. Washington, D.C.: National Education Association, 1950.

Los Angeles City Health Department. Printed Listing of Communicable Diseases, Issued July 1956.

Los Angeles County Superintendent of Schools. *Appreciation Curriculum Supplement: The Arts.* Los Angeles: Office of the Los Angeles County Superintendent of Schools, June 1957.

Stoops, Emery, and John Dunworth. *Classroom Discipline.* 3d ed. Los Angeles: California Teachers Association, Southern Section, 1958.

Taba, Hilda, and Deborah Elkins. *With Focus on Home Relations.* Washington, D.C.: American Council on Education, 1950.

Willcutt, Gladys. "Informal Talks with Children and Parents." *Fostering Mental Health in Our Schools.* 1950 Yearbook, Association for Supervision and Curriculum Development. Washington, D.C.: National Education Association, 1950.

Applied Educational Psychology for the Supervisor: Growing, Learning, and Testing

Society in America is particularly conscious of children, and children differ from each other in a variety of ways. This chapter supplement presents an outline of applied educational psychology for the supervisor, with special attention to the principles of growth and development and the psychology of the learning process for supervisors; how to help the teacher in testing; assigning marks; and understanding statistical measures; and a look at the future.

Principles of Growth and Development for the Supervisor

Studying Individual Development

THE INTUITIVE UNDERSTANDING OF CHILDREN. Any firsthand dealings with children have a concrete quality. It therefore is vital that those who have dealings with them understand children as children. The study of how children behave and how this behavior differs from that of adults might well be called the psychology of childhood, as opposed to psychology of adulthood. There is additionally the psychology of development, which examines the process of becoming mature, the influences of the child's environment, his personality, and his potentials.

INTUITIVE UNDERSTANDING AS OPPOSED TO SCIENCE. The reason that children seem so inconsistent to the adult observer is that he is likely to interpret their behavior from an adult point of view. The child's behavior may therefore, at times, make no sense at all. To understand children, there is no substitute for direct experience. We must develop some explanation of child behavior that goes beyond intuitive understanding if we are to effectively communicate our understanding and account for those aspects of behavior which are beyond the present understanding of our wisest parents and teachers.

If our understanding of behavior is completely intuitive, we shall have difficulties in communicating this understanding. Our explanations may tend to be in the form of analogies and metaphors. If we speak of behavior in terms of objective detachment instead of in analogies and metaphors, the concepts derived will be useful in explaining a variety of child behavior. These concepts may be testable.

The difference between intuitive understanding and a scientific explanation is, therefore, that a scientific explanation permits behavior to be observed or deduced logically. The explanation applies to a wide range of child behavior. Superficially, the range does not resemble the original incident, while an intuitive understanding is more limited to actual incidents, although intuition is also somewhat generalizable to some new situations. The most important difference between an intuitive understanding and a scientific explanation of child behavior is that the latter may be tested and may be applied to further hypotheses, suggesting further areas of research.

Major Concepts of Growth and Development

All members of the professional staff should know and understand certain basic factors about human growth and development. In human development there are four areas that are always to be considered in understanding the growth and development of the child: physical, intellectual, emotional, and social. Each of these areas of development in the child follows a schedule from birth until death.

On the biological or physical level this cycle is easily seen when the child first sits up, then crawls before walking, and so on. There are certain tasks at each level that must be mastered, so that the tasks at the next level can be mastered. Where development is too deviant or uneven, certain problems arise. Every developmental task may pose a problem for some children. Some children spend more time on one phase of development than do others. For example, in the development of motor skills, research has shown that some children never crawl; they progress immediately from the standing stage to the walking stage. Others will spend a long time in the crawling stage, while some will crawl for only a short period of time. Provision for, and recognition of, these differences by line, staff, and instructional personnel is imperative.

An example of misunderstanding in this area would be the practices of some educators in the past that were based upon the finding that "large" muscles develop and are usually controlled before "smaller" muscles. These well-meaning individuals gave children extremely thick pencils and crayons of grotesque proportions, in the belief that the muscles of the hand and fingers were "small" muscles and were not sufficiently developed to control smaller objects. Actually, these finger and hand muscles, both extensors and flexors, are relatively large muscles and are sufficiently well coordinated to permit the efficient use of normal-sized crayons and pencils in even the lowest grades.

Such research findings, and their educational implications, should be evaluated continuously by supervisory personnel. Channels for communications concerning this topic must be kept open and active.

Major concepts relating to growth and development, which can help teachers in working with individuals and groups, are:

1. Growth is determined by capacity and experience.
2. There is a continuous, predictable pattern of growth even though any student may be accelerated or retarded within this pattern.
3. Growth or development follows a sequential order, and students are not likely to skip a stage of growth.
4. All aspects of growth are interrelated.
5. Growth creates needs. All students have certain basic needs even though the intensity of the needs will vary.
6. Growth proceeds at different rates.

Table Supp. 11-1 contains an outline of the stages in the growth and development of a child and what the supervisor can suggest to the teacher concerning each stage.

EMOTIONAL DEVELOPMENT AND IN-SERVICE EDUCATION. A child first learns to listen by imitating others. He watches adults, and if they listen to one another with interest and respect he comes to sense the rightness of having a give-and-take relationship with people. Even more important to the person he will become is how his parents and teachers listen to him. If at home he finds talkers but no listeners, he may take his problems elsewhere, or worse, seal them inside himself. The supervisor should help the teacher to realize that the little child who is talking so big, and with so much bravado, may well be seeking security and attention.

An example of two areas that were discussed by the school psychologist

TABLE SUPP. 11–1

	Physical Factors	Reaction Patterns	Supervisors Stress How Teachers Can Help
EARLY CHILDHOOD Ages 5, 6, and 7	1. Growth is slower, more stable than during infancy and preschool years.	1. These children are active, vigorous, and noisy. They tire easily.	1. Ample provision should be made for active, vigorous games as well as simple group work and play. Rhythmic and dramatic activities are important. Because of short attention span, work periods must be short and frequent change of pace is important. Teachers should be aware and help parents to become aware that academic progress, particularly in reading and writing, can be affected by perceptual immaturity, by immaturity in eye muscles, and by poor eye-hand coordination.
	2. By age six, girls are likely to be a year or more ahead of boys in physical maturation.	2. They have short interest span and will become restless and fidgety if activities require concentration over long periods.	
	3. Motor skills will continue to develop during this period, although large muscles of the arms and legs are more developed than the small muscles of the hands and fingers.	3. There is great interest in activity. Increasing motor control gives them increased ability in skipping, hopping, keeping time to music, catching and throwing balls.	2. Adequate rest is vital. Provision should be made for quiet, relaxing activities and rest periods at school as well as cooperative planning with parents. Children need from eleven to twelve hours of sleep.
	4. Eye-hand coordination is improving but may still be incompletely developed throughout this period. Children are likely to be far-sighted as they enter school; eyes still are not ready for much close work at age seven.	4. They will be interested in other children as they enter school but will also be highly individualistic. Many will play "along side of" not *with* another child at first, then with one or two children before developing skill in team and group activities. Usually they are sensitive to the opinions of both adults and classmates by age seven.	3. Encourage independence at home and school while permitting the child to fluctuate between self-sufficiency and extreme dependence upon adults. At home he can brush his teeth, dress himself, and help with household chores. But he will need some help. At school, with the teacher's help, he can assume monitor duties, learn to observe safety precautions, and help to plan and evaluate his own work.
	5. There is great susceptibility to childhood diseases. There is particular need to guard against strain during convalescence.	5. There is gradual growth toward greater independence although they will fluctuate between apparent self-sufficiency and extreme dependence upon adults. They may seem more cooperative at age five because of greater dependence upon adults. At ages six and seven they are likely to be more interested in being first, more self-assertive, more competitive. Growing ability in self-evaluation is apparent. By age seven the child is likely to be quite self-critical.	4. The teacher can help by planning her daily program in accord with children's need for routine and by giving children opportunity to help with the planning and setting up of their own standards.
		6. There is beginning awareness of fairness and justice.	

TABLE SUPP. 11-1 (Continued)

	Physical Factors	Reaction Patterns	Supervisors Stress How Teachers Can Help
EARLY CHILDHOOD Ages 5, 6, and 7 (continued)		7. Concrete, first-hand experiences and active participation promote effective learning at this time.	
		8. They like the familiar, the routine. They like a great deal of repetition and will play the same game, tell the same joke, or listen to the same story over and over.	
		9. Their sense of humor may seem silly and "slapstick" to adults.	
		10. Boys' and girls' interests usually are beginning to differ by ages six or seven.	
MIDDLE CHILDHOOD Ages 8, 9, and 10	1. There is slow, steady physical growth with a growth lag occurring just before adolescence.	1. They usually have boundless energy. They are eager and enthusiastic and may seem careless and hurried.	1. There should be ample provision for active team games. Competition is likely to be strong and teams should be evenly matched. The need for group approval creates increasing need for him to "hold his own" with the group. The teacher can help and can encourage parents to help them develop skills which will enhance their prestige with the group.
	2. Some girls, because of more rapid physical development, may reach a period of rapid (preadolescent) growth by the age of ten.	2. There is a longer interest span and ability to work for longer periods, independently. Wider interests are developing.	2. Adequate rest is very important. During this period they often are fatigued if special provision is not made for rest periods. They need ten to eleven hours of sleep.
	3. Large muscle control and coordination improve rapidly and are excellent during the latter part of this period. The control of very small muscles as well as eye-hand coordination continue to	3. There is great interest in organized team games and at this age they will work hard to develop specific skills.	3. Encourage growth in independence. Ample provision should be made for many group activities. Clubs, committees, and special group projects are valuable and all require different skills and
		4. There is greater sensitivity to the opinion of peers and increasing participation in peer society. During this period approval of age-mates begins to be more important than approval of adults. Peer loyalty results in extreme interest in "gangs" and clubs in most nine and ten year olds. Best friends are of the same sex; "gang" loyalty is likely to be stronger in boys.	

SUPPLEMENT A

11

TABLE SUPP. 11–1 (Continued)

	Physical Factors	Reaction Patterns	Supervisors Stress How Teachers Can Help
MIDDLE CHILDHOOD Ages 8, 9, and 10 (continued)	improve and usually become well developed during this period. 4. By eight years of age the eyes of most children accommodate both near and far vision; by age ten the eyes usually function as well as at the adult level. 5. They normally will be energetic and in good health; toward the end of this period they will have had most contagious diseases.	5. There is increased ability in self-evaluation. They not only are critical of themselves but are developing a critical attitude toward adults. 6. A strong sense of justice and fairness is developing. 7. There is a growing ability to learn through vicarious experience though concrete, first-hand experiences are still necessary for all children. 8. Interest in routine develops into conscious appreciation of a well-organized program which they can help plan. 9. A definite sense of humor may manifest itself in rough-house activities, much poise, and giggling. This is particularly apparent at the beginning of this period. 10. Close friends and "gangs" are of the same sex. Differences in interests are widening. They are learning to assume their masculine and feminine roles.	abilities and serve to meet differing interests. At these ages they are capable of effective committee work and need practice in being a good leader and a good follower. 4. Increased provision should be made for them to set up their own standards and help in planning their activities. Reasonable explanations to their questions from teachers and parents are particularly important at this period in keeping with their sense of justice and fairness. They need, at school and home, to feel that they are in on the plans.
LATER CHILDHOOD (PREADOLESCENCE) Ages 11, 12, 13	1. There is a growth lag prior to a very rapid growth spurt. Growth, at this stage, is uneven. 2. Girls mature, physically, as much as two years ahead of boys.	1. Rapid and uneven growth is likely to result in awkwardness and restlessness. Poor posture may develop during this period. There is a wide range in both physical and emotional maturity among children of this age. 2. Interests are more mature and increasingly more diversified.	1. There should be provision for more highly organized games like handball and softball, although competition is keen and they will be self-conscious about trying any activity in which they lack skill. 2. Adequate rest is important. From nine to ten hours of sleep are needed.

TABLE SUPP. 11-1 (Continued)

3. Muscular growth is very rapid. Rapid, uneven growth may result in poor muscular control.

4. Eye function is usually well established.

5. During the transitional period there may be more minor illnesses. There is susceptibility to fatigue.

6. Secondary sex characteristics are developing.

3. There is increased interest in highly organized games, particularly among boys.

4. Peer codes are extremely important although there tends to be a shift from "gang" interest to interest in one or two close friends. There is increasing ability to sacrifice personal desires and self-interest for the good of the group.

5. There is increased ability in self-evaluation and much interest in self-improvement which includes improving personal appearances. The "rift" between children and adults is widening so that children nearing adolescence are likely to seem highly critical and uncooperative toward adults.

6. There is increased need to feel that adults are just and fair but a tendency to feel that they are not. They want to feel that they are in on the planning which involves them, that they are sharing in the decision-making.

7. There is rapid growth in ability to see relationships between ideas; to generalize.

8. Their growing independence increases their need to help plan and evaluate their activities. At these ages they are able to effectively analyze situations and problems.

9. Sense of humor is becoming more "adult" and will likely manifest itself in verbal cleverness. There is much giggling, however, when boys and girls are together.

10. Closer identification with masculine and feminine role is developing. While interests are different, at the same time their interest in each other may lead to a "scornful," antagonistic attitude between sexes. Considerable teasing can be expected.

3. Encourage and provide opportunity for many self-directed activities both on an individual and a group basis. They are ready now, if they have had practice, to assume real leadership roles. They can engage in effective committee work and learn to become good group members. They want to and are able to assume real responsibility. Membership in student councils or other self-governing groups at school is helpful as is membership in a "family council."

4. Teachers can help greatly by providing opportunity for them at this age to discuss problems either in a teacher-student conversation or with their group. They can and want to evaluate their plans and decisions but resent being told what to do or "talked down to." Above all, teachers realize that they, at this age, are growing away from dependence upon adults. Their efforts to establish independence will be clumsy at first and they will seem antagonistic and uncooperative.

11 SUPPLEMENT A

in an in-service education program planned by the supervisor in one school system in the midwest follows:

1. Recent developments in research related to three causes of reading retardation, including sensory immaturity, where the perception areas of the brain have not yet reached maturation; emotional difficulties; and brain damage.
2. Recognition of the overaccepted (overprotected), rejected, and dominated child; the brain-damaged child, who exhibits the action-for-action's sake pattern; and the behavioral-epileptic child, who may respond with aggressive movements which are intense and which the child does not remember after the occurrence.

IMPLICATIONS FOR THE SCHOOL. Since all students approach the task of maturing in a unique fashion, all students will not master specific learnings at the same chronological age. The interrelatedness of all phases of growth makes it possible to help students progress in one phase of development and reinforces growth in other areas.

While teachers are aware of the tremendous variation among the students they teach, they also observe that no student differs completely from all other students. No student, however puzzling he may be, is entirely baffling to a teacher because of what he knows and understands about *all* students.

SIMILAR PATTERNS. Noting specific capacities, interests, experiences, and needs of children emphasizes the differences among them. However, as the *total* child is viewed in light *of his basic needs and stages of growth, similarities among children are apparent.* An understanding of normal growth and development, along with an awareness of the total sweep of the developmental processes, provides the framework or context within which teachers interpret the behavior of individuals and lends perspective and direction to educational planning.

Psychology of the Learning Process for Supervisors

Learning for the sake of learning is not a child's attribute, for learning is work. To learn, the child must subordinate the pleasure principle, play, to the reality principle, work. An immature child needs understanding and time to move in the direction of learning. Since children identify with their families and carry this relationship into the classroom, the teacher must know what feelings the child has brought with him. If he feels disliked at home or dislikes the teacher, who may be a parent-surrogate, he does not have the motive to learn. Positive feelings stemming from his home influence and develop his attitude toward learning.

The understanding educator is aware of the child's wish to please his parents and his teacher, and depends on this motivation. He attempts to direct, stimulate, and gratify the student's curiosity and his wish to learn and know. Before a supervisor can attempt to help teachers to improve instruction he must be aware of the basic principles concerning the learning process.

Theories of Learning

William James, eminent anatomy teacher, turned to philosophy, becoming the first exponent of the pragmatic philosophy that was later to influence the works of John Dewey. William James conducted no research work except in the area of memory training. To James, learning was a matter of forming connections within the nervous system. Then connections resulted in the formation of habit.

Wilhelm Max Wundt, whose initial psychological laboratory in Leipzig in 1879 has become famous as the first laboratory in the field of psychology, saw cortical action as the basis for the mental act. David Hume (1711–1776) previously had developed a theory that there was a principle of connection between various thoughts and ideas; while David Hartley, in approximately the same era, perceived a factor of association in learning. Alexander Bane, an evolutionist, probably was of great influence in the development of the theories of trial and error learning as set forth by the great psychologist Thorndike.

EDWARD LEE THORNDIKE. Edward L. Thorndike, undoubtedly a true genius in all the ramifications of the term, originally worked with William James at Harvard, after which he moved to Columbia University where he worked with J. McKeen Cattell, a student of Wundt. Thorndike's initial work was in the field of animal intelligence, which was the topic of his doctoral dissertation. Thorndike was the first teacher of statistics in the United States. After turning from the study of animals to the study of children, he wrote a three-volume set in psychology. This work was followed by the famous *Briefer Course*.

From 1913 to 1930, Thorndike's stimulus-response connectionism was omnipotent in the field of educational psychology. Some outstanding points of view of Thorndike that have implications for the supervisor are those concerning stimulus-response bonds which are fixed and made permanent by success or pleasure.

Thorndike's three laws of learning were readiness, effect, and use. The law of *readiness* stated that if the organism was ready to act, being permitted to act would be satisfying, while not being permitted to act would be quite dissatisfying. The law of *effect* stated that the success of trial and error learning is dependent upon the effective and satisfying result of the successful movements. The law of *exercise* or *use* brought forth the idea that—other items being equal—learning is a factor of repeating a response over and over again.

The supervisor should be acquainted with the supplemental principles of Thorndike, such as the laws of multiple response, set, partial activity, analogy, and associated shifting, and should realize that Thorndike has shown us that we must teach for transfer, making our materials more lifelike. This transfer theory has proven a most valuable lesson to educators.

Thorndike helped us in the field of discipline. He showed us that, if we must punish, the undesirable character of behavior must be eclipsed with a new positive, acceptable behavior response which is made available to the child. It is easier to obtain a more desirable outcome with a positive response in the form of acknowledgment from the teacher in the first place, with undesirable reactions not being rewarded.

He has shown us that with no knowledge of results, there is no motivation. Thorndike considered motivation as essential to the learning situation. Thorndike also stressed that there is to be drill, but only in the form of meaningful practice, with materials proceeding from the simple to the more complex, and from the specific to the general.

On the negative side, one must admit that this system is atomistic, with the whole being developed by a synthesis of the parts—a view not held today by many educational psychologists. In spite of this limitation, one inevitably must return to the completeness of the system and to the logic with which it has been developed.

The supervising principal also must be familiar with the theories of those psychologists who developed the theory of contiguous conditioning. This theory was propounded by Edwin R. Guthrie in 1935. If one applies the teaching of this school to the classroom, he will find it is unnecessary to apply reward for correct behavior responses. *We learn what we do,* and in the situation where we have a series of movements we learn the last thing we do. Therefore the child must be informed that he is through with a particular impinging stimulus he has been working on, and that he has learned the particular item.

Material must be presented in a variety of ways in a variety of situations, such as on the blackboard, on paper, vocally, kinesthetically, and through various audio-visual media. Clues must be given by the teacher which will assist the child in discovering the correct answer, provided the child is sufficiently mature to make the desired reactions.

The supervisor should be familiar, also, with the works of Clark L. Hull and E. R. Hilgard, who developed a behavioral system which stressed that the child must be taught how to live in this social world, for inadequate learning would result in maladjustment. Since *learning occurs by doing,* there must be an emphasis on the activities of the student. Problems must be presented so as to insure reinforcement of the habit hierarchy needed for adequate response.

DESCRIPTIVE BEHAVIORISM AND THE SUPERVISOR. Of special interest to the student of programmed learning are the implications for education of the system developed by B. F. Skinner termed "descriptive behaviorism." If one utilizes Skinner's system of education, he will wait until the child does the correct thing in the classroom and then will reinforce the response. He always will reinforce a positive reaction. Skinner said that punishment will not reinforce a reaction that is desired.

One must build up another response with reinforcement, thereby building up *operant strength* in desired directions. In the classroom one must reinforce the appropriate moves, building operant strength, and must show the correct moves in the case of adverse response. The appropriate move must be reinforced when it is made.

According to Skinner, the selection of stimuli is of optimum importance. The individual's growth and development should be taken into account. Skinner's theories and findings are valuable when applied to the area of programmed learning, which is treated in Chapter 14.

GESTALT PSYCHOLOGY. The supervisor should familiarize himself with the works of Kurt Koffka, Wolfgang Koehler, Max Wertheimer, and Kurt Lewin. These scientists treated learning as a problem in figure and ground, as traces upon the cerebral cortex, as sudden flashes of insight, and as field forces with valance and vector potentials, respectively. They did not view learning as atomistic nor as trial and error behavior. Insight was stressed.

When one learned something new he modified the whole trace system; he did not add a new part. When two or three learnings came at the same time, there would be a more complex change in the trace system than if they came at one time. Instruction must be geared to the maturity of the learner, with individual differences being taken into account.

The instructor must take into account the learner's intellectual level, provide for motivation, and present the curricular materials in a pattern rather than an atomistic form. Periodic checks of each child's growth and development must be accomplished. The gradual development of discernment as the organism matures is considered as the prime measure of the learning that has taken place.

It would seem that some background of material or experience of a trial and error nature would be needed in at least some of the learnings that occur, but this has been negated by Koehler. Lewin, the field psychologist who emphasized the importance of the student's level of aspiration, stated that the individual must become ego involved with the task presented. The instructional materials, therefore, must be neither too difficult, nor too simple.

FUNCTIONALISM. The psychologists James R. Angell, John Dewey, Harvey Carr, Charles H. Judd, Edward F. Robinson, and Robert S. Woodworth were the leaders in the school of functionalism. Experiments of Robinson seem to indicate that the teacher must present the learner with a series of tasks that are evenly spaced and that will not result in interference with prior learning. The materials selected must not be so similar as to result in retroactive inhibition. The teacher must watch for trophism and be very aware of the four basic laws of *contiguity, frequency, assimilation,* and *intensity* in the presentation of material; he must be certain that the correct associations are emphasized.

One must, according to the functionalists, teach the *whole child.* Schools must assure that habits that have gone through a previous stamping-in process are retained. Continuous supervision on the part of a teacher who assumes an active role in a learning environment is essential.

John Dewey, who has been identified with the functionalists of the University of Chicago, which he left for a position at Columbia University, was a pragmatic philosopher as well as a functionalist with a touch of Gestalt in him, and he did not care for the functionalist idea of Stimulus-Organism-Response (S-O-R). He stated that the organism *learns by doing,* and was convinced that there is not the slightest worth in Herbartian pouring in of subject matter. He felt that a large amount of isolated facts and figures are of little value in our social world. Education must be the child's becoming aware in his own right, thereby acquiring the ability to solve his own problems in the society which is his environment. The child must have the freedom needed to be peripatetic and to solve his problems collectively, thereby gaining a sense of self-reliance and adequacy.

Dewey stated in 1938, in his *Experience and Education,* that there must be a curriculum with objectives, law, and order, but without the ancient pouring in that, to Dewey, was valueless. To him the only truisms were the facts that would accrue from experimental work, with the eternal verities thus being cast in disrepute except as they have been verified in the laboratory.

While Guthrie had stated that we learn what we do, Dewey said that we learn by doing. Dewey's project method, which took into account the basic needs of the learner, included the five steps of learning which he identified as follows:

1. Realization of the problem—locate the problem;
2. Search for clarity—specifications and size;
3. Statement of the proposal or hypothesis—for solving the problem;

4. Rational application—an attempt to solve the problem;
5. Experimental verification—ascertain what has happened in the attempted solution of the problem.

If there were no solution, one would start again with number (3), pragmatically trying hypotheses after hypotheses until the desired results were obtained, or another alternative was accepted as a solution.

Dewey saw learning as an item that must be founded upon the everyday problems of social democracy, and as a procedure by which the organism was to be guided in life by ascertaining the solutions to problems that inhibit personal and social growth.

IMPLICATIONS FOR THE SUPERVISING PRINCIPAL. Dewey's five steps in learning, and the project technique, may be employed by the classroom teacher in the education of the "whole child." Teachers should utilize the method that works, no matter what it is, with no pet beliefs or detriments to location of new knowledge.

The teacher must act as a guide and counselor in the learning environment. Individual differences must be taken into account, for the individual is all-important in the learning situation. Dewey said that stimulation and motivation, especially of the intrinsic variety, are essential, for children learn best from activities and materials in which they are actively interested.

The critics of Dewey may have overlooked the statements regarding the curriculum and other related matters in 1932, although one must admit that the system apparently falls short in the area of the formation of habits in the child. One may criticize the concept of discarding all of the so-called eternal verities, except those that can be experimentally proved in a laboratory.

One should, therefore, take this concept of truth along with Dewey's pragmatically extreme views in a buffered fashion for optimum classroom results. Again, one must remember that Dewey was angered by the manner in which many of his ideas were being stretched and compressed, especially by the followers of the child-centered wing of the Progressive Education Association. He was most emphatic in stating that he considered reading, studying, experimenting, and purposeful practice as activities that constituted "doing," just as surely as did such enterprises as dramatic representations and construction. Surely, such activities as dramatic play, construction, and playing and working with blocks may have certain social values in the primary grades. Their extensive use in the middle and upper grades is to be questioned seriously. If it is true, as we have seen, that play *is* a natural expression of childhood, should the student spend extensive time receiving instruction on how to play when this time could have been spent in studying mathematics, oral and written language, health, science, spelling, reading, and even foreign languages?

A positive answer to the question would seem both to be inaccurate and illogical, and the supervisor of tomorrow is cautioned lest the temptation to have the classroom turned into a showcase rather than a learning laboratory be too much to withstand. It may be more entertaining to visitors to the classroom to see children engaged in dramatic activity than in learning certain processes in mathematics. The temptation on the part of the supervisor to force the teacher to utilize such techniques as dramatic representation, block play, and construction is to be avoided when there is no real need for their utilization, or when the class or the teacher does not work best with these techniques.

The patrons of the school at the lower grade levels, for instance, have the right to expect that the students are being taught reading, mathematics, spelling, grammar, science, geography, history, and, in some instances, a foreign language. Instruction in other areas certainly has a place, but there is no justification for spending several hours per week from the regular instructional program preparing for a "culmination" show for parental consumption in the name of public relations, as has been the practice in certain elementary schools of this country, any more than there is for spending hours in dramatic play or "free rhythmic representation" activities with children who probably would benefit more from direct instruction in the so-called eternal verities.

Summary of Learning Principles for the Supervisor

When one studies the theories of the psychology of learning as espoused by Skinner, Thorndike, the Gestaltists, and the functionalists, it becomes evident that there is a need for an eclectic point of reference for the supervisor. The following summary is an attempt to provide a brief outline:

1. Learning has been defined as the modification and development of those tendencies which govern the psychological function.
2. Learning takes place when there is a felt need on the part of the individual. Reinforcement apparently is important.
3. Learning is greatly influenced by frequency and distribution of practice, generalization, opportunity to transfer. and sensory modality (the use of various colors, sounds, odors, and tactile stimulations).
4. Learning must be stimulated. It should be noted that stimulation may be accomplished by the teacher, but motivation is from within. We should, therefore, refer to that which we do to influence the learner as *stimulation*, which is done with the hope that the learner will be *motivated* to respond.
5. Many different theories have been advocated to explain learning phenomena, but no one of these theories accounts for all of the phenomena and all of the research findings. Among the theories most widely discussed are those of Koffka, Koehler, Lewin, Wheeler, Robinson, Dewey, Thorndike, Guthrie, Hull, Skinner, and Tolman.

We must stimulate, but we must keep the stimulating material at the proper maturity level, and the material must be patterned. This material which we are stimulating the individual to learn must be adjusted to the level of maturation.

It is essential that we evaluate progress that is being made by the individual, otherwise motivation will lag. Knowledge of results, then, is essential to learning. Finally, we must work toward a broad integrated development for basic skills, mental health, physical health, understandings, appreciations, hobbies and interests, and social development, including the essential social skills and the amenities. It is the job of the supervisor to assist the teacher in becoming increasingly familiar with the more basic teachings of the psychologists in the field of learning.

EVALUATION OF LEARNING. The findings of educational psychology in the area of tests, measurements, and evaluation should be brought to the attention of the certificated staff. These findings and developments should be interpreted to the staff. Recommendations for the utilization of selected methods and techniques of measurement and evaluation should be made on an individual basis. Clearly, techniques applicable to Grade 6 or Grade 9 may not be applicable to Grade 1.

The supervisor must use due caution when working with teachers in the area of measurement and evaluation. The difference between measurement and evaluation should be understood clearly by both teacher and supervisor. As used in this text, measurement refers to a mathematical determination. This determination may be either exact, as in the case of three correct answers, or approximate, as in the case of a line three inches long. In the former, it should be noted that one may count accurately how many answers are correct according to an answer key. However, even with the highly advanced electronic measuring devices of the space age, one may never be absolutely certain that a line is EXACTLY three inches long. There will be an error, even though this error may be only in the millionths of an inch.

The second case discussed is that of evaluation. Unlike measurement, evaluation implies a comparison or a subjective judgment of worth. While evaluation will usually include measurement as a preceding step, measurement does not necessarily include evaluation.

Teaching through understanding is the heart of the learning process. It is a skill developed only through discipline and constant practice. The supervisor must aid the staff in developing this skill. Regardless of the individual behavioral manifestations, there are certain general principles that apply to the understanding of all children. Everyone has certain basic needs that must be met, no matter how different the surface behavior may be. All need a fairly comfortable opinion of the self with which to live. This may be achieved in a variety of ways. Regardless of the behavior differences, all children need a good opinion of themselves. The psychological integrity of the individual must be preserved. The following seven items are guides to the preservation of individual integrity:

1. *Acceptance.* Students need to be accepted as they are.
2. *Consistency.* Consistency can be used effectively to contribute to a student's security.

3. *Negative emotions.* Students need to be allowed to express negative emotions. This expression, however, should be routed into positive channels.
4. *Reassurance.* Reassurance must be given by interest in the student as a person.
5. *Routine.* An explanation of routine assignments and plans should be given on the student's level of understanding.
6. *Force.* Verbal and physical coercion should be avoided as much as possible.
7. *Objectivity.* Objectivity should be a goal in understanding the student and should contribute to the effective employment of the principles of interpersonal relationships.

A basic tenet is that no two students are exactly alike. Supervising principals are reminded constantly, as they observe students, of the countless ways in which they differ. In any class students vary in height and weight and amount of energy output. They differ in capacities, interests, and background of experiences. They differ in how they feel about themselves, how they feel about others, and in what they think is important. These latter are subtle forces not readily observable perhaps, but powerfully influencing the way a student acts and learns, thereby affecting the rate and manner in which he masters the task of "growing up."

How to Help the Teacher Test, Assign Marks, and Understand Statistical Measures

Testing provides basic information regarding the student's ability to learn and his educational achievement, personality, needs, and interests. This information should be considered in relation to information about his health and physical development, his reactions to daily learning activities, his social relations, and his attitudes. As no one test successfully defines the student, the teacher should be encouraged to compare the results from many tests in order to secure a more valid profile.

Test results help the teacher to better understand and plan for the class as a whole and to spotlight the student who may merit special attention. Groups of teachers representing one grade level or subject matter area can meet to study certain tests, evaluating their ideas and impressions with each other. The school psychologist can help the teachers in analyzing the significance of the intelligence or achievement test scores, the aptitudes, and the relations between tests. The principal, assistant principal, director of curriculum, counselor, specialist-consultant, and other specialists should help in evaluating test results.

The Use of Tests

The teacher who knows how to administer, use, and interpret tests will have a better understanding of the students in his classroom. He will be able to give them better counsel. Principals should assist teachers to a better understanding of tests and measurements. Standardized tests, including the following, should be made available to the staff by the principal. Recommended—(1) intelligence tests, group and individual; (2) achievement tests; (3) aptitude tests. Optional—(4) interest inventories; and (5) personality tests.

The following is a listing of just a few of these tests:

1. Intelligence tests—group
   a) Kuhlman-Anderson Intelligence Test (Grades 1–9)
   b) Otis Classification Test
   c) Otis Group Intelligence Scale
   d) Otis Quick-Scoring Mental Ability Tests
   e) California Tests of Mental Maturity (all levels)
   f) Terman-McNemar Test of Mental Ability
   g) Thurstone SRA Primary Mental Abilities (ages five through seven, seven through eleven, eleven through seventeen)
   h) Progressive Matrices (Lewis and Company, London)
2. Intelligence tests—individual
   a) Latest Stanford Revision of the Binet-Simon Intelligence Scale
   b) Wechsler Intelligence Scale for Children (WISC) and the WASC

11 SUPPLEMENT A

c) Gesell Development Schedules

d) Arthur Point Scale of Performance (cubes, form board, maze)

3. Interest inventories

   a) Kuder Preference Record (occupational interests)

   b) Pressey Interest-Attitude Test

   c) Guilford Interest Survey

4. Achievement tests

   a) Metropolitan Achievement Test

   a) Gates Modern Scholastic Achievement Tests

   c) SRA Iowa Tests of Educational Development

   d) Stanford Achievement Test

   e) SRA Achievement Series by Thorpe, Lefever, and Naslund

   f) American School Achievement Tests (reading, arithmetic, language)

   g) Diagnostic Reading Test

   h) California Achievement Tests (reading, arithmetic, language)

   i) Monroe Reading Aptitude Tests

   j) Iowa Silent Reading Tests

   k) Iowa Every-Pupil Tests of Basic Skills (silent reading, study skills, arithmetic, language)

   l) SR/SE Survey of Reading and Study Skills (SRA)

   m) Sequential Tests of Education Progress (STEP)

   n) California Phonics Survey

   o) Lee-Clark Arithmetic Fundamentals Test

5. Aptitude tests

   a) Differential Aptitude Tests (verbal reasoning, numerical ability, abstract reasoning, space relations, mechanical reasoning, clerical speed and accuracy, language usage)

   b) Lee-Thorpe Occupational Interest Inventory

   c) Detroit Mechanical Aptitudes Examination

   d) Clerical Aptitude Test

   e) Seashore Tests of Musical Aptitudes

   f) Employment Survey Tests

   g) SCAT and SAT

6. Personality tests

   a) Ohio Guidance Tests for Elementary Grades

   b) California Test of Personality

c) Allport A-S Reaction Study
d) Vineland Social Maturity Scale
e) Kuder Preference Record—Personal
f) Mooney Problems Test Sheet

Test Functions and Factors

Reading readiness tests assist teachers and principals in ability grouping for reading instruction and in preparing individuals for reading programs (kindergarten and first grade). Achievement tests assist teachers in diagnosing individuals' and classes' strengths and weaknesses for planning instruction, assessing progress (student and class), and reporting to parents.

Teachers and principals also should consider achievement test results in class placements. These tests provide measures (in grade-placement or percentiles) of reading vocabulary, reading comprehension, total reading, arithmetic fundamentals, arithmetic reasoning, total arithmetic, spelling, and English (punctuation, grammar, and usage).

Tests of mental maturity, or "intelligence tests," normally provide a "verbal," a "performance" or "nonverbal," and a "total" I.Q. The major purpose is estimating intellectual or scholastic capacity and expected achievement. These tests help indicate "overachievement" (a misnomer, at best), "underachievement," and potential superior intelligence which should be tested individually.

The *Iowa Tests* often are given the second semester of the eighth grade to assist students, staff, and parents in planning a program for high-school years. Evaluating overall academic knowledge, they compare the student with local class average and with national average.

A good test is readily and easily scored; is objective, valid, reliable, easily administered; and is as free from contaminating factors as possible.

Assigning Marks, Statistical Concepts, and Interpreting Statistical Measures

The supervising principal should aid the teacher in becoming familiar with such basic statistical tools for test interpretation as the *median, mode, mean, average deviation, standard deviation, correlation, chi square,* and with the basic methods of assigning marks. The supervising principal may wish to recommend the following technique utilizing the average deviation from the median (middle) score of the distribution for use in assigning marks.

Assuming five raw scores for illustrative purposes:

	Raw Scores		Deviation from Median (Midscore)
	30		12
	20		2
Median or Midscore	18		0
	17		1
	10		8
N = 5		Σ (sum) of deviation =	23 all deviations are treated as positive

1. Arrange the test scores in sequence, with the highest score first.
2. Calculate the median or midscore. If there is an even number of cases (N) go up and down the distribution of scores $\left(\dfrac{N}{2}\right)$ scores, and find the average of the two middle scores. If there is an odd number of cases (N) go up or down the distribution $\left[\left(\dfrac{N\text{-}1}{2}\right) + 1\right]$ scores, where N = the number of cases (the number of scores in the distribution). In the event that N is even, it is possible to round off the median to the nearest whole number as follows:
   a) If the fraction is less than 0.5, delete it;
   b) If the fraction is more than 0.5, round up;
   c) If the fraction is exactly equal to 0.5, round up if one would obtain an *even* number in so doing. If one would have obtained an *odd* number in rounding up, delete the fraction and *do not* round up. In this manner the calculations that result in fractions exactly equal to one-half are rounded up and down approximately the same number of times, and should, by chance, result in no significant differences in the quantities obtained. *Example:* 3.4 would be rounded to 3; 3.5 would be rounded to 4, since 4 is an even number; 3.7 would be

rounded to 4; 2.5, however, would be rounded down to 2, since rounding up would have resulted in an odd number. Note that one need not be concerned whether the resulting rounded number would be even or odd *except* where the fraction is exactly equal to one-half.

3. Calculate the deviation of each score from the median. All deviations are treated as positive. A raw score minus the median equals the deviation.

4. Obtain the sum of the deviations.

5. Obtain the average deviation (AD): the sum of the deviations divided by the number of scores, or $\left(\dfrac{\Sigma d}{N}\right)$ where Σ = sum, d = deviations, and N is as above. In our example AD = $\left(\dfrac{\Sigma d}{N}\right) = \left(\dfrac{23}{5}\right) = 4.6$. To facilitate computations, one should always round off the AD to the nearest tenth.

6. Obtain the *scale unit* or range of each letter mark. Assuming a letter-grade assignment of five letters, as A, B, C, D, F, the scale unit is equal to the average deviation multiplied by the constant figure 1.5. In our example SU = (4.6) × (1.5) = 6.9, rounded to the nearest tenth. It should be noted that 1.5 is a constant, and is always used as a multiplier when five letter marks are to be assigned.

7. Find the range of the C marks: one-half of a scale unit above and one-half below the median.

a) $\dfrac{SU}{2} = \dfrac{6.9}{2} = 3.45 =$ one-half of a scale unit in our example.

b) The median plus and minus one-half the scale unit equals the lower and upper limits of the mark C:

18 + 3.45 = 21.45 = upper limit of C.
18 − 3.45 = 14.55 = lower limit of C.

8. Find the upper limit of B by adding one scale unit to the upper limit of the mark C:

$$21.45 + 6.90 = 28.35$$

9. Find the lower limit of D by subtracting one scale unit from the lower limit of C:

$$14.55 - 6.90 = 7.65$$

10. What is left equals the marks A and F:

> A = 28.36 and up
> B = 21.46 to 28.35
> C = 14.55 to 21.45
> D =   7.65 to 14.54
> F = Lower than 7.65

The extremes of each letter mark may be indicated by plus and minus marks. The score 21.45 would be a C+, and 14.55 a C−.

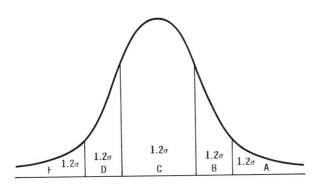

FIGURE SUPP. 11–1   Sample Curve Showing Five Letter Marks Assigned Within the Normal or Standard Distribution.

Since it is assumed that there will be approximately six standard deviations (σ) under the curve of the normal or standard distribution, if there are five letter marks to assign, each will occupy 1.2 (6 divided by 5) standard deviations along the baseline of the curve. About 3.9 percent of the population would receive a mark of A, and the same percent would receive F's; 23.84 percent would receive a mark of B, and the same percent would receive D's; while 45.14 percent would receive a mark of C. It should be noted that these percents change from class to class; often there will be no F's, or no B's, and so forth.

Since 1.2σ is approximately equal to 1.5 average deviations, a constant of 1.5 was used as a multiplier in the example given in the text. In the event that there are more than five letter marks to assign, the amount of σ to assign to each letter mark is determined by dividing six σ (constant) by the number of marks to assign. One then determines the percent to be assigned to each letter mark by referring to Table Supp. 11–2, which gives the percent of the distribution under the normal curve in terms of standard deviations from the mean of the distribution.

The material that follows demonstrates a few of the methods commonly used to calculate standard statistical measures.

Three Measures of Central Tendency

1. THE ARITHMETIC MEAN—The total of all measurements or scores divided by the number of such measurements. For grouped data, see the example included below:

ci	MP	Tally	f	d	fd	x(x = MP − True Mean)	fx
90–94	92	1	1	4	4	25	25
85–89	87	11	2	3	6	21	42
80–84	82	111	3	2	6	16	48
75–79	77	111111111	9	1	9	11	99
70–74	72(am)	–5–5–1–1	12	0	0	6	72
65–69	67	5–5	10	−1	−10	16	10
60–64	62	5–1111	9	−2	−18	4	36
55–59	57	1111111	7	−3	−21	9	63
50–54	52	1111	4	−4	−16	14	56
45–49	47	111	3	−5	−15	19	57
40–44	42	11	2	−6	−12	24	48
35–39	37	1	1	−7	−7	29	29

$$N = 63 \quad \Sigma\, fd = \overline{-74} \qquad \Sigma fx = \overline{584}$$

ARITHMETIC MEAN for grouped data = AM =

$$am \pm \left[\frac{\Sigma\, fd}{N} \cdot ci \right] = 72 - \left[\frac{(74)}{(63)} \cdot (5) \right] = 66.15$$

ci—class interval. (Orginally determined as follows:

$$\frac{\text{Highest Score} - \text{Lowest Score.}}{\text{Number of Intervals Wanted}}$$

am—assumed mean (mispoint of ci with most tally marks)

d—number of intervals away from the interval containing the assumed mean.

TABLE SUPP. 11–2   Table of Areas Under the Normal Distribution Curve

$\frac{x}{\sigma}$	0.00	0.01	0.02	0.03	0.04	0.05	0.06	0.07	0.08	0.09
0.0	0000	0040	0080	0120	0160	0199	0239	0279	0319	0359
0.1	0398	0438	0478	0517	0557	0596	0636	0675	0714	0753
0.2	0793	0832	0871	0910	0948	0987	1026	1064	1103	1141
0.3	1179	1217	1255	1293	1331	1368	1406	1443	1480	1517
0.4	1554	1591	1628	1664	1700	1736	1772	1808	1844	1879
0.5	1915	1950	1985	2019	2054	2088	2123	2157	2190	2224
0.6	2257	2291	2324	2357	2389	2422	2454	2486	2517	2549
0.7	2580	2611	2642	2673	2704	2734	2764	2794	2823	2852
0.8	2881	2910	2939	2967	2995	3023	3051	3078	3106	3133
0.9	3159	3186	3212	3238	3264	3290	3315	3340	3365	3389
1.0	3413	3438	3461	3485	3508	3531	3554	3577	3599	3621
1.1	3643	3665	3686	3708	3729	3749	3770	3790	3810	3830
1.2	3849	3869	3888	3907	3925	3944	3962	3980	3997	4015
1.3	4032	4049	4066	4082	4099	4115	4131	4147	4162	4177
1.4	4192	4207	4222	4236	4251	4265	4279	4292	4306	4319
1.5	4332	4345	4357	4370	4383	4394	4406	4418	4429	4441
1.6	4452	4463	4474	4484	4495	4505	4515	4525	4535	4545
1.7	4554	4564	4573	4582	4591	4599	4608	4616	4625	4633
1.8	4641	4649	4656	4664	4671	4678	4686	4693	4699	4706
1.9	4713	4719	4726	4732	4738	4744	4750	4756	4761	4767

EXAMPLE: between the mean and a point 1.96 σ ($\frac{x}{\sigma} = 1.96$) are found 47.50 per cent of the entire area under the curve.

NOTE: $x = X - M$, where $X = $ a score and $M = $ the mean of the distribution. σ = a standard deviation. Therefore, $\frac{x}{\sigma} = $ the distance from the mean in terms of σ ;

Note that in reality we compute the *algebraic sum* of the assumed mean and the correction factor (which is derived from the formula) in order to obtain the true mean. In the example we subtract because Σ fd is negative.

2. THE MEDIAN—The frequency above or below which is found 50% of the total frequency; the score above and below which 50% of the scores fall. Determined by counting up the distribution to find $\frac{N}{2}$

TABLE SUPP. 11–2 (Continued)

2.0	4772	4778	4783	4788	4793	4798	4803	4808	4812	4817
2.1	4821	4826	4830	4834	4838	4842	4846	4850	4854	4857
2.2	4861	4864	4868	4871	4875	4878	4881	4884	4887	4890
2.3	4893	4896	4898	4901	4904	4906	4909	4911	4913	4916
2.4	4918	4920	4922	4925	4927	4929	4931	4932	4934	4936
2.5	4938	4940	4941	4943	4945	4946	4948	4949	4951	4952
2.6	4953	4955	4956	4957	4959	4960	4961	4962	4963	4964
2.7	4965	4966	4967	4968	4969	4970	4971	4972	4973	4974
2.8	4974	4975	4976	4977	4977	4978	4979	4979	4980	4981
2.9	4981	4982	4982	4983	4984	4984	4985	4985	4986	4986
3.0	4986.5	4986.9	4987.4	4987.8	4988.2	4988.6	4988.9	4989.3	4989.7	4990.0
3.1	4990.3	4990.6	4991.0	4991.3	4991.6	4991.8	4992.1	4992.4	4992.6	4992.9
3.2	4993.129									
3.3	4995.166									
3.4	4996.631									
3.5	4997.674									
3.6	4998.409									
3.7	4998.922									
3.8	4999.277									
3.9	4999.519									
4.0	4999.683									
4.5	4999.966									
5.0	4999.997133									

the number of σ's. This table gives the percent of the area under the distribution curve between this $\frac{X}{\sigma}$ point and the mean. Fractional parts (10,000ths) of the total area under the curve are shown. It should be recalled that $\frac{X}{\sigma}$ = how many standard deviations you want from one side of the mean. To obtain both sides, multiply by two.

(use $\frac{N + 1}{2}$ if there is an odd number of scores.) $\frac{N}{2}$ = one-half of the total number of scores. For grouped data, use the formula

$$L + \left[\frac{\frac{N}{2} - F}{fm} \right] \cdot (i \text{ or } ci)$$

where F = the sum of scores for all intervals *below* the interval upon which the median falls

fm = frequency (number of scores) *within* the interval
upon which the median falls

i = the length of the class interval

3. THE MODE—The score which occurs most often in a distribution of scores; the "fashion."

Two Measures of Deviation from the Arithmetic Mean (AM) (All Deviations Treated as Positive)

1. AVERAGE DEVIATION (AD)—The sum of the deviation of each score from the arithmetic mean, ignoring positive and negative signs, divided by the number of such scores:

$$AD = \frac{\text{Sum of fx}}{N}, \text{ where } f = \text{ the frequency (number of scores), and}$$

$$x = \text{ the difference of the midpoint of a class interval minus the mean (AM) of the distribution}$$

Referring to the example given under Arithmetic Mean, above, especially to the two right hand columns,

$$AD = \Sigma \frac{fx}{N} = \frac{584}{63} = 9 \frac{17}{63}$$

2. STANDARD DEVIATION (σ)—The square root of the sum of the squared deviations of each score from the mean divided by the number of scores. A more powerful measure of deviation than the average deviation, but somewhat more difficult to calculate.

$$\sigma = \sqrt{\frac{\Sigma d^2}{N}}$$

Correlation Analysis

Correlation analysis focused upon the determination of whether two variables are related to one another in ordering individual differences between people. The maximum correlation index is = 1.00, with both variables ordering people in the same way. An index of -1.00 indicates an ordering in reverse directions. An index of 0.00 indicates no relationship between the variables. In no instance can we draw a conclusion concerning cause-effect relationship based upon correlation analysis and none is implied.

SPEARMAN RHO CORRELATION: Rank the scores of individuals within the two sets of data— 1, 2, 3, 4, 5. Then apply the formula

$$\text{RHO } \rho = 1 - \frac{6 \Sigma d^2}{N(N^2-1)}$$ where d^2 = the difference between the individual's rank on one test and his rank on another test $(r_1 - r_2)$.

The advantage of the average-deviation method, as well as that of the chi square method, described below, over the correlation and the more complicated (but increasingly popular) analysis of variance methods, is the ease with which the calculations may be performed. The teacher may, of course, use the above system in combination with others, such as finding the so-called natural breaks in a distribution. It should be noted that the latter, when used in isolation, gives data, generally, that are not treatable statistically.

Chi Square

The supervising principal may wish to recommend the use of the chi square statistic to the teacher who wishes to research some problem within the classroom where chi square may prove a helpful tool. J. P. Guilford[1] noted that chi square is a general purpose statistic with many diverse applications. It is intended to test the hypothesis of no relationship between two variables.

H. E. Garrett noted that the chi square test represents a useful method of comparing experimentally obtained results with those to be expected theoretically on some hypothesis:

The differences between observed and expected frequencies are squared and divided by the expected number in each case, and the sum of these quotients is x^2. The more closely the observed results approximate to the expected, the

[1] J. P. Guilford, *Fundamental Statistics in Psychology and Education* (New York: McGraw-Hill Book Company, Inc., 1956), pp. 229–239.

smaller the chi square and the closer the agreement between the observed data and the hypothesis being tested. Contrariwise, the larger the chi square the greater the probability of a real divergence of experimentally observed [results] from expected results.[2]

Further discussion of the properties of this statistic may be found in Ruch[3].

Interpreting Statistical Measures

Certainly honesty is essential in dealing with statistical data. One over-zealous school system in the midwest, in the struggle for enhanced public confidence in the educational program, printed inaccurate norms to the achievement test used locally. The students obtained scores which indicated that they were ahead approximately one to two years of where they really were in educational achievement. What was forgotten in this little bit of educational dishonesty was that such procedures definitely do delimit the scope, or universe of application, of the examination results.

One must bear in mind, also, when interpreting examination results, that those scoring in the so-called average range would have scored there only two-thirds of the time, while those in the far extremes would have scored these extreme scores approximately but one-sixth of the time. This is illustrated in the normal distribution curve (Figure Supp. 11–2).

Again, it is the supervisor's rightful role to do all in his power to aid the teacher and administrator in interpreting examination results, and to assist in the maintenance of honesty in this interpretation.

A Look at the Future

As supervisors help teachers plan educational experiences for students, continuous attention to the ways in which students differ and are alike is vital. Thus teachers, through observation, conferences, and the various other techniques described in this text, will do a better job on the instructional firing line. In the future, teacher training institutions will stress not the

[2]Henry E. Garrett, *Statistics in Psychology and Education,* 5th ed. (New York: Longmans, Green and Company, 1958), pp. 253–254.
[3]Floyd L. Ruch, *Elementary Statistics in Psychology and Education* (Columbia, Missouri: Lucas Brothers, 1957), pp. 1–14.

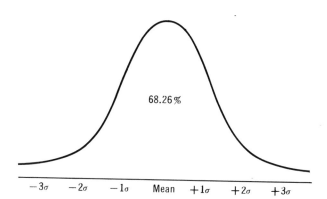

68.26%

-3σ -2σ -1σ Mean $+1\sigma$ $+2\sigma$ $+3\sigma$

FIGURE SUPP. 11–2   Normal Distribution Curve.

fundamentals of educational philosophy, psychology, and sociology, but rather the *application* of these principles.

As the various states increase the requirements for the license or certificate authorizing service in school supervision, the preparing institutions will require the completion of additional professional course work in scientific research methods. Such courses will help to prepare the supervisor for advanced research which, it is hoped, will help solve many of the problems of his chosen profession. Advanced work in research design for the school supervisor who elects to obtain training beyond that required for the basic license or certificate in school supervision will become the rule rather than the exception, with such a program being required of all who enter the doctoral program in educational administration and supervision.

Information Covered by Case Studies

The case study should include the following material:[1]

I. Identifying Data
  A. Referral
    1. Source of referral_____
    2. Procedure of referral_____
    3. Date study initiated_____
    4. Date of report_____
    5. Name of person or persons to whom report is directed

    _____

  B. Subject
    1. Name_____
    2. Age_____
    3. Birthdate_____
    4. Sex_____
    5. Subject's counselor or teacher_____
    6. School_____
    7. Grade_____
II. History
  A. Developmental History
    1. Prenatal condition of mother and child_____
    2. Postnatal condition of mother and child_____
    3. Description of illnesses_____
    4. Description of infections_____
    5. Description of injuries_____
    6. History of speech and language development:_____
      a) Age at which child babbled_____
      b) Age at which child used jargon_____
      c) Age at which child uttered first words_____
      d) Age at which child uttered first phrases_____
      e) Age at which child uttered first sentences_____
    7. History of development of gross motor control
      a) Age at which child held bottle_____
      b) Age at which child sat up_____

[1]For further information that should prove helpful see Louis E. Harper and Benjamin Wright, "Dealing with Emotional Problems in the Classroom," *Elementary School Journal* LXIII (March 1958): 316–325.

      c) Age at which child crawled⎯⎯⎯⎯⎯⎯⎯⎯

      d) Age at which child pulled up⎯⎯⎯⎯⎯⎯⎯

      e) Age at which child walked⎯⎯⎯⎯⎯⎯⎯

  8. History of social development

      a) Feeding⎯⎯⎯⎯⎯⎯⎯⎯

      b) Toilet control⎯⎯⎯⎯⎯⎯⎯

      c) Dressing⎯⎯⎯⎯⎯⎯⎯

      d) Bathing⎯⎯⎯⎯⎯⎯⎯

B. Family History

  1. Parents' occupation⎯⎯⎯⎯⎯⎯⎯

  2. Parents' education⎯⎯⎯⎯⎯⎯⎯

  3. Parents' religion⎯⎯⎯⎯⎯⎯⎯

  4. Parents' marital status⎯⎯⎯⎯⎯⎯⎯

  5. Socioeconomic status ⎯⎯⎯⎯⎯⎯⎯

  6. Nationality⎯⎯⎯⎯⎯⎯⎯

  7. Racial background ⎯⎯⎯⎯⎯⎯⎯

  8. Language background of family ⎯⎯⎯⎯⎯⎯⎯

  9. Ages of siblings ⎯⎯⎯⎯⎯⎯⎯

 10. Sex of siblings ⎯⎯⎯⎯⎯⎯⎯

 11. School record of siblings⎯⎯⎯⎯⎯⎯⎯

 12. Emotional climate of home ⎯⎯⎯⎯⎯⎯⎯

 13. Quality of parent-sibling-child relationships:

      a) Mother-infant relationship ⎯⎯⎯⎯⎯⎯⎯

      b) Disciplinary measures used⎯⎯⎯⎯⎯⎯⎯

C. Educational History

  1. Date of entry into kindergarten or first grade⎯⎯⎯⎯⎯⎯⎯

  2. Record of schools attended ⎯⎯⎯⎯⎯⎯⎯

  3. Summary of progress in school:

      a) Retentions ⎯⎯⎯⎯⎯⎯⎯

      b) Special learning difficulties ⎯⎯⎯⎯⎯⎯⎯

  4. Summary of social adjustment in school:

      a) With teachers⎯⎯⎯⎯⎯⎯⎯

      b) With classmates⎯⎯⎯⎯⎯⎯⎯

D. Results of Previous Studies

  1. Summary of results of previous
    group intelligence tests⎯⎯⎯⎯⎯⎯⎯

2. Summary of results of previous
   achievement tests _____
3. Names of tests_____
4. Grade test was administered_____
5. Date test was administered_____
6. Summary of previous contacts with:
   a) Special services in the school _____
   b) Community agencies _____
   c) Other professional persons _____ _____
      Include in above
      (1) Name of agency or person_____
      (2) Grade of study_____
      (3) Date of study_____
      (4) Findings_____
      (5) Recommendations _____

III. Test Data
  A. Intelligence
    1. Names of tests administered_____ on _____
                                                                      (dates)
    2. Indication of measured intelligence in terms of:
      a) I.Q. _____ on _____
                                      (test)
      b) Mental age_____
      c) Grade placement norms _____
      d) Other descriptive classifications _____
    3. Analysis of student's performance on a specific type of test
       item _____
    4. Description of range of abilities_____
    5. Description of patterns of abilities_____
    6. Basic strengths included in description of range of abilities_____
      _____
    7. Basic strengths included in description of patterns of abilities_____
      _____
    8. Basic weaknesses included in description of range of abilities _____
      _____

9. Basic weaknesses included in description of patterns of abilities
_____

10. If test results are of questionable validity, evidence and supportive reasoning has been provided, such as:
    a) Variability in success _____
    b) Variability in failure _____
    c) Educational deprivation _____
    d) Social deprivation _____
    e) Sensory handicap _____
    f) Physical handicap _____
    g) Lack of rapport _____
    h) Lack of cooperation _____

11. Indication of the student's expected level of academic achievement on the basis of measured intelligence _____

B. Achievement
    1. Names of tests administered _____
    2. Skill areas tested _____
    3. Results in terms of grade placement norms _____
    4. Analysis of the types of errors committed _____
    5. Discussion of the implications for remedial classroom instructional technique _____
    6. Comparison of the student's achievement scores with his actual grade placement _____
    7. Discussion of the implications for selection of the level of instructional materials _____
    8. Discussion of the achievement scores in relation to measured intelligence _____
    9. Implications concerning:
       a) Educational placement _____
       b) Classroom instruction _____
       c) Types of materials _____

C. Personality
    1. Names of tests administered _____
    2. Discussion of personality structure _____

3. Discussion of dynamics
   a) Self concept _____
   b) Perception of others _____
   c) Interpersonal relationship _____
   d) Inner conflicts _____
   e) Defense mechanisms _____
   f) Techniques for dealing with frustration _____
4. Discussion of the possible causes for emotional disturbances___
5. Discussion of the possible causes for social disturbances_____
6. Estimation of the seriousness of the problem_____
7. Attempt to predict future adjustment_____

IV. Test Observations
   A. Student's physical appearance _____
   B. Speech and language characteristics _____
   C. Physical activity _____
   D. Motor coordination _____

12

How to Help the Staff Study and Improve the Curriculum

"Curriculum" is the term for the sum total of the means by which a student is guided to the attainment of the intellectual and moral discipline requisite to the role of an intelligent citizen in a free society. The curriculum, therefore, is not merely a course of study, nor is it a listing of goals or objectives; but rather it encompasses all of the learning experiences that students have under the direction of the school.

Any school system is a part of, and consequently reflects, the unique cultural setting of its society. The school is an integral part of community life, rather than an institution set apart from that life:

> The curriculum is all that goes on in the lives of the children, their parents and their teachers. The curriculum is . . . everything that surrounds the learner in his waking hours. In fact, the curriculum has been defined as the "environment in motion." It is this concept which we try to put into practice . . . and which, of necessity, makes us a community school . . . which recognizes that everything which happens to the learner is educative either for good or for ill . . . since only in that way can the total curriculum be seen in action. Reading, writing, and arithmetic are not the curriculum, though they are part of it. Freedom, self-direction, and social growth are not the curriculum, but they are part of it. Books, tools, supplies, and material are not the curriculum, but they are used by it. School rooms, school buildings, and teachers are not the curriculum; neither are homes, churches, stores, and parents. Yet all of these are part of it.[1]

A school springs from the cultural soil of the community, and its fruits return to enrich that soil. Although the school reflects its society, it still has a responsibility to raise that society to better things. The effective curriculum is one that capitalizes upon the everyday lives of students being served by it, and the job is to move these students as far as possible up to the limit of their capabilities. The cultural values of education must be set in terms of the

[1] Hollis L. Caswell et al., "Curriculum Concepts in a Community School—Glencoe, Illinois," in *Curriculum Improvement in Public School Systems* (New York: Bureau of Publications, Teachers College, Columbia University, 1950), p. 173.

culture in which the student lives, rather than in terms of the culture of the past.

H. Spears[2] indicated that the conception of education which the local community has is more compelling as a curriculum determinant than is the conception of the curriculum that the superintendent brings from the graduate school. Further, the layman's complaints about the schools' accomplishments usually represent too much rather than too little faith in education.

It is entirely within reason to believe that many present-day curricula are entirely out of harmony with modern objectives of education, and hence make it relatively impossible to attain the goals which have been assigned to the modern school.[3]

Experience has shown that failure to keep abreast of social, industrial, and scientific advancements results in a form of cultural lag which may be a factor in social unrest, and even revolution or war. But the public has always been slow to accept changes in education. Campus problems such as those of the Columbia, Berkeley, and San Francisco State variety in the late 1960's have not made it any easier for the truly sincere, modern educator who is in search of progress. Parents often judge schools with reference to what they recall school was like when they were students, and will many times accept deviation from these recollections only in time of crisis.

This chapter includes a discussion of the following topics:

Basic principles and evolving changes in curriculum development

The supervising principal's role in curriculum change

How to use the systems analysis cycle in curriculum development

How to determine resources

The supervision of cocurricular activities

Do—don't

"In-Basket" supervisory problems

Chapter Supplement

[2]Harold Spears, *The Teacher and Curriculum Planning* (Englewood Cliffs, New Jersey: Prentice-Hall, Inc., 1951), pp. 31–59.
[3]Henry J. Otto, *Elementary-School Organization and Administration* (New York: Appleton-Century-Crofts, 1954), p. 78.

Basic Principles and Evolving Trends in Curriculum Development

The following basic principles concern the role of the supervising principal in improving the school curriculum

1. All curricula, instructional guides, and courses of study need improvement and adaptation.
2. The supervising principal should help teachers in improving the techniques utilized in their attempts to improve individual student growth.
3. The principal should help teachers in understanding that curriculum modification is reflected in the students' future.
4. The principal can help teachers in developing fundamental skills and creative abilities in students.
5. Supervisory personnel may help teachers in adapting the curriculum to the life and conditions in which the student lives and learns.
6. Adequate time, specialist-consultant help, and appropriate facilities and materials must be provided if teachers are to improve and adapt the curriculum successfully.
7. Teachers should participate in curriculum evaluation and subsequent revision.
8. Supervisors in intermediate unit offices can help school systems keep their courses of study and instructional guides up-to-date.
9. Research findings add needed knowledge to curriculum improvement.
10. Out-of-class activities concern the supervisor as well as does the regular course of study.
11. Accelerated change in the world hastens the need for curricula revision and makes revised plans and materials less permanent.
12. Teachers should participate in continuous curriculum evaluation and subsequent revision.

Evolution in Curriculum Design

The last quarter of the nineteenth century began a period of expansion and reform which was to last until 1929. Some of the changes which occurred during this period were:

1. Teacher education quality was improved;
2. Private schools were established;
3. Individual evaluation procedures were developed;
4. Modern testing practices were introduced;
5. Individual differences were recognized with curricular implications;
6. High schools developed rapidly.

Since 1929 there has been much progress in the basic reorganization of the school curriculum. The areas include the introduction of greater unity, reality, and democracy into the school experiences of students.

The major types of curriculum organization which have developed include: (1) the subject-centered curriculum; (2) the broad fields curriculum, including the integrated type of organization; and (3) the core program. It is in the *broad fields curriculum* that such terms as social studies, general science, and language arts are used, and that the individual subjects tend to lose their separate identities but still maintain subject matter area boundary lines. In the *core program* broad fields of subjects are combined. As an example of the latter type, language arts and the social sciences could be integrated. It is at this point that we encounter *fusion*—a process whereby broad fields or core subjects completely lose their separate identities and are no longer recognizable.

Leading educators have agreed to the need for curriculum change. The public wants the best possible program of education. This desire was reflected in the passage of the National Defense Education Act of 1958, which came about largely as an answer to the Soviet Union's orbiting Sputnik in October 1957. The Eisenhower administration answered the popular call for America to "catch up" by pushing for passage of the act, which provided for financial aid to educational institutions on a matching basis for advancement in science, mathematics, foreign languages, teacher education, and guidance.

TODAY'S INTERESTING DEVELOPMENTS. Courses which may be termed "nonacademic," except for vocational education programs (especially at the community college and adult-school levels), such as supervised play and manual training, appear to be due for de-emphasis in the school curriculum.

Such interesting developments as the ungraded primary system and grouping according to social maturity have implications for the school supervising principal in the area of curriculum development.

Today's state codes affecting curriculum tend generally to be permissive, with certain subjects specified as required. Prohibited is instruction that would reflect upon citizens of the United States because of race, color, or creed. Generally, no sectarian, denominational, or partisan material is permitted in the public schools; and no bulletin, circular, or any other publication intended to propagandize or indoctrinate may be used in public schools.

Today, lay people, as well as educators, look at educational institutions and strongly criticize the activities they see—or think they see. They criticize courses of study, realizing that curricular inadequacy may mean the despair of the nation's future. Although some of these criticisms are not logical, they are indices of the interest of the people in education and the realization, on the part of the public, of the importance of the role of educational curricula in shaping the destiny of the nation.

Some leading educators have proposed a national curriculum. They have argued that such a curriculum will provide the children and youth in schools throughout the country with the highest possible standards of education. The public is slow to accept this proposal.

DETERRENTS TO CONSTRUCTIVE CURRICULUM CHANGE. Unfortunately, four basic deterrents to curriculum change are existent.

1. Lack of adequate budgeting of time and money for curriculum change;
2. Lack of a common philosophy and agreement upon objectives;
3. Lack of a sound program of public relations which involves the public;
4. The unwillingness of teachers, supervising principals, specialist-consultants, and superintendents to discard that which is familiar.

SUPERVISING CURRICULUM PLANNING. The organization and design of the curriculum will emerge somewhat naturally when the basic goals and beliefs of the school system have been determined. A decision must be reached as to what the school system should do for students. This decision should be presented to the governing board by the superintendent and should be based upon advice and counsel of his administrative assistants, the teachers, and the community.

DERIVING THE CURRICULUM DESIGN. H. J. Otto[4] stated that the design of the curriculum is derived from decisions relating to the scope and nature of the school's objectives, the psychological principles of learning to be used in teaching, the basic orientation of the curriculum, and the types of teaching-learning situations to receive major emphasis.

Supervisory functions should be planned to serve or to further the instructional program. Some implications for supervisors include:

1. Supervision should assist in providing a balanced program of living for students.
2. Supervision should assist in securing a curriculum which will aid students with their needs, interests, and concerns and help them relate these to broader social problems.
3. Supervision should foster a curriculum which builds competence in the basic tools and methods of work.
4. Supervision should encourage student planning and self-direction.
5. Supervision should aid in using the community as a laboratory.
6. Supervision should be adjusted to the type of curriculum planned.

The foregoing statements emphasize the importance of these basic supervisory policies: (1) supervision and administration are important means for the attainment of effective curriculum; (2) supervisory and administrative plans and procedures should be developed cooperatively by the educational staff, the parents, and the students; and (3) the educational program should be conceived, planned, supervised, and administered as a whole.[5]

How to Focus the Forces of Supervision in Curriculum Planning

Some suggested guides for curriculum planning are:

1. Curriculum planning should focus directly on the improvement of student learning experiences.

[4]Ibid., p. 291.
[5]Ibid.

2. Programs for curriculum improvement should be products of cooperative staff activity.
3. Programs for curriculum improvement must be flexible.
4. These programs should be included within the regular school day of the employees involved. Staff members must be freed of some regular duties if they are to participate effectively.
5. Continuous planning for curriculum improvement should be recognized as an integral part of the ideal school program.
6. The responsibilities of the administration in curriculum development should be clearly defined.

In-service education is necessary to supplement the preservice training of many teachers in order to help them in curriculum development. In a well-planned program the administration consults the teachers about the type, variety, and quality of curriculum programs.

HOW TO USE STAFF MEETINGS AND WORKSHOPS IN CURRICULUM IMPROVE-MENT. Frequently, curriculum improvement programs are planned around a series of staff meetings and workshops. If utilized to their fullest advantage, workshops should:

1. Center about the needs and ideas of the staff;
2. Enhance the social, emotional, and professional development of the individual;
3 Provide opportunities for the faculty to contribute to the body of knowledge of the profession;
4. Facilitate access to the assistance of specialist-consultants in curriculum improvement;
5. Provide a stimulus to continued professional growth.

USING ALL AVAILABLE ASSISTANCE AND STIMULATING THE STAFF. The superintendent should make use of all local resources. Usually there are colleges and universities upon which he can rely for assistance. Other local specialists should be enlisted. Curriculum planning, experimental pilot studies, and study groups will serve to stimulate and encourage continued professional growth in a school system.

The Supervising Principal's Role
in Curriculum Change

While most economic, industrial, and scientific changes are out of the control of the supervising principal, other factors can be controlled. High morale and good human relations facilitate curriculum development at the building level.

Human Dynamics and Curriculum Improvement

The supervising principal must work to develop a creative climate within the local school. Skill in human dynamics is the essential ingredient for success in curriculum improvement.

Leadership in curriculum research and design must not be identified as a position of status; the principal must assume the role of a member of the group. He must have the capability to guide his fellow staff members to gain new insight into the problem on which they are working. He should create an atmosphere conducive to curriculum improvement through encouraging faculty members to use their abilities, interests, and aptitudes to the end of cooperative solving of curricular problems.

By helping the staff in this way, the principal discovers the talents and resources of each individual member. When these elements are put to proper uses, curriculum improvement can be achieved smoothly and successfully.

Techniques

It must be understood that in treating the problems of improving the quality of curriculum there is no one *best* way to proceed. The staff might be helped in proceeding through the steps presented by exploring a number of avenues:

1. Workshops in which the leader, who would be a person who has had a great deal of work in the area of curriculum, would draw ideas from the group as well as have opinions of his own to contribute may be employed.

2. It may be desirable to form a community-teacher committee to decide upon what things are most important in these changing times and agree on how best to include them in the curriculum. Due caution must be observed here, however.
3. Faculty committees should be organized to develop new instructional guides in a designated area or to change existing guides which seem outmoded.
4. Specialists need to be consulted. This can be done in terms of a survey, observation, and consultation, or a series of lectures in specific problem areas.
5. The department or grade-level meeting should be a source of great strength if the teachers can be made to understand that their opinions are of great importance and will be given true and honest consideration.
6. The maintenance and improvement of curricular efficiency can be expedited by the promotion of high staff morale. These two go hand-in-hand and must be maintained if an effective program is to be carried through.

THE SUPERVISOR EMPLOYS THE WORKSHOP TECHNIQUE IN CURRICULUM IMPROVEMENT. By the process of leading the participants into various areas of exploration as to possible curriculum change or improvement, several things may be accomplished. This does not imply that the members of the group act in a sponge-like manner. Rather, it implies that most teachers can profit from the ideas of specialists and, properly directed, these ideas can be put into operation.

In the absence of a recognized specialist, a group of teachers may conduct their own workshop or study group under the direction of the supervising principal. This participation would be more in the nature of an exchange of ideas.

THE PROJECT METHOD APPROACH TO CURRICULUM DESIGN. In either of the foregoing situations the possibilities for change of a positive nature are unlimited. The changes which evolve from the types of meetings which have been described can be of major importance and of long-standing significance, provided the supervisor serves in the capacities of leader, specialist, and coordinator. It might be helpful to use a project-method approach. Some guidelines for the use of this technique are:

1. This procedure would be initiated by the various staff members choosing to work in an area in which change is contemplated.
2. With several groups involved, the ideas and suggestions which would be forthcoming should be helpful and meaningful. The supervisor must give the necessary direction to make the project worthwhile.
3. During the process of executing the proposed plan of action the supervising principal must act as a counselor or adviser, insuring that the groups or committees, and their discussions as a whole, do not become too labored nor stray too far afield.
4. Of necessity, the principal must serve as both director and consultant. In conjunction with this role, certain areas developed by the staff may be incorporated into particular areas of the curriculum on an experimental basis in order to see the possible reactions to the changes.
5. After a trial period the proposals can be evaluated and reorganized to strengthen areas of weakness.
6. The revised plans, with recommendations as to their use, then can be presented to the committee-of-the-whole. While there would be nothing binding on the committee, the possibility of new areas which have been explored with some degree of detail could have nothing but a beneficial effect on the studies of the committee.

Figure 12–1 presents a pictorial representation of the program for curriculum change.

In planning for curriculum improvement the supervisor should aid the faculty in (1) identifying school objectives, (2) deciding what learning experiences will best achieve these objectives, (3) organizing experiences for teaching and learning, and (4) appraising and judging. Generally, the steps involved include:

1. Identification of an existent curriculum program with which there is considerable dissatisfaction;
2. Survey and assessment of the curriculum as it presently exists;
3. Identification of a specific difficulty on which to work;
4. Search for ways and means of improving the program;
5. Selection and trial of promising solutions;

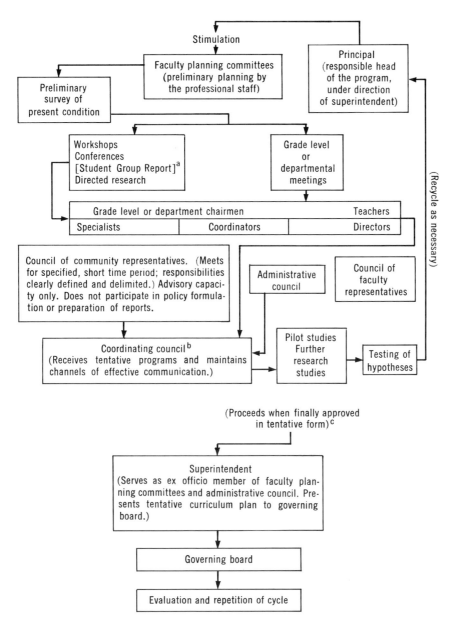

FIGURE 12–1   The Program for Curriculum Change.

[a] If school serves pupils of grade eight or above, may include student group report.

[b] The Coordinating Council is composed of representatives from community, administrative council, outside consultants, and faculty. It resubmits preliminary progress reports and preliminary plans to all participating above that level in the chart for evaluation, review, and revision, in addition to function noted above.

[c] Reports on curriculum improvement are considered tentative rather than final, since the latter implies a closed issue or an ultimate answer.

6. Careful appraisal of consequences;
7. Reconstruction of practical values;
8. Suggestions put into action;
9. Cycle starts again with another difficulty.

HOW TO INVOLVE THE COMMUNITY IN CURRICULUM DEVELOPMENT. The parent's association and recognized local service organizations (Kiwanis, Lions, Masonic organizations, and other fraternal, social, and service groups) should be invited to send representatives to serve as members of a lay advisory committee on curriculum design. The committee should identify an area within the curriculum as a starting point for its work. The committee then systematically attempts to discover what is being taught in the given area and what steps need to be taken in order to include those items which are deemed important but are not yet a part of the curriculum. In this type of situation, people from the community can be of great help by letting the educators know what they feel is important.

Within any community the people can be of assistance in the development of any program, and of even greater value in insuring the acceptance of the program. The supervisor can be especially helpful here, serving both as the representative of the superintendent and as specialist in current practice, recent research, and legal requirements. A group of this kind should be made up of a number of lay and professional people to insure the best results in implementing the program.

COMMUNITY PARTICIPATION. The discussion method must, of necessity, be a contributing part of any community-professional staff relationship, and will be discussed in Chapter 13. The method of community participation should be utilized with extreme caution, and only when definite objectives as well as delimitations of committee functions are established. A definite date of termination should be prescribed.

How to Use the Systems Analysis
Cycle in Curriculum Development

The supervisor may wish to employ the systems analysis approach to curriculum design. The Task Group on the Systems Approach to Education and Training[6] has developed a simplified approach which might be employed in the design of a program for curricular improvement. The systems analysis cycle is represented graphically in Figure 12–2.

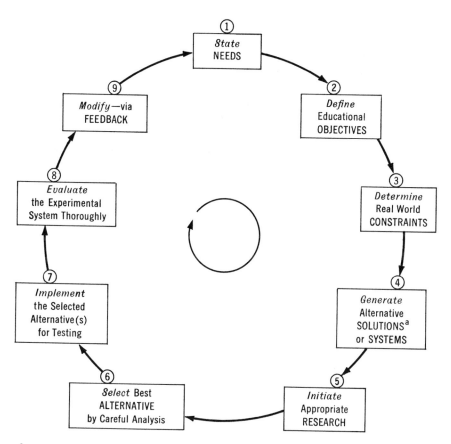

^aLook at each alternative in terms of restraints and potential for accomplishing objectives.

FIGURE 12–2   The Systems Analysis Cycle.

[6]The Task Group on the Systems Approach to Education and Training, Henry Lehmann, Chairman, *Eight Steps in the Design of an Education and Training System* (Washington, D.C.: The Group, 1967).

Step 1: How to State the Problem

The operational statement of the real problem being faced by the society under consideration is that statement which initiates consideration of an educational system as a potential solution.

1. Start with an expression of the *generalized* need; e.g., "our society needs better medical care."
2. Determine whether education constitutes at least a partial satisfaction of the need.
3. Determine, in the light of present state-of-the-art, what type of manpower and what skills are needed (e.g., in a community college, the training of more knowledged medical technologists).
4. Define more specifically and in greater depth the group of people and skill areas required to satisfy the need.
5. Verify the need and the delineation of the group concerned through the judgment of knowledgeable people in the real world involved.

Let's evaluate and consider the following hazards:

1. Have you specified the real problem, or are you addressing a synthetic subproblem which may presuppose a favored solution? (Have you considered the need for improved, modernized equipment, rather than additional personnel?)
2. Have you based the problem too heavily on assumptions and too little on verified findings?

Step 2: How to Define the Educational Objectives

Defining educational objectives involves the determination and specification of the terminal capability desired of students after having successfully completed a learning experience. Figure 12–3 compares objectives stated operationally and subjectively.

The supervisor should:

1. Define that portion of the need which can be satisfied by the education system.

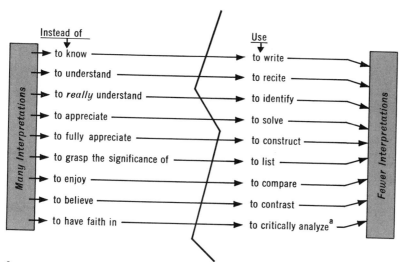

[a] After Robert F. Mager, *Preparing Instructional Objectives* (Palo Alto: Fearon Publishers, 1962), p. 11.

FIGURE 12–3   Using More Precise Terminology in Stating Curricular Objectives.

2. Describe in measurable terms the observable act(s) which will be accepted as evidence that the learner has achieved the objective.
3. Describe the environmental (stress) conditions under which the desired end behavior must be demonstrated.
4. Define the minimum acceptable criteria for demonstrating terminal behavior objectives.

Let's evaluate:

1. Are you sure that your objective contributes significantly to satisfying the real need?
2. Are your objectives stated in specific measurable terms (must be able to identify themes from Beethoven and Mozart piano concerts) as opposed to qualitative statements (must develop an understanding and appreciation of romantic music)?

3. Is your definition of the test conditions realistic and valid in light of the true need?
4. Have you confined your statement of objectives to "should be able to . . . ," or have you mixed in references as to how the student will in fact acquire these capabilities?

Step 3: How to Identify Limiting Constraints

Constraints are those real-world limiting conditions which must be satisfied by any acceptable system designed to attain the educational objectives.

1. Identify the applicable constraint families (initial student behavior, facilities, financial, timing, staff limitations, administrative, political, others).
2. List specific constraints within each family and establish the source of the constraints.
3. Label the constraints by severity (physical law, short-term but inviolate, financial or political; psychological or political, subject to change).
4. Rank constraints, in order, upon the system design.

Let's evaluate:

1. Have you separated:
   Findings from assumptions?
   Constraints from variables?
   Intuition from bias?
   Need from unwarranted special interests and pressures?
2. Have favorite solutions introduced unwarranted constraints?
3. Have you eliminated all but a favored answer by seeing constraints which are, in reality, nonexistent?
4. Have the constraints been validated carefully?
5. Has the prerequisite or presupposed student *entry behavior* been identified and defined with accuracy sufficient to permit the design of a system to bring about the required change in behavior?

Step 4: How to Generate Alternatives

Proposing alternatives involves the generation of candidate systems which could achieve the objectives for consideration:

1. Gather data based on current and expected state-of-the-art with respect to potential means toward the specified ends.
2. Solicit ideas from a wide spectrum of sources.
3. Keep a written list of all suggested ideas. *Record all ideas,* even if they appear to be impractical or seem to violate constraints.
4. Gather more data if the ideas are insufficient in quantity or scope.

Let's evaluate:

1. Are ideas solicited only from a favored few?
2. Have ideas which seem impractical or inappropriate been rejected? (If "yes," refer to item 3 above!)
3. Are you inhibiting contributors from proposing solutions which could be termed as "radical" or unusual?

Steps 5 and 6: How to Initiate Appropriate Research and Select the Best Alternative Proposal

The systematic evaluation of all alternatives in terms of objectives and constraints in order to select the one which is considered the most desirable requires that supervisors:

1. Define the criteria which will be used to select the most promising system.
2. Establish a quantitative method for rating each alternative against the selection criteria.
3. Evaluate the relative importance of the selection criteria.
4. Gather data pertinent to each alternative.
5. Relate all possible *constraints and limitations* (hazards and defects) to each alternative.

6. Utilize analytical methods (anything from logical thinking to mathematical models) to select the best alternatives.
7. Review the results of the analysis against mature judgment.
8. Make final selection of alternative(s) for testing.

Let's evaluate:

1. Have you considered all pertinent selection criteria?
2. Is your evaluation system producing bias in the answer?
3. Do you balance systematic analysis and considered judgment as you proceed?
4. Are radical solutions automatically, if unintentionally, eliminated so as to avoid possible problems?
5. Has a predetermined conclusion been rationalized?
6. Is there objective evidence that the means selected really are effective?

Step 7: How to Implement the Selected Alternative

Implementation implies the first adoption of the selected alternative to meet the specified objective. The supervisor should:

1. Delineate the activity elements, schedule of events, and resource requirements.
2. Plan a program to evaluate the selected alternatives(s) in utilizing a *pilot program* as a test phase, *if possible*, so as to minimize the risk factor.
3. Establish a controlled experiment and/or establish machinery to collect data (performance, financial, others) to use for evaluation.
4. Implement the program with conviction.

Let's evaluate:

1. Has the system been implemented in sufficient depth so as to permit success?
2. Have you planned to continue the experiment over a sufficient length of time (so that valid results may be obtained)?
3. Are you considering alteration of the original plan without sufficient justification?

4. *Are you ready to demonstrate active resistance to those who would have you stop after one or two early faltering steps?*
5. Are you prepared to go ahead if reasonable success is demonstrated or to repeat earlier steps if results are unsatisfactory?
6. Are you willing, and endowed with sufficient courage, to try something new?

Step 8: How to Evaluate the Results of Your Curriculum Development Program

Evaluation implies the determination of the conformance or discrepancy tween *all* of the objectives initially specified and the performance that was actually obtained. The supervisor should:

1. Review his original statement of operational objectives, noting particularly the statements concerning specific, measurable behavioral outcomes.
2. Review his original statement of operational objectives, noting the statements that concern the environment within which the behavior is to be demonstrated.
3. Develop as many reliable and valid procedures as may be required to determine which objectives are being met.
4. Incorporate in the procedures diagnostic features that provide definite guides for corrective action.
5. Apply the procedures to the tentative-experimental system.
6. Interpret the results of applying the procedures. Both quantitative and qualitative approaches are appropriate and are called for.
7. At regular, specific intervals review and reevaluate the problem and *all* elements of the system.

Let's evaluate:

1. Are you evaluating with a mind to the originally specified behavior?
2. Are quantitative measures valid and reliable, and do they measure characteristics of the same parameters specified in the objectives?
3. Have you avoided subjective (it seems great!) responses?
4. Have you provided for evaluation of the *temporal stability* (lasting quality) of the behavior?

5. Have you reexamined the statement of *assumptions* to determine if they are both explicit and tenable?

Step 9: How to Use Feedback to Modify the Curricular Learning System

The final step in the systems design approach to curricular improvement involves the process of modifying the designed learning system based on deficiencies in meeting the objectives as determined through evaluation. The supervisor should:

1. Examine discrepancies between the specified system, or objectives, and the obtained system performance as determined by thorough evaluation so as to determine probable cause for deficiencies.
2. Analyze the entire system to ascertain where the correction can best be made.
3. Develop a specific plan for correction.
4. Make the correction during the next system cycle.
5. Conduct a new evaluation and continue this cycle until the specified performance is attained.
6. See to it that general feedback leads to continuous analysis and evaluation.

Let's evaluate:

1. Are you willing to admit that you had discrepancies which need corrective action or are you blaming it on problems "which are normal at this early phase of our operation?"
2. Are you sure the system has actually been implemented the way you thought it would be?
3. Do not be fooled by initial success, but continue the evaluation to detect the degradation of system performance with time, and to evaluate the quality of education under real-world conditions.

Figure 12–4 depicts the process diagrammatically.

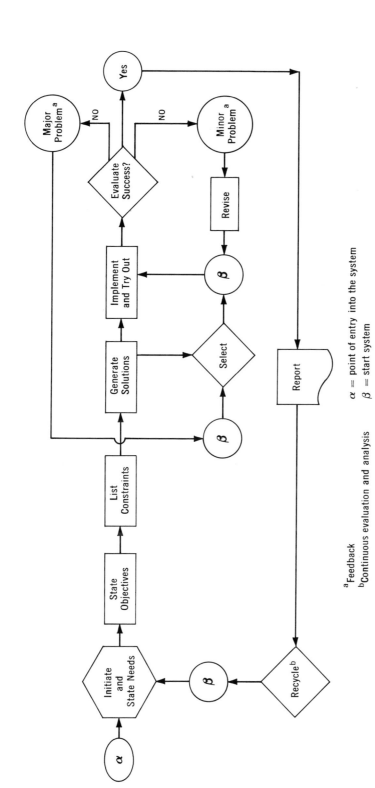

FIGURE 12–4   Diagrammatic Representation of the Systems Analysis Approach to Curriculum Development.

[a]Feedback

[b]Continuous evaluation and analysis

α = point of entry into the system

β = start system

How to Determine Resources

The supervisor should seek out teachers, consultants, students, administrators, and parents in order to gather information on any phase of the curriculum.

The program of evaluation must be extended to include a wide variety of evidences of student growth. The school psychologist can be of great assistance in the evaluation of a given program or a suggested change. The opinion of the school nurse must be considered, for she probably has had an opportunity to view the present program and its accompanying effects on the students. In any case, the supervisor should determine if the program seems to be doing the desired job and how, if at all, a proposed change would help to improve the educational program.

The Council of Faculty Representatives and the Coordinating Council

The council of faculty representatives is the advisory board selected by the teachers through which teachers are represented at scheduled meetings with the administration and community leaders via the coordinating council.

Since the trust of the rest of the faculty is placed in these agencies, the possibility of having suggestions considered with a good chance for action is greatly enhanced. No group will function with any degree of success unless there is some indication that their suggestions at least will be considered. Good staff morale is an important part of any curriculum change or improvement.

PRACTICAL ESSENTIALS. There must be great consideration given to the practical possibilities for curriculum amendments, the economy of such changes, the good which is expected from such changes, the policies which have been in practice up to this time. All of these things must be taken into consideration if real progress is to be achieved.

REQUISITE ESSENTIALS: FACULTY PARTICIPATION AND SUPPORT IS ENHANCED THROUGH EFFECTIVE COMMUNICATION. Let us consider the possibilities for success of an addition to the curriculum:

1. If this change is to be successful, it must first have the support of the faculty. This goal can be accomplished only by a full explanation of the reasons for making the change and the additional procedures for putting this change into action. If this petition for support has been preceded by actual contributing effort on the part of the faculty, the chances for general acceptance will be greatly enhanced.
2. A second factor to be considered is the need for economy in putting the program as changed into action. The public has the right to expert efficiency and economy and quality in curriculum development.
3. Finally, the community must be informed and must understand the need for and the procedures involved in implementing the proposed change, although it is the professional staff that ultimately should decide what change is to be made.

How to Use Outside Specialists Effectively

Although the use of outside specialists for the *total* program of curriculum development has fallen into disuse in many situations, the need for such experts has not entirely disappeared. There are certain areas in which an expert can provide great benefits to the program. These areas include:

1. The specialist in a given subject area who can bring new ideas to the teachers is valuable. Also, the matter of techniques and methods can be greatly supplemented if a person from outside the school brings in suggestions.
2. The specialist also has his place in the area of advice and/or judgment concerning a particular problem area that may be causing great concern within the total structure. This person may work in various ways, such as talking to teachers, students, and administrators and making personal observations; and then bringing together all of the information in terms of a report. The specialist has the advantage of not being hampered by superficial problems; he can evaluate without concern for individuals.
3. The third area of expertness involves a team of specialists to evaluate the curriculum. Generally, the survey method used by this group involves the opinions of specialists in the various fields of curriculum. This may

be accomplished over a period of days or weeks, but a study of this kind can be of great help in pointing out areas that need consideration.

Another source of valued opinion is that of the law enforcement and probation officers who have direct contact with students. Will this program, as proposed, help to solve any problem in the area of concern?

No matter what the change, whether it be of major consequence or a change in the smallest order of business within a given subject area, the importance of making the proper choice for maximum benefit is of primary significance.

Beware the Pseudo-Experts in Curriculum Change

There have been many views concerning the best way to improve curriculum. There was a time, not long ago, when the pseudo-expert emerged in the field of curriculum. Many changes which occurred were the result of imitation, opportunism, and pressure from special interest groups. Although this was progress, it was of a negative quality. There is a weakness in relying on outside "experts" for the introduction of subjects into the curriculum. This phase has passed, and a more realistic approach to the problem now is pursued.

OTHER CONSIDERATIONS. Certain subjects must be taught in the public schools, and any change must be within the prescribed limits by law.

The danger of special interest groups needs some consideration since many pressure groups seek benefits for a minority. It need only be remembered that the general interests of the public at large must, of necessity, be given first consideration.

Curriculum Improvement and Teacher Growth

During recent years curriculum improvement has been recognized as a chief vehicle of teacher growth. Attention has been directed toward achieving change in the experiences of students with change in teachers.

Curriculum change involves what we know about students and how they learn. Public interest now is focusing on educating the talented, or gifted. Individual needs have made the classroom a laboratory for learning.

Schools must be kept up-to-date if teachers are to accept curriculum commitments. Each teacher should have some professional help in utilizing research.

The continuing study of the curriculum in American schools is highly important. Not only is it essential that prospective teachers have a good understanding of curriculum principles and procedures, but also it is important that teachers in service continuously review and refine these curriculum essentials.

Research reveals that curriculum improvement involves many people—teachers, principals, parents, students, and others. Curriculum development is a complex social enterprise demanding the highest skills in human relationships, guidelines, respect for personalities, mutual responsibilities of individuals and groups, and good reflective thinking.

The curriculum content of the public schools constantly is being evaluated. Faculty committees, curriculum specialists, and citizens advisory committees are concerned with the courses offered and their content.

If the program for curriculum improvement has been carried on successfully, the professional staff should have:

1. Surveyed the present situation;
2. Decided on school objectives;
3. Decided what learning experiences would best achieve those objectives;
4. Organized the experiences for teaching and learning;
5. Judged the entire program and its outcomes;
6. Made a plan for further action.

The Supervision of Cocurricular Activities

Basic Beliefs Regarding Student Activities

There are three basic attitudes concerning cocurricular activities operating in American schools:

1. *The strictly academic viewpoint* views the curriculum as "only those subjects for which unit credit is offered and marks are assigned," and does not recognize the activities program as a part of the curriculum.

2. *The all-inclusive viewpoint* views everything students do or accomplish while under supervision of teachers as "curricular." Nothing advocated or sponsored by the school is considered to be "extra" or outside the curriculum.
3. *The combination* views selected allied activities, such as debate and dramatics, for which credit is not assigned as considered to be part of the curriculum.

The type of program implemented depends upon the school's location, background, traditions, and the attitude of the staff and the community.

THE SUPERVISING PRINCIPAL DELEGATES RESPONSIBILITY UNDER EACH TYPE OF PROGRAM. Under the academic viewpoint there is no delegated responsibility as a rule, unless specifically assigned by the administration. Under the combination program there are limited responsibilities to those assigned to sponsor groups. The all-inclusive program results in maximum responsibility since no real delineation is made between classroom duties and activities; both are considered vital to student learning.

CHARACTERISTICS OF THE ALL-INCLUSIVE PROGRAM. The all-inclusive program embraces the entire school community—the students, the parents, the administrators, the teachers, and the classified staff.

The program provides a natural and wholesome outlet for the energies and interests of students. With the supervision and guidance of interested teachers, students are provided with a laboratory in which to practice and test ideas taught in the classroom.

The following evaluation checklist may prove helpful in improving cocurricular activities.

1. Does the principal have control of the leadership of the activity?
2. Is a definite meeting time allotted for the activity?
3. Is the activity sponsored by a member of the faculty?
4. Are the meetings attended by a sponsor?
5. Are the students allowed to elect their activities under proper supervision?

6. Is activity membership governed by approved rules of the school?
7. Is membership limited to regular students?
8. Are the meetings held on the school grounds?
9. Is the money (if any) audited by the sponsor?
10. Is there money in the school budget for defraying the expenses of the activity program?
11. Does the activity fill a social need?
12. Are students selected to office on a fair basis?
13. Is the number of organizations to which a student may belong limited?
14. Does the activity have a written constitution?
15. Is an activity record kept for each student?
16. Are the meetings and events of the activity arranged for in advance?
17. Are faculty members trained in directing student activities?
18. Does the activity fulfill definite stated objectives?
19. Does it grow out of the needs and interests of the students?
20. Are democratic group processes emphasized?
21. Is interest the primary membership requirement?
22. Does it place any other activity above it on the scale of importance, or is it equal?
23. Does the activity have educational value?
24. Is mental activity considered a form of action?
25. Is there provision for evaluation?

See Figures 12–5 and 12–6 for two devices which may prove helpful in evaluating cocurricular activities.

FIGURE 12–5   Evaluation Sheet for Activity Adviser

1. Am I interested in my activities assignment? _____
2. Do I attempt to inspire student interest in activities? _____
3. Do I believe that activities participation can be of great value? _____
4. Do I yield my "teacher" role to become a partner in the activity? _____
5. Do I provide ideas and leadership subtly? _____
6. Do I attend meetings regularly and arrive promptly? _____
7. Do I earn and keep the respect and confidence of the group? _____

8. Am I following administrative policy and decisions, and at the same time aiding students in understanding and respecting these decisions? _____

9. Do I maintain an adequate personality at neither extreme? _____

10. Do I keep a sense of humor and good nature at all times? _____

11. Do I exercise a good sense of relative values; stress only those things really important and valuable? _____

12. Do I give adequate preparation, time, and thought to my group's activities; keep aware of their progress and needs? _____

13. Do I try to expand my effectiveness in activities? _____

14. Do I try not to become discouraged easily, even if students do?_____

15. Do I ever consider when I might be wrong and admit it? _____

16. Do I have the courage to try something new? _____

17. Do I try to understand and observe regulations and procedures related to activities? _____

18. Do I evaluate activities constantly with a view toward change where the need is indicated? _____

FIGURE 12–6   Student Evaluation Sheet for School Organizations

Directions:

Do not sign your name. Make your statements concise and to the point.

1. Did you attend all the meetings of this club?_____

2. Have you participated in the activities of this club as much as you would like to? _____

3. Would you like to be a member of this club next semester: _____

   Why? _____

   Why not? _____

4. Among the activities of the club, which have you enjoyed the most? _____

5. Regarding the meetings of the club, check the answers you think best apply to each of the statements below:

   a) Too long _____

   b) Too short _____

   c) The right length _____

   d) Held too often _____

e) Not often enough _____
f) At correct intervals _____
g) Very interesting_____
h) Fairly interesting _____
i) Boring _____

6. What suggestions might the club adopt in order to be a more effective organization?

_____
_____
_____

How to Supervise the Organization of Play Days and Sports Days in the Cocurricular Program

The California Association for Supervision and Curriculum Development reported the following committees to be of assistance in carrying through the activities of cocurricular education:

1. Planning Committee
2. Reception Committee
3. Registration Committee
4. Public Relations Committee
5. Rules and Regulations Committee
6. Officials Committee
7. Communication Committee
8. Field and Equipment Committee
9. First Aid Committee
10. Refreshment Committee
11. Evaluation Committee

The following techniques should be used in a program for the improvement of the curriculum in the school:

[7]California Association for Supervision and Curriculum Development, *Organizing and Conducting Intramural Programs, Play Days, Sports Days, and Field Days* (Sacramento: The State Professional Committee on Health, Physical Education, and Recreation, 1962), p. 7.

DO

1. Determine the degree of readiness for curriculum change through opinionaires, parents' association meetings, conferences, surveys, teacher reactions, editorials, results of standardized tests, and research.
2. Encourage laymen, administrators, teachers, and other certificated personnel to participate in curriculum development committee work.
3. Employ a curriculum specialist to facilitate the work of teacher committees.
4. Send a "kit" containing a statement of objectives and pertinent materials to teachers participating in curriculum revision.
5. Maintain a professional library containing books on curriculum, copies of other school systems' courses of study, and curriculum records to aid teachers in curriculum improvement.
6. Budget time for teachers to work on curriculum committees.
7. Keep a current card file on outside consultants available for help in curriculum revision.
8. See that curriculum revisions are in harmony with the education code.
9. Help teachers establish, supervise, and evaluate a tentative curriculum revision before it is adopted.
10. Encourage teachers to work jointly with other teachers of the grade behind and the grade ahead to achieve continuity in the course of study.
11. Organize staff meetings and individual teacher conferences to discuss curriculum adaptation and revision.
12. Facilitate curriculum committee work by making pertinent materials, equipment, secretarial assistance, and consultants available.

DON'T

1. Lose sight of the axiom that improving the school curriculum requires the professional capabilities of the highly skilled educator. Although the pulse beat of the community must be taken, it is the professional educator who must prepare policies concerning the curriculum.
2. Fail to allocate sufficient time, facilities, and finance so that these activities do not become a burden to the participants.

Supervisory Problems

Problem 1

Playground supervision is the responsibility of the teaching staff. The supervision of students begins when they arrive on the school grounds, includes recesses and noon hour, and does not end until the departure of the school bus at the end of the day.

A special problem involved in this area is the early arrival at school of students whose parents begin work at 8:00 A.M. Another problem is that many primary students eat hot lunches in the cafeteria. These students are on the playground before 12:00 noon, as it is necessary to stagger the lunch hour in order to accommodate the remaining students. A third problem occurs after the primary grades are dismissed at the close of school. The local students can go home, but the bus students must remain either in their respective rooms or on the playground.

How can a really effective schedule be arranged for the supervision of these students without jeopardizing the preparation time of the teacher?

How could appropriate cocurricular activities be identified and initiated?

Problem 2

Doris Hamilton, supervising principal of the St. Andrews High School, has been under pressure by the superintendent since St. Andrews High had not been participating actively in the school system-wide curriculum study and revision committee. Although Doris was interested in working closely with her fellow administrators and with the Citizens Advisory Committee for Curriculum Study, when she announced the existence of the curriculum study program and requested volunteer assistance on the part of the faculty, only one teacher from the staff indicated any interest.

What should Doris do? How should she proceed?

Problem 3

A meeting of the supervising principals advisory committee (the membership of which included the two assistant principals, the coordinators of counseling and cocurricular activities, and three teachers elected by the faculty) met to discuss the school's general curricular subject pattern. Miss Rose, the principal, began the meeting by reviewing several changes made in course offerings and graduation requirements during the immediate past years. She concluded by saying, "This year's curriculum, or at least its basic pattern, can hardly be changed now. Any proposals which we make at this meeting should be for the coming school year, or perhaps even later." It was early in the fall semester.

Mr. Lewis, the science teacher, said, "I'm very concerned about the students who may complete their high school program without a course in science. Unless a student has to take science for college preparation, we have no required science course."

Miss Muriel, the guidance counselor, said, "That is true, but we have encouraged all students to have at least general science or nonlaboratory biology. Also, many noncollege students elect the applied science course in their eleventh or twelfth years."

The science teacher responded, "Perhaps all of us should review the records of our last two graduating classes to determine how many enrolled in a science course."

Mr. Hart, the mathematics teacher, responded, "Regarding our requirement of one year of mathematics, noncollege students usually meet this requirement by enrolling in general math in the ninth grade. Actually, a good review course in mathematics would do them more good in their senior year. We might excuse some students from the course if they made sufficiently high scores during the junior year. If this were done, it would be easier to require a science course at the ninth-or tenth-grade level."

The counselor added, "I have often wondered why any mathematics necessary for noncollege students cannot be incorporated in the shop, homemaking, science, commercial, or other course where the mathematics is applied."

Mr. Hart responded, "Does this group have any authority to alter existing graduation requirements?"

After further discussion, it was agreed that the pattern of graduation requirements should be reviewed.

What should the supervising principal do at this point? What plans should he make? What should his answer be to Mr. Hart's question?

Selected Bibliography

Books

Anderson, Vernon E. *Principles and Procedures of Curriculum Improvement.* New York: The Ronald Press Company, 1956.

Beck, Robert, Walter Cook, and Nolan Kearney. *Curriculum in the Modern Elementary School.* 2d ed. Englewood Cliffs, New Jersey: Prentice-Hall, Inc., 1960.

Benne, Kenneth D., and Bozidar Muntyan. *Human Relations in Curriculum Change.* New York: The Dryden Press, 1951.

Dewey, John. *Democracy and Education.* New York: The Macmillan Company, 1916.

Hutchins, Robert M. *The Higher Learning in America.* Cambridge: Yale University Press, 1936.

Kelley, Janet A. *Guidance and Curriculum.* Englewood Cliffs, New Jersey: Prentice-Hall, Inc., 1955.

Krug, Edward A. *Curriculum Planning.* New York: Harper and Brothers, 1950.
_____. *Curriculum for Elementary School Children.* New York: Harper and Brothers, 1950.

Lee, J. Murray, and Doris May Lee. *The Child and His Curriculum.* New York: Appleton-Century-Crofts, 1960.

Mager, Robert F. *Preparing Instructional Objectives.* Palo Alto: Fearon Publishers, 1962.

Miel, Alice. *Changing the Curriculum: A Social Process.* New York: D. Appleton-Century Company, 1946.

Neagley, Ross L., and N. Dean Evans. *Handbook for Effective Curriculum Development.* Englewood Cliffs, New Jersey: Prentice-Hall, Inc., 1967.

Otto, Henry J. *Elementary-School Organization and Administration.* New York: Appleton-Century-Crofts, 1954.

Pritzkau, Philo T. *Dynamics of Curriculum Improvement.* Englewood Cliffs, New Jersey: Prentice-Hall, Inc., 1959.

Ragan, William A. *Modern Elementary Curriculum.* Rev. ed. New York: Henry Holt and Company, 1960.

Smith, B. Othanel, William O. Stanley, and J. Harlan Shores. *Fundamentals of Curriculum Development.* New York: The World Book Company, 1950.

Sowards, G. Wesley, and Mary Margaret Scobey. *The Changing Curriculum and the Elementary Teacher.* San Francisco: Wadsworth Publishing Company, 1961.

Spears, Harold. *The Teacher and Curriculum Planning*. Englewood Cliffs, New Jersey: Prentice-Hall, Inc., 1951.

_____. *Curriculum Planning through In-Service Programs*. Englewood Cliffs, New Jersey: Prentice-Hall, Inc., 1957.

Periodicals

Beauchamp, George A. "The Elementary School Principal's Responsibility in Curriculum Improvement." *Educational Administration and Supervision* XL (February 1954): 103.

Cunningham, Ruth, and Alice Miel. "Research in Elementary School Curriculum Development." *Journal of Educational Research* LX (January 1947): 365–392.

Dewey, John. "Education and Social Change." *The Social Frontier* III (May 1937): 235–238.

Lyda, Wesley J. "Suggested Conceptual System for Decision Making in Curriculum Developing." *Educational Record* XLI (January 1960): 74–83.

Olson, Arthur R. "Organizing a Faculty for Curriculum Improvement." *National Association of Secondary School Principals Journal* XII (September 1961): 178–184.

Other Sources

American Association of School Administrators. *American School Curriculum*. Departmental Thirty-First Yearbook. Washington, D.C.: The Association, 1953.

American Society for Curriculum Development. *Learning and the Teacher*. 1959 Yearbook. Washington, D.C.: The Society, 1959.

California Association for Supervision and Curriculum Development. *Organizing and Conducting Intramural Programs, Play Days, Sports Days, and Field Days*. Sacramento: The State Professional Committee on Health, Physical Education, and Recreation, 1962.

Caswell, Hollis L. et al. "Curriculum Concepts in a Community School—Glencoe, Illinois," in *Curriculum Improvement in Public School Systems*. New York: Bureau of Publications, Teachers College, Columbia University, 1950.

Floyd, Earl Howard. "The Organization and Administration of Curriculum Programs in Selected City School Systems." Doctoral dissertation, University of Southern California, 1954.

The Task Group on the Systems Approach to Education and Training, Henry Lehmann, Chairman. *Eight Steps in the Design of an Education and Training System*. Washington, D.C.: The Group, 1967.

Educators, Philosophers, and Sociologists Influence School Supervision

Philosophers such as Socrates, Aristotle, Locke, and Descartes, who expounded the philosophy of Cartesian rationalism, have made contributions to school supervision.

Herbart, Froebel, Pestalozzi, Hand, Hutchins, Maritain, and other famous educators and sociologists of the past have been vitally important to the development of the curriculum and its supervision.

This chapter supplement outlines briefly the lives of these educators and the philosophies and sociological constructs that have had the most influence upon education.

The Educators

The Empiricists

Included among the early Empiricists whose philosophies did much to implement supervision and instruction were John Locke (1632-1704) and Immanuel Kant (1724-1804). Locke believed that the mind contained no content except experience—that the mind was a passive receiver; Kant believed that although the mind contained nothing except experience, it did have forms of its own in order to classify or order that which was received through experience.

Johann Friedrich Herbart (1776-1841), also an Empiricist, denied the existence of anything peculiar to the mind itself that could manufacture ideas without experience. He opposed Locke and Kant on this matter. He believed that no content, except that of experience, mediated by the senses, was present in the mind. It was false to assume that the mind had some sort of mysterious faculties.

Herbart was successful in attacking faculty psychology, but did not succeed in establishing psychology as a true science. He believed that the power to form knowledge from experience was a function of the ideas themselves. This was closely allied to what was termed by others as "associationism." Herbart believed that the mind itself gave nothing. He did believe that contiguity was a very important factor in learning. He believed that if two ideas were contiguous in time and space, that is, if they were learned together, they would stay together.

According to Herbart, the power to create knowledge was in ideas themselves, which would seek out in the mind other ideas that were related to them. These ideas, then, would enter the conscious mind, pass through it to the *subconscious mind,* where they would continue to be active rather than passive.

William James' concept that even after one ceases in his attempts to learn something, he continues learning it, goes back to the Herbartian idea of the subconscious mind. When new ideas are similar to the idea in the subconscious, the old idea can easily ascend to the conscious mind. This process was termed "apperception," which was defined as the quality of perception plus something from previous experience with which to interpret, greet, welcome, or combat the new idea or experience.

Herbartian Theory and Method

Herbart was without question the greatest educational philosopher of his time. He was honored with a chair in philosophy at the University of Leipzig, and established the experimental school. His theories had applications in the field of aims or goals of education and educational instructional methods and procedures. As a result of the influence of Herbart, the schools of Germany in the 1800's were the best in the world. Herbart integrated the curriculum with a central core of history. The method that was used in Germany at the time was the Herbartian method. In one lesson the famous five steps would be accomplished:

1. *Preparatio*n of students;
2. *Presentation* of new ideas;
3. *The assumptio*n of new ideas to old in the conscious and the subconscious;
4. *Generalization,* or the extension of meanings; and
5. *Application* to the new situation.

Rousseau

Jean Jacques Rousseau (1712–1778), a follower of Locke, believed that all learning was based on experience. He thought that direct firsthand experience without intervention of communication, coupled with removal of the child from civilization, and returning him back to nature where he could learn from firsthand experience, would produce the optimum in education.

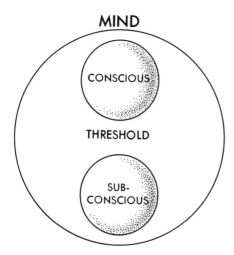

FIGURE SUPP. 12–1   The Mind: The Theater of Action for Ideas.

In his famous book *Emile* he presented an attack on French aristocracy and its practice of wet-nursing and the lack of identification of child with father.

The earliest of John Dewey's writings were written when he was a disciple of Rousseau, around 1900. In *Emile,* the tutor of Emile provided experience leading to learning without really telling Emile anything. Emile learned by himself, the hard way.

Some have criticized Rousseau for his concepts as presented in *Emile,* which stated that it is society, not the individual, that is fundamentally important, that education may modify the social medium, and that education really cannot occur in a social vacuum.

Pestalozzi

In Switzerland the work of Johann Heinrich Pestalozzi (1746–1827) with pseudoferal orphans received much attention. He adopted the philosophy of Kant for his own, stating that the three forms that would fit into Kant's philosophy of the mind giving form to what the mind received were language, for the classification or naming of things; form, itself; and number.

Pestalozzi claimed that without classification, sorting, and identification the human intellect was of no use. He believed that the mind needed constant practice, and that to improve its capacity, to give adequate expression in language, experience was needed.

Pestalozzi hung tapestries on the wall and would ask the student what he saw there. He would emphasize that what the child was seeing was a representation of a line brought about through an arrangement of colors of threads that looked like a line. He believed in training students to do certain exercises that would improve the minds of people in giving forms to experience.

The purpose of education, according to Pestalozzi, was to train the mind in giving forms to broad categories of materials. Pestalozzi attempted to train the individual to observe the actual shape of things in nature by having him draw these things. He taught drawing by producing a geometric design that he claimed had all the degrees and elements of drawing. His students would practice the figure over and over again. This practice was to become the basis for our own education in the twentieth century.

Pestalozzi also believed that children should be prepared for vocational life as well as being prepared to better organize and interpret experience. At Yverdon, in Switzerland, Pestalozzi would strike his desk with a long, heavy stick and ask his students to shout their lessons louder than his banging.

In summary, the main concept that Pestalozzi introduced was that of firsthand experience being essential for education, with reality in learning being essential so that one may give form to new experience.

Around the time of the Civil War, Edward A. Sheldon, who had gone to Canada where there was an exhibit of the objects used in the Pestalozzian school in England, brought Mrs. M. E. M. Jones from England to teach and started the first training school for teachers at Oswego, New York. The institution was called the Oswego Normal School and was open to all during the last quarter of the nineteenth century.

Froebel

Friedrich Froebel (1781-1852) established the first kindergarten in Germany. Froebel, a mystic, believed in development of the spirit. He further believed that, through the use of sensory experience, spiritual growth could occur. Froebel painted a circle on the floor that was to represent the unity of mankind and God.

The students in Froebel's first kindergarten would sit around the circle holding hands. Theoretically, they were thus unified in spirit. He introduced "gifts" or playthings for the students in the kindergarten. Such gifts included the round ball (for from such contact an appreciation of the uniformity existent in universe could result), a cube (to demonstrate the strength and power of God), a pyramid, and various other solid wooden forms for a total of twelve "gifts." Froebel's curriculum consisted of playing, pleasure, learning, much sensory stimulation and contact, thinking about the forms or gifts, drawing, music, and the like.

The name "kindergarten" was first given in 1840, and the first German kindergarten was established on the American continent in 1855. The teacher was Mrs. Schurz. The first English kindergarten in the United States was in Boston in 1860. The teacher was Elizabeth Peabody. This institution was later to become the first teacher training school.

The great thinkers and pioneers in educational thought enunciated concepts upon which modern supervision has been built. These concepts fashion the design for an evolving democratic program.

The Philosophies

The philosophies which have had the most influence on education in general, and supervision in particular are those of pragmatism, realism, and idealism. Although not new, existentialism is still in the proving laboratory.[1]

---

[1] For an interesting comparison between pragmatism and existentialism, the philosophy which teaches that philosophy is for everyone, that everyone can decide on the kind of person he wishes to be by identifying the assumptions and choosing the values by which he wishes to govern his life—that it is the individual, not external forces or environment, who is responsible for making decisions and taking action, see Nancy Gayer, "Will Existentialism Triumph Over Pragmatism?" *Phi Delta Kappan* XLIII (October 1961): 20–24.

Pragmatism: James, Peirce, and Dewey

William James reported that the term "pragmatism" was derived from the Greek words pragmatikos and praktikos, meaning "action."[2] Our own words *practical* and *practice* are of the same origin. James noted that the term pragmatism was first introduced by Charles Peirce in the year 1878 in an article that appeared in the *Popular Science Monthly* for January 1879, and that was translated in the *Revue Philosophique* for January 1879, Volume VII. The article was entitled "How to Make Our Ideas Clear."[3]

After noting that beliefs are really rules for action, Peirce observed that in order to develop a thought's meaning we need only determine what conduct it is fitted to produce; "that conduct is for us its sole significance."[4]

Peirce emphasized the importance and meaning in solving problems, complaining that the absolutely unknowable was unmeaningful. To Peirce, in order to have meaning, a problem must be logical, literal, and have the quality of public understanding. He emphasized the scientific method, the standard of objective intelligibility, and stressed emphatically that meaning was equal to the sum of the verifiable consequences; that is, consequences that were verifiable through investigation. By this Peirce meant that whether a statement was true or false was irrelevant. What was important was what difference the meaning of the statement would have in the experience of the individual if it were true, as opposed to the different state of the universe that would exist if the statement were not true.

While statements were significant to Peirce if the consequences of the meaning of the statements were capable of experimental investigation, for William James[5] statements were significant if the meaning of the statements could influence human conduct. The nature of meaning to William James could be explained on a psychological basis.[6]

---

[2]Joe Park, ed., *Selected Readings in the Philosophy of Education* (New York: The Macmillan Company, 1958).
[3]For a lucid treatment of the terms "logical positivism," "rationalism," and the application of analytical philosophy to educational supervision, see Nancy Gayer, "How to Get the Fly Out of the Bottle," *Phi Delta Kappan* XLIII (April 1962): 276–283.
[4]Park, *Selected Readings*, p. 57.
[5]Ibid., pp. 8, 12, 151, 163, 172, 228, 231–232, 238.
[6]For a brief biological sketch of William James see Park, *Selected Readings*, pp. 55–56.

John Dewey[7] thought of ideas as instruments and denied antecedent reality. Dewey noted that the kind of knowledge that was present was derived partly from the means of obtaining this knowledge. If knowledge was not from a problem, it was mere verbalism.

To both James and Peirce an idea would produce satisfaction because the idea was true; the idea would not be true because it was satisfying. To the pragmatists, truth was scientific truth; verified experimentally for social and public value. For Peirce two different moments, separate in time and space, were required for knowledge. The first moment was the problem, the act of looking or searching for something; and the second moment was the determination of whether that which was predicted was actually found. If so, there was knowledge.

To Dewey, only the second moment was required; that is, once involved with a problem did research lead to what was predicted? If so, it showed that we have knowledge. Dewey stressed that experiences must be firsthand, and that an idea worked if it would achieve goals in practical life. Therefore students, according to Dewey, first must encounter a problem. Generalization was all right, if the generalization helped to solve a specific problem. Those working in school supervision have been much affected by the pragmatic approach.

Educational Implications of Pragmatism

Pragmatism has broad implications for education. Some scientists have claimed that pragmatism includes some of the best concepts of the philosophies of subjective idealism and realism. Yet pragmatism is certainly a philosophy unto itself, for it has both external and internal consistency.

If one were to follow the philosophy precisely, there would be fewer lecturers in the classroom; circumstances would be arranged to make the child see the need for learning to read and to foresee all consequences of desired

[7]Ibid., pp. 73–74; John Herman Randall, Jr. and Justus Buchler, *Philosophy: An Introduction* (New York: Barnes and Noble, Inc., 1942), pp. 119, 130–132; and Merritt M. Thompson, *The History of Education* (New York: Barnes and Noble, Inc., 1951), pp. 51–52, 57. The latter reference includes an outstanding comparison between the philosophy of John Dewey and that of Giovanni Gentile and Plato.

12 SUPPLEMENT

actions. The teacher would change students so that they would not misbe-
have by helping them to see the consequences of their actions. Punishment,
to pragmatists, was merely a stopgap. Effort and discipline follow interest;
therefore discipline would result from cooperatively chosen goals. Since the
learner's behavior changed constantly, the educator must create an optimum
condition for growth and development through insight and understanding.
Individual interests, value, and behavior are important. Education is to take
place through experience; and through the modification of experience one
would gain power, which is knowledge. If one has knowledge, one might
predict the consequences of his act. Education is, then, a reconstruction
process, and learning is equal to the consequences of perceiving the effects of
an action.

The pragmatic supervisor would certainly operate within the scientific
frame of reference. He would stress obtainable objectives that are of value
to the individual and to society.

Realism

Bertrand Russell[8] was opposed to the pragmatic philosophers, including John
Dewey. To Russell, when one truly *knew* everything was all right, the
real state of affairs of the world was satisfactory. To the realist, reality
existed before we came to know it, and our knowing it did not change the
environment. This concept was in direct opposition to the ideas of the
pragmatists.

According to realism, the perfect idea existed in reality. Such an abstrac-
tion as the perfect circle, or as the square root of minus one, existed in
reality as the perfect idea. Moral law, to the realist, was a part of reality.
The realist educator could possibly, as a first course of action in the case of
disciplinary action in the classroom, send the child to the principal, for the
real world was independent to be learned about—the same for all people
universally. The realist educator would not be worried about the individual
child as such; he would, however, attempt to aid his charges through instruction of the great classics.

[8]Park, *Selected Readings*, pp. 295, 352, 367.

Educational Implications of Realism

Some educational implications of realist philosophy would certainly have to include the instruction of the content of the great classics, in order to put the student in cultural touch with the heritage of the race. The task of the school, according to the realist, is to help children understand the world in which they live, for they were born into a culture not of their own making.

To the realist, administrators and supervisors along with boards of education have the legal right to manage education but should certainly refrain from doing so. Those who study the human mind come to know the world as it really is; therefore, specialists are better qualified than laymen concerning specialties in education. The realist educator would teach art for art's sake; the art object would possess quality all by itself. If a beautiful painting were held in a dark room with no one looking at it, it would still be beautiful and have the qualities of beauty.[9]

A further purpose of the school is to help the learner to identify rationally with the world in which he lives. One branch of the realist school of philosophy stresses role-playing and molding the mind and soul of the individual. Realists of this branch of the school of philosophy would control behavior in order to gain acceptance into the group. Unfortunately, the methods and objectives of this group dynamics branch of the realist school of philosophy are at once both undemocratic and totalitarian. The reader should not confuse those individuals who are sincerely interested in promoting better human relations through group and individual dynamics with the group dynamics branch of the realist school of philosophy. Realism has had some impact upon supervision.

Idealism: Subjective and Objective

The *subjective idealist* stressed the principle *esse est percipi*—"to be is to be perceived." According to John Locke's successor, George Berkeley (1685–1753),[10] the notion of material reality behind ideas was superfluous. Only ideas in our minds existed. Whatever exists does so only when

[9]Robert L. Brackenbury, *Getting Down to Cases* (New York: G. P. Putnam's Sons, 1959), pp. 58–74.
[10]Randall and Buchler, *Philosophy: An Introduction,* pp. 101, 103, 208–220.

thought of. What we can think of, we can speak of without mere verbalism. The unexperienced is the inconceivable; for everything was created within experience, and could not exist without experience. Only minds or spirits were real; there was no event and an idea of an event, for they were the same thing. The danger here was solipsism, that *self* was the only existing reality.

According to Berkeley, what we get through sensations is equal to ideas in the mind. This latter thought was in conformity with the ideas of John Locke. The only thing we know, however, according to Berkeley, is the idea of an object. In the individual mind, one is different from the world at large.

The *objective idealist,* on the other hand, emphasized the presence of a universal mind, while the *absolute idealism* of Hegel (1770–1831)[11] stressed the idea that human processes were the reflection of the universal process and absolute universal reason. The objective, real world is mental. So, to the objective or absolute idealist, each individual mind was part of the universal mind. There is just mind.

Hegel's extreme historianism—the idea that everything eventually is a result of history—led, eventually, to the evil concept of the master race, for such historianism had as its goal the remaking of the world. The world, according to these philosophers, had a history that went on working toward some later outcome. To evaluate experience Hegel stressed the dialectic technique of thesis-antithesis-synthesis. The *thesis* is an established but inadequate system or idea, the *antithesis* is the clash aimed at the correction of the inadequacy, and the *synthesis* is the final molding of the best elements of each viewpoint. Karl Marx was one of Hegel's disciples.

Hegel said that a kind of soul was present in humanity and it was necessary for us to promote that soul above all. This idea was somewhat similar to the ideas of objective idealists, who talked about a universal soul.

The aims and objectives of the subjective idealist would be to develop the inner self in the most healthful way possible. In the Middle Ages the philosophy of *personalism* and *humanism* were essentially subjective idealism.

If the misbehaving child were to be treated by the subjective idealist he

[11]Ibid., pp. 222–225.

probably would be sent to the nurse. Undoubtedly he was not feeling well emotionally. Self-realization, then, is vital to those who believe in this mystical philosophy of subjective values.

Educational Implications of Idealism

The subjective idealists placed one's personal experience in prime focus To change one's interior self for the better and to help a person know himself better and achieve social approval through education would be prime goals of education for the subjective idealist. Each person in the classroom possesses traits, tenderness, talent, and desires that are constantly undergoing modification.

The game of life in schools should help children realize their potentials; to see themselves as others do. If a child is misbehaving in the classroom, the problem exists because there is something wrong with the environment, not with the child. Know thyself would be the creed of the educational subjective of the educator who believed in this philosophy.

To the subjective idealist it would be the children of the classroom who would determine what is to be taught. The school exists to help perfect the individual. As Emerson stated, what children do is foreordained; we must respect the child. Aesthetic experience was all right because such experience would lead to self-realization. The child would learn when he would relate the subject matter to his own goals. He must see significance to be stimulated to learn. Probably the dominant and objective idealist and scholasticist would want to emphasize one major goal for education, that being that one must learn to suppress urges. The manner in which the same sentence might be interpreted by subjective and objective idealists, pragmatists, and realists is presented in Table Supp. 12–1.

The following cases may assist the reader in understanding further the major philosophies that have influenced education.

Case 1

Mary entered Mr. Books' classroom after the tardy bell rang. Mr. Books listened patiently to Mary's explanation of the reasons for her tardiness. He

TABLE SUPP. 12–1   How Subjective and Objective Idealists, Pragmatists, Realists, and Scholasticists Might Interpret the Same Sentence

The Statement	The Philosophies
You	Subjective idealist stresses
should not	Scholasticists and objective idealists stress
destroy	Pragmatists stress (consequences)
school property.	Realists stress

then decided that Mary had to learn that there were certain things that she had to do and certain things that she could not do, as was stressed in the tales of chivalry in Sir Thomas Malory's *Morte d'Arthur*. He therefore sent Mary to see the principal, Mr. Lawrence.

Mr. Lawrence, after listening to Mary's story, decided that Mary's problem was that she had not learned the consequences of arriving late at school. He therefore explained these consequences to her, and helped her to foresee what would happen in the future should she be tardy again, miss the beginning of the lesson, and disturb the class on her late arrival. He showed her how having missed the beginning of the lesson meant that she would miss the day's work and that she probably would not understand what had happened for the whole school year.

He convinced Mary that she should try and try again to arrive at school on time in the morning. He then asked Mary to return to class.

As he stressed the importance of the cultural heritage of the literary works of the past, as well as the existence of certain moral laws that were outside of oneself and to which one must adjust, the teacher had emphasized certain ideas with which many who followed the realist philosophy would not argue. The principal, in stressing the consequences of the act, had attempted to proceed in a more scientific and cautious manner, and had been able to convince Mary of the foreseeable consequences of arriving tardy at school. He was acting as would many pragmatists. He could have determined the cause for Mary's late arrival, had he been better versed in the finer aspects of the philosophy.

Case 2

Tom had been getting into a great deal of trouble this past semester. He had been caught attempting to steal the only flute owned by the school music department, but fortunately for him he had been caught by Miss Alan.

Miss Alan had decided that Tom's real problem was that he was ill. She therefore proceeded to treat him to the best of her ability, trying to bring forth from within that which was really and truly virtuous; for the individual was all-important to Miss Alan, who followed the philosophy of the subjective idealists.

Tom was lucky, however, for Miss Moffitt, the school secretary, was able to convince him that he needed to learn to suppress his urges.

In the latter case the clerk performed as would the objective idealist, while Miss Alan had performed in a manner to which many who followed the subjective idealist's cause would not object.

The Sociologists

The viewpoints of leading figures in the field of sociology have had a definitive influence on the role and function of the supervising principal. John Dewey, a liberal, stressed the idea of teaching for social change. Dewey's theory was not that of life adjustment; he did not hold that we should adjust to what *is,* but rather that we should *change* that which presently exists. Dewey and the famous sociological trio Smith, Stanley, and Shores[12] agreed that schools have a social function.

Harold Hand[13] stressed the need for a core program of common learnings that would include the techniques of solving problems dealing with the individual's developmental tasks. The curriculum would also include instruction in the requisites to citizenship in a democratic society.

[12]John Dewey, "Education and Social Change," *The Social Frontier,* III (May 1937), 235–238; and B. Othanel Smith, William O. Stanley, and J. Harlan Shores, *Fundamentals of Curriculum Development* (New York: Harcourt, Brace & World, Inc., 1950), pp. 186–192, 726–727.
[13]Harold C. Hand, "The Case for a Common Learning's Program," *Science Education* XXXII (February 1948): 5–11.

12 SUPPLEMENT

The developmental tasks are functions of the individual's sociological and psychological needs. Some developmental tasks, therefore, are common to children everywhere, but not all tasks are common to all children. The problems incident to this approach result from the inherent value judgments that must be exercised.

Hand disagreed violently with the theories of John MacDonald, which are explored below, and attacked a curriculum composed exclusively of traditional subjects. Hand did say, however, that value judgments enter here, and that if we are looking for traditional learnings we should employ someone who is skilled in teaching traditional subjects.

Warner, Havighurst, and Loeb[14] stressed that education should serve as a social elevator, and must exclude all implications of the caste system. They emphasized that it most assuredly is democratic to have high standards and to select. They noted that value judgments must occur, but that indoctrination need not take place.

Philosophically, MacDonald[15] was a realist. He believed that the world is as it is and that there is a universal cycle of psychologically expanding worlds. He defended the traditional subjects and was opposed to the ideas espoused by Harold Hand. MacDonald stressed that no subject by itself will do the job of education; the teacher serves an equally important function. He thought that the job of education is to produce a liberally educated individual.

The intellectual virtues were emphasized by Robert Hutchins.[16] He believed that it is the job of education to cultivate the mind, and that the curriculum must be organized to accomplish this task. Since the school's sole responsibility, according to Hutchins, is to develop the mind, other functions must be left to other institutions, and training must not be confused with education. There must be no "how to" in school; there should be no shop or industrial arts courses.

Hutchins believed that all men are rational to some extent. As a realist, he stressed the study of the great books. He also believed that initially we

---

[14]W. Lloyd Warner, Robert J. Havighurst, and Martin B. Loeb, *Who Shall Be Educated?* (New York: Harper & Row, 1944), see especially pp. 141–158.

[15]John MacDonald, *Mind, School, and Civilization* (Chicago: University of Chicago Press, 1952), especially pp. 85–94.

[16]Robert M. Hutchins, *The Higher Learning in America* (New Haven: Yale University Press, 1936), especially pp. 59–70.

must reach an agreement on philosophy, following which we would be able to oust the problems of education. This latter belief is not concurred in entirely by the authors of this textbook, who believe that theory has a *reciprocal* relationship to practice.

Hutchins would build the mind from a study of the great books, grammar, rhetoric, logic, and Euclidean mathematics.

The new humanism of Jacques Maritain[17] stressed the need to liberate the individual so as to produce the man. Leisure time education, the development of personality, and the meeting of the needs of life in community civilization were central in Maritain's system.

Smith, Stanley, and Shores were close to Dewey[18] in their beliefs concerning social change and education. They placed social change in primary focus as an objective of education. The sources of educational authority, according to Smith, Stanley, and Shores, are derived from the capabilities of professional experts and from the local and the national good. Professional educators, including supervising principals and teachers, determine the means, and society determines the ends.

A summary of the beliefs of these sociologists is included as Table Supp. 2.

Supervisory Implications

The supervisor should seek:

1. The maximum development of individuals and groups for participation in a democratic society;
2. Provision for participation of each individual in all decisions, issues, and problems;
3. The development of respect for intellectual integrity and differences of opinion on educational problems;
4. The cooperative participation by all staff members in the program for school supervision;

[17]Jacques Maritain, *Education at the Crossroads* (New Haven: Yale University Press, 1943), see especially pp. 85–100.
[18]John Dewey, *Democracy and Education* (New York: The Macmillan Company, 1916).

TABLE SUPP. 12–2   Sociological Influences on the Role of the Supervisor in Curriculum Development in Terms of Goals

The Sociologists	Goals of the Curriculum
Dewey	Social change—liberal.
Hand	Traditional subjects should be de-emphasized. Common learnings. Developmental tasks. Core program. Social and psychological needs.
Warner, Havighurst, and Loeb	Social elevators; values but not indoctrination.
MacDonald	Traditional subjects—the teacher is equally important (versus Hand).
Hutchins	Intellectual virtues. The cultivation of the mind is the only job of the school. Great books. No social amenities.
Maritain	New Humanism. Religion. The individual.
Smith, Stanley, and Shores	Social change—reconstruction for the national good, with development of the individual.

5. The recognition of individual differences among staff members as well as among students;
6. Initiation of the supervisory program at the attainment level of the staff;
7. The utilization of scientific evidence and experimentation within a workable philosophy to secure answers to problems;
8. Support for a continuous evaluation of supervisory objectives, procedures, and accomplishments.

13

How to Measure Teacher Effectiveness and Improve Methods and Techniques of Instruction

If civilization is to advance and our nation to develop, improvements in teaching are essential. Teachers must employ the most effective instructional techniques. If this goal is to be realized, those who direct the efforts of others in the field of education continuously must evaluate the effectiveness of teaching and must be aware of the results of modern research and current, up-to-date, best practice which might present implications concerning the methods and techniques of those whom they supervise.

It is the purpose of this chapter to indicate several of the techniques and methods available for evaluating teacher effectiveness and for assisting teachers in the improvement of instruction. The following topics are covered:

Basic principles
How to get started in measuring teacher effectiveness
How the principal should initiate the evaluation program
How to encourage teacher self-evaluation
How to select criteria
How to evaluate instructional efficiency
Do—don't;
"In-Basket" supervisory problems
Chapter Supplement

Basic Principles

The several supervisory techniques are not applicable to all teachers, nor are they effective to the same degree. E. O. Melby, in 1929, made an inventory of the various supervisory techniques. He concluded:

... it must be admitted that the plan of [supervision] ... for any school system will depend upon those factors of school organization, teacher training, and educational objectives which ... [prevail] in that system. These factors are dynamic rather than static. It is, therefore, to be expected that ... [continuous] modification must be made in the organizations charged with the responsibility for the improvement of teaching, as well as in the [techniques].[1]

It is necessary for supervisors to be aware of all applicable techniques. The supervising principal has a responsibility to provide leadership and to apply in practice the following basic principles:

1. Teaching methods can be improved through adequate and appropriate supervision.
2. All certificated personnel have degrees of responsibility for improving classroom methods and should function as a supervisory team.
3. Supervisory personnel should practice effective democratic methods in supervision if they expect teachers to use such methods in the classroom.
4. The merit of all methods of classroom instruction should be weighed in terms of desirable student growth.
5. Good supervision promotes methods that bring about a classroom climate of satisfaction and accomplishment.
6. Supervision should provide help for individual teachers and a general methodology improvement program.
7. Supervision of methods should include preplanning, observation, and a follow-up conference.
8. Wise supervision should include freedom for teacher initiative in classroom experimentation of methods.
9. Suggestions of methods should utilize the capabilities of the entire staff.
10. All supervisors, in recommending methods, should consider the individual differences of teachers as to personal, physical, mental, and social capabilities.
11. A primary approach to methods revision is acquaintance with late research in the field.

[1]Ernest O. Melby, *Organization and Administration of Supervision* (Chicago: Public School Publishing Company, 1929), p. 37.

12. Supervision should produce in teachers a genuine interest in professional improvement of teaching methods.
13. A good supervisory program of methods revision grows out of the classroom and leads to further improvement.
14. Effective supervision provides for a cooperative program, of continuous evaluation and improvement, of all methods used.

How to Get Started in Measuring Teacher Effectiveness

Before a program for measuring and improving teacher effectiveness can get under way, there must be general agreement on a school system-wide basis that the chief function of modern supervision is the evaluation and improvement of the factors affecting learning. This major function clearly necessitates certain subsidiary functions.

1. We cannot evaluate except in terms of an accepted philosophy, an accepted and understood statement of aims. The cooperative formulation of this statement is a function of school supervision. Common purposes, goals, and standards are thus established.
2. A process has to be developed for carrying on an educational program aimed at achieving the objectives.
3. A staff and organization, varying in size, complexity, and relationships, must be established for implementing and improving the program. The policy, process, and organization should be of such nature as to protect and stimulate the individuality and creativity of persons included. Human relations are far more important than the mechanical efficiency of any process or organization.
4. A policy and process for community relations must be devised, stressing cooperative participation in policy making and planning.
5. A theory and practice of evaluation must be developed which is consistent with the accepted goals and philosophy.[2]

---

[2] A. S. Barr, William H. Burton and Leo J. Brueckner, *Supervision* (New York: Appleton and Company, 1938), p. 3.

How Supervision May Differ in Definition and Practice

The historical development of school supervision explains many difficulties and strengths in modern supervision. Supervision, properly defined and understood, often differs widely from supervision as it is practiced. It is at this point that the educational worker who relies solely on experience makes his greatest blunder, both in his own actions and in his interpretation of what he observes. What he, with pride, frequently calls the "practical" view as distinguished from the "theoretical" is neither practical nor theoretical, but merely the result of a lack of information.

The experience upon which the naive practical man relies is usually fragmentary and inadequate, and usually incorrectly interpreted. Experience, if it is to become a basis for conclusions, must be enlightened and illuminated by knowledge of basic principles and facts derived from philosophic reflection and from controlled research. *Critically analyzed experience* and the critical analysis of wide observation of practice are valid bases for conclusions.

The aim of supervision in the abstract has been the same throughout history—the improvement of instruction. But if one includes in this definition the connotations with respect to methods and processes that were accepted in the past, one will see how different the old definition really is from that of the present.[3]

The Implications of Current Knowledge for Evaluation and Improvement Programs

The avoidance of errors resulting from outmoded principles and practices may be insured partially by the use of new principles and practices.

1. Education is recognized as a basic social force affecting the development of human personality and of a stable democratic social order.
2. A consensus must be developed within the group as to the ends and values of life, hence of education, before details of education, hence of supervision, can be developed.

[3]Edwin H. Reeder, *Supervision in the Elementary School* (Boston: Houghton Mifflin Company, 1933), p. 15.

3. Change is recognized as a principle of the universe, affecting all phases of life and of social organization.
4. The process of social change is recognized and used.
5. Supervision is recognized as a social process; in our country it is a cooperative democratic process.
6. The chief function of supervisors is leadership and the stimulation of leadership within the group.

How the Principal Should Initiate the Evaluation Program

The principal should be able to identify good and poor teaching and be able to assist individuals in making their own evaluation of instruction. He should be able to make positive recommendations for improvement or to enlist the aid of those who can be of help. Through observation and participation, he should keep in close touch with classroom activities in order that he may be better able to give assistance to each individual.

The Principal and Teacher Appraisal

There are various types of teacher appraisal forms. Some of these forms are based on the supervising principal's expectations which list, for the most part, desirable qualities. Rating scales, observation forms, the predictive appraisal of teacher training institutions, studies of student opinion, and other diagnostic techniques are used. All of these devices provide *subjective measurement of no more than a sample portion of total performance.*

An evaluation procedure should be used *with* teachers, rather than *on* teachers. Evaluation must be viewed as *a cooperative attempt to solve a professional problem.* Discussion of the items on evaluation forms may serve as an effective stimulus to desirable classroom results. An evaluative scale could be used well by teachers for self-evaluation and subsequent conferences with the supervising principal. Teachers must be encouraged to use whatever self-appraisal techniques are suitable.

If teachers feel that the results of evaluation will be used against them, they will be unwilling to reveal weaknesses and problems. They will be eager to participate in evaluations, however, which strengthen their own professional status.

A First Step in Teacher Appraisal

One of the first steps in teacher appraisal is to accept criteria for effective teaching. Administrators and staff members should be responsible for the selection of these criteria via a cooperative process. In fact, cooperative planning and joint effort hold the key to any successful evaluation program. Evaluation should be purposeful. Too often it is considered as an end in itself. True evaluation is for improvement and growth through analysis of an individual's strengths and weaknesses, and thus it should be the basis for guidance and constructive criticism.

How to Assume Supervisory Responsibility

For a successful evaluation program the principal *must* accept the responsibility for acquainting the teacher with what is expected of him and what appraisal techniques are being used. Teachers must think in terms of the constructive concept of evaluation and must consider it a source of help. The principal must avoid giving the impression that the evaluation is the final verdict on the teacher's work and worth.

Teacher appraisal should be continuous rather than periodic. It should be accompanied by, and followed with, helpful supervision. The *purposes* of evaluation may be for retention or dismissal; for promotion, tenure, or merit pay; or for improvement of instruction. The most vitally important of these purposes is the improvement of instruction.

How to Determine the Appraisal Task Functions of the Supervisor

A. S. Barr and others[4] have listed the appraisal and improvement task functions of the supervising principal:

1. Evaluating the data related to the educational products in terms of the accepted goals of education and the objectives of instruction.
   a) Determining cooperatively critical analysis of goals.

[4] A. S. Barr et al., *Supervision* (New York: Appleton-Century-Crofts, 1947).

b) Selecting the means of appraisal and applying them.

c) Analyzing the data so as to discover strength and weakness in the product.

2. Conducting a critical analysis of the entire teaching-learning situation so as to determine the antecedents of satisfactory (anticipated) and unsatisfactory student growth as reflected in observable behavioral changes and operationally defined capabilities.

a) Studying the course of study and the curriculum-in-operation.

b) Studying the materials of instruction, the equipment, and the sociophysical environment of learning and development.

c) Studying the factors related to instruction (the teacher's personality, academic and professional training, organization for instruction, use of materials, methods and techniques of instruction, and other factors).

d) Studying the factors present in the learner which may be investigated (capacity, interest, work habits, and others).

3. Improving the entire teaching-learning situation.

a) Improving the course of study and the curriculum-in-operation.

b) Improving the materials of instruction, the equipment, and the sociophysical environment of learning and development.

c) Improving those factors relating directly to instruction which may be dealt with by the supervisory team.

d) Improving such factors as may be present in the learner which may affect his development and achievement which may be attacked in the school situation.

4. Evaluating the objectives, methods, and outcomes of supervision.

a) Discovering and applying the techniques of evaluation.

b) Evaluating the results of given supervisory programs, including the factors which may tend to limit the success of those programs.

c) Evaluating and improving the performance of all who compose the supervisory team.

In performing these functions, the supervisor should call upon specialists from the intermediate and state units. Local system supervisors in a given geographical area should cooperate in area meetings and in the sharing of materials.

Some Contrasts in Traditional and Modern Appraisal Techniques

The characteristics of modern appraisal and improvement techniques, as opposed to the more traditional programs, are summarized:

1. Modern supervision directs attention toward the fundamentals of education and orients appraisal and improvement programs within the general aim of education.
2. The aim of supervision is the appraisal (analysis) and improvement of the total teaching-learning process—the total setting for learning—rather than the narrow and limited aim of improving teachers in service.
3. The focus of appraisal is on a situation, not on a person or group of persons. All persons are co-workers aiming at the improvement of a situation. One group is not superior to another, operating to "improve" the inferior group.
4. The teacher is removed from his embarrassing position as the focus of attention and the weak link in the educational process. He assumes his rightful position as a cooperative member of a total supervisory team concerned with the improvement of learning.

Traditional supervision too efficiently did well what should not have been done at all. The attention of modern appraisal and improvement program supervision is focused more upon the aims, structure, and fundamental processes of education, and on how well we meet our objectives, than upon the minute, specific, day-to-day devices for the improvement of trivial aspects of classroom procedure. With improved levels of teacher and supervisor training the invention, selection, administration, and application of devices should become more and more a question of individual initiative based upon understanding of basic principles. The sphere of modern supervision is the whole range of elements affecting learning.

How to Encourage Teacher Self-Evaluation

THE IMPORTANCE OF SELF-SUPERVISION. The move away from imposed supervision, coupled with the desirable modern emphasis upon cooperative group endeavor, sometimes obscures the possibilities for self-direction, self-supervision, and self-guidance. The supervising principal may wish to present the teaching analysis sheet which appears as Figure 13–1 and the checklist, included as Figure 13–2 to his staff as aids in teacher self-evaluation.

FIGURE 13–1   Teaching Analysis Sheet

Student: Your cooperation is sincerely desired in filling out this questionnaire. The following, when completed, will aid the instructor in obtaining an evaluation of the success of the methods that he has employed and the classroom environment that he has created. Because of the benefit to both instructor and future students, please be sincere in answering these questions. *Do not sign your name!* Explain items marked D and F; make any other comments on reverse side of sheet. Indicate your opinion by encircling the appropriate letter before each item.

A—Excellent   B—Good   C—Average

D—Below Average   F—Poor   O—Does not pertain to this course

INSTRUCTOR EVALUATION

A B C D F O   Knowledge of subject matter.
A B C D F O   Is willing to admit error or lack of knowledge about a certain area.
A B C D F O   Interest and enthusiasm for subject.
A B C D F O   Interest and attention of class.
A B C D F O   Ability to stimulate your interest in subject.
A B C D F O   Definite, clear-cut presentation of subject matter.
A B C D F O   Criticizes students' efforts on a constructive basis.
A B C D F O   Voice qualities (pleasant, easily heard, etc.)
A B C D F O   Awareness of students' failure to understand.
A B C D F O   Understanding attitude toward students' efforts and problems.
A B C D F O   Approachability of instructor.
A B C D F O   Freedom of student to express his own ideas.
A B C D F O   Preparation for class meetings.

COURSE EVALUATION

A B C D F O   Clarity of course objectives.
A B C D F O   Use of recent research and material in this field.
A B C D F O   Logical arrangement of topics and material.

FIGURE 13–1 (Continued)

A	B	C	D	F	O	Clear examples and illustrations.
A	B	C	D	F	O	Use of examples that make course interesting.
A	B	C	D	F	O	Effective use of class time.
A	B	C	D	F	O	Clarity and readability of text.
A	B	C	D	F	O	Value of text for course.

MARKING EVALUATION

A	B	C	D	F	O	Value of exams for measuring your knowledge.
A	B	C	D	F	O	Clarity of assignments and exams.
A	B	C	D	F	O	Fairness of grading system.
A	B	C	D	F	O	Is the amount of work required appropriate for credit received?
A	B	C	D	F	O	Uses tests for actual learning situations, after they have been returned.
A	B	C	D	F	O	Prompt return of assignments and exams.

FIGURE 13–2 A Checklist for Teachers

HOW DO I RATE AS A TEACHER?

KEY: Indicate A for excellent
B for very good
C for passable
D for poor, needs improvement

1. Do I create, a happy, relaxed, but business-like atmosphere? _____

2. Is order and control inherent in my approach to classroom management? _____

3. Am I conscious of each student's potentials and needs? _____

4. Do I avoid judging students by adult standards? _____

5. When a student does not reach my standards do I search for causes? _____

6. How do I encourage initiative and originality? _____

7. Has every student confidence that I will try to see his problem from his point of view? _____

8. Do I have conferences with each student as often as possible? _____

9. Do students come to me for advice voluntarily? _____

10. Do I recognize symptoms of withdrawal, timidity, unsociableness, and discouragement as being especially serious? _____

FIGURE 13–2   (Continued)

11. Am I impersonal in dealing with behavior problems? _____

12. Do I analyze behavior problems through a systems analysis approach? _____

13. Are specific instructional objectives, stated in terms of observable changes in behavior and performance, definitely formulated? _____

14. Do I stimulate my students by scheduling field trips, audio-video-presentations, motion pictures, special reports, open-forums, guest speakers, and other attention-getting and interest-stimulating techniques? _____

15. Do I consider both students and subject matter as I plan for instruction? _____

16. Do I use the materials of instructional technology, including the simplest audio-visual aids, regularly and with purpose? _____

17. Do I capitalize on each student's personal environment? endowments? _____

18. Am I aware of each student's interests? _____

19. Am I mindful of individual differences, abilities, and needs? _____

20. Do I give all students equal opportunities and equal attention? _____

21. Do I help students to form good work habits? _____

22. Do I teach students how to study effectively? _____

23. Are students assuming more and more responsibility for their own improvement? _____

24. Is each student's attention span increasing? _____

25. Is there evidence that students are increasing in self-control, initiative, and originality? _____

26. Do students attack difficult problems eagerly? _____

27. Does a large percentage of students participate in class discussion? _____

28. Do I summarize ideas and generalization regularly? _____

29. Do I supply each student with knowledge of results? _____

30. Do I make the subject so clear and vital that students are highly stimulated? _____

31. Do I begin each class session promptly and keep things moving without appearing to hurry? _____

32. Do I encourage students to assist each other? _____

FIGURE 13–2   (Continued)

---

33. Do I expect to be more than a **good** teacher?   _____

Consider yourself as a superior teacher if you scored 25 or more items as excellent or very good. If you marked less than 15 items as excellent or very good, you may do well to enroll in a graduate course in professional education and/or psychology, to seek the aid of your colleagues in education, to consult professional texts and journals, and/or to enroll in in-service education programs.

The mature individual will not only serve as a leader in group enterprise and make contributions to group discussions and decisions, he often will engage in individual improvement.

Specialists do this when working independently on a frontier problem. A member of the rank and file does this when he engages in a study of his own needs or in tryouts of new methods in his classroom, or pursues a problem of his own through the available literature. Self-initiated attention to any problem often grows out of group activities.

How to Select Criteria

Selecting the criteria for the measurement of teacher effectiveness is probably the most difficult and most important task in the development of the appraisal program. A well-rounded program might include such items as teacher behavior and relationships with the staff, student growth, student-teacher relationships, student reaction, room control, participation in programs for community relations, professional growth, teaching techniques, and the like. These statements, however, are more general than they may at first appear to the reader.

R. F. Mager[5] indicated that instruction should be evaluated in terms of evidence the teacher has concerning the extent to which the objectives established by the teacher have been realized:

[5]Robert F. Mager, *Preparing Instructional Objectives* (Palo Alto, California: Fearon Publishers, 1962), especially chapters III–IV.

1. Identify the terminal behavior the educator is seeking by name; he should specify the type of behavior that will be accepted as evidence that the learner has achieved the objective.
2. Attempt to define the desired behavior more precisely by describing the important conditions under which the behavior will be expected to occur.
3. Specify the criteria of acceptable performance by describing how well the learner must perform to be considered as having mastered the task at hand and as having succeeded in reaching the desired objective. "You can test whether . . . [an] objective clearly defines a desired outcome by answering 'yes' to the following question: Can another competent person select successful learners in terms of the objective so that you, the objective writer, agree with the selections?"[6]

Criteria for evaluation, then, must clearly communicate and be related to intended educational outcomes, and as the statements are written they must describe all intended results. Statements as to criteria are useful only to the extent that they specify what the learner must be able to *do or perform* when he is demonstrating his mastery:

Since [no one is able to] see into another's mind so as to determine what he knows, [the supervisor] can . . . determine the state of the learner's development [and infer instructional effectiveness] only by observing behavior.[7]

Appraisal of instructional outcomes, then, is perhaps a more accurate description of how the supervisor should operate than is *appraisal of teacher effectiveness.* Appraisal, then, is not limited to the application of a single test of value to one simple, predetermined criterion. It is a comprehensive process. Characteristics of appraisal are:

1. It is an integral, complex part of education.
2. Instructional effectiveness is determined best by appraisal of growth as related to goals in the individual situations.
3. The total personality and all aspects of individual development and behavior are evaluated.

[6]Ibid., p. 12.
[7]Ibid., p. 13.

4. Many tools and procedures and many types of evidence are utilized in the evaluative process.
5. Evaluation means not only appraising, judging, and diagnosing but it also means determination as to whether the results are adequate and desirable.
6. The evaluation process is not completed by the teacher alone; cooperative efforts by many participants are indicated.

How to Evaluate Instructional Efficiency

General questions to be answered in evaluating instructional efficiency are suggested:

1. Is there an organized instructional program?
2. Is the program known to the teachers?
3. Is the program organized to provide for continuity and completeness?
4. Is the teacher competent, well prepared, and interested in the area?
5. Is the program apparently geared to the student and his program of learning (e.g., stimulation, individual differences, and readiness)?
6. Are the supplies, equipment, texts, and audio-visual aids readily available for an adequate program?
7. How much time is given to the area, and how is it distributed?
8. Is the classroom environment conducive to learning?
9. Is the class size reasonable?
10. Do the students apparently enjoy and respect the program?
11. How do the teachers plan for instruction?
12. Do teachers apparently know the various approaches to learning the subject?

Questions concerning instruction in mathematics:

1. Is mathematics taught as a drill subject, is it taught incidentally, or is it taught meaningfully?

2. Is mathematics taught for generalization or as a series of individual means of working examples?
3. How is problem-solving taught?
4. What provision for teaching technical reading is there?
5. What concrete materials are used?
6. Do the students use mathematics intelligently in practical situations and when appropriate in other subjects?
7. Are there subgroups within the class? How are they formed?
8. What do objective test results show concerning learning in mathematics?
9. Are the more capable learners allowed to go beyond the customary subject matter of the grade?

Questions concerning instruction in reading:

1. How many learning groups are there within the class, and how are they determined?
2. Are there sufficient books for recreational reading?
3. What do objective test results reveal about the program?
4. Are both oral and silent reading skills developed?
5. How do upper-grade teachers adapt to the previous readiness program?
6. What provisions are there for remedial reading?
7. Does the reading program coordinate reading activities with all the other subjects depending upon reading?
8. How is reading taught? Is there an emphasis on specific instruction in word attack skills?

Questions concerning instruction in social sciences:

1. Does student behavior in the classrooms and on the school grounds offer evidence of learning citizenship and democratic behavior?
2. Are the students competent in the skills of locating data; reading charts, pictures, graphs, maps, diagrams, tables; and reading for social science understanding?
3. What objective data, other than teacher-made tests, are there to describe achievement in the social sciences?

4. What activity units have been accomplished, and how successful were they?
5. Is the emphasis on cooperative and democratic participation, as well as on the learning of facts in history, geography, and civics?

Questions concerning instruction in science:

1. Is the program balanced between biological and physical science?
2. Is the learning directed toward understanding scientific generalizations?
3. Is there development of scientific attitudes and the use of scientific method?
4. Is there sufficient firsthand experience to develop functional understanding of science?

Questions concerning instruction in handwriting:

1. What objective scales (Ayres, Freeman, Thorndike) are used to evaluate handwriting? Are goals and standards known to the students and the teachers?
2. What directed learning of handwriting is there after the third grade?
3. When and how is cursive writing taught? What becomes of manuscript writing?
4. What follow-up of handwriting is done throughout the day?

Questions concerning instruction in spelling:

1. How does the teacher now evaluate spelling? (Spelling lesson only? Spelling throughout the day? Or?)
2. What provisions are made to teach students to attack a previously unstudied word? Are the skills of phonetic and structural analysis taught?
3. What provisions are made for individual difficulties in spelling?

Questions concerning instruction in grammar and composition:

1. What is the range of activities and/or media utilized in teaching oral and written communication skills?

2. What do objective test results indicate as to the strengths and weaknesses of the program?
3. What follow-up is there?

Questions concerning instruction in art:

1. What are the objectives of the program (technical excellence, understanding, appreciation, production, enjoyment)?
2. What is the range of media experienced?
3. How is art used throughout the rest of the curriculum?
4. Is technical assistance in art available to the teacher who feels insecure?
5. How does the instructor evaluate art learnings?
6. Does the room environment reflect the art philosophy?

Questions concerning instruction in music:

1. What music activities are available for students?
2. What evidence of enjoyment and/or appreciation by the students is there?
3. What technical assistance is available to the teacher who feels insecure?
4. What provisions are there for musically talented children?
5. How is music correlated/integrated with other subjects?
6. How is the instrumental program coordinated with the academic time schedule?

Questions concerning instruction in physical education:

1. Is the course one of physical education and of physical exercise? How is it distinguished from recess or after-school recreation?
2. Does each teacher have a knowledge of the physical and health conditions of the students so that each one may have appropriate activities?
3. How are the learning outcomes evaluated by the classroom teachers?
4. Does the teacher diagnose difficulties as she does in academic subjects and give appropriate remedial instruction?

Figures 13–3 through 13–6 illustrate some forms which have been used in evaluating teacher effectiveness.

FIGURE 13–3   Teacher Evaluation

Circle the words or phrases which most nearly describe the classroom spirit and the influence of the teacher.

Teaching Materials and Procedures	Textbooks, dictionaries, reference material, maps, globes, wall charts
Adequate supplies	Provision for levels of abilities of students, grouping, adequate chalk-board, bulletin board space
Student-Teacher Relationships	Type of leadership, respect for students, respect for teacher, discipline-control
	Student leadership
	Stimulates students to work up to their capacity
Interest and Activity of Students	Students are nervous, fidgety, squirmy; free, relaxed; mobility about room; evidence of student activities, group activities; students courteous and mannerly
	Students appear to have a sincere desire to learn
	Students listen with interest
Classroom Management	Student responsibilities and leadership, traditional teaching, rigid control—line up and march in
	Reading center, library books, movable desks, carpet, dittoed material, student creative work, flexibility in organization
General Appearance and Poise (Teacher)	Modern, conservative, appropriate, appealing
Clothing Hair, grooming	Modern, conservative, pleasant appearance
Room Appearance and Physical Condition	Well organized, poorly organized, bulletin board materials properly displayed; adequate lighting—heating; room adjusted to curriculum or grade level taught; clean room, student work on display

FIGURE 13–3 (Continued)

Attitude toward Teaching	Professional attitude; loves to teach; enjoys class and students; encourages students to want to be teachers by actions
Command of Language	Speaks at level of students, clearly, distinctly, does not have to repeat assignments, grammatical usage correct, enunciates clearly
	Handwriting *legible and of acceptable style*

FIGURE 13–4 Teacher Evaluation Report

(Teacher)   (Department)

(Subjects taught)

Points of strength _____

_____

_____

_____

_____

Points where improvement might be made_____

_____

_____

_____

_____

Principal's Signature

FIGURE 13–5   Analysis Report

REPORT ON PRINCIPAL'S TEACHING
EFFECTIVENESS ANALYSIS VISIT
(To be retained in school files)

SCHOOL_____   Report for:

                                                    Sem. 1 _____

                                                    Sem. 2 _____

                                                    Sem. 3 _____

                                                    Sem. 4 _____

TEACHER _____CLASS _____ HOUR _____

DATE OF VISIT _____

I. *Physical Characteristics of Classroom:*
   (Satisfactory or not satisfactory)
    1. Ventilation and lighting
      (if within control of
      teacher) _____3. Displays _____
    2. Seating arrangements _____4. Orderliness _____

II. *Teaching and Learning:*
    1. What work was actually in progress?

      _____

      _____

    2. What were the apparent student reactions to this work?

      _____

      _____

    3. Were classroom activities in line with stated objectives?

      _____

      _____

    4. General evaluation for this visit:
      Satisfactory or better _____
      Not satisfactory_____
    5. Comments: _____

      _____

      _____

(Continue on other side if necessary)

(Teacher's signature does
not necessarily mean complete
agreement on part of teacher.)
_____   _____
    Teacher's Signature   Principal's Signature

_____   _____
         Date   Date

FIGURE 13–6   Teacher Evaluation Report

PROBATIONARY TEACHER EVALUATION SUMMARY REPORT

(To be filed with Personnel Division—for instructions,
refer to Principal's Circular No. _____)

Teacher's Name (Last first)   School

Subject and/or Grade

REPORT FOR: *First Year*
1st Prob. Sem. (Internship or Regular)   _____
2nd Prob. Sem.   _____

Second Year
3rd Prob. Sem. _____   4th Prob. Sem. —————

POINTS OF STRENGTH:

POINTS OF WEAKNESS:

SUMMARY:

	Is performing satisfactorily or better as a probationary teacher at this time	_____
1st, 2nd or 3rd Semester Report	Should not be offered new contract	_____
	Should be dismissed immediately	_____
	Cannot make a judgment at this time (A judgment must be made in the 4th semester)	_____

It is my carefully considered professional
opinion that this teacher:

4th Semester Report	Should be granted tenure	_____
	Should not be granted tenure	_____

(Teacher's signature does not
necessarily indicate agreement)

Teacher's Signature   Date

Principal's Signature   Date

Evaluation and Morale

Evaluation cannot achieve its objective unless it is cooperatively approached by both teacher and principal. It seems that supervision's main tasks, therefore, are determining ways of stimulating teachers, attempting to fit methods and techniques to teacher personality, and encouraging self-evaluation with stress of strengths and weaknesses.

It must be recognized that teacher evaluation is a very potent process. If it is incorrectly handled, it can destroy staff morale, and high morale is an essential prerequisite to optimal teacher effectiveness. Cooperative planning of a beneficial program offers opportunities for better understanding and stronger relationships.

Factors Which Influence Teacher Morale

Factors related to staff morale include:

1. Security on the job and with groups;
2. Status, prestige, and recognition;
3. Adequate salary, professional level, and advancement;
4. Satisfying social relationships and working conditions;
5. Successful achievement of objectives;
6. A feeling that one has the support and loyalty of his supervisor;
7. Superior leadership, with confidence in this leadership; and
8. Recognition for a job well done.

Environmental factors which tend to generate a high teacher morale response include:

1. Teamwork
2. Positive school relationships
3. Availability of personnel
4. Superior performance by one's teaching colleagues.

Areas in which morale response is relatively low include:
1. Required cocurricular activities supervision

2. Personal security (lacking)
3. Recognition (lacking)
4. Negative student relationships
5. A feeling that one does not have adequate possibilities for advancement in the profession
6. Inadequate salary and/or fringe benefits
7. An excess of extra-instructional duties
8. Below standard physical facilities
9. Lack of freedom from distractions
10. Poor, ineffective communications
11. Undersirable contacts with parents and/or with community pressure groups and their representatives.

Morale is contagious; in time it permeates the whole staff and is influential in determining the quality of instruction. Certainly, without high morale the teacher cannot operate with maximum effectiveness.

How to Organize for Instruction

FLEXIBLE GROUPINGS AND INDIVIDUAL INSTRUCTION. There seems to be a trend toward the utilization of large group, medium-sized group, small group, very small group, and individualized instruction for an identified group of students within the school. An example of one program for the use of this technique of organization is included as Figure 13–7a, 13–7b, and 13–7c.

If such schemes for instructional organization are to be effective, the principal should insure that:

1. The teacher is given adequate time for lesson preparation and for gathering material;
2. Groupings remain flexible and the professional judgment of the teacher(s) concerned determines the placement and reassignment of students within each of the groupings;
3. Adequate time and physical facilities are made available for staff conferences;
4. Adequate physical facilities are available for teacher use with each of the groupings;

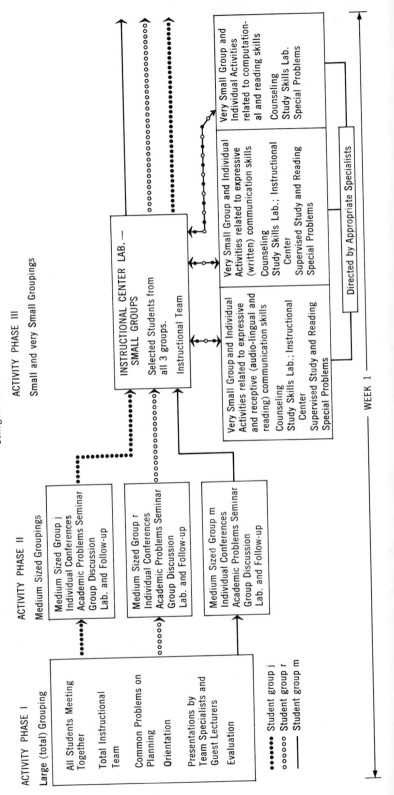

INSTRUCTIONAL TEAM PROGRAM, West Community College
College Basic Skills

ACTIVITY PHASE I

Large (total) Grouping

All Students Meeting Together

Total Instructional Team

Common Problems on Planning

Orientation

Presentations by Team Specialists and Guest Lecturers

Evaluation

•••••• Student group j
oooooo Student group r
——— Student group m

ACTIVITY PHASE II

Medium Sized Groupings

Medium Sized Group j
Individual Conferences
Academic Problems Seminar
Group Discussion
Lab. and Follow-up

Medium Sized Group r
Individual Conferences
Academic Problems Seminar
Group Discussion
Lab. and Follow-up

Medium Sized Group m
Individual Conferences
Academic Problems Seminar
Group Discussion
Lab. and Follow-up

ACTIVITY PHASE III

Small and very Small Groupings

INSTRUCTIONAL CENTER LAB.—SMALL GROUPS

Selected Students from all 3 groups.

Instructional Team

Very Small Group and Individual Activities related to expressive (audio-lingual and receptive (audio-lingual and reading) communication skills

Counseling
Study Skills Lab.; Instructional Center
Supervised Study and Reading
Special Problems

Very Small Group and Individual Activities related to expressive (written) communication skills

Counseling
Study Skills Lab.; Instructional Center
Supervised Study and Reading
Special Problems

Very Small Group and Individual Activities related to computational and reading skills

Counseling
Study Skills Lab.
Special Problems

Directed by Appropriate Specialists

WEEK 1

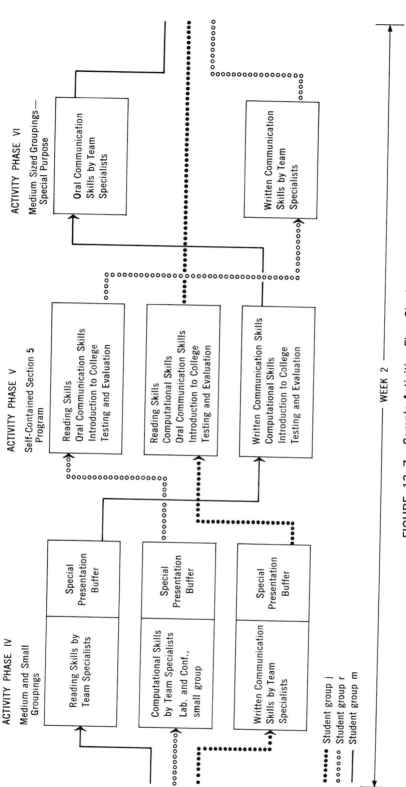

FIGURE 13-7 Sample Activities Flow Chart.

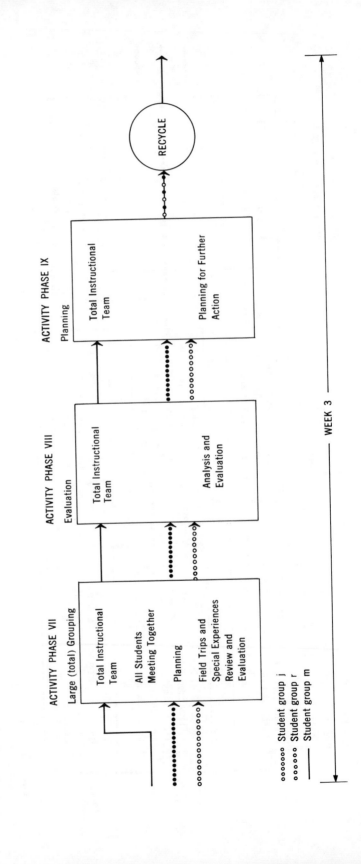

5. The large-sized grouping is used for presentations which are not better given in medium, small, very small, or individualized sessions, such as seeing a motion picture, or listening to a guest speaker or a specialized lecture;

6. The materials of instructional technology are made available to the teachers concerned, and that these materials are strategically placed so that it is very easy for the teacher to obtain them;

7. That small discussion groups are not used to go over again that which has been covered in the large groupings, but rather that students bring to the discussion groups materials and notes from outside research and, in seminar session, further the points that had been developed in the large groupings;[8]

8. Individualized instruction and independent (programmed or not) work is initiated gradually, following very small group instruction.

STODDARD'S PLAN. D. G. Stoddard, of New York University, operating under Ford Foundation sponsorship, challenged the concept of the self-contained classroom by offering the semidepartmentalized dual progress plan.

In the dual progress plan all teachers are full-time specialists in one of six curricular areas. Students progress in the language arts, social studies, and physical education according to the usual graded ability system, while these same students progress in science, mathematics, and the arts on a nongrade level basis. All students study both the *cultural imperatives,* which constitute the graded section of the plan; and the *cultural electives,* which are seen as occupying an area in which mastery cannot be expected of all students.

If such a program, which actually is a combination of several plans for school organization for instruction, including many of the key aspects of the platoon school, of departmentalization schemes, of nongraded plans, and of special student grouping formulations, is incorporated into the curriculum, there will be a greater need for specialists in given fields. The need for

[8]See Herbert W. Wey, *Handbook for Principals* (New York: Shaum Publishing Company, 1966), p. 31.

consultant assistance and for further physical facilities will have budgetary implications.[9]

HOW TO ORGANIZE FOR "NONGRADED" INSTRUCTION. Many faculties are experimenting with deparmentalization and/or with "team teaching" techniques. While the student will be with one teacher for the major portion of the day, he well may be with different teachers for physical education, music, art, foreign language, or other subjects. We should look for greater experimentation in this area in the future, along with further employment of the "nongraded" plans, which first were proposed shortly after the Quincy Grammer School opened its doors in 1848 with the first "graded" organization in the New World. There have been arguments, incidentally, that the first nongraded school existed in the colonies as the dame school.

The type of nongraded program which is most successful seems to be that program which is based upon the use of a variety of groupings simultaneously. Such groupings have been developed according to achievement, abilities, talents, interests, and work-study skills. In reality, it seems that many of the schools experimenting in this area have merely substituted twelve or more grade groupings for three, although, theoretically, at least, individuals as well as groups may move from one achievement level to the next as soon as readiness for the higher level is indicated. Students are then identified as being enrolled in the primary division rather than in grades one, two, or three.

Progress in reading comprehension seems to be the primary criterion for advancement to grade four from the primary division. In a truly nongraded situation, grade levels should not become a matter for concern until the student is about to enter grade four, and *flexible mobility* must be the keynote of the system.

There has been a great deal of conflicting—but little significant—research concerning the value of the nongraded organization. Further experimentation in this area seems indicated.

[9]For a discussion of plans of the past concerning instructional organization with which the supervisor should be familiar, see Emery Stoops and James R. Marks, *Elementary School Supervision: Practices and Trends* (Boston: Allyn and Bacon, Inc., 1965), pp. 166–168.

STAFF UTILIZATION: TEAM TEACHING PLANS. In essence, a team is an instructional unit within a school. This unit is a combination of (1) a distinct student group, (2) a small faculty group responsible for teaching the student group, and (3) individuals who assist the teachers and students.

A *team leader* is a mature, experienced, certificated teacher of unusual talent and extensive training who has been elected or appointed to serve as the leader of a teaching team and whose major responsibilities are teaching and coordinating the team's efforts. He should be paid a stipend above his normal pay for this latter responsibility. Moreover, he receives time to plan and to coordinate team activities.

A *team teacher* is a fully certificated member of a teaching team, while an *intern teacher* is a beginning teacher, not yet fully certificated. The intern teacher is given a regular teaching assignment on the team and receives supervision from both the employing school system and the sponsoring college or university.

A *student teacher* is a college student assigned to a school to observe and to teach directly under the supervision of a master teacher within that school. The *master teacher* is an experienced, regularly certificated teacher who possesses considerable advance study, unusual knowledge, and great skill in teaching.

A classified (noncertificated) individual from the community who works with the team on a paid, part-time basis is termed a *teacher's aide*. He relieves the teachers of clerical and other routine work so that they may concentrate on instructional activities.

An *auxiliary teacher* is a fully certificated teacher who is called in upon team request. A *community resource person* is a skilled individual, not ordinarily affiliated with the school. He can, under supervision of a teacher, assist in some specific aspect of the instructional program, or can lead student study groups in his special area of competence.[10]

If team teaching is to be successful it must not be a thinly-disguised plan for departmentalization. In team teaching all members of the team share, in varying degrees, responsibility for the entire instructional program for the individuals within the class group. The supervisor must aid team mem-

[10]John A. Brownell and H. A. Taylor, "Theoretical Perspectives for Teaching Teams." *Phi Delta Kappan* XLIII (January 1962): 150–157.

bers in increasing their abilities to solve instructional problems through their individual skills, abilities, talents, and insights. The supervisor should do all in his power to enhance effective communication between team members and between teams. He must encourage the free exchange of experiences, ideas, and information.

While research in the area of team teaching is limited in quantity, it does seem that members of the team must share the common abilities of being able to adapt readily to new and varied situations, of being highly efficient in self-elevation, in working well with other adults in a coopera-tive endeavor, and in organization, in addition to the usual attributes of the outstanding educator.

The supervisior should encourage the team to experiment with new ma-terials, ideas, and techniques, He must aid the team members in analyzing evident deficiencies in team instruction, but he must not discourage team members from making decisions based upon sound judgment and experi-ence. Rather, he must encourage the development of the strengths of the members both as individuals and as members of a functioning instructional team. While adequate facilities and time must be made available to the teaching team, adequate supervisory assistance is even more essential.

A grouping schema used in an instructional team program is illustrated in Figure 13–7, the Sample Activities Flowchart.

How to Help the Teacher Plan for Instruction

D. O. Weaver's[11] guidelines or "tricks of the trade" for the teacher may prove especially helpful in discussion groups studying organization and planning for effective instruction:

1. By assigning seats and keeping a copy of the plan in front of him, the teacher quickly learns the names of students. Calling a student by name makes the class a personal affair rather than a cold, formal, and impersonal experience.
2. Good questions stimulate interest and promote initiative among stu-

[11]Reprinted with permission from David O. Weaver, "The Instructor's Relationship to His Students." *Training Directors Journal* XIV (January 1960): 40–70. This Journal has much to offer the educational supervisor.

dents. They also secure cooperation and give the teacher an idea how each student is progressing. The teacher also gets an idea as to how effective his instruction is. Make questions definite and state them clearly.

3. Remember to ask questions that will make the students think. If questions can be answered simply by a "yes" or "no," the class will not be stimulated. When a student has answered a question, ask him to explain his answer. Then request another student to comment on his explanation. In this way each student will follow every word that is being said, knowing that he may be called upon at any moment. By probing into a topic in this way, the teacher will not fall into the habit of saying, "Are there any questions?" Most students will not be willing (or able) to say whether they are in doubt or not. It is up to the teacher to find out, by proper questioning, whether the class is getting the material.

4. Take plenty of time making definite assignments. Before giving an assignment, the teacher should explain to the class what it is about and why it is being given at that time. The teacher should be specific—from page such and such to page so and so. He also should be definite about the work to be undertaken—telling the students that they are to read, memorize, outline, or whatever. The home assignment should not be put off until the end of the period when it might have to be dealt with in a hasty and inadequate manner. The competent instructor is definite about study assignments. Knowing the value of repetition and review, he gives his students frequent tasks, tests, and examinations.

5. Unless the teacher shows his students that he himself is enthusiastic about the subject matter and about teaching it, they will not attack their lessons with vigor and determination. Every good instructor is, to some degree, a salesman. He is convinced he has the finest product in the world to sell. His salesmanship will largely determine the readiness with which his class accepts the product. Enthusiasm is caught, not taught.

6. Students learn by trial and error, by observation, by "transfer," and by *doing*. Trial and error is the inefficient way; doing is the most effective. The capable instructor knows that theory is good, but, as Dewey told us, theory divorced from practice is ineffectual.

7. Demonstration and illustration—appealing to the eye (or mind's eye) —are the best means of teaching as they make the most vivid impres-

sion upon the learner. Mock-ups, models, and similar teaching aids are employed by the competent instructor whenever available.

8. The good teacher shows "how" and explains "why."
9. The capable teacher does his best to arouse the students' *will to learn.* He convinces the students that the subject is worthwhile and acquirement of that particular knowledge or skill will be of immediate benefit to the students.
10. The competent teacher keeps his students informed as to their progress. He is liberal with encouraging commendation and sparing with reproof. The good teacher knows that the principle of immediate feedback of results to the student is a primary tenet of education.
11. The able teacher does his best to maintain good classroom and study periods, and keeps an eye on the physical welfare of his students.
12. The good teacher never plays Professor Know-It-All, never tries to bluff. *If he does not know the answer, he says so.* If he makes a mistake, he acknowledges that fact. He does not pose as an infallible authority.
13. At all times the competent teacher encourages student initiative and intellectual curiosity.

How to Plan for Instruction

One of the most important factors in successful instruction is a careful, thorough preparation on the part of the teacher. For many reasons a written lesson plan, at least in the early part of the professional career, is a must.

The supervising principal should stress that a lesson plan first helps to insure that the material is covered completely; and second, it keeps the teacher pointed in the right direction—toward a definite goal—and helps to insure sequence and organization. The lesson plan acts as a guide and refreshes the memory.

There are several possible methods and combinations of methods and techniques for teaching, and there will be many differences among lesson plans.

FORMULATION OF THE PLAN. The first problem encountered in planing a lesson is the determination of clearly defined objectives, for they give a purpose and direction to teaching efforts.

Next, the teacher must determine the method or combination of methods and techniques of instruction which he will use for a particular lesson. Several factors would determine this choice: classroom facilities; the age level, maturity, and needs of the students; time available for instruction; and the objectives of the lesson.

A further step is the selection and organization of the supplies, equipment, and materials to be used in instruction. The teacher must study the texts, teacher supplements, and instructional guides to acquire as broad a background of information on the subject as possible. Then the information to be presented is selected. This selection will be determined by considerations similar to those which govern the selection of the method of teaching.

Normally, students will not be able to retain more than two or three major ideas, so the lesson material should be contained within this number of headings. The teacher should (1) determine the headings, and (2) on one-half of a folded piece of paper lay out notes under these headings so that each heading follows logically the previous one and each thought within the headings logically follows the preceding one. (The best criterion for arrangement of headings is that which makes the most sense from the student's point of view.) The supervising principal should encourage the teacher to complete the blank side of the plan by indicating, at the appropriate points, the supplementary material to be used—references, teaching aids, or quotations.

The entire content material outline should then be incorporated into a plan, such as that which appears as Figure 13–8. The amount of material in the plan will need to be adjusted according to the teacher's experience with the class.

FIGURE 13–8   Sample Lesson Plan Form

I. Introduction: Objectives (Specific!)
II. Materials to Be Used
III. Procedure:
    A. Building readiness, including stimulation
    B. Body—all steps in lesson
    C. Review and evaluation (with students)
IV. Evaluation by Teacher of His Lesson

Content Material:
A. Introduction
B. Body
C. Summary

In the majority of cases the content side of the lesson plan should have a set overall pattern. It should have three main parts:

1. The introduction
2. The body of the lesson
3. The summary

These three parts of the lesson plan are illustrated in Figures 13–9, 13–10, and 13–11.

INTRODUCTION

WHY	HOW
1. To establish contact; to stimulate.	1. Good opening statement.
2. To arouse interest.	2. Stories or examples.
3. To secure attention.	3. Quotations
4. To disclose and clarify the subject.	4. Questions, skits and demonstrations. Tell and show what, why and how.

FIGURE 13–9   Introduction.

Unit Plans

The unit plan is an effective way to plan a program for instruction within the classroom. A unit is planned for a period longer than a day, and it may extend for several weeks. Because the students' attention span is related to age, units in the lower grades are usually short—about one or two weeks. Attention spans become increasingly longer in the upper grades, lasting from four to eight or more weeks.

At any grade level, the learning process is implemented more efficiently when the unit is organized for more than one instruction period or one

BODY

 WHY   **HOW**

1. To present teaching points.
2. To explain knowledge.
3. To develop understanding.
4. To stimulate appreciation. To change behavior. Behavioral objectives should be stated clearly.

1. Sound organization.
2. Smooth transitions.
3. Repetition, frequent summaries.
4. Vital and interesting presentation.

FIGURE 13–10   Body.

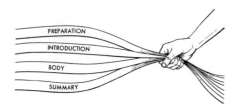

SUMMARY

 WHY   **HOW**

1. To provide an over-all view.
2. To emphasize.
3. To summarize, clarify, and conclude instruction.

1. Clear up questions.
2. Recap main points.
3. Close with a strong statement.

FIGURE 13–11   Levels of Planning for the Improvement of Instructional Materials.

day. It is extremely difficult, if not impossible, to use teaching time efficiently when planning is on a day-to-day basis. The students cannot discover the relationship between each day's work when the teacher does not know how it fits into a larger plan.

Units may be planned on a basis of content in a single area, such as reading, mathematics, English, or science; content extending beyond a single area, such as "How Desert People Live"; a unit in the social studies in which history and geography are combined; and projects or problems which cross subject lines completely, as in a unit called "Understanding Our South American Neighbors," which involves reading, the teaching of music and art, the working of mathematics problems, the building of science concepts, and the study of history and geography.

Unit teaching provides for many student activities, such as reading from several books, telling stories, listening to teacher or classmates, individualized study, group projects, group discussion, visits outside the classroom, construction activities calling for creative and artistic talent, listening to records, and seeing and discussing films. For any grade, student activities and the order in which they are taken should be determined by the organization of instruction for that grade and by the successive steps required to achieve the desired outcomes.

Units are classified as resource units and as teaching units. Each has characteristics which make it adaptable to certain planning situations.

RESOURCE UNITS: A resource unit usually is planned by a group of teachers. For example, in a seventh-grade class, where special teachers provide instruction in music, art, and physical education, the homeroom teacher and the three special teachers work out a series of resource units for that grade.

A resource unit typically has the following features:

1. A title or topic and an indication of the grade or age levels for which it is designed;
2. An introductory statement;
3. A statement of proposed objectives;
4. A content guide;
5. Suggested student activities;
6. A list of teaching aids books for both students and teacher, pamphlets, music records, films, community resources;

7. Suggested evaluation procedures.

The resource unit gives much attention to student activities and instructional materials. Organizing a resource unit is helpful to the teacher in planning activities for a given class, in preparing a teaching unit, and in gaining a more comprehensive idea of the instructional techniques used by other teachers.

TEACHING UNITS. A teaching unit is a unit organized by a teacher for a given class. It is usually outlined prior to actual instruction and it has the same features as the resource unit except that the teaching unit includes only the activities, materials, and evaluation techniques which are to be used with a particular class. Thus, a resource unit might list many stories about Indian life, whereas the teaching unit, which is organized by a teacher for given class (prior to actual instruction), would list only the ones that are to be read. Materials and activities—the variety necessary to meet student needs—are listed in the teaching unit in the order in which they will be presented in the class.

Good teaching generally requires the teacher to plan in advance, especially by writing a statement of objectives, suitable learning activities, instructional materials, and evaluation techniques. After this task is completed the teacher may ask the students to share in choosing from among the various activities. Too often, when this advance planning has not been done, a great deal of class time is lost unnecessarily because the teacher does not know what can be done to good advantage and what cannot.

FRAMEWORK FOR A UNIT. The following outline may be considered as a basic framework for a unit:

1. Title or topic of the unit, appropriate age or grade level, and approximate time allotted;
2. Introductory statement, formulation of general purposes, and clarification of topic;
3. Objectives, including major understandings, skills, and attitudes to be acquired by the students;
4. Content guide, including the major subject matter content, problems to be solved, and suggested class activities;

5. Student activities required to achieve the objectives, including initiatory activities and developmental activities and the estimated time required for them;
6. Culminating activities, such as a summary activity or group of activities to which each student can contribute, toward which the class will direct its effort throughout the unit, which will best satisfy each student's need for approval from classmates and teacher, and which will promote favorable attitudes toward classmates, teacher, and school; and the estimated time required for these activities;
7. Materials and resources, including printed materials: the materials of instructional technology, including programmed material, single concept films and tapes, other audio-visual aids, and materials for demonstration, experimentation, or display; facilities outside the classroom which may be used; and procedures for bringing people from the community to the classroom and for taking the students on visits to the community;
8. Evaluation procedures, including ascertaining where students are when they begin work, helping students measure their own progress, and evaluating student grown in terms of demonstrated changes in behavioral changes.

Instructional Methods

There is no such thing as one method of teaching or supervision that is effective for all teachers, all students, all subjects, and all situations. Furthermore, method, considered apart from purpose, lacks direction and meaning. Method must be conceived, applied, and appraised in terms of the stated objectives. For a discussion of general teaching methods with which the supervising principal should be familiar the reader is referred to the supplement to this chapter. For specific techniques which the supervisor may wish to refer to in recommending procedures in the several subject areas, see Appendix D.

DO

1. Establish a healthy working relationship with co-workers by approaching problems on a democratic and cooperative basis.

2. Strive to enhance each individual's position by delegating responsibility for instructional improvement to members of the certificated staff.
3. Evaluate continuously your own professional competencies, seeking to build upon your strengths and overcome your weaknesses.
4. Work for the emerging concept of "the supervisor as a chief of staff" which will designate the principal as a staff instructional leader as opposed to a dominantly administrative figure.
5. Be aware of the changing needs of the staff and be adept at devising or adapting new plans or procedures to meet those needs.
6. Employ staff meetings as a source for stimulating interest in in-service education programs.
7. Work for the cooperative study of school problems as an efficient and effective way to improve instruction.
8. Attempt to create an atmosphere in the school which will encourage experimentation.
9. Provide opportunities for teachers to share new techniques, and to observe good teaching practices.
10. Rotate the personnel of subject matter and grade-level committees frequently so that each teacher has a wide familiarity with current developments.
11. Recognize and reward excellent individual teacher performance.
12. Encourage teachers to share their successes with other members of the staff.
13. Be alert to new techniques and materials, and keep teachers informed.
14. Establish a professional library and encourage teachers to use and contribute to it.

DON'T

1. Rebuke any teacher in the presence of students or any other persons.[12]
2. Fail to praise teachers, and, in the fields of their special preparation, walk humbly.

[12]Unfortunately, it is frequently this first item that is broken in this listing of commandments. When a teacher is rebuked or corrected by the supervising principal in the presence of students or adults, the principal is guilty of a gross breach of professional ethics.

3. Deal lightly with any person's problem, but treat it as if it were your own.
4. Forget the days of your youth; keep a sense of cheer.
5. Fail to honor your custodians and your teachers that your days may be long on the job that the governing board has given you.
6. Let any student be judged by his behavior alone, but seek the causes of such behavior that they may be corrected.
7. When you have a teacher who is old in the service so that he no longer teaches well fail to deal with him tenderly and understandingly (teachers do grow older—and they don't just fade away).
8. Fail to develop a sensitivity to the needs of your whole community, and a faith in its people, for in that faith you will find your strength to improve instruction.
9. Fail to develop vision as well as devotion, so that instruction may truly be improved and that you may use your talents for the benefit of all humanity.[13]

Supervisory Problems

In Basket

Problem 1

Recently a rural school district in Wyoming passed a bond issue for the construction of a new school. Members of the board of education, administrators, and several teachers visited many schools in an attempt to view the most modern buildings. A building designed for flexibility to meet educational needs for future years was desired.

The staff hoped to move into a team-teaching situation and eventually a truly nongraded school. The staff at present consists of fifty classroom teachers, with approximately eight teachers in each grade division. None of the teachers has been trained in team teaching, and very few have observed team teaching in action. All of the present staff have taught in a most traditional setting.

How should the supervisor proceed in selecting personnel from the present staff for participation in the team-teaching situation?

[13] After Douglas E. Lawson, Ten Commandments for the Humane Principal in Improving Instruction," an Address at Southern Illinois University, Carbondale, Illinois, 1955.

Problem 2

The problem developed at Joseph Senior High School which has an enrollment of near 2,000 in grades ten, eleven, and twelve. (A second public high school, Charlotte, has a similar enrollment—no problems!) At Joseph mathematics students are placed within one of three levels of ability. At each grade level there are two sections of "honors" or advanced mathematics. Mr. Chinn has fifteen years of successful teaching experience and has been praised for his outstanding work with the "slow learner." He requested an assignment to the junior-level "honors" sections and taught them for two years with few, if any, complaints from parents or students. To avoid a father-son teaching relationship, he kept only one section the following year.

Ronald, the particular student involved, is from a divorced home where the economic status is extremely low. He is enrolled in the lower performance section.

The principal soon received complaints from students and parents relating to "boring routine" and "lack of opportunity to be creative in thought and approach to a problem," in the lower performance section. Ronald asked to be transferred to the advanced section. This request was refused, since school policy dictates that students shall be transferred to another section only in EXTREME cases. The principal praised the teacher's past performance to parents and students and assured them that the situation would not continue. He did not confer with Mr. Chinn, and for a time complaints stopped. This afternoon, however, Ronald and his mother have arrived in the principal's office, insisting that he, Ronald, be permitted to transfer to the other section.

What do you, as supervising principal, propose to do?

Problem 3

The instructional effectiveness of the sixty-year-old teacher with tenure seems to be inadequate, boring, and causing ridicule from parents and students. His marking system apparently hinges largely on how well students get along with him.

Mr. Doe uses the formal lecture technique all period, each period, in world history. He says that after teaching thirty years, his memory is infallible, but facts, dates, names, and chronology are often wrong. Students work on mathematics, shorthand, and other subjects during his classes.

At a final year's end National Honor Society farewell banquet, which was an emotional session, a girl tearfully and emotionally gave a testimony of thanks to faculty members present. Coming to Mr. Doe, she thanked him for never bothering her and allowing her to practice her shorthand during his class time. Realizing what she had said, the girl was most embarrassed. The audience was amused.

On the credit side, the teacher is a fine gentleman. Generally, he is liked and respected by other faculty members.

How can the principal approach this individual and help him to become a more efficient teacher, respected by his students?

Is the problem solvable, and to what degree?

Selected Bibliography

Books

Anderson, Richard C. et al. *Current Research on Instruction.* Englewood Cliffs, New Jersey: Prentice-Hall, Inc., 1969.

Anderson, R. H. *Teaching in a World of Change.* New York: Harcourt, Brace and World, 1966.

Barr, A. S. et al. *Supervision.* New York: Appleton-Century-Crofts, 1947.

Barr, A. S., W. H. Burton, and L. J. Brueckner. *Supervision.* New York: D. Appleton and Company, 1938.

Burton, William H., and Leo J. Brueckner. *Supervision: A Social Process.* New York: Appleton-Century-Crofts, 1955.

Davis, Harold S. *How to Organize an Effective Team Teaching Program.* Englewood Cliffs, New Jersey: Prentice-Hall, 1966.

Hicks, Hanne J. *Educational Supervision in Principle and Practice.* New York: The Ronald Press Company, 1960.

Kyte, George C. *How to Supervise.* Boston: Houghton Mifflin Company, 1930.
————. *The Principal at Work.* Boston: Ginn and Company, 1952.

Mackenzie, Gordon N., and Stephen M. Corey. *Instructional Leadership.* New York: Bureau of Publications, Teachers College, Columbia University, 1959.

Mager, Robert F. *Preparing Instructional Objectives.* Palo Alto, California: Fearon Publishers, 1962.

Melby, Ernest O. *Organization and Administration of Supervision.* Chicago: Public School Publishing Company, 1929.

Myers, George R., and William J. Walsh. *Student Teaching and Internship in Today's Secondary Schools.* New York: Charles E. Merrill Books, Inc., 1967.

Reeder, Edwin H. *Supervision in the Elementary School.* Boston: Houghton Mifflin Company, 1953.

Stoops, Emery, and James R. Marks. *Elementary School Supervision: Practices and Trends.* Boston: Allyn and Bacon, Inc., 1965.

Weber, Clarence A. *Personnel Problems of School Administrators.* New York: McGraw-Hill, 1954.

Wey, Herbert W. *Handbook for Principals.* New York: Shaum Publishing Company, 1966.

Periodicals

Adams, H., and C. R. Hollenbach. "How Can Supervisory Practices Contribute to Teacher-Pupil Growth?" *National Association of Secondary School Principals Bulletin* XXXVIII (April 1954): 151–156.

Bradfield, Luther E. "Basic Principles Underlying Techniques of Supervision." *American School Board Journal* CXXVIII (June 1954): 21–23.

Brownell, John A., and H. A. Taylor. "Theoretical Perspectives for Teaching Teams." *Phi Delta Kappan* XLIII (January 1962): 150–157.

Coombs, Arthur W., and Harold E. Mitzel. "Can We Measure Good Teaching Objectively?" *N.E.A. Journal* LIII (January 1964): 34.

Drummond, William H. "The Meaning and Application of Performance Criteria in Staff Development." *Phi Delta Kappan* LII (September 1970): 32–35.

Gronamon, A. H. "Improving Classroom Instruction." *Educational Administration and Supervision Bulletin* XXXIII (May 1947): 300–309.

Kirby, David. "An Administrator Looks at the Human Side of Teaching." *Educational Forum* XIV (March 1950): 351–356.

Pearson, Evelyn. "Making Use of Teachers' Talents." *Minnesota Journal of Education* XL (September 1959): 19–20.

Stoddard, D. G. "Team Teaching for the Elementary School." *Educational Leadership* XVIII (November 1960): 89–91.

Unruh, Adolph. "Has Your School Changed?" *Educational Forum* XVIII (May 1954): 470.

Weaver, David O. "The Instructor's Relationship to His Students." *Training Directors Journal* XIV (January 1960): 40–47.

Weber, C. A. "Promising Techniques for Educating Teachers in Service." *Educational Administration and Supervision Bulletin* XXVIII (December 1942): 691–695.

Other Sources

Association for Supervision and Curriculum Development. *Creating a Good Environment for Learning.* Washington, D.C.: National Education Association, 1954.

Bennion, Adam S. *Principles of Teaching.* Salt Lake City, Utah: Deseret News Press, 1958.

Brighton, Stayner F. *Increasing Your Accuracy in Teacher Evaluation.* Successful School Management Series. Englewood Cliffs, New Jersey: Prentice-Hall, Inc., 1965.

Department of Superintendence. *Improvement of Teachers in Service.* Eighth Yearbook. Washington, D.C.: National Education Association, 1930.

Department of Supervisors and Directors of Instruction. *Newer Instructional Practices of Promise.* Twelfth Yearbook. Washington, D.C.: National Education Association, 1940.

_____. *Scientific Method in Supervisory Programs.* Washington, D.C.: National Education Association, 1934.

Deseret Sunday School Board. *Teacher Training.* Salt Lake City, Utah: The Board, 1955.

Gage, N. L., ed. *Handbook of Research on Teaching.* Chicago: Rand McNally, 1963.

Hamacheck, Don E., and Joseph A. Callaman. *Evaluating Your Teachers.* New York: Croft Educational Services, 1967.

Lawson, Douglas E. "Ten Commandments for the Humane Principal in Improving Instruction." An Address at Southern Illinois University, Carbondale, Illinois, 1955.

Trump, J. Lloyd. *Images of the Future.* Commission on Experimental Study of the Utilization of the Staff. Urbana, Illinois: The Commission, 1959.

Instructional Methods

There is no such thing as one method of teaching or supervision that is effective for all subject matter, all teachers, and all students at all times and places. The teaching method used in any specific case must be geared to such factors as the maturity and capacity of the students, the size of the class, the length of the class period, the facilities and materials available, the teaching situation, and the lesson to be taught.

Method, considered apart from purpose, lacks both direction and meaning. Method must be conceived, applied, and judged in terms of the purpose to be achieved. Although a given method may not be a good one for achieving a particular purpose, it may, nevertheless, be an excellent method for use at another time to achieve a different purpose.

The adjustment of students to teachers and to each other, and the overall social climate in the classroom, are more important than the method of instruction.

With these fundamental ideas in mind, let us consider the various patterns of instruction or, in other words, methods of teaching.

Teaching methods can be classified under three general headings:

1. Teacher-centered patterns;
2. Student-centered patterns;
3. Cooperative-group patterns.

However, any such classification is somewhat artificial and another grouping may be preferred. It is recognized that there is so much overlapping between methods that to classify them strictly or to define them rigidly is an oversimplification. But, for the sake of a starting point, let us consider various teaching methods that are used widely and successfully throughout the profession.

Although teacher-centered methods of instruction are perhaps the most widely used, the more formal of these methods are, at the same time, the least successful when measured in terms of changing the attitudes, understandings, and behavior of students. As the name implies, the focus of attention is on the teacher rather than the students. All too frequently student motivation is taken for granted, when in reality the student may be attending to anything but the lesson being presented in spite of an apparent attitude of interest on his part.

These teacher-centered methods, then, must be used with caution. Nevertheless, they do have value and may be employed successfully to accomplish certain objectives under certain conditions.

The basis of the *lecture method* is that the teacher relates information vocally. It is obvious that in any lesson one is going to present he must do some talking. The supervising principal must not withdraw in horror at the mention of the term "lecture." Rather, he must understand the value and strengths of this method, as well as its weaker points.

The amount of talking on the part of the teacher during a lesson varies from brief remarks interjected to guide the course of the discussion right up to the *formal lecture*, where students merely listen.

The *informal lecture* is of greater value because:

1. Students may ask questions and participate in other ways.
2. This type of lesson presents to the class the best and most well considered thoughts of the lecturer.

It is extremely difficult to become proficient in the effective use of the informal lecture and only those who are well above the average in gifts of personality, speech, and teaching abilities should think of attempting it. Even then, they should think again before they make it their exclusive method of presentation in a classroom.

In connection with this method, as well as with all the talking one does as a teacher, it would be well to remember the following words quoted from Bennion: "Aimless talking which indulges in the main in vague generalities can never be justified."[1]

All this is not to say that a teacher should never occupy the class time with a short lecture. Indeed, the teacher must always be ready:

1. To clear up a point;
2. To draw the loose ends together into a meaningful picture;
3. To impart facts and explain concepts to the group, always being guided by the capacities and general abilities of the group.

[1]Adam S. Bennion, *Principles of Teaching* (Salt Lake City, Utah: Deseret News Press, 1958), p. 131.

In other words, the lecture, especially the informal variety, should be used along with other methods, in a happy combination which leads the group logically and conclusively to the goal sought—the objective of the lesson.

The *discussion method* includes the techniques of the panel, the open forum, and the symposium. It should *never* be used unless all participants have acquired a common body of knowledge pertinent to the topic to be discussed. This common body of knowledge *must* have been acquired *prior* to the discussion.

1. The *panel* type of discussion is a preset technique with panel members using prepared speeches. These are followed by audience participation at the end through questions, answers, and challenges.
2. In a *symposium*, set speeches are utilized. No audience participation is permitted.
3. The (open) *forum permits audience participation and audience reaction to set speeches* during the presentation.

Discussion utilizes the question as a technique. The directed question, with someone's name attached to the end of it, is preferred. The teacher asks the question and then states the name of the individual who is to respond.

If the teacher is asked a question he either responds to it, sends it back in a different form, or sends it to another student.

The discussion method utilizes the following problem-solving techniques:

1. The problem is defined.
2. The aspects of the problem that must be investigated are located.
3. Possible solutions (hypotheses) are suggested.
4. The hypotheses are sifted and eliminated.
5. One solution is chosen.
6. The solution is applied and tested.

The *recitation method* is the procedure by which:

1. The teacher assigns certain material to be studied.
2. The students, having completed the assignment either in or out of the class, in response to the teacher's questions or directions, recite the information covered in the lesson.

The recitation method is sometimes called "lesson hearing." It is of doubtful value and traditionally employed. It probably has little place in the modern nation's classrooms.

In the *project method* student interest is focused on the completion of a particular project or the solution of a special problem:

1. This focus of attention provides the stimulation for a wide variety of purposeful activities and learning experiences.
2. Instruction leans away from the teacher-centered types, which rely more on the authority of the teacher.
3. The students develop the lesson in terms of their own experiences, carrying the lesson forward by their contributions.
4. The supervisor may note that the problem to be solved, or the project to be completed, usually is posed by the students under the guidance of the teacher, rather than being imposed by the teacher himself.

To employ the *laboratory method* the teacher creates a situation in which the classroom becomes a laboratory wherein students experiment with various ideas and theories to test their validity. For example, the students may wish to experiment with different methods of committing to memory the various classifications in the animal kingdom, or basic atomic numbers, or other material. By testing several methods, such as writing the material several times, using programmed devices, responding to tape recordings, reciting aloud, or reading silently, they not only may learn the desired material but also may find a method, or a combination of methods, that produces the best results for them.

The *dramatic* or *role-playing method* fulfills Shakespeare's statement, "All the world's a stage, and all the men and women merely players." Adults and children alike seem to have a strong desire at times to "play a part" other than their own. A supervising principal may capitalize on this

desire for the purpose of helping teachers, as well as students, to understand and appreciate another's point of view.

The method consists of having members of the class assume various roles
and play the parts of others, then try to "project" themselves into the roles
they are playing. For example, a group of children are studying ancient
history. The lessons to be learned are meaningful and important to them
only when the characters and incidents studied are made to "live" in their
lives. A planned or an impromptu dramatization of the events being studied, wherein each student plays the role of one of the real-life characters of
a bygone age, is more apt to make such lessons "come to life" than if the
story is merely read or told.

The role-playing method may be used effectively in in-service education,
and in teaching adults. For example, one successful teacher in an adult
evening school class on early American history assigned various members
of the class to play the parts of characters being studied. Whenever a quota-
tion was to be read, the person playing the part of that particular character
would read it. Whenever questions came up concerning the policies of
Cortez or of Montezuma, the "player" tried to answer them as if he were
that person. Appendix D includes specific techniques in several subjects
and should prove helpful to the supervisor, especially in working with
teachers who are new to the subject matter area or grade level.

14

How to Select, Organize, and Facilitate the Use of Instructional Technology Materials

The modern educator, whatever his level of involvement may be, must meet an almost unprecedented challenge. We live in a world where exponential expansion of knowledge and scientific breakthroughs are commonplace. Each day our professors and teachers are faced not only with the problem of transmitting the new knowledge, but also the awesome responsibility of guaranteeing that the young people in their trust actually understand it all. The educational problems are so complex, and the needs so intense, that we no longer dare allow the teacher to work alone and unaided. Devotion to the profession is not enough.

The unique problems of individual students and of special groups (e.g., the socially and/or academically disadvantaged, the high-school dropout, the highly gifted, and the "average" student) are inadequately solved by the usual present-day educational facilities. A carefully formulated educational plan must provide for such heterogeneous inputs. The plan must avoid arbitrary curricular standards and decisions; it must reject the word "rejection" and substitute the concept of words such as "preliminary," "tentative," "alternate," and "auxiliary."

A systems analysis approach is implied, but whatever the approach:

1. It must match the inventory and the potential of the individual to his present and future academic and/or career environment;
2. It must provide the means for transformations toward a goal with a high probability of attainment;
3. It must furnish the resources to develop human talent in an optimal way;
4. A program with such dimensions must be self-improving, and therefore, flexible.

Without the application of sophisticated technology, it is difficult to see how the teachers of today, small in number in proportion to the tremendous student population, would be able to lead each student to explore, to learn, to evaluate, and to master the prodigious quantities of evolving knowledge. The transforms, or paths, through which these objectives may be realized may range from the use of a combination of media for mass instruction (including components such as video tape) to selected media for small group and individual instruction such as the language laboratory, the speech laboratory, the reading center, computer assisted learning and computer managed instruction, audio assisted learning, and other individual response systems. A coordinated complex, which includes and integrates the library and the instructional technology and media center (which subsumes a programmed instruction center, a study center, and audio-visual instructional technology) is implied, so that the many facets of a subject may be explored and researched meaningfully. It may require the integration of machines and information-retrieval systems (both audio and video) with teaching teams. The reader must keep in mind, however, that the most intricate system of automated learning aids and systems of programmed instruction is irrelevant without reference to the clarity of the instructional program(s).

Materials of instruction include all books and printed matter, the more traditional audio-visual and other teaching aids, and the materials of programmed instruction (including digital, dial, and audio-manual access information retrieval and instructional technology distribution systems and computer-oriented, assisted, and managed learning) which are utilized to enhance student learning in the classroom.

The selection and organization of materials and resources for instruction are schoolwide problems that should be considered by the entire staff. Teachers, principals, and specialist-consultants cooperatively should establish definite policies as to the selection of various instructional materials and equipment and enumerate the steps to be taken in acquiring them. There are no short cuts to the wise selection of books, films, and other materials.

What procedure should be used in choosing instructional materials? Should textbooks be selected on a school system-wide basis or by individual schools? What part should the supervisor play in selecting books and other instructional materials? Who should decide what texts are to be purchased? How extensively shall community recources be utilized? There are the types of decisions that must be made in selecting materials and resources.

This chapter includes a discussion of:

Principles and practices
Curriculum improvement through the use of instructional materials
How to evaluate instructional materials
How to evaluate and improve the media center
How to improve the use of instructional materials
Do—don't
"In-Basket" supervisory problems

Principles and Practices

The selection of instructional materials should follow a study of the educational program and its objectives. Specialists in the various subject areas long have considered their main problem to be the choice of texts and the materials of instructional technology. The selection of materials without true knowledge of their purpose is a blindfolded process. If we wish to secure the best assortment of pertinent learning materials for students we should spend considerable time in cooperative planning as a faculty, under the leadership of the supervising principal. The purposes of the instructional program, and the kinds of materials that will give the students desirable experiences and serve those purposes, must be determined.

Basic Principles

The following may be considered as a set of basic principles in this area:

1. Student learning can be accelerated by the use of better instructional materials.
2. Materials promote good teaching when they fit the curriculum and are adapted to the needs, interests, and abilities of students.

3. The supervising principal should keep teachers informed about new and better materials.

4. Materials should be purchased early, be kept readily available for use, and be maintained in adequate supply.

5. The program for securing materials should permit representatives of all involved to participate in varying degrees in the selection.

6. Each school staff should help to select its own materials, assist with storage, evaluate effectiveness, and make recommendations for improvement.

7. A Materials of Instruction Committee should make recommendations as to the appropriate grade level and subject area use of teaching aids.

8. Teachers, specialists, and supervising principals should be trained in the proper use of materials of instruction.

9. The annual appropriation per student for materials of instruction should meet some acceptable standard, such as the recommendations of experts or the findings of research.

10. There is no short cut to the wise selection of books and the other materials of instructional technology.

A Source of Difficulty

One source of difficulty in planning for the improvement of the materials of instruction in individual schools and school systems is securing the cooperation of those involved. Each teacher has a contribution to make to the total program of the school. Materials of instruction for a particular group of learners may improve as a result of the participation of the entire staff in cooperative planning, study, and experimentation.

Planning Levels

Four levels of planning for the improvement of the program of instructional materials may be identified:

1. *Teacher planning.* Of first importance is the teacher's own planning of the curriculum for his class. It is at this level that planning directly af-

fects the experiences of students. Regardless of how sound planning at
other levels may be, it serves little purpose unless it it implemented at
the classroom level. Curriculum planning at this level is basically a matter of making choices within a flexible curriculum framework.

2. *School unit level.* Second, there is the school unit level. The local school
faculty, under the direction of the supervising principal, is responsible
for planning the total program of the school for effecting desired learnings. Here planning may proceed through the total faculty, grade level
and special committees, and through cooperative school councils.

3. *System level.* Third, there is the system level, as may be seen in Figure
14-1. Such representative or composite groups of status leadership as
may be designated are responsible for planning general policies concerning the programs of all the schools for effecting desired learnings. Representative councils, grade level and special committees, individuals or
groups having particular interests, and sometimes the whole group may
carry on this planning, with the legally responsible body, the board of
education, having final responsibility. There may be a hierarchy of planning groups at this level; that is, the local school system may need to
work out plans which are consistent with those of the intermediate unit
authorities and the intermediate unit with those of the state. All these
plans may be affected by state laws and regulations of the state board of
education.

4. *The external level.* Fourth, there is a level we may classify as external.
Although having no legal or administrative relationship with the school,
an accrediting association may have considerable influence on local curriculum planning. Through research studies and publications, and
through curriculum materials, professional associations frequently contribute very directly to local planning groups.

Planning that affects local groups indirectly, but sometimes quite forcibly, is done by various organized groups throughout the nation who seek to
influence what is taught in school in relation to their interests. They may
work through:

a. Direct publications;
b. Speakers, and films for school;

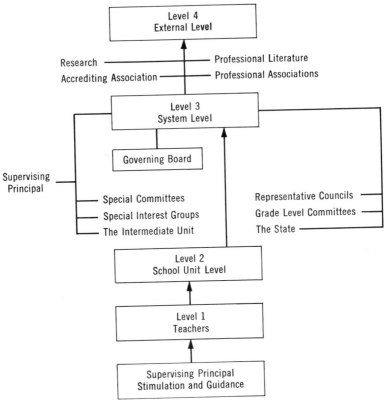

FIGURE 14–1   Levels of Planning for the Improvement of Instructional Materials.

c. Pressure on legislatures;

d. Pressure on governing boards and school curriculum planning groups;

e. Pressure on publishers and/or textbook writers.

How to Determine the Responsibilities for Planning

The teacher may participate in each level of planning: he is the major participant at the first level and one of the group of planners at the second level; and he is represented, if not personally involved, at the third level.

The supervising principal should be involved at all levels. His participation at the latter two upper levels may be in connection with in-service education activities and cooperative experimentation and research in addition to membership in faculty planning groups. So far as the fourth level is concerned, participation usually is as a consumer of materials from the various groups although he may work actively with professional organizations in planning.

THE SELECTION OF MATERIALS. To the greatest extent possible, the choice of materials and resources should be the responsibility of those who use them. In school systems both large and small the common practice has been centralization of responsibility in the selection of instructional materials. In small schools, superintendents have chosen books through their contacts with book salesmen; in larger school systems, in the interest of economy, the textbooks have been adopted on a system-wide basis for a period of three to five years. A number of states have some form of textbook adoption by a state agency. In Texas, Oregon, and California, textbook commissions have been established by the state legislature for statewide adoption of textbooks.

Some larger school systems, in recent years, have been moving away from the standardization and centralization of purchasing of all instructional materials. The purchase of such standard items as pencils, paper, and notebooks may be done more economically and efficiently through a central purchasing agency; but choosing textbooks and other supplementary materials is too closely related to local curriculum problems to be relegated to a central agency. Some schools have found that the individual in charge of purchasing may become involved in policy-making through the selection of instructional materials.

PRINCIPLES OF PURCHASING. The real reason for the change, however, is the desire of educators to choose materials that will be best suited to the individual school and community. In terms of adapting materials to curriculum needs, there is a real advantage in allotting each school its own budget for the purchase of instructional materials, including textbooks. Actual purchasing can still be done in the central office without increasing expenses, but the selection should be the responsibility of the individual school.

The supervising principal and the teachers can work together in choosing the types of materials that will best suit their needs and purposes. In any school system there is variation from school to school in ideas concerning the use of materials. Certainly no teacher who wants to use a variety of materials rather than a single text should be handcuffed by restrictive, outmoded policies.

The job of the supervising principal is to facilitate the choice of better, appropriate materials, and to maintain lines of effective communication. Above all, his responsibility is to see that choices are made wisely in terms of the purposes for which the instructional materials are to be used.

If this principal is applied seriously, the teacher, in cooperation with his students, will have an important part to play in the selection of materials. One of the more powerful incentives to experimentation is the encouragement given to the teacher through furnishing the necessary means for such experimentation in the classroom. Certainly the teacher must play a major part in the selection of materials for his classroom.

Where there are restrictions imposed by the state or by the board of education, some school systems have followed the practice of giving greater flexibility through adopting a list of books from which the individual school faculty may choose. This is the practice in a number of the states that require textbook adoption at the state level.

Curriculum Improvement through the Use of Instructional Materials

As the scope of the school curriculum continually widens, the recitation method of instruction must increasingly be supplemented. In using present-day curricular vehicles to guide students to worthy goals, appropriate instructional aids must be selected out of the countless materials of instructional technology made available.

THE SCHOOL LIBRARY AS A DISTRIBUTION CENTER. In a small school, just as in the larger institutions, the materials accumulate, and it is impossible for the teachers to keep all of these items in their classrooms. The central library may be the only suitable place in the school to gather all of the materials required by the instructional program.[1] The library, especially in the elementary schools, is becoming, therefore, the distribution center in the school, not only for books but also for the other various materials of instructional technology. In the larger secondary schools and in the colleges the instructional technology centers and libraries may be combined in a larger instructional media complex, each area being coordinated and supervised by a professional specialist.

Unless the librarian has received special, advanced training, and is well acquainted with these materials and able to give adequate, technical information concerning the application and use(s) of the types of materials and devices which are available for the various school activities, keeping all the instructional aids at this centralized place will not serve its intended purpose.

Since small schools are not in a position to employ a top-notch specialist who can perform in the role of *materials counselor*, it is the job of the supervising principal to make certain that the proper types of teaching aids required for proposed lessons are supplied. Instruction in the use of the materials also must be provided. The supervising principal also should help teachers by keeping them informed. This may be accomplished by furnishing a list of materials available both in the school and in the central office.

VIDEO- AND AUDIO-TUTORIAL SYSTEMS, AND OTHERS. Video- and audio-tutorial systems, television, and single concept films and tapes are coming to the front as supplementary educational aids. There are many experiments under way dealing with educational programs. They may prove to be especially useful in the fields of science, communications, mathematics, and foreign languages. Many school systems are employing television in the program for in-service education.

Teachers should be alert to the latest audio-visual and other mechanical devices which may be employed to deal with the newly enriched curriculum. The principal should encourage them to keep in touch with the latest periodicals, and with books on education, including state and federal publi-

[1] See National Education Association, Department of Elementary School Principals, *Elementary School Libraries Today*, Thirtieth Yearbook (Washington, D.C.: The Department, 1951), p. 415.

cations. Only then will instruction be presented in the most effective and efficient manner.

THE INSTRUCTIONAL MATERIALS LABORATORY. In many schools of education in the large universities, in some state departments of education, and in some community colleges and large school systems there are centers which are equipped with instructional materials. These materials may include such items as:

1. Courses of study from other states and from local school systems;
2. Curriculum pamphlets and bulletins of all types;
3. Resource materials and units for the use of teachers within the system;
4. Textbooks and professional books concerning various aspects of the curriculum;
5. Materials of instructional technology.

While most of the instructional laboratories provide the materials only as a reference service to teachers, some provide guidance and assistance in becoming acquainted with the techniques for utilizing newly developed aids and in the construction of teacher and student made materials.

On the community college level, and also at the university level, an instructional technology and media center such as was described in the introduction to this chapter would include all of the items listed above plus provision for individual information retrieval and response systems including audio-and/or video-assisted (audio-tutorial) instruction, computer assisted and managed learning, and the utilization of the other materials of instructional technology, including provisions for single concept films, tapes, sound filmstrips, and similar programs.

How to Select Criteria for Evaluating Instructional Materials as Aids for Instruction

According to J. M. Gwynn[2] the instructional materials should:

1. Suit the age level and experience of the student.
2. Bring realities to the student, building upon previous experience.

[2]J. Minor Gwynn, *Curriculum Principles and Social Trends* (New York: The Macmillan Company, 1960), p. 561.

3. Be introduced after careful preparation based upon thorough study and investigation.
4. Contribute to, rather than substitute for, the learning process.
5. Be of reasonable length.

Further standards concerning the use of instructional aids are:

1. The use of more than one type of material at the same time is of doubtful value.
2. The effectiveness of the use of the materials should be evaluated by both teacher and students.
3. The materials should be utilized within a well-balanced program, with one type of teaching aid being used at one time, and a different teaching aid being used at another time.
4. The materials must present an air of reality, not an artificial setting which cannot be understood by the students.
5. The objectives of instruction in each case must have been determined in advance before the materials will be of maximum value to the learner.
6. Materials must be used which take into account the differences in students, where one student sees a relationship much more quickly than another, and yet all students see some relationship.

The major problem faced by the supervising principal in attempting to select, organize, and improve instructional materials is that varied materials are needed to provide for the individual differences of students. Most specialists tend to agree with the American Textbook Publishers Institute's definition of a modern textbook as "an assistant teacher in print."[3]

The major criticism to be made with regard to the present manner of textbook utilization is that one such "assistant teacher" is not enough for the variety of needs, interests, and abilities of the typical learning group. The solution, therefore, is to increase the effectiveness of the use of this resource, and wherever possible to add other resources—not to do away with a most important resource. The methods by which these solutions are realized constitute part of the job of the supervising principal.

[3]American Textbook Publishers Institute, *Textbooks in Education* (New York: The Institute, 1949), p. 5.

The choice of materials and resources should be based upon the purposes, maturity, and background of the group. Too often books and other materials for use in the classroom are selected on bases other than the objectives to be achieved and the students to be taught. A particular book may appear to be "teachable," it may have an attractive format, or the teacher may find that other teachers are using it. Objectives become empty statements when textbook selection is based on criteria such as the aforementioned objectives.

How to Evaluate Instructional Materials

Positive Characteristics

The first characteristic to be considered by the supervising principal in selecting any learning aid is its relevancy to the goal-seeking activity involved. Thus one turns to the assignment specifications to learn about his duties and responsibilities; to the dictionary to find the meaning of a word; to the microscope to examine microbes. This seemingly obvious criterion of selection is abused, however, by such practices as:

1. Use of textbooks and other printed materials as sole sources of information about problems which have changed materially since the materials were published.
2. Use of films and other visual aids as time fillers, without relation to the subject at hand.
3. Use of persons as speakers because they are entertaining, without regard to their subject matter.
4. Use of the same field trips from year to year, without relation to particular units of work.

The Criterion of Usability

The criterion of usability has at least two connotations of significance:

1. *The resources must be accessible at the time needed.* The most relevant materials can be selected from book and film catalogues, but may not be

usable because of lack of funds or time to secure them. The resource file may yield names of persons who can help on projects, but inquiry reveals that these persons are not available when needed. The problem of timing is a particularly complex one in relation to the selection of visual aids, which frequently must be ordered (on a rental basis) weeks in advanced.

2. *A learning aid must be usable in terms of its appropriateness to the particular group*. Relevant materials are available on almost any topic, but they may be appropriate only to mature readers. Similarly, competent persons may have a wealth of information bearing on students' questions, but may be completely unable to explain this information to students. The matter of appropriateness ultimately is answered in terms of individual learners, and so far as possible supervisors and teachers must select a range of resources which provides for each individual. This criterion is violated most generally in regard to instructional materials, the selection of which may be completely out of the teacher's hands.

NEED FOR ACCURATE INFORMATION. The resources for learning must give as accurate information as possible. This criterion is of special significance in relation to printed sources, particularly pamphlet materials. However, films, programmed materials, and even visiting specialists may give inaccurate information. Materials prepared with particular biases, such as those used for advertising, may be helpful resources, but the teacher is obliged to point out the biases and inaccuracies and to use any other available materials to show differing viewpoints.

THE SUPERVISOR SELECTS ECONOMICAL RESOURCES. Other things being equal, the most economical resources should be used. Often other things are not equal and teachers have difficulty in estimating the costs in time and money of different tools. However, good judgment will rule out:

1. Using expensive sound, color films, *if* more economical slides, pictures, single-concept cartridge film loops or tapes, or pamphlets are available and would be as effective.
2. Purchasing expensive motion pictures (when only one teacher wants to

use the film one time per term) if rental (and even free) films are available, or renting films which are used several times each term when purchase would be more economical.

3. Taking a group of students to see a resource specialist who could come to the school and is willing to do so.
4. Sending an entire class to a set of reference books to check on the same topic if one person could present the information effectively.

The principle of economy is violated, contrary to common assumption, by using the same materials for all members of a class, when perhaps half of the group finds these materials too difficult or too boring. The same funds could be spent for materials developed at different levels of difficulty for varying interests.

In addition, the maturity and the background of the group must be taken into consideration. Students who have grown up on a farm cannot be expected to profit most from reading books that are based on life in the city. In recent years more attention has been given to this problem in the development of readers for the schools.

HOW TO SELECT MATERIALS DEALING WITH BASIC ECONOMIC AND SOCIAL ISSUES. More books and materials should be produced that are based on the backgrounds of the students. Many kinds of free and inexpensive materials are available. The Joint Council on Economic Education in the Greater Hartford (Connecticut) area,[4] through one of its committees, developed the following criteria for selecting materials dealing with basic social and/or economic issues:

1. The source and sponsorship of literature and teaching aids should be clear, so that students may make judgments as to probable bias.
2. Resource materials should arouse interest in our economic life. They should give insight into problems inherent in our economic society, including those of human relationships.

[4]Greater Hartford Council on Economic Education, *Aids in the Improvement of Education for Economic Understanding,* Bulletin No. 1 (Hartford, Connecticut: The Council, 1950), p. 2.

3. In the overall selection of materials there should be a wholesome balance among the various points of view. However, the fact that an individual piece of literature has a one-sided point of view does not disqualify it as a useful aid to economic understanding.
4. Materials should be on the students' level of understanding and interest. In most classes there will be students with mature abilities and interests and others whose abilities and interests are immature. Attempts should be made to secure a variety of materials in order to meet the varied needs of a variety of students.
5. The above criteria should be considered in the use of various types of resource materials including speakers, films, recordings, and field trips, as well as pamphlets and other printed materials.

Students can participate in the selection of free materials through writing for them as a committee or class project, searching for the kinds of information that will be helpful in the solution of their problems. The fact that material is free may make it attractive to those operating on restricted budgets.

How to Evaluate the Classroom Use of Materials of Instruction

The need for materials and equipment to take care of a variety of individual interests, development, and abilities should be considered for every classroom. Generally, if a rich environment is provided, learning will be facilitated. Students tend to choose the more appropriate kinds of materials, if given the opportunity, through a process of self-selection. Modern classrooms should have flexible self-instructional (tutorial) carrels equipped with audio and visual input terminals reading centers, music centers, science centers, and equipment for art and for practical arts. Classrooms should serve as instructional laboratories. The classroom laboratory is essentially a *flexible* collection of the materials and equipment useful in connection with particular purposes of the learning group. Classroom laboratory materials are unique only in respect to location.

How to Establish Criteria for Supervising
Selection of Instructional Materials

The members of the staff should establish criteria cooperatively for the selection of materials to be purchased for the school. When a committee has the responsibility for choosing materials for the study of geography, it should determine the criteria for selection before it begins to study the books, maps, transparencies, or globes themselves. The establishment of criteria means that the program will have to be studied to see what kinds of experiences are desirable in view of the objectives. Such matters as authenticity, vocabulary, organization, consistency, teaching and study aids, style, and format should be considered.

HOW TO IMPROVE THE SELECTION OF TEXTBOOKS. The following criteria for evaluating books, pamphlets, and periodicals were established by one city school system:[5]

In terms of instructional merit:

1. How well does the material cover the essentials in this field?
2. How suitable is the vocabulary for the grade students' level of achievement?
3. How adequate is the material in scope and in interest appeal? Should it meet teacher and student needs at the grade level for which it is being considered?
4. How factually correct is the material?
5. How up-to-date is the material?
6. How well does the material suggest and discuss applications to everyday life?
7. If an anthology, how genuinely representative of the thought and the culture of the period and area to be studied are the selections?
8. How well do the problems of life presented stimulate students to meaningful consideration of right and wrong behavior?

[5]Adapted from Form 113-8, used in the evaluation of materials, in "Procedures in the Selection and Adoption of Learning Materials in Pasadena City Schools," duplicated material (Pasadena, California: Pasadena City Schools, 1953).

In terms of the loyalty factor, judged on the basis of the purpose for which the particular publication is to be used:

1. How adequately presented is that aspect of American civilization with which the book deals?
2. How well does the author support his generalizations with reliable information and logical deduction?
3. In the study of democracy, how well are both its accomplishments and problems considered?
4. How well does the material offer means and methods for arriving at solutions to the problems?
5. In dealing with the individual American's relationship to government, are his obligations stressed as well as his rights?
6. How adequately does the material help pupils to develop sound methods of propaganda analysis to be applied to all situations?
7. For judging basic texts: if controversial issues are considered, how adequately are representative points of view included and treated objectively?
8. For judging supplementary materials: how well does this material contribute to an appropriate balance of all representative points of view in your school or library?
9. For judging plays, newspapers, and other periodicals; how sound is the reputation and integrity of the editorial board?

In terms of format:

1. How clear, readable, and attractive is the type?
2. How suitable is the paper for this type of textbook?
3. Is the binding attractive but still durable for extended school use?
4. Is the size of type appropriate for the students of the grade for which the material is being considered?
5. How clear, well designed, and meaningful are the illustrations?
6. How adequate for student reference work is the index?

In terms of instructional aids and authorship:

1. How well does the bibliography encourage and aid the students in carrying on research?
2. How well qualified in the field and grade level is the author?
3. How effectively are such reading aids as variations in type, center heads, side heads, and italics used?
4. How challenging and stimulating are study aids such as self-tests, summaries, reviews, and suggested activities (including instructional trips, films, tapes, and others)?
5. How adequate and practical are such instructional aids as suggested problems or projects, tests, bibliographies, appendices, glossaries, and maps?

The supervisor must ask himself questions, such as:

1. Does the book develop the kind of ideas that are important?
2. Does it clearly distinguish between propaganda and factual information?
3. Is it suitable for use in developing the kinds of attitudes, skills, understandings, and appreciations that are important?

These are the type of questions that grow out of concern for the purposes of instruction.

Practices in Selection of Textbooks

Practices in the selection of textbooks vary widely in the United States. In general, the supervising principal should insure that the competent, experienced teacher has the freedom to decide whether the needs of the learning situation require the use of a basic textbook (that is, the same book for each student) and, if so, the additional materials that are required. If not so, the teacher should participate in selecting cobasic textbooks (that is, multiple sets of books) and other materials. The teacher should determine which materials he will use with his class. With freedom to make this decision, teachers may find it advantageous to select particular books from a list already screened or adopted.

In practice, textbooks sometimes are chosen by state or local authorities and distributed to classrooms without any consultation of teachers' preferences. In such situations there may be freedom for teachers to select additional materials, or even to arrange exchanges.

Authors, professional committees, and school systems have prepared extensive lists of criteria, scoring sheets, and other guides for selecting textbooks. Although these may be valuable in making selections, the principal always must bear in mind the unique needs, interests, and abilities of the teacher, the particular group of learners involved, and the general goals planned for this group.

HOW TO AVOID UNDUE INFLUENCE. In selecting instructional materials principals must guard against being influenced by outside pressures, direct or indirect, that would limit the freedom to teach and to learn. There is no doubt that the atmosphere of regarding new ideas with suspicion has influenced the selection of textbooks and other instructional materials. One unfortunate result appears to have been a tendency in some schools toward greater centralization of the process of selection. The safeguards can become so formalized that it becomes difficult, or at least discouraging, for a principal or a teacher to secure the necessary current materials on up-to-date problems and issues.

Two steps in avoiding undue influence by such pressures to the extent that learning is adversely affected are: (1) to work with regularly established citizen groups in the study of the kinds of materials that instruction for living in a democratic society needs, and (2) by developing written policies for the selection of materials.

HOW TO EVALUATE THE UTILIZATION OF AVAILABLE RESOURCES. In a study of twentieth-century schools a hundred years from now, undoubtedly the researchers will be puzzled by the great homage paid to written materials as resources for instruction. Written materials are only one kind of resource; in fact, the human elements in the learning situation are the most important kinds of resources.

Not so generally accepted or understood is that valuable resource of the students themselves. There will be students who have traveled to various parts of the country or who will have lived in other countries, and there will be students of varying backgrounds.

Attending an in-service education course are teachers from all levels of education. So many times we overlook these most valuable resources that are immediately at hand. When workshops consider resource people they ought first to look at the resources that are contained within the group.

There are opportunities for varied experiences in the school, such as:

1. The lunchroom or cafeteria
2. The halls
3. The school grounds
4. The books to be taken care of
5. The traffic to be regulated
6. The supplies to be inventoried and stored

There is the community, with its rich resources in:

1. Governmental institutions
2. Service organizations
3. Places of business
4. Industries
5. Homes
6. Farms
7. People who have interesting backgrounds and hobbies
8. People who have ideas that may differ from those of other people
9. People engaged in various occupations
10. Natural resources in the form of trees, soil, rock formations
11. Illustrations of erosion and conservation practices
12. Wild life
13. Tame animals

All of these are rich and wonderful resources which are at hand for almost every school.

HOW TO EVALUATE PICTURES. The criterion of accuracy is important in the selection of pictures since distorted, one-sided, or untrue concepts may result from a single picture that fails to tell the whole story or misrepresents what it does tell. This caution is applicable particularly to the attractive pictures appearing in the advertisement sections of magazines. Series of pictures, and contrasting pictures on the same topic, are most helpful. Also consider size, clarity, color, and composition.

HOW TO EVALUATE SLIDES, FILMSTRIPS, TRANSPARENCIES, AND RELATED EQUIPMENT. Slides, filmstrips, and transparencies may be prepared, rented, or borrowed from distribution agencies. Like pictures, they have extensive utility in learning. Filmstrips are not as flexible as slides and transparencies since they have to be shown in a fixed series, but they are more convenient to handle. Simple concept cartridge film loops are, according to many who have used them, at least as convenient as filmstrips. In any event, the operator should be able to pause to discuss any frame as the material is projected.

Various types of projection equipment may be used for showing slides, filmstrips, transparencies, and pictures on the projection screen. The opaque projector is a particularly usable resource. The work of the students, as well as pictures and printed material, may be projected by using this projector.

Several types of equipment for projecting slides, filmstrips, "single concept" cartridge films, and transparencies are available. The overhead projector is becoming lighter and its light source more flexible; *technamation* introduces a sense of motion to the projected transparency through polarization. Slides, filmstrips, and transparencies, and equipment for their projection, offer the advantage of considerable economy over motion pictures.

The screen may be of the glass beaded lenticular type which affords a distortion-free image to those sitting anywhere at the sides of the room. Certainly adequate room-darkening equipment should be provided, and the screen should be permanently mounted rather than portable. Two screens, one in the front of the room and one in a rear corner, angled toward the center of the room, are recommended.

HOW TO EVALUATE SPECIMENS AND MODELS. Collections, relics, specimens, models, and other items brought from home, bought from commercial agencies, or loaned by museums, serve valuable instructional purposes. Generally these items are used in connection with the preparation of exhibits and displays which serve both to stimulate learning and to provide information.

Problems of space, storage, and the preservation of these materials sometimes are acute. Unless a central school museum is practicable, it probably
is best to prepare exhibits or displays when needed and then return the
pieces to the original sources. Consider size and portability, as well as
application.

HOW TO EVALUATE MAPS, GLOBES, AND CHARTS. A great variety of maps,
globes, and charts are available from commercial agencies. These should
be selected with particular concern for their practicability in the classroom,
as well as their appropriateness for the students' achievement level and
maturity. Fixed equipment has the disadvantage of taking up needed space
when not in use. Central school facilities for the storage of maps, globes,
and charts would seem desirable, provided these can be readily and easily
moved into classrooms when the need arises. Wise curriculum planning will
make available a number of the most relevant, usable, and accurate maps,
globes, and charts, and will provide for getting adequate information about
their availability and use to teachers.

HOW TO EVALUATE THE MOTION PICTURE. Possibly the most widely used
and misused instructional technology resource is the motion picture. Lack of
careful planning and problems of distribution frequently result in the
showing of films to learning groups without relation to the classroom experiences and maturity levels of the students. In fact, the criteria for selecting
and using this resource are violated by practices which permit the unecono-
mical use of learners' time in seeing films irrelevant to their goals, inappropriate to their interests, or inaccurate in film content. It clearly behooves
supervisors to help teachers to plan carefully for the wise use of a most
valuable resource.

The selection of films is eased by curriculum guides which suggest relevant
film resources. In the absence of such guides, the teacher may find aid by
annotated guides to films prepared by the distribution agencies.

There is no adequate substitute for a preview of the film by the teacher
concerned. In using the film various steps should be planned for, but essentially they are similar to those used in connection with any other learning
experience:

1. Formulating questions to be answered; that is, learning goals;
2. Understanding the goal-seeking activity of seeing the film;
3. Answering the questions, and reviewing information, evaluating the learning experience, and planning the next steps.

Properly used, the motion picture perhaps is the resource which can give to the largest number of learners the most intelligible information on the greatest variety of problems in the shortest period of time, with the possible exception of video tape and costly and complex computer-assisted learning. Hence, we may well hope to see its proper use greatly expanded.

A sample film evaluation form is included as Figure 14–2.

FIGURE 14–2   Sample Motion Picture Evaluation Form

Film title _____ Length _____

                                                              Sound _____

Source _____ Date _____ Silent _____

                                                              Color _____

Cost _____   1. Rent ( )   Black and White _____
                     2. Purchase ( )   Age Level
                     3. Free for   or Grade _____
                        Evaluation ( )

Subject area(s)_____

General category_____

1. Is empathy on the part of the viewer probable?
   Yes _____ No _____ Don't know _____
Comments _____

2. Does the content flow and progress smoothly?
   Yes _____ No _____ Don't know _____
Comments _____

FIGURE 14–2   (Continued)

3. Is the dialogue clear and well presented?

Yes _____ No _____ Don't know _____

Comments _____

4. Is the film modern in content and presentation?

Yes _____ No _____ Don't know _____

Comments _____

5. Was an adequate musical background provided?

Yes _____ No _____ Don't know _____

Comments _____

6. Was the sound track adequate as to volume, clarity, and tone?

Yes _____ No _____ Don't know _____

Comments _____

7. Would you commend the film for its photography?

Yes _____ No _____ Don't know _____

Comments _____

8. Was this a good print?

Yes _____ No _____ Don't know _____

Comments _____

9. Were special photographic techniques used?

Yes _____ No _____ Don't know _____

Comments _____

10. Was animation used?

Yes _____ No _____ Don't know _____

Comments _____

11. Was there any attempt to indoctrinate the viewer?

Yes _____ No _____ Don't know _____

Comments _____

FIGURE 14–2   (Continued)

12. Was the content accurate?

Yes _____ No _____ Don't know _____

Comments _____

13. Was the content clearly presented?

Yes _____ No _____ Don't know _____

Comments _____

14. How would you rate this film?

Excellent_____Good _____ Average _____ Poor _____
Not suitable for school use_____

Comments _____

General comments and recommendations: _____

_____

_____

HOW TO EVALUATE PHONOGRAPH TRANSCRIPTIONS AND AUDIO AND VIDEO
TAPE RECORDINGS. In addition to the usual phonograph records and audio
tapes widely in use, several other types of recorded resources are available:

1. Transcriptions and video tapes of television and radio broadcasts make
   possible the repetition of the program material at more convenient times
   and as frequently as desired.
2. Video and audio tape and phonograph recordings of dramatizations,
   stories, poetry, and historical events are available commercially.
3. Various recording devices owned by schools now make possible the
   recording of class activities, individual student endeavors, and other
   events in the school and in the community.

Stereo cassette recorders offer maximum ease of use, flexibility, and the
cassette cartridges have the advantage of protecting the tape within. Video
and audio tape recordings of classroom sessions, speeches, assembly programs, and similar happenings may serve many purposes. These resources

offer excellent help for learning experiences in almost every curricular area. Community colleges, university bureaus, schools, and school systems maintain libraries of records and recordings, frequently as a part of a complete resource center. If such libraries are not available, the supervising principal should help the teacher to make selections from whatever listings can be found.

If a video tape recorder is to be purchased, one which is compatible with another in a neighboring school would permit sharing program materials. In spite of the comparatively moderate cost differential, a color signal video tape recorder should be given due consideration. The supervisor should give maximum assistance in the selection and use of recordings and transcriptions, along with other learning resources.

HOW TO EVALUATE RADIO AND TELEVISION RESOURCES. Radio and television are resources of unique significance because of their inherent values and because of their possible uses both in and out of school. Figure 14–3 illustrates a sample brochure presented to students concerning television program selection.

FIGURE 14–3   Brochure Presented to Students on the Topic of
Television Program Selection

TV!

As a study resource, your television set at home is somewhat like your school library. It can provide a great deal of helpful and stimulating material if you know how to use it to good advantage. In the library, you first study the card index to find out what's available on the subject in which you are interested. For TV, you study the program schedules.

In addition to following the daily schedules in newspapers, TV guides are available where offerings are divided under drama, music and arts, public affairs and history, and science and exploration.

Try to choose programs that:

- Are specifically related to something you'll be studying during the week.

- Will assist you in special assignments.

- Will help you have a better understanding of today's world.

- Will fit in with your own personal interests.

Curriculum planning for in-school use of these materials introduces the practical problem of utilizing broadcasts at scheduled times which may or may not coincide with convenient times in the school schedule. Taped program materials (video and audio) help overcome this disadvantage. The primary problem in directing the out-of-school use of educational television and radio is found in the difficulty of controlling students' home schedules. Perhaps one major goal to be sought with regard to out-of-school radio and television is cooperative planning with parents as to appropriate programs for children and youth.

The selection of in-school programs involves considerable day-by-day study of program announcements. Frequently some program can be found that bears directly on current units of work and the daily program, especially in nondepartmental schools, can be adjusted accordingly. Some school systems and broadcasting stations arrange programs in series for use in schools, and plans for instructional units may be built around these series. One effective way of using telecasts and broadcasts is through small group or individual reports. A group of students may see a program and report to the class in the same way as might be done with respect to work in the library or a field trip. This plan is useful particularly for out-of-school programs.

Television sets equipped to handle the *electronic video recording* system, produced initially by the Columbia Broadcasting System, should receive due consideration. The electronic video recording system (EVR) was specifically designed for schools, industrial training programs, hospitals, and other institutions where education, training, and in-service improvement programs are emphasized.

EVR utilizes a professionally produced and edited minifilm which has the appearance of a round cartridge with the diameter of a 45 rpm phonograph recording. It can be inserted into a player which is, in turn, connected to any number of ordinary television receivers. The cartridges contain two tracks for a total running time of fifty-two minutes. The pictures are sharp, clearly defined, and free from interference. The teacher can accelerate or slow the action, stop to examine a specific frame, and proceed manually frame-by-frame.

In any event, the supervising principal should remember that television, motion pictures, and the newer programmed learning devices are teaching *aids* only. They cannot take the place of the teacher, nor should a telecast schedule be allowed to dictate the daily program for a class except at the discretion of the teacher.

HOW TO MAKE BEST USE OF AUTOMATED AND PROGRAMMED LEARNING. A radio program broadcast over the Columbia Broadcasting System began with a somewhat startling passage:

> There's a group of . . . school children who can give surprisingly accurate answers to some rather technical questions about molecular theory. These children are in the first grade![6]

A Case in Point

In a school not too long ago a very nervous, excited little girl peeked through the door of her classroom. With a startled look at a mysterious array of gadgets and machines and strange people, she drew back shyly and clutched tightly at the girl friend beside her. The students finally gathered enough courage to slip into the room, and one of the monitors led the youngest child to a screened off cubicle. The girl climbed onto the chair before a mechanical device with a viewing screen and brightly colored push buttons. Earphones were placed over the child's head, and she was told how to operate the machine and answer its questions. She was so frightened that pushing the first button to answer a question took all the courage she could muster. But as she pushed the buttons a few more times, getting the answers right each time, a very friendly voice would say through her earphones, "Fine, good for you." This would happen repeatedly as she pressed the buttons for the correct answers.

So, gradually, the little girl relaxed and settled down to enjoy her first success with the funny "teaching machine." If she made an error, the ma-

---

[6]University of California: Radio-Televsion Administration, "The Overrated Machine," Broadcast No. 4057—University Explorer 1771, over the Columbia Broadcasting System, Sunday, June 4, 1961. Mimeographed. Much of the material in this section has been influenced by this broadcast.

chine explained the source material carefully, showed her an illustration on the viewing screen, and asked her to point to the correct drawing with her "light pencil."

The little girl also had her first science lesson that day—a carefully programmed sequence of thirty-six items about molecular theory. This little girl was quite different from the other children, however. Most of them were fascinated by the gadgets from the very start and were full of eager attention and delight in this new kind of classroom exercise. They were all first-graders.

Although the girl and her classmates learned something about science, even more important perhaps was what the supervising principal learned about this technique. Similar experiments have been going on in increasing numbers in classrooms across the country, though this does not mean an educational revolution. Automation has not taken over the classroom. The real, live human teacher still is required. The significant change is that the teacher has some new tools which, hopefully, will make it possible for him to teach more effectively. It is certain that the educator has another valuable technique for scientific research which may aid in the improvement of instruction.

Nevertheless, these mechanical devices are called computer-assisted learning terminals (or "teaching machines," despite the fact that they do not really teach). As is true of any computer, the machine can do no more than the program with which it has been provided.[7]

Summary of Terms Related to Instructional Technology

AUTOINSTRUCTION. Autoinstruction is a term which denotes a process involving the utilization of carefully planned materials and machinery which are designed to produce learning, without necessarily requiring the immediate presence of a human being other than the student.

---

[7]The programmed materials may be words on tape, or pictures presented on a screen, or images transmitted through a video tube. Many of the devices and techniques employed by teaching machines are described in a book coauthored by Dr. A. A. Lumsdaine and Dr. Robert Glaser, *Teaching Machines and Programmed Learning* (Washington, D.C.: National Education Association, 1960).

BRANCHING. Branching is a generic term indicating a type of programming wherein students are sent to alternative items depending on their responses to a question. In intrinsic programs, the branch usually consists of a single item explaining why a particular answer is incorrect. The branch then returns the student to the original item for another attempt at the problem. A branch that would permit the student to skip over intervening material he had already mastered would be called a *wash ahead* branch. If the student were ordered to repeat a portion of the program that he has inadequately mastered, the branch would be termed *wash back*.

PROGRAMMED TEXT. A programmed text is a program presented in book form. In the programmed text, pages may be "scrambled"; that is, successive pages need not contain successive content material. If the individual is successful in mastering the contents of one page, he is then given instructions as to the proper page to turn to. A scrambled text, then, is a special type of programmed book or text. Students are directed to pages which are not in consecutive order in terms of alternate choice or successes and/or failures. A programmed book or text need not be scrambled, but all scrambled texts are programmed. In any event, a programmed book presents material in a step-by-step fashion, each step being composed of an infinitesimal body of knowledge.

The Teaching Machine

There are many different types of machines designed for a wide variety of purposes. Generally, utilization of a teaching machine is as follows:

1. The student reads assigned material.
2. He is asked to answer multiple choice or completion questions that follow immediately while the material is still fresh in his mind.
3. Answers may be written onto a tape, "drawn" on a cathode-ray tube with a "light pencil" (if a computer terminal is available), or recorded by selecting and pushing buttons on the machine. The materials are organized carefully in a sequence of information. Simple statements follow, idea by idea and step by step.

4. The student is led carefully by the program, much like the author of a book draws his reader progressively through a chain of developments. Unlike the conventional book, in programmed instruction the student is asked to respond continuously.

REMEDIAL LOOP. A remedial loop consists solely of an explanation of an error that a student has made in selecting one of the answer choices available to him. The frame will refer him back to the item he has just left so that he may have another chance to answer the question inherent in the item, but the frame itself contains no question. In some textbooks the remedial loop is referred to as the *first order branch*.

SUB-SEQUENCE. When a student has made an error on a mainstream frame, he may be directed to a sequence of standard intrinsic frames which contain both new material and questions on that material. New frames will provide for further remedial instruction if necessary. The sub-sequence returns the student to the mainstream upon its completion.[8]

The teaching machine is a mechanical device which presents a program to a learner, as may be seen in Figure 14–4. The major features of such instruments include:

1. They usually present a one-item frame at a time.
2. They provide some method for the student to indicate an overt response.
3. They indicate whether a response is correct or not.
4. They may or may not provide branching.
5. They maintain a record of student responses.
6. They provide for feedback.

In the homemade "machine," if one electrode is touched to the question and the other electrode to the proper response, a buzzer and a light are activated. On the map, for example, if one touches the proper city name below the map with the contact point representing the city on the map, a circuit is completed, and a buzzer sounds (or lights flash). See Figure 14–5.

[8]See Susan Meyer Markle, *Good Frames and Bad* (New York: John Wiley & Sons, Inc., 1964), p. 275.

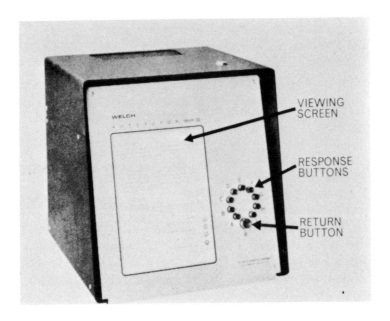

FIGURE 14–4   The "Autotutor" Teaching Machine.
(Photo by Irving Galzen)

Programmed learning marks a renaissance of the method of dialectic question-based teaching which was used so brilliantly by Socrates. This approach of learning is available in several formats, but the teaching machine probably is the best known of the various types of mechanical devices that make use of the programmed materials.

The machines fundamentally are independent of the program material. Any type of machine that presents the program frame by frame or as distinct items, and provides an opportunity for the student to respond, may be adequate. Such machines can be built for less than $50, and it hardly need be said that the machines will not use all of the student's time. A child may make a simple machine using the plan presented in Figure 14–5.

As program availability increases, the total amount of the student's time spent with the teaching machine will amount to about one-third, which means that one machine (the "hardware") is needed for every three to five students. The cost of the program material ("software") is something

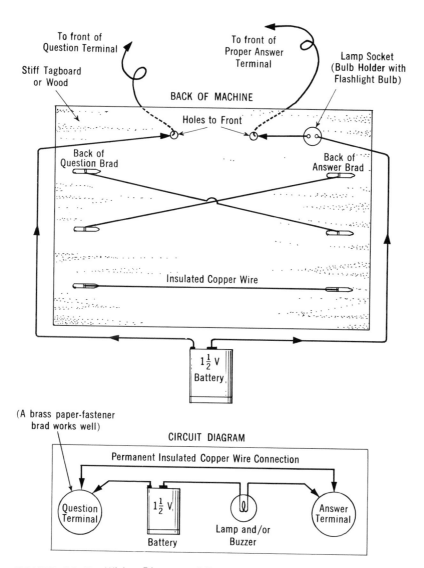

FIGURE 14–5   Wiring Diagram of Teaching Machine.

else again. In one estimate made recently it was calculated that the production of the manuscript for a single program would amount to about $50,000.

"Audio- and/or Video-Tutorial," Computer-Supported Instruction, Computer-Assisted Learning, and Computer-Managed Instruction

The supervisor should be familiar with the following characteristics of "audio-and/or video-tutorial," computer-supported instruction, computer-managed instruction, and computer-assisted learning. In *computer-managed instruction* it is the management dimension which is important. A student would complete one unit of work and then obtain, perhaps, the next three instructional "units" or "modules," in response to the computer's direction. The computer would have reached the "necessary" decision by analyzing the first test completed by the student. The "units" or "modules" may be programmed texts, standard textbooks, various illustrated materials or guided activities, and others.

Computer-supported instruction permits the use of the power of the computer for rapid test scoring interpretation and evaluation; keeping students continuously apprised of their progress and standing in the class; giving prompt feedback as to what the teacher and, perhaps, what his fellow students consider as the weak and strong points of a presentation he has made; for permitting rapid, complex calculations; for rapid information retrieval including multi-media programming and switching; and for meeting similar demands.

In *computer-assisted learning,* the computer is used as a compiler of educational texts.[9] The computer permits a true interaction, and in many cases a dialogue. The student is presented with information at the terminal, to which he responds by pushing a button, applying a light pen (a computer input device) to a cathode-ray tube (CRT) screen, by using the teletype terminal, or in some other manner. Such instruction tends to provide for:

1. Individualization of instruction, in that it provides for:
   a) Self-pacing—there is a pacing component which tells the student, in effect, words such as "You have an hour."

[9]Lawrence M. Stolurow, *Computer Assisted Instruction* (Detroit: American Data Processing, Inc., 1968), p. 25.

    b) Diagnostic preimposed testing
    c) "Modules"—unitized materials (especially in *computer-managed* learning).
2. Continuous participation through:
    a) Overt responses
    b) Varied environment
    c) Review and tutoring.
3. Evaluation and knowledge of results through:
    a) Continuous feedback
    b) Performance testing.
4. Unit revision ("module alteration") based on feedback.

Audio- and video-tutorial instruction attempts to do what has been outlined above, with audio information predominating; visual display materials are kept to a minimum. In *video-tutorial* situations the opposite is true. In *audio-video-tutorial* programs there is a balance of visual and auditory information. The medium used in the latter two situations would be video tape. The supervising principal may wish to review the scheme developed by Norman E. Rich and Hayden R. Williams at Golden West College in California. The TRAILS project (*Total Receptive Access, Independent Learning System*) operated under the weekly format described below.

GENERAL ASSEMBLY SESSION. All students in the course assembled at a scheduled time one hour early in each week. (Almost all of the traditional lecture content was incorporated into the TRAILS experience.) The general assembly session was used to heighten interest, provide historical and theoretical perspective, show longer motion pictures than was possible in the independent study session, provide guest speakers, and provide time for lectures.

INDEPENDENT STUDY SESSION. Students had access to carrels in a center for independent study for several hours daily. This center was called the "Trails lab." In the "Trails lab" students proceeded at their own rate, worked the period of time required to master a unit, and work at their own individual efficiency peak, independently. Each week of the semester was devoted to a major concept or principle of biology. For each concept there had been prepared a program on magnetic tape. This program included the material usually found in the traditional lecture, except that the unit was programmed to include whatever combination of techniques proved most appropriate to each unit. These techniques included short tape-lectures, taped introductions to laboratory materials, study of demonstration materials, examination of specimens under taped direction, the performance of experiments, reading and study of texts and pictures, viewing brief single-concept films, studying microscope slides, and other activities of this nature. An instructor was on duty at all times to provide special assistance to those who needed it, personalizing the tutoring and maintaining the study atmosphere.

SMALL ASSEMBLY SESSIONS. Once each week students met in groups of twenty-five or fewer in a scheduled session, always with the same instructor. During this session questions were answered; assignments were given and collected; course mechanics such as enrollments, withdrawals, absences were handled; and examinations were given. The instructor was an experienced discussion leader and functioned here as such. Students identified this instructor as their teacher in the course.

STUDENT PROJECTS. The small assembly session instructor assigned each student two projects to be completed during the semester. There was a laboratory provided for those projects which required laboratory facilities. For the first project, the student was told what to do, how to do it, what data to gather, and how to use the data. For the second project the student was counseled as to what to do and how to do it. He decided what data to gather and how to use the data. This practice was to give the student an appreciation of the scientific approach to problem-solving and a taste of the excitement of discovery.

HOME STUDY SESSIONS. The students did the usual amount of outside study. Assignments were made during the small assembly session.

THE DECISION MAKING, THE AUDIO-INSTRUCTIONAL SYSTEM, AND TEACHING MACHINES. The tutorial decision-making process is graphically illustrated in the systems analysis chart included as Figure 14–6.

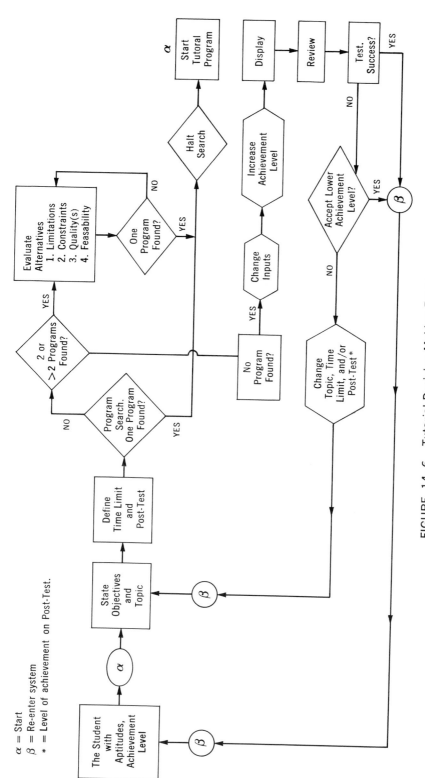

α = Start
β = Re-enter system
* = Level of achievement on Post-Test.

FIGURE 14–6 Tutorial Decision-Making Process.

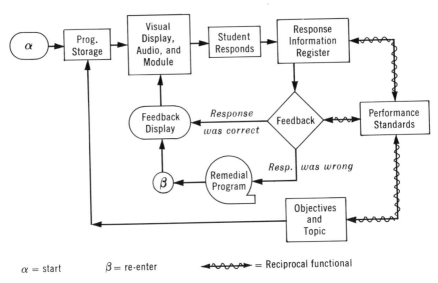

α = start β = re-enter   ◄~~~► = Reciprocal functional

FIGURE 14–7   Audio-Tutorial Program Selection Process.
(After Lawrence M. Stolurow, *Computer Assisted Instruction*, Detroit:
American Data Processing, Inc., 1968, p. 25.)

The audio-instructional system, which would follow the start of the tutorial program, is diagrammed in Figure 14–7.

Machines provide a *medium* for teaching, but the actual information is presented by the programmed material. Investigators are using teaching machines:

1. To test concepts that are at the heart of the educational process;
2. To assist in the teaching of many procedures that can be broken down into some sequence;
3. To train for a variety of skills in industry and in the Armed Forces.

One large factory uses a teaching machine to introduce workers to its assembly line procedures (see Figure 14–8).

FIGURE 14–8   Teaching Machines and Programmed Learning: C.A.L.? C.M.I.? AUDIO-WOW!

How to Assess Programming and Its Advantages

The use of self-instructional programmed learning materials represents a potential contribution of great importance to American education. The supervising principal must be prepared to assist teachers in the proper utilization of such devices.

A variety of programmed material is becoming available, but not all programs will fit all machines. Just any set of question and answer material does not constitute a self-instructional program. Self-instructional materials are designed to adapt to individual differences by allowing each student to proceed at his own rate (see Figure 14–9).

THE JOB OF THE PROGRAM. The program's job, then, is to present to the learner an infinitesimal series of steps which lead from one behavior repertoire to the next. The program must be divided into small, equally assimilated segments. The construction of the sequence of segments of the subject matter being presented constitutes program development. Three popular programming techniques which the supervisor should bring to the attention of interested teachers are:

FIGURE 14–9   Students Using Self-Instructional Materials and Devices.

1. Linears with sublinears;
2. Linears with criterion frames;
3. Intrinsic programming.

These three paradigms are illustrated in Figure 14–10.

Programming requires the process of dividing a complex area of knowledge into a finite series of unitary facts that may be understood and mastered without error. Certainly the supervising principal must assure that there is no premature use of experimental materials that have not been tested through scientific research.

One interesting advantage of the program is that the student can arrive in the learning situation with some knowledge of the subject to be analyzed by the entire class. Bright students generally take about one-third as long to go through complex program material as do average and below average students. While both bright and dull students are able to solve problems presented by the program, the more gifted students are better able to formulate concepts and generalizations than are the average and duller students. In any event, it has been said that if a teacher can be replaced by the machine, then that teacher needs replacing.

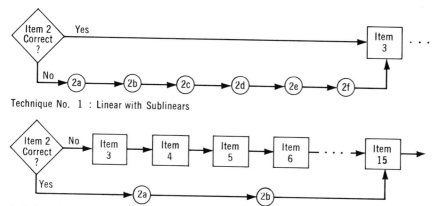

Technique No. 1 : Linear with Sublinears

Technique No. 2 : Linear with Criterion Frames

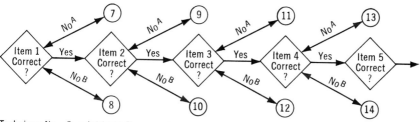

Technique No. 3 : Intrinsic Programming

No^A = Answer incorrect because of (or in direction of) condition A
No^B = Answer incorrect because of (or in direction of) condition B

FIGURE 14–10   Three Program Branching Paradigms.

ADVANTAGES OF PROGRAMMED INSTRUCTION. Some of the advantages of programmed instruction include:

1. Immediate knowledge of results is recorded and the effectiveness of the program can be readily assessed;
2. Distraction is cut to a minimum;
3. The instruction is individualized to a high degree;

4. Provision may be made for students to hear a lecture missed, to receive ancillary information, or to hear an instructor describe a course in which he might wish to enroll.

The reader will recognize the difference between the program and a workbook. A workbook does not provide for a large number of extremely minute, carefully designed steps. The teaching machine and programmed instruction industries are based upon the work of Professor B. F. Skinner of Harvard. Skinner stressed the importance of the development of *operant strength* which was constructed through having made a successful *overt response,* but there is some question as to the value of overt response. In recent experiments conducted at a large western university, two groups of students worked with teaching machines. One group responded overtly to questions, while the second group merely observed the program as it progressed. No significant difference in the amount of information absorbed was found.

HOW TO WRITE THE PROGRAM. The process of program writing is very expensive. It is estimated that a semester's program must consist of about 3,000 or 4,000 frames, which would cost about $50,000 to write. A sample of the charting and diagramming symbols which are used in the preparation of flow charts and block diagrams for program systems is presented in Figure 14–11.

One frame may take approximately three or four hours to write. The procedure followed is:

1. Try out the question with the students
2. Rewrite the question
3. Try out again
4. Rewrite
5. Try out again
6. Rewrite
7. Try out the question once more
8. Final rewrite
9. Preliminary writing on tentative program tape

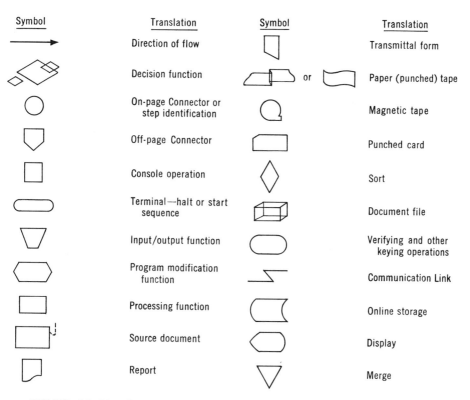

Symbol	Translation	Symbol	Translation
	Direction of flow		Transmittal form
	Decision function	or	Paper (punched) tape
	On-page Connector or step identification		Magnetic tape
	Off-page Connector		Punched card
	Console operation		Sort
	Terminal—halt or start sequence		Document file
	Input/output function		Verifying and other keying operations
	Program modification function		Communication Link
	Processing function		Online storage
	Source document		Display
	Report		Merge

FIGURE 14–11   Programming Flow Chart Symbols.

10. Try out
11. Final editing and writing
12. Reproduce on program tape

HOW TO PREPARE TAPES FOR THE AUDIO-TUTORIAL PROGRAMS. The supervising principal should recommend the following steps to teachers who wish to use the audio-tutorial approach to instruction;

1. Define each goal in measurable terms;
2. Establish a hierarchy of goals for greatest emphasis in the course;
3. Determine the time to be allowed to each unit or goal;

4. Arrange the units (and/or modules) in sequence—weekly wherever possible;

5. Determine the best method of achieving the objective for each unit without regard to mechanics of budgeting, scheduling, or staffing;

6. Assess realistically the real world constraints and proceed to achieve the objectives within the limitations which are inherent in the possible choices;

7. Decide what experiences a student should have to achieve most efficiently and effectively the objectives of the unit-module;

8. Assemble all equipment and materials, whether hardware or software, needed for the experiences agreed upon;

9. Using a cassette-type tape recorder, follow a prepared outline of the program and instruct a student lab assistant in the learning experiences. (Some reports seemed to indicate that recording the instructions in shorthand rather than recording them on tape may save time.)

10. Transcribe the tape (or shorthand notes) onto the script, which is triple spaced to permit easy editing;

11. Edit the script; the instructor who produced the initial recording of the material should do the initial editing;

12. Edit the script again with another instructor, reading the script as a doublecheck for clarity and content;

13. Retype the script (at one college this step was accomplished by a student typist while another student typist was transcribing tapes for additional units);

14. Read the script onto a master tape;

15. A systems analysis flow chart, which pictures graphically the general steps in program revision is included as Figure 14–12.

The supervisor is referred to the *Program Evaluation and Review Technique (PERT)* for information concerning program analysis and revision.[10] Figure 14–13 includes the directions for using an audio-tutorial program. These directions were developed by N. E. Rich and H. R. Williams[11] at

[10]See Federal Electric Corporation, *A Programmed Introduction to PERT* (New York: John Wiley & Sons, Inc., 1967).
[11]Norman E. Rich and Hayden R. Williams, "Western Trail Stories," duplicated material (Huntington Beach, California: Golden West College, 1968), p. 2.

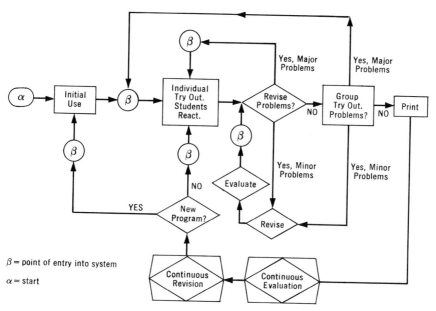

FIGURE 14–12 General Program Revision System.

Golden West College in California. The reader should note that the instructions given imply a relatively unsophisticated tape recorder as being the "teaching machine." The instructions for using a dial or digital (logic) random access system would be much *simpler*. In a random access system developed by Ampex Corporation, the student is able to select any number of programs by punching a predetermined program address number in a touch-tone remote console located in a carrel in the study center. The transistor-logic digital switching system (whose number of sources and output potential is virtually unlimited) can deliver an audio signal and any preprogrammed, recorded video signals within thirty seconds, which is almost in real time. The video portion of the program in this system is limited to still pictures which are recorded on video buffer discs. If desired, the system can permit the student to duplicate the audio portion of the signal on a special cassette duplicator. A forty-five minute program can be recorded in thirty seconds. A student could patch in his own tape recorder and take a copy of the audio information with him for further study.

FIGURE 14–13   Directions for Using Audio-Tutorial Laboratory.

1. Check with the laboratory assistant and fill out attendance time card.

   a) Neatly print last name and initial in space provided and provide other pertinent information indicated.

   b) Take time card by one of the upper corners and insert the bottom of the card into the time clock firmly enough to engage the clock and record the time of entrance.

   c) Follow the same procedure as in "b" above when leaving the laboratory.

   d) Remember to total the number of hours spent in laboratory at the end of each week.

   e) The time card is to be used only for the school's records and will in no way affect your grade.

2. Become familiar with the tape recorder.

   a) To turn on the recorder, push "A.C. Power" switch to "On" and the "motor" switch to "Normal."

   b) Put on the headset, being careful not to twist or otherwise mishandle it. It will break under excessively hard use. Do not use only one side as this is the most frequent cause of breakage!

   c) Note the three small windows in the lower lefthand corner of the recorder. These give you a reference footage on the tape so that you can return to the same place on the tape at a later time.

   d) Turn on the recorder by turning the left selector to the "Play" position. Stop the machine *only* by turning this lever to "Stop." If you use the on-off switch the machine will have to warm up each time you return to the tape.

   e) Follow directions on the tape.

   f) If you wish to backspace a short distance, depress the foot pedal. When you have gone back the necessary distance on the tape, release the foot pedal and the recorder will resume normal play.

   g) When finished for the day, you should record the tape footage in your notes then rewind the tape to "000." (Turn the righthand selector to RWD—Rewind.) ALWAYS REWIND THE TAPE BACK TO "000."

   h) If you wish to play a portion toward the middle or end of the tape, turn the right selector to "FWD" (Fast Forward) until you reach the count at which you wish to begin, using the footage numbers.

   i) Follow directions on the tape, and then remember to rewind when finished.

   j) Turn off recorder toggle switches at bottom of the machine when you have finished and wish to check out of the laboratory. (Note: the "Stop"

FIGURE 14–13   (Continued)

lever only stops the *tape*. The *Power Switch* and *Motor Switch* turn off the electricity and recorder motor, respectively.)

k) *If you have any problems, turn off the recorder and ask for help from the Lab. Assistants, tutors, or instructors.*

3. To check out, take your card from the file and record your time of departure. At the end of the week, total the time spent in the TRAILS laboratory during the week. Place the card back in the alphabetical file.

If there is class work to be turned in, don't forget to turn it in on time! ! ! ! !

Figure 14–14 describes the study center, where program materials are available at a community college in the midwest. The form was presented to each student who entered the study center.

FIGURE 14–14   The Instructional Technology and Media Center.

WEST COLLEGE

The Instructional Technology Media Center is designed to help meet the needs of the instructional program—both for faculty and for students. Offices are in _____. Instructional aids for faculty and students are listed in a later section of this catalog. In addition to the films in our own film library, Center personnel order films for faculty members on a loan or rental basis. As literature on new instructional aids is received, departments are notified and previews arranged.

SERVICES AVAILABLE: THE INSTRUCTIONAL TECHNOLOGY AND MEDIA CENTER TEAM

The Media Center team consists of an illustrator, an electronics or television technician, an instructional media technician, an instructional technology clerk, a laboratory assistant, and the Instructional Technology and Media Center Coordinator, _____ . While the Media Center staff operates as a team, major areas of specialization have been identified. The illustrator assists faculty in the preparation of charts, posters, display cases, and graphic materials for classroom use. The instructional media technician assists faculty in the maintenance, operation, and mechanical repair of equipment; duplicates slides or tapes; and prepare photographic materials, including making slides from pictures or illustrations. The instructional technology clerk orders films for faculty use, and issues filmstrips, records, tapes and equipment for student listening or classroom use.

THE CENTER SERVES THE COLLEGE

1. Services are available to students of four levels: (1) Basic Skills (2) Corrective (3) Standard Progress and (4) Developmental (Advanced)
2. Those served include:

FIGURE 14-14   (Continued)

a) Entering students referred by a counselor or instructor for assistance in study skills and to make use of the programmed materials in the basic skills areas;
b) Small or intermediate sized groupings or entire classes may be scheduled by faculty members on a regular or intermittent basis to use the available programmed learning materials, the random digital (transistor logic) access information retrieval equipment, the language laboratory, the reading center, the typing and transcription laboratory, or the adjunct media located in the College Library;
c) All students of West College who wish to make use of the programmed materials which are available and/or who desire assistance in areas of study skills and the psychology of success in college;
d) Other groups, as indicated by student and faculty needs and desires;
e) The College as a whole, for:
   (1) Research
   (2) Study
   (3) Experimentation
   (4) Consultation
   (5) Assistance in solving instructional problems
   (6) Assistance with non-clinical scholarship problems
   (7) Assistance in the selection, preparation and use of instructional media.

PROGRAMMED RANDOM DIGITAL (TRANSISTOR-LOGIC) ACCESS INFORMATION RETRIEVAL SYSTEM FACILITIES:

Adjacent to the Instructional Technology and Media Center Offices is the Programmed Instruction and Study Center, which contains random digital access equipment, as do the College Library and the speech, reading, foreign language and the typing and transcription laboratories. Students are able to enter, select specific programs through the use of special touch-tone equipment by entering a predetermined program address number and listen and respond to recorded audio and video taped programs in several subject areas. Buffer disc video recording permits monitoring of single frame recorded pictures in all carrels. These locations include a total of fourteen INSTRUCTIONAL CENTER PROGRAM DECK REMOTE CONTROL CONSOLES. Multiple-channel closed circuit television programming is available.

Programmed materials are available for student use. These materials are self-instructional and students either use them in the Programmed Instruction and Study Center or, with faculty authorization, check them out. They are designed for remedial or corrective help, supplementary information, or for enrichment.

PREVIEW OF NEW FILMS:

New films may be previewed at the Center or in department offices.

HOURS OF OPERATION:

The Center Offices are located in (_____). The Center is open from 7:00 a.m. to 3:00 p.m., and (with student help) from 5:00 p.m. to 8:45 p.m. The Coordinator is available from 7:00 a.m. and is on duty during the noon hour. Stop in and become acquainted with the services that are available to students and to faculty members!

One programmed study center and its control room, which may be described as the heart of the media center, are pictured in Figures 14–15, 14–16, and 14–17.

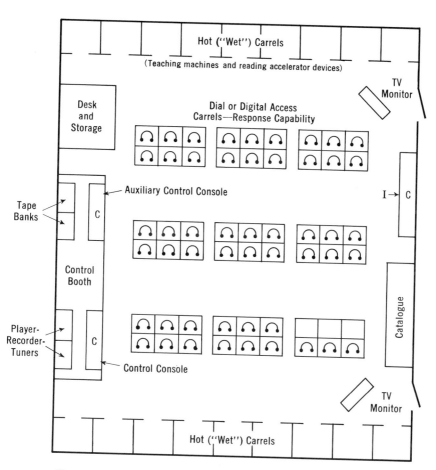

$\cap$ = Dial or Digital Access Carrels with Student Response Capabilities
C = Control Console(s)
I = Instructions and Dial or Digital Access Program Information
(Digital access is preferred.)

FIGURE 14–15   The Programmed Instruction and Study Center.

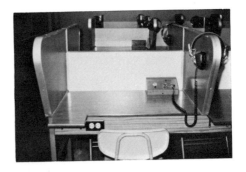

FIGURE 14–16   View of the Programmed Instructions and Study Center.
Closeup of a Carrel Showing the Audio-Access Console.

How to Evaluate and Improve the Media Center

Many large school systems and colleges have an "Instructional Technology
and Media Center," "Instructional Center," "Learning Center," or "Audio-
Visual Center" which provides services to students, teachers, and classrooms. In some very large schools and in several colleges an instructional
media center has been developed in the individual school unit. According to
the modern concept of the materials of instructional technology, the center
should be concerned with all instructional media (except basic course texts
and most library books), including films, filmstrips, audio and video tapes,
exhibits, slides, specimens, objects, pictures, maps, globes, charts, recordings, television, teaching machines and programmed materials, radios, recorders, projectors, posters, information concerning field trips, and others.

When materials are costly or scarce, they should be kept in a central pool.
An adequate, efficient distribution system should be developed. In this case

FIGURE 14–17   Heart of the Instructional Center: The Program
Distribution Control Room.

the center would supplement the materials regularly kept in the classroom, and would be a central coordinating agency.

Small schools need someone to perform this coordinating function. Even
though a plan for distribution is established on a county-wide basis, every
school building should have someone who serves as a coordinator. The
principal should delegate this responsibility to a teacher. He should be provided with some clerical assistance and should be allocated released time as
well.

Improving the Performance of the Coordinator of the Media Center

Smaller school systems, as a rule, have a part-time audio-visual director, and
larger systems and colleges generally have a full-time supervising-director.
Such a person is not trained to repair equipment, but serves as a specialist-
ist-consultant who works with teachers to help them to improve instruction
under the direction of the local supervising principal.

A listing of the duties of the instructional technology (audio-visual) consultant in one school system[12] indicates how a coordinator of the media center is actually a consultant to teachers in the improvement and utilization of the materials of instructional technology, in establishing courses of study, in setting goals, and in developing the curriculum by:

1. Arranging sessions at which equipment can be evaluated and making recommendations to schools on the basis of these evaluations.
2. Arranging for preview of instructional materials by teachers and purchasing materials for the media center on the basis of these teacher recommendations.
3. Ordering rental and free instructional materials as requested by teachers.
4. Organizing and distributing a catalogue of owned instructional technology materials.
5. Booking materials as requested by teachers.
6. Organizing a workable system for distribution.
7. Working with the teachers who have been delegated the responsibility of serving as instructional coordinators at the local school level in planning for the future of the audio-visual program and in providing types of in-service help that can be carried back to teachers.
8. Making recommendations to teachers regarding audio-visual materials that will help them teach specific units.
9. Working with teachers to help them learn how to operate equipment, how to obtain materials, how to make materials, and how to use the materials effectively.
10. Working with principals and their representatives on problems specific to their schools.
11. Encouraging and working with teachers who are interested in producing materials for the audio-visual collection.
12. Advising community groups regarding the materials of instructional technology that will meet specific needs of these groups.
13. Interpreting the instructional technology program to school personnel, the board of education, and the community.

Since the main function of an instructional technology director is that of specialist-consultant, clerical service should be provided for handling the

[12]Ford L. Lemler, *Audio-Visual Programs in Action* (Ann Arbor: Michigan Audio-Visual Association, 1951), pp. 18–19.

details. Assistance is needed in booking and distribution, and in maintenance repair.

How to Improve the Use of Instructional Materials

The following is a list of current practices which may lead to improvement in the use of instructional materials:

1. The supervising principal should work continuously with teachers in providing and improving instructional materials.
2. The teacher should continuously evaluate instructional materials in the light of student programs.
3. Consultant services should assist and instruct principals and teachers in the correct use of special materials, audio-visual equipment, and new devices.
4. The librarian should catalogue and provide care for all materials stored in the library, and serve as consultant regarding their selection and use.
5. In large school systems a purchasing agent should procure materials and supervise a central warehouse where supplies are received, stored, and inventoried in readiness for distribution to schools.
6. Purchases should be made in quantity when possible, either through the system office or a central purchasing service in the intermediate unit superintendent's office.
7. Classified personnel should be given responsibility for receiving, storing, and caring for instructional materials as a means of lightening the clerical load on teachers.
8. Lay persons should be invited to help in selecting some instructional materials, such as supplementary tapes, films, and other nontechnical aids.
9. The supervising principal should provide a workroom where teachers can construct and adapt their own instructional materials.
10. Free and inexpensive materials should be procured from commercial, civic, and service organizations.
11. The supervising principal should help teachers instruct students in the careful use of materials as part of their education in the conservation of public property.

A sample checklist, developed by one supervising principal to aid the teacher in evaluating the effectiveness of his use of the materials of instructional technology, appears as Figure 14–18.

FIGURE 14–18   Sample Checklist for Evaluating Use of the Materials of Instructional Technology[a]

HOW'S YOUR I-T-Q?*

Score one point for each "yes."

1. Do you utilize the materials of instructional technology in regular classroom situations, avoiding auditorium showings whenever possible? _____

2. Do you utilize only those materials which are pertinent to, and serve the needs of your particular class? _____

3. Do you discuss, review, and maintain good "listening and viewing standards" as needs arise? _____

4. Do you build a readiness for viewing by establishing purposes, goals, or questions which the film will help to satisfy? _____

5. Do you, after viewing, utilize the material content for actual classroom learning by relating it to established purposes? _____

6. Do you operate all instruments of instructional technology carefully in order to avoid damage? _____

7. Do you preview the material in advance to determine content and its relationship to the specific ability of your class? _____

8. Do you check your audio-visual equipment in advance to make certain that it is in proper working condition? _____

9. Do you know where to locate your school's supply of replacement parts such as the various lamps required in your projector? _____

10. Do you return immediately all material to the proper location? _____

Total Score _____

*Instructional Technology Quotient

HOW DO YOU RATE:

10 points = Genius
9 points = Definitely gifted
8 points = Capable
7 points = Inconclusive
6 points and
  below = Hide your score

[a]Based upon Los Angeles City Schools, Instructional Aids and Service Branch, "How's Your A-V-Q?" *Audio-Visual News* IX (May 2, 1960): 1.

DO

1. Accept the responsibility for working with the rest of the school staff in setting up policies for the selection materials.
2. Ensure that teachers are involved in the selection of materials. Selections should not be made on the basis of friendships, of political expediency, or of unconsidered arbitrary personal opinion. Such decisions are not as efficient as are those which result from the combined judgment of several people who reach a decision after careful analysis.
3. Make every effort to educate the board of education as to the necessity for giving schools within the school system the opportunity to purchase materials on their own. In drawing up the budget, call upon teachers for advice. Work with all of those who are concerned with using equipment.
4. Work for the allocation of a good proportion of the budget to instructional materials each year.
5. Assist teachers in finding materials that will be of help to them in the classroom.
6. Help to establish curriculum laboratories which will serve as resource centers for teachers. One may begin with small collections secured through an exchange with other school systems, as well as through purchases.
7. Assist teachers in learning how to use a variety of materials. Many teachers may be afraid of taking that step since they have always depended upon the security of a single textbook.
8. Give teachers an opportunity to evaluate materials that are available, to send for materials, and to select materials for the classroom from the central library and from the community library.

DON'T

1. Fail to study the community to determine its potential resources for learning—its institutions, its people, and its industries.
2. Assume the total responsibility yourself. Encourage teachers to study written materials themselves in order to find out what types will be suited for the needs and interests of different students.
3. Fail to find out all possible about the students—their abilities, skills,

needs, interests, and problems—so that suitable material may be made available for each student.

4. Purchase materials too late.

5. Let material stores fall below an adequate supply level.

6. Assign responsibility for receiving, storing, and caring for instructional materials to certificated personnel. These responsibilities, along with the associated clerical work, should be assigned to classified personnel.

7. Attempt to teach *all* instructors how to use *all* of the equipment and materials available to them. Consultant services should be available to assist and instruct principals and teachers in the correct use of special materials, audio-visual equipment, and new devices developed through instructional technology.

8. Fail to encourage the development of an instructional center and an educational materials laboratory which would facilitate teacher experimentation.

Supervisory Problems   In Basket

Problem 1

A school, with an enrollment of approximately 1,400, is located in a small city school system which has been quite aggressive in the areas of curriculum improvement and the purchasing of equipment and materials through its own efforts and those offered through various federal aid programs. The department with which we are concerned has obtained tape recorders, record players, audio notebooks, overhead projectors, filmstrip projectors, and motion picture projectors. Also provided have been materials such as records, transparency materials, classroom sets of various books, additional copies of resource materials, and subscriptions to various periodicals. In addition, the library staff has made an effort to provide a good supply of reference materials for this department.

The group of teachers involved (called a department for the sake of the problem) consists of five men and one woman, is described briefly below:

1. Male, comparatively young, dynamic as a teacher, efficient, interested in improving his teaching as well as that of the whole department. In many

respects acts as a department head without remuneration, authority, or released time.

2. Male, young, interested, willing to cooperate, wants to improve his teaching but still lacks some sophistication in his field.
3. Male, has been known as a good teacher, has health problems, nearing retirement age, has little interest in helping to improve the department.
4. Male, older, fairly well adjusted, in a rut so far as his teaching methods and materials are concerned.
5. Female, middle-aged, excellent background, makes students think and work, border-line in the use of new techniques and materials but does try to keep up-to-date in her field.
6. Male, young, member of coaching staff, possibly background in subject area somewhat weak, does not show great interest in using new materials and techniques but has shown fleeting glimpses of his ability to do so, coaching of greater interest than teaching.

Only three of the members of the department show consistent interest in improving the curriculum or their teaching. The other members seem to have no resentment toward these people, but register little interest in joining with them. Much of the teaching of the latter three is formal lecture, end of the chapter questions, notebook development, and tests. In the meantime, equipment and materials are not used as they should be, students are aware of the differences in the class structures, and those students who care openly ask for assignment to the more "progressive" teachers' rooms. The problem has been brought to the attention of the principal. The principal realizes that many similar problems exist in several departments having a number of teachers.

How can you, as a supervising principal, provide the leadership that will help improve this department and provide for the use in the proper way of the costly educational aids available? What would you do?

Problem 2

A school system-wide committee had been organized to select the basic textbook for the new required semester course in health education at the ninth-grade level. Mr. Douglas, Assistant Superintendent for Instructional Services, convened the organizational meeting and suggested that the group elect a chairman for the remainder of the work period. Following the election of one of the science teachers, the question was raised as to procedure. Mr. Douglas reported that his staff had already surveyed the available materials and had requested samples from the several book companies with textbooks in this area of the curriculum.

Mr. Lawrence, science teacher from Isadore High, asked, "Is it absolutely necessary that we adopt one book for all three high schools, or may we consider different textbooks for different schools?"

Mr. Douglas replied, "Up to now we have held to school system-wide use of textbooks for equivalent courses. However, if this committee desires to come up with any recommendations, they certainly will be considered carefully. It seems to me that this required course may call for the use of two levels of textbooks in each school. Let me suggest that perhaps the committee should establish criteria for an evaluation of the books and then should score each book in the light of these criteria."

As supervisor, you are a member of the committee.

How would you proceed to develop the criteria as suggested by Mr. Douglas? What recommendations would you make concerning:

1. Whether all schools in a single school system should be required to use single, dual, or multiple textbook adoption policies, and
2. Whether all students or classes in a single school should be required to use the same textbook or whether the policy of dual or multiple textbook adoption should extend to the individual school and/or to the individual classroom.

Selected Bibliography

Books

Bartky, John A. *Supervision and Human Relations.* Boston: D. C. Heath and Company, 1953.

Beck, Robert H., Walter W. Cook, and Nolan C. Kearney. *Curriculum in the Modern Elementary School.* Englewood Cliffs, New Jersey: Prentice-Hall, Inc., 1953.

Briggs, T. H. *Improving Instruction.* New York: The Macmillan Company, 1938.

Dale, Edgar. *Audio-Visual Methods in Teaching.* Rev. ed. New York: The Dryden Press, 1954.

DeYoung, Cris A. *Introduction to American Public Education.* New York: McGraw-Hill Book Company, 1950.

Faunce, Roland C., and Nelson L. Bossing. *Developing the Core Curriculum.* Englewood Cliffs, New Jersey: Prentice-Hall, Inc., 1951.

Federal Electric Corporation. *A Programmed Introduction to PERT.* New York: John Wiley & Sons, Inc., 1967.

Gwynn, J. Minor. *Curriculum Principles and Social Trends.* New York: The Macmillan Company, 1960.

Kinder, James S. *Audio-Visual Materials and Techniques.* New York: American Book Company, 1953.

Kinney, Lucien, and Katharine Dresden. *Better Learning through Current Materials.* 2d. ed. Palo Alto, California: Stanford University Press, 1952.

Lawson, Douglas E. *School Administration.* New York: Odessy Press, 1953.

Markle, Susan Meyer. *Good Frames and Bad.* New York: John Wiley and Sons, Inc., 1964.

Melchior, William T. *Instructional Supervision.* Boston: D. C. Heath and Company, 1950.

Olsen, Edward G. *The Modern Community School.* New York: Appleton-Century-Crofts, 1953.

Reeder, Edwin H. *Supervision in the Elementary School.* Boston: Houghton Mifflin Company, 1953.

Saylor, J. Galen, and William M. Alexander. *Curriculum Planning for Better Teaching and Learning.* New York: Rinehart and Company, Inc., 1954.

Stolurow, Lawrence M. *Computer Assisted Instruction.* Detroit: American Data Processing, Inc., 1968.

Wiles, Kimball. *Supervision for Better Schools.* Englewood Cliffs, New Jersey: Prentice-Hall, Inc., 1950.

Periodicals

Corey, Stephen M. "Imperatives in Instructional Materials." *Educational Leadership* V (January 1948): 211–214.

Eakin, Mary K. "Educational News and Editorial Comment." *The Elementary School Journal* LI (November 1950): 115–125.

Galanter, Eugene. "The Mechanization of Learning." *National Education Association Journal* L (November 1961): 16–19.

Norberg, Kenneth D. "A New Instructional Materials Center." *The Elementary School Journal* LII (January 1952): 256–257.

Trillingham, C. C. "Selecting Books and Materials for Schools." *School Executive* LXXI (February 1952): 19–22.

Other Sources

American Textbook Publishers Institute. *Textbooks in Education.* New York: The Institute, 1949.

Association for Supervision and Curriculum Development. *Creating a Good Environment for Learning.* 1954 Yearbook. Washington, D.C.: National Education Association, 1954.

Greater Hartford Council on Economic Education. *Aids in the Improvement of Education for Economic Understanding.* Bulletin No. 1. Hartford, Connecticut: The Council, 1950.

Lemler, Ford L., ed. *Audio-Visual Programs in Action.* Ann Arbor: Michigan Audio-Visual Association, 1951.

Los Angeles City Schools, Instructional Aids and Service Branch. "How's Your A-V-Q?" *Audio-Visual News* IX (2 May 1960): 1.

Lumsdaine, A. A., and Robert Glaser. *Teaching Machines and Programmed Learning.* Washington, D.C.: National Education Association, 1960.

Merritt, Eleanor, and Henry Harap. *Trends in the Production of Curriculum Guides.* Nashville: Division of Surveys and Field Services, George Peabody College for Teachers, 1955.

National Citizens Commission. *How Good Are Our Teaching Materials?* New York: The Commission, 1955.

National Education Association. "Selecting and Appraising Library Materials," *The National Elementary School Principal.* Thirtieth Yearbook. Washington, D.C.: The Association, 1952.

_____, Department of Elementary School Principals. *Elementary School Libraries Today.* Thirtieth Yearbook. Washington, D.C.: The Department, 1951.

National Society for the Study of Education. *Audio-Visual Materials of Instruction*. Forty-Eighth Yearbook. Chicago: University of Chicago Press, 1949.

"Procedures in the Selection and Adoption of Learning Materials in Pasadena City Schools." Duplicated material. Pasadena, California: Pasadena City Schools, 1954.

Rich, Norman E., and Hayden R. Williams. "Western Trail Stories." Duplicated material. Huntington Beach, California: Golden West College, 1968.

University of California: Radio-Television Administration. "The Overrated Machine." Broadcast No. 4057—University Explorer 1771, over the Columbia Broadcasting System, Sunday, 4 June 1961. Mimeographed.

15

How to Improve the Work of Classified Personnel

How often have we heard:

"Everything seems to run smoothly when the principal is out of the office, but let his secretary be ill and utter chaos breaks loose."

"The most important member of our whole staff is the custodian. We couldn't function without him."

"Those bus drivers certainly can be counted on to get our children here on time each morning—and happy."

"The staff members who contribute the most to faculty and student morale are those cafeteria workers. *Good food, served with a smile, certainly helps!*"[1]

The contributions made by these behind-the-scenes staff members are immeasurably vital to the success of each individual school. It is fitting that consideration be given to assisting them with their respective assignments and to helping them continuously to improve their job performance. Some of the ways in which this can be accomplished is the primary purpose of this chapter, which includes a discussion of:

1. Principles of classified service improvement
2. How to select, assign, and orient classified personnel
3. How to improve the quality of office management
4. How to improve the morale of classified personnel
5. How to evaluate classified personnel performance
6. How to do it: techniques which work
7. How to plan for more efficient classified personnel performance
8. How to get the most out of in-service education programs for classified personnel
9. Do—don't
10. "In-Basket" supervisory problems

[1] Leo B. Rotter—*connoisseur*, military tactician, and noted expert in criminal *modus operandi*.

Principles of Classified Service Improvement

A. N. Galluzo[2] listed the following basic principles concerning the improvement of the performance of classified school personnel:

1. The most important aspect of a well-rounded personnel program is the people in it.
2. Written personnel policies should be maintained by all school systems.
3. The classification plan is the heart of the personnel program.
4. Recruitment is the responsibility of the personnel office of the school system. Selection should be a shared responsibility of the personnel office and the line supervisor.
5. Tests are valuable tools in the selection process.
6. Transfers should not be used as a means of eliminating problem employees.
7. Disciplinary action should be positive rather than destructive.
8. If an organization expects loyalty from its employee and special effort during pressure periods, the employee, in turn, is entitled to a proper claim to a similar loyalty during times in which he is having personal difficulties.
9. It is poor practice to demote employees for disciplinary reasons.
10. Turnover is expensive. Every effort should be made to salvage a trained employee rather than to terminate his employment and hire a substitute employee.
11. The classified personnel system should be based on a principle of recognition of employee competence and performance through assignment and promotion.
12. All school systems should establish policy statements and rules governing the administration of classified personnel.
13. Each school system should have an administrative manual and a handbook for employees.
14. All school systems should establish a classification plan.
15. All school systems should establish positive recruitment programs.

[2]A. Neil Galluzo, "Practices in the Administration of Classified Personnel in California" (Doctoral dissertation, University of Southern California, 1955).

16. School systems should develop, utilize, and continuously evaluate assignment specifications[3] for classified school personnel.
17. A selection of personnel should be on the basis of competitive examination. A promotional examination should be given regularly with a civil service plan developed for large school systems. In small school systems a semiformal plan is suggested. Examinations should be followed by a personal interview of the prospective employee.
18. Thorough preemployment examinations should be given all applicants concerning new developments in their specialized fields. The results of these examinations should serve as a basis for planning the in-service education program. Periodic physical examinations should be required of all employees.
19. Promotion should not be on the basis of seniority alone; however, some consideration should be given to seniority, especially if other factors are equal.
20. The orientation program should have as its main objective the establishment of a feeling of belonging on the part of the new employee.
21. The following factors should be taken into account in determining the general level of the salary schedule for classified personnel:
    a) Local-market rates;
    b) Cost-of-living indices;
    c) Supply and demand factors;
    d) Financial condition of the school system.
22. Grievances should be settled as near to their point of origin as possible.
23. Suggestion systems should be utilized.

How to Select, Assign, and Orient Classified Personnel

Selection and Assignment

Desirable human relations begin with initial contact at the time of application or first interview. First impressions are lasting. Thus, a prime considera-

[3]James R. Marks, "An Analysis of Assignment Specifications for Certificated School Personnel in the United States" (Doctoral dissertation, University of Southern California, 1962).

tion must be the general atmosphere in which this meeting is held. It should be friendly but businesslike and to the point, and should invite questions. There should be a mutual exchange. Many times classified personnel are not too experienced in such situations. Every effort should be made to put them at ease immediately.

It is important that the principal, or the person doing the selecting, be thoroughly familiar with the job in question. He should be able to clarify duties, hours, and special training needed. An assignment specification, which will be discussed later, should be in his possession. He should discuss personnel policies and working conditions to the point that the applicant understands the job situation. A tour of the school grounds, including equipment and facilities, is helpful.

While discussing the assignment, the supervising principal must be able to make a valid judgment about the character and capabilities of the applicant. Both are essential for efficiency, economy, and dependability on the job. Selection, then, is finding a man to do the job, rather than attempting to fit a job to the man.

A major factor is the total plan of application and selection. If steps are defined and carried through, the job will seem important. The casual manner in which many members of the classified personnel are selected is one of the main reasons for low morale in this group.

If selection has been made in a warm atmosphere and in a businesslike manner, if the assignment has been explained thoroughly, and if placement has been made in a position appropriate to training, the new staff member is off to a good start and looks forward to his new job with enthusiasm.

How to Prepare Assignment Specifications

Perhaps no single factor contributes more to a feeling of well being and security on the job than does knowing what is expected and possessing the skills for optimum performance. Obviously, the principal cannot be an authority in all areas of operation, but he does carry the responsibility for supervising all personnel on his staff. Some of the most important tools which can be used to accomplish this are concise and complete assignment specifications, well-planned orientation programs, in-service education programs, constructive supervision, and frequent evaluation. Each technique should be considered for the contribution it can make to the effectiveness of each staff member.

ASSIGNMENT SPECIFICATIONS. These documents should be available at the time of the initial interview so that each applicant may know exactly what is to be expected of him. Other purposes of assignment specifications are to make sure that necessary duties are performed, to eliminate overlapping, to upgrade efficiency, and to increase employee satisfaction. They are the basis for supervision and evaluation.

With these purposes in mind, the checklist in Figure 15–1 can be used in preparing specifications for classified personnel. The preparation of assignment specifications is an excellent way in which to involve staff members in the recruitment-selection process. No one knows the job of the maintenance man better than the head of buildings and grounds.

FIGURE 15–1   Classified Personnel Specifications Checklist

---

1. Is it in writing?_____   Is it complete? _____

2. Is it clear?_____   Is it written in language understandable to the person applying for the position?_____

3. Are **all** major requirements for selection included?_____
4. Are staff relation responsibilities listed?_____
5. Are community relation responsibilities included?_____
6. Are hours of work and the salary schedule included?_____
7. Are line and staff relationships noted?_____
8. Are all "extra" assignments which the employee might be called upon to do from time to time included? _____
9. Are fringe benefits and tenure requirements listed?_____

A complete, to-the-point assignment specification can best be used by personally reviewing it with the new staff member, by clarifying questions orally at that time, and by giving him a written copy. A sample assignment specification for the school secretary was found to include a list of duties and minimum requisites for obtaining the position. The following qualifications were listed: neat appearance, pleasing personality, tact, ability to work well with others, skill in typing, skill in taking and transcribing dictation, filing, skill in written and oral English, emotional stability, poise under stress, and ability in handling general office tasks. These characteristics were spelled out specifically, as may be seen in Figure 15–2.

FIGURE 15–2   Qualifications for the Position of Educational Secretary

1. Either twelfth-grade education supplemented by a standard secretarial course, or an equivalent combination of education and similar experience.

2. For higher classifications the qualifications are twelfth-grade education, including or supplemented by courses in stenography and typewriting, and two years of experience in stenographic or clerical work involving contact with the public.

3. General knowledge of office methods and procedures, some knowledge of business letter-writing and business forms, knowledge of and ability to operate a mimeograph and duplicating machine, ability to perform clerical work, ability to spell correctly and use good English, ability to follow oral and written directions, aptitude and liking for office work, neatness, accuracy, pleasing personality, orderliness, good health, and mental and physical ability to do the work required.

4. Higher classifications will be required to acquire knowledge of and be able to administer first aid; and also to be able to size up situations and people accurately to adopt an effective course of action, and to get along well with students as well as with adults.

5. Ability to take dictation at a speed of not less than eighty words per minute and to transcribe it accurately at a rate of not less than twenty words per minute; ability to type at a rate of not less than forty words per minute from ordinary manuscript or printed or typewritten material.

6. For higher classifications the qualifications are the ability to take difficult dictation at a speed of 100 words per minute and to transcribe it accurately at a speed of not less than twenty-five words per minute, ability to type at a speed of not less than forty-five words per minute from ordinary manuscript or from printed or typewritten material.

How to Conduct an Orientation Program for Classified Personnel

Orientation programs vary greatly. Ordinarily orientation programs for classified personnel are handled poorly. The following are some items that should be on the agenda of all orientation meetings:

1. The total school program should be one of the first considerations. *All* staff members should be acquainted with *all* phases of the organization and its operation.
2. Such facts as the number of students attending, size of the staff, budget totals, and certainly the general philosophy of the school system and the school are important and should be discussed briefly. A tour of the school grounds and all facilities should be taken as soon as possible, unless this was done at the time of application.
3. The classified personnel should have the opportunity to meet as many of the certificated personnel as possible. Introductions can be made at staff meetings or by personal contact, but should be accomplished as soon as possible.
4. Personnel policies should be covered in detail during the orientation period. Salary schedules, advancement possibilities, causes for dismissal, job benefits, hours of work, provisions for health and emergency leaves, and grievance procedures should be discussed at the outset.
5. Line and staff relationships must be clarified.
6. Information should be given as to what to do in cases of accident or emergency, whom to call, and what reports to make. All bus drivers, the secretary, and at least one of the cafeteria staff should be trained in first aid. This training may be given at the school or arrangements may be made for staff members to attend courses given in the community.
7. Some suggestions should be made concerning community relations responsibilities. Although this is most important to the secretarial group, all staff members come in contact with parents and taxpayers. Because of the importance of the impression they make, it is well to discuss this at some length during orientation. It is especially important to extend information on how to handle visitors, what should be dis-

cussed with them, what questions may be answered, and what questions should be referred to the supervising principal or to other employees.

8. Information regarding use and care of equipment will vary with each group, but must not be overlooked.

9. Appearance, neatness, cleanliness, and appropriate dress should be stressed. Bus drivers and cafeteria workers usually decide upon a uniform, and maintenance personnel in many schools are doing likewise.

10. Relationships with students require a fine line between being friendly and helpful or being too personal. Classified personnel should, at all times, earn the respect of pupils.

11. Staff members new to the community should learn something about it —its people, its organizations, and its services.

According to W. A. Yeager,[4] a program for orientation in a school system should include the following areas:

1. Orientation to the school, such as its philosophy, objectives, organization, program, rules and regulations, and the physical plant, together with general information such as enrollments, calendar, and the like;

2. Orientation to the position, such as specific duties, routine, equipment, schedule, salary, and increments;

3. Orientation to the persons with whom one will be associated, such as the superintendent or principal, both certificated and classified personnel, and the students;

4. Orientation to the community, including its social activities.

If the orientation program has been helpful and meaningful, staff members will look forward to beginning their assignments with a feeling of confidence and security.

How to Improve the Quality of Office Management

The efficiency of a school or school system depends to a large degree upon an expeditious and otherwise efficient performance of numerous office

[4]William A. Yeager, *Administration of the Noninstructional Personnel and Services* (New York: Harper and Brothers, 1959), pp. 169–170.

duties.[5] An introduction to the techniques of office management should be a part of the orientation program.

EQUIPMENT. The equipment with which an employee is provided is a significant factor in determining the quality, the quantity, and the cost of the work which he accomplishes. These materials have much to do with the mental and the physical condition of the employee, and that condition is reflected in the employee's output. In every school system, therefore, considerable attention should be given to the selection of adequate equipment and comfortable, functional furniture.

MINIMUM CLERICAL SERVICES. It is pennywise policy for boards of education to employ teachers, specialist-consultants, and principals at high salaries and then require them, or permit them, to spend their time and energy in performing tasks which clerks could perform more cheaply and, perhaps, more efficiently.

Every school needs some clerical service. A minimum standard is one full-time clerk for each 400 students. This would mean a half-time clerk for each 200 students.

The following is a list of some of the chief ways in which a clerk or secretary can assist the principal:

1. Taking and transcribing dictation, and copying matter on the typewriter;
2. Mimeographing;
3. Filing correspondence and other materials, keeping financial records, and making out payrolls, checks, and vouchers;
4. Writing purchase orders and requisitions;
5. Keeping inventories of equipment, books, and supplies;
6. Looking after the bookkeeping for internal funds;
7. Making appointments for the principal, and reminding him to keep them;
8. Meeting callers;
9. Answering the telephone;
10. Sending and receiving telegrams;

[5]Ward G. Reeder, *Fundamentals of Public School Administration* (New York: The Macmillan Company, 1951), p. 726.

11. Making out contracts for teachers and for other school employees;
12. Selling textbooks and supplies to students;
13. Issuing supplies to teachers and keeping supply records;
14. Recording the minutes of school board meetings and of faculty meetings;
15. Recording memoranda of conferences of the principal;
16. Opening and distributing the mail;
17. Typing certificates of experience for teachers;
18. Posting the mail;
19. Keeping the office in order;
20. Receiving and sending parcel post, express, and freight;
21. Receiving notes from, and making notes for, the attendance officer, the school nurse, and other employees;
22. Posting school announcements;
23. Completing transcripts of record of employment certificate completion.

How to Improve the Morale of Classified Personnel

The quality of service rendered by the classified personnel is directly related to their sense of belonging to a team and the awareness of their importance on this team. Each member must recognize and respect the role of the other before the degree of cooperation and teamwork necessary for the smooth running school can be attained. Each must be dedicated to the total job to be done and feel his task is a vital one.

HOW TO GET A POSITIVE RESPONSE. Nothing brings a positive response faster than does a friendly smile. This is particularly true of the relationship between professional and classified staff members. It is easy, in the rush of busy days, for either principal or teacher to pass by the faithful custodian in a haze of preoccupation without so much as a glimmer of recognition. And yet a warm "Hi, Rochelle! How's the new grandson?" can make a world of difference in the spirit with which the next assignment is fulfilled. Almost as important as the greeting is knowing the name; Rochelle immediately becomes a "recognized" staff member.

The inclusion of *all* staff members, or representatives from each group, in the process of planning the school program is essential to the development of team spirit. A special school function or activity might well affect all staff members:

1. Responsibility for the students—the faculty;
2. A special setup in the multipurpose room—the custodian;
3. A change in schedule—the cafeteria staff and the bus drivers;
4. Interpretation and clarification (to staff as well as to parents and community)—the secretary.

Aside from understanding the *what, when,* and *how,* each group might contribute important and helpful suggestions.

Most important is the fact that if classified personnel are brought into planning two things happen: (1) they will act more efficiently because of better understanding, and (2) they will develop a sense of pride and a feeling of worthwhileness.

Including the classified personnel in faculty activities whenever possible is another way of keeping them on the team. This is, at times, more difficult to schedule with the maintenance staff than it is with the office workers, but is none the less important. Joint coffee breaks, the Christmas breakfast, and end of the year get-togethers can be planned to include all groups. Big dividends could accrue.

Greeting by name, inclusion in democratic planning, and inclusion in staff activities are the most obvious ways to strengthen classified personnel morale. Surveys have shown that more important than salary to these individuals is a spirit of friendliness and cooperation.

HOW TO MEASURE THE NATURE AND EFFECTIVENESS OF MORALE FACTORS. Since morale is so essential in staff personnel administration, methods must be utilized to measure its nature and effectiveness. H. H. Remmers[6] has given us five methods for determining morale:

1. The "listening in" or general impression method, in which impressions are gathered by all those in contact with personnel and cleared through the central office or individuals;

[6] H. H. Remmers, "The Analysis of Employee Attitudes," *Proceedings of the First Personnel Institute* (Columbus, Ohio: State University, 1938), p. 4.

2. Unguided interviews, in which persons are encouraged to talk freely to reveal the true situation about themselves or others;
3. Guided interviews, in which key individuals are interviewed through a series of carefully prepared questions designed to reveal a given situation;
4. Questionnaire blanks, previously prepared and submitted to large groups requesting both information and opinion;
5. Attitude scales, either specific or more general in nature.

How to Evaluate Classified Personnel Performance

Continuous Evaluation and Supervision

Orientation programs and in-service education, no matter how well planned, cannot take the place of close personal supervision. Whether this is done by the principal himself or by someone delegated by the principal, the important thing is that it be positive and creative, not negative and critical. It must be both systematic and sympathetic.

The relationship between the principal, as the supervisor, and the employee must be one of mutual respect based on sincerity of purpose. The employee should feel free to go to the supervising principal for advice and help at any time. Complete honesty is vital, for these contacts will become an important factor in evaluation and, pehaps, in the settlement of grievances.

The supervising principal, then, must have the ability to analyze situations quickly and accurately, and be helpful before it is "too late." He must be frank yet tactful, friendly but impartial. He must know the job he is supervising—its skills, materials and equipment, and methods.

Frequent Evaluation

If evaluation primarily is to be done for the purpose of helping the staff, then it should be done frequently. This especially is true during the probationary period of employment. It should be made on the basis of the same basic beliefs that underlie teacher evaluation. It should be:

1. Democratic
2. Fair
3. Specific
4. As objective as possible
5. Continuous

The two major considerations of evaluation should be the correction of weaknesses and the improvement of services. Evaluation of all staff members can easily fall into three major areas:

1. The individual as a person;
2. The individual as a staff member;
3. The individual as a skilled worker.

The evaluation itself may take one of several forms:

1. A rating scale
2. A checklist
3. An outline
4. A written essay

Ideally, the form should be planned and developed cooperatively by members of the classified personnel and their immediate supervisors. Samples of checklist and rating forms are included as Figures 15–3 and 15–4.

More important than the form, however, is the fairness of the evaluation and the use to which it is put. Opinions based on one specific instance should be avoided. Each evaluation should be discussed with the individual rated in a personal conference. The primary purpose and end result of the evaluation must be more effective service.

How to Do It: Techniques Which Work

In a recent study, T. Jackman reported fifteen items which were rated most effective by at least 50 percent of the principals questioned:

1. Special job instruction for new employees prior to starting work, or shortly thereafter.

FIGURE 15-3   Classified Personnel Evaluation Checklist Form

_____   _____ Probationary Report

                    Principal
                          SERVICE REPORT

                          Date Due _____

(Name)_____ Classification_____

In each group place a check mark ( ) before the descriptive phrase which most nearly typifies the employee's performance.

Promptness in   ( ) Nearly always late
Reporting for Work   ( ) Often tardy
                           ( ) Usually on time
                           ( ) On time more than average
                           ( ) Rarely if ever late

Knowledge of Work   ( ) Inadequate comprehension
                           ( ) Limited knowledge of job
                           ( ) Adequate knowledge; knows job fairly well
                           ( ) Well informed; has mastered most details
                           ( ) Thoroughly familiar with all phases of his work

Work Attitude   ( ) Complains or acts unconcerned
                           ( ) Sometimes indifferent; goes about
                               work half-heartedly
                           ( ) Average interest; likes most phases of his job
                           ( ) Definite interest in work
                           ( ) Enthusiastic, wholehearted active interest

Initiative   ( ) Needs frequent direction, or prodding
                           ( ) A routine worker; usually waits to be told
                           ( ) Reasonably alert to opportunities
                           ( ) Resourceful; completes suggested
                               supplementary work
                           ( ) Seeks and sets for himself additional tasks;
                               shows ingenuity

Capacity to Develop   ( ) Has very little future growth; has about
                               reached limit
                           ( ) Future growth doubtful
                           ( ) Moderate development ahead
                           ( ) Great latent possibilities
                           ( ) Bright future growth; shows promise

FIGURE 15–3   (Continued)

Attitude Toward Other Employees	( ) Surly, touchy or quarrelsome; does not cooperate
	( ) Sometimes difficult to work with
	( ) Normal self-restraint
	( ) Tactful and obliging; good self-control; cooperative
	( ) An unusual and strong force for group morale
Quality of Work	( ) Poor work; frequent errors; unsatisfactory
	( ) Not always satisfactory; sometimes careless
	( ) Satisfactory; does fair work; few errors
	( ) Work usually well done; practically no errors
	( ) Work very satisfactory; quite carefully done
Quantity of Work	( ) Puts out very little work; unsatisfactory
	( ) Does not do his share of work
	( ) Average amount of work
	( ) More than average amount of work
	( ) Turns out unusually large amount of work
Ability to Understand Directions	( ) Carries out only the simplest directions, with help
	( ) Often misunderstands or bungles orders
	( ) Occasionally requests simple instructions to be repeated
	( ) Readily understands most orders
	( ) Requests additional information on only most complex orders
Appearance	( ) Usually unkempt, slovenly, or careless
	( ) Often neglectful of appearance
	( ) Presents a favorable appearance
	( ) Well groomed
	( ) Takes genuine pride in his appearance

Check the following only if employee has contacts with the public which are considered a necessary part of his duties:

Contacts with Public	( ) Surly, touchy or quarrelsome; antagonizes others
	( ) Lacks certain requirements of common courtesy
	( ) Complaints occasionally received; usually maintains courteous effective relations

FIGURE 15–3   (Continued)

( ) Tactful and obliging; good self-control
( ) Exceptionally courteous and well-mannered

Give percentage rating according to the rating guide below: _____

Rating Guide:

1. *Superior*—exceptionally qualified for the position in every way; 96 to100 percent
2. *Good*—could do the job better than most and has several positive and desirable qualities; 86 to 95 percent
3. *Average*—could do the work and has no outstanding undesirable qualities; 76 to 85 percent
4. *Passable*—probably could do the work, but some one else probably more desirable; 70 to 75 percent
5. *Failure*—either could not do the work or not desirable in the position; below 70 percent. (Not recommended for permanency.)

Signed: _____ Date _____
                        Principal

Signed: _____ Date _____
                        Employee

2. Opportunity for classified employees to work with experienced personnel during probationary period.
3. Participation of classified employees in evening or extension courses pertaining to their work.
4. Basic training course for classified employees.
5. Meetings stressing employees' part in school health and sanitation.
6. Opportunities to attend job conferences, with expenses paid.
7. Opportunities to have individual conferences with the principal
8. Meetings devoted to job skills or problems of classified employees.
9. Planning of training programs on the basis of the results of performance evaluations of classified employees.
10. Demonstrations by commercial representatives of the use of equipment and materials.
11. In-service . . . [education] meetings for supervisors of classified employees.

FIGURE 15–4   Evaluation Rating Form

The following evaluation form is used for the rating of educational secretaries. It is to be made out in triplicate by the person for whom the secretary works.

NAME OF SCHOOL

Copy for:

( ) Employee
( ) Principal or
    Director
( ) Personnel Office

Name of Employee_____ Office _____

Rating[a]

Points on Which Rated	Excel-lent	Good	Aver-age	Below Average
1. Punctuality				
2. Accuracy				
3. Responsibility				
4. Initiative				
5. Tact				
6. Cooperation				
7. Efficient planning of work				
8. Ability in the necessary skills				
9. Completing work at the proper time; productive output				
10. Neatness of desk, files, records, reports, etc.				
General or Average Rating				

[a]Some supervisors recommend terminology such as, "Exceeds Work Standards," "Meets Work Standards," and "Below Work Standards" or "Fails to Meet Minimum Acceptable Work Standards."

12. Opportunities for classified employees to participate in salary committee meetings.
13. Opportunities for classified employees to visit other schools to observe job skills.
14. Handbooks or manuals for the use of classified employees.
15. Performance ratings for classified employees.[7]

How to Evaluate Working Conditions

Each school has specific problems, but the principal always should give consideration to: (1) physical facilities and equipment, (2) health and safety precautions, and (3) cooperation from faculty and students. Examine the checklists under each of these headings in Figure 15-5. These, then, are some of the techniques used to help staff members understand their jobs, learn how to do them more efficiently, and therefore help them to feel more secure.

Noise is a disturbing factor. It can not only disturb, but also decrease efficiency. It is helpful to:

1. Place typewriters and other machines on rubber or foam pads;
2. Soften all buzzers and bells;
3. Oil squeaky metal hinges or wheels;
4. Use such items as staplers quietly;
5. Close cabinet doors softly;
6. Keep voices quiet;
7. Line boxes and desk and file drawers with blotter pads;
8. Cover desk surfaces;
9. Play soft background music, if desired.

How to Communicate Effectively with Classified Personnel

Without adequate communication the best plan of classified employee supervision can be totally ineffective. One of the most important and immediate

[7]Taylor Jackman, "The In-Service Training of Classified Employees in Elementary School Districts of Southern California" (Doctoral dissertation, University of Southern California, 1959), pp. 154–155.

FIGURE 15–5   Working Conditions Checklist

Physical Facilities and Equipment

1. Is there adequate room for equipment, for storage, for operation?   _____
2. Are light, ventilation, and heat appropriate for the job?   _____
3. Is equipment satisfactory? If it is not new, has it been kept in good repair?   _____
4. Are supplies adequate?   _____
5. Are restrooms, lunchroom, and sanitary facilities adequate and pleasant?   _____

Health and Safety Precautions

1. Are machinery and equipment safe?   _____
2. Have potential hazards been eliminated?   _____
3. Are first-aid facilities and services available?   _____
4. Are workloads equalized? Are adjustments made under extenuating circumstances (peak loads and overtime)?   _____
5. Is there an adequate sick leave plan?   _____
6. Is there a health insurance program?   _____
7. Are there health advisory services?   _____

Cooperation from Faculty and Students

1. Are rooms left in good order—straightened up and picked up?   _____
2. Are lunch bags thrown on the school grounds or in the trash can?   _____
3. Is the cafeteria neat after the lunch hour?   _____
4. Is reasonable care taken of the restrooms?   _____
5. Do students evidence self-discipline and courtesy in the office, in the cafeteria, on the school grounds, and on the school bus?   _____

---

jobs of the principal is to establish lines of communication and to keep them open. If communication is to be effective it must: (1) be well written and continuous, and (2) flow in both directions. If the purpose is to impart information, such information should be timely, pertinent, and helpful. If it is a directive, the communique should be clear and concise and should be capable of fulfillment. It also should imply confidence.

Written Classified Personnel Policies

Every school system should have its own set of classified personnel policies which should be in writing and in the hands of every staff member. The extent to which staff members are satisfied with these policies, and the degree of their effectiveness, will be related closely to how much of a part the members had in their making. Salary schedules, fringe benefits, grievance procedures, and tenure, dismissal, and promotion policies constitute a minimum content.

REALISTIC SALARY SCHEDULES. The topic of personnel salaries is too lengthy to discuss in detail here. The most important point to be made, however, is that classified personnel should be on a regular salary schedule, and that it must be designed just as carefully as is the schedule for the certificated personnel. It continuously should be reviewed and revised in a democratic and cooperative manner, and it should provide for advancement.

A school system, even one of moderate size, soon becomes big business. Hiring employees at substandard wages results in substandard efficiency. Salary schedules should compare somewhat favorably with the rates being paid in industry for the same work. There is, naturally, some prestige attached to a position in the school system, but the amount is not sufficient to overcome an extremely low salary schedule.

It is not resonable to place a million dollar school plant in the hands of a fifty dollar a week custodian; nor is it wise to allow expensive office machinery, cafeteria equipment, and transportation facilities to be used or maintained by comparatively unskilled labor.

The hiring of skilled, interested, enthusiastic, and loyal employees is the first step in improving the standards of the classified personnel. The increased salary rate necessary to the procurement of such personnel will be offset by their capabilities, and in many ways economies will be affected by their more efficient work habits.

Salaries vary greatly with the type and location of the community, the size of the school system, and the assignment specifications. Professional organizations make continuous studies of trends and publicize results. Two of the best sources of guideline information are school systems of comparable size and situation, and local industries which employ for comparable jobs.

FRINGE BENEFITS. As large a factor in personnel morale as they are a head-
ache to the business office are fringe benefits, which should be as carefully
conceived and provided for classified personnel as they are for certificated
personnel. The most important of these benefits are listed:

1. *Sick leave.* A minimum of twenty days per year at full pay, plus ninety
   days at half pay, is recommended. Unused sick leave should be partially
   cumulative and partially repaid to the employee, according to a set
   formula.
2. *Compensation insurance.* Most school systems participate in a state compensation program, but definite protection against on-the-job accidents
   must be provided.
3. *Vacations.* All full-time employees should be given vacations. It is
   important that no preference be given to one group over another when
   planning for vacations.
4. *Health insurance.* Health insurance, including dental, medical, optical,
   and hospitalization coverage, should be paid for by the school system. If
   necessary, permissive legislation should be sought.
5. *Substitutes.* Substitutes must be provided for all departments, and they
   must be trained. Knowing that one will not have to "double" every time
   a fellow worker is ill can be a big factor in personnel morale.
6. *Retirement.* Retirement provisions should be developed carefully, and
   should be stated clearly in the personnel policies handbook.

HOW TO HANDLE GRIEVANCES. Matters of misunderstandings or discontent
will arise in even the most highly trained and efficient groups. The dimensions to which these dissatisfactions grow will depend upon the procedures
established to take care of grievances and the manner in which they are
handled. If from the first day on the job the worker knows to whom to go
for help with dissatisfactions, and if he feels free to do so, a large percentage
of such problems can be solved in their infancy. Approachability, absolute
fairness, and impartiality are essential qualities which arbitrators must
possess. The better the arbitrator knows all staff members as individuals,
the more effectively he can function.

How to Handle Problems Related to
Dismissal, Tenure, and Promotion

Perhaps no single factor contributes as much to the security and morale of staff members as does knowing the exact terms of, and reasons for, dismissal, promotion, and tenure.

DISMISSAL. Dismissal procedures must be governed strictly by state laws and local regulations and policies. Local regulations should be established cooperatively, with classified personnel participating. The dismissal procedure itself is of vital importance, for such action may well throw the morale of the whole group off balance.

1. Action toward dismissal should be taken only after careful and complete investigation in which all facts have been gathered;
2. Suggestions should be offered;
3. The worker should be given the opportunity to improve;
4. The employee should be taken into the supervisor's confidence as soon as possible;
5. If dismissal becomes necessary, advance notice should be given, and the manner in which it is done should be as friendly as possible.

It is advisable to help the employee to find another job for which he is qualified.

It is necessary that a list of the causes for dismissal be included in the written personnel policies. This list should be adapted specifically to each department and to each job classification. It must cover specialized skills for each job. It is important that the causes for dismissal be reviewed carefully during orientation and in-service meetings. Prior to initiating dismissal procedures, the supervisor should schedule several *control interviews* with the employee. See Chapter 9 for specific suggestions concerning such conferences.

PROMOTION. Knowing the possibilities for promotion helps lead to increased effort and a desire to do better work. Practical suggestions for the administration of promotion are listed:

1. The basic concerns in promotion and transfer are, in rank order, betterment of the school and betterment of the employee. The career concept should be stressed, with sufficient incentives other than monetary prevailing. Employees who cannot be adequately remunerated for their services should be given due recognition and aided in finding appropriate positions outside the school system, if that be their desire.
2. The basis for promotion and transfer should be found in the classification system of positions as adopted by the governing board.
3. Assignment specifications should be adopted.
4. Evidence of growth in service should be established before promotion.
5. Advantage never should be given to the more ambitious employee to the detriment of the more timid, but competent, worker. To seek out and reward the faithful and efficient employee after years of service is perhaps, in itself, a morale builder of great consequence.
6. Personal favoritism or prejudice has no place in the supervision of a program of promotion and transfer.
7. Promotion and transfer always should be made upon recommendation of the principal to the superintendent. In this respect it is akin to selection and appointment.

Promotion which is not based on merit can lead to the loss of initiative on the part of employees who see that increased effort and industry are not rewarded. Promotion based on personal friendship or political expediency will lead to loss of morale and a high rate of turnover. It is helpful for school systems to institute a policy of promotion from within.

TENURE. It is good practice to offer employment to classified employees on a contractual basis. This should be done, however, only after an adequate probationary period has been served during which both competency and loyalty have been demonstrated. Many school systems have adopted a probationary period of six months for classified employees.

The terms of any tenure agreement, and reasons for removal, must be explicit. The fact that there are even limited provisions for a tenure status will add greatly to personnel security and morale.

How to Plan for More Efficient Classified Personnel Performance

Efficiency and skill of all personnel help to save money, time, and materials. Every economy which the governing board is able to affect leaves the way clear for the provision of some additional service for the students.

In developing more efficient methods it first is necessary to determine the present state of affairs with regard to classified service in the school system. The program must be studied carefully and its strengths and weaknesses noted. Once the facts are ascertained and analyzed it is possible to decide upon a plan of action and to set such a plan in motion.

Any plan considered by the school system must be formulated after careful study and knowledge of the legal requirements and governing board rules and regulations. They must be developed in the light of sound business procedures. Efficient and economical business management are necessary in order to conserve time, money, and energy. As a matter of fact, practices in school supervision are indicating a trend toward the hiring of business management specialists, rather than leaving such matters for the attention of the school system superintendent.

Store System Purchase of Supplies Can Increase Employee Efficiency

A sufficient quantity of high quality materials immediately available for use by classified personnel helps to increase efficiency. There is no time lost in waiting for the purchase of needed supplies, nor loss of quality in work by employing substitute materials.

The purchase of supplies on a store system basis would have the following advantages:

1. A quantity discount would be possible;
2. Standard supply requisitions would be filled promptly;
3. Efficient storage of standard items would be possible.

Materials which may be purchased economically in this manner are those standard items used by the school system in large quantities, such as instructional materials, office and custodial supplies, and maintenance and equipment items.

Adequate storage facilities should be provided, a cataloguing system for standard stock items should be developed, and a running supply inventory system with periodic physical inventories should be maintained. A definite procedure for issuing and receiving supplies will save time and money.

Neatly and accurately completed standard order forms will save clerical time and school system funds and will avoid duplication of effort. Verification should be made that there are sufficient funds in the budget to cover the order of any supplies.

Daily Schedule of Activities for all Classified Employees

A daily schedule, when made, should be uncrowded and should be used as a general guide only. The schedule should be flexible and should allow for interruptions and emergencies, which are the rule rather than the exceptions.

At the end of the year, all such schedules should be evaluated in the light of the quality and quantity of work done, possibilities for increased efficiency, and changes necessary to allow for additional tasks which have been noted.

Information as to the advisable starting dates of any long-range jobs should be noted so as to insure their completion on time. A day-by-day suspense calendar, noting job due dates, should be employed.

How to Get the Most Out of In-Service Education Programs for Classified Employees

Planned instruction and help must not stop with the orientation program. In-service education provides an opportunity for the continuous growth of the classified staff member, as well as for improved efficiency in the operation of the school. The content of the program will vary with the job category, but there are two major topics common to all:

1. *New ideas, new techniques, new equipment.* From a new directive on attendance accounting, to a new wax finish, to a new dishwasher—there

constantly is something new. Staff members using new equipment first
of all should have a part in the decision whether to purchase the item,
and then should be acquainted thoroughly with both its operation
and care. New ideas for method and organization of work will come
constantly from the group if the mechanics for exchange of ideas are
established.

2. *The total school program and plans.* An advance knowledge of coming
   activities will help staff members to anticipate peak work periods and
   plan ahead more efficiently.

Methods Employed in Classified Personnel In-Service Education

There are many methods by which in-service growth can be accomplished.
Again, no single method should be used to the exclusion of all others, but
rather a combination of several of the ones most applicable to each group.
The following are the most commonly used:

1. *Staff meetings.* Staff meetings are a must, if only for the value of fellow
   workers meeting together and exchanging feelings and ideas. Such
   meetings can include discussions of common problems at the local level,
   an outside speaker, a demonstration of new equipment, or a motion
   picture illustrating a new method.
2. *Workshops.* It often is profitable for staff members to spend a longer
   period of time together—a day or several days—reviewing their jobs
   and discussing how to perform them more efficiently.
3. *Personnel handbooks.* These policy handbooks should include general
   information about the school which pertains to the job and specific duties to be done, assignments, hours, schedules, methods, and materials.
4. *Faculty meetings.* Classified personnel should attend certificated personnel faculty meetings when practical and possible.
5. *College and evening adult-school courses.* While classes for secretarial
   training long have been available, there are now a growing number of
   colleges and schools that are offering both workshops and classes for
   the training of custodians or maintenance engineers, and for cafeteria
   managers.

6. *Professional literature.* Pertinent material found in professional books or periodicals should be routed to classified personnel.
7. *Special bulletins.* Printed materials may call attention to specific problems or ideas. They can help to keep classified personnel up-to-date with a minimum of time and effort.
8. *Professional organizations.* Professional organizations help to raise performance standards and should become more involved.

How to Improve the Performance of Bus Drivers

In student transportation there are three types of positions: (1) supervisory, (2) driving, and (3) maintenance. The largest number of employees constitute the driver category. The drivers are responsible for the safety and for some control ("discipline") of the students. Public relations become especially important where bus drivers are concerned since they are in constant contact with homes, parents, and students. Bus drivers should wear attractive, clean uniforms provided, at least initially, by the school system.

Standards for the position of school bus driver frequently are set too low, since the work is considered a part-time job with consequent low pay and low prestige. There is a trend toward better selection, higher standards, higher pay, and higher prestige.

In-service education programs should be available for bus drivers in both basic duties and first aid. Courses concerning basic maintenance procedures as are necessary should be provided if the school system uses drivers in this capacity.

The greatest responsibility of the bus driver is the safety of the students he is transporting. This responsibility demands skill not only as a driver but also as a mechanic-inspector, for the bus driver is responsible for the bus that he drives.

As in the case of other classified personnel, it is well to establish written standards in the selection of bus drivers. Certainly more care should be taken than is usually required by the various states in granting licenses to drivers. Aside from recommendations regarding character and experience, the record of the applicant should be studied carefully and application denied to the driver who has been proven to be reckless or has been in accidents due to bad judgment or failure to comply with the law. No individual connected with the school system has more to do with the safety of students than does the driver of the school bus.

Although the driver is responsible for the conduct of the students on his bus, teachers can help by discussing with the students the importance of proper conduct to and from school. Dangerous, improper conduct must not be tolerated on school buses.

Most school systems require as qualifications for drivers:

1. A minimum age of twenty-one;
2. Physical fitness (determined by physical examination);
3. Experience in driving;
4. Proper certification according to state and local requirements;
5. Knowledge of first aid;
6. Good character and habits.

It is most helpful, in addition, if the driver has a sense of humor, enjoys being with children, and is an unobtrusive disciplinarian.

In-service education should be continuous for the purpose of keeping up-to-date on such items as:

1. Changes in the motor vehicle code;
2. Route changes and new assignments;
3. Condition of the buses and maintenance problems;
4. School programs or events which will affect transportation schedules;
5. Handling emergencies or accidents;
6. Supervision of student behavior.

Because of the safety factor involved, it is essential that the bus driver has complete administrative and supervisory backing in the control of behavior. Transportation rules for students should be developed cooperatively, be covered thoroughly in the classroom, and be strictly enforced by the principal.

Many school systems employ part-time personnel for work as school bus drivers. Such personnel have more outside interests, and special care must be taken to create enthusiasm for the part they play in the educational system.

How to Improve the Performance of Cafeteria Employees

The organization of the cafeteria staff is dependent upon the size and type of the school. There is a definite trend toward requiring a bachelor's degree, with special training in nutrition and management, for all cafeteria supervisors. Other cafeteria employees must possess the qualifications of good health, regard for children, skill in cafeteria work, a pleasant personality, and neatness.

Where housewives are employed part time, the cafeteria consultant or "line supervisor" must be skilled in giving both formal and informal on-the-job training. Areas requiring special attention include the ability to:

1. Read written instructions accurately;
2. Prepare food in quantity;
3. Learn to operate the expensive equipment with skill and safety;
4. Serve the food attractively;
5. Keep accurate records;
6. Prepare reports.

Cafeteria workers must stress cleanliness of person and of the lunchroom.

It is important that provision be made for compensation for extra functions. Attention to the safety factors in the kitchen is vital. The supervisor should be aware of the adequacy of facilities for:

1. Food preparation;
2. Food service;
3. Dishwashing;
4. Storage;
5. Refrigeration;
6. Receiving;
7. Space;
8. Dining area;
9. Management space.

How to Improve the Work of Custodians

If a custodian works well, appreciation should be expressed and deserved praise should be rendered. A "that's fine," or "I'm glad you thought of that," is helpful. No one, including members of the classified staff, should be criticized in the presence of *anyone* else.

HOW THE CLASSIFIED EMPLOYEE ACQUIRES A BODY OF CUSTODIAL KNOWL-EDGE. Custodians acquire a knowledge of the care of the school plant mostly through experience. If they are encouraged to read and study in the areas of their problems, intelligent custodians make great improvement in their services. Thus they come to know reasons for doing things in certain ways, and to learn about new materials and techniques.

One of the first problems encountered in the use of school equipment and materials is that of training custodians to use them properly. Most manufacturers are happy to display and discuss their products with the people who use them. The manufacturer's representative should be invited to participate in the in-service education program. Such participation must be delineated carefully, however.

Since the custodians are the ones who will be using these materials, they should have some say in their selection. This practice tends to give them a feeling of belonging to a team, rather than just having a job.

WHAT TO LOOK FOR WHEN SELECTING A CUSTODIAN. The custodian is an important representative of the school and is in close contact with students. His character and reputation must be above reproach. It is necessary that he be physically healthy and strong, sure-footed, and have good sight and hearing. He must be good in housekeeping.

One of the first steps in securing, keeping, and interesting good personnel in their jobs is providing for adequate salary schedules. Higher salary schedules lead to improved custodian status and morale.

RESPONSIBILITIES OF THE CUSTODIAN. Custodians are responsible for the health and safety of both students and teachers, and for the care of costly property. Additionally, since visitors often judge the entire school by the appearance and actions of the custodian, the custodian can do great service or harm to the school in the field of community relations. The custodian is asked questions regarding school policy and members of the staff. A careless remark can be most harmful.

The custodian is the key to making any plant functional for those who use it. His job of maintenance essentially includes four items:

1. Cleanliness and sanitation—of classrooms, drinking fountains, cafeteria, restrooms, and grounds;
2. Safety—from fire hazards to loose handrails;
3. Preservation of buildings—good care adding to life expectancy;
4. Attractiveness—resulting in better student and teacher morale and better community impressions.

HOW TO DETERMINE CUSTODIAL LOAD. The principal must give particular attention to the work load of the custodial or maintenance staff. In order to avoid disagreements and dissatisfactions, and to get the job done efficiently, a detailed work schedule should be developed. Such a schedule is included as Figure 15–6.

The following factors should be taken into consideration when determining the custodial load:

1. Administration of the school and student control factors;
2. Size of the school;
3. Age and state of repair of the buildings;
4. Attendance area location, including its general category such as residential or industrial;
5. Climatic conditions;
6. Type of building structure and number of windows;
7. Kind of school and its age level;
8. Social background of students and home cleanliness;
9. Enrollment;
10. Type and arrangement of rooms and desks;
11. Amount and kind of floor area;

FIGURE 15–6   Sample Custodial Schedule[a]

LEVINE JUNIOR HIGH SCHOOL

_____

Name of Custodian

School Year: 1984–85
Hours Assigned: 12:00 Noon through 8:00 P.M.

Time	Activity	Completed Check When
12:00–12:15 (15 Min.)	Prepare and check custodial equipment	_____
12:15–1:15 (1 Hour)	Sweep Kindergarten A and clean[b] and sweep Rooms 1A, 1B, and Instructional Center	_____
1:15–1:45 (45 Min.)	Cafeteria cleanup	_____

[a]See Lowell G. Keith, S. Robert Infelise, and George J. Perazzo, _Guide for Elementary School Administration_ (Belmont, California: Wadsworth Publishing Company, 1965), p. 122; and Emery Stoops and Russell Johnson, _Elementary School Administration_ (New York: McGraw-Hill Book Co., 1967), p. 165.

[b]Includes: 1. Clean sinks, sink counters, drinking fountains, chalk trays, and chalk board
              2. Clean inside of both exit doors

---

12. Type and condition of heating, ventilation, and plumbing facilities;
13. Amount and kind of playground and yard;
14. Workshop area—location and adequacy;
15. Convenience of storerooms and supply areas.

In-service education for the custodial staff must include information concerning the use of new techniques, new materials, and new equipment. "New," however, does not necessarily imply "improved." Wise planning and wise use of materials and supplies can save money for the school system.

The custodian's responsibilities for maintaining proper sanitation and for safety can be made more meaningful by providing speakers, filmstrips, transparencies, and audio materials.

FIGURE 15–6   (Continued)

1:45–2:00 (15 Min.)	Coffee break	_____
2:00–3:30 (1½ Hours) 3:30–4:30	Clean all restrooms; clean Rooms 6, 11, 17, 18 Lower flag, secure flag; continue to clean rooms, clean faculty lunchroom, lock offices, deliver and set out clean trash cans	_____
4:30–5:00 (30 Min.)	Lunch	_____
5:00–7:00 (2 Hours) 7:00–7:30 (30 Min.)	Clean all ballrooms; bring in equipment left out; clean rooms 5, 8, 9, 13, 17 Clean cafeteria kitchen area	_____
7:30–8:00 (30 Min.)	Clean lower and intermediate level restrooms	_____
8:00	Secure facilities and leave	

3. Empty waste containers and remove miscellaneous articles from floor
4. Sweep floors, return chairs to floor, where applicable
5. Dust counter tops, and all other flat surfaces including desks
6. Where applicable, clean and fill soap and towel dispensers
7. Check room again, noting general room maintenance, lights, windows
8. Lock doors (each Friday clean all erasers and spray special solution on chalkboard after dusting it.

Safety precautions listed by J. E. Barbour[8] included:

1. Checking playgrounds for safety hazards;
2. Proper storage of inflammables, acids, and combustibles.

He urged:

1. Formal training in the use of power equipment;
2. Building inspection for faulty or dangerous rundown conditions;

[8]Julius Ervin Barbour, "The Selection and Instruction of Public School Custodians in Selected School Districts" (Doctoral dissertation, Michigan State College, 1954), p. 39.

3. Practice in the use of fire extinguishers, electrical apparatus, and extension cords.

The school plant inspection report form, included as Figure 15–7, may prove useful.

FIGURE 15–7   School Plant Inspection Report

School _____ Date _____

I. *Grounds Report*

    A. Condition of surfaced area: _____

    B. Condition of nonsurfaced area: _____

    C. Please check—grounds were _____ littered

                                   _____ fairly clean

                                   _____ clean

    D. Condition of trees, shrubbery, flowers: _____

    E. Are there any conditions, problems, or requisitions that we should bring to the attention of the central office? _____

II. *Playground Equipment*

Please note carefully any unsafe conditions, broken equipment, or anything else which we might wish to call to the attention of the students, the teachers, and possibly the superintendent of schools: _____

In your opinion, what is the most important thing we should do to have a safer playground for students? _____

III. *Lavatories*

    A. Condition of urinals and commodes: _____

    B. Condition of wash basins: _____

    C. Condition of floor: _____

    D. Condition of ventilation: _____

    E. Mirrors: _____

    F. Lavatory room doors: _____

    G. Other: _____

IV. *Classrooms*[a]

Please check or answer as specifically as possible:

A. Chalkboards: (condition?)_____

Are chalk trays clean?_____

B. Floors: Condition _____Clean? _____Waxed? _____

C. Windows: When last washed?_____

Are window blinds working?_____

D. Desks and furniture: Clean? _____Dusted? _____Waxed? _____

E. Locker space: Floors? _____ Shelves? _____

F. Are teachers' closets clean?_____

G. Condition of room lighting? _____

H. Are thermostats working properly? _____

I. When have seats been adjusted in this room? _____

[a]This kind of report would have to be used for each classroom.

V. *Gymnasium and Stage*

A. Note here any unusual or poor condition: _____

_____

B. Condition of gymnasium lighting: _____

C. Condition of gymnasium floors: _____

D. Condition of windows, shades, and screens: _____

E. Condition of walls and ceiling: _____

F. Are there any hazards to student's safety in the gymnasium? _____

VI. *Offices and Storage Areas*

A. Floors: _____ Windows: _____

B. Condition of equipment and furniture:_____

C. Items which need repair or replacement:_____

D. Condition of public address system: _____

VII. *Boiler Room*

Are there any conditions, safety hazards, unfilled requisitions, etc. that the central office or the superintendent of schools should know about?

_____

_____

Signed _____

Head Custodian

HELPING THE BEGINNING CUSTODIAN. If the custodian is new to the school, he will require more of the principal's time and attention. All advice given to the custodian should be given tactfully.

It will be necessary for the principal to stress every situation which may prove detrimental to human welfare. For a while the principal may find it necessary to make certain inspections which a beginning custodian may overlook, such as checking to see that all lights are out at the close of school, and that all windows, doors, and gates are closed and locked.

THE CUSTODIAN AND THE STUDENTS. The students should be informed about the activities and responsibilities of the custodian and the importance of his work. The custodian's pride in his work in connection with the school buildings may become a source of inspiration.

WHAT SUBJECTS TO COVER. It is felt by most educators and custodians alike that meetings devoted to the job skills or problems of classified employees are a helpful addition to formal in-service education programs. Subjects pertaining to retirement law, school rules and regulations, employment practices, and explanations of the need for additional funds are handled more easily when one instructional session for all custodial employees is held It is possible to maintain a feeling of unity when the total school membership is kept informed regarding school issues and problems.

A well-trained custodian can affect savings through conservation of water, electricity, fuel, and supplies. There should be a definite program of in-service education to help custodians in this area. Such a program should not only teach abilities and skills, but also develop desirable habits and attitudes.

WHAT THE SMALLER SCHOOL SYSTEM CAN DO. Smaller school systems sometimes find it difficult to provide an adequate in-service education program for their custodial staff. In order to help these school systems, as well as the larger school systems wishing to take advantage of such courses, some states offer a three-to five-day intensive training course. School systems wishing their employees to attend usually pay the expenses involved.

These courses are of short duration because most of those attending are unaccustomed to long periods of intensive study. In addition, most are family men and unable to stay away from home too long without hardship to their families. Smaller school systems frequently work together, cooperating with the county superintendent to provide a more adequate training program.

SPECIAL PROBLEMS FACED BY ALL CUSTODIANS. New employees must understand their duties in regard to safety emergencies, fire prevention, and civil defense drills. As mentioned earlier, a daily schedule of the custodian's work should be defined clearly. Time must be allocated in the schedule for emergency and periodic duties, and for special repairs.

In addition, the principal should assure that:

1. Extra duties are fairly and equitably distributed among employees. All employees should be encouraged to suggest needed improvements in equipment or procedure.
2. All special or extra work desired by teachers is cleared through the principal's office. No teacher should ask a custodian to run errands. A custodian can have only *one* boss.
3. All custodial personnel are provided with a handbook. A good handbook might be *The School Custodian's Housekeeping Handbook* by H. H. Linn, or *The Custodian at Work* by N. E. Viles.

How to Improve the Work of the Educational Secretary

If you ever come into a school office and find that the secretary is home with a cold, you realize her importance. The office has that empty, lost feeling.

The secretary performs services which give balance and tone to the school. Her work requires skill and finesse, tact and personality. Her responsibilities are of a detailed and routine nature, and it is obvious that these essentials contribute greatly to the smooth functioning of the school organization.

The following are identifying characteristics of a good secretary:[9]

[9]National Association and Council of Business Schools, *Secretaryship as a Career Field* (Washington, D.C.: The Council, 1959), p. 5.

1. A close personal contact with the immediate supervisor and a knowledge of business routines;
2. A decrease in the time spent typewriting or performing stenographic duties;
3. An increased reliance upon personal initiative, judgment, and knowledge of business;
4. The ability to direct and supervise clerical workers;
5. The ability to carry responsibility for the most important details and to assume many minor administrative duties.

HOW TO ELEVATE THE QUALITY OF THE EDUCATIONAL SECRETARY'S WORK. The techniques listed here may be employed in upgrading secretarial services:

1. Provide for guided observation tours through the office so the secretary may learn what equipment is in use and may see central storage facilities, observe the system of distribution, and examine the record-keeping system.
2. Arrange for a tour of the school to which the secretary has been assigned.
3. Require that beginning secretaries attend workshops or institutes planned for them; arrange the calendar so that experienced secretaries may attend such in-service programs if they so desire; and insist that such in-service education classes be attended by the secretary as one of the prerequisites to promotion.
4. Arrange for school system funds to pay for transportation and registration fees at the Secretarial Association's regional conferences.
5. Use available standardized and informal tests to appraise English usage, office procedure knowledge, general information, and achievement in office skills including stenography and typing.
6. Schedule regular on-the-job observations of the secretary at work.
7. Schedule routine examinations of files, stockrooms, and the secretarial work area.
8. Work toward a secretarial salary schedule based on preparation, experience, and performance.
9. Arrange for demonstrations, obtain motion pictures, sound and silent film-

strips, video tapes and slides, and make available publications that are pertinent.[10]

HOW TO KEEP SECRETARIAL PERSONNEL PROBLEMS TO A MINIMUM. A good supervising principal, with his secretary, will maintain good relations between the school office and teachers, other personnel, students, and the various publics. Some problems unique to the secretary may develop because of the very nature of her job. The principal must be alert to the problems and do all he can to prevent them from hindering the secretary's growth. Such problems include:

1. The secretary may identify with the principal, and therefore may tend to feel "superior" to the faculty. It may help to emphasize that she is *ex officio* the secretary of the entire faculty, although actual secretarial duties are assigned only by the principal. She must *never* even *appear* to give orders to a teacher!
2. Teachers become suspicious of an aloof secretary and lose confidence in her.
3. The attitudes of the students may create problems.
4. She may be "in the know" concerning problems and therefore "on the spot" with the faculty.
5. Cliques may develop among the clerical personnel. Where these cliques exist, much of the spirit of cooperation is lost.

HOW TO FACILITATE THE SECRETARY'S WORK DURING TIME OF PEAK LOAD. Another task of the principal in relationship to his secretary is awareness of work load and overtime. Some hints are listed below:

1. To discover bottlenecks in job routine, a secretary may list on cards all of her activities and the amount of time spent on each. In this way it is possible, over a period of time, to discover if she is spending too much time, or not enough, on the various tasks for which she is responsible.
2. A monthly or annual schedule will indicate the times of peak load and allow the secretary to plan so that nonessential duties are scheduled for

[10]National Association of Educational Secretaries, *Plan Your Work* (Washington, D.C.: The Association, 1959).

times other than the peak load time. It helps to schedule ahead as new emergency work is added to the schedule.

3. In planning for peak load periods, a well-established routine, which allows for paper work to be done quickly, is necessary to ensure that time is available for the all-important job of taking care of people.

4. When load reduction can be accomplished during peak periods, accuracy and efficiency can be increased.

5. Some part-time help can be employed to handle routine tasks.

6. Where two or more secretaries work in one office, encourage them to help one another with tasks during peak loads, even though a task may be the sole responsibility of one of them.

7. Student help may be used.

8. Have all work delegated by one person.

One principal prepared the following list of suggestions for the secretary:

About yourself—

1. The educational secretary's position is a key position in the school. Since you often give the public its first impression of the school, a smile of welcome is always appreciated.

2. Poise and dignity must be maintained at all times. Cultivate a quiet, well-modulated voice. Dress carefully and in good taste.

3. You should notify the principal immediately if it is necessary for you to be absent or late.

4. Your relations with the principal, the teachers, the students, and parents should be pleasant. Learn to make adjustments with cheerful readiness. It may seem easier at times to give orders to teachers. Don't do it! It is the principal's job to supervise and administrate.

5. Accept your responsibilities willingly. Be kind and generous but do not assume more than a secretary's responsibility.

6. Loyalty is a characteristic which helps to make a secretary valuable to the principal, the teachers, and the community.

7. Interruptions often are necessary and should be accepted graciously.

8. Plan your work carefully and look ahead. A last-minute rush does not enable you to perform your duties efficiently.

About the students—

1. All information concerning students in the school is confidential. Inquiries regarding them must be referred immediately to the principal.
2. Discipline and control problems are the responsibility of the principal.
3. Students may be excused to leave the school grounds only under certain conditions, as indicated by the principal.

About good office practices—

1. Your office should be neat and attractive, and all materials should be kept in the proper places.
2. All information concerning the faculty and other employees of the school is confidential, and inquiries regarding them should be referred immediately to the principal. Matters pertaining to teachers and their personal business and salary ratings should not be discussed with others.
3. Acquaint yourself with the names of members of the board of education, the superintendent's office, and particularly the administrative and clerical employees of surrounding schools with whom you frequently communicate.
4. Telephone conversations are numerous. It is well to remember that your telephone voice is often your first introduction to people. Learn to know whom to call for specific information. Extend a word of thanks to those who assist you.
5. Keep your calendar up-to-date! Check the "calendar of reports" which is sent to the schools each term and record the dates when reports are due. Remind the principal of appointments and meetings to be attended.
6. All bulletins and school mail should be read by you. Make arrangements with the principal to have incoming materials reach your desk as soon as they are received at school.
7. All notices and materials to be circulated within the school must have the approval of the principal.
8. School supplies and equipment are strictly for the use of the school.
9. Filing is important. Organize and mark all materials before you place them in the files. Cross index if desirable. Check out communications,

reports, or other materials which are loaned to anyone. Keep your files up-to-date so that you can be proud of them. Remove obsolete materials annually in order to make space for records of next year.

10. Your work area should be clear, with only necessities out on the desk. Other materials should be put into the desk so that you are closest to those used most often. All supplies should be kept as close as possible to the area of use, with the things used most often being the easiest to reach. Use an organizer.

THE SECRETARY'S DESK: A MOST IMPORTANT TOOL. The desk has two work areas; i.e., the one reached by moving the forearm in an arc with the elbow close to the body, and that reached by moving the entire arm. Any space beyond this reach can be utilized only by changing the position of the body.

Instead of the conventionally styled desk, a modular type is available which increases efficiency. If both desks use the same amount of floor space, the modular design will almost double the available working area.

SHARED EQUIPMENT CAN CREATE PROBLEMS. When other personnel or faculty members are using some of the office equipment it helps to have certain hours reserved for this purpose so that interference is avoided. All personnel using equipment should be trained carefully in its proper use. Perhaps additional secretarial help should be provided to eliminate the necessity for the faculty's using such equipment.

A handbook for the educational secretary should be prepared by the superintendent and the professional staff, and should be presented to the governing board for official adoption. Such a handbook should provide for the necessary degree of administrative efficiency required for sound school system management and operation. The handbook for educational secretaries of one public school system includes:

1. Philosophy of the (*Name*) Public Schools
2. The Secretary's Position in the Educational Picture
3. National Association of Educational Secretaries
4. (State) Association of Educational Secretaries
5. (Local) Association of Educational Secretaries

6. Basic Technical Skills
7. Personal Growth and Development
8. Public Relations
9. Rating of Secretaries
10. List of Reports
11. Educational Terms
12. (Assignment Specifications)

DO

1. Be concerned about good working conditions, and make that concern known.
2. Provide for well-planned orientation and in-service education programs.
3. Provide for written personnel policies.
4. Provide for definite work schedules for all classified personnel, and involve the personnel concerned in developing the schedules.
5. Provide adequate equipment and supplies to do the job.
6. Remember to express appreciation for a job well done.
7. Introduce all classified staff members to visiting personnel when they are encountered in the course of the visit.
8. Encourage students to address all members of the classified staff as Mr., or Mrs., or Miss.
9. Work for adequate remuneration for the classified staff.
10. Provide adequate facilities (not just the boiler room!) for personal needs of the classified staff.
11. Keep lines of communication alive between the principal and members of the classified staff and remember to invite all members of the classified staff to the "staff meetings" held with the certificated staff.
12. Measure success in terms of the quality and quantity of output, the promptness with which duties are performed, individual initiative and suggestions for improvement, and cooperation with the entire staff.
13. Develop self-confidence in each classified staff member by recognizing him as an individual, encouraging creativeness, and expressing appreciation.

14. Work for the assignment of the bus driver as a full-time employee of the school system.
15. Work with other supervising principals to establish a policy wherein in-service education meetings for classified personnel will be held on school time, when the meetings are intended to improve job performance. If special meetings are held for job advancement, these may be held on the employees' time.
16. See to it that the instructional methods employed at these in-service education meetings are those preferred by the classified staff, to wit: meetings with demonstrations, video tapes, films, and which use conference techniques.[11]

DON'T

1. Assume that the new classified employee knows his job.
2. Assume that the work of the classified employee is being satisfactorily done unless you have evidence to that effect.
3. Assume that the work of the classified employee is not being satisfactorily done unless you have evidence to that effect.
4. Allow salesmen to sell a bill of goods to your secretary or custodian.
5. Disregard the problems of the custodian, the cafeteria worker, or the bus driver.
6. Permit your classified employees to attempt to repair equipment which they are not trained to repair.

Supervisory Problems

 In Basket

Problem 1

The custodial service at Jessie Junior High was not satisfactory. The classrooms and halls were poorly swept and very little dusting was done. There was a "don't care" attitude developing among teachers and students concerning the appearance of the building. It was called to the attention of the

[11]Lowell G. Keith, S. Robert Infelise, and George J. Perazzo, *Guide for Elementary School Administration* (Belmont, California: Wadsworth Publishing Company, 1965), pp. 57–59.

supervising principal that the custodian was not doing a satisfactory job. Teacher morale was reflected in the appearance of the classrooms. Students were becoming careless in disposing of gum wrappers and other waste materials. There was a noticeable lack of pride in the looks of the building.

Then finally one morning, after an especially messy paper cutting art lesson the preceding day, Miss Samantha's room was practically untouched by the custodian's hands. Paper scraps lay scattered about, a wastebasket remained filled to the brim, and bits of this and that were even outside the door. This scene greeted Miss Samantha when she entered her room at 8:10 A.M. Miss Samantha wrote a letter of complaint to you, the supervising principal.

What should you, as the supervising principal, do?

Problem 2

Thornwood School has been having its share of difficulties. The educational secretary, who has been employed at the school for twenty years, had as her supervisor the former principal for nineteen of those twenty years. Miss Dundy, the former principal, was of the old school; her manner was as gruff as it was insulting.

As supervising principal, you have been receiving complaints from teachers and parents alike that the educational secretary seems to think that she is *ex officio* assistant principal. Teachers complain that they are not able to obtain supplies when they needed them for instruction because "she says she's too busy!" They have further complained that the educational secretary has demanded explanations as to why certain requests have been made or certain actions taken, when the teachers believe such decisions to be in the realm of their professional domain. Yesterday a parent complained that in your absence the secretary had administered corporal punishment in the form of a "light paddling" to her child. The custodian has complained that the secretary is treating him in a manner which is unbefitting his skill and competence.

This secretary is going to retire in two years. She is a good typist and is most efficient in handling office routine.

How should you, as the supervising principal, proceed so as to rectify the situation?

Selected Bibliography

Books

Brainard, Alanson D. *Handbook for School Custodians.* Revised by A. E. Goedeken. Lincoln: University of Nebraska Press, 1961.

Chandler, B. J., and Paul V. Petty. *Personnel Management in School Administration.* New York: The World Book Company, 1955.

Grieder, Calvin, Truman M. Pierce, and William E. Rosenstengel. *Public School Administration.* New York: The Ronald Press Company, 1961.

Keith, Lowell G., S. Robert Infelise, and George J. Perazzo. *Guide for Elementary School Administration.* Belmont, California: Wadsworth Publishing Company, 1965.

Linn, H. H. *The School Custodian's Housekeeping Handbook.* New York: Bureau of Publications, Teachers College, Columbia University, 1958.

———. *School Business Administration.* New York: The Ronald Press Company, 1956.

Mosher, William E., and J. Donald Kingsley. *Public Personnel Administration.* New York: Harper and Brothers, 1941.

Reeder, Ward G. *Fundamentals of Public School Administration.* New York: The Macmillan Company, 1951.

Shane, Harold G., and Wilbur A. Yauck. *Creative School Administration.* New York: Henry Holt and Company, 1954.

Stoops, Emery, and M. L. Rafferty, Jr. *Practices and Trends in School Administration.* Boston: Ginn and Company, 1961.

Viles, Nelson E. *The Custodian at Work.* Lincoln, Nebraska: University Publishing Company, 1941.

Walter, J. E. *Personnel Relations.* New York: The Ronald Press Company, 1945.

Weber, Clarence A. *Personnel Problems of School Administrators.* New York: McGraw-Hill Book Company, Inc., 1954.

Yeager, William A. *Administration of the Noninstructional Personnel and Services.* New York: Harper and Brothers, 1959.

Periodicals

Carlin, M. M. "The Role of the Educational Secretary." *Teachers College Journal* XXX (March 1959): 75–79.

Carson, T. E., Jr. "Is Your Janitor Work Fair?" *Nation's Schools* XXXIV (September 1944): 58.

Essex, M. W. "Practical Personnel Policies." *National Education Association Journal* XXXVII (March 1948): 159.

Handel, H. "Mr. Custodian, Partner in Education." *New York State Educator* XLV (April 1958): 492–494.

Kern, E. "On Secretaries in Particular." *National Education Association Journal* XXXVII (March 1948): 159.

McIntosh, Charles. "The ABC's of Training." *National Custodian* V (March-April 1968): 14–15, 36, 39–40, 43–44.

Melfi, Vincent A. "8 Steps to Cleaning Management Efficiency." *National Custodian,* I (January-February 1968): 22–26.

Ogden, L. K., and E. Stoops. "Staff Morale: What Is It? How Do We Get It?" *Education Administration and Supervision* XLIII (December 1957): 487–491.

Saxe, R. W. "No Office Should Be Without One." *National Elementary Principal* XL (October 1960): 37–38.

Other Sources

Barbour, Julius Ervin. "The Selection and Instruction of Public School Custodians in Selected School Districts." Doctoral dissertation, Michigan State College, 1954.

Evansville Public Schools. *Handbook for Educational Secretaries.* Evansville: Public Schools, 1955.

Galluzo, A. Neil. "Practices in the Administration of Classified Personnel in California." Doctoral dissertation, University of Southern California, 1955.

Jackman, Taylor. "The In-Service Training of Classified Employees in Elementary School Districts of Southern California." Doctoral dissertation, University of Southern California, 1959.

Marks, James R. "An Analysis of Assignment Specifications for Certificated School Personnel in the United States." Doctoral dissertation, University of Southern California, 1962.

National Association and Council of Business Schools. *Secretaryship as a Career Field.* Washington, D.C.: The Council, 1959.

National Association of Educational Secretaries. *Plan Your Work.* Washington, D.C.: The Association, 1959.

Remmers, H. H. "The Analysis of Employee Attitudes." *Proceedings of the First Personnel Institute.* Columbus, Ohio: State University, 1938.

The Association of School Business Officials of the United States and Canada. *Proceedings of the Association of School Business Officials of the United States and Canada.* Thirty-Eighth Yearbook. Washington, D.C.: The Association, 1952.

16

How to Provide Supervision of Auxiliary Services

While not always directly a part of the instructional program, the aims of auxiliary services are to aid, supplement, and enhance the instructional program, and thus require careful, competent supervision. This chapter includes a discussion of the following topics:

How to supervise student transportation
How to improve food services
How to supervise attendance and welfare services
How to improve health services
How to improve library services
Do—don't
"In-Basket" supervisory problem

How to Supervise Student Transportation

Organizing Student Transportation

School system ownership of the transportation system and the employment of responsible personnel for its operation are recommended. Both school buses and auxiliary transportation equipment must provide for efficiency in the transportation of students for regularly scheduled classes, as well as the transportation of students for field trips and other approved transportation needs.

HOW TO APPRAISE THE TRANSPORTATION SYSTEM. To facilitate the appraisal of the transportation system for the school system, Melbo et al. have established standards as portrayed in Table 16–1. These standards should be applied to organization, personnel, equipment, and operating procedures.[1]

[1]Irving R. Melbo et al., "Report of the Survey, Taft City School District," duplicated material copyrighted by the author. (Los Angeles: July 1960), pp. 269–272.

TABLE 16–1 Evaluation of the Transportation System

Number	Item	Superior	Average	Poor
1.	The school system (if large enough) should operate its own transportation system rather than contract for major services.			
2.	The transportation program should be directed by an employee who has the ability, and who is allowed sufficient time, to supervise adequately all operations.			
3.	Only modern equipment in excellent condition should be used.			
4.	Inspections by the . . . highway patrol should be welcomed and a certificate of inspection must be posted in the bus showing approval within the previous year.			
5.	Under *no conditions* should anyone other than a properly licensed bus driver operate the vehicle while transporting children.			
6.	Classified employees rather than teachers should be used as bus drivers.			
7.	Classified employees not regularly used as bus drivers should be licensed to act as substitutes when necessary.			
8.	A utility bus or buses should be available for use in case of an emergency and for special field trips.			
9.	An adequate plan for doing the repair work and servicing the buses in the school system should be followed.			
10.	The school system should try to standardize its transportation equipment. This simplifies repair work and other procedures. It is then possible to carry a minimum stock of needed parts.			
11.	The school system should provide safe and adequate storage facilities for gasoline and oil, and should purchase these items according to specifications on open bid.			
12.	Adequate insurance protection should be carried.			
13.	Controls regarding the dispensing of gasoline should be exercised the same as if cash were involved.			
14.	Adequate cost and other statistical records should be maintained.			
15.	Definite regulations regarding pupil transportation should be adopted by the board and made available in written form to certificated and classified employees.			

TABLE 16-1 (Continued)

Number	Item	Superior	Average	Poor
16.	Bus drivers should wear uniforms. The school system should provide caps equipped with bus drivers' badges. The use of uniforms increases the dignity and authority of the bus driver in dealing with pupils as well as with the general public.			
17.	No person other than public school pupils, or adults assigned for supervision, should be permitted to ride on school buses.			
18.	The bus capacity should never be exceeded by even one pupil. A card furnished by the . . . highway patrol must be posted in each bus giving the maximum seating capacity.			
19.	Loading of the buses at school should be accomplished at established safety zones under proper supervision.			
20.	Buses should not be backed up on school grounds.			
21.	The cost of transportation should compare favorably with transportation costs in other similar school systems.			
22.	All state regulations and all laws enacted by the state legislature should be adhered to rigidly.			
23.	All bus routes should be approved by board action.			
24.	Continuous study should be given to bus routes to make sure that changes are made as needed so the routes will be laid out in the most efficient manner.			
25.	Each bus driver should possess a valid first aid certificate issued by the American Red Cross or United States Bureau of Mines.			
26.	Each bus driver should make daily written reports and weekly or monthly reports showing the condition of his bus and recommending any necessary repairs.			
27.	No bus driver should require any pupil to leave the bus as a disciplinary measure before the pupil has reached his destination.			
28.	No person should be permitted to serve as a bus driver for more than ten hours in any twenty-four hour period. Neither should the bus driver be permitted to do more than fifteen total hours of any kind of work in a twenty-four hour period when driving a bus with children.			

TABLE 16-1 (Continued)

Number	Item	Superior	Average	Poor
29.	Each school bus should be kept clean at all times and should be thoroughly cleaned after each day's use.			
30.	No use of tobacco, other narcotics, or stimulants in a school bus should be permitted when pupils are aboard.			
31.	No animals should be transported in a school bus.			
32.	The bus driver should turn on red blinking lights and escort school pupils across the street or highway when traffic controls are lacking.			
33.	No school bus stop along the highway should be approved unless a clear view of the bus, when stopped, is available from a distance of 400 feet in each direction.			
34.	The driver should bring the bus to a full stop at all railway crossings not closer than ten feet and not more than fifty feet from the nearest rail. He should not proceed until he has opened and closed the entrance door of the bus and has, by hearing and by sight, ascertained that the tracks are clear in both directions.			
35.	No bus stop should be approved that is closer than 200 feet from the nearest railroad grade crossing except at regular railroad stations or on highways which parallel the railroad.			
36.	In general, large and heavy transportation equipment should be used rather than small, light equipment. This practice is recommended in the interest of efficiency and economy.			
37.	Unless unusual traffic hazards exist, school systems should transport only those pupils for whom state aid reimbursement will be received. All pupils who qualify for state aid reimbursement should be transported.			
38.	Each school bus must be equipped with one or more fire extinguishers.			
39.	Each school bus must be equipped with a buzzer which will give audible warning when air brake pressure drops to less than sixty pounds per square inch.			

Total overall rating

OPERATIONAL PROCEDURES. Generally, students in kindergarten and grades one through three may ride school buses if they live more than three-fourths of a mile from school, and students in grades four through eight may ride the bus if they live more than one mile from school. Exceptions may be made where students would have to pass through busy intersections where no crossing-guard services are available or when other physical hazards are present. Such exceptions, however, should be noted in written policies governing the operation of the school transportation system, and should be delimited clearly.

Maintenance and servicing equipment should be handled by transportation section employees in school system shops. Supplies of gasoline, oil, and greases should be carried in inventory by the school system and should be subjected to careful accounting procedures. A spare bus should be available to fulfill special needs.

TRANSPORTATION PERSONNEL. Transportation personnel should be full-time employees who work on a school-year basis rather than on a calendar-year basis. Assignment of part-time drivers to other tasks during portions of the day is to be questioned. Nondriving work assignments as gardeners, custodians, or maintenance men bring doubtful returns. Part-time service in the bus garages is better.

The principal should help specify that the driver of each bus is held responsible for the safety and welfare of the students and for the care of school-system equipment. Lights, windshield wipers, horns, directional signals, brakes, glass, flashers, first aid equipment, and fire extinguishers should be inspected each day.

Drivers must maintain good discipline on buses. One principal recommended that mischievous students be warned three times. If a fourth warning was forthcoming, a report was made to the principal. If this procedure was not effective, the parents were called into the principal's office. Here the discipline problem was resolved, or, in extreme cases, the student was refused transportation privileges.

In all cases the principal should see to it that students are delivered to classes (1) on time, (2) safely, and (3) in a calm and relaxed mood that makes immediate learning possible.

How to Improve Food Services

Organizing Food Services

Responsibility for food services at the local school level should be delegated to the principal. He should receive technical help from the specialist in food services and cafeterias. All equipment and supplies should be owned by the school system.

How to Evaluate the Program of School Food Services

Food services should be evaluated regularly by the principal and the school system specialist. Table 16-2 is a checklist for use in the evaluation.[2]

Since food service operation is not run for profit but rather for the welfare of students, the highest quality of food at the lowest cost should be served. The principal must insure that:

1. Teachers are free from the time-consuming task of collecting lunch money;
2. Cash registers with totalizers replace money boxes;
3. Adults handle the collection in each cafeteria and deliver total receipts to a messenger who will take the money, in locked bags, to the bank for deposit;
4. The deposit slip is reconciled with cash totals at the bank;
5. A duplicate deposit slip is sent by the bank to the auditing section of the school-system office and to the cafeteria;
6. No money is counted in the school cafeteria.

If students are used as cafeteria assistants, they should pass a health clearance by school system health services, and they should be paid in cash for their services.

How to Supervise Attendance and Welfare Services

School-age children are subject to many kinds of physical defects, and they have many kinds and degrees of educational, psychological, and sociological

[2]Ibid., pp. 280–282.

TABLE 16-2 Appraisal of Food Services

Number	Item	Superior	Average	Poor
Organization				
1.	Every school should provide cafeteria service for pupils.			
2.	The school system should operate its own cafeteria rather than depend upon some private or public agency to handle the concession.			
3.	When three or more cafeterias are in operation the program should be headed by a properly trained and experienced classified employee, with the title of head of food services.			
4.	Cafeteria facilities should serve 50 per cent or more of the pupils enrolled.			
5.	The food service should be correlated with the health program of the school.			
6.	The school system should take advantage of federal food surplus commodities as a means of passing on the economy to pupils.			
7.	The food service program should be continued upon a nonprofit basis, but without serious loss to the school system.			
8.	Food service for pupils should be the primary aim of cafeterias, as opposed to service for community groups or even employed personnel.			
9.	The food service program of the school system should be operated upon a policy basis. All policies having been approved by the governing board and subject to review as conditions change.			
Personnel				
1.	From twelve to fourteen plate lunches should be served for each hour of employee labor.			
2.	All selections and terminations should be recommended by the superintendent and be approved by the governing board. These actions should appear in the board minutes.			
3.	The school system should make provision for an adequate in-service training program and an impartial appraisal of food service personnel performance.			
4.	Prior to service, all those who handle food should be given a general health examination by a school system physician and at school system expense.			
5.	Food service personnel should be provided with equitable benefits, including salary, leaves, vacations (per monthly employees), health insurance, and the like.			
6.	Pupil help, when used, should be shielded from the operation of machines with moving parts, or other types of danger. Pupil work in cafeterias should be a learning experience and should not interfere with study programs. Such work should be paid for at an hourly rate rather than the provision of "free" meals.			

TABLE 16-2 (Continued)

Number	Item	Superior	Average	Poor
7.	Cafeteria workers should wear appropriate white costumes.			
8.	Food service personnel should be given priority to earn overtime when the facilities are used by school-connected associations.			
9.	Food service personnel play an important role in the nourishment and well-being of pupils and faculty, and should receive appropriate recognition orally and in writing from the administration.			

Operation

Number	Item	Superior	Average	Poor
1.	All disbursal of funds and the payment of bills should be made by check through the business office.			
2.	Cash registers with tapes and totalizers should be used in the collection of money at cafeterias and candy counters.			
3.	All receipts should be subject to a double check and deposited in the local bank each day.			
4.	A financial report of food service operations should be submitted to the governing board at the close of each month, and at the close of each fiscal year.			
5.	Charge accounts are illegal in some states, and free meals should be provided by welfare agencies, and by parents' associations.			
6.	The cafeteria account should be audited at the close of each fiscal year.			
7.	Central purchasing and warehousing of staple food and supplies is recommended.			
8.	A standard replacement policy for equipment should be approved by the governing board.			
9.	Dishes, utensils, and equipment should be kept clean and hygienic by cafeteria workers. Floors, windows, and the like should be cleaned by custodians.			
10.	Periodic inspections by the county health department and other agencies should be welcomed.			
11.	Every effort should be made to decrease the length of lines and other delays at the cafeteria and the snack bars.			

Total overall rating

Quality of Food service _____

Economy _____

handicaps. These handicaps may interfere with a successful adjustment to their school environment and also to the community in which they live. Unfortunately, it is not uncommon to find instances where parents are unable to provide the minimum essentials required for healthful living.

Schools, however, cannot be all things to all people. I. R. Melbo et al, cautioned:

It must be remembered that the public schools are not a social agency for the indigent, although many offer some temporary aid to individual children. The obligation for furnishing medical or surgical services, clothing, food, or financial assistance to parents or children in a community is generally assigned to agencies other than the school, as for example, the Parent-Teacher Association, . . . [charitable associations], and other . . . child welfare agencies.

This does not mean that the public schools are completely relieved of any responsibility with respect to child welfare. School personnel, particularly teachers, . . . are in a very excellent position to observe . . . [students] during the school day and to identify health, nutritional, and other welfare needs. Thus, the primary responsibility for identifying . . . [students] with welfare needs, and for referral to appropriate community agencies, . . . generally [has] been assigned to the public school system. Many school districts have, in addition, assumed responsibility for setting up certain programs or activities designed to meet certain welfare needs of . . . [students], as for example, special programs for the physically or mentally handicapped.[3]

Attendance Supervision

The supervising principal should ascertain the degree to which absences are recorded and the accuracy with which verification of illness is made. He also must see that compulsory education laws are enforced and that attendance activities are coordinated with state and intermediate unit agencies. Additionally, he must be ever watchful for ways in which attendance-accounting can be facilitated.

SPECIAL ATTENDANCE-RECORDING. Many school systems throughout the nation are switching from the old style method of recording individual attendance in a register to central attendance-accounting. Five advantages advanced for the central attendance-accounting system are:

[3]Ibid., pp. 308–309.

1. Central attendance-accounting relieves the teacher of register-keeping and allows him this time for his educational pursuits.
2. Central attendance-accounting provides a more accurate record system. It is under the direct supervision of the principal and an attendance clerk.
3. Central attendance-accounting results in economies in pay hours (teachers' professional salaries contrasted with the pay of clerical personnel), and in the total amount of time spent in maintaining these records.
4. Central attendance-accounting provides for a ready reference.
5. Central attendance-accounting provides a more efficient filing procedure in a central location by eliminating the necessity for maintaining state register books.

Principals should check carefully the requirements of state law concerning central attendance-accounting systems. Sufficient clerical time must be provided in each of the schools to handle the routine matters involved in central attendance-accounting. Usually at least a one-quarter time clerk in each school is required. The coordination of problems of child welfare and attendance should be the function of the coordinator, whose office is located in the offices of the school system. The school supervising principal, however, must maintain responsibility for the supervision of child welfare and attendance services in the school to which he is assigned.

The Legal Status of Public School Attendance

C. R. Ahee[4] examined the status of the public school student and his parents with respect to school attendance. He concluded that:

1. The purpose of compulsory attendance laws is to uphold a philosophy of government rather than to accomplish an immediate need of society.
2. The courts have rendered decisions which have been upheld which state that it is a state obligation to provide for the education of all on equal terms, that is, to provide for equal educational opportunity for all children in the state.

[4]Carl R. Ahee, "The Legal Status of the California Public School Pupil and His Parent with Respect to Attendance" (Doctoral dissertation, University of Southern California, 1959).

3. Where rules and regulations adopted by a governing board of a school system are found to be oppressive or violative of any fundamental right of a student or his parents, they will be nullified by the court.
4. Statutes requiring compulsory school attendance within certain ages are constitutional if they include reasonable exemptions from otherwise absolute requirements of the state.

How to Improve Health Services

Generally, three areas are included in the total school health program: (1) health and safety instruction, (2) health services, and (3) the maintenance of a healthful school environment. Research has shown that one out of every three children of school age has defective hearing, three out of every ten have defective vision, one out of every four is suffering from malnutrition, and three out of every four have dental defects.

The Development of School Health Services

Unfortunately, school health services have developed in many communities without definite planning or definite consideration of the reasons for their existence.

A student's physical well being is a necessary factor when considering overall adjustment problems in our ever-changing society. As a student's health improves, so do other phases of his educational program.

A good school health program should be appraised according to the extent that it meets the following criteria:

1. Partial fulfillment of a student's educational goals should be accomplished. With proper diagnosis, teachers may become more familiar with students' health problems and will be in a better position to assist them in solving individual problems.
2. Through proper instruction, students should become better informed about their own physical characteristics and gain new attitudes toward the medical profession as a whole.
3. Proper diagnosis should be accomplished and disease prevention measures should be taken. Many students enter schools each year with un-

detected health problems, and perhaps with inadequate and often a complete absence of necessary immunization.

4. The school program should be adapted to students' needs. Through physical examination teachers are in a better position to place a student in the right activity and location according to his physical limitations.
5. School absences should be reduced to a minimum. Proper health services should provide for immediate detection of illness which, in turn, reduces the probability of long absences.

Points in Appraisal of the School Health Program

The school health program should provide for the following minimum services and organizational details:

1. Establishment of case study referral techniques.
2. Establishment of school-system policy statements concerning procedures to be followed in the emergency care of injuries and sudden illnesses of students.
3. Development of policies which detail the responsibilities of teachers with respect to the school health program.
4. Maintenance of a school health council which will coordinate the whole area of school health education. The membership in the council should include representatives from the administrative staff of the school system, the teachers, the custodial staff, parents, professional medical and dental personnel, and other community agencies concerned with the health and welfare of children. Officers of the council should be elected for a fixed period of time and the council should meet at regularly designated times with a prepared agenda. The accomplishments and recommendations of the council should receive adequate publicity.
5. Provision for adequate supply of health facilities and equipment.
6. Provision for facilities for handicapped students.
7. Planning for adequate communicable disease control, including immunization services.
8. Employment of medical consultants for examinations, within the delimitations noted above.

9. Scheduling dental inspections. (Although the services of a dental hygienist are desirable, they are not essential. The school nurse should serve as a consultant to teachers in the dental health education activities.)
10. Encouragement of the participation of students in health and safety clubs.

How to Improve Library Services

The need for good library services in a modern school is recognized by effective principals and specialist-consultants. Schools that have superior library services usually seem to have a superior educational program. In a sense, the nature and scope of library service may serve as a partial index to the character and quality of curriculum and instruction.

How to Supervise the Organization of Library Service

CENTRAL OR CLASSROOM LIBRARIES? In some circles there still is a controversy whether a centralized library or separate collections in each classroom is the better plan for elementary schools. In schools without a central library, practically every teacher gradually gathers a few books which form the nucleus of a classroom collection. Some school systems make a beginning in strengthening their library resources by providing each teacher with a small annual appropriation for purchasing new books for the classroom. No doubt such a plan has merit as a way to begin; such beginnings may develop into more adequate service.

Separate permanent classroom collections have several limitations when viewed from the standpoint of library needs in a modern school program. Where teachers oppose the establishment of a central library because they are reluctant to give up their room collections, some supervising principals have used the strategy of assuring teachers that they could keep their personal collections as long as they wished. The central library merely would provide additional materials which they could borrow to augment their room collections.

The present attitude of librarians and other educational leaders is that there is no point in continuing the controversy whether a central library or classroom libraries is the better plan for elementary schools. Both are essential parts of a comprehensive plan for library service in a school.

The temporary classroom collection should serve as a reservoir that feeds breadth of content into the instructional program in the classroom, provides recreational reading for students during spare moments, and equips the teacher with materials of different levels of difficulty to suit many and varied student interests.

The central library is the service agency that helps teachers to maintain classroom collections which may be adjusted continuously to the evolving instructional program. The central library and the temporary classroom collections operate as partners that provide comprehensive library services to the school.[5] The services are diagrammed in Figure 16–1.

ESSENTIALS OF THE CENTRAL SCHOOL LIBRARY AS A TEACHING AGENCY. One's approach to the organization of library service in a school primarily hinges upon whether one views the library as a direct teaching center or as a service agency.

Those who consider the library as a great teaching agency will assign the librarian responsibilities for:

1. Aiding the teacher in instruction in the use of books and libraries;
2. Developing in students strong motives for and permanent interests in reading;
3. Guiding individual students in the selection of reading materials;
4. Developing literature appreciation;
5. Promoting the habit of using reading as a wholesome way of engaging one's leisure time.

It is doubtful whether a librarian should assume sole responsibility for guiding students in the selection of reading materials unless it is done under the guidance of the student's classroom teacher.[6]

[5]R. T. Calhoun, "Why Not a Central Library in Elementary Schools?" *Illustrated Elementary English* XXXVIII (January 1961): 37–40.
[6]B. T. Williams, "Why an Elementary School Library?" *California Journal of Elementary Education* XXIX (August 1960): 19–23.

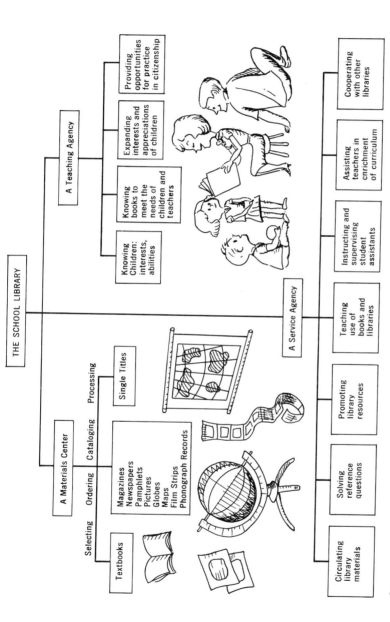

THE SCHOOL LIBRARY

A Materials Center

Selecting   Ordering   Cataloging   Processing

Textbooks

Single Titles

Magazines
Newspapers
Pamphlets
Pictures
Globes
Maps
Film Strips
Phonograph Records

A Teaching Agency

Knowing Children: interests, abilities

Knowing books to meet the needs of children and teachers

Expanding interests and appreciations of children

Providing opportunities for practice in citizenship

A Service Agency

Circulating library materials

Solving reference questions

Promoting library resources

Teaching use of books and libraries

Instructing and supervising student assistants

Assisting teachers in enrichment of curriculum

Cooperating with other libraries

a From Deparment of Education, *Hawaii School Libraries: A Manual for Organization and Service* (Revised edition; Honolulu: The Department, 1964).

FIGURE 16—1   The Function of the School Library. (From Department of Education, *Hawaii School Libraries: A Manual for Organization and Service*, Revised Edition, Honolulu: The Department, 1964.)

HOW TO EVALUATE THE EFFECTIVENESS OF THE SCHOOL LIBRARY AS A SERV-
ICE AGENCY. A centralized library which functions appropriately as a
service agency must meet certain requirements, such as concerns:

1. Room size and arrangement;
2. Equipment;
3. The basic collection of books, pamphlets, visual aids, and recordings;
4. Financial support;
5. The qualifications of the librarian.

The library must operate in accordance with procedures appropriate to a
service unit. The library also must relate itself wisely and fruitfully to local
system-wide supervision, and state and national groups and agencies.[7]

EVALUATING THE SUFFICIENCY OF LIBRARY EQUIPMENT. Every library needs
good equipment. The following list is a guide for principals and librarians:

	Quantity
Cabinet, card catalogue, 15 tray	1
Chairs, 14 inch	8
Chairs, 16 inch	30
Chairs, 18 inch	2
Desk, teacher's, and chair	1
Filing cabinet, 2 drawer	1
Globe	1
Stand for unabridged dictionary	1
Table, round	2
Table, work (seats 6)	5
Truck, book	1
Built-in equipment:	
Shelves, adjustable, 5 feet standard, and	
section partitioned for picture books	
Bulletin board	
New libraries in established schools	
may require movable bookcases	

[7]Calhoun, "Why Not a Central Library?" pp. 37–40.

Equipment in a library should be arranged so that it is both attractive and functional, and provides ease of supervision. It is helpful to:

1. Use all available wall space for shelving.
2. Arrange tables and chairs to allow at least five feet of aisle space for ease of movement and for the best possible light.
3. Place the charging desk near the entrance.
4. Arrange low tables and chairs near primary book shelves.
5. Place the card catalogue where it is easily accessible, but where it is away from regular traffic aisles.
6. Arrange for bulletin boards and display tables in prominent positions.

The following supplies are needed to open a school library:

1. Holder, label, sheet steel with flange: one per shelf (except bottom shelf). (If library is newly built, check plans to see if label holders are built in.)
2. Labels, shelf, plain, buff (100 to a package)—two packages;
   or
   Labels, shelf, forty printed titles, 5 x 3/4 inches, printed on buff card stock (forty to set)—one set.
3. Book card, ruled, 3 x 5 inches, white (500 to a package)—two packages.
4. Dater, small, Crown No. 0—two.
5. Pad, stamp, purple—two.
6. Cards, catalogue, blue, 3 x 5 inches (for shelf list).
7. Book ends—twenty-five pairs.
8. Tray, charging, wood—one.

The following supplies should be purchased for cataloguing, shelf listing, and processing books:

1. Book pockets, plain, folded and glued, 3 1/2 x 3 3/4 inches (250 to a package).
2. Cards, catalogue, medium weight, 7.5 x 12.5 centimeters, plain (white), punched, red edged (100 to a package).

3. Cards, catalogue, light weight, 7.5 x 12.5 centimeters, plain, salmon, punched (100 to a package), (for shelf list).
4. Ink, waterproof, black (3/4 ounce).
5. Ink, waterproof, white (3/4 ounce).
6. Paste, bookbinder's—one jar.
7. Book card, ruled, 3 x 5 inches, salmon.
8. Stamps, for library books, rubber, 5/16 inch, set of three, one each: star, dot, and triangle.

How to Supervise the Teaching of Library Use Techniques

All children need to learn to appreciate the content and value of books and how to handle and care for books. They also need to learn how to use the library to find most quickly the things they seek, and to develop independent habits and skills of study and research and the routines essential for keeping a library in good working order. There is considerable disagreement, however, even among librarians, as to how library instruction should be organized. Some insist that there should be a graded series of lessons taught by the librarian in accordance with a predetermined schedule. This plan has the advantage of guaranteeing that the lessons will be taught.

Dynamic stimulation arises out of needs developed in classroom instructional activities. It is for this reason that many librarians are beginning to advocate the "integration plan," whereby classroom teachers assume responsibility for instruction concerning library use.

FUNDAMENTAL BOOK AND LIBRARY SKILLS. Students at different levels need to know some fundamentals concerning the use of books and libraries. Mastery of these skills is a step toward independence.

Students need to know that:

1. Care of books is important.
2. Books are arranged in a library according to a system as an aid to the user of the library in finding the book he needs.
3. Nonfiction books are shelved numerically from left to right and section by section.

4. Fiction books are shelved alphabetically by the last name of the author from left to right and section by section.
5. Shelf labels are guides to books on those particular shelves.
6. The card catalogue is an index on cards of all books in the library. It records books according to author, title, and subject.
7. Various parts of a book have distinctive and important uses.

Students need to know how to:

1. Find books in a library through use of the card catalogue.
2. Use encyclopedias and dictionaries and understand what kind of information they contain.
3. Use special reference books.
4. Take notes.
5. Make and use bibliographies.

TEACHING THE CARE OF BOOKS TO ALL GRADES. The signs of normal wear on a book over a period of time are indications that a book has been read and enjoyed. This is expected, and efforts to preserve books should never prevent students from handling them themselves. However, it is of the greatest importance that children be taught how to handle books from the first moment they are exposed to them.

The following rules help students learn how to handle books:

1. Have clean hands before handling books.
2. Put away pencils, crayons, chalk, and ink before handling books.
3. Do not eat while reading a book.
4. Keep books out of the reach of very small children and pets in the home.
5. Use only paper book marks.
6. Open a *new* book properly so that the back will not break and it will lie flat when open:
   a) Place the spine of the new book on a clean flat surface.
   b) Hold the book with its spine on the table and press the front cover down until it touches the table.
   c) Hold the leaves of the book up right in one hand and press down the back cover.

    d) Open a few pages in the front and press down gently.

    e) Open a few pages in the back and press down gently.

    f) Repeat this process with a few pages near the front, then a few pages near the back, until all pages have been opened.

7. Open a *large* book by placing it flat on a clean table, front cover up. Open the cover carefully so that the book lies flat on the table. Open a *small* book by holding it securely in one hand and opening the cover carefully so that the weight of the book does not fall on the binding.

8. Turn the pages of a book by picking up each page with "dry" fingers at the *upper* right corner and turning it carefully. This practice prevents tearing inner edges.

9. Hold books *away* from the body to avoid rubbing and tearing the lower edges of the pages on clothing.

10. Avoid creasing or folding back of pages.

The library itself should come to be accepted as a source of enjoyment. Students will feel secure in knowing that a corner of the library is reserved for them and their books, and that "going to the library" means a new adventure with each visit.

One supervising principal suggested activities for primary, middle, and upper grades as shown in Table 16–3.

HOW THE PRINCIPAL SUPERVISES THE LIBRARY SERVICES. The principal must take the initiative in improving library services in his school.[8] Faculty cooperation must be encouraged so that the curricular needs of the entire school will be balanced appropriately in the orders placed for books.

Another area in which leadership will be expected from the supervising principal is the actual organization and operation of the library program within the school. The organization, and the schedule under which the library operates, will need to be determined in the light of sound principles of library service.

Since the library is a service agency, its prerogatives should be subordinated to those of the instructional program. There should be no occasion for

[8]See A. Farelli, "Library Is a Must," *Illustrated Instruction* LXIX (November 1959): 75–76.

Primary	Middle	Upper

Primary

1. Bring the kindergarten class to the library for visits. Explain the library's purpose as part of the school community.

2. Bring the class to the library for story hours. Point out the picture book section and read favorite books from the collection. Make the time spent in the library pleasurable.

3. Use library books to answer students' questions whenever possible.

4. Encourage students to look at picture books and ask them to share their favorites by showing and talking about them. The teacher may select picture books before the class visit and spread them about on tables before students arrive.

5. Call their attention to displays, bulletin boards, and the like. Display work of the class in the library at least once each semester. Tie it in with books, if possible.

6. Teach students the rules for the care of books.

7. Teach students that a library is a friendly place where people are quiet and courteous so that each student may enjoy his own book.

8. Appoint library assistants to straighten shelves and leave the room in order for the next class.

9. Show beginning readers in the primary grades where to find their books and allow small groups to browse. Increase their desire to read independently.

Middle

1. Repeat activities of the kindergarten and primary grades.

2. Show students where to find middle grade books.

3. Show them how to take a book from the shelf carefully without scraping the bottom of the book. Have them make cardboard markers with their names on them. When a book is removed from the shelf, the marker is inserted in the spot. When the book is returned to the shelf, the book is replaced in that spot.

4. Talk about different kinds of books and different kinds of stories.

5. Learn to make and use a simple bibliography.

6. Practice skills in using books:
   a) Finding the title;
   b) Finding the author;
   c) Finding and using the table of contents;
   d) Finding and using an index.

7. In the fourth grade the better readers will be using all of the library shelves and it will be necessary to teach them to locate books on these shelves. Take one section of shelves at a time and explain how the books are arranged:
   a) Explain "fiction" and "non-fiction" sections. Explain what each means.
   b) Emphasize that each book belongs on a particular shelf and in a particular place on the shelf.
   c) All books are "named" in some way, either by a number or a letter, before they are put on the shelves. This number or letter is like a house and street number. It places the book on the shelf and makes it possible for the book to be found quickly and easily.
   d) Nonfiction is numbered according to the Dewey Decimal Classification, which divides all knowledge into ten major divisions. A book is assigned a number which stands for the subject of the book. Books with the same subject will be shelved together.
   e) Fiction is shelved alphabetically by the first letter of the last name of the author. Books by the same author will be shelved together.
   f) Show how to use the card catalogue. Teach the use by actually locating a book by author, by title, and by subject. Emphasize the fact that a catalogue is an index to the library and is used much in the same way as the students use an index to a book. Choose a title of a book and show how it can be located by noting the alphabetical arrangement of the catalogue, using the guide letter on the catalogue tray, and choosing the correct tray; finding the title card, discussing the arrangement of books on the shelf, using the labels on the shelf, finding the correct shelf, and finding the book.

8. Have students keep simple records of the books they have read.

9. Discuss the Caldecott Medal books.

10. Have students give very short book reviews.

Upper

1. Review the activities of the earlier grades.

2. Supply material for practice in using the card catalogue and finding books in the library.

3. Introduce the Newbery Medal books.

4. Encourage students to give short book talks and have group book discussions.

5. Teach students to take notes on informational reading from reference materials.

6. Encourage students to make book lists on favorite subjects for others to use.

7. Promote wise book selection.

8. Promote correct use of reference materials.

9. Discuss authors and gather material on them from sources in the library.

teachers to say that they desire materials from the library, but the hours and "red tape" rules of the library are such that it is impossible to utilize the resources which are there.

HOW TO LOCATE RESOURCES FOR THE PROFESSIONAL LIBRARY. Most school systems have some kind of a school library containing professional materials. The supervisor should evaluate the present status of the professional library. Gaps may be filled from several sources:

1. The public library may provide valuable assistance.
2. Free and inexpensive pamphlets and other materials may be obtained.
3. The school system may subscribe to various professional periodicals.
4. Individuals in the profession may donate college texts.

It is well worth the effort to develop a collection of helpful books and professional periodicals at the school. Some publications will sell themselves to the teacher, *if* they are readily available. The supervisor may wish to promote other publications, especially in conjunction with individual problems.

The results of recent research should be interpreted to teachers, and professional journals which emphasize such findings should be included in the library. Resources which may prove valuable in filling the gaps in the professional library are summarized in Figure 16–2.

Evaluating Library Services

Usually the book collection is the first item to which most supervisors turn their attention in evaluating the school library. The American Library Association has made the following recommendation regarding the book collection for public school libraries:[9]

School Enrollment	Number of Titles	Number of Volumes
200 or less	1,700	2,000
500	3,500	5,000
1,000	5,000	7,000
3,000	7,000	12,000
5,000	8,000	15,000

[9]Mary Peacock Douglas (chairman), *School Libraries for Today and Tomorrow* (Chicago: American Library Association, 1945), chapter V.

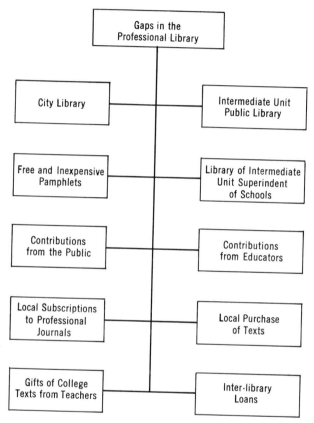

FIGURE 16–2   Resources for the Professional Library.

The figures cited above are more generous in number of titles for smaller schools than previously published minima found in bulletins of state departments of education. Figure 16–3 represents an evaluation form applicable to community college libraries. For small rural schools the latter quotas ran as low as 250 to 500 titles for one-teacher and two-teacher schools.

Theoretically, a small school should own or have access to as wide a range of titles as a large school. The range of individual student needs and the breadth of the curriculum do not depend upon size of school. Those who have recommended smaller book collections for small schools have done so as a practical adjustment to the more limited financial resources of

FIGURE 16–3   Appraising Library Services in the Community College

	Recommended	Actual
A. *The Book Collection*		
Basic Collection, Volumes	20,000	
Plus 36 Volumes per Staff FTE[a]		
Plus 4 Volumes per Student FTE		
Plus 120 Volumes per Subject Field of Study Beyond Standard Programs		
Total Book Collection		
B. *Periodicals*		
Basic Collection, Titles	300	
Total Periodical Collection	300	
C. *Staff*		
Technical Services	4	
Staff Ratio: 2 clerical to 1 professional (Recommend service by Brodart Books, Inc., which provides processing and cataloguing according to Library of Congress system)		
No technical service position provided		
Public Services		
None; present facilities inadequate		
Administrative Staff		
Total professional and secretarial positions: range from 1 in college of 1,500 to 2 in college of more than 7,500 (FTE)		
D. *Space*		
.10 assignable square feet per anticipated volume		
Reading Stations for 18 per cent of full-time enrollment, with 25 assignable square feet provided for each station		
A basic complement of 400 assignable square feet plus 140 assignable square feet per FTE staff member		
Total Space		
Additional Areas		No Formula

[a]Full-time equivalent

small schools. Although this is a noble recognition of reality, it is not the wisest approach to the problem.

Instead of being satisfied with the meager library resources which the local school system can afford, small schools should strive to affiliate themselves with larger library service units (such as the intermediate unit library) so that they may have access to as diversified a collection of books as the large school.

Variety of titles and total number of volumes are not the only criteria by which one judges the adequacy of library services. Recency of publication often is important for books in the content fields. A book collection which consists largely of out-of-date textbooks and volumes discarded by parents who cleaned closets or attics has little merit.

Paper-bound bulletins and pamphlets with accurate content usually can be obtained free or at little cost from the state and federal bureaus and departments, and sometimes from commercial firms. The library should provide a vertical file in which such materials can be preserved for repeated use. Teachers and the librarian should cooperate in a plan whereby the school can acquire a rich reservoir of pamphlets and bulletins over a period of a few years.

Adequate records, such as a shelf list and a card catalogue, are essential if the library is to serve the school adequately. An annual inventory should be made of the materials on hand. Books that are getting out-of-date or are worn beyond repair should be eliminated. Some items should be discarded, others repaired, while still others will need replacement. Replacement of worn-out titles becomes a part of the annual plan for new purchases.[10]

Most school libraries make inadequate use of the resources of other libraries. Frequently the teachers of a school never have set foot inside the door of the public library in the community, and librarians in the public library are equally unfamiliar with the activities of the school library. Often students make no contact with the public library during their entire school career.

Absence of an extensive cooperative relationship between the school library and the public library is inexcusable. A union or joint catalogue would

[10]M. V. Gaver, "Needed: More and Better Elementary School Libraries," *American Association of University Women* **LIII** (January 1960): 96–100.

facilitate greater use of the materials of both agencies. The time has come
when those responsible for the administration of public services no longer
can tolerate the loss of public funds such as is represented by lack of cooperative planning, financing, and utilization of a community's library resources.

HOW TO ORGANIZE THE PROFESSIONAL LIBRARY. Whether a school has a
professional library for teachers and how it is used depends largely on the
supervising principal. The recent interest in faculty participation in curriculum revision and other phases of school management and supervision indicates the necessity for each school system having *an adequate professional
library for teachers*. The local professional library frequently can be augmented by loan collections from the intermediate unit library, the state library, the state department of education, or the state university. Again, it is
the principal who must take the leadership in creating the faculty organization through which these materials are utilized in study and in meeting local
problems. Table 16–4 contains a summary evaluation of library services
supervision.

How to Supervise Recreation Programs

Wholesome recreation opportunities which are provided adequately and
attractively throughout the school year should assist in the development of
high standards of safety, health, and moral and mental development. These
activities also help to assure adequate social adjustment of future citizens:

Experience has shown that sound recreation programs have been a powerful
force in the prevention of juvenile delinquency. The adequacy of a recreation
program, whether it be school or community sponsored, will depend upon how
well it meets the following criteria:
1. The school or community should provide all . . . [students] with the opportunity to benefit from participation in recreation of a suitable type for each
   individual.
2. There should be an equitable allocation of time, staff, space and equipment
   between physical education classes and after-school recreation programs.
3. Leadership is an important factor and therefore a professionally trained
   person should be responsible for the planning and supervising of a coordinated program which attempts to meet the recreational needs of all . . .
   [students].

TABLE 16-4 Evaluation of Library Services: A Summary

A. The Library and Its Staff

1. The frequency of use of the library by students, classes, teachers, and other members of the professional staff should be determined.

2. Special subjects should be supervised by an assistant librarian who has special interest in the field.

3. There probably should be one librarian, two or three parent volunteer helpers, a clerk, and student assistants, depending upon the size of the school population.

4. Student assistants should be assigned different work from time to time so that each may gain from rich experience in the many library services. They should participate eagerly (this is a sign of a successful librarian).

5. The librarian should have a pleasing personality and should possess the ability to get along with others and to understand individual needs and interests. She should be able to deal effectively with both children and adults, and must know books, other library materials, and how to select, organize, and interpret the books and other materials present.

6. The school librarian must organize the materials for service, promote an effective and attractive reading program, serve in a teaching capacity, aid in curriculum development, and contribute to guidance services.

B. The Library Facilities

1. Books should be organized according to topics or departments. They should be selected carefully in order to satisfy various interests, and should be chosen according to subject and vocabulary level.[a]

2. It should be determined whether the card catalogue is used by the students. A chart should be present showing the Dewey Decimal System.

3. There should be an adequate reference section.

4. The library should present an inviting, home-like atmosphere. Pictures and other audio-visual materials, including museum specimens, should be provided. There should be an attractive bulletin board display. The general environment should be pleasing to the eye, restful, and conducive to relaxed, quiet reading. Students should check out their own books within delimitations.

5. Adequate ventilation should be provided.

6. There must be adequate lighting, with thirty to thirty-five candle-power being recommended.

7. The library should be located centrally on the ground floor, accessible to both primary and intermediate classes, and away from the noise of practical arts activities in classrooms and from the playground. The reading room should have a minimum of twenty-five to thirty square feet per reader, but in no case should it be less than 1,200 square feet.

8. Overall seating capacity should be large enough to seat the largest class expected, plus not less than ten additional students.

9. Adequate electrical outlets should be provided on all four walls.

10. Acoustical tile should be present on the ceiling, while floors should be of a rubber tile or other noise-deadening material.

11. The library should be painted a color which is light and attractive, such as light green.

12. Adequate furniture, including tables of both twenty-five inch and twenty-seven inch length, with a surface area of five by three feet, should be provided. Chairs should be both sixteen and fourteen inches in height. There should be easy chairs, table lamps, and attractive reading nooks.

13. There should be adequate working room for the library staff, and for the storage of library materials, supplies, and equipment. A ten by twelve foot clear working space for the library staff should be provided.

14. If a separate office or workroom is provided, adequate ventilation, lighting, electrical ventilation, lighting, electrical outlets, furniture, and equipment, including telephones, paper cutter, a typewriter with library keyboard, a portable standard chair, a bulletin board, files, rack case, a sink with hot and cold water, a coat locker, adjustable shelving, and cupboards must be present.[a]

[a]See School Library Association of California, *Recommended Standards*, Bulletin of the Association (Sacramento: The Association, March 1955. See also California Teachers Association, *Survey of Elementary School Library Practice*, Research Bulletin No. 91 (San Francisco: The Association, April 1956).

4. The recreation program should include a wide variety of activities, as well as seasonal sports . . . .
5. The usual type of . . . activity associated with . . . school children should be coordinated with the total recreation program of the community.[11]

Legal Aspects of the Recreation Program

Several laws in the various states give school systems the legal authority to participate in community recreation, either as the sole participating agency or as a cooperative of contributing agency. N. O. Tallman[12] studied opinions of the state attorney general, court cases, and responses to a checklist questionnaire concerning the nonschool use of public school buildings, grounds, and equipment. His findings indicated governing boards:

1. Generally seek to determine whether a proposed use of the school or its grounds for recreation purposes is consistent with or might interfere with the regular school use and program;
2. Generally require that the use satisfy public interest, and may make reasonable rules concerning such use;
3. May determine what constitutes recreational activities, charity, and the welfare of the students;
4. Can deny facilities if the meeting's purpose is immoral or for purposes of beliefs, values and goals of the school system and of our democracy.

Statutes authorizing the use of school property for nonschool recreational purposes generally have been upheld by the courts in all states, and there is a trend toward the wider use of school facilities for collateral purposes in the absence of specific statutes. Tallman concluded that public school facilities may not be used for religious or sectarian purposes of any kind, and that the larger school systems have better and more clearly defined policies concerning recreation programs in general and the nonschool use of school facilities for recreation programs in particular.

POLICIES ARE NEEDED. Clear, concise, liberal policies must be adopted by the governing boards regarding the operation of the recreation program.

[11]Melbo, "Report of the Survey," pp. 311–312.
[12]Norman O. Tallman, "The Nonschool Use of Public School Buildings, Grounds, and Equipment" (Doctoral dissertation, University of Southern California, 1951).

These policies should include statements regarding:

1. Application
2. Law
3. Acceptable use and prohibitive use
4. Supervision and proper use
5. Delimitations as to hours and days
6. Delimitations concerning smoking and the use of alcohol
7. Responsibility for loss or damage
8. The right of the governing board to revoke permission to use the facilities of the school at any time.

Certainly the meaning of the word "recreation" must be clarified. At present the participation of the public school systems in community recreation is highly diversified. The various recreation activities, and the planning necessary in their implementation, should be so integrated and coordinated as to assure adequate coverage and to avoid duplication of efforts.

DO

1. Work toward adequate staffing which will permit a central attendance-accounting system.
2. Emphasize the importance of the health services program.
3. Make a special effort to encourage parents to devote more attention to child health and to acquaint them with health problems of which they may be unaware.
4. Encourage parents to utilize the services of a family physician, the dentist, and other local community health agencies since school health services can be supplemental only.
5. Work toward school-system owned transportation services.
6. As supervising principal, evaluate the transportation services from the school level vantage point.
7. Work toward a library with an adequate collection, adequate shelving, periodical rooms, reading or study areas, a reference room, and a reserve section.
8. Work toward a coordinated complex which includes and integrates the library and the instructional center (which subsumes audio-visual in-

structional technology), each supervised by a professional specialist, so that the many facets of a subject may be explored and researched meaningfully.

9. Work toward an adequate staff for the library.
10. Work toward adequate clerical assistance for the professional library staff, and for the instructional center coordinator.
11. Familiarize the librarian with systems such as have been developing by book processing companies such as Brodart, Incorporated, which would facilitate circulation, order, and information retrieval services.
12. Work toward a more realistic money handling system in the school cafeteria.
13. As supervising principal, retain the ultimate responsibility for the supervision of the food services program *within the school.*

DON'T

1. Permit too many organizations to become involved in setting up recreation programs.
2. Permit recreation programs to fall into the pattern of being delimited primarily to availability during the summer vacation period. There should be an organized year-round recreation program for school students which should be located at various school grounds or buildings.
3. Fail to play a dominant role in establishing and coordinating the recreation program.
4. Be satisfied with inadequate library cataloguing systems.
5. Fail to encourage teachers to send individual small groups and to take entire classes to the library as well as to the instructional center.
6. Fail to establish a schedule for the supervision of the several auxiliary services.

Supervisory Problem   In Basket

Ruben Junior High School has an enrollment of 600 students. Traditionally, English classes are scheduled by the English department head to visit the library one day per week. The school system does not have local library consultant-specialists, but the state library supervisor is available periodically.

Sources of the problem include:

1. An approach to education that provides little stimulation or time for student use of the library.
2. A study hall concept of the library which discourages the development of an affection for reading, and turns the library into a forbidding den.
3. A physical setting for the library that is not only isolated from the main stream of student traffic, but also inadequate in size and ventilation.

   How will you, as supervising principal, provide leadership that will result in the teachers' wanting a flexible library in their school?

   How could you, as supervising principal, improve the quality of library services in the school?

   Through what steps would you proceed in accomplishing this improvement?

Selected Bibliography

Books

Arbuthnot, May H. *Children and Books*. Glencoe, Illinois: Scott, Foresman, 1947.

Brown, Frank B. *Education by Appointment—New Approaches in Independent Study*. West Nyack, New York: Parker Publishing Company, 1968.

Chase, Mary E. *Recipe for a Magic Childhood*. New York: The Macmillan Company, 1952.

Duff, Annis. "Bequest of Wings." *A Family's Pleasure with Books*. New York: The Viking Press, 1944.

_____. "Longer Flight." *A Family Grows Up with Books*. New York: The Viking Press, 1955.

Ellsworth, Ralph E. et al. *The School Library Facilities for Independent Study in the Secondary Schools*. New York: Educational Facilities Laboratories, Inc., 1966.

Mahoney, Bertha (compiler). *Illustrators of Children's Books, 1744–1945*. Boston: Horn Book, Inc., 1947.

Periodicals

Brewer, M. L. "Elementary Library." *School and Community* XLVI (January 1960): 22–23.

Calhoun, R. T. "Why Not a Central Library in Elementary Schools?" *Illustrated Elementary English* XXXVIII (January 1961): 37–40.

Dobson, M. "Elementary School Library—An Essential." *Teachers College Journal* XXXII (January 1961): 92–93.

Farelli, A. "Library Is a Must." *Illustrated Instruction* LXIX (November 1959): 75–76.

Foy, R. N. "Any School Can Have a Library." *Illustrated Instruction* LXIX (November 1959): 73–74.

Gaver, M. V. "Needed: More and Better Elementary School Libraries." *American Association of University Women* LIII (January 1960): 96–100.

McMahan, Marie. "Educational Media Center—the Library's New Look." *American Annals of the Deaf* CXII (November 1967): 46–47.

_____. "Problems in School Library Supervision." *American Library Association Bulletin* LXII (February 1968): 14–19.

Silver, E. F. "School Library for Every Child." *Elementary English* XXXVII (March 1960): 164–166.

Williams, B. T. "Why an Elementary School Library?" *California Journal of Elementary Education* XXIX (August 1960): 19–23.

Other Sources

Ahee, Carl R. "The Legal Status of the California Public School Pupil and His Parent with Respect to Attendance." Doctoral dissertation, University of Southern California, 1959.

Alexander, Elenora. *School Library Supervision.* Los Angeles: Immaculate Heart College, 1958.

————. *Standards for School Library Programs.* Washington, D.C.: American Library Association, 1969.

Association for Childhood Education. *Adventuring in Literature with Children.* Washington, D.C.: The Association, 1953.

California Teachers Association. *Survey of Elementary School Library Practice.* Research Bulletin No. 91. San Francisco: The Association, April 1956.

Department of Education. *Hawaii School Libraries: A Manual for Organization and Service.* Rev. ed. Honolulu: The Department, 1964.

Douglas, Mary Peacock (chairman). *School Libraries for Today and Tomorrow.* Chicago: American Library Association, 1945.

Melbo, Irving R. et al. "Report of the Survey, Taft City School District." Duplicated material copyrighted by the author. Los Angeles: July 1960.

National Education Association and the American Medical Association. *School Health Services.* Washington, D.C.: National Education Association, 1953.

School Library Association of California. *Recommended Standards.* Bulletin of the Association. Sacramento: The Association, March 1955.

Tallman, Norman O. "The Nonschool Use of Public School Buildings, Grounds, and Equipment." Doctoral dissertation, University of Southern California, 1951.

West's California Education Code. St. Paul, Minnesota: West Publishing Company, 1969.

17

How to Provide Better Physical Facilities

The school plant constitutes a major factor in instruction and in satisfying the educational and social needs of the members of the community. The specific purpose of the school plant is to develop the best architectural expression of the curricular needs and the educational ideals of all the people. The plant should not only perform its physical purpose efficiently, but also serve as a visible symbol of learning and of culture. Consideration should be given to architectural design, physical setting, landscaping, and good housekeeping.

This chapter includes a discussion of the following topics:

Principles of physical facility improvement
How to supervise school plant improvement
How to secure optimum utilization of space and content
How to plan for adequate instructional facilities
How to improve classroom design
What the supervisor should consider in a physical facilities improvement program
Do—don't
"In-Basket" supervisory problems

Principles of Physical Facility Improvement

How to Determine Responsibilities

BOARD RESPONSIBILITY. The governing board, operating as a policy-making and appraising body, officially confirms the educational needs, standards, and plans as presented by the superintendent. The board makes provisions for financing the school plan program according to law.

FIGURE 17-1   Sample Monthly Plant Inspection Form

School _____ Date _____

Area	G	F	P	Comments	Date Corrected
Classroom					
Office					
Library					
Cafeteria					
Kitchen					
Custodian: Supply Rm.					
Closet					
Entrances					
Stairways					
Walks					
Grounds					
Fencing					
Playgrounds					
Lavatories					
Drinking Fountains					
Fire Extg.					

Other _____

Principal _____

Custodian _____

SUPERINTENDENT'S RESPONSIBILITY. Control of the school plants is the superintendent's responsibility. He determines the need for and location of new buildings, and the size and location of sites. He must translate the curricular and social needs of students and the community into the number, size, type, and location of rooms. He develops standards for equipment, material, and construction.

RESPONSIBILITIES OF THE PRINCIPAL AS SUPERVISOR OF PLANT OPERATION. The principal of a school, in the role of supervisor of plant operation, has the responsibility for being aware at all times of the internal and external condition of the school plant. He should delegate to the custodian the responsibility for completing a monthly inspection form, such as appears in Figure 17–1. Additionally, he must be aware of the classroom needs of individual teachers so that they may function more effectively in their roles as directors of classroom instruction. A diagrammatic representation of the organization of school plant operations and maintenance is included as Figure 17–2.

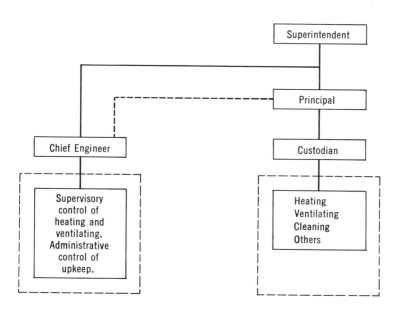

FIGURE 17–2 Organization of School Plant Operation and Maintenance in a Medium-Sized City School System.

The principal is responsible for the successful operation of the school plant, just as he is concerned with the continuous improvement of educational services. He continuously should study the needs of the school, teachers, students, and parent groups, and should use physical facilities to meet these needs.

Generally speaking, the supervising principal strives to provide for the continuous improvement of space and facilities. This improvement is necessary if the essential elements of high quality education are to be realized, as may be seen in Table 17–1.

OPERATION AND SPECIAL PERSONNEL. All operating personnel should be under the administrative control of the principal and responsible to him for all standards of cleanliness and comfort.

Special personnel include the consultants in educational planning who usually perform required surveys and educational designing, the architects and engineers who prepare technical drawings and specifications according to approved standards, and the contractors who construct the buildings. Their work should be inspected and approved by the superintendent and trained specialists.

Basic Principles concerning Physical Facility Improvement

The following may be considered as a listing of basic principles:

1. The physical environment for teaching should be considered as including the school site, its location and buildings, the classrooms, multipurpose rooms, administration rooms, health and food facilities, mechanical facilities such as lighting, heating, ventilating, plumbing, and sanitary equipment.
2. The school plant should be designed, operated, and maintained so that it will contribute to the education, health, safety, and happiness of the students, and to the development of higher aesthetic, cultural, and civic ideals in the students and adults of the community.
3. The plant should be capable of being modified as the educational program changes.

TABLE 17–1[a] Adequate Facilities Reflect Instructional Needs

OUR BASIC FOUNDATIONS	help us determine	ESSENTIAL ELEMENTS OF HIGH QUALITY EDUCATION	which require	ADEQUATE SPACE AND FACILITIES
American Democratic Values Faith in the use of reason and intelligence for solving problems Respect for the dignity, worth, and potential of every human personality Willingness to face the responsibilities which go with freedom Faith in living and working together for the common good		*Clear Goals to Give Direction* Intellectual development to fulfill the highest potential of individuals: facts, skills, understandings, problem-solving ability, and creative capacity Democratic citizenship and public morality—loyalty to nation and mankind Physical and social development to strengthen intellectual growth and contribution to citizenship		*Adequate Space for Activities and Groupings* Basic rooms for individual study and research, small group and whole group activities Specialized rooms for specialized activities and for combining basic groups Work areas for listening, recording, viewing, construction projects, library work—in basic or special rooms, or both
Demands of Living Scientific and technological advances that create profound changes in way of life Basic physical and psychological needs of human beings that remain constant		*Practices Designed to Achieve Goals* Optimum challenge provided so each individual can develop at his own best rate A meaningful world created for the child by relating school and out-of-school experiences and by providing a base of operations in school The child's school day planned with balance between the child and his parents and time spent with specialists Individual study, small and large group experience, use of community resources, and full use of all media provided by the learning environment Learning carried on as an active process, with pupils participating in planning and evaluating the experiences which affect their growth The school environment created to be attractive and stimulating—healthful and safe—for both children and adults		*Adequate Materials and Equipment* Books, magazines, newspapers, films, filmstrips and slides, pictures, maps, globes, and construction materials—to name a few Chalkboards, bulletin boards, easels, sinks, laboratory equipment for subject fields, radio, TV, projection equipment, tape recorders, and record players
Essentials of Growth and Development Maturation and accompanying needs Individual differences Emotional needs for achievement, belonging, varied experiences Needs for social and spiritual values				*Characteristics of Building(s) as a Whole* Facilities for social learnings to nurture personal development, pride in school Instructional center, including science, A-V, and construction materials, plus the normal library materials Offices and equipment for guidance, health services, and administration Conference and work stations for individual teachers and for small groups Space for staff relaxation A functional architectural design which provides beauty, health, and safety School grounds which contribute to both function and beauty
Essentials of the Learning Process Full use of all senses required Motivation through having interests and goals Balance of firsthand and vicarious experiences		*Evaluation of the school program* Cooperative problem-solving activities based on an analysis of needs and objectives.		

[a]La Franchi, Edward H., "Schoolhouse Program and Plans." Los Angeles: 1958. (Duplicated material copyrighted by the author.)

4. The plant's design should be developed from the cooperative planning of professional employees, civic leaders, parents, and the intermediate unit and state departments of schoolhouse planning.
5. The service facilities of a school plan—heating, ventilating, lighting, sanitary equipment, and acoustical apparatus—should be designed and operated to create a stimulating environment in which maximum learning can take place.
6. Aesthetic planning should take into account the geographical and architectural components of the area.
7. The ultimate in safety, comfort, and adaptability is fundamental and basic to an efficient educational plant.
8. School plant operation, management, and maintenance are matters of concern to the supervisor when they are viewed as a part of the learning environment.
9. All playground space and equipment should be determined on the basis of their value to the educational, recreational, and citizenship training program. Physical facilities should fit the needs, age, and development of students.
10. The design of the physical environment should reflect the instructional program, including all that happens in and about the school aimed at helping students to meet and to solve problems intelligently, to understand personal strengths and weaknesses, to discover and cultivate interests and abilities, to understand the physical and social environment, to recognize dependence on others, and to grow in an understanding of democracy.[1]

How to Evaluate

For the purpose of evaluating the school plant, the supervising principal should ask himself the following questions:

1. Is the physical setting in harmony with the objectives of the program?
2. How do the students respond to it?

[1]National Council on Schoolhouse Construction, *Elementary-School Plant Planning* (Nashville, Tennessee: George Peabody College for Teachers, 1958), p. 2.

3. Does it encourage flexibility and stimulate interest?
4. Do conditions facilitate rather than hinder the educational use of the school plant?

A good physical setting:

1. Provides safe, sound sanitary conditions;
2. Encourages learning about people and their activities through flexible class space and equipment suitable for individual and group work;
3. Is a background for an activity and accentuates or complements what goes on (the perfect room or building is one which is apparent only to the extent that it facilitates the conduct of a desired activity or process);
4. Gains the confidence of the students through its size and style;
5. Uses scale, texture, color, and shape to bolster the student's desire to enter and use school facilities.[2]

The physical environment sets the stage for social, emotional, and intellectual growth and constitutes an important base upon which is built an effective school program. Only recently has the psychological impact of the environment upon the student been given any real consideration in public education in the United States. There are many situations where the physical environment is a decisive factor in a student's behavior. Most of all, a student should perceive of space in ways that make him feel happy, at ease, or, at times, stimulated.[3]

In a school plant beauty makes itself felt in many ways:

1. The student feels happier, learns more quickly, and has a feeling of pride in his school;
2. The teacher has more stamina, and is more patient and more relaxed;
3. The need for discipline is lessened, and vandalism may be negligible;
4. Custodial and maintenance costs diminish.

[2]National Association of Elementary School Principals, "Basis for Effective Learning," *The National Elementary Principal,* Thirty-First Yearbook (Washington, D.C.: The Association, 1952), p. 253.
[3]National Association of Elementary School Principals, "Elementary School Building —Design for Living," *The National Elementary Principal,* Thirty-Eighth Yearbook (Washington, D.C.: The Association, 1959), p. 14.

The modern school helps the instructional process by providing a clean, functional, simple, light, colorful, and properly air-conditioned environment in which students work with attractive, functional materials. Appreciation of beauty develops from living in and with it. The building and its furnishings encourage and help students, and people in the community are encouraged through their young people. Students, as a result of school activity, take a more aesthetic approach to living. Schools cease to be "institutions" and become centers of learning.[4]

How to Supervise School Plant Improvement

When a supervising principal is assigned to a school he has little choice but to accept the facilities given him and to do all he can to adapt, alter, and supplement them for the welfare of the teachers and the students. The principal must combine his talents with those of teachers, other school officials, parents, architects, educational theorists, psychologists, sociologists, and many others if he is to give all students the best possible educational experiences.[5]

In each school in which facilities are inadequate the principal and others are faced with the decision whether existing facilities can be adapted to current needs or whether extensive alterations and structural changes will be required.

One of the first prerequisites to an improved school plant is a clear-cut statement of the community's beliefs regarding public education. It is proper that the professional educator should lead the community in the formulation of educational aims and objectives. It is the function of supervision to provide leadership for the professional staff in the undertaking. It is the responsibility of the superintendent and the supervising principal,

[4]James D. MacConnell, *Planning for School Buildings* (Englewood Cliffs, New Jersey: Prentice-Hall, Inc., 1957), p. 4.
[5]Marion Jordan and David Jackson, "The Schools We Already Have," *The National Elementary Principal,* Thirty-Eighth Yearbook (Washington, D.C.: The Association, 1959), p. 172.

as a team, to take the lead in the formulation of a community's educational philosophy.[6]

How to Evaluate Existing Facilities

In evaluating existing facilities the following questions should be answered:

1. Which buildings are inadequate for the program?
2. Which buildings can be adapted for limited use?
3. What improvements are necessary to make buildings functional?
4. What major alterations, expansions, and rehabilitation should be made?
5. What land should be acquired for site expansion?[7]

A school plant survey must be made in order (1) to know the available space, (2) to plan the utilization, (3) to determine the substandard features, (4) to estimate costs, and (5) to plan an orderly adjustment within the master plan. A survey should be conducted using the competencies of an educator, an engineer, and an architect. An inspection record is desirable so that the adequacies and inadequacies of the plant may readily be evaluated by others. The instruments consist of simplified plan sketches, a school-plant survey score form, and checklists. The school site is evaluated, usually, separately from the improvements.[8]

The supervising principal should consider as criteria points such as those included in the checklist identified as Figure 17–3.

The survey data are used to reach decisions concerning: (1) the existing plant, (2) its long-range need and usefulness, (3) its contributions to the educational program, (4) its convertibility, and (5) any proposals for additions, alterations, or modernization. The final evaluation of existing

[6]American Association of School Administrators, *American School Buildings,* Twenty-Seventh Yearbook (Washington, D.C.: The Association, 1949), p. 525; see also Helen Heffernan and Charles Bursch, *Curriculum and the Elementary School Plant* (Washington, D.C.: National Education Association, 1958), p. 71.
[7]MacConnell, *Planning for School Buildings,* p. 42.
[8]Wallace H. Strevell and Arvid J. Burke, *Administration of the School Building Program* (New York: McGraw-Hill Book Company, Inc., 1959), p. 146.

FIGURE 17–3   Physical Facilities Checklist

The Site

1. Are the grounds adequate for conducting a proper physical education program? _____
2. Is additional play area available? _____   Where? _____
3. Are there provisions for adequate on-site parking? _____
4. Are service drives properly located for student safety? _____
5. What is the general condition of the grounds? _____

Educational Requirements

1. Are the existing facilities adequate for conducting a proper school program? _____
2. Can adequate provisions be made by remodeling or additions? _____
3. After remodeling, what normal student capacity could be housed? _____
4. Can existing special subject areas be increased in size without extensive structural changes? _____ Mechanical changes? _____

Existing Construction

1. Are there any signs of deterioration or failure of footings, foundations, or piers? _____
2. Are structural steel members adequate? _____ Are there signs of rusting in crawl spaces? _____   In attic spaces? _____
3. Are wood floor joists adequate? _____   Are there any signs of dry rot or termite damage? _____
4. Has there been any cutting and altering of floor joists or have additional loads been imposed? _____   Has there been any damage by water?
   _____
5. What is the condition of the exterior masonry? _____
6. What is the condition of interior walls and partitions? _____
7. What is the condition of roof and roofing surfaces, roof drains, and skylights? _____
8. What is the condition of flashings, gutters, downspouts? _____
9. What is the condition of doors and windows, wood door frames, ornamental trim? _____
10. What is the condition of hardware—door closers, panic bolts? _____

FIGURE 17–3   (Continued)

Mechanical and Electrical Facilities

1. What are location, number, type, and condition of plumbing fixtures? _____

2. What are condition and capacity of water supply and drainage piping? _____

3. Has extensive pipe replacement taken place recently (indicating possible complete replacement of system in event of alterations)? _____

4. Is present heating system adequate to provide economy of operation and room comfort? _____

5. Is the ventilation system adequate to provide proper air exchange in winter? _____ In summer? _____

6. Are vertical vent flues adequately protected against fire? _____

7. Does the ventilation system have proper controls? _____

8. Is the ventilation system in special areas—auditorium, gymnasium, shops, kitchen, and cafeteria—adequate and fire safe? _____

9. What is the condition and capacity of light and power distribution wiring? _____

10. Does wiring meet present-day standards? _____

11. Is wiring in older portions fire safe? _____

12. Do fixtures provide adequate foot-candle illumination in all areas? _____

Fire Safety

1. Are stair halls and exits adequate and properly located? _____

2. Do corridors and stair halls provide safe egress from the building for students? _____ For the public? _____

3. Are exits from auditorium and balcony adequate and properly located? _____

4. Are there any areas not adequately served by corridors or fire exits? _____

5. Is location of boiler room, kitchen, auditorium, and balcony a problem with respect to fire safety? _____

6. Is sprinkler system maintained in operating condition at all times? _____

7. What is present state of fire alarm, intercommunication systems? _____

8. Within the rooms, is at least twenty-two inches allowed between desks and thirty-six inches for exit aisles? _____

school facilities should reveal how adequate the plant is in terms of the phases of the community's approved educational program.

After the decision for modernization of an existing plant has been reached, it should be administered in an orderly manner:

1. Priorities must be assigned to each of the modernization needs;
2. The administrator must recommend a program of requirements (usually he is the person responsible for the business arrangements to get the work completed);
3. Financial arrangements should be handled by the chief business administrator of the school system.[9]

The variety of circumstances under which modernization is conducted depends on the part that such projects have in the long-range master plan.

How the Supervising Principal Manages Planning Within the School

The adequate involvement of the professional staff is the responsibility of the principal. He should insure that:

1. Teachers participate in planning.
2. Each employee makes a worthwhile contribution.
3. Credit is given where credit is due.
4. Teamwork is developed.
5. Primary emphasis is placed upon the educational program.
6. People are put at ease.
7. Community goals are defined.
8. Responsibilities of teachers and administrative staff members for school planning are clarified.
9. Effective use is made of the specialist.
10. Students are involved where possible.

[9]For the role of the school system employee who is in charge of the supervision of school planning and construction, see Robert E. Welling, "The Role of the District Employee in Charge of School Planning and Construction" (Doctoral dissertation, University of Southern California, 1960).

11. The custodial and maintenance staffs are involved.

Early appointment should be made of the principal-elect, especially if the school is new. This practice constitutes a wise investment of school funds.

Nothing is more demoralizing to good planning and more devastating to good architecture than to have one creative approach after another ruled out by a custodian or a maintenance man on the basis of its seeming to be difficult to maintain or hard to operate. Their contributions should come in the form of suggestions rather than vetoes of new ideas and insistence on the perpetuation of existing features of buildings merely because they are familiar.[10]

How to Predict Enrollment

The following sources of evidence concerning future enrollment factors should be considered by the supervising principal:

1. *Trend studies and comparisons*[11]
   a) Population
   b) School
   c) Residential housing
   d) Economic factors
2. *Sociological factors*
   a) Opportunities and facilities for students
   b) Recreational facilities
   c) Local traditions and community history
   d) Trade and cultural service centers
   e) Religious composition
   f) Community services
3. *Area maps*

[10]National Council on Schoolhouse Construction, *Elementary-School Plant Planning*, p. 103.
[11]New York Commission on School Buildings, *Classrooms for How Many?* (Albany: The Commission, 1952).

4. *Local sources of information*
   a) Municipal offices
   b) Real estate agencies and utility companies
   c) Tax assessor's office, county planning boards, local building inspec-
      tors, county and municipal engineers
   d) Metropolitan newspapers
5. *State sources of information*
   a) State health department, office of vital statistics
   b) State department of commerce
   c) State department of education
   d) State public works department
6. *National sources of information*
   a) United States Department of Health, Education, and Welfare, Public
      Health Service, National Office of Vital Statistics, Washington, D.C.
   b) United States Department of Commerce, Bureau of the Census,
      Washington, D.C.
   c) United States Department of the Interior, Coast and Geodetic
      Survey, Washington, D.C.
   d) United States Department of Health, Education, and Welfare, Office
      of Education, Washington, D.C.

Numerous studies have revealed that approximately 80 percent of all new urban dwelling units initially are occupied by couples during their first five years of marriage. It is important for the supervising principal to realize that the initial impact of new housing developments is not the maximum impact. Most of the children will be of preschool age, and thus the maximum student yield may be expected in five to ten years after the completion of the housing development.

After the first cycle, which lasts about fifteen years and is characterized by high birth rates with maximum impact at the elementary school level, the development will enter the second cycle. This phase, lasting about fifteen years, is characterized by relatively low birth rates, and the maximum impact on schools is at the secondary level. Toward the end of the second phase, high-school enrollments also tend to decline.

Phase three is characterized by sociological and economic changes. Older families tend to migrate out of the community and are replaced by persons of a somewhat lower cultural-economic level. These new families tend to be younger, and the number of children begins to rise.

The fourth and last cycle is characterized by a deterioration of the property and the emergence of blighted areas and slums. School enrollments tend to mushroom in a short period of time.[12]

How to Secure Optimum Utilization of Space and Content

Essential Functions

The job of the school building has changed and is changing. The school plant has several special functions:

1. It should provide facilities needed by the entire community.
2. It should provide facilities particularly planned and designed for the full-time use of a particular segment of the community.
3. It should provide facilities for the types and kinds of activities for the instructional program which will occur.

The community service concept of the schools has made them available not just for learning but for recreation as well. School buildings no longer stand idle after three o'clock. More and more they are called upon to supply the needs of an adult population with greater leisure time and the desire for group recreation and part-time education. The neighborhood school can become the service center for many important community activities. Rooms can be provided for meetings, cooking, and conferences. Ample parking space and uncrowded waiting spare are needed.[13]

Since economy is an important consideration in improving the school plant, many systems call upon financial, legal, and other specialists for

[12]Metropolitan School Study Council, School Buildings Committee, *Forecasting School Enrollments* (New York: The Council, 1953).
[13]*The Cost of a Schoolhouse* (New York: Educational Facilities Laboratories, 1960), p. 29.

advice. Published school surveys have demonstrated that efficient, prudent scheduling of building space is a major source of economy.

Supervision in the modern school demands a tremendous amount of time and energy as well as versatility, imagination, and ingenuity. Careful planning to reduce effort and increase efficiency in terms of time and motion will free the supervising principal's time for utilization in essential functions.

Traffic and Accessibility

Internal student traffic can become a disturbingly serious problem unless proper planning has gone into the use of the plant. Accessibility of the playground, cafeteria, offices, and other plant units should receive major consideration. The location of the administrative unit should be convenient to teachers, parents, and students.

The Administrative Unit

The administrative unit should be planned functionally in terms of the persons who use it and the services it renders.[14] The principal's office should be located near the reception room and the secretary's work area. It should be accessible to the public, yet should have a quiet atmosphere that is conducive to concentration.

The office should be designed to permit private conferences without interfering with or being disturbed by activities in other parts of the administrative suite. Adjustable shelves should be provided for books, periodicals, and curriculum materials. The secretary's work area should be large enough to permit the efficient performance of her many duties.

The Health Suite

The clinic or health room should be adjacent to the secretary's work area so that she, in the absence of the school nurse, can be responsible for its

[14]Some of the data presented by Harold C. Tomini, "Space Requirements of the High School Administrative Unit" (Doctoral dissertation, University of Southern California, 1959) may prove helpful in supervising the improvement of the school administrative unit.

use. Two small beds, a desk, a filing cabinet, and shelves usually are ample for the room. Both open and closed shelves are desirable. First aid supplies should be readily available for emergency use. The health suite should contain facilities for dental and medical examinations, first aid, resting, dressing, reception, and conferences. Its completeness and location are determined by school policy.

Guidance Facilities

Schools increasingly are giving attention to the provision of guidance facilities. Many of the emotional problems of students can be lessened by providing warm, attractive counseling areas. Office space, files, testing rooms, observation rooms, and consultation rooms are needed.

Library Design Requirements

A library is a necessary part of the school program. It may be located in a specifically designed room or it may be placed in a multipurpose room. Through cooperative efforts parents and members of the school staff can provide library facilities in any well-lighted and properly ventilated room. A large but little used corridor also could serve as a library. If a library can be obtained by remodeling a school, it should be centrally located and should occupy an area at least equal to a classroom and a half. In elementary schools, space and equipment for students in the primary grades should be included, along with space for work, references, periodicals, and exhibits.

Assembly and Multipurpose Rooms

Each school should have suitable facilities for student assemblies and for adult groups. Some schools have complete auditoriums with slanted floors, fixed seats, a large stage, and acoustically treated interiors. Others may utilize areas which actually were designed for other purposes. For example, in recent years there has been increasing adaptation of cafeterias and gymnasiums for this purpose with fairly satisfactory results.

Where a smaller assembly area will suffice, a *multipurpose room* is quite satisfactory, especially if it is equipped with a stage. It usually is advisable to use tables and chairs that may be folded and stacked, both for flexibility and convenience.

The *auditorium* is one of the major areas of the school devoted to "large group" activities. The seating capacity and the shape of the auditorium should be determined by the curriculum and the instructional program. The relationship of the school building to the role it is expected to assume in the community also should be considered.[15]

A cafeteria or lunchroom is considered as one of the essential features of a school. Some systems utilize a *cafetorium,* a type of multipurpose room that may be used for other activities, such as assemblies. Some systems prefer not to have a lunchroom but cart the food from a central kitchen to each classroom, or to several strategically located multipurpose rooms. These rooms should be convenient to classrooms, and entrances and exits should be easily accessible. They should be self-contained to the extent that utilities, heat and light, can be controlled apart from the whole of the plant.

Faculty Lounge and Workroom

The lounge should be so located and accommodated that the staff members can relax in comfort. Comfortable furniture should be provided. Chairs, a desk, and a sofa should be part of the furnishings.

The faculty workroom is one of the most important rooms in the school. It serves many purposes and should be planned accordingly. Furnishings will influence greatly the usability of the room. Both open and closed shelves should be installed. A sink and waterproof cabinet top are indispensable. In addition, a typewriter, a paper cutter, and duplicating equipment including duplicator master paper and duplicator bond should be available for use.

Instructional Center

The supervising principal must see to it that the instructional center and its materials are advantageously located. The degree of centralization of materials and facilities is a matter to be decided upon by each school system.

[15]National Education Association, *Planning the Schools for the Use of Audio-Visual Materials* (Washington: The Association, 1953), p. 183.

In some schools and colleges the instructional center and the library form an instructional media complex.

Language, Speech, and Reading Laboratories

A number of schools are giving consideration to the provision of special rooms to serve as laboratories for the introduction in speech, reading, and foreign languages. Various specialized instructional aids are provided, including control consoles which offer audio connections to headphones. Whether the school that has such a laboratory receives full value is a function of the extent of educational use to which the laboratory is put.[16]

How to Improve Maintenance and Operation Facilities

Maintenance and operation facilities should consist of areas for keeping records and making assignments, storerooms for supplies and equipment, custodial workrooms with sinks and repair equipment if needed, and lavatory facilities for custodians.

In general, school equipment should be:

1. Safe and healthful;
2. Light in weight and easily movable;
3. Readily regroupable and storable;
4. Rugged and durable;
5. Comfortable and conducive to good posture;
6. Student-scaled;
7. Pleasing in form;
8. In keeping with functional requirements.

How to Improve Visual Conditions

Light is something more than a means for aiding the student in the recognition of words and objects. It is a force in his environment that can shape or distort his eyes, muscles, and well-being, currently or permanently.[17]

[16]Frank G. Lopez, "Automation in the Schools," *Progressive Architecture* XL (November 1959): 144.
[17]D. B. Harmon, "Light on Growing Children," *Architectural Record* XCIX (February 1946): 79.

To obtain a visual environment that meets minimum standards it is necessary to balance reflected brightness within the normal field of vision:

1. Ceilings must be white or near white.
2. Walls should reflect at least 60 percent of the light that hits them.
3. Wainscot should reflect 40 percent or better.
4. All trim should reflect not less than 40 percent.
5. Floors, desks, and other equipment should reflect 30 to 40 percent.
6. Chalkboards should reflect 20 to 25 percent.

Any good light source can be used, but the source should be shielded as to the amount of direct glare and to light uniformly throughout the room, with no dark spots or shadows on the ceiling.[18]

The proper distribution and adequacy of the light is important. No unshielded lighting fixtures or highly polished surfaces should be allowed in the normal field of vision. The light fixtures should not require a specific seating pattern.

CURRENT PRACTICE IN SUPERVISING LIGHTING FACILITIES. Many methods and devices are used in attempts to produce a glare-free classroom as well as one with an adequate level of daylight evenly distributed:

1. Continuous windows on both sides of the room help to distribute daylight evenly;
2. Extended eaves overhanging the window heads, louvers, and northerly facing of main windows will keep the sun off the glass;
3. Low angle sources of brightness constitute the most difficult conditions to control—sand, concrete, and whitish walls are highly reflective;
4. A low light transmission glass is the most promising method to control low-level glare, but it requires studious and skilled use for effectiveness.[19]

High placement of windows has been found to reduce glare, prevent breakage, and facilitate the use of audio-visual aids in the classroom. However, the preference for a view and its educational value must be considered.

[18]Paul Seagers, "Providing an Environment for Learning," *The National Elementary Principal* XXXII (September 1952): 248.
[19]Heffernan and Bursch, *Curriculum and the Elementary School Plant*, p. 52.

The most common methods of light control are drapes, opaque shades, full closure Venetian blinds, adjustable louvers, and jalousies. In selecting methods of light control to be used in any situation, planners should consider the method's effectiveness in controlling light as well as initial and maintenance costs, durability, and ease of installation and maintenance. Surveys revealed that the use of room-darkening equipment to control light in classrooms is more economical than is the provision of an audio-visual room. Regulations regarding the hanging of draperies or other light controlling devices should be developed cooperatively.

USE OF COLOR. The use of color within a school will not only make lighting more efficient and effective, but also have an effect on personality. The balancing of color in order to avoid an institutional scheme or monotony of color is highly desirable. A predominant color should be selected for a room on the basis of the age of the occupants, the use of the room, the orientation of the room, and the desired psychological atmosphere.[20]

Color on the walls and ceilings, as well as elsewhere, may affect greatly what happens to the available illumination. Quiet color, with little contrasts, will tend to improve a room for classroom use if the room is situated on a noisy street. Light colors will reflect light in dark rooms and make small rooms look larger. Glare may be minimized by the use of flat paint and by avoiding the use of glass over pictures and cupboards. The proper scientific use of color throughout the school plant is essential to the development of a learning environment of the highest caliber.

How to Improve Acoustical Conditions

The conditioning of classroom space for ease and efficiency of hearing and for control of noise becomes more significant as the learning situations become less formal and more noise-producing. Basic to noise control is the location of the school in quiet surroundings. The principal knows the importance of noise control near the classrooms.

A compact shape reduces speaking distances from the center of the room

[20]National Education Association, *Planning the Schools for the Use of Audio-Visual Materials* (Washington, D.C.: The Association, 1953), p. 253.

as the floor area is increased. The application of acoustical materials to the ceiling and high walls; installation of quiet floors, door stops, and controls; and quietly operating heating and ventilation equipment contribute to less noise.[21]

The audible environment derives its sounds from two sources: those outside the classroom and those inside. Some suggestions are listed:

1. Trees can soften some of the noise from outside; the sounds within the classroom are easier to cope with.
2. Lightweight aggregate concrete block, now left exposed in many school-rooms, has acoustical properties.
3. Partitions, screens, drapes, tackboard, suspended lighting fixtures, room irregularities, and movable cabinets cut down reverberation of sounds.
4. The elimination of plaster walls, reduction of chalkboard areas, increase in classroom size, reduction of ceiling heights, and the new integral sound absorbing roof structures contribute to better acoustical conditions.
5. An acoustical engineer can determine the amount and placement of sound absorbing materials to provide for conditions that approximate the optimum reverberation time.

There are indications that the effective acoustical treatment in classrooms eases audio communication—a basic instructional media—and decreases the hearing differences between students in the front of the room and those in the rear.[22] In larger areas, such as the corridors and the auditorium, sound control of flutter and echoes is effected by delimiting the use of parallel surfaces.

How to Improve Interior Ventilation and Heat Control

Much of the heating problem is a negative one: heat must be removed. The job normally must be accomplished by the ventilating system which, many times, consists of an open window and a corridor ventilator. This traditional

---

[21]Heffernan and Bursch, *Curriculum and the Elementary School Plant*, p. 50.
[22]MacConnell, *Planning for School Buildings*, p. 95.

system, never effective even in yesterday's high ceiling rooms, becomes grossly inadequate in today's buildings that have fewer cubic feet for each student. The next step up the line in effectiveness, to unit ventilators, is a big one, and to the heat pump an even bigger jump.

The principal must assure that the efficiency of the teaching staff is not impaired because of inadequate heating and ventilating equipment. Whether the health and educational values to the teacher and to the students justify the expense of air conditioning will depend upon many factors, including: (1) the extent of utilization of the classroom throughout the school year, (2) the number of days in the year in which cooling is needed, and (3) local conditions affecting cost and operation.[23]

How to Plan for Adequate Instructional Facilities

It is commonplace to hear educators say that school-building design must arise from the needs of school children and the needs of a good educational program. What does this really mean?

As our knowledge of subject matter and of child development and the learning process increases, changes in the evolving instructional program become apparent. A well-designed school plant provides facilities for a wide range of teaching techniques. Provision must be made for small and large groups, individuals, the materials and equipment of instructional technology, remedial work, guidance services, and for the large number of other activities and functions.

Is school design keeping pace with the changes in our educational programs? Are buildings being designed with the needs of school children and the needs of a good educational program given paramount attention?

F. J. Flynn[24] listed the following interesting developments in classroom planning and design as a result of answers to questionnaire replies received from 190 school systems.

[23]Harold B. Gores, "The Case for Controlled Environment," *Architectural Record* CXXX (July 1961): 185.
[24]Francis Joseph Flynn, "An Appraisal of Innovations in Elementary Classroom Planning and Design" (Doctoral dissertation, University of Southern California, 1951).

General plans:

1. The curriculum was a determining factor in the design of classrooms in 81 percent of the schools studied.
2. A trend toward the utilization of the services of all concerned with the ultimate school plant was shown.
3. The single-loaded corridor is the predominant type of new construction, with 87 percent of the schools reporting this innovation.
4. Flexibility in design is increasing.
5. The innovation of the outdoor classroom adjacent to the regular room was shown.

Lighting problems:

1. Bilateral lighting was reported in 89 percent of the cases.
2. North window daylighting was in use by 81 percent of the school systems.
3. Only 4 percent of the schools were using fluorescent lighting.
4. Photoelectric controls were practically nonexistent.

Service features:

1. Twenty-five percent had individual gas-fired hot air units.
2. Natural ventilation led considerably over mechanical systems, with 87 percent using this method.
3. Ninety percent reported having electric outlets in two or more walls. Only 4 percent had television service outlets.
4. Forty-nine percent reported having an intercommunication system.
5. School planners have done a fine job of site selection insofar as isolation from noise is concerned.
6. Ceilings have been treated acoustically with perforated tile by 67 percent of those reporting.

Flynn framed the following recommendations:

1. More acoustical treatment should be given to wall areas.
2. Those who are responsible for classroom planning and design should become better acquainted with the latest developments in the use of materials of construction, various devices, and techniques of design.

3. More consideration should be given to the use of modular, movable storage facilities.

Built-In Obsolescence

Of the thousands of schools being built, almost all are obsolete before their doors are opened. The march of change in education has speeded to a quick step, while progress in school design, despite acres of glass, progresses at a tortoise pace.

Most of the new school buildings are of the typical egg-crate form—identical boxes thirty by forty feet, strung along both sides of an exterior corridor. Rooms within these buildings do not allow for large sized grouping, nor do they permit individual instruction. The typical classroom has few, if any, fittings for modern electronic devices—closed circuit television terminals, for example.

Educators should realize that the revolution which radically has changed our kitchens, living rooms, and other rooms in our homes can make a contribution to the classroom. School facilities which make no provision for laboratories, instructional organization such as that which is offered by the various team-teaching plans, and for the use of the materials of instructional technology, aptly have been dubbed *lock-step*. They form a triangular confine consisting of the student, the teacher, and the course of study or instructional program.

Many schools have been planned without adequate educational specifications. Frequently schools have been planned in an atmosphere of crisis. While a community may argue for years whether or not a school is needed, once they have decided and money has been committed they expect work on the school to begin immediately. This squeeze on time for planning makes it difficult to draw up good educational specifications.

Often the specifications of a school are described solely by formula and index numbers. Until very recently, description by formula was acceptable practice. Uniformity, rather than diversity and functional adaptability, has been characteristic of our schools.

Many school buildings in use today were built fifty or more years ago. It is reasonable to expect that buildings constructed recently, utilizing modern, durable materials, will be in use for comparable periods. It is of great importance that these buildings be designed so that they meet adequately the needs of the present and of the future. Flexibility and adaptability should be built into the school plant.

Architects and educators, as well as the public, have a responsibility that they do not maintain inadequate ideas concerning style that will hinder the designing of schools with a future. The supervising principal has a responsibility to keep the public informed regarding the reasons for change in school building design.

How to Improve Classroom Design

The Supervisor Stresses Functional Design

A properly designed, well-equipped, and self-contained classroom makes a definite contribution to the curriculum. To make the greatest contribution it must be spacious, informal, flexible, equipped for a wide range of learning experiences, and conditioned for safety, health, comfort, efficiency, and the convenience of the occupants.

An adequate amount of space is essential. Most specialists agree that from twenty-five to forty square feet of floor space should be provided per student. The elimination of structural columns, unnecesary furniture, and doors adjoining other work areas may extend the classroom space.

The teacher and the students should be able to arrange the classroom to accommodate varied activities.

Each classroom should have a work area or a counter covered with smooth, waterproof material and be equipped with a sink. The counter height should be governed by the size of the students who are to use it. A drinking fountain is desirable. Most teachers like to have extra tables in the classroom for the display of materials. Extra chairs are needed so that students may work in small groups.

Sixteen to twenty linear feet of bulletin board space should be installed in each classroom. It should be arranged in large units rather than in small areas so as not to limit display space. Large bulletin boards provide ample space for the display of murals, samples of work, and any number of materials. Through these samples the interests, concerns, and achievements of the students may be shown.

It is becoming common practice, wherever possible, to extend the indoor space to the outdoors. It is not uncommon to have two classrooms per teacher: one, the conventional one-story indoor; the other, the outdoor, separated by glass doors and low windows. With a little ingenuity and a slightly increased budget for extra paving, shelter, space separators, outdoor sink, and storage space, the school has another teaching area which is rich in educational opportunity.

A Special Problem: How to Plan for Improved Kindergarten Facilities

It is desirable that the kindergarten be completely self-contained and of a size—usually 1,200 to 1,500 square feet—sufficient to care for the children enrolled. Lighting should be uniform and glare-free. Since it provides a transition between home and school, the kindergarten should retain as much of the home atmosphere as possible. It should have an easily accessible play area. It should be isolated from the rest of the plant both as to its building and its play area, but should be readily accessible to the administrative offices and multi-use area.

Among the areas provided in the kindergarten are the teacher's area, the music center, the food preparation and serving area, the lavatory area, the storage area, the reading corner and science center, the art and construction center, and the play and rest areas. A sink must be provided with both hot and cold water. The drinking fountain should be a separate unit. It is necessary to have a warm floor, and adequate ventilation is required.[25]

Kindergarten walls and ceilings should reflect a sufficiently high degree of light, and the lower wall should be washable. There should be no dangerous protrusions from walls or equipment.

Factors to Be Considered by the Supervising Principal

The supervising principal should see to it that classrooms are sufficiently flexible to accommodate the varied activities that make up a day's work.

[25]MacConnell, *Planning for School Buildings*, p. 179.

Room for small groups to work, a place for individual study, an area for working with a reading group, and room for guided, independent work are a few of the activities for which provision must be made. The classroom should be able to meet each of these situations with a maximum of ease and a minimum of control on the part of the teacher.

Structural flexibility within the building should be provided for whenever possible. The reorganization of areas inside of a building, including changes in room sizes and space allocations, are possible only when the number of structural load-supporting walls are kept at a minimum. Team teaching and varying grouping schemes may call for retractable walls.

Rapidly changing conditions and new knowledge make it difficult to forecast the future. The supervising principal has to be well informed about building trends and materials, as well as constantly being aware of the demands of the educational program.

What the Supervisor Should Consider in a Physical Facilities Improvement Program

The following points should be considered in developing a program of school construction:

1. The governing board should adopt policies and initiate the program. Policies should include a policy statement, planning principles, and proposed program procedures.
2. The public should be kept informed concerning the proposed school plant development program.
3. The curriculum, the instructional program, the type of school, the school population to be housed, accessibility, traffic, environment, and availability including size and cost should be considered in site selection and purchase.
4. Early planning, master plan layout, building location, playground planning, walks, landscaping, drives, service lines, and community use areas should be included in school site layout planning.
5. Architectural service should be provided under governing board policies which state basic functions, relationships, services, methods of architec-

ture, methods of employment, payment of fees, supervision, and final authority.

6. Building drawings and specifications should provide for preliminary studies, educational demands and needs, preparation of tryout sketches, approval of preliminary drawings, advertising for bids, governing board acceptance, method contracts, inspection by the appropriate supervisor, construction, final inspection, and acceptance.

Generally, the individual in charge of planning for the school site purchase should:

1. Survey the rights of all parties to the impending land ownership transfer;
2. Obtain a legal description of the property;
3. Determine ownership and property rights involved;
4. Determine the property cost and obtain information concerning mineral rights;
5. Employ an attorney.

DO

1. Secure the interest and cooperation of the community in the construction or acquisition of new physical facilities.
2. Secure the advice of specialist-consultants with respect to needed revisions or maintenance.
3. Consider hearing ease and noise abatement and organize a committee for that purpose.
4. Conduct a survey, to be made by outside experts, for better planning and utilization of all buildings.
5. Establish an evaluation committee to determine whether or not the building and facilities are being utilized to best advantage.
6. Train students, with the assistance of the teachers, to protect school property through self-control and involvement.
7. Have the custodian make periodic inspections of the total school plant in order to insure the optimum control of lighting, heating, ventilation, cleanliness of lavatories and drinking fountains.

8. As principal, with the cooperation and aid of the teachers and the students, formulate rules and regulations to insure the safety and welfare of those who use the physical facilities.
9. As part of supervisory services, encourage teachers to take responsibility in practicing good housekeeping.
10. Work with the custodian, as a specialist, to insure proper use, operation, and ordinary care of the mechanical equipment used for the heating, lighting, ventilating, and operation of the school building.
11. Encourage the community, parents, civic leaders, and all qualified, interested groups to work closely with teachers and supervisors in determining the kind of school plant best suited to student learning.

DON'T

1. Fail to keep the several publics continuously informed as to the growing needs of the school system for new school sites of adequate size.
2. Proceed on a hit or miss basis in selecting sites, rather, insure that good evaluation procedures are followed.
3. Attempt to play it by ear; the need for sites must be anticipated several years in advance, and appropriate plans made and policies established.
4. Select sites without carefully entering them first on the school attendance area maps.
5. Accept inflexible classroom planning without a fight. Classrooms in the future will be flexible and not of the *lock-step* variety.
6. Go it alone. Rather, encourage the community, parents, civic leaders, and all interested groups to work closely with teachers and supervisors in determining the best kind of school plant for student learning.

Supervisory Problems   In Basket

Problem 1

At a meeting with the superintendent, it was decided that all supervising principals should participate in establishing the features that should be included in a particular instructional unit of the school plant.

As supervising principal, what educational specifications would you propose for a particular instructional unit such as an elementary school classroom?

What policy decisions must be made by a school system before any long-range educational developments may be planned?

Problem 2

Assuming the same background situation as that posed in Problem 1, how many units, of what square footage, would you recommend for a junior high-school plant designed to house 750 students in grades seven through nine? (You may assume any pattern of curricular programs you wish.)

Problem 3

Assuming the background environment and problem as posed in Problem 2, how would you, as supervising principal, proceed to answer the questions posed for a high-school plant designed to house 1,565 students in grades nine through twelve?

Problem 4

Answer Problem 2, above, with reference to a community college plant designed to house 5,000 students. Again, you may assume and specify any curricular program you wish.

Selected Bibliography

Books

Hagman, Harlan L. *The Administration of the American Public Schools.* New York: McGraw-Hill Book Company, 1951.

Landes, Jack L. *Citizen's Workbook for Evaluating School Buildings.* New York: Harper and Brothers, 1951.

MacConnell, James D. *Planning for School Buildings.* Englewood Cliffs, New Jersey: Prentice-Hall, Inc., 1957.

Pierce, David A. *Saving Dollars in Building Schools.* New York: Reinhold Publishing Corporation, 1951.

Schneder, Raymond C., and Jon S. Peters, eds. *Improving the School Environment.* Palo Alto, California: Stanford University Press, December 1956.

Strevell, Wallace H., and Arvid J. Burke. *Administration of the School Building Program.* New York: McGraw-Hill Book Company, Inc., 1959.

The Cost of a Schoolhouse. New York: Educational Facilities Laboratories, 1960.

Wiles, Kimball. *Supervision for Better Schools.* Englewood Cliffs, New Jersey: Prentice-Hall, Inc., 1950.

Periodicals

Essex, D. D. "Basic Principles of School Building Design." *American School Board Journal* CXVI (January 1948): 19–20.

Gores, Harold B. "The Case for Controlled Environment." *Architectural Record* CXXX (July 1961): 185.

Harmon, D. B. "Light on Growing Children." *Architectural Record* XCIX (February 1946): 79.

Lopez, Frank G. "Automation in the Schools." *Progressive Architecture* XL (November 1959): 144.

Mitchell, M. A. "Classrooms Need Movable Equipment." *School Executive* LXIX (November 1949): 61–63.

Raubinger, Frederick. "Kind of Information Needed for a Survey of School Building Needs." *American School Board Journal* CXVI (January 1946): 24–28.

Reese, Jack. "Unusual Design in a One-Story Building." *School Management* XIX (March 1950): 4–11.

Seagers, Paul. "Providing an Environment for Learning." *The National Elementary Principal* XXXII (September 1952): 248.

Woolf, Kenneth. "Improved Working Conditions for Teachers." *American School Board Journal* CXVI (March 1948): 45.

Other Sources

American Association of School Administrators. *American School Buildings.* Twenty-Seventh Yearbook. Washington, D.C.: The Association, 1949.

Association for Supervision and Curriculum Development. *Creating a Good Environment for Learning.* Washington, D.C.: National Education Association, 1954.

Flynn, Francis Joseph. "An Appraisal of Innovations in Elementary Classroom Planning and Design." Doctoral dissertation, University of Southern California, 1951.

Heffernan, Helen, and Charles Bursch. *Curriculum and the Elementary School Plant.* Washington, D.C.: National Education Association, 1958.

Jordan, Marion, and David Jackson. "The Schools We Already Have," *The National Elementary Principal.* Thirty-Eighth Yearbook. Washington, D.C.: National Education Association, 1959.

LaFranchi, Edward H. "Schoolhouse Program and Plans." Duplicated material copyrighted by the author. Los Angeles: 1958.

Melbo, Irving R. et al. "School Housing for Our Children." Duplicated material copyrighted by the author. Los Angeles: 1950.

———. "Report of the Survey, Laguna Beach Unified School District." Duplicated material copyrighted by the author. Los Angeles: 1961.

———. "Report of the Survey, Bear Valley Unified School District." Duplicated material copyrighted by the author. Los Angeles: 1962.

Metropolitan School Study Council, School Building Committee. *Forecasting School Enrollments.* New York: The Council, 1953.

National Association of Elementary School Principals. "Basis for Effective Learning," *The National Elementary Principal.* Thirty-First Yearbook. Washington, D.C.: The Association, 1952.

———. "Elementary School Buildings—Design for Living," *The National Elementary Principal.* Thirty-Eighth Yearbook. Washington, D.C.: The Association, 1959.

National Council on Schoolhouse Construction. *Elementary-School Plant Planning.* Nashville, Tennessee: George Peabody College for Teachers, 1958.

National Education Association. *Planning the Schools for the Use of Audio-Visual Materials.* Washington, D.C.: The Association, 1953.

New York Commission on School Buildings. *Classrooms for How Many?* Albany: The Commission, 1952.

Tomini, Harold C. "Space Requirements of the High School Administrative Unit." Doctoral dissertation, University of Southern California, 1959.

Viles, N. E. *School Building, Remodeling, Rehabilitation, Modernization, and Repair.* United States Office of Education Bulletin No. 17. Washington, D.C.: Government Printing Office, 1950.

Welling, Robert E. "The Role of the District Employee in Charge of School
Planning and Construction." Doctoral dissertation, University of Southern
California, 1960.

18

How to Supervise the Program for Obtaining Community Support

Our country has traveled a long way since the days when pioneer settlers built their own schoolhouses and the schoolmaster lived with one of the families as a boarder. Today our society is one of sophistication, but there is a real need for people to renew their pioneering interest in the schools.

This country's future sits at the desks of today's classrooms. To protect America's heritage of individualism, freedom, and the right of each person to develop to his highest potential, the citizens must become working partners with school personnel in initiating supervisory programs that strengthen the schools.

The question in this area that is most urgently in need of an answer concerns the supervising principal and how he may function best in supervising the program for obtaining increased community support for the educational program in general, and for the program of school supervision in particular.

This chapter includes a discussion of the following topics:

Definitions and functions
Basic principles
How the staff can participate
How to build a community relations program
How to evaluate the community relations program
Do—don't
"In-Basket" supervisory problems
Chapter Supplement

Definitions and Functions

Community Relations Defined

Broadly conceived, community relations refers to the harmony of understanding that exists between any group and the publics it serves. Thus any institution or organization affected by the will of these publics gives some consideration to public attitude and understanding, and to the influence certain of its activities have on the public viewpoint.[1]

The public relations of any institution are the sum total of all the impressions created by the institution and by the various persons connected with it. A strong supervisory program can exist only when it has faculty and community support.

Nucleus and Essence

The substance of any program for improved community relations is a continuous duologue with the several publics involved concerning the achievements, status, objectives, and desires of the schools.

In essence we are seeking the understanding and cooperation of the entire community. The relationship of the supervising principal with the community should not be centered on the *justification* or *defense* of a program —this is the task of the board of education and the administrative units within the school system. Rather, community relations should seek to *inform* and *present* to the public the "educational program," and plans concerning that program, as they exist.

Why Community Relations?

Public education, by its very nature, is an area of public concern. Since funds and students are furnished by the several publics, the school owes those publics an accounting of its stewardship.

In a time of rapid technological change that, in turn, encourages just as rapid a change in the school's educational programs, community under-

[1]See Jefferson N. Eastmond, *The Teacher and School Administration* (Boston: Houghton Mifflin Company, 1959), p. 250.

standing is vital. The publics generally are suspicious of new instructional programs. Most adults view education in terms of what they experienced in their youth. An innovation may be considered a frill, and therefore unnecessary.

The main goal of supervision is the improvement of the quality of education. Public relations may be viewed as the means for obtaining community support and understanding that are essential to the success of the supervisory program.

Basic Principles

The following basic principles apply to the tasks of planning, organizing, implementing, evaluating, and improving the supervision of the program for community relations:

1. The school is founded upon the good will of people who support it. The main purpose of the community relations program must not be the gaining of financial support for the schools.
2. The most important factor in gaining support for the supervisory program is developing and maintaining an instructional program which people like. Stress this factor, along with the value of facilities and improvements; not the money involved.
3. The key to sustained community support of supervision is the instructional program which is responsive to the changing needs of the community.
4. In planning a successful community relations program, the principal must be well acquainted with all aspects of the local community.
5. To be effective, the principal must understand the power structure of the community and establish working relationships with individual and group opinion leaders.
6. The principal knows that parents react to what they *think* the supervisory program is, rather than what it *actually* is.
7. Gaining support for the supervisory program is the responsibility of all members of the school team: board of trustees, administration, fac-

ulty, classified employees, students, and parents. The school principal should provide leadership.

8. In developing support for the supervisory program, the teacher-supervisor relationship is the focal point.
9. The basis of effective community support from parents, taxpayers, and businessmen is participation through shared responsibilities in the plans, goals, and activities of the school.
10. The principal should establish two-way communications concerning the plans, purposes, and results of the supervisory program with the school and the community.
11. The student is the key to effective communications because he is the vital link between the home and the school.
12. The projection of a positive attitude by the school team is an indispensable factor in gaining support for the supervisory program.
13. Besides assuring that all employees know their community relations duties, responsibilities, opportunities, and limitations, it is well to appraise their effectiveness at regular intervals.

Through adequate planning one is able to exploit all available avenues leading to the goal of enhanced public relations in the most efficient, effective, and economical manner.

Information must be geared to the several publics that are the intended receivers. This means that both the wording and the instruments used must be aimed at reaching these publics. Good publicity will not substitute for poor public relations. Good public relations involves the ability to take criticism, admit faults, and rectify shortcomings. The best road to tread in community relations is the one that has been paved by the achievement of excellence in the instructional program.

The necessity for keeping the publics well informed is recognized by all well-run organizations. School officials should help the people to become intelligently and completely informed and thereby guided into sympathy and understanding toward school problems. The responsibility of the school supervisor is: (1) to gather, (2) to organize, and (3) to present information.

Honesty is the best and only policy in supervision, as well as in all other areas of the educational enterprise. We must be prepared to present all of the facts that are pertinent in a truthful and sincere manner. No effective school-community relationship can exist without this prerequisite. Education is big business, but it must be differentiated from commercial big business. The goals of the school are not reached by way of the "hard-sell" of its commercial brothers.

An essential fact in public relations is that once the community supports school employees, support for the supervisory program will follow. This is a necessary outgrowth if we wish to advance the general educational program in general, and the supervisory program in particular.

WHAT THE PRINCIPAL CAN DO WITHIN THE SCHOOL ATTENDANCE AREA. The principal in each school is the catalyst that makes the supervisory program sparkle with action and use. If the principal is aware of the personality of the school's neighborhood and understands its many facets, then the supervisory program can be geared to meet these needs:

1. Each school-community has needs to be met as each has its own pattern of social, religious, commercial-industrial, and recreational life.
2. Each community, though individual, has an obligation to relate itself to the local school system, to the state, and to the nation.

The supervising principal has a unique position in today's society. He can become a modern-day town crier and reawaken the people to the needs of educating their children, who are afloat in the sea of demands of a volatile world.

THE SCHOOL AS A REFLECTION OF THE COMMUNITY. Each school is a mirror of the community. The school's curriculum reflects what the citizens desire for their children. If there is no participation by the citizens in the school's life, then the activities within its walls are static and unchallenging.

Community relations seek harmony between any groups and the publics served. The supervising principal enhances this harmony by (1) informing, (2) rallying support, (3) developing an awareness of the importance of education in a democracy, (4) developing the partnership between parents and the school, (5) integrating the program for community relations, (6) evaluating the status of the program, and (7) correcting existing misunderstandings.

If well planned such a program will be truthful, unselfish, intrinsic in the instructional program, positive, continuous, comprehensive, interesting, and sensitive to the needs and desires of the patrons of the school. It will be expressed clearly so that it is easily understood.

THE GOVERNING BOARD AND COMMUNITY RELATIONS. The governing board should develop an adequate statement concerning public relations, which should be placed in the official handbook. Suggestions for implementing the provisions should be listed.

Definite board policies should be developed that will (1) facilitate co-operation with other community agencies, and (2) insure working conditions which will attract and hold competent employees.

The governing board can further public relations by:

1. Planning community programs;
2. Erecting schools that have areas for meetings;
3. Maintaining open channels of effective communication between industry and the school;
4. Providing adequate financial support for the program for school supervision.

THE SUPERINTENDENT AND PUBLIC RELATIONS. The person responsible for planning and coordinating public relations for supervisory programs must be the superintendent. Under his leadership the supervising principal performs to the best of his ability. The superintendent must encourage the supervising principal to adapt activities to suit his own personality, the personalities of the teachers and students of the school, and the personality of the community. In-service education courses for the superintendent and for the supervising principal are recommended. Technical assistance is essential.

In many school systems one person is assigned the task of coordinating news releases. The superintendent, as well as the supervising principal, should stress the importance of every member of the staff participating in the program for community relations. The educators should maintain broad, professional contacts outside of the school system. All must work to eliminate the teacher stereotype, and to hold to high professional standards in the selection of school employees.

HOW SCHOOL MANAGEMENT INFLUENCES COMMUNITY RELATIONS. Generally speaking, planning and managing school business should be done at such a high level that public confidence will be created and maintained. Up-to-date instructional materials must be provided. Organizing and pre-planning help to avoid confusion. The amount of direct lay participation in educational planning, even in an advisory capacity, should be delimited sharply in amount and kind. The community is represented through its elected representatives on the governing board.

WHAT THE PRINCIPAL CAN DO IN THE AREA OF SCHOOL FINANCE AND COMMUNITY RELATIONS. The supervising principal has definite responsibilities in maintaining the community's confidence in the fiscal management of its educational enterprise. Several suggestions are:

1. The supervising principal should have national, state, and local school finance data available at all times;
2. He should be ready to interpret the relationship of financial support to the quality of education;
3. Generally speaking, the principal should insure that no fees are charged to parents or to students, nor should teachers be encouraged to purchase materials from their own funds;
4. If a piece of equipment or material has a place in the instructional program, the school system should purchase the item.

HOW TO ORGANIZE AND ASSIGN PRIORITIES FOR PUBLICITY. A listing of criteria for organizing a publicity program follows:

1. Unfounded attacks by "taxpayers" organizations should be met with a counterattack of facts.

2. Reports should be issued to the public concerning what is happening with bond funds which have been voted.
3. Easy to read, interesting financial reports should be published regularly.
4. All publicity should be accomplished through selected media.
5. As many types of media should be utilized as possible.
6. Selected material should be distributed throughout the year, with a few good stories released each week.
7. One individual should be in charge of school publicity.
8. The material produced should be checked by a second staff member.
9. All material should be simple, honest, direct, and up-to-date.

Some priorities for publicity, listed in descending order, follow:

1. Student programs and welfare
2. The instructional program
3. Guidance and health services
4. Attendance, discipline, and control
5. Enrollment trends
6. School staff members and the administration
7. The building program
8. School management and finance
9. Parents' association
10. General student activities.

How the Staff Can Participate

The Supervising Principal Obtains
Participation of the Staff Members

In developing support for the supervisory program the principal must work not only with the community, but also very closely with the professional staff. He must insure that each person on the staff understands and sees the need for improvement through supervision and discerns its relationship to the total school program. The school program should be planned cooperatively with the total staff. Specialists[2] know that sharing in formu-

[2]Robert E. Wilson, *The Modern School Superintendent—His Principles and Practices* (New York: Harper and Brothers, 1960), p. 422.

lating decisions concerning one's working world contributes to the realization of the goals of the profession.

How to Educate the Members of the Staff

The supervising principal should develop, in cooperation with the members of his staff, a program for keeping parents and citizens informed. He also must acquaint his staff with the techniques of good public relations. Certainly it is beneficial for the students to arrive at home happy and excited about their class, but all this can come to a halt if the parents have unsatisfactory experiences with the school. Many unpleasant situations and misunderstandings can be avoided if the professional staff of the school is well versed in basic public relations methods.

The principal, in planning his in-service program, should devote much time to making his total staff aware of the need for successful relations with the public. The use of forms, such as those which appear as Figures 18–1 and 18–2, should be discussed with the teaching staff. No school employee, nor any correspondence emanating from such employee, can be disregarded. "Every employed member of the school system must know every aspect of the program well enough to believe in it and to interpret it in its proper perspective to the public."[3] All have a very important part to play in obtaining the community's respect and support.

How the Custodian and the Secretary Can Help

Many times the first person that a visitor to the school sees or talks with is the custodian or the school secretary. Their appearance, tone of voice, and knowledge of the school's program frequently will determine the visitor's opinion of the school. If one is met at the school by a person of careless grooming and uninteresting personality, and who lacks knowledge of the school plant and its personnel, one constructs a negative mental picture of the school.

Many times lasting impressions are made by the telephone voice of the school secretary. Is it sharp, listless, annoyed in tone, or is it warm, pleasing,

[3]Howard Stephenson, *Handbook of Public Relations* (New York: McGraw-Hill Book Company, Inc., 1960), p. 739.

FIGURE 18–1   Home Assignment Data Form

Name of School

Date _____

To the Parents of _____

    Homework which was due today was not turned in by _____.
_____ . As it is the policy of the Board of Education
that homework be assigned according to individual and class *needs*, his/her
achievement in the subject area within which the homework was assigned
may suffer considerably.

_____   This is the first time he/she has failed to complete a home
assignment in this class.

_____   This problem has occurred in the past.

_____   He/she has failed repeatedly to turn in home assignments.

_____   An appointment has been made for a conference at school on
_____ , at_____ . Please
notify me if this time is not convenient.

    Thank you for your kind attention to the above matter.

Sincerely,

_____
(Principal)

FIGURE 18–2   Exceptional Progress or Improvement Form

Name of School

Date _____

Dear _____ ,

    I am pleased to inform you that _____ 's progress has been
most satisfactory this past week.

Sincerely,

_____
(Principal)

and helpful? These qualities do much to create displeasure or good will toward the school program. H. Stephenson emphasized the importance of secretarial contacts, "for a system is constantly judged by the way its telephones are answered and visitors are received, and by the quality of its correspondence."[4]

The supervising principal should offer reminders such as the following to school secretaries in connection with the community relations program:

1. Remember that the child comes first.
2. Avoid generalizing, whether at school or away from it. Weed out of your conversations such phrases as "trouble with parents is . . ." or "kids now-a-days . . . ."
3. Be loyal to co-workers. A negative comment about one reflects upon all. Positive comments foster higher public respect for the secretary as well as for all the teachers and administrators in the school.
4. Do not breach a confidence whether it is about a student, parent, teacher, or other co-worker.
5. Again, avoid, however, giving the impression that the school has any "secrets" to be kept from the public. While there may be confidential information about an individual, it should be made clear that the overall public information policy is frank, honest, and forthright.
6. Remember that a telephone voice must be friendly, cheerful, interested, and helpful. Avoid sounding busy. Be a good listener.
7. Be cordial to visitors. Show that you are concerned with whatever the visitor is inquiring about. Make the visitor feel that the school welcomes his call and appreciates his visit.
8. Do not procrastinate or stall. Handle complaints and requests promptly.
9. Do not presume to answer for the principal or for the governing board.
10. Remember that there is no individual who is a true *enemy* of the school. There are critics and there are cranks; the well informed, uninformed, and misinformed; the biased and the prejudiced. You must operate on the premise that everyone's views, no matter how haywire they may sometimes sound, are aimed toward the improvement of education.

[4]Ibid., p. 740.

11. Treat every school patron alike, no matter how troublesome some of them seem to be. Be willing to listen. Be patient and friendly.

How Cafeteria Workers Can Help

In addition to the custodian and the school secretary, the cafeteria workers can help in the public relations program. These staff members are instrumental in creating positive or negative feelings toward the school and its supervisory program. They can help by being (1) courteous to all, (2) scrupulously neat and clean in appearance, (3) skilled in their craft, (4) the recipients of the benefit of continuous supervision, (5) made to feel that they are an important, integral part of the total school family, and (6) made aware of the vital part they play in community relations.

The School Nurse and the Community

The duties of the school nurse take her into the homes of many of the students. She can be a positive force for the good of the school. Through knowledge of the supervisory program, and through an understanding of public relations techniques, she can create positive reactions to the school. The principal must arrange time for this staff member to be present at many of the in-service meetings.

How Teachers Can Provide Fuel for the Program's Progress

The principal must be alert to the latest knowledge and information in education. His public relations program for teachers must be complete and must cover various techniques for communicating with parents; it will have to be interlaced with thoughtful, professional guidance, for teachers provide a window through which the public can view the supervisory program. Teachers must be made to realize that the school is evaluated in the minds of the parents by their response to the teachers' relationships with the home. Corrected papers, homework assignments, notes reporting on how well a student is doing in school, and person-to-person contacts have impact upon the parents. The supplement to Chapter 18 contains specific suggestions on how the supervising principal can assist the teacher in planning for more effective conferences with parents.

From the Principal's Desk

The principal can do much to gain parental support through bulletins and notices. Many parents are unable to attend the parents' association meetings. Printed information from the principal's desk is of great importance.

A monthly newsletter, dealing with some area of the curriculum or with some unmet need, is a valuable device. The letter should be well written, readable, informative, and brief. This friendly information missive may stimulate parents to participation.

By having a perforated tear-off section on the lower part of the letter a principal can ask for questions and suggestions. These topics can be discussed in the following month's letter. This is a contact that can benefit both home and school.

Everyday Visiting Day

Each classroom should have a planned program for inviting parents to visit the school. Parents share their children with teachers for a school year. They should feel comfortable in visiting their children's classrooms.

In the past a teacher and the curriculum were classified information as far as parents were concerned. In many cases parents were never given such basic information as their children's reading levels. Fortunately, due to the impact of Sputnik I on the American parent, more parents became interested in what was happening in the schools. The challenge of the future demands that educators establish and maintain a close understanding and working arrangement with the parents. Without it the program for supervision will be ineffective.

How to Build a Community Relations Program

Major steps in building a community relations program follow:

1. A competent person should be employed to organize and direct the public relations work.
2. The public relations director should be utilized in a counseling capacity.

3. The publics involved should be located and defined.
4. The reactions of the various publics to the objectives, services, policies, and ideals of the program involved should be analyzed.
5. The needs of the schools should be examined.
6. All public relations activities should be coordinated.
7. The efforts of the schools and the institutions of higher education should be coordinated.
8. Every policy proposal should be considered carefully in order to decrease the possibility of hasty or unwise action.
9. All possible procedures for improving relations between the schools and each of the various publics should be analyzed.
10. All possible sources of adequate funds and personnel should be examined.

To create an interest that eventually will lead to community participation in educational activities, a supervising principal should proceed through four basic steps:

1. The supervising principal should publicize and support the local parents' association.
2. The supervising principal should know the desires of his school and community. He should form a joint parents-community information committee. This joint group would represent better home-school coordination. It would involve both professional people and civic leaders contributing.
3. The supervising principal should utilize student help. Students provide the community with living proof of the merits of the educational program. Teachers should be encouraged to conduct a ten-minute review of "what we learned today" just prior to dismissal each day.
4. The supervising principal should encourage attendance at board meetings. By introducing lay citizens to the benefits gained from attending school board meetings, the supervising principal will have a group with greater understanding of the many problems confronting the schools.

Once these fours areas are explored, they should provide a breeding ground for many new approaches aimed at inducing a high level of positive citizen participation.

One sees in this analysis that good public relations are the result of a well-planned and well-defined program. Emphasis is placed on the need for an awareness of the various publics and their characteristics, desires, and beliefs.

How to Make Use of the Instruments of Communication

Those in charge of the program for bettering public relations should be aware of the fact that there are several vehicles that should be used. These media should be used when and where they will be most effective, and as informative or preventive media, not as crisis media.

W. G. Reeder[5] divided public relations activities into four major categories: (1) written, (2) visual, (3) oral, and (4) social. One can readily see, in the following list of communications media, that many of the activities overlap, and thus may fall into more than one of the categories.

1. The press
2. Radio and television
3. Exhibits
4. Commencement exercises
5. Report cards
6. Alumni gatherings
7. Debates, panels, and open forums
8. Excursions
9. Personnel
10. Bulletins
11. School newspapers
12. The local parents' association

In dealing with the vast number of media the supervising principal must realize that, if he is to reach the general public, he must not rely on any one method of presentation. He must decide which media will transmit the message to the greatest number of people in the most satisfactory manner.

[5]Ward G. Reeder, *An Introduction to Public-School Relations* (New York: The Macmillan Company, 1937), p. 13.

To rely on one medium could prove disastrous, not only because of the limited publics that may be reached but because of certain limiting characteristics inherent within the medium.

E. Stoops and M. L. Rafferty[6] cited just such an example in the relationship between a local newspaper editor and a superintendent. The study cited below, while limited in the number of respondents is, never the less, of interest. It illustrates how the two disagreed on the relative importance of items included in a list of thirteen topics, in rank order:

The Editor Rank No.		The Superintendent Rank No.
1	Co-curricular activities	12
2	Parents' Association	11
3	Board of education and administration	8
4	Student progress and achievement	2
5	Teachers and school officers	9
6	School buildings and building program	4
7	Courses of study	5
8	Business management and finance	7
9	Discipline and behavior of students	13
10	Health of students	3
11	Value of Education	1
12	Methods of instruction	6
13	Attendance	10

How to Work with the Press

Generally the press serves as the publisher of releases issued by the local governing board, and as an observer and interpreter. For the most part, educators are aware of the need for a good working relationship with the press. The question is how to set about establishing and maintaining good press relations. L. W. Kindred[7] offered the following points as suggestions for improving newspaper publicity:

[6]Emery Stoops and M. L. Rafferty, Jr., *Practices and Trends in School Administration* (Boston: Ginn and Company, 1961), p. 524.
[7]L. W. Kindred, *School Public Relations* (Englewood Cliffs, New Jersey: Prentice-Hall, Inc., 1957), p. 336.

1. In planning the publicity program, discuss with the newspaper editor the types of stories in which he is interested and the style in which news should be presented.
2. One person should coordinate the news service. He should be available to the newspaper as needed.
3. Daily contact with the press should be established. Report possible news stories and supply requested copy.
4. Reporters should be treated with professional courtesy.
5. Honesty and frankness are essentials of news releases.
6. Confidence in the reporter is essential and advisable. Background information should be provided.
7. All copy should have news value.
8. A directory of the names, addresses, office hours, and telephone numbers of city editors, department editors, reporters, and photographers should be kept up-to-date.
9. A weekly calendar and future events ("suspense") book should be maintained. These may be shared with reporters and photographers.
10. Reporters should be permitted a reasonable amount of freedom to interview the professional staff.
11. Reporters should be briefed in advance of governing board meetings. They should know what problems and issues will be brought up for discussion.
12. A press conference should be held when something significant and newsworthy occurs.
13. All newspapers must be treated alike, even though one may feel a dislike for the personnel and editorial policies of a particular paper.
14. Editors and reporters should receive deserved praise for the way they have written and presented a story, but *not* for having published the story.
15. The *community press* also should be employed as a means of gaining support for the supervisory program. This vehicle provides an excellent source for focusing community attention on the school.

It is important that the educator be aware of the impact of the press upon his community. It long has been known that the press is one of the boldest molders of public opinion. The press reaches almost all segments of the population and can serve education well.

How to Make Use of Radio and Television

In recent years radio and television have served as vocal arms of community-school relations. Radio and television broadcasts reach segments of the population that normally might be missed by other media. Federal law requires that the commercial stations devote a certain portion of their broadcast time to public service programs. A recent trend has been to have numerous "specials" that deal with education—in both local and national surroundings. Some educational television stations have been approved by the Federal Communications Commission.

A combination of public interest and school effort has brought these programs to the air waves. A point well worth considering here is that much of the public will listen to or view these broadcasts although they would not take the time to read articles conveying the same information.

Television has a unique quality about it that the educator would be foolish to overlook. Through television several devices may be incorporated into one. Thus many current programs may have speakers, slides or filmstrips, live performances, charts and graphs, and a host of other techniques, all in one program.

Some Inherent Limitations of Broadcast Media

Although radio and television can serve the educator, certain difficulties are inherent in the uses of these media. For one, the problem of time is of major importance. Since radio and television are highly commercial, the desirable hours usually are devoted to commercial programs. Additionally, television time is sold in increments of fifteen, thirty, sixty, or ninety minutes. The script may be padded or overedited, thus becoming distorted or losing its force.

Television offers an additional drawback in terms of production. It is a highly technical medium. Production of a television script may require the use of technically trained personnel whose sympathies lie in producing an "entertaining" product.

How to Evaluate the Community Relations Program

Public education, by its very nature, is an area of extreme public concern. Since funds for its maintenance are taken from the public pocket according to set formulas, it is essential that the various publics feel that their monies are being spent in an appropriate and wise manner.

A publication of the American Association of School Administrators[8] suggested the following set of criteria which may be employed in evaluating factors that influence the community relations program:

1. The governing board should develop and constantly improve the educational program, provide adequate personnel for staffing the school program, provide and maintain an educationally efficient physical plant, secure adequate financial resources, maintain a two-way contact with the adult community and the schools, and choose the chief executive and work harmoniously with him.
2. The superintendent should serve as a partner and executive officer of the board as well as a member and leader of the professional staff, and should keep open the lines of communication between the board, the co-workers, and the community.
3. The superintendent's dual role as champion of the teachers' needs and representative of the governing board provides a challenge to administration which must be faced explicitly and honestly.
4. Due deliberation should precede any policy decision.
5. Ignorance of school problems on the part of the press frequently is the cause for poor public relations. An explanation should be provided for the press in order to avoid unjustified criticism.
6. Schools should have an open board press policy.
7. Board members cannot escape being identified with schools twenty-four hours per day, and people expect them to give answers to questions. These questions can be answered only on the basis of stated board policy.

[8]American Association of School Administrators, *School Board-Superintendent Relationships,* Thirty-Fourth Department Yearbook (Washington, D.C.: National Education Association, 1956).

8. Supervising principals must be wise listeners also, and confine answers to questions to stated board policy and professional levels.
9. Board members, superintendents, and supervising principals must be able to "take the community pulse" and evaluate pressures.
10. Potential value of all local professional associations should be tapped.
11. Economical use of funds and assurance of value received are major responsibilities.
12. Awards earned by students of the school system, such as appear in Figures 18–3 and 18–4, should be publicized.

FIGURE 18–3   Sample Service Award Form

(Name of School System)

SERVICE AWARD

This is to certify that _____

is presented this

AWARD CERTIFICATE

in recognition of outstanding service.

_____
Date

_____
Teacher

FIGURE 18–4   Sample Attendance Record Certificate

CERTIFICATE

This certificate is hereby awarded to

_____

who has an outstanding record of attendance and promptness, and whose citizenship
has been commendable at all times
during the term.

_____
Date

_____
Teacher

---

13. A booklet indicating when and where governing board meetings are held, the usual pattern of board procedure, and how one may have a subject included on the agenda should be readily available to all patrons of the school and should be presented to all who visit board meetings. Excerpts from such a booklet are included as Figure 18–5. Such a booklet should contain:

   a) A message of welcome;
   b) A card which may be utilized to ask questions from the floor and/or to request that an item be put on the agenda;
   c) Instructions for utilizing the card noted in "b" above;
   d) A list of school system facilities;
   e) A summary of usual board procedure;
   f) A summary of the duties and sources of authority of the governing board;
   g) A list of board meeting dates.

FIGURE 18–5   Sample Booklet of Information for Board Meetings

---

WHAT TO DO IF YOU WISH TO ADDRESS THE BOARD OF EDUCATION

If the Item is on the Agenda—

If you wish to speak on an item which is on the agenda, fill out the attached card, indicate the item number, and hand the card to the secretary prior to the start of the meeting. You will be called upon by the chairman at the time this subject is under consideration. He will grant you a maximum of ten minutes in which to make your comments.

If the Item is not on the Agenda—

It is impossible for the Board to make intelligent decisions on important questions without complete information. It will not act on an item which is not on the agenda.

If there is a subject which you wish the Board to consider, you may fill out and submit the attached card stating your desires. When the chairman reaches the topic, "Questions from the Floor," he will call upon you. You may have the floor for a maximum of five minutes to make your presentation and to re-

FIGURE 18–5   (Continued)

quest that your problem be placed on the agenda for a subsequent meeting. The Board will act on this request following your comments.

Board Procedure:

Adoption of the agenda for the meeting is the first item of business acted upon by the Board. The agenda then becomes the scheduled order of business.

The agenda, with its extensive background material, has been studied by each member of the Board for at least three days preceding the meeting. Board members have had an opportunity to call the district offices for clarification of items on the agenda. This procedure enables the Board members to handle more efficiently the many, many items which come before them.

[Sample Card]

Agenda Item —————————————————— Date ——————————

Subject, if not on the agenda: ——————————————————

—————————————————————————————————

—————————————————————————————————

Name ————————————————————————————

Address ————————————————————————————

Telephone ——————————————————————————

(If additional space is necessary, use reverse side)

What the Supervising Principal Should Consider

Every supervising principal and community relations committee should consider:

1. Specific yearly *goals.*
2. Some sort of *publication,* annual report, etc.
3. *Good relations* with the local press.
4. *Contact with local service clubs* and other community organizations.

5. A *plan* for a continuous community relations project at each of the pre-Area Council meetings.
6. A *"leadership membership"* in the National School Public Relations Association.
7. *Representation* at the Public Relations Conferences.
8. During the fall season, representation at the public relations session of the nearest state professional association field conference.
9. Purchasing subscriptions to *Report Card,* published by the California Teachers Association, Southern Section, Los Angeles, California, for members of the local board of education, parents' association presidents, presidents and/or education committee chairmen of chambers of commerce and service clubs, and other lay leaders.
    a) Subscription prices are more advantageous when one purchases in packets and handle mailings himself (committee members could help here).
    b) Many local associations precede the first issue with a letter explaining the complimentary subscription and indicating the hope that the publication will be helpful.
    c) At the end of the term, some groups follow up with a questionnaire.
    d) Some member of the public relations committee might be designated to submit news or feature stories of broad interest for inclusion in *Report Card.*
10. *Assuming leadership* in United Way, Community Chest, Salvation Army, Blood Bank, and other such drives; and arranging to have publicity in local newspapers when large association checks are presented to such agencies.
11. *Cooperation* with other supervisors and the administrators of the local school system in setting up regular channels for collection of articles, or ideas for articles, in school system or association "house organs" and community newspapers.
    a) Each teacher should be alerted to the need for a continuous flow of such ideas in order to give complete coverage and proper balance to news about school activities.
    b) One person in each school might be delegated to contact others, on regular deadlines, for such contributions.

    c) Emphasis might be on future events and human interest stories, rather than past events. Care should be exercised in selection of human interest materials.

    d) A specialist familiar with journalistic writing may be appointed to edit copy in conformity with the style sheet of publications to which stories are submitted.

12. *Four elements which contribute to good community relations are:*
    a) A fundamental belief in public education;
    b) A questioning attitude of "Why is this so?";
    c) Belief in the democratic process;
    d) *A sense of humor!*

13. *Cooperation in publicizing* and promoting school system participation in American Education Week and Public Schools Week observances.

14. *Purchasing* leaflets produced by state associations, such as the California Teachers Association, for mass distribution during Public Schools Week (sold at or below cost—from one to two cents per copy).

15. *Cooperation with parents' association leaders* and unit organizations as fully as possible.

16. *Strong and continuing emphasis* on the fact that every teacher, in and out of the classroom, is contributing (consciously or otherwise) to public attitudes toward schools.

    a) Reporting (regardless of the type used in the district) presents a problem and a challenge. Insofar as possible, some good words should be a part of every report about student progress.

    b) The latest NSPRA publication on this subject is "Person to Person." Its contents would be helpful to many teachers.

    c) There is a high rate of turnover in the "publics" in many school systems. Teachers should be genuinely hospitable to newcomers.

17. *Cooperation with the National Professional Associations,* the state associations, and, the state legislature, in initiative and other campaigns.

18. *Urging educators (and others) to register and vote* at all elections.

19. *Purchasing,* for members of the committee, copies of "Freeways to Friendship" (a handbook for local associations public relations committees). Price: twenty-six cents. Order from Field Service, CTA, 1125 West 6th Street, Los Angeles, California 90017.

Some Further School-Community Relations Aids

Some sources of materials and services are:

1. *Trends*—a monthly digest of important developments in school public relations in all parts of the country.
2. *It Starts in the Classroom Newsletter*—a monthly roundup of classroom-inspired, classroom-tested public relations ideas developed by teachers.
3. *Public Relations Leads for the Elementary School Principal*—a quarterly report on outstanding public relations case studies and how to-do-it techniques written expressly for the elementary school principal.
4. *Public Relations Leads for the Secondary School Principal*— a quarterly review of successful public relations projects designed to help the secondary school principal plan his overall public relations program.
5. *Public Relations Leads for the Local Association Leader*—includes case studies, techniques, and publicity tips especially planned for use by local association leaders.
6. "Public Relations Research Memo"—a quarterly service of the National School Public Relations Association and the National Education Association Research Division designed to channel to subscribers new findings and background data on significant public relations topics and trends.
7. "Public Relations Guide"—a quarterly listing of new public relations books, pamphlets, films, and television and radio programs designed to spark the school public relations program.
8. "Exchange File"—a monthly mailing of outstanding printed materials produced by school and nonschool sources.
9. NSPRA handbooks:

   Let's Go to Press—a guide to better school news reporting

   Contacts Plus—a handbook of ideas for improving school-community relations

   Janie Learns to Read—a handbook to help parents understand the school's reading program, and how they can help.

The aforementioned listings may be obtained through the National School Public Relations Association (a department of the National Education Association), 1201 Sixteenth Street, N.W., Washington, D.C. 20006.

The California Teachers Association, Burlingame, California and 1125 West Sixth Street, Los Angeles, can provide, in quantity and at minimum cost, a number of helpful pamphlets for distribution to the public. Among these publications are:

1. *There's a Flag Flying at Your Public School*—tells how schools are teaching American history, government, and citizenship.
2. *Assignment for Today: The 7 R's*— shows ways in which schools are teaching the "3 R's" plus reasoning, responsibility, resourcefulness, and respect for law.
3. "The Truth About Our Public Schools"—a reprint of an article in *Changing Times,* the Kiplinger magazine, showing factually that modern children are getting a better education today than they ever could have received in the public school before. (This is one of the most effective articles written for showing the strong points of public education in the United States.)[9]
4. *Freeways to Friendships*—an entertaining and informative guide to beginning a public relations program.

Other sources:[10]

1. National Association of Manufacturers, 532 Emerson Street, Palo Alto, California. *This We Believe About Education*—a booklet published in the interest of greater education-industry cooperation. *National Association of Manufacturers News,* August, 1954, "Our Public Schools and Their Financial Support"—a statement of the problem, and how businessmen may help.
2. United States Chamber of Commerce, 1615 H Street, N.W., Washington, D.C. 20006. "Education—An Investment in People"—a research

[9]See also C. W. Scott and C. M. Hill, *Public Education Under Criticism* (Englewood Cliffs, New Jersey: Prentice-Hall, Inc., 1954). This is a comprehensive anthology of three parts: major criticisms of public education, analyses of such criticisms, and suggested procedures used in meeting the criticisms. Contains over 100 pertinent excerpts from a wide range of authors.
[10]See also R. F. Campbell and Elaine A. Ramseyer, *The Dynamics of School-Community Relationships* (Boston: Allyn and Bacon, Inc., 1959). This is an excellent approach to working with citizens' committees.

brochure which documents the interdependence of business and education; probably the finest and most complete publication in its field. (Due to its cost this publication is not for quantity distribution, but is invaluable when strategically placed.)

DO

1. Distribute periodically prepared materials, brochures, newsletters, and special notices concerning the school to the several "publics."
2. Arrange for speeches before community organizations by qualified school personnel to help to gain support for the supervisory program.
3. Encourage the use of research programs, studies, tests, and surveys to build an understanding of the school program and the way in which supervision has helped.
4. Encourage citizens' advisory committees to participate actively in support of the instructional program.
5. Arrange for demonstrations and exhibits by teachers and students to be used to present the school program in a positive light.
6. Make information available to the local press regarding all school functions, including supervisory activities and educational accomplishments.
7. Plan for a program of teacher and supervisory conferences with the parents to share student progress and educational accomplishments. This is an excellent medium of public relations.
8. Invite the parents' association and other organized groups to participate in the responsibilities of the school program as an effective technique in gaining community support for supervision.
9. Use Open House activities to present the school program to the community.
10. Have supervisors present radio and television programs (and encourage teachers to do the same) to publicize outstanding features of the educational program.
11. Encourage school forums on important issues as a service to promote the community-school concept and draw attention to its program.
12. Use governing board (trustees) meetings to create understanding of the role of supervision in the educational program.

13. Encourage special curriculum area gatherings, such as Business Education days, which reach an important public.
14. Stress the importance of making sure that each student leaves school with a clear idea of what he has learned that day.
15. Take steps to strengthen staff relations. Money and time spent in this manner are investments, not an expense. They could pay enormous dividends in improved community relations.

DON'T

1. Threaten, denounce, or bring pressure on an editor to print or to withhold a story.
2. Employ *destructive* criticism or become emotional when the facts of a story are reported incorrectly, when headlines give the wrong impression, when individuals are misquoted, when unfavorable news stories are published, or when a story is not published.
3. Refuse to release timely information to the press and broadcast media or pretend to be unacquainted with the details of a story.
4. Send out many news releases that really do not have news value.
5. Be drawn into controversies on a personal basis when the school is criticized or attacked in a news story.
6. Play favorites with television and radio stations, nor with the morning or evening (or daily or community) newspapers.
7. Create the impression that you know more about listener, viewer, or reader interests than the commentator, the reporter, the producer, the director, or the editor.
8. Fail to invite representatives of all communication media (press and broadcast) to special school affairs which should be reported or, having invited them, fail to show them the courtesy and hospitality that is expected.
9. Cause the commentators and reporters to wait for a long time for an interview with a school official.
10. Always be on the "asking end" in your relations with the press.
11. Fail to obtain support for the community relations program through a functional in-service education plan, strengthened by a professional staff which practices good public relations every day.

12. Neglect pushing for an adequate budgetary provision for the program for community relations.
13. Neglect the professional associations, which can be of great help in planning your program for improved community relations.
14. Plan for improved community relations on the basis of a particular past experience in a stable present, for the materials, content, and procedures of the requirements of education are changing so rapidly that these changes must be taken into account if the program for school-community relations is to have validity.

Supervisory Problems

In Basket

Problem 1

Candy machines have been placed in five of six secondary school buildings. Carbonated soft drink vending machines are available to students in the senior high schools. In one junior high school there is a milk and orange drink dispenser. Students have access to the machines throughout the school day.

This practice is in violation of district policy. The policy, written and in effect before candy machines were installed, stated:

During regular school hours candy and soda pop shall be sold only in the school cafeterias and only during regular lunch hours. This policy does not prohibit the sale of milk in vending machines.

Teachers have complained that accessibility of vending machines during the school day increases *a permissive attitude* and affects adversely the discipline in the school. It has been charged that educational objectives are being ignored by "not practicing what we preach about dental and personal health practices." The state administrator of federal hot lunch programs has registered a complaint that the sale of candy is contrary to regulations of federal hot lunch programs. Five principals have stated that revenue from the machines is essential to help pay for increased costs of student activities. The revenue from the candy machines is significant.

The local distributor who supplies the machines and keeps them stocked has an investment in the machines. He has said that he would resist removal of his machines and the ensuing loss of business.

As supervising principal, would you decide that the existing policy be enforced and the vending machines removed? If so, how should this be done? What would you do?

Problem 2

At a recent meeting of the administrative council, the superintendent presented his views concerning community relations. He indicated that he felt that good community relations should be within the skill and scope of the school community; that is, that it should be attainable. He stressed that community relations should be a continuous effort, based upon truth and honesty, which would unfold and develop naturally. He emphasized the importance of interest and the stimulation of enthusiasm and good will, and of the importance of good two-way, open channels of communication. He said that he felt all available avenues should be used so that the program could be comprehensive, and concluded by saying that the community relations program should be balanced in time and emphasis as well as planned, guided, and flexible. At the following meeting of the administrative council, the superintendent reported that he believed that the success of a community relations program depends, to a large extent, upon the school personnel and the students. He assigned various tasks to the individuals attending the meeting.

Your task, as supervising principal, is to prepare a checklist to be used in evaluating the community relations program with respect to the local school, the classroom, and the teacher association group.

How would you proceed?
Whom would you involve in solving your problem?
What would you do?
What checklist would you come up with?

Problem 3

The superintendent of schools, once again, has become concerned about the adequacy of the community relations program. He indicated that he felt that time and/or money spent in fact-finding research could well prove to be good insurance in a community relations program. He indicated that he felt that the power structure and decision-making machinery in the community was difficult to discern; that some facts were deeply imbedded and required especially careful study.

Although you know that you will not have to go to the public in the near future to ask for a tax rate increase or for a bond issue to be passed, nevertheless the superintendent has indicated that he feels it is necessary to know more about how the public feels about its schools. Your assignment is to gather that information.

How would you proceed?
What would you do?

Selected Bibliography

Books

Adler, Irving. *What We Want of Our Schools—Plain Talk on Education, from Theory to Budgets*. New York: The John Day Company, 1957.

Arnold, William E. et al. *The Administration of Public Education*. New York: The Ronald Press Company, 1952.

Bennett, Margaret E. *Guidance in Groups: A Resource Book for Teachers, Counselors, and Administrators*. New York: McGraw-Hill Book Company, Inc., 1955.

Bernays, Edward L. *Public Relations*. Norman: University of Oklahoma Press, 1957.

Campbell, R. F., and Elaine A. Ramseyer. *The Dynamics of School-Community Relationships*. Boston: Allyn and Bacon, Inc., 1959.

Cook, Lloyd. *School Problems in Human Relations*. New York: McGraw-Hill Book Company, Inc., 1957.

Davies, Daniel R., and Kenneth F. Heller. *Citizens Committees*. New London, Connecticut: Arthur C. Croft Publications, 1954.

Eastmond, Jefferson N. *The Teacher and School Administration*. Boston: Houghton Mifflin Company, 1959.

Frey, Sherman H., and Keith R. Getschman, *School Administration: Selected Readings*. New York: Thomas Y. Crowell Company, 1969.

Jones, James J. *School Public Relations: Issues and Cases*. New York: G. P. Putnam's Sons, 1960.

Kindred, L. W. *School Public Relations*. Englewood Cliffs, New Jersey: Prentice-Hall, Inc., 1957.

McCloskey, Gordon. *Education and Public Understanding*. New York: Harper and Brothers, 1959.

Reeder, Ward G. *An Introduction to Public-School Relations*. New York: The Macmillan Company, 1937.

Scott, C. W., and C. M. Hill. *Public Education Under Criticism*. Englewood Cliffs, New Jersey: Prentice-Hall, Inc., 1954.

Stearns, Harry L. *Community Relations and the Public Schools*. Englewood Cliffs, New Jersey: Prentice-Hall, Inc., 1955.

Stephenson, Howard. *Handbook of Public Relations*. New York: McGraw-Hill Book Company, Inc., 1960.

Stoops, Emery, and J. L. Rafferty, Jr. *Practices and Trends in School Administration*. Boston: Ginn and Company, 1961.

Wilson, Robert E. *The Modern School Superintendent—His Principles and Practices*. New York: Harper and Brothers, 1960.

Zirbes, Laura. *Spurs to Creative Teaching.* New York: G. P. Putnam's Sons, 1959.

Periodicals

Mauro, Carl. "Partners in Education." *Educational Leadership* XV (April 1958): 401–406.

Other Sources

American Association of School Administrators. *Public Relations for America's Schools.* Twenty-Eighth Department Yearbook. Washington, D.C.: National Education Association, 1950.

_____ . *School Board-Superintendent Relationships.* Thirty-Fourth Department Yearbook. Washington, D.C.: National Education Association, 1956.

Educational Policies Commission. *Strengthening Community Life: Schools Can Help.* Washington, D.C.: National Education Association, 1954.

Mass Media in Education. Fifty-Third Yearbook of the National Society for the Study of Education. Chicago: University of Chicago Press, 1954.

National Citizens Commission for the Public Schools. *How Can Citizens Help Their Schools?* New York: The Commission, 1954.

National School Public Relations Association. *Public Relations Gold Mine.* Volume II. Washington, D.C.: National Education Association, 1959.

_____ . *Public Relations Gold Mine, Brightest Ideas of 1957.* Washington, D.C.: National Education Association, 1957.

_____ . *No News Is Bad News Where Schools Are Concerned.* Washington, D.C.: National Education Association, 1955.

_____ . *Person to Person—The Classroom Teacher's Public Relations.* Washington, D.C.: National Education Association, 1956.

_____ . *Contact Plus—A Handbook of Ideas for Improving School-Community Relations.* Washington, D.C.: National Education Association, 1954.

_____ . *Action and Reaction—Public Relations for Educational Secretaries.* Washington, D.C.: National Education Association, 1957.

How to Assist the Teacher in Planning for More Effective Conferences with Parents

It is the teacher to whom parents come, or should come, to learn about the child and the school. The program for community relations will falter and, perhaps, be doomed to failure if conferences with parents are not properly handled. Only the teacher can tell the parents what his plans are for the student's program; only the teacher knows how he will attempt to help the student to learn. A child, in relating school happenings to his parents, sees such details from a child's viewpoint, and for this reason the teacher should attempt to schedule frequent interviews with parents.

It is commonly agreed that the home and the school must work closely together if a good educational program is to be developed for students. Yet the establishment of constructive, positive relationships between teachers and parents is often a slow business. One circumstance which may advance or hinder good parent-school collaboration is the manner in which contact between home and school is planned. The importance of satisfactory school-parent contact is directly related to teaching and to understanding children.

How to Help the Teacher Plan for Productive Parent-Teacher Conferences

Purpose of Conferences

The purposes of the conference or interview with the parent are reciprocal, and involve gaining information, acquiring insight, and communicating needs, status, and progress. A. Fenlason[1] noted that the interview was a purposeful conversation. The objective of the parent-teacher interview are fourfold:

1. To help parents develop an objective concept of the student's capacities and abilities.
2. To acquaint the parents with the student's present status in his plan.
3. To establish cooperatively specific objectives for the student's growth at the present time.
4. To make plans cooperatively for the achievement of the objectives.

Further purposes of the parent-teacher conferences may be:

[1]Anne Fenlason, *Essentials in Interviewing* (New York: Harper and Row, Publishers, 1952), p. 15.

1. To interpret to the parent the student's experiences at school and how he is responding to them.
2. To acquaint the parent with the school, its facilities, its personnel, and its work, and thus to further the community relations program.
3. To learn about the student's home environment and relationships important to his development—his feelings, his interests, his friends, his health, his parents' hopes and desires concerning him.
4. To foster positive relationship between teacher and parent.
5. To discuss ways in which teacher and parent can help each other to help the student.
6. To give the student a sense of confidence and security through the friendship of parent and teacher.
7. To discuss common goals for the student appropriate to his stage of development.
8. To share observations about the student which parent and teacher interpret together.
9. To plan cooperatively with the parent so that consistent guidance may result, and so that the student may meet the same kinds of demands at home and at school.

Most students welcome this planning, and give valuable information and clues into their feelings and attitudes.

How to Plan for the Interview

The number of interviews or parent conferences will depend on the problem situation. For each student, if feasible, there should be several interviews. The first contact is usually the initial brief encounter, perhaps with the student present, at the beginning of the school year. Rapport should be developed in the first meeting, regardless of the brevity of the initial contact. Student and parent should feel understood and accepted.

The teacher should encourage the parent to return, but the teacher must take the initiative in planning future conferences according to his schedule. Students enjoy having their parents come to school, unless teacher-parent-student relationships have been strained. If negative factors have entered into the picture, the teacher or staff member must rebuild rapport and understanding. This rebuilding process will be slow.

SUPPLEMENT 18

The supervising principal should stress that, in planning interviews with the parent, it is advantageous first to consult the student and discuss with him what his parent and the teacher will be covering. The following outline is a summary of steps in preparation for parent-teacher conferences. These steps should be stressed by the supervisor, and ample opportunity should be given the teacher to ask questions concerning each point.

A. *Preparation by the teacher:*

1. Review the student's school records such as cumulative record card, health card, anecdotal record.
2. Confer with principal, school nurse, or other school personnel to secure most recent information.
3. Secure samples of student's work from his folder which is kept throughout the term.
4. Give consideration to the physical factors involved when the conference is held, such as light, temperature, comfort, the privacy— free from interruptions.
5. R. H. Hatch[2] intimated that most parents want the same type of information about their children:
   a) What are the strengths and weaknesses of the student?
   b) What special aptitudes does he have?
   c) What is his learning potential?
   d) What are his interests and plans?
   e) What special problems does he face?
   f) How does his achievement compare with his ability?
   g) What can be done for him at home?
   h) How may certain home problems be *solved?*
6. Attempt to make a positive statement concerning the student.

B. *Preparation by the parents:*

Encourage parents to:
1. Note questions they would like to ask.
2. Note observations about the student which they feel would help the teacher.

[2]Raymond H. Hatch, *Guidance Service* (Dubuque, Iowa: William C. Brown Company, 1953).

3. Note unusual health factors, family situations, etc., which may have affected or do affect the student.
4. List experiences that may explain present behavior.
5. List special interests or abilities.

These steps in preparation serve as a base from which good parent-teacher conferences may develop. Implied is careful interpretation so that the information will be *objective* and *acceptable*. It is offered that perhaps the most important preparation which both the parent and the teacher can make is the development of an attitude of accepting the other as a true partner in the joint task of helping the student to enjoy school and his social relationships, and of creating a happy and stimulating environment in which he will want to learn.

The Conference

Acceptance and Empathy

The first element of expertness in interpersonal relations is respect for the other person and awareness of the other person's feeling of security.[3] The teacher must be able to accept and understand individual differences in heredity, background, experience, and attitude as the basis of acceptance and understanding of both parent and student.

The teacher must be particularly aware of the parent's feelings as the parent faces the authority figure of his own childhood. For many parents, school has meant (and still means) a threatening place with many traumatic events and scars on the memory. There are certain limits set on the student through the behavior of parents and other people in his life, as they relive their early school experiences once again through their children.

Some have found it wiser to play the role of naive observer when interviewing parents. The teacher should allow the parent to be the expert regarding his child. For example, the teacher may say, "I noticed that Paul seems to be less interested in . . . and I wondered if something might have

---

[3]See H. S. Sullivan, *The Interpersonal Theory of Psychiatry* (New York: W. W. Norton & Company, Inc., 1953).

happened that you feel has caused this trouble?" For the most part, the parent will react to this invitation to be the one who knows most about the student. Parents believe they know their children better than anyone else, and perhaps they do, unless they are too emotionally involved. It is important for the teacher to remember that it is unwise to play the role of the expert with people who may feel insecure. What happens when the parents face the authority figure of their childhood?

One supervising principal listed some techniques for the conference, which appear in Table Supp. 18–1.

TABLE SUPP. 18–1   Some DO's and DON'T's—Meeting with the Parent

1. Try to arrange the conference so that there will be no interruptions.

2. The teacher's greeting should be warm and friendly, with a warm-up topic to open the conversation.

3. Begin with a positive statement of the student's abilities. The parent is less defensive, and it conveys interest and liking for the student.

4. Share observations about the student, comparing responses at home and at school before making an interpretation or judgment.

5. Let any advice grow out of mutual discussion and a growing insight on the part of the parent into the reasons for the behavior.

6. Discover how the parent is thinking and feeling about the student. The teacher cannot understand the student's behavior until he knows the parent's attitude.

7. Listen to the parent's complaints or criticisms of the school, accept-ing them as evidence of interest or suggestions to be considered.

8. If a parent gives his reason for the student's behavior, accept it, and, if possible, lead the discussion on to other possible causes. Behavior is a result of many causative factors.

9. Listen, and then listen some more. The teacher did not invite the parent in so he could lecture to him, but to obtain as well as give help. *Encourage the parent to talk, and listen to what he has to say.*

10. Try to close the conference with a constructive, hopeful statement.

11. It is easier to build a cooperative relationship if the teacher is not behind a desk. (Use a table if available.)

12. The educator should *not* argue with a parent. Arguing will arouse resentment.

13. He should *not* try to push his thinking onto a parent. Con-

TABLE SUPP. 18–1 (Continued)

clusions and recommendations should be reached through a process of discussion and mutual thinking.

14. He should *not* criticize harshly or negatively. Destructive criticism may be fatal to the building of a cooperative relationship in parent-teacher conferences since most parents cannot be objective about their children. The emotional involvement is too great.

15. The educator should *not* give direct advice unless it is requested, and never as the single successful solution.

16. Do *not* imply that the parent or home is to blame for the student's behavior.

17. Do *not* overlook influences other than the home on the student's life.

18. *Avoid* discussing other children in the school. Such comments direct attention from the problem at hand, encourage competitiveness, and often harm school and neighborhood relationships.

19. Do *not* use blanket words such as immaturity and insecurity.

20. Do *not* assume that the parents want help or advice. Such assumption usually brings resistance because it implies a form of criticism.

21. Do *not* criticize or blame past school experiences or teachers because such comments tend to destroy confidence in all education. Attention should be centered upon present needs and on plans for the future, not on past mistakes.

Communication in Parent-Teacher Conferences

The supervisor may wish to encourage the teacher to have a set of carefully prepared questions which he introduces into the conversation tactfully at the appropriate time.

The way a question is formulated has a definite bearing on responses. It is important for the teacher to realize that human beings are always protecting their egos. There is a desire to protect one's psychological integrity in all interpersonal contacts. Teachers must be sensitive to the desire of parents to impress and to repress. An attempt should be made to get the parents to say what is necessary without their feeling that their psychological integrety is in danger. The parents may have difficulty in accepting an idea they interpret as reflecting upon them in a socially undesirable manner. The chief barrier to communication in such situations may be anxiety.

The supervisor should help the teacher to be alert to the many factors which may detract from the interview situation. Among these are hesitancy, indecisiveness, tenseness, fatigue, apathy, sadness, overdramatics, elation, contradictory statements, mannerisms, gestures, and others. The teacher should attempt to establish some congruity between verbal and nonverbal behavior in his search for clues to understanding the child he attempts to teach.

Successful interviewing is an art and requires experience for optimum results. It must be a relationship that permits the parent to express his thoughts and his feelings with the knowledge that he will be listened to and understood by a sympathetic and accepting person who, in understanding and accepting, helps him in turn to understand and accept both himself and the student.

How to Evaluate a Supervisory Program

S. H. Moorer[1] reported that an effective supervisor continuously seeks to narrow the gap between what is and what might be in the supervisory program.

This chapter includes a discussion of the following topics:

Principles for the evaluation of supervision
Teachers and principals view supervision in action
Evidence of an effective supervisory program
Some questions the principal can ask himself
Do—don't
"In-Basket" supervisory problem
Chapter Supplement

Principles for the Evaluation of Supervision

Supervising principals have suggested the following criteria for the evaluation of a supervisory program:

1. Supervisors must accept the principle that supervision is a cooperative service activity (specific, cooperative planning being at its heart), and that its goal is to help teachers perform more efficiently and more effectively.
2. Supervision must release the energies of the professional staff in creative ways to solve both individual and common problems.[2]
3. The evaluation of a supervisory program should be a fundamental part of the program itself.

---

[1]Sam H. Moorer, *How Good Is Your Supervisory Program?* (St. Augustine: Florida State Department of Education, 1950).
[2]See Jane Franseth, *Learning to Supervise Schools,* Circular No. 289 (Washington, D.C.: Office of Education, n.d.), p. 3.

4. Evaluation is continuous—and occurs at regular, frequent intervals.
5. The aim of evaluation is to improve supervision and, ultimately, instruction for students.
6. A supervisory program should be evaluated in terms of its own objectives and the instructional improvement which it achieves.
7. Evaluation should encourage improvement of the school's organization for supervision.
8. The evaluation of a supervisory program aids in forming harmonious relationships between school staff members.
9. Statistical data-gathering and interpretation form the basis of supervisory evaluation.
10. Evaluation considers the total teaching-learning situation.
11. Outside consultants occasionally are needed to make more objective evaluations and to bring new points of view.

The Department of Elementary School Principals of the National Education Association[3] has defined four minimum essentials for the program of supervision which may be considered as evaluation points. To what extent does the supervisory program provide for:

1. The appraisal of specific learning situations to ascertain the needs of students and the efficiency of instruction?
2. Technical service to teachers in the form of instructional aids, specific suggestions for the improvement of instruction, and assistance in diagnosis and measurement?
3. Research for the purpose of curriculum construction and revision, and for the improvement of materials, techniques, and methods of instruction?
4. Professional leadership of and cooperation with teachers through individual and group conferences, through stimulation to further professional study, and through cooperative development of a program of in-service education?

[3]Department of Elementary School Principals, *The Elementary School Principalship —Today and Tomorrow*, Twenty-Seventh Yearbook (Washington, D.C.: National Education Association, 1948), p. 104.

In the search for ways to evaluate the supervisory program emphasis is placed upon an effective, cooperative approach to a professional problem. School supervision, however, usually does not begin with cooperation and democratic action, but that is where it may arrive under proper guidance. In the end "supervision" will constitute something slightly different for each one who supervises and for each one who is supervised.[4]

Good supervision is based upon a belief in democracy and uses the scientific method, continuously improving and evaluating its products and processes. It proceeds by means of an orderly, cooperatively planned and executed series of activities and is judged by its results. Effective supervision seeks to evaluate (1) personnel, (2) procedures, and (3) outcomes.

How to Appraise the Written Evaluation

The written characterization must be a true record of evaluation based on measurement which is as objective as possible. Evaluation must be a positive critique; it should not be laudatory anymore than it should be defamatory. Deserved praise should be included. In the case of a beginning teacher, the individual must be evaluated in terms pertinent to the experience of the individual, but the issues should not be evaded.

If the written characterization is to serve its purpose, an account of performance should be provided that includes the whole truth uninfluenced by personal motives, fear, or pity. A frank appraisal of the strengths and weaknesses of the individual should be included so that a program of professional growth may be planned.

If a check sheet is used the principal should be sure that any written comments apply to professional competencies, and that they are not duplications of phrases included in the checklist. Written comments may explain, but they also should amplify the check sheet section of the evaluation so that a clearer picture of the individual and his needs will be provided.

Specific information that should be found in the evaluation form includes:

1. Personal characteristics
2. Professional competence and knowledge of subject matter

[4]Harold Spears, *Improving the Supervision of Instruction* (Englewood Cliffs, New Jersey: Prentice-Hall, Inc., 1953), p. 17.

3. Ability to work with and control students
4. Classroom management and instructional efficiency
5. Interpersonal relationships
6. Needs (specific)
7. Recommendations
8. Prognosis

The important consideration is that written records, and supervisory conferences as well, will be helpful to teachers. If they are not, recommendations should be made to alter the written record form (and/or the conference procedure).

How to Describe and Appraise the Status of the Supervisory Program

The supervising principal will not be satisfied to know merely the adequacy of the product; rather, he will want feedback concerning the status of the many conditions that limit or facilitate educational outcomes.

Knowledge of status is important. Not only is feedback concerning present conditions and effectiveness of the supervisory program important in itself, but it may serve to assist in the interpretation of the many kinds of data that may be received by the principal concerning his program for supervision. Furthermore, such knowledge can lead to revision, innovation, and subsequent improvement, continuous evaluation, and further feedback which is so vitally important to educational supervision.

Normative Survey of the Effectiveness of Supervision

Generally speaking, the supervising principal should proceed through following ten steps in conducting a normative survey of the supervisory program in order to determine present status.

1. Prepare statements of the objectives of the normative survey;
2. Define the population to be sampled;
3. Decide as to the nature of the data to be collected;
4. Delineate techniques for collecting the data;
5. Delimit the study and the sampling unit;

6. Select a method for determining the sample;
7. Decide upon methods for treating nonrespondents;
8. Conduct exploratory of pilot surveys, follow with the final study;
9. Prepare a summary and analysis of data received;
10. Prepare the survey report.

When the supervising principal asks questions of opinion concerning the supervisory program, every effort should be made to formulate wording that is not going to invoke bias in the respondent. Some opportunity should be given in the survey to permit respondents to record general remarks on special points. These remarks should direct attention to facts that are relevant to the problem at hand, but that were not included in the list of questions.

In reporting the results of the sampling survey the supervising principal should take into account the following list of suggested material.

1. A general description of the survey should be included. Purposes of the survey, descriptions of the material covered, methods used in collecting the data, nature of the information collected, sampling method, accuracy, repetition, period of time, responsibility, and basic references should be indicated.
2. The design of the normative survey should be presented carefully, with limitations and delimitations of design reported.
3. The method of selecting sample units should be noted.
4. All materials and personnel utilized in conducting the supervisory survey should be included in the report.
5. The cost of conducting the evaluative survey should be noted.
6. Precision and the efficiency of the survey, as indicated by the degree of agreement observed between independent investigators and from a comparison with other sources of information, should be reported.
7. A summary of the findings, conclusions, and recommendations for further study should be included.

It should be remembered that the ultimate purpose in studying causes is to be able to predict the effects of certain causes with a view to the control of the cause-effect continuum. The collection of enumerative data may provide important source data for analytical investigation of the effectiveness of the program for school supervision.

The purpose of the normative survey in an analytical problem situation is to inquire into the underlying factors or causes that may have given rise to an observed condition or situation, whereas in the enumerative problem situation the objective of the normative survey is to determine certain characteristics of the population without inquiring into the reason as to why these characters appear as they do. The latter situation does not appear to have as much value as does the former in the evaluation of the program for supervision.

FIGURE 19-1   Which Is Worse?

Teachers and Principals View Supervision in Action

D. Benjamin[5] reported teachers' and principals' reactions to supervisory techniques, listed in rank order and based upon frequency of occurrence.

[5]Dayton Benjamin, "How Principals Can Improve Instruction," *American School Board Journal* CXXXII (May 1956): 37–39.

Teachers and principals differed widely concerning their concepts of helpful supervision. A combination, however, is possible.

TEACHERS' VIEWS. Teachers viewed the following as effective supervisory behavior:

1. Occasionally relieving the teacher of classroom duties so he may attend to pressing professional commitments; respecting plans made by the teacher.
2. Building the teacher's confidence by demonstrating knowledge of teaching procedures.
3. Observing the class and conducting follow-up with a clear, direct evaluation of the teacher's work.
4. Using the formal evaluation conference as an objective agreement concerning strengths and weaknesses previously discussed.
5. Supporting the teacher in his relations with children and parents.
6. Relieving the teacher of clerical details to allow more time for preparation and actual teaching.
7. Granting teachers' requests for help from outside specialist-consultants.

PRINCIPALS' VIEWS. Principals viewed the following as effective supervisory behavior:

1. Becoming thoroughly acquainted with the teacher's capabilities before suggesting a new procedure; observing for a length of time to assess the teacher's capabilities.
2. Waiting until the beginning teacher becomes acquainted with the students, the philosophy of the school system, and its routines before suggesting major changes in routine.
3. Waiting until the teacher is emotionally ready to accept suggestions for change.
4. Listening sympathetically to the teacher's personal problems and offering assistance when asked for it.
5. Arranging visits to other classrooms, making certain that no stigma is attached to a visitation, and discussing the visitation thoroughly.

TEACHERS AND PRINCIPALS COMBINE THEIR VIEWS. A combination of views of both teachers and principals is possible.

1. Continuing to work with the teacher in the development of new techniques and procedures; continuing to bring new ideas to the teacher.
2. Helping the teacher improve classroom control by giving suggestions that apply directly to the problem area.
3. Providing direct assistance in the utilization of instructional materials.
4. Considering the teacher's preferences and ideas when making suggestions.
5. Demonstrating teaching procedures in such a way that the students' respect for the teacher is preserved.
6. Giving direct praise for specific accomplishment.
7. Giving reassurance when possible that the teacher is doing a good job.
8. Giving the teacher an assignment in which he feels important before other school and community adults.
9. Complying with the teacher's request for expediting additional plant facilities and instructional supplies.

Evidence of an Effective Supervisory Program

The symptoms below may be indicative of a supervisory program that works. There is evidence of:

1. Increased understanding of the nature of the student.
2. Increased knowledge of skills and techniques of directing, improving, measuring, and recording the intellectual and social growth of the student.
3. Increased knowledge and skill in the planning and adaptation of learning materials and activities to individual (and group) abilities and interests.
4. Increased knowledge in the subject matter fields.
5. Understanding and skill in the use of "newer" classroom procedures and devices of worth.
6. Knowledge of modern concepts dealing with the problems of discipline and control.

7. Increased understanding and skill in counseling young people.
8. Construction of a curriculum related to local, state, and national needs, pertaining to present and future needs of the student.
9. The establishment of better relationships with students, professional colleagues, and members of the community.
10. The development of greater interest in reading, in research, and in professional writing.

Evidence as to the effectiveness of the supervisory program may be gathered through the review of tests and inventory results as well as through the survey technique. The following should be investigated:

1. Results of achievement tests;
2. Results of intelligence and aptitude tests;
3. Results of adjustment inventories;
4. Anecdotal records of student behavior;
5. Records of teacher's estimate of student achievement;
6. Records of the reactions of students, parents, and the community to the school program;
7. Classroom visits and supervisory conferences.

A general survey of supervisory organization and administration by outside consultants should be completed occasionally. A committee composed of local staff members should be appointed and given the function of evaluating the program of supervision. The evaluation committee should compare the budget expenditures for supervision with those of other school systems.

Some faculty meetings should be devoted to the evaluation of supervisory services. An unsigned opinionnaire, answered by teaching personnel, is a technique for uncovering attitudes toward supervisors and supervision.

The supervising principal should determine if goals have been met and whether or not the goals were desirable in the first place. He should examine the validity of the instruments or records used to conduct the evaluation. All results must be recorded and, if the evaluation is to be worthwhile, it should result in some sort of action. Evaluation per se is worthless!

Some Questions the Supervising Principal Can Ask Himself

The following listing of questions to be answered by the supervising principal may prove helpful in evaluating the supervisory program:

1. Do I maintain cordial relationships with teachers?
2. Is communication with the staff on a personal basis?
3. Do I seek out the strong points in teachers and build upon these?
4. Do I seek and accept the contributions of all members of the staff, no matter how inconsequential the contribution may seem at the time?
5. Do I provide opportunities wherein teachers can make decisions in matters in which they are vitally concerned?
6. Do I seek to uncover and encourage the development of leadership on the part of staff members? (It is the supervisor who knows that the more people who feel a personal responsibility for the supervisory program, the more successful it probably will be.)[6]
7. Do I pretend to be expert in all subjects and grade levels, or am I a specialist in working with teachers on the requirements of successful instruction?
8. Do I provide an ample supply of textbooks and supplementary materials and equipment, and then make sure that it is very easy for teachers to obtain these materials?
9. Do I keep teachers informed about free and inexpensive materials which are available?
10. Do I facilitate the participation by teachers and students in educational field trips?
11. Are my plans for supervision concrete and specific?
12. Are my plans for supervision consistent with the aspirations, goals, and level of development of the teaching personnel and the citizens of the community?
13. Do I base planning, so far as possible, upon the realities of the situation that are discovered through the use of the techniques of research and careful experimentation?

[6]Moorer, *How Good Is Your Supervisory Program.*

14. Do I consult parents to find out what they think the school should be doing?
15. Do I contribute to and help coordinate and integrate the efforts of all agencies and institutions in the community that are interested in the improvement of education?
16. Do I actively cooperate with, and draw upon, the available local, state, national, and international departments that are interested in the improvement of education?
17. Do I establish a schedule for my supervisory activities on a yearly, monthly, weekly and daily basis?
18. Do I judge my success by the progress of the school program toward goals accepted by the group?
19. Do I encourage teachers to assume more responsibility for self-supervision?
20. Have I been successful in elevating the quality and quantity of cooperative planning among staff members?
21. Have I been successful in stimulating more teachers to experiment and do research related to the instructional program and the curriculum?
22. Am I flexible, making changes easily when pertinent and qualified data indicate changes are in order?[7]
23. Do I realize that self-evaluation is the real key to the effective analysis of my contribution to the improvement of instruction?

DO

1. Recommend a general survey of supervisory organization and administration by outside consultants periodically.
2. Seek the appointment of a staff committee from the local school system and give it the task of evaluating the supervision program.
3. Make certain the supervisor and all personnel engaged in the process of supervision are encouraged to make observations concerning the effectiveness of the supervisory program.

[7]Harvey L. Roach, Lieutenant, Los Angeles Police Department, in the Leadership Training Conference Series, Los Angeles, September, 1970.

4. Conduct interviews with the teachers, students, parents, and others to determine the effectiveness of the program.
5. Evaluate the supervisory range, scope, and function in the light of research findings.
6. Use an unsigned opinionnaire filled in by teaching personnel as a technique for uncovering attitudes toward supervisors and supervision.
7. Institute a suggestion box. (Such a device, utilized by teachers and supervisors, may aid constructive evaluation.)
8. Employ preschool workshops in the evaluation of aims, objectives, plans, purposes, and goals with respect to the supervisory process.
9. Remember that evaluation should accompany and follow each supervisory activity.
10. Invite intermediate unit (county) or state consultants to help evaluate the school's supervisory program.
11. Examine records and note what changes have occurred in the curriculum.[8]

A FINAL DON'T

DON'T OVERDUE IT!

Supervisory Problem

The existing policy for supervision has been enforced in School District No. 35 for the past eight years. A university evaluation study of the total district organization and program resulted in a series of faculty and administrative council meetings.

All concerned seemed to agree that there is a need for some revision in the policy for supervision for the district.

How would you, as supervising principal, determine what additions, changes, or deletions you might suggest?

---

[8]See Kimball Wiles, *Supervision for Better Schools* (Englewood Cliffs, New Jersey: Prentice-Hall Inc., 1955).

Selected Bibliography

Books

Barr, A. S. William H. Burton, and Leo J. Brueckner. *Supervision: Democratic Leadership in the Improvement of Learning.* New York: D. Appleton-Century Company, 1947.

Barr, Arvil S., Robert A. Davis, and Palmer O. Johnson. *Educational Research and Appraisal.* Chicago: J. B. Lippincott Company, 1953.

Collings, Ellsworth. *School Supervision in Theory and Practice.* New York: Thomas Y. Crowell Company, 1927.

Crosby, Muriel. *Supervision as Co-operative Action.* New York: Appleton-Century-Crofts, 1957.

Knudsen, Charles W. *Evaluation and Improvement of Teaching.* New York: Doubleday Doran and Company, 1932.

Lucio, William H., and John D. McNeil. *Supervision—A Synthesis of Thought and Action.* New York: McGraw-Hill Book Company, Inc., 1962.

Spears, Harold. *Improving the Supervision of Instruction.* Englewood Cliffs, New Jersey: Prentice-Hall, Inc., 1953.

Wiles, Kimball. *Supervision for Better Schools.* Englewood Cliffs, New Jersey: Prentice-Hall, Inc., 1955.

Periodicals

Benjamin, Dayton. "How Principals Can Improve Instruction." *American School Board Journal* CXXXII (May 1956): 37–39.

Kyte, George C. "This Is the Kind of Supervision That Teachers Welcome and Appreciate." *Nation's Schools* XLVIII (July 1951): 33–34.

Maier, Norman R. F. "Leadership Principles for Problem-Solving Conferences." *Michigan Business Review* XIV (May 1962): 8–15.

Other Sources

Arkansas State Department of Education, Division of Instruction. *Guide to Effective Elementary School Supervision.* Little Rock: The Department, n.d.

Department of Elementary School Principals. *The Elementary School Principalship—Today and Tomorrow.* Twenty-Seventh Yearbook. Washington, D.C.: National Education Association, 1948.

Franseth, Jane. *Learning to Supervise Schools.* Circular No. 289. Washington, D.C.: Office of Education, n.d.

Harris, Lewis E., and Clyde B. Moore. *Keys to Quality—Quest for Quality.* Washington, D.C.: National School Boards Association, American Association of School Administrators, 1960.

Moorer, Sam H. *Supervision: The Keystone to Educational Progress.* Tallahassee: Florida State Department of Education, 1952.

_____. *How Good Is Your Supervisory Program.* St. Augustine: Florida State Department of Education, 1950.

Reavis, William C. "Evaluating the Work of the School," *Proceedings of the Ninth Annual Conference for Administrative Officers of Public and Private Schools.* Volume III. Chicago: University of Chicago Press, 1940.

Texas Education Agency. *Work-Conference on Educational Leadership and Supervision.* Austin: The Agency, 1949.

_____. Curriculum Division. *Supervisor's Exchange.* Austin: The Agency, 1951.

B. M. Bass[1] presented a valuable analysis of the psychological aspects of supervisory decision-making in industry. He reported that according to classical principles of organization, conflict can be eliminated or resolved by programs of rules which can be applied to each problem as it arises to provide appropriate answers. Conflicts over returned goods can be resolved, for instance, if the firm has a routine, standard operating procedure for handling customer complaints. An applicable rule might be that refunds are automatic for all merchandise returned within a year costing less than $100. Other refunding is on a pro-rata basis reflecting cost and use. All problems about refunds can be categorized and decisions made according to rules for each category.

While it often is possible to apply such programming, particularly for the simpler problems, a variety of human judgments and discriminations are involved when the problem becomes more complex and is not subject to routine solution. For example, before appropriate rules can be applied to the problem of whether or not to discontinue a particular instructional procedure, it is necessary to classify the problem or to see if the problem can be classified according to acceptable categories for which rules are available. Even before this, someone may have to decide whether or not there is a problem—whether there is dissatisfaction with the current procedure.

Problem-solving proceeds in three stages: perceiving the problem, searching for or inventing solutions, and evaluating the solutions. Various characteristics of the problem and the problem-solver affect outcomes at each of the three stages. At each stage it is seen that despite his intention to be rational, various attitudinal and motivational factors limit the decision-maker, but much can be done at each stage to reduce these restrictions on creativity, inventiveness, and accuracy of decision.

Decisions on how to handle problems may be reached through discussion, persuasion, delegation, or by accident, and/or executives from two different divisions of an industrial concern may happen to meet in a hallway and decide, as a consequence, on a subsequent production plan. If they had not been in the same hallway at the same time, they might never have decided on such a plan.

Decisions may be *random*. Administration might be indifferent as to

[1]The authors are grateful to Bernard M. Bass, *Organizational Psychology* (Boston: Allyn and Bacon, Inc., 1965), for much of the data in this section.

which of two departments will switch to a new plan first, so a coin might be tossed to decide the matter. Sometimes random decisions are a rational or best possible solution to a problem. But organizations are unlikely to survive if all their decisions are made accidentally, randomly, or as a consequence of power.

Stages in Problem-Solving

Three broad stages complete the decision process. (1) First, the problem must be sensed and analyzed. Applicable elements must be discerned. (2) Then, solutions must be discovered, invented, or identified. To do this, known information is appraised and corrected for bias. Unknown factors are isolated. (3) Third, the solutions must be evaluated to identify the one or more that best copes with the problem. For this to be done, we need to (1) establish criteria for evaluation, (2) weigh the pertinent alternatives and unknowns, (3) project expectations of the impact on objectives, and (4) synthesize our findings with a course of action.

Figure Supp. 19–1 displays a flow chart of logical steps which might be involved in a complete or ideal problem-solving process. The problem-solvers, if they act like a computer, can proceed from one step to the next only if the test of whether they have completed the step permits them to pass on to the next.

The process usually begins with a sense of dissatisfaction with the current state of affairs. A memorandum may be written to the safety director viewing with alarm the increasing number of minor accidents to employees. If the safety director can assure the dissatisfied memo-writer that the rise in accidents is only a random departure from expectations and that the alarm is not warranted, the process may stop. If he agrees that the situation is unsatisfactory, he may call an *ad hoc* committee of his staff to define the problem. They may raise numerous questions. Is the unsatisfactory situation due to a change in reporting methods? Is it due to the opening of a medical first-aid center nearer to the workplace? Are only major accidents increasing? Are the definitions of minor and major accidents in terms of days work lost meaningful and do they help clarify the nature of the current

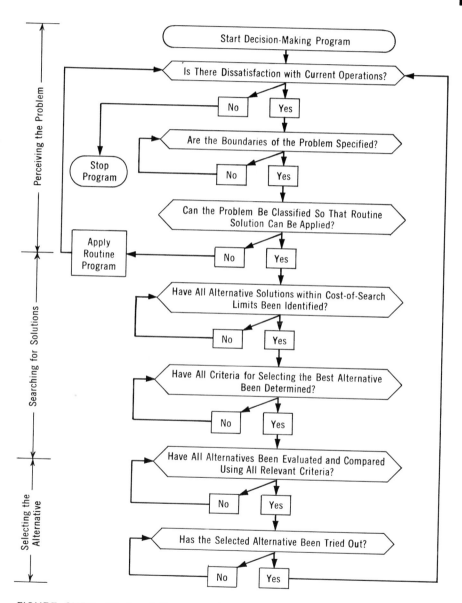

FIGURE SUPP. 19–1   A Program of Tests of Logical Steps in the Decision
Process.

problem? Are minor accidents on the increase in all or only selected departments and shifts? Has there been any recent change in worker morale? Has there been a slackening in the safety program? Are new employes more prone to accidents, or is the introduction of new, faster equipment with more risks for operators confusing the issue?

Following this examination, are we in a position to classify the problem? For example, can we say that the increase in minor accidents is due specifically to faster equipment. If it is, then we have a routine solution for the problem. We have available a special employee training program to be used when new equipment causes difficulties for employees. Therefore we can follow standard operating procedure and end the decision process at this time by contacting the training department about the matter.

But suppose our analysis suggests that rather than being routine, the problem is due to several causes. Moreover, it is judged to contain considerable uncertainty and therefore remains outside the bounds of routine classification and treatment. Therefore we now must search for alternatives until we can pass the test that all options have been identified or that continued exploration for solutions is not worthwhile. We may generate such alternatives as starting a special safety campaign, providing special programs for supervisors on attitudes toward supervisors, hiring a consulting psychologist to counsel individual employees who are accident-repeaters, hiring an engineer to redesign the equipment, and so on.

The criteria for evaluating the alternatives must be established. Efficiency, cost, and feasibility might be adopted as the three criteria to use in evaluating each option. As a consequence, the proposal to launch a supervisory training program might be judged as best in meeting the selected criteria. The supervisory program then will be tried out. A follow-up evaluation may eventually report favorably on the success of the new project, and the decision process will end with the conclusion that the accident problem no longer exists. Of if it is reported that the project failed to reduce minor accidents, then there still is dissatisfaction with current operations and the problem-solving cycle is repeated as shown in Figure Supp. 19–1.

AN ILLUSTRATION. A staged process of problem-solving similar to the hypothetical one just described was seen in a detailed account of how a medium-sized school system examined the feasibility of introducing electronic data-processing equipment into its accounting operations. First, for example, there was a considerable period in which a special assistant to the controller explored the problem by corresponding with experts, talking with salesmen and users, and reading journal articles before moving into the next stage.

Problem-Solving by Computer

Step-by-step logical description of problem-solving makes it possible to stimulate this heuristic process by computer programs. A General Problem-Solving Program has been written by a Carnegie Tech-Rand research group, which develops its own network of instructions to detect differences between the present situation and a goal, retrieves from its memory or through search and analysis alternative ways of reducing the discrepancy, and then applies the alternative which will reduce the discrepancy between current state and objective. Similar programs have been designed which prove mathematical theorems and play checkers or chess. The computer model indicates that relatively straightforward step-by-step procedures are sufficient.

Left to their own devices, humans usually follow somewhat less orderly procedures. For example, analysis of four cases of educational decision-making at the community college level suggests, unfortunately, that the actual human decision process is not as rational or orderly as it might be. First, rough expectations apparently screen out obviously inappropriate alternatives. Thus one alternative to cutting costs might be to eliminate the continuation of high-cost-low-enrollment classes. But such elimination immediately brings on many new unwanted problems such as unfulfilled student major curriculum needs; unmet requirements for graduation; failure to complete specialized course sequences demanded by the community and/or required for more advanced college-level work; and decreased use of full capacity. Second, the feasibility of implementing a particular decision is considered, as well as ways it can be evaluated. Most important is whether the solution is within budgetary constraints. There is some examination of the expected costs and returns of alternative solutions to the problem but

19

little attempt to demonstrate that the expected net return on the chosen alternative will equal or exceed the expected return on alternative investments. But when forced into more orderliness, humans become more successful problem-solvers.

While computers *must* adopt such orderly processes, humans may find it efficacious to do so also for there is some evidence that a step-by-step orderly attack on problems increases the effectiveness of human problem-solvers. Orderly problem-solving proceeds in three stages: (1) delineating the problem, (2) creating and/or searching for alternative solutions, and (3) evaluating prospective solutions. Problem-solvers are most effective when they thoroughly consider one stage before moving to the next.

Staging More Likely Among More Effective Supervisors

Further evidence on the profitability of outlining the problem and screening alternatives before taking action is seen in the results of "in-basket" tests given to 232 supervisors. These tests were a collection of facsimiles of letters, memoranda, and other contents likely to be found in a typical supervisor's in-basket. The supervisor responded to the 32 problems posed by the contents of his in-basket by placing in his out-basket instructions for his secretary memos, letters, reminders, and appointment calendars.

The contents of each out-basket could be scored on 68 aspects, such as number of unusual actions, number of superiors involved in action taken, or amount of information given to subordinates. Eight primary factors emerged in a factor analysis, showing the dimensions along which these supervisors varied consistently. They varied in how much information they exchanged with others, how often they discussed matters before acting, how often and under what conditions they complied with the suggestions of others, to what extent they analyzed the situation before acting, how concerned they were with maintaining organizational relationships, how much care they took to specify in advance when work was to be done, to what extent they were responsive to outsiders, and how often they gave orders to their subordinates in writing.

Two higher-order factors accounted for the correlations found among the primary factors. Some executives did more work than others, making for higher or lower scores on the eight primaries. Most significant for our discussion of staging was the second higher-order factor, which suggested that these supervisors vary on what stage of the decision process they concentrate. On the one extreme, some supervisors concentrate on trying to clarify the problem. They spent somewhat less time on scheduling and organizing facts and even less on taking action. At the other extreme were supervisors who were most likely to take action, paying less attention to alternatives and with even less concern about clarification of the problem or organization of facts about it. Further analyses disclosed that it was the supervisors with more ability (as measured by aptitude tests) and supervisory knowledge (as measured by a special achievement examination) who were most likely to concentrate on preparing for a decision rather than on taking immediate action.

Searching for Solutions

Effective Versus Ineffective Approaches to Perceiving the Problem

More and less effective ways of viewing a problem can be suggested from studies of successful and unsuccessful problem-solvers. Those likely to succeed almost immediately, perceive through some familiar stimulus, word, or phrase, a point at which they begin their attack. They break the problem into smaller parts, parts with which they are likely to have had some past experience. They eliminate redundancies while retaining the important points and tend to sharpen and bring the major elements of the problem into focus. They systematically reorganize the problem into a series of sub-problems, extracting key terms and ideas and simplifying their perceptions without losing the essentials. They handle each part of the problem methodically.

Unsuccessful problem-solvers fail to understand the statements of the problem they are given. They become confused about the requirements. They cannot fill in gaps in understanding with guesses at the possible

19 SUPPLEMENT

meanings of elements that are unfamiliar to them. Worse still, unsuccessful problem-solvers are more likely to distort the problem and attack a newly perceived problem—one that is so dissimilar from the original that the solution has no relation to it. Often their failure to solve a problem lies mainly in this misinterpretation of the issue through unwillingness to devote the needed time to this first stage of problem-solving. These prospective failures often possess the knowledge necessary to solve a problem, but they cannot perceive it as being solvable with their knowledge. At the same time they believe that reasoning as such is of relatively little value in answering problems—either one has all the necessary information and therefore knows the answer, or he does not. Unlike the potentially successful problem-solvers, those likely to fail refuse to break up a problem into its parts.

In generating solutions those who ultimately fail to solve a problem satisfactorily have no logical plan of attack. They jump from one part of a problem to another and from one stage to another, neglecting the important details; they become sidetracked by external considerations; they wander off on tangents when some word suggests an irrelevant idea or an interesting incident. Before they have sufficiently engaged in considering alternatives, the failing problem-solver selects one on the basis of feeling that it "seems right." Often some trivial or irrelevant point is used to justify such a selection. Even if he begins with a systematic plan to generate solutions, such as one based on the criteria that the correct answer must fulfill, he fails to follow through with the plan and loses sight of it when difficulties occur during the reasoning process.

For ultimate success in solving a problem, alternatives need to be identified, classified, discovered, and invented. Many of the perceptual tendencies which describe how problems are recognized also describe what happens in the search for solutions. Particularly important is the *set* one adopts.

Increasing Search for Alternatives by Using a Set

THE BRAINSTORMING SET. Fundamental to improving the search process is promoting a set to increase the number of alternatives to be considered. As has already been discussed, decisions reached are better when stage-by-stage problem-solving forces problem-solvers to spend more time searching for alternatives before making a decision. If the cost in time for such searching is minor, then it will be profitable to *brainstorm,* to delay criticism, and to generate as many alternatives as possible before considering the quality of the proposals.

Brainstorming has been offered as a generally useful method for improving the quality of decisions by forcibly increasing the quantity of alternatives generated by the problem-solvers. Four rules are prescribed to create a brainstorming set. Evaluation and criticism of any presented idea is withheld during brainstorming. Idea generation as such is unrestricted in this search phase. "Wild" ideas are as acceptable as pedestrian solutions more easily seen as relevant to the problem. Quantity of output is stressed. Preceding ideas are reviewed only to generate new combining solutions; new ideas are synthesized from earlier ones presented to solve the problem. With this frame of mind it is possible, for example, to generate literally a hundred ways of, say, using a wire clothes hanger, many of which are both creative and original. Inhibitors to creative output are avoided, criticisms such as: "it's not part of our job, we've never done it that way, we haven't the time, we tried that before, our situation is different, it's too hard to administer, what will our customers think, or somebody would have used it before if it were any good."[2]

To demonstrate the value of brainstorming, one sample of subjects was told to produce freely ideas for solving two problems. A control group was told to produce only high-quality ideas. The control group also was to avoid poor ideas because they would bring penalties for them. Those free to brainstorm without fear of penalty for inadequate solutions actually produced more good ideas than those restricted by fear of penalties for poor proposals. Moreover, subjects who brainstormed without previous exposure to the riskier situation, where poor ideas were penalized, generated better solutions than subjects who freely brainstormed after first experiencing the need to avoid poor ideas. An earlier experience of restriction adversely affected idea production even after the restrictions were lifted.

[2]C. H. Clark, *Brainstorming* (New York: Doubleday, 1958).

GROUP VERSUS INDIVIDUAL BRAINSTORMING. It was thought that group participation would facilitate brainstorming, that members could build on each other's ideas and generate more good ideas collectively as a consequence of their interaction than they could alone. However, 48 Yale students who brainstormed in real, functioning groups of four failed to match in number or quality the ideas of 48 students who worked alone but whose isolated contributions were assembled in nominal groups of four to eliminate duplications. Even after these duplications were subtracted, the nominal groups produced almost twice as many different ideas as the real groups.

Similar results were found for 48 research scientists and 48 advertising personnel of Minnesota Mining and Manufacturing, although the latter, at least, might have been expected to do better in groups. Nor was personal orientation or group homogeneity important. Results continued to favor individual brainstorming when groups were formed according to the self-, interaction-, or task-orientation of members. Neither when members were all different in orientation, nor when they were all alike did the real groups produce little more than half the different ideas that the individuals in those groups could produce when working alone. However, some research points to the possibility that real groups do become as effective or more so than isolated individuals if they continue to practice as groups and as members become more familiar with each other. Presumably members can learn to become more effective in groups; in building on each other's ideas.

A QUESTIONING SET FACILITATES SEARCH. The search process is facilitated if the decision-maker adopts a *questioning set*. To help generate alternatives, he may ask in a systematic sequence: Why? Where? When? Who? What? How? What current resource could be adapted? Modified? Substituted? Transformed? Combined? Omitted? Reversed? Along the same lines, merely adopting *a set to be original* increases the originality of ideas generated. That is, if we are given instructions to try to discover or invent unique solutions rather than just any solutions, we increase our production of such out-of-the-ordinary alternatives. If we adopt a *constructive set* rather than a negative or critical set towards ideas, it helps to promote greater and more successful search for creative solutions.

In the search for alternatives a number of tests can be made on how well the search has proceeded. Is the search broad enough and clear in its directions? Have some alternatives been ignored because they customarily are solutions to different problems? Has there been a failure to consider alternatives considerably different from the initially proposed solution? Have some alternatives been rejected without full consideration or because they are misunderstood? Are we holding onto one alternative because it has worked successfully before on a different problem or in a different situation?

The frame of reference the organization sets for its problem-solvers is of particular importance. Venturesomeness and wide-ranging search for new and better ways of doing things are likely to be inhibited if emphasis in the organization is always on rules, clearances, and reviews, or if the payoff is to those who maintain stability and order rather than to those who innovate. Search will be inhibited if jurisdictional lines are stressed, so that one executive avoids making suggestions to another about the other's area of responsibility. On the other hand, creativity will be enhanced when the organization approves attempts to experiment, to innovate, and to challenge old ways of operating.

Divergent Versus Convergent Search

So far we have concentrated primarily on the *divergent* search for alternatives. That is, we have been concerned with the production of as many diverse solutions to a problem as possible, assuming that many solutions may work although the best one is likely to be uncovered if the search is broad enough and continues long enough. In many situations the search becomes *convergent,* starting with many possibilities available and continually narrowing the range of alternatives or creating the best alternative out of some or all of the available possibilities.

Divergent search is usually involved when one is considering publishing a catalog of products for wheat farmers or formulating an advertising campaign for a client. Convergent search is usually involved when one is seeking to discover the proof of a mathematical theorem, what move to make next in a game, or at what point there has been a communication breakdown in one's organization:

In . . . convergent thinking there almost always is one conclusion or answer that is regarded as unique, and thinking is to be channeled or controlled in

19 SUPPLEMENT

the direction of that answer. . . . In divergent thinking, on the other hand, there is much searching about or going off in various directions. This is most easily seen when there is no unique solution . . . [3]

Individual differences in success in convergence have been assessed by tests of picture or sentence arrangement, synthesizing objects from parts, identifying hidden figures embedded in more complex patterns, reasoning with forms, and completing numerical operations. Convergent thinking occurs when one tries to find the answers to multiple-choice questions. All alternatives are provided, but only one answer is correct or best. Individual differences in success in divergence have been assessed by symbol production tests, creating plot titles, planning air maneuvers, work listing, and inserting similes. Divergent thinking occurs on any completion test requiring the generation of as many correct answers as possible. The distinction is not always clear on some problem-solving tests. However, a number of factor analytic studies support the proposition that convergent and divergent search are logically and operationally distinct.

CONVERGING BY COMPUTER. In trying to understand the step-by-step ways human beings deduce theorems, or detect and discover the answer to a problem through convergent thinking, it may be helpful to examine how computer programs must be written to obtain such a solution, for studies of convergent human problem-solving are often obscured because so much of the connected process is internalized. Even where the subject verbalizes what he thinks he is doing, one cannot be sure that his verbalizations are accurate portrayals of the actual process. Only indirect experiments can provide objective guides as to what is happening. For this reason, it may be that computerized models will provide a needed catharsis in the study of problem-solving. The models are sufficient. They may or may not do what human beings do, but they suggest that human beings might well look to the computer to see how much of what they are doing is unnecessary or inefficient.

ACTIVE INSTEAD OF PASSIVE. While most neurological descriptions see the neurons of the brain as passive switchboards, acted on and modified by stimuli, and behaving subsequently as modified, the computerized information-processing system suggests that for problems to be solved there

[3] J. P. Guilford, *A Revised Structure of Intellect,* Reports from the Psychological Laboratory, No. 19 (Los Angeles: University of Southern California, 1957), pp. 6–7.

must be developed and stored complex strategies which are evoked by a problem stimulus. In the same way, to be effective the human problem-solver must take an active role in the formulation of hypotheses and to realize that one does not need complete conviction that a particular hypothesis is the correct one before considering it.

Such activity is necessary for a solution to be invented which is a creative synthetization, a fresh approach to handling a problem, one which often combines previously disassociated ideas. First a number of potentially acceptable alternative ways of solving the problem need to have been generated. The willingness to reserve judgment and continue searching, discussed earlier, is a necessity. If only one ready-made solution stands out and is quickly seized as the only way, problem-solving will be at an end. On the other hand, if none of the proposals uncovered after continuing search carry much support, apathy may ensue. And if they balance each other in support and are in conflict, they may produce a stalemate. At this point for a creative solution to occur, the elements in conflict among the acceptable solutions need to be identified. Then the variations in these elements which are compatible can be searched for so that a new solution can be formulated which encompasses what has been acceptable among older, partial, answers to the problem.

Computerized thinking is closer to these kinds of approaches to understanding of problem-solving which emphasize organizing operations into strategies, step-by-step, where each subsequent step depends on the outcome of the preceding one. A problem is described as a "schematic anticipation" for which means of solution must be found and applied. Priorities must be assigned to provide the order in which methods and evaluations will be tried. Long sequences of solution-methods are chained in a variety of ways. All of this convergent search can occur if the problem-solver has a memory, primitive information processes, and programs of rules for substitution, replacement, detachment, and chaining along with an executive controlling matching, testing, and priorities.

Evaluating and Choosing

Following the search process, particularly the divergent kind which has generated many solutions to the problem at hand, how does supervision evaluate the alternatives it has assembled? How does it decide on which alternative or alternatives to select to apply in solving the problem?

Evaluation is affected by how orderly and systematically it proceeds. Evaluation is affected by the error of the estimates of the cost of each alternative as well as the potential utility of each alternative. Evaluation depends on the *risk* and *uncertainty* of each prospective outcome. (We are involved in a 50 percent risk if we bet that a coin will land as a head instead of a tail; we are involed in 50 percent uncertainty when we have only half the information about what is affecting a particular outcome while the other half is unknown.)

Subjective rather than objective perceptions of risk, uncertainty, and confidence govern evaluations. Persons differ in their preferences for avoiding such risk and uncertainty, although most people share certain preferred risks. Groups will risk more than individuals, but the quality of the final decision will not depend on whether it is made by the group or the group chief after group deliberation.

An Orderly Approach to Evaluation

It appears profitable to adopt a systematic screening procedure. Failure to maintain an orderly approach leads to accepting answers to problems on vague feelings about their rightness rather than logical, rational, or objective considerations. First, the *criteria* need to be examined upon which evaluation will be based. Weights may be attached to each of these criteria. A series of questions about risk preferences may guide our choices: Do we seek the anticipated outcome yielding the greatest probability of gain? Are we interested in the least risk of loss? Do we prefer the greatest gain regardless of risk or the least loss regardless of probabilities? What material, monetary, and human constraints limit what we may do? What are the consequences of implementing each alternative? What new problems will be generated by each particular solution?

WEIGHING ALTERNATIVES. After screening out obviously unfeasible or irrelevant alternatives, an orderly evaluator proceeds to examine and weigh the advantages and disadvantages of each alternative, using the selected criteria. Often, a checklist of pros and cons is advisable. Each criterion in the checklist need not be given the same weight, but the checklist forces the decision-maker to be systematic in evaluating every alternative by means of each criterion. No one alternative is treated with favoritism. Wherever possible, supporting evidence and the confidence in evaluations is examined. A choice matrix may be worked out and game mathematics applied in a search for an optimum choice.

INTEGRATING SOLUTIONS. Often such systematic exploration makes it possible to see ways of combining and integrating solutions, particularly if one makes an effort to do so. To promote such integration, it appears more profitable to look at each alternative solution with a positive constructive attitude rather than with a negative set. When a college staff, for instance, reviewed ideas by asking, "What's good about these proposals?" they were more likely to incorporate the suggestions in the final solution. When they focused on what was wrong with the proposals, the ideas were likely to be rejected completely.

QUALITY OF FINAL DECISION BY SUPERVISOR OR SUPERVISOR AND STAFF. One supervisor may believe that he should obtain the advice and consent of his subordinates about the problem at hand and possible solutions to it. Yet he still feels he alone must make the decision about which alternative to adopt. Another executive does not stop in his use of his group of subordinates after alternatives have been discussed. He collaborates with his group in making the final decision. Is one approach better than another?

If the executive is trying to capitalize on the values of group consensus, if he reserves the last step, the final decision, for himself, he risks selecting an unfavored one through misunderstanding how the problem and the solutions to it were seen by his group in his deliberations with them. On the other hand, if he maintains the group approach to the end of the process, hammering out a jointly constructed agreement, he risks obtaining a decision which he personally regards as less than the best.

Actually, if the supervisor and his staff are pursuing similar goals with knowledge of similar constraints, have achieved agreement on the problem, and have searched and evaluated the various alternative solutions to the problem, the final choice is likely to be very similar whether the executive alone makes it or it is made by the executive and his group. One experiment suggested that the quality of the decision will be about the same under both circumstances. Simulated *ad hoc* staffs of Air Force officers wrote decisions after discussion of a particular problem. The commanders of the groups also wrote a decision following a review of the opinions of the *ad hoc* staff. There were no significant differences in the quality of the commanders' decisions and those of their staffs. Of course, quality was better for both staffs and commanders who reviewed staff opinion than for commanders who did not have the benefit of staff consultation.

Factors Affecting the Final Choice

Classical economics assumed that a decision-maker was completely informed about the choices available to him as well as about their consequences. He was infinitely sensitive to this information and was completely rational. As such, he chose that alternative whose consequences would give him the greatest value or utility with the least cost. Where utilities for different alternatives were the same, the decision-maker became indifferent about his choice. If these assumptions were correct, then there would be no need to study the behavior of the decision-maker, for we would only need to understand the decision-maker's environment and the choices available to him. Then we could determine mathematically what his choice would be.

Unfortunately most organizational decision-makers are not completely informed, are not infinitely sensitive, and exhibit only limited rationality. Therefore, to understand how decisions are reached we must examine the decision-maker's expectations and his values. Although the decision-maker sees himself as orderly, systematic, and rational, he must estimate the likely consequences of each prospective choice, how much it will cost, whether it will work, and how much utility lies in making the given choice. In making these estimates he displays certain cognitive tendencies and judgmental errors. To understand fully what decision will be made we need to appreciate some of these propensities when human beings are faced with choices. The logical mathematics of the *economics of expected utility* do apply to understanding choice, but only in relatively simple situations.

Although the quality of the decision may not differ after the group has deliberated, the group's decision is likely to involve taking more risks than would the decision made by a lone individual. In comparison to a control group of individuals making risky decisions in isolation, individuals who discussed decisions and reached consensus but remained personally responsible for the decisions increased risk-taking by about 5 percent. When their group as such became responsible, they collectively increased their willingness to risk by 12.5 percent. Thus discussion, consensus, and the diffusion of responsibility led to increased tolerance for risk. We may infer that bank committees are likely to approve more risky loans than are individual loan officers.

AN IRRATIONAL GROUP DECISION MAY EMERGE FROM RATIONAL CHOICES OF ITS MEMBERSHIP. A purely rational person is transitive in his choices. If Mr. Black prefers apples to bananas, and bananas to cherries, then he will also choose apples over cherries. (If $a > b$ and $> c$, then $a > c$.) Consider that Mr. Black, Mr. Brown, and Mr. Green prefer the fruits in the following order:

	Members		
	Black	*Brown*	*Green*
First Choice	Apples	Bananas	Cherries
Second Choice	Bananas	Cherries	Apples
Third Choice	Cherries	Apples	Bananas

For Mr. Black, $a > b > c$; for Mr. Brown, $b > c > a$, and for Mr. Green, $c > a > b$. Suppose the trio votes on which fruit to choose. In each case a majority of two of three voters can decide the outcome. Apples are favored over bananas by Mr. Black and Mr. Green; so for the trio, if a vote is taken, $a > b$. Bananas are favored over cherries by Mr. Black and Mr. Brown; so for the trio, $b > c$. If the trio vote is completely rational it should be transitive. Since $a > b$ and $b > c$, then $a > c$; apples should be voted for over cherries. Yet in such a vote both Mr. Brown and Mr. Green favor cherries over apples ($c > a$) and so the trio majority would be irrational or intransitive despite the fact that each of its members, Black, Brown, and Green, are completely rational.

SYSTEMATIC DISTORTION OF OBJECTIVE PROBABILITIES. Understanding of choice is made more difficult by the increasing distortions which occur in individual's subjective estimates as the objective odds rise. There seems to be a general tendency to overestimate the size of low objective probabilities of success. In the same way we tend to underestimate probabilities of success of those choices with high probabilites. Slot machine players in particular are usually playing against impossibly unfavorable odds. Classical economics would suggest that no one would play a slot machine after he observed the pattern of payoff, for the player should act completely rational. He would maximize his holdings by not playing at all and keeping what money he had. But the 24-hour-a-day casinos of Nevada prove otherwise.

Confidence of Decision

Our willingness to risk is obviously directly related to our confidence that we know what outcomes are likely as a consequence of our choice. Studies of confidence provide clues as to how we move to reduce the uncertainty in situations before making final decision.

As might be expected, we tend to be more confident that an alternative will work as a direct consequence of our previous experience of success or failure with that alternative. For example, when subjects must guess whether a light will signal and whether it will be a right or left light on a panel, they decide on the right light fastest when the right light responds 75 percent of the time, more slowly when the right light signals 50 percent of the time, and most slowly when it works 25 percent of the time. As should be equally obvious, our confidence and how long we take to decide is directly affected by the real physical or social differences in the alternatives from which we must choose. Certainty and speed of decision of laboratory subjects is greatest when they must judge among physical differences which are likewise greatest. Certainty and speed of decision also depend upon the intensity with which one emotionally favors one alternative over another. One is less likely to deliberate over choices about which he already has strong attitudes, regardless of the reason for the development of those attitudes.

We tend to be more confident when we receive more information about an alternative and when the information is more constant. We will attempt to increase our confidence before making a decision which could prove expensive by reviewing the probable costs and projected gains. Thus subjects were given two packs of cards. Each card had a number on it. The subjects had to decide which pack came from a population of cards with a higher mean number. Subjects made more confident decisions about bigger packs and packs of card on which the numbers did not vary greatly. In this situation when prizes were given for correct decisions and costs attached to receiving more cards before deciding, subjects behaved quite rationally. When the prize was large, they requested and paid for more information before deciding. Conversely, when the cost per card was small, they were more likely to ask for more cards before deciding.

Judgment is fraught with other errors. We have mentioned before the general tendency to accept or agree rather than to object or disagree. Such a tendency becomes more pronounced if we are confronted with more uncertainty and ambiguity. We also become more acquiescent if we are bored or indifferent.

Our judgment of one alternative will be affected by its contrast to other alternatives. It may look good simply because other solutions look bad. In the same way we may accept an alternative because it is embedded in a context of optimistic and hopeful statements, or because it is connected to other actually more promising solutions which are to be tried.

Following Up a Final Decision

The decision process is not complete even after we have made our final decision. We must follow up the decision to see whether the consequences were as expected. If the outcomes have occurred as predicted, then the problem is solved. Otherwise a reexamination of the problem may be needed, initiating again the cycle of steps in the decision process.

In the follow-up phase, a particular judgmental phenomenon which is likely to affect accuracy adversely is the tendency to seek justification and validation of one's decisions rather than an objective appraisal of the decision.

THE TENDENCY TO CONFIRM RATHER THAN REJECT DECISIONS. Francis Bacon noted 350 years ago,

19
SUPPLEMENT

The human understanding when it has once adopted an opinion . . . draws all things else to support and agree with it. And though there be a greater number and weight of instances to be found on the other side, yet these it either neglects or despises, or else by some distinction sets aside and rejects; in order that by this great and pernicious predetermination the authority of its former conclusions may remain inviolate.

Once we have made a decision we tend to concentrate on corroboration of its correctness rather than take equal note of subsequent contradictory evidence. We become blind to contrary evidence, particularly if the after-effects of decisions are ambiguous or difficult to evaluate. Since cognitive balance is favored over cognitive dissonance, if the evaluation of the wisdom or efficacy of a decision which has been made depends on subjective judgment, it is likely that we will perceive the decision to have been beneficial rather than detrimental when actually it may have had no utility for us. Errors of judgment in reaching the final decision are thus reinforced, and our subsequent evaluations biased accordingly. For instance, most executives, when queried about the effects of some special training they have received, will respond favorably about the effects on them. And if they must decide on whether the program should be continued, they are more likely to vote to continue than to suspend it regardless of its actual worth or lack of value.

Confucius said, "The superior man understands what is right; the inferior man understands what will sell."

Publications and Films Related to
Human Relations for the Supervisor

1. Publications of the National Institute of Leadership[1]

   a) *The Identification, Education, and Evaluation of Leaders*—a 100-item checklist for determining the training needs and evaluating the executive's, manager's, or supervisor's performance of his leadership functions, by Russell H. Ewing and Nadine R. Ewing. Price $2.00.

   b) *The Leadership Functions of Executives and Managers*—an evaluation of current leadership theory and practice, by Russell H. Ewing and Nadine R. Ewing. Price $2.00.

   c) *Leadership, Principles, and Practices Chart*—a series of charts which contain over 500 items of information about leaders and leadership training, by Russell H. Ewing and Nadine R. Ewing. Price $1.00.

   d) *Sensitivity Training for Permissive Leadership—A Critical Analysis and Evaluation,* by Russell H. Ewing and Nadine R. Ewing. Price $2.00.

   e) *Train Future Leaders Today—Tomorrow May Be Too Late,* by Russell H. Ewing and Nadine R. Ewing. Price $2.00.

   f) *Management by Motivation—Checklists, Questionnaires, and Bibliography,* by Russell H. Ewing and Nadine R. Ewing. Price $2.00.

   g) *Training by Motivation–Checklists, Questionnaires, and Bibliography,* by Russell H. Ewing and Nadine R. Ewing. Price $2.00.

   h) *The Motivation of a Nation—Production, Distribution, and Consumption,* by Russell H. Ewing and Nadine R. Ewing. Price $2.00.

   i) *The Crisis in the Colleges and Universities—Causes, Consequences, Cost, and Cures of Student Riots,* by Russell H. Ewing and Nadine R. Ewing. Price $2.00.

   j) *Checklist for Evaluating Fraternity Leadership Training Programs,* by Russell H. Ewing and Nadine R. Ewing. Price $2.00.

   k) *The Education, Training, and Evaluation of Fraternity Leaders— A Fraternity Personnel Performance Checklist,* by Russell H. Ewing and Nadine R. Ewing. Price $2.00.

[1]National Institute of Leadership, 9015 Wilshire Boulevard, Beverly Hills, California 90210.

A APPENDIX

1) *How to Conduct Successful Seminars, by Russell H. Ewing.* Price $3.00.
2. *Explorations in Human Relations Training: An Assessment of Experience, 1947–1953.*

3. Selected readings series—approximately 100 pages each:

   a) *Group Development,* edited by Leland P. Bradford, 1961.
   b) *Leadership in Action,* edited by Gordon L. Lippitt, 1961.
   c) *Human Forces in Teaching and Learning,* edited by Leland P. Bradford, 1961.
   d) *Forces in Community Development,* edited by Dorothy and H. Curtis Mial, 1961.
   e) *Issues in Human Relations Training,* edited by Edgar Schein and Irving Weschler, 1962.
   f) *Conferences for Learning, Planning, and Action,* edited by Richard Beckhard, 1962.

4. Research-training series:

   a) *Interpersonal Perceptions of Teachers, Students, and Parents,* by David H. Jenkins and Ronald Lippitt. 119 pp. An action-research project for teacher in-service education.
   b) *Emotional Dynamics and Group Culture,* by Dorothy Stock and Herbert A. Thelen. 314 pp. An interpretation of research concerned with factors of group productivity and with personality changes occurring in groups, which was conducted over a five-year period at the Human Dynamics Laboratory of The University of Chicago and NTL sessions in Bethel, Maine.
   c) *Interdisciplinary Team Research: Methods and Problems,* by Margaret Barron Luszki. 384 pp. A study of problems arising when researchers from various disciplines attempt to work together—made possible by a grant from the National Institute of Mental Health. (Books 2 and 3 in this series were published for NTL by the New York University Press, Washington Square, New York 3, New York.)

5. Research reprint series:

a) *Bibliography of Research*—NTL—1947–1960. Compiled by Lewis E. Durham and Jack R. Gibb. 10 pp. Free.

b) *An Annotated Bibliography of Research*—NTL—1947–1906. Compiled by Lewis E. Durham and Jack R. Gibb. 22 pp. An annotated listing of forty-nine publications resulting from research performed entirely or in part at the National Training Laboratories.

c) *Defense Level and Influence Potential in Small Groups,* by Jack R. Gibb. 25 pp. (This, and the following four items, result from Office of Naval Research sponsorship.

d) *Some effects on Group Problem Solving of an Enforced Separation of Problem-Solving Stages,* by Jacqueline Goodchilds, Jacob Schonfield, and Jack R. Gibb. 17 pp.

e) *Group Effects on Perceptual Behavior,* by Dorothy Stock. 23 pp.

f) *Effects of Group Activities upon Member-Performance,* by Jack R. Gibb. 24 pp.

g) *Effects of Group Goals upon Personal Goals,* by Alvin F. Zander. 20 pp.

6. NTL *Trainers Workbooks,* each approximately 100 pages:

a) *Group Observation and Recording.*

b) *Sample Group Evaluation* (Post-Meeting Reaction) *Forms.*

c) *Large Group Meetings, Conferences, and Institutes.*

7. Free Materials

NTL distributes without charge such items as the following:

a) "Brand-New Breakthrough in Management Development" by George A. Hoy, reprinted from *Factory* magazine. 8 pp.

b) "New Thrust for Community Leadership Training" by Edward E. Moe and H. Curtis Mial, reprinted from *Adult Leadership.* 5 pp.

c) "Partial List of Resources in the Field of Human Relations Training," 2 pp.

d) "What Makes a Small Group Tick?" reprinted from *Business Week.*
    4 pp.

8. *Supervisor's Survival Kit.* (By Elwood N. Chapman, published by Science
   Research Associates, 259 East Erie Street, Chicago, Illinois 60611.)

Films

1. "Laboratory Training for College Student Leaders and Faculty." 12
   minutes.
2. "Our Invisible Committees." A 25-minute training film.
3. "Role Playing in Human Relations Training." A 25-minute training film.

Major Published Sources for Educational Research

1. *The Encyclopedia of Educational Research*—published in 10-year
   cycles by the American Educational Research Association.
2. *The Education Index.*
3. *The Review of Educational Research.*
4. Professional journals.
5. *The Journal of Educational Research.*
6. Professional books.
7. *Theses and Dissertations Accepted by the United States Office of Education*—published biennially.
8. Dissertations.
9. *Monograph Series*—Teachers College, Columbia University; University of Chicago; University of Southern California; and others.
10. Publications of organizations—such as the American Association of
    School-Administrators, The National Society for the Study of Education,
    The Department of Elementary School Principals, The National Asso-
    ciation of Secondary School Administrators, The Association for Child-
    hood Education International.
11. *The Vertical File Index*—a bibliography of pamphlet materials.
12. *Books in Print*—published annually.

Educational Bibliographies

W. S. Monroe and L. Shores[2] compiled a summary of over 4,000 published bibliographies and summaries in education. Annotations indicate the number and character of references, degree of completeness, format, kind of annotations, and further material.

Educational Dictionaries

The Dictionary of Education[3] is a scholarly and accurate work of more than 16,000 technical and professional terms covering the entire area of education. Foreign educational terms most frequently employed in a discussion of education, and significant in educational psychology, philosophy, and sociology, are included. The work is an indispensable part of the library of a professional school supervisor.

Educational Encyclopedias

The Encyclopedia of Modern Education[4] presents a concise treatment of basic items as well as some biographies. *The Cyclopedia of Education*[5] presents excellent bibliographies, and is extremely useful for bibliographical and historical research purposes. The *Encyclopedia of Educational Research*[6] is indispensable in its field, for it presents a critical and evaluative synthesis of the literature of educational research arranged alphabetically by subjects. Each topic is presented with a critical summary and evaluation of research, as well as a list of needed research in the area.

[2]Walter S. Monroe and Louis Shores, *Bibliographies and Summaries in Education to July 1, 1935* (New York: H. W. Wilson Company, 1936).
[3]Carter V. Good, ed., *The Dictionary of Education* (New York: McGraw-Hill Book Company, Inc., 1945).
[4]Harry N. Rivlin and Herbert Scheuler, eds., *The Encyclopedia of Modern Education* (New York: Philosophical Library, 1943).
[5]Paul Monroe, ed., *The Cyclopdedia of Education* (New York: The Macmillan Company, 1911–1913).
[6]Walter S. Monroe, *Encyclopedia of Educational Research,* rev. ed. (New York: The Macmillan Company, 1950).

A APPENDIX

Educational Yearbooks and Government Publications

The yearbooks of the National Society for the Study of Education[7] and The Year Book of Education[8] are valuable, the latter containing annual surveys of educational developments in most European countries. Major educational problems throughout the world and attempts at their solutions are indicated.

All educators should be familiar with the publications of the United States Government.[9] Access to most special documents is available through the Government Printing Office.

Alexander and Burke[10] presented an outstanding listing of government publications and documents in the field of education. They recommended bringing a government list up-to-date by listing important publications only, and through exhaustive searching.

Periodical Sources

The following is a list of major professional journals and their content. These sources should be helpful in determining present status as well as recent developments and practices in the field:

1. *American School Board Journal*—presents problems of public school administration, and attempts to promote better administration and supervision.
2. *Art Education Bulletin*—designed for teachers; presents new developments.
3. *Curriculum Bulletin*—reports current, timely curriculum materials; each issue is complete in itself.

[7]National Society for the Study of Education, *Yearbook* (Chicago: University of Chicago Press, 1902 ff.).
[8]*The Year Book of Education* (Yonkers-on-Hudson, New York: World Book Company, 1932–1940 and 1948 ff.).
[9]United States Government Publications, Superintendent of Documents, *Decennial Cumulative Index,* 1941–1950 (Washington, D.C.: Government Printing Office, 1953).
[10]Carter Alexander and Arvid J. Burke, *How to Locate Education Information and Data* (New York: Bureau of Publications, Teachers College, Columbia University, 1958). Access to federal documents, as well as to the documents of state and local governments, is treated on pp. 272–283.

4. *Educational Outlook*—presents trends as well as a discussion of broad issues and problems.
5. *Educational Research Bulletin*—presents summaries of research in education.
6. *Elementary English Review*—reports modern methods.
7. *English Journal*—presents teaching techniques and content material.
8. *Health, Physical Education, and Recreation*—an outstanding summary of news, especially in the area of health education. Administrative problems also are treated.
9. *Hygiene*—developments in medicine are treated.
10. *Journal of Education*—presents problems of elementary and high schools.
11. *Journal of Educational Research*—a scientific study of education.
12. *Journal of Experimental Education*—reports statistics and scientific investigations concerning curriculum and methods.
13. *Journal of Girls' Physical Education*—especially helpful to those teaching physical education to girls or to coeducational classes.
14. *Journal of School Health*—emphasizes coordinated activities of the school nurse, the principal, and the teacher.
15. *National Education Association Journal*—presents suggested solutions to classroom problems.
16. *National Elementary Principal*—attempts to keep members informed.
17. *Nation's Schools*—attempts to improve school administration and public education through presentation of research, current practice, and theory.
18. *School and University* (formerly *Overview* and *School Executive*)— presents school news, practices, and advanced thinking in connection with educational problems.
19. *Research Quarterly*—presents abstracts of research in health, physical education, and recreation.
20. *Review of Educational Research*—includes an excellent bibliography and summaries of research in education under fifteen topics in a three-year cycle. Published five times per year.[11]

[11]For an outstanding review of recent research concerning instruction, see Richard C. Anderson, et al., *Current Research on Instruction* (Englewood Cliffs, New Jersey: Prentice-Hall: Inc., 1969).

A APPENDIX

21. *School Administrator*—a news bulletin.
22. *School Business Management*—promotes efficient business procedures within school systems.
23. *School Management*—keeps school administrators abreast of new developments in school administration, maintenance, equipment, supply, and building construction.
24. *Phi Delta Kappan*—an invaluable resource in educational research, supervision, administration, curriculum, and instruction.

Other valuable periodicals include:

1. *Audio-Visual Instruction*
2. *Audubon Book*
3. *Bulletin of the National Association of Secondary School Principals*
4. *Current History*
5. *Education Digest*
6. *Educational Leadership*
7. *Grade Teacher*
8. *Journal of Health, Physical Education*
9. *Journal of Higher Education*
10. *Journal of Home Economics*
11. *Journal of Research in Music Education*
12. *Journal of the National Society for Programmed Instruction*
13. *Life*
14. *National Geographic*
15. *Personnel and Guidance Journal*
16. *Quarterly Journal of Speech*
17. *Scholastic Coach*
18. *School Activities*
19. *School Arts*
20. *School Life*
21. *School Shop*
22. *Speech Teacher*

TABLE B–1 Categories for Interaction Analysis

TEACHER TALK	*INDIRECT INFLUENCE*	1.* *ACCEPTS FEELING:* accepts and clarifies the feeling tone of the students in a non-threatening manner. Feelings may be positive or negative. Predicting or recalling feelings are included.
		2.* *PRAISES OR ENCOURAGES:* praises or encourages student action or behavior. Jokes that release tension, but not at the expense of another individual; nodding head, or saying "go on" are included.
		3.* *ACCEPTS OR USES IDEAS OF STUDENTS:* clarifying, building, or developing ideas suggested by a student. As teacher brings more of his own ideas into play, shift to category five.
		4.* *ASKS QUESTIONS:* asking a question about content or procedure with the intent that a student answer.
	DIRECT INFLUENCE	5.* *LECTURING:* giving facts or opinions about content or procedures; expressing his own ideas; asking rhetorical questions.
		6.* *GIVING DIRECTIONS:* directions, commands, or orders to which a student is expected to comply.
		7.* *CRITICIZING OR JUSTIFYING AUTHORITY:* statements intended to change student behavior from non-acceptable to acceptable pattern; bawling someone out; stating why the teacher is doing what he is doing; extreme self-reference.
STUDENT TALK		8.* *STUDENT TALK—RESPONSE:* talk by students in response to teacher. Teacher initiates the contact or solicits student statement.
		9.* *STUDENT TALK—INITIATION:* talk by students which they initiate. If "calling on" student is only to indicate who may talk next, observer must decide whether student wanted to talk. If he did, use this category.
		10.* *SILENCE—CONFUSION:* pauses, short periods of silence and periods of confusion in which communication cannot be understood by the observer.[a]

[a]Ned Flanders, "Intent, Action, Feedback: A Preparation for Teaching," *Journal of Teacher Education* XIV (September 1963), no. 3. Reprinted by permission.
*There is NO scale implied by these numbers. Each number is classificatory; it designates a particular kind of communication event. To write these numbers down during observation is to enumerate, not to judge a position on a scale.

B   APPENDIX

CLASS CODE NO. _____ OBSERVER _____ DATE _____

CATEGORY	1	2	3	4	5	6	7	8	9	10	TOTAL TALLIES
1											
2											
3											
4											
5											
6											
7											
8											
9											
10											
TOTAL TALLIES											
Percent of Total											

Teacher Total: Student Total: Silence

I/D =   Steady State =
i/d =   Content Cross =

FIGURE B–1   Observation Matrix.

FIGURE B–2 Scatter Sheet—Working Matrix.

Health Information for Teachers and Parents

The supervising principal should make available to teachers information concerning certain health problems that are attributable especially to school-aged children.[1] The general categories that the supervisor should cover would include nutrition, rest and sleep, cleanliness, dental health, posture, mental hygiene, and disease prevention. A form used by one school system to acquaint parents and teachers with these health points included the following topics:

1. Food
2. Rest and sleep
3. Cleanliness
4. Tooth care
5. Posture and foot care
6. Other health habits
7. Mental hygiene
8. Disease prevention
9. Adolescent development problems

Readmission of Students After Illness

State and local laws and regulations concerning the readmission of pupils after illness, which vary widely, should be covered in the meetings scheduled prior to the first day of classes. The readmission of students who have been absent from school because of illness is generally governed by the provisions included in Figure C–1 in most states.

Since most school systems do not use central attendance-accounting procedures, it is the teacher who often must make decisions concerning readmission of students. It is, therefore, the job of the supervisor to improve the teacher's knowledge and understanding of the laws, rules, and regulations in this area.

[1] For a discussion of the sources of information concerning health factors see chapter 8.

FIGURE C–1   Sample Readmission Form

READMISSION OF STUDENTS AFTER ILLNESS
West School District

1. Students who have been absent from school because of a disease subject to full quarantine, such as diphtheria, smallpox, cholera, or bubonic plague, usually may be readmitted to school only after they have been released from quarantine by written consent of the local health department. Students with ringworm of the scalp may be readmitted to school only with written consent from the local health department.

2. Students who have been absent from school on account of a reportable communicable disease but who were not quarantined and did not have ringworm of the scalp must obtain permission, in most school systems, to return to school from the school physician or nurse, or from the local health department. In certain instances the individual's personal physician may approve such readmission.

3. Students absent from school because of communicable diseases, such as chickenpox, German measles, influenza, pneumonia, skin diseases, common cold, or other nonreportable or noncommunicable diseases, may be readmitted to school by the principal, providing that any health department regulations concerning the period of exclusion have been met, and also, that the child appears to have recovered fully.

4. If the principal is doubtful whether the student is well enough to return to school, he may refer the student to the school physician or nurse for readmission, or request the parents to obtain a readmittance statement from the student's personal physician.

5. Absences due to dog bites should be reported to the Department of Animal Regulations, while absences due to food poisoning should be reported to the local health department.

Exclusion from School

The supervising principal should assist teachers, especially those who are new to the school system, in becoming familiar with the reasons for which a student may be exempted from attendance. He also should acquaint the teachers with the various forms that are used to report such exemption. A sample of such a form appears as Figure C–2. Essential information concerning communicable diseases, which should be made available to the teacher by the supervising principal, is included in Table C–1.

FIGURE C–2   Sample Exemption Form

RECOMMENDATION FOR EXEMPTION FROM REGULAR SCHOOL ATTENDANCE
Because of Physical Condition

Date _____

Student's Name _____ Birthdate _____

Male _____ Female _____

Student's Address _____

City _____ Zone _____ Phone _____

Student's School _____ Grade _____

Parent's Name _____

Parent's Address _____

City _____ Zone _____ Phone _____

As provided under Section _____ of the _____ Education Code, I recommend that the above-named student be exempted from full-time regular school attendance for a period of _____ days because of the physical condition described below:

Physician's Diagnosis: _____

(To Physician: Please check one of the following)

I further recommend that this student:

_____ Attend a regular school for _____ hours per day.

_____ Attend a school for physically handicapped.
(Bus transportation is provided, if necessary.)

_____ Be provided services of a home teacher.

_____ Refrain from exertion.

Signed _____ M.D.

Address _____

City _____ Zone _____

Phone _____

Approved by: _____
Supervisor of Attendance

TABLE C–1   Communicable Diseases, and Exclusion from School

Disease	Incubation Period	Period of Exclusion of Patient	Period of Exclusion of Contacts
Chickenpox	13 to 21 days	At least 7 days after appearance of 1st crop of vesicles until primary crusts off exposed surfaces	None, if patient properly isolated
Conjunctivitis	1 to 2 days	Until recovery	None
Diphtheria*	2 to 7 days	Until 2 negative cultures from throat and 2 from nose, 24 hours apart not less than 7 days after antibiotic	7 days from last contact and 1 negative nose and throat culture, not less than 7 days after antibiotic if given
Dysentery, Bacillary (Shigella infections)	2 to 7 days	Until recovery and 2 negative fecal cultures, one week apart, beginning at least one week after discontinuance of specific therapy.	Food handlers at discretion of Health Officer
Encephalitis (Infectious)	4 to 21 days	7 days from onset	None
German Measles (Rubella)	14 to 21 days	Until recovery	None
Gonococcus infection	2 to 14 days	None if under adequate treatment	None
Hepatitis (Infectious)	21 to 35 days	Until recovery	None
Influenza	1 to 3 days	Until recovery	None
Impetigo contagiosa	2 to 5 days	Until recovery	None
Measles	10 days to onset of illness. 13 to 15 days to onset of rash	During catarrhal symptoms and 7 days after appearance of rash	None, if susceptible contacts inspected daily at school

TABLE C-1 (Continued)

Disease	Incubation period	Isolation period	Quarantine period
Meningococcus Meningitis; Meningococcemia	2 to 10 days	Until recovery	At discretion of local Health Officer. Intimate contacts under 3-day medical observation.
Mumps	12 to 26 days	Until swelling of salivary glands has subsided	None
Paratyphoid (Salmonella infections)	1 to 10 days	Until recovery and 2 negative fecal and urine cultures, one week apart, one week after discontinuance of specific therapy	Food handlers at discretion of Health Officer
Pediculosis	7 to 14 days	Until under adequate treatment	None
Plague*	3 to 6 days	Until 2 days after all symptoms have subsided	At least 7 days after last exposure in case of pneumonic plague and until Health Officer is satisfied infection was not contracted
Pneumonia, viral (Infectious)		Until recovery	None
Psittacosis	6 to 15 days	During acute stage	None
Poliomyelitis	7 to 14 days	7 days from onset or for duration of fever if longer	None, if patient properly isolated
Ringworm of scalp		Until under adequate treatment	None
Streptococcal infections (incl. scarlet fever, strept. sore throat, and "septic" sore throat)	2 to 5 days	At least 7 days from onset and until clinically well	None, if patient properly isolated and contact inspected daily at school. Restriction at discretion of Health Officer.
Smallpox*	7 to 16 days	Until recovery and scabs separated and scars completely healed	At least 16 days after last exposure or immunity established by successful vaccination and released by Health Officer

TABLE C–1 (Continued)

Disease	Incubation Period	Period of Exclusion of Patient	Period of Exclusion of Contacts
Syphilis (primary and secondary)	10 to 45 days	Until under adequate treatment or noninfectious	None
Tuberculosis		Until disease is in noncommunicable stage	None
Typhoid	3 to 38 days	Until recovery and 2 negative fecal and urine cultures, at least one week apart, beginning at least one week after discontinuation of specific therapy.	Food handlers at discretion of Health Officer and under his restrictions
Typhus, Murine (flea-borne)	6 to 14 days	Until recovery	None
Epidemic (louse-borne)	6 to 14 days	Until recovery	Household contacts must be louse-free
Whooping Cough	7 to 10 days	During early catarrhal period and for 21 days after appearance of paroxysmal cough	None, if contact inspected daily at school
Yellow Fever	3 to 6 days	During clinical phase of the disease in a room satisfactorily protected against mosquitos	None, if contact under observation for 7 days after last exposure

*Quarantinable diseases

This appendix contains step-by-step lesson-plan samples. These plans present only one approach in each area and must be adapted, amended, or ignored by the supervisor according to the requirements of the particular community, school, class, group, and teacher. The plans contain the type of materials that supervisors will wish to keep handy in their top desk drawers, for they should refer to them continuously in assisting beginning teachers (particularly in the lower elementary grades and in intermediate or junior high schools) in detailing the specific steps in a lesson.

How to Help the Inexperienced Teacher
Plan for the First Week of Classes

Suggested topics for the supervisor to cover in meeting with beginning teachers:

1. Advance preparation for the school year
2. Nature and resources of the community
3. School location and building facilities
4. Reports and records available
   a) Cumulative records
   b) Tests results
   c) Previous teachers
   d) Health records
   e) Enrollment data
5. School regulations, policies, and facilities
   a) Special schedule for the first day
   b) Finding out about textbooks and library facilities
   c) Getting supplies and equipment ready, e.g., sharpen pencils
   d) Making a seating chart and name cards
   e) Ordering instructional technology (audio-visual) materials
   f) Knowing duties and missions
   g) Bus schedules
   h) Announcements and reminders

The Course of Study

1. Curriculum
2. Instructional guides
3. Supplementary bulletins

The First Week

1. Meeting parents
2. Planning room procedures
   a) Seating
   b) Attendance
   c) Discussion
3. Distributing books and materials
4. The first day
   a) What is special about the first day?
   b) Planning for the first day: *Read!*
   c) Suggested daily programs
   d) Items to be considered in the daily schedule
   e) Activities to be included in a weekly schedule
   f) Trends in program planning
   g) Initiating routines, activities, and procedures
   h) Techniques: Starting the teaching of subjects
   i) Establishing Control (teacher-student relationship)
   j) Providing for a functional environment
      (1) Managing routines
      (2) Stressing functional design
      (3) Lighting
      (4) Ventilation
      (5) Temperature control
      (6) Furniture arrangement centers, displays, bulletin boards
      (7) Learning centers
      (8) How can the teacher evaluate the effectiveness of my room environment?

Sample Steps in Art and Practical Arts Lessons

Art and Practical Arts Work Period

The teacher should:

1. Review
2. Stimulate, building readiness
3. Relate present tasks to previous lessons
4. Have students select a standard (of classroom behavior) which is to be emphasized
5. Provide for planning—by committees, if desired
   a) Stimulate; review needs
   b) Procedures
   c) Problems that must be solved prior to going to work
6. Review standard, signal-to-stop-work
7. Guide students as they work
8. Help one group or committee at a time in planning and working. The teacher must cover the entire classroom and observe entire classroom even when working with one individual.
9. Have students clean up. Chairmen only, after a 5-minute warning.
10. Encourage sharing and problem-solving
    a) Problem-solving
    b) Needs felt by students
    c) Relate
    d) Evaluation of work period
11. Supervise final clean up, if necessary

Steps in Production Lessons In Art

An hour should be allotted to the art production lesson. It is not practical to attempt five 20-minute lessons per week; rather, one 50- or 60-minute lesson per week should be scheduled in the elementary school.

Using Water Colors

The teacher should:

1. Ensure that all materials are ready prior to the lesson. Students should be given an opportunity to distribute brushes, water, newspaper, art paper. A paper towel should be available to every two students.
2. Stimulate by showing paintings which demonstrate special objective for the day.
3. Note on the chalkboard how the artist achieved the desired effect. For example, a center of interest could be painted in bright, light colors; could be the largest object in the picture; could be in sharp focus; and could be near the center foreground.
4. Demonstrate, using student helpers.
5. List steps to be followed on chalkboard.
6. Review the objective; give assignment: "You may paint anything you wish, as long as you have a definite center of interest and ————."
7. Guide students in a discussion of special water color lesson standards. Students should:
    a) Put name in lower left-hand corner, front side of painting.
    b) Put a drop of water in each color. (It is not necessary to measure exactly *one* drop.)
    c) Mix colors in lid of water color box, not in paints themselves.
    d) Start with light colors (yellow). If a mistake is made it is easy to change light colors. (Indicate time element—ten minutes for 1 through 7d?)
    e) Paint (35 minutes)
    f) Receive five minute warning
    g) Clean up (5 minutes)
    h) Share and evaluate (10 minutes)

Sample Steps in Group Painting

1. Stimulate interest.
2. List items to be included in picture.

3. Note the most important item to be included. Remind students that it should be the biggest item.
4. The teacher marks bottom and top of most important subject.
5. Students will put in most important figures in chalk, between lines drawn by teacher, and:
   a) Practice most important subject.
   b) Correct most important subject.
   c) Using variously colored construction paper, determine most important color. Pin it in place on the butcher paper.
   d) Fill in other colors.
   e) Paint in the colors.
6. For city buildings, one could start with sponge-applied rectangles of color, to correct size. One person to a color.
7. The teacher should suggest that students close their eyes and open them fast. If they do not see ONLY the major color, more of that color may be needed.
8. Students may outline in black or read something into the painting. There may have been no definite subject prior to this time.
9. Students add figures, planes, birds.
10. Decide on a title.

Further Sample Steps in Simple Art Procedures

1. Using liquid starch:
   a) Paint starch onto paper with brush.
   b) Apply colored chalk—flat edge for wavy lines; point for dots, crooked lines, and others.
   c) Go over the page with thin tempera or water color.
   d) Scrape picture with a stick or cardboard comb or plastic straight-edge to produce designs.
   e) Apply colored tissue paper instead of paint. If one decides to do so, he should apply more liquid starch on top of tissue, brushing from center to outside of each small piece of tissue paper. Usually not more than four colors of tissue paper should be utilized for the production.

2. Using finger paints:
   a) Mix liquid starch plus some dry tempera paint powder.
   b) Put a spoonful of the mixture on one corner of heavy manila or hard surface paper divided into four sections.
   c) Spread the mixture. A design may be made by using a tongue depressor.
   d) Fold over the paper so as to print the design onto the other corner.
   e) Could fold paper further.
3. Using gadgets in art education:
   Gadgets may also be used as printing devices. One could use a sponge, if starch is used. See item 1d, above, for additional suggestions on using gadgets.
4. Crayon resist:
   a) Use edge of crayon to put colors on paper.
   b) Apply dark tempera which has been mixed with starch, or apply dark water colors.
   c) The wax in the crayon will resist the paint.
5. Scraffito:
   a) Apply colors to paper with crayon or watercolors.
   b) Cover colors with heavy, dark crayon.
   c) Scrape with comb, cardboard, or gadgets.
6. General design techniques:
   a) A good design has the same qualities that a good picture has. It includes a dominant subject or center of interest.
   b) Variations in thickness of lines opposition and repetition have a place in the various design processes.
   c) One game design process includes drawing two horizontal lines, one vertical line, and so forth. No two areas should be the same.
7. Further techniques include printing from colors painted onto a piece of glass and using a brayer with a string around it to roll paint onto newsprint. Practice in the use of charcoal should also be provided.

Sample Steps in an Art Appreciation Lesson

1. Show art work or picture of artist to stimulate.
2. Build background. Provide information regarding the artist; write his name on board.

3. Introduce vocabulary: landscape, junctions.
4. Show the work of art. Write title on board.
5. Discuss the medium used.
6. Discuss art principles such as texture, colors, center of interest, perspective, hue, brightness, value.
7. Discuss what is particularly enjoyable in the picture: shadows, sizes, shapes, background, foreground, texture, repetition of colors, contrast, perspective, brightness.
8. Review.
9. Evaluate.

Sample Steps in Teaching Art

The teacher should:

1. Organize procedures to avoid wasting time:
   a) Make sure materials and supplies are available. (TV plates make good pallets, clear pint plastic containers good for paint.)
   b) Use newspapers (classified ads) to protect desks (or, use oilcloth or plastic sheeting).
   c) Have shelves organized and labeled with a place for all supplies.
   d) Have a place for drying painting that won't clutter room.
2. Plan effectively so that he might:
   a) Know and teach basic art objectives and principles.
   b) Provide many varied experiences with many media.
   c) Stay within the capabilities of the students.
3. Consider the teacher's Evaluation Checklist:
   a) Is there a point to the picture?
   b) Is there fresh, clear color?
   c) Is there a dominant center of interest?
   d) Are there sufficient subordinate interests to bring out the dominant interest?
   e) Is there sufficient dark and light contrast?
   f) Is there a variety of size, texture, and color?
   g) Is there perspective? How is it achieved?
      (1) By diminishing size?

(2) By graying color?

(3) By lessening of detail?

h) Is the student showing growth in his art expression? Is he trying? Is he creative? (Assign at least an average mark unless child does not try or annoys others.)

4. Help the student evaluate his own work:

a) Was he creative or original?

b) Did he fill the space well?

c) Are colors clean, rich, and interesting?

e) How has he improved?

d) Is there sufficient contrast?

Sample Steps in Teaching Current Events

Elementary Grades

1. Standards

2. Stimulation

3. Directions

a) "Reading leaders" distribute current events classroom newspaper.

b) Students skim newspaper and decide which articles to share with the class.

c) Working with three ability groups: teacher works with the lowest group first week, second group second week, lowest again third week, and highest fourth week. The teacher should first help the group he is *not* working with to select articles. Students give three suggestions, vote on one article, then begin reading and, possibly, outlining. They finish reading and outlining and work on an assigned exercise.

d) Low ability group: teacher helps students to develop the skill of outlining (using the chalkboard), guides students to select main topics, lists on chalkboard the supporting details given by the students, chooses students to be on the panel, and directs students to return to seats and finish work.

4. Presentation of news item by the panel (up to 25 minutes)

a) Students are selected for each article

b) Participants are seated accordingly

c) A chairman presides and introduces the speakers

d) Speakers from each group present the selected article from the outline—reporters discuss names, events, and places; reporters illustrate material, locating places on maps and globes; the class may add information after each group completes presentation.

e) Audience may ask pertinent questions.

5. Evaluation with students

a) Chairman or member of group may summarize content.

b) Students evaluate new presentation.

c) Evaluate relevant and important news and procedures.

d) Establish standards for improvement.

e) Students collect papers (clean up).

Grades 7, 8 and 9

1. Objective: To review current history of the world
2. Materials: Globe, maps, classroom or daily newspaper, agenda, chart
3. Preliminary Details

a) Attendance accounting, announcements

b) Students begin reading front page story in classroom newspaper (e.g., *Jr. Review*) (5 minutes only)

4. Stimulation

a) Show headline of interest to teenagers

b) Use map

5. Procedure

a) Class president calls on individuals (e.g., those whose names begin with the initials I–R) to serve on current events panel.

b) After each topic has been discussed, the president calls for participation by the class in an open forum.

6. Review and Evaluation

a) Student relates most important points covered. The discussion is guided by the teacher.

b) The class president calls on one panel member to evaluate the audience; one person in the audience to evaluate the panel. President evaluates participation by audience. If time allows, students continue reading in the newspapers or periodicals.

7. Assignment
   Read . . . .
   Study for . . . .

Sample Steps in Teaching Dramatic Representation

Related to a Study of the Colonies

1. Stimulate; review.
2. Students discuss life, customs, food, games, ways to make a living in the colonial home (the fireplace).
3. Students discuss several possible scenes and choose one to do (e.g., a breakfast scene).
4. Students choose standards or plan a scene set up. (speak loudly, clearly)
5. Students plan action to take place. (List on chalkboard).
6. One particular standard for the day is chosen.
7. Students chosen as chairmen arrange materials and props (could be done prior to lesson).
8. Students act out the scene. One child may introduce the scene in upper grades.
9. Five minute warning signal, if appropriate.
10. Players and audience evaluate. Constructive criticism is emphasized; praise as deserved.
11. Needs are noted.

Sample Steps in an Examination
Lesson Plan in Grades 7 and 8

1. Objective: To evaluate progress through test
2. Materials: Test sheets, answer sheets, pencils
3. Preliminary Details:
   a) Attendance accounting
   b) Return marked papers

   c) Necessary announcements
4. Procedure:
   a) Review test standards
   b) Distribute tests
   c) Give directions
   d) Performance by students; teacher proctors
5. Evaluation and Review:
   a) Students pass papers to front, putting down paper on top of stack.
   b) Teacher marks papers, noting individual and group needs.
6. Assignment: Four terms . . . to identify . . .
7. Directed Study: Students begin assignment. Teacher assists those having difficulty starting.

Sample Steps in Teaching a Modern Foreign Language

1. Stimulate interest.
2. Begin work with a review of phrases formerly learned.
3. Use recordings for practice in correct pronunciation of new words and phrases.
4. Use pictures, slides, motion pictures, video tapes, and audio tapes to present and practice new vocabulary.
5. Encourage dialogues and dramatization of phrases when possible. Use videotaping devices.
6. Practice words and phrases in class whenever an opportunity presents itself.

Oral-Aural or Audio-Lingual Approach

1. This approach seems to be especially valuable in elementary and junior high schools and is applicable to *all* levels.
2. Although the oral approach is good, best practice seems to indicate the student should see (and write) the words also.
3. The teacher should be sure to use some other approach too, such as the written word.

4. The teacher should try many approaches and be able to use and discard as necessary.

INTRODUCTORY PHASE

1. Repetition drill—students repeat what teacher says.
2. Saturation drill—the teacher says sentence, students repeat. The teacher changes the subject, verb, or object, saying only the item that is to be changed in the practice sentence, making the change. Students repeat the sentence, accommodating the change.

PRACTICE PHASE

1. General practice (subject or verb change; others)—the teacher says entire sentence, students repeat.
2. Two-part drill—questions are asked by the teacher, answered by individual students. The teacher then gives cue to student who asks question of another student, using cue. Second student answers question. The procedure is termed *directed dialogue* if students are told *what* to ask. All two-part drill is not directed dialogue, but all directed dialogue is two-part drill.

Sample Steps in Teaching Handwriting

Specific Procedure (10-minute lesson)

1. The teacher should obtain a music staff liner, and draw 3 lines on the board by putting a piece of chalk in spaces 1, 3, 5. He should explain and *stress* that the middle line is the interline, or is imaginary, to aid in finding the halfway point between the top and bottom lines. The teacher could make the top and bottom lines heavier.
2. The student should keep a piece of handwriting paper in a special place in the handwriting book.

Steps in Teaching

1. The teacher should stimulate interest, build readiness, and review standards.
2. Demonstrate on chalkboard:
   a) Slant
   b) Special characteristics of letter.
3. Students should be instructed to make a line of "_____" (a certain letter). The teacher may ask the student to have the book or chart open to a specific page.
4. The largest practical unit to teach is the single letter.
5. Students practice the letter, check and evaluate.
   a) The teacher should help the students check or evaluate their own work by circling the best letter they have made.
   b) The teacher should say, "Circle the "_____" you have made. I will mark only the one you have circled."
6. The teacher demonstrates again.
7. The students check again.
8. The teacher discusses letters and the special aids, e.g., letters with similar strokes may be grouped and presented together. Many teachers feel that it is just as well to present them as a unit. The letters *a, e, r, t,* and *s* should be stressed.
9. Letters may be isolated for drill.
10. The teacher should ask for a short word containing the letter.
11. After the teacher writes the word on the chalkboard, the students can be instructed to make a "line" of the word. It should be written at least 4 or 5 times.
12. The students write a line of the word, check and circle the best one. Again, the teacher marks only the circled one.
13. The students evaluate their own progress:
    a) Letter forms
    b) Spacing
    c) Alignment
    d) Slant (uniformity)
    e) Speed and facility
    f) Related to other work

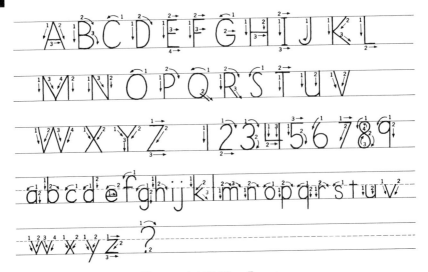

FIGURE D–1   Sample Manuscript Writing Forms.

Steps in Changing from Manuscript to Cursive (First Half of Grade 3)

The teacher should:

1. Have the students read simple cursive writing from the chalkboard. The teacher can use their names for these words. Put about 5 each day on board.
2. Build background, set standards. Attempt to stimulate the students stressing that cursive handwriting is:
   a) More efficient
   b) Easier
   c) Faster (sometimes)
   d) The way grownups write
3. Select some easy word like "it" or "cat." Don't use the letters *r, s, e.*
4. Write the word on the board in manuscript, straight up.
5. Write the word, slanting it.
6. Join the letters together.
7. Write the same word in cursive.

8. Describe the similarities and differences. (Drawn from the students with teacher's help.)

9. Demonstrate each step again while the students follow and *write, at each step, as the teacher does it on the chalkboard.* Give specific directions.

10. Have the students transcribe some of their own manuscript papers into cursive form.

Figures D–1 and D–2 illustrate recommended cursive and manuscript letter forms. Figure D–3 includes an evaluation guide for marking handwriting.

Sample Steps in Using the Materials of Instructional Technology

Using Instructional Technology (Audio-Visual) Aids

1. Assume the lesson involves the use of a film or filmstrip: The students list questions they would like to have answered in the film, or read questions on the board (four, more or less). Students note hypotheses: "What We Think." Students are told to keep these questions in mind while watching filmstrip.

2. New vocabulary is discussed.

3. The film is shown. If it is a filmstrip, the teacher should discuss each picture, asking guiding questions; pointing out important facts, adding additional relevant information.

4. Students read the printing after class has read silently. The teacher should clarify different words and concepts through questions.

5. Students answer questions. Check to see which questions were answered by the filmstrip, depending on which method was used.

6. The teacher should say, "Tell one thing you learned." The items elicited should be listed on the chalkboard, following which the students should be encouraged to compare *What We Think (Hypotheses)* with *What We Know.*

7. Evaluate.

FIGURE D-2   Sample Cursive Writing Forms.

Sample Lesson Plan: Using Instructional Technology Materials

1. Objective: To review history of measures, especially cups.
2. Materials: Texts, filmstrip, projector, chart
3. Preliminary Details:
   a) Attendance accounting
   b) Short quiz
   c) Return papers.

SAMPLE	GRADE LEVEL
first	Low 3 I
any	Low 3 II
glass	Low 3 – High 3
first	High 3
any	Low 4
glass	High 4
first	Low 5
any	High 5
glass	Low 6
first	High 6 – Low 7
any	Low 8 – High 8
glass	Low 9
first	High 9
any	Low 10
glass	High 10

Courtesy California Test Bureau

FIGURE D–3   Sample Evaluation Guide for Marking Handwriting.

4. Stimulation: Show chart regarding . . . tell story.
5. Procedure
   a) List, "What We Want the Filmstrip to Show."
   b) Following stimulation as in 4, above, instruct students to take notes on filmstrip, especially noting vocabulary. All should be ready to ask and answer two questions regarding the filmstrip. Discuss standards for behavior.

c) Show filmstrip.
d) Following showing of filmstrip, class president calls on individuals to ask and answer questions about filmstrip.
6. Evaluation and Review: President calls on one student to indicate most important points covered. Compare what was in filmstrip to above list (5a).
7. Assignment: Identify five terms regarding . . . . (These terms have been written on the chalkboard.)

Sample Steps in Teaching Language—Written and Oral

Sample Lesson Plan: Creative Writing

(One day)
1. The teacher develops final stimulation for writing lesson with the class.
2. The student's ideas may be recorded on the chalkboard.
3. Teacher may list commonly needed words on the chalkboard and provide vocabulary charts.
4. Students begin to write. Dictionaries used by students to find needed words.
5. The teacher circulates and gives individual help with words, and notes quality work that may be shared later with class.
6. Students write for about fifteen minutes and are reminded when writing period is almost over.
7. Papers are collected.
8. The teacher should read dramatically some stories or parts of stories that are of good quality.
9. The teacher or both teacher and student may correct and rewrite these stories *if* they are to be kept.
10. Evaluation:
    a) Were the students given freedom to express their creative ideas?
    b) Were all ideas given equal consideration?
    c) Were students given an opportunity to write freely?
    d) Were the stories shared for enjoyment by the group?
    e) Did the students seem to feel a sense of achievement?

Sample Lesson Plan: Work-Type Writing

PLAN ONE. The whole class works together.

1. First Phase (Monday, or Monday and Tuesday): stimulate; write (see Figure D–4 for a sample weekly block form).
   a) The whole class writes as group, or
   b) Two groups alternate for writing experience.
   c) The independent group may illustrate or do review language assignment.
2. Second Phase (Wednesday): teach skill; follow up drill
   a) A needed skill as determined from student's work is taught.
   b) Students reinforce skill with followup drill.
3. Third Phase (Thursday): edit papers
   a) Review of skills previously taught
   b) Students edit their papers
4. Fourth Phase (Friday): rewrite, or additional drill, or personal writing lesson

FIGURE D–4   Sample Weekly Block Plan Form—Language

1st Day	2nd Day	3rd Day	4th Day	5th Day
Objective—Stimulate story-writing	Continue writing	Skill lesson based on common errors	Review with students, editing especially for skill taught	Students write final copy
List suggested titles	Teacher collects papers and skims for common errors	Objective_____	3rd day	Teacher collects papers
List words *all* will need		Pages_____	(Have chart ready)	
		Follow up_____		
(Teacher writes maximum of ten words on board)		Teacher collects papers		

a) Stories are rewritten.
b) There is additional drill on review skills; or
c) There may be a personal writing lesson.
5. Fifth Phase
   a) An oral language skills lesson is taught, or
   b) Background is built for future written language experiences.

PLAN TWO. Two Groups

1. First Day (Monday): Groups I and II—stimulation. Group I—write; Group II—language work or illustration
   a) Class writes as two groups; alternate days.
   b) Independent group may illustrate or do review language assignment.
2. Second Day (Tuesday): Group I and II—stimulate again. Group I— language work or illustration; Group III—write. Procedure same as 1(a) and 1(b) above.
3. Third Day (Wednesday): Teach skill; followup drill. The procedure is the same as the Second Phase in Plan One.
4. Fourth Day (Thursday): Edit papers. Procedure same as Third Phase in Plan One.
5. Fifth Day (Friday): Rewrite or oral language
   a) Rewrite stories, or
   b) Teach oral language skills lesson.
   c) Build background for future written language experience.

Further Sample Steps in Phase I of Work-Type Language Lesson: (Monday, or Monday and Tuesday)

First Phase—stimulation and writing.

1. The teacher should stimulate to develop readiness
   Every writing lesson is introduced (use pictures, sounds, experiences, stories, charts, others).
2. The teacher should encourage students to discuss topic for writing to clarify and exchange ideas. The teacher may note some of these ideas on chalkboard.

3. Common words, when needed by group, may be listed and numbered on chalkboard.
4. Students write freely for about fifteen minutes.
5. If students need words they:
    a) Refer to word books
    b) Refer to word charts (social studies, science vocabulary)
    c) Refer to spelling books or list
    d) Use standard dictionary
    e) Ask the teacher
    f) Find page in word book and teacher writes word on the page
       (The teacher writes on chalkboard words needed by several students.)
6. As the teacher circulates to help students, he should make notes of phases of the student's stories that illustrate the purpose of writing.
7. The teacher reminds students of time left to finish their stories; tells them to skim through and correct stories.
8. Students complete their thoughts.
8. The teacher or the students read parts of stories noted by teacher.
10. Papers are collected. If more time is needed to write, use Tuesday. Re-stimulate. Note needs.
11. After the writing period, the teacher reads the stories to determine a common need for learning by the class.
12. Papers should be collected every day.
13. Evaluation:
    a) Was the stimulation adequate?
    b) Did the children express themselves effectively?
    c) What needs for future skill lessons were evident?

Further Sample Steps: Phase II Skills Lesson (Wednesday)

1. Stimulation. The teacher indicate type of common error in work. He should not return the compositions.
2. An example of the correct skill is written on the chalkboard on chart.
3. Students and teacher discuss skill.
4. Types of errors made by students on this skill also are written on chalkboard or chart.

5. Corrections are made with the students.
6. The correct form is left on the chalkboard so that students can see the correct copy as the last form. Students make up examples: call on each other.
7. Students and teacher define a rule (or rules) for this skill.
8. The rule is written on chalkboard (to be added to permanent chart).
9. Books are opened, the selection read, and example discussed.
10. Review
11. A followup practice lesson is introduced—students work from charts, workbooks, duplicated papers, books, or chalkboard.
12. Students check papers.
13. All papers are collected for teacher evaluation (including stories, if passed back). The teacher should determine if the skill was understood by the students; and if reteaching is necessary on this skill.
14. Evaluate

Further Sample Steps: Phase III Work-Type Writing Editing Lesson (Thursday)

1. The teacher should return the students' first draft papers.
2. The students edit for one skill (10 minutes).
   a) Papers are returned to students.
   b) Students edit own papers after review of skill taught previous day.
   c) The teacher guides correction period and should circulate to give individual help where needed.
3. Editing for other skills (10 minutes)
   a) The teacher and students review skills from fundamental skills chart.
   b) The students correct papers for skills just reviewed and spelling.
   c) The teacher circulates to guide students in correcting papers and gives individual assistance where special needs have been noted.
   d) Papers are collected and the teacher edits for errors overlooked by students and skills not taught.
4. Evaluation:
   a) How well did the student remember skills previously taught?
   b) What reteaching is necessary?

Further Sample Steps: Phase IV
Rewrite Lesson (Friday)

1. Edited stories that have been corrected by the teacher are returned to the students.
2. Students copy stories and make corrections as indicated.
3. Teacher gives assistance with handwriting and mechanics.
4. Papers are collected
5. Teacher checks the corrected form. Teacher assigns marks. Possible mark distribution:

20) A	15)	11)	Sample score:
19)	14) C	10) D	19 (Story mark)
	13)	9)	B (Handwriting mark)
18)	12)		
17) B		F	
16)			

Note: A definite marking system should be used. An academic areas supervisor in the southeast suggested the following plan, which he had recommended to the teachers new to his school system:

a) Twenty points were alloted if the required number of paragraphs were completed. For instance, if two paragraphs were assigned, but only one was completed, only ten points were allotted.
b) One point was subtracted for each *type* of error in grammar, usage, sentence structure, spelling, punctuation.
c) A three point bonus was given for a truly outstanding *story,* regardless of grammar and punctuation. Three points were subtracted for a lack of effort. In no case was the total number of points greater than twenty. (If, with bonus points, the total was twenty-one, it was indicated as a score of 20+.) A handwriting grade was assigned at the same time.

6. Rewritten stories should be:
   a) Filed in student's files;
   b) Placed in student's notebooks;
   c) Filed in class story folder, author's box, or social studies or science file;

d) Displayed on bulletin board;

e) Taken home for definite purpose.

7. Evaluation:

a) How accurately were the papers copied?

b) Were there spelling and handwriting needs for future lessons?

(If the sequence is completed by Thursday, use Friday for teaching oral language skills *or* for building background for future written language experience.)

Steps in Teaching Choric Verse Reading

1. The teacher should read the poem to students.

2. The teacher then rereads the poem; students softly tap out rhythm with their hands.

3. The students fill in last word of each line as teacher recites the poem.

4. The teacher and students recite the poem together.

5. The teacher and students recite the poem together again, working on "expression."

6. The students recite the poem alone.

7. Characters are chosen (e.g., soldier, Jonathan Bing,[1] archbishop) to act out the poem, class narrating all parts other than lines of the characters chosen.

   Expressive pantomimic movements may be used.

Steps in Teaching Poetry Writing

The teacher should:

1. Stimulate. Note beauty in the immediate environment.

2. Discuss ideas, feeling.

3. Read poems by others. Discuss.

4. Write, to express student's own feeling and ideas.

5. Evaluate (own ideas, thoughts, picture words, rhyme, rhythm, repetition.

[1]Beatrice Curtis Brown, "Jonathan Bing," in *Anthology of Children's Literature* by Edna Johnson, Carrie E. Scott, and Evelyn R. Sickels (2d edition; Boston, Mass.: Houghton Mifflin Company), p. 878.

Does the poem tell a story? Paint a picture? Stimulate the imagination?)
6. Read a few poems orally. The group should assist in obtaining rhythm, picture words, and so forth.
7. Tell the student to edit. The teacher may suggest that perhaps a better word could be used, or the rhythm improved.

Steps in Teaching Letter Writing

The teacher should:

1. Stimulate. Note importance of letter writing.
2. Discuss purpose for particular letter-writing lesson. For example, inviting parents to open house.
3. Discuss proper form, including return address, greeting, body, closing. Stress proper indentation and punctuation.
4. Discuss facts to include in the letter:
    a) What will be seen and what will happen (work samples, meet teacher).
    b) Ask questions: the invitation.
    c) Make time, place, and date clear.
5. Write needed words on the chalkboard.
6. Have the form of the letter on the chalkboard. Stress good letter-writing posture.
7. Direct the students to write.
8. Direct the students to edit the letter.
9. Have the students repolish the letter.
    a) Were the written items of interest to the addressee?
    b) Did the writer say what he intended to say?
    c) Were the points listed in the best order? Was the letter concise?
    d) Was the correct form used? Correctly written? (Good grammar and usage, and proper capitalization, punctuation, and spelling?)
10. Discuss plans for forwarding letter(s).
11. Review.
12. Evaluate.

Steps in Teaching Informational Expository Writing—The Essay

1. Contents of a good essay:
   a) Descriptive words: vocabulary control;
   b) Good topic sentences;
   c) Paragraphs containing one main idea;
   d) An interesting beginning;
   e) A good ending;
   f) Data—lots and lots of facts!
2. Plan of attack:
   a) Decide upon the subject matter; delimit the topic.
   b) Obtain materials.
   c) Scan materials.
   d) Choose interesting phase(s); organize and reorganize.
   e) Rewrite the statement of purpose; further delimit the topic.
   f) Select the title.
   g) Take notes of important and interesting facts.
   h) Write the outline by rearranging the notes (use of 6 x 8 index cards).
   i) Write the essay by using the outline as a blueprint. Remember documentation.

Sample Steps in an Oral Language Lesson: Correction of Speech Difficulties

The teacher should:
1. Find out what the difficulties are.
2. Start with the least difficult sound.
3. Stimulate with "speech stories" that stress the sound or element needed.
4. Have student read words that contain the speech element.
5. Avoid repeating the incorrect sound as the student says it. If necessary, write it on the board.
6. Drill for recognition of the incorrect form.
7. Use pictures, stories, and poems that stress the element.
8. Have the student raise his hand every time he hears the element.
9. Teach the student how to produce the sound correctly; show the correct placement of tongue, and so forth. Let him see how it is done.

10. Connect the sound with the environment, such as the *sss* heard when steam escapes from a kettle or the *hmmm* of a motor.

Procedure for Teaching Remedial Speech

The teacher should:

1. Start with a sentence from a story that has the phoneme in it.
   a) Have the student read it silently first.
   b) Have the student then read it aloud.
2. Have the student read a phrase containing the phoneme.
3. Have the student say the word containing the phoneme.
4. Have the student say the syllable containing the phoneme.
5. Have the student say the phoneme.
6. Have the student repeat the steps in reverse order if the sound is produced correctly anytime during the first five steps.
7. Have the student practice in front of the mirror and with a tape recorder. The best type of recorder to use is the sound-on-sound type that allows the teacher to record on one channel and the student to listen to it while he records on another channel without erasing the first channel. A special laboratory equipped with "Dolby" stereo cassette decks and video taping equipment should be available.
8. Encourage the student to begin using a correctly produced sound in different words and with vowels.
9. Enlist the parent's help if possible. Practice is a very important element. Five two-minute or three-minute sessions per day are all that are needed or advised.
10. Use the phoneme to form nonsense syllables.
11. If the difficult sound is a consonant, have it practiced in all three positions.
    a) Initial   *b*ye
    b) Medial   a*b*a
    c) Final   ab*b*
12. Always use the syllable-phrase-sentence-story procedure.
13. Remember, in the case of problems that include stuttering and stammering:

a) Stuttering is the repetition of the initial consonant.
b) Stammering is difficulty in getting a beginning sound out.
c) The stutterer usually has a less severe emotional problem than the stammerer.
d) Help the stutterer and the stammerer to relax; suggest that they take deep breaths; do not interrupt them; suggest that they practice in private.
e) The classical *Beta* hypothesis may be employed. According to this plan, the stutterer is encouraged to *practice his defect* a certain number of times each day. It is hypothesized that the student will, therefore, learn to control the muscles and end the problem.
14. People who talk too quickly often are helped by reading *group poetry*. Tape recordings, listening to one's own voice, and reading are helpful, too.

Some Sample Steps in Teaching Mathematics

The teacher should:

1. Build readiness: drill, practice. (See Figure D–5 for an overview.)
2. Stimulate using social setting problem/picture/realia/other.
3. List steps in development of lesson: concrete, semiconcrete, semiabstract, abstract, practice.
   a) Flannel board or other teaching visual or audio aid (teacher guides)
   b) One student does the problem on the chalkboard in numbers, or the teacher works the problem on the chalkboard and calls upon students to relate steps in calculation.
   c) If available, use individual place value charts or fraction kits to work some problem.
   d) One student does the problem on the chalkboard in numbers, or the teacher works problem on the chalkboard and calls upon students to relate steps in calculation.
   e) Carry the same problem through all steps from step 2 through step 3.
4. List all content material to be developed in (a) through (d).
5. One-half of the students may work at the chalkboard and one-half at their seats on practice problems.

FIGURE D–5   Sample Flowchart, Mathematics Lesson

Flowchart Mathematics—Two Directed Lessons Per Day*

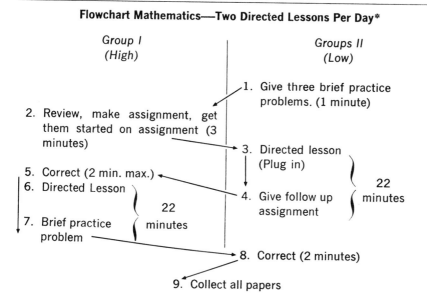

Group I
(High)

Groups II
(Low)

1. Give three brief practice
problems. (1 minute)

2. Review, make assignment, get
them started on assignment (3
minutes)

3. Directed lesson
(Plug in)

5. Correct (2 min. max.)

6. Directed Lesson

22
minutes

4. Give follow up
assignment

22
minutes

7. Brief practice
problem

8. Correct (2 minutes)

9. Collect all papers

Flow Chart Mathematics—One Directed Lesson Per Day

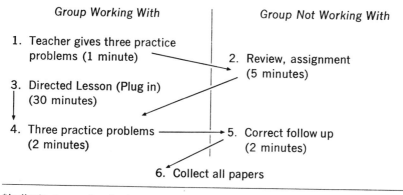

Group Working With

Group Not Working With

1. Teacher gives three practice
problems (1 minute)

2. Review, assignment
(5 minutes)

3. Directed Lesson (Plug in)
(30 minutes)

4. Three practice problems
(2 minutes)

5. Correct follow up
(2 minutes)

6. Collect all papers

*Indicate arrows teacher's route

6. Teacher and class review, clinch.
7. Plan follow-up, evaluate assignment, extra credit work provided.

Entire Procedure, When Using One Directed Lesson Per Day Only

Teacher's route if directed lesson is with Group I:

1. The teacher goes to Group I. He assigns three practice problems.
2. The teacher goes to Group II. He reviews, makes assignments, provides extra credit work, assists students in beginning assignments.
3. Assume the lesson concerns Venn diagrams in set theory, and lends itself to the use of a flannel board. The teacher goes to Group I, and:
   a) Builds readiness, directs a brief drill-practice.
   b) Stimulates, using social setting problem.
   c) Lists steps in lesson-on-lesson plan.
   d) Directs step-by-step use of flannel board; one student at a time participates.
   e) Directs use of individual set theory demonstration kits. All steps through (d) above repeated using individual kits.
   f) Allows one student to do work on chalkboard. If entirely new material, teacher does work on board, calling on individual students to relate each succeeding step orally.
   g) Has one-half of students work at chalkboard, one-half at seats on practice problems. Teacher talks the students through the first of these problems, step by step.
   h) Reviews the material.
   i) Plans follow-up—evaluates.
4. The teacher goes to Group II to correct follow-up, after giving Group I three practice problems.
5. Papers are collected.

Steps in Learning to Solve Verbal Problems in Mathematics

The teacher should:

1. Stimulate, using a social setting problem. For example, "We are going to have a paper drive. If all 30 children in room 11 bring 25 pounds, how many pounds of paper will be brought by room 11?"

2. Review steps in working a verbal problem. Make a chart of these steps:
   a) Read carefully.
   b) Reread the question part. Exactly what is asked?
   c) What are the facts? (numbers with labels)
   d) Decide which process to use. Discuss "process." Discuss meaning of plus (+), minus (−), division (÷), and multiplication (×) signs. Note that if the answer will be larger than the facts given, the process used will be addition or multiplication; if the answer will be smaller than the fact which has the greatest value, the process used will be subtraction or division. Division is used to group, or to find *one*. Note that the word "each" means one. It should be seen that if we are *given* the value of one, and asked to find many, we probably use that process which is the opposite of division, i.e., multiplication. Generally, we may add if the labels of the facts are the same, but if the labels are different we may multiply. If working with measures, it may be well to note that in changing a large unit measure to a smaller unit of measure we multiply, while in changing from a smaller unit of measure to a larger unit we divide. Note especially that the latter two rules apply ONLY in the changing of measures.
   e) Estimate the answer.
   f) Work the problem. Perform needed calculations.
   g) Label the answer. (Reread the question part of the problem to determine the label.)
   h) Check: (1) Are calculations correct? (2) Does the answer make sense?
3. Use appropriate steps to solve the problem, calling on one student per step.
4. The teacher could go through steps (a) through (e) above for all problems to be assigned.
5. Review; evaluate.
6. Assign problems and extra work.

Remember: stress, especially to beginning teachers, that one must uphold high (but realistic) standards. Even first-graders have been out of the crib for some time! The maxim "we get just about what we expect" is, within reason, valid.

D APPENDIX

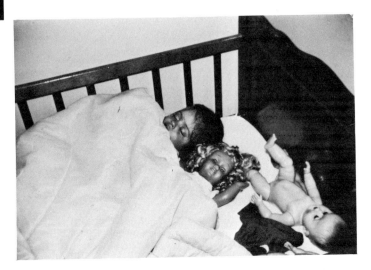

FIGURE D–6   Supervisors Must Help Teachers Realize that High but Reasonable Standards are Essential. Even First Graders Have Been Out of the Crib for Some Time.

Sample Lesson Plan: Mathematics in Grades 7 and 8

1. List of objectives:
    a) Grade 7—to introduce measurement of temperature
    b) Grade 8—to review reading and writing of decimal fractions
2. List of materials:
    a) Place-value charts
    b) Large cardboard "thermometer"
3. Preliminary details:
    a) Attendance
    b) Announcements
4. Stimulations:
    a) Social setting story involving temperature (Grade 7).
    b) Involving decimal fractions (Grade 8)
5. Procedure:
    a) Stimulation, as in (4) above
    b) One pupil uses materials noted in (2) above; teacher guides
    c) One student works problem from (4) above at blackboard; teacher guides

d) One-third of class to blackboard; practice

e) Students turn to text; follow development in text

6. Review and evaluation:

a) One student to board; review steps

b) Teacher asks guiding questions

7. Assignment:

a) Grade 7—pages . . . .

b) Grade 8—pages . . . .

8. Directed study: Begin assignment.

Some Sample Steps in Teaching Music Lessons

Steps in Singing (The Record Player Should be Set up and Ready)

The teacher should:

1. Build readiness

a) Set standards, using general standards chart.

b) Sing a familiar song first.

c) Stimulate interest in the new song. Use the whole-part-whole method on song introduction.

d) Spend half music time singing, half listening.

2. Have students take out music books. Teach them to put books in the same spot on the desk, and leave them closed. Never teach to inattention. With books closed, listen quietly to get the feel of the music. (Play records at a sufficiently high volume setting.)

3. Have students describe briefly the characteristics of the song by asking them leading questions.

4. Listen to the song again, for a purpose—something specific such as indicating phrases, ends of phrases.

5. Call on students to answer the question.

6. With books open, have them follow the words and music as the song is played again.

7. Have the students find similar phrases, tonal patterns, rhythms, and so forth, and frame them with their fingers. Charts, blank notation, and other matters related to the topic may be introduced.

8. Compare phrases and find differences. (Start simply.)

9. Give the starting note with a pitch pipe and have the students hum it.

10. Direct the students to sing with the record. Use song bells if a record player is not available. (Have a student practice in advance using a pencil with a larger rubber eraser for a clear, soft tone.)

11. Give the starting note again, have the students hum it, then have the students sing without the recording.

12. Correct mistakes by listening to difficult portions of the melody. Use blank notes if needed, and be sure students are looking at the correct part by asking them to "frame" it in the book with their forefingers.

13. Direct the students to sing the entire song again without the recording.

14. Have free choice of songs already known to students.

15. Evaluate. Singing should be a pleasant experience for teacher and students, but if the teacher does not enjoy singing, the students will not either.

Steps in Teaching Two-Part Songs

1. The teacher should briefly review some known songs to give a feeling of security.

2. The whole group sings the song together, following steps 1–15, above, and works on difficult parts.

3. The teacher works on the alto part with altos, while the sopranos study their parts without help. If possible, a transcription which has a separate alto part recorded should be used.)

   a) The teacher sings or plays the record while students listen.

   b) Teacher and students sing alto part together, at least twice.

   c) The students sing without the aid of the teacher or record.

   d) The teacher helps the students with difficult parts.

   e) The alto part is sung again.

4. The whole group sings together, in two parts, with the teacher singing with the altos.

5. If there is time, the students choose two familiar songs.

How to Review Unison Songs

1. Have the whole group sing with the teacher or a record.
2. Vary the singing in some way—half sing one verse, the other half the next, etc.
3. Have the whole group sing without the teacher, perhaps letting a student lead.

How to Review Two-Part Songs

1. Have the entire group sing soprano with the teacher.
2. Discuss and sing the alto part with the altos.
3. Have the whole group sing in two parts with the teacher singing with the altos while a student leads the sopranos.

Rhythm

Rhythm is so integral a part of the total musical concept that it is best to feel and learn it with the melody and harmony of the song. Suggestions for acquiring a feeling for the rhythm of the song are listed. The teacher should:

1. Chant the words of the song in the rhythm of the melody.
2. Clap or play rhythm instruments in the rhythm of the song as the words are chanted.
3. Play the chords of the song on the autoharp in the rhythm of the melody as the teacher or students chant the words.
4. Listen to a recording of the song.

When it is necessary to analyze the rhythm of a song more carefully, the teacher should:

1. Ask students to "feel" the number of beats in a measure while listening to the song; recognize the kind of note which gets one beat; and relate the meter signature to that which has been experienced.
2. Clap, tap, or play on rhythm instruments the underlying beat and rhythm patterns.

3. Put the characteristic or difficult rhythm patterns on the chalkboard in blank or drum notation, and chant and play them.
4. Determine the number of beats each note and rest receive, and count or name each note according to its time value.

Steps In The Use of Song Recordings

Approaches in Learning New Songs:

1. An audio approach without a book may be employed.
2. An audio-visual approach with a book or song chart may work well.
3. Interest in the song may be stimulated by an appropriate picture, a poem, personal experience, brief and by authentic information.
4. A leading question to guide attention to the predominant musical characteristic of the song might relate to its rhythm, melody, harmony, tempo, mood, range, words, accompaniment, and so forth.

Procedures in Presenting the Whole Song:

1. Playing the song without interruption;
2. Discussing briefly the initial impression it made on the class;
3. Directing attention to some musical aspect of the song:
    a) Its phrase structure: How many, any repetitions, and others
    b) Its melodic structure: Outstanding tonal patterns, melodies that go up or down, others
    c) Its rythmic structure: Predominant rythm patterns;
4. Replaying the song to study one of the aspects mentioned above;
5. Inviting class participation with the recording in: clapping, showing melodies, direction, phrasing;
6. Singing with the recording to develop confidence;
7. Eliminating parts of the recording by lowering the volume;
8. Encouraging independent singing, using the recording only as an introduction;
9. Listening to the class's singing without the recording and evaluating the performance;
10. Correcting any mistakes by repeated listening to difficult portions;
11. Singing the entire song with pleasure.

Some Steps In A Consumer's Enterprise: Music Listening and Appreciation

The teacher should:

1. Set standards, stimulate, relate to earlier work.
   a) Talk about the composer, have his name and the title of the song on the chalkboard (perhaps keep a notebook).
   b) Show a picture of the composer.
2. Direct the students to listen to the song. (A recording).
3. Have the students listen for one or two things, such as tempo, theme, and what section of the orchestra or what instrument predominates.
4. Call on a student to answer the question.
5. Ask students to listen to the recording again, if there is time.
6. Have free choices of available recordings if time permits.
7. Evaluate.

Some Steps in Teaching Physical Education

How to Proceed on the First Day

The teacher should:

1. Divide the class into several groups for more effective game participation. Do this in the classroom.
   a) Have the class "count off" quickly to make up the game groups (4 squads): 2 squads of boys, 2 of girls
   b) Appoint a member of each group to serve as captain.
2. Select a simple team game or game of low organization which holds the interest of the class.

Sample Lesson Plan for Introducing a Game

The teacher should:

1. Stimulate; obtain students' attention.
2. Have a sketch of the court or play area on the chalkboard or flannelboard.

3. Teach only the basic rules of the game.
4. Teach during the first lesson only those rules that all participants must know before playing the game. Answer questions during the play period as they arise.

FIGURE D–7   Sample "Batting Order" Rotation Schedule

Names	1st and 3rd Weeks of School Month					2nd and 4th Weeks of School Month				
	M	T	W	T	F	M	T	W	T	F
1.	1	2	3	4	5	6	7	8	9	1
2.	2	3	4	5	6	7	8	9	1	2
3.	3	4	5	6	7	8	9	1	2	3
4.	4	5	6	7	8	9	1	2	3	4
5.	5	6	7	8	9	1	2	3	4	5
6.	6	7	8	9	1	2	3	4	5	6
7.	7	8	9	1	2	3	4	5	6	7
8.	8	9	1	2	3	4	5	6	7	8
9.	9	1	2	3	4	5	6	7	8	9
10.	10A	10B	10A	10B	10A	10B	10A	10B	10C	10C
	10C	10C	10C	10C	10C	10C	10C	10C	10A	10B

NOTE: All have a chance to play all positions

1	Catcher
2	Pitcher
3	1st Base
4	2nd Base
5	3rd Base
6	Left Field
7	Center Field
8	Right Field
9	Left Short Stop
10A	Right Short Stop
10B	Assist at 2nd Base
10C	Assigned by Captain

Substitute starting with Number 10 if player 1, 2, 3, 4, 5, 6, 7, or 8 is absent, Numbers 1–5 must be filled. Substitute first Number 10, then 9, then 8, and so forth.

Team Number_____
Team Captain _____
Assistant Captain_____
   Approved: _____
                    Class President

5. Encourage discussion.
6. Determine what supplies are needed and which areas on the playground are to be used (should be scheduled ahead of time). A sample batting-order rotation schedule is included as Figure D–7.
7. Set standards with the students.
    a) Skill performance
    b) Conduct
    c) Safety (essential)! See Figure D–8 for a safety memorandum prepared by one supervising principal.

FIGURE D–8   A Memorandum Concerning Safety in Play Prepared by One Supervising Principal.

Safety Education and Practice in Softball

The following suggestions are offered to teachers for the specific purpose of helping them provide for the student's safety in all ballgames in which bats are used.

1. To teach the game of softball properly, and all other games which require the use of a bat, the first several lessons should be devoted to safety instruction. Students should be taught where and how to use the bat, proper location of the batter's bench, and the correct place for spectators.
2. Only one bat should be permitted for each game. The bat should be the standard elementary school bat.
3. All ballgames in which a bat is used should be played only where regulation softball backstops are availabe. It is suggested that principals confer with the physical education supervisor regarding the use of a backstop that is other than regulation or the substitution of a facility for the regulation backstop.
4. A batter's bench (also used for spectators) should be located at each diamond, behind safety fencing.
    a) On blacktop surfacing, the location is indicated by a painted diagram.
    b) On dirt surfacing, the bench should be at least 21 feet from home plate and 15 feet from the baseline.
5. "Hard" ball, "hard" baseball bats, and "hard" baseball games are not permitted on the elementary school grounds during the regular school session, after school playgrounds, or at any other time. The use of leather mitts is permissible provided the principal approves.

FIGURE D–8 (Continued)

6. All bat handles should be taped. The taping should extend approximately 9 or 10 inches up the handle.
7. The home plate shall be 10 or 12 feet from the backstop. Players should *drop* the bat (not throw it) on the ground near the home plate before starting for first base or returning to the batter's bench.
8. All students should be given specific instruction as to the hazards of crossing through game areas.
9. Players on the team at bat should remain seated on the bench until it is their turn to bat. Many schools have adopted a rule which we recommend to you: *All members of the batting team, with the exception of the batters, shall be seated on the batter's bench. The penalty for violation of this rule shall be "one man out."*
10. The safety elements in all ballgames that involve the use of the softball bat should be stressed as often as necessary by the director.
11. Evaluate:

Do not permit students:

a) To use a bat other than the school bat.
b) To use a bat that does not have the handle taped.
c) To use a bat in any place other than on a softball diamond.
d) To play with the ball and bat on the way to the diamond or while returning it to the playground box.
e) To have more than *one* bat at each playing area.
f) To leave the batter's bench while there is a batter in the batter's box.
g) To move the batter's bench any place other than the place designated for it.
h) To climb or sit on the backstop.
i) To walk or stand in front of the backstop (the catcher excepted).

8. Have students move outside in two lines. If more talking is necessary, have them form a *U* or *L, not a circle,* so that all may hear. A short exercise period should precede the game. Two of the four teams can play the new game while the other two teams play a known game. Evaluate!

Steps in Teaching Singing Games

Singing games are comparatively simple rhythmic patterns danced to traditional songs. They are relatively easy to perform and have particular appeal to younger students, or less skilled groups, because of their simple melodies and strong rhythmic accent. They usually involve much repetition. Even adults enjoy performing many of the traditional singing games as they usually have entertaining and often humorous implications, as well as the always appealing game element.

Suggestions for teaching singing games are listed. The teacher should:

1. Select and know the singing game before presenting it to the class.
2. Build a background.
   a) Play the music for the students.
   b) Explain briefly the origin of the singing game, if known.
   c) Teach the song.
   d) Explain briefly the meaning of any of the words with which the students might not be familiar.
   e) Encourage questions and comments from the students.
3. Teach the singing game.
   a) Play the first part of the music for the students.
   *b) Encourage them to suggest movements they think suitable for the first part or phase. (optional)
   *c) Try the movements suggested by the students. (optional)
   d) Present the singing game in its traditional form.
   e) Repeat the game from time to time for thorough learning and enjoyment.
   f) Most singing games may be accompanied by the singing of the dancers themselves, but groups may be formed, if space is limited— one group sings while the other dances.
   g) Divide the class into smaller groups for more active participation.
4. Evaluate the dance or the rhythms period.
   a) Evaluate the lesson with the students in terms of:
      (1) What we liked about the individual singing game or the whole rhythm period.
      (2) What we did well. A video tape recording would help.

*If the teacher feels that the *creative aspect* of the rhythmic activities has been given sufficient emphasis in other phases of the rhythmic program (Interpretative Rhythms, Rhythmic Pantomime and Dramatization, and Class-composed Dances), steps (b) and (c) under *Teach the singing game* may be omitted.

(3) What improvement is needed.
(4) What we can do next time we dance.
(5) How we conducted ourselves as good citizens.
   b) Evaluate the lesson in terms of the teacher's own objectives:
     (1) Did the students have wholesome fun?
     (2) Were appropriate rhythmic skills developed?
     (3) Was there evidence of physical, mental, and social growth of the students during the period?

Steps in Teaching Folk Dances

The teacher should:

1. Stimulate; build readiness and background; set standards.
   a) Play enough of the music to establish the mood.
   b) Tell stories related to music.
   c) Show pictures related to music.
   d) Teach vocabulary or words in the song.
   e) Discuss the people and their heritage.
2. Play music, asking students to listen for a purpose such as recognition of parts, themes, and so forth.
3. Assemble students into starting position.
   a) Put 1/3 of the class in the position at a time.
   b) Have rest of the class sit and watch.
4. Explain and demonstrate figure.
   a) Have students walk through first figure without music.
   b) Have students dance through first figure with music.
   c) Explain and demonstrate next figure.
   d) Continue adding new figures using same procedure.
5. Present the entire dance as soon as possible, at least in the same period, even though the last steps are not perfected. (Put whole back together.)
6. Work on needed figures. Put the remainder of class in figures.
7. Evaluate standards and dance performance.
8. Choose freely from other available dances already learned.

Steps in Teaching Square Dances

Before attempting to introduce a new square dance, the student should have been instructed in square dance terminology and formations (names and positions of couples, corners, etc.), and should have had practice in the fundamentals of square dancing (Promenade, grand right and left, allemande, dos-a-dos, sashay, swing, honor, circle, and others).

The procedure for teaching a square dance is basically the same as for any folk dance, whether the calls are on the recording or the teacher does the calling or prompting. The teacher should:

1. Know the dance in advance.
   a) Ensure that the calls fit the recording (opening, figures, choruses, ending, others).
   b) Know the pattern of the calls on the recording.
   c) Teach the dance to a "demonstration square" of students in advance.
2. Build a background with the students (e.g., the meaning of the title).
3. Play enough of the music to establish mood.
4. Explain the opening figure, and have one square walk through it to demonstrate.
5. All squares then walk through the opening figure.
6. All squares then dance the opening figure to music. (If there are calls on the recording, they are for prompting purposes, *not* teaching purposes.)
7. Repeat steps 4, 5, and 6 (4, explain and demonstrate; 5, walk through; 6, dance to music), with each new figure and chorus and ending, *adding* the new figure to the preceding each time it is done to music, until the whole square dance is learned.
8. Repeat the whole dance.
9. Practice parts that need drill separate from the rest of the dance.
10. Evaluate with the students.

Simple Classroom Games the Supervisor May Suggest to the Elementary School Teacher

SEVEN-UP: Seven students are chosen to stand side by side in front of the room. The appointed leader of this group gives the command, "Heads down!" On this command, the seated students close their eyes, lower their heads, and leave one forearm extended in the air.

At this time, each of the seven players quietly circulates among the tables or desks and touches one of the seated students on the arm. Each student touched immediately lowers his arm, and the player who touched him returns to his original position in front of the room.

When all seven players return to the front of the room the leader says, "Heads Up, Seven Up." On this command, all students raise their heads, and the seven tagged students stand beside their desks. Each tagged player is asked by the leader to guess who tagged him. If the tagged player guesses correctly, he exchanges places with the player who tagged him. If he guesses incorrectly, he stays in his seat. When all tagged players have had an opportunity to guess who tagged them and the exchanges have been made, the game continues as before.

Teacher suggestions: The leader should check carefully to see that the seven seated players have been tagged and have lowered their arms. Students who continue to "peek" should be eliminated from the game. In succeeding games tagged students who have guessed incorrectly should hold up one finger to avoid being tagged again. In this way, no one student will be tagged twice before other students have been tagged once.

BUZZ: The players sit in a circle, or any place where each player can easily be heard, and begin to count in turn. When the number 7 or any number in which 7 occurs, or any number which is a multiple of 7 is reached, the player says, "Buzz" instead of that number.

Let us suppose the players have counted up to 13. The next player will say, "Buzz" because 14 is a multiple of 7. The next would say 15, the next 16, and the next would say, "Buzz" because the figure 7 occurs in the number 17.

The game continues in this way until the count reaches 70 (which is "Buzz"). From here it goes on as "Buzz 1," "Buzz 2," etc., up to 77, which is "Buzz, Buzz." These higher numbers are seldom reached until the students thoroughly know their multiplication tables and are very familiar with the game. When a player says "Buzz" at the wrong time or does not say "Buzz" when he should, he is out of the game. The game continues until only one player remains.

A variation of "Buzz" is "Fizz" in which students count beginning with one. When five is reached or any multiple of five, such as 10 or 20, the students says "Fizzo." Fifties are handled by saying "Fizzo-o," "Fizz-one," and so forth.

APPENDIX

D

GHOST: The first player thinks of a word and calls out the first letter of that word. Then the second player calls out the second letter of some word that begins with the first letter that was called. The players take turns until a complete word has been spelled out. Each player tries to keep adding letters already called without completing a word. Let us say that the first player calls an "S," the second player a "P"; the first player on his second turn continues with an "O." If the second player should now call "T," he would lose the round because he would be completing the word SPOT. If, however, he calls another O, making the letters SPOO, his opponent would probably have to complete that word with an "L," forming the word SPOOL, or an "N," SPOON, or a "K," SPOOK. If he used any of these letters, he would lose the round.

The first time a player loses a round he becomes a 'G," then an "H," then an "O," then an "S," and finally a "T." In other words, if he loses five rounds, he becomes a GHOST, and loses the game; 3-letter words do not count. A word can never be completed until the fourth letter is called.

During the play, if one player has an idea that his opponent has called a letter that really does not form a word, the opponent may be challenged to tell what word he has in mind. If the challenged player cannot give the word which begins with the letters that have already been called, then he loses the round; but if he does have such a word, the challenging player loses the round. When a new round is begun, the old word is dropped and a new word is started.

COFFEEPOT: One student leaves the room while the class thinks of some activity. The student returns and asks questions of other students he chooses that must be answered truthfully. In asking the questions, he must use the word "coffeepot" to represent the activity. Likewise in answering, the word "coffeepot" must be used. The questioning continues until the student names the activity. The person who makes the remark that enabled him to guess is next to leave the room. Sometimes an object is selected to be identified instead of requiring some specific action.

For example, if the student who is IT is supposed to write his name on the chalkboard, the dialogue could begin somewhat as follows:

IT: Is the coffeepot in the front of the room? Student: yes
IT: Is the coffeepot something I have to do? Student: yes

IT: Should I coffeepot with one hand? Student: Yes

IT: Should I coffeepot the map? Student: No.

The dialogue continues until IT is successful or exhausts his previously agreed upon number of questions. The student or team which is most successful in identifying the coffeepot wins.

SIMON SAYS: One player is selected as the leader. He stands in the front of the room and the other players stand in the aisles facing the leader. The leader gives the commands, some of which are prefaced by "Simon says." Any player who complies with a command which is not prefaced by "Simon says" must sit down in his seat if the leader sees the error and calls his name. After the leader has caught three players making such errors, another leader is selected, the three players get into the game again, and the game starts over.

GUGGENHEIM: Each player has a paper and a pencil, and draws a table. A four letter word such as "Card" is written across the top, one letter in each column. In compartments on the left, write objects, such as automobiles, cities, countries, flowers. The students must write in each compartment the name of an object of the type mentioned to the left, beginning with the letter indicated at the top. Score: 10 points for a word no one else has, 9 points for a word two players have, 8 points for a word three players have, etc. The player with the highest score wins.

WORD MAKING: The teacher states a long word and tells each of the students to write it at the top of a sheet of paper. It should be a word with many vowels. Then he gives ten minutes to see who can write the longest list of words, using only the letters found in the word and in no instance using any letter more often than it appears in that word.

HANGMAN: One person thinks of a word and can go to the chalkboard or take a sheet of paper and put a dash for each letter in the word. The rest guess one letter at a time that may be in the word. If the guessed letter appears in the word, the leader puts it in the proper space. If it is not, the leader puts a head on the hanging man; the second miss and the body is drawn; third, one arm; fourth, the other arm; fifth, one leg; and sixth, the other leg. In such cases the leader wins and may put up another word.

JACKS: The player places the jacks in a circle on the ground. He bounces the ball, and must pick up one jack before he catches the ball, which must not bounce more than once. He puts the jack down and bounces the ball again. This time he picks up *two* jacks before he catches the ball, which—as before—must not bounce more than once. Players take turns going through the series. The first player keeps playing until he makes a mistake. The winner goes through the series first. Students can suggest various series.

BUTTON-BUTTON: All the players except IT sit in a row with clasped hands extended in front of them. IT goes to each of the others in turn placing his own clasped hands which contain a button over the others. He must drop the button from his clasped hands to those of another without allowing anyone else to see the transfer. When he reaches the end he points to one of the other players and says, "Button-Button, who has the button?" The player pointed to in turn makes a guess. If he guessed correctly, he becomes IT; if not, the person who has the button becomes IT. There are other versions.[1]

Steps in Teaching Reading

GRADE I, READING READINESS ACTIVITIES AND CHART READING

1. Readiness activities include:
   a) Developing left to right and top to bottom progression and using picture stories.
   b) Using small books with pictures and, perhaps, arrows to point.
2. Chart reading. The teacher should:

[1]See Gladys Andrews, Jeannette Saurborn, and Elsa Schneider, *Physical Education for Today's Boys and Girls* (Boston: Allyn and Bacon, Inc., 1962) and Winifred Van Hagen, Genevieve Dexter, and Jessie F. Williams, *Physical Education* (Sacramento: State Department of Education, 1951) for some excellent suggestions for game rules.

   a) Write an experience or creative story on a chart.

     (1) The students dictate the story and the teacher writes it on the chalkboard.

     (2) The teacher reads the story to the students, underlining words with his hand.

     (3) Someone can usually remember and "read" the story.

     (4) The teacher then writes the story on the chart. (It is a good idea to have a related picture at the top.)

     (5) Three lines are sufficient, and some—but not too much—repetition is useful.

   b) The next day, produce the chart.

     (1) Discuss the picture in relation to the students' experiences: "what color," "where did we see it," and so forth.

     (2) Ask a stimulating question; have students read chart to themselves. Direct them to look up when done. The teacher should note strengths, weaknesses.

     (3) Call on a student to answer the question and read the story aloud to prove he is right. (The teacher should move his hand along each line to help the student keep his place.)

     (4) Following the chart lesson, an activity directly involving reading might be to:

       a) Direct children to illustrate an idea of the story;

       b) Find similar stories in supplementary readers;

       c) Discover related stories in library books;

       d) Listen to a record that is related to the chart story;

       e) Explore books for new adventures.

GRADE I WORD ATTACK SKILLS LESSON SUGGESTIONS

1. Have the student frame a word or sentence that shows a certain element or idea and find if it is repeated anywhere else.

2. Have a pocket chart with sentence strips for the students to put in order or match.

3. Have a phonetic analysis drill, probably an initial consonant for the first few lessons.

GROUP THE CHILDREN AS SOON AS POSSIBLE INTO THREE GROUPS. Factors in selecting the first reading group include:

1. *Physical factors*
   a) Ability to respond as a member of a group through listening and discussing.
   b) Ability to hear like and unlike sounds.
   c) Ability to hold a book properly.
   d) Ability to turn pages in sequence.
   e) Ability to sit in a group for at least ten minutes.
   f) A chronological age of at least six years.
2. *Intellectual factors*
   a) Ability to listen to teacher's questions.
   b) Ability to discuss ideas.
   c) Mental age of approximately six years, six months.
3. *Social factors*
   a) Genuine desire to read.
   b) Interest in books.
   c) Enjoys working with other students.
4. *Emotional factors*
   a) Generally happy and cheerful.
   b) Has patience in completing a project.
   c) Is not easily annoyed.
   d) Not self-conscious or over aggressive.
5. *Linguistic factors*
   a) Adequate vocabulary.
   b) Speech easily understood.
   c) Correct usage of language.
   d) Good articulation.
   e) Expresses himself in complete thought sentences.

The teacher should:

1. Use sources of information;
   a) Cumulative records; mental age; books read, if any, and mark in reading
   b) Records of teacher observations and marks, if any
2. Schedule the reading period;
   a) One hour a day
   b) Reading time may vary according to group needs

3. Identify groups;
   a) Student's name
   b) Name of current reader
   c) Others
4. Plan for flexible grouping;
   a) Provide equal learning opportunities
   b) Rotate as often as the need is indicated.

Three-Group Organization: Procedures in Instruction

1. When the three groups have been formed:
   a) One group reads with the teacher
   b) Two groups are engaged in guided independent work. See Figure D–9 for a sample weekly block form.
2. Procedure for an initial reading lesson to develop skills:
   a) Relate the story, through discussion, to the children's experience.
   b) Involve the new words in this oral discussion as often as possible.
   c) Locate the story in the book.
   d) Discuss the picture and title.
   e) Pose a directed question for silent reading.
   f) Encourage students to answer questions orally in their own words (not words of the book).
   g) Read orally to prove the answer.
   h) Read a complete story in one period, if possible, so students gain the idea and sequence of events.
   i) Practice new words introduced in the story to strengthen basic vocabulary.
   j) During this period the teacher notes:
      (1) Words that give difficulty;
      (2) Word attack problems;
      (3) Problems of phrasing or smooth reading.
      (4) Ability to anticipate.
      (5) Ability to interpret what is read;
      (6) Pleasure and ease of the student's experience in the story;
      (7) Expression in oral reading.

FIGURE D–9   Sample Hourly Block Activities and Weekly Plan Forms

Ability Group	3 Group Reading: Hourly Block Activities Outline		
	First	Second	Third
Top I	Follow Up	Guided Independent Work	T
Middle II	T With Teacher in Circle	Follow Up	Guided Independent Work
Lowest III	Guided Independent Work	T With Teacher in Circle	Follow Up

Weekly Plan Form: Reading, History, Geography, and Art

Name _____ Key: W.A.S. = Word Attach Skill
F.U. = Follow Up
Week of _____ Object. = Objective

Subject	M	T	W	T	F
Reading III	Object. ___ pp. _____ W.A.S. _____ F.U. _____	Current Events	Object. ___ pp. _____ W.A.S. ___ F.U. _____	Object. ___ pp. _____ W.A.S. ___ F.U. _____	Library Reading, Self selection; Book reviews _____
Reading II	Object. ___ pp. _____ W.A.S. _____ F.U. _____	Same as above	Object. ___ pp. _____ W.A.S. ___ F.U. _____	Object. ___ pp. _____ W.A.S. ___ F.U. _____	Same as above _____
Reading I	Object. ___ pp. _____ W.A.S. _____ F.U. _____	Same as above	Object. ___ pp. _____ W.A.S. ___ F.U. _____	Object. ___ pp. _____ W.A.S. ___ F.U. _____	Same as above _____

    k) Following the lesson, activities directly involving reading might be:
       (1) To summarize the main ideas of the story;
       (2) To organize the ideas in sequence;
       (3) To direct the group to illustrate the ideas in sequence or select one idea for each student to illustrate and reconstruct the story the next day with summary statements and student's illustrations;
       (4) To direct the students to read a similar story in another book one or two levels lower than their reader to answer motivating questions;
       (5) To encourage any other activity that will strengthen this skill such as using a listening center with a similar recorded story and related book, or reading charted or duplicated materials geared to the writing ability of the group or other ideas;
       (6) To reread story independently to prepare for an audience situation;
       (7) Recreational reading.
  3. Procedures for a rereading lesson to strengthen one specific skill.
    a) The teacher prepares:
       (1) Five or six sentence strips, each containing one word emphasizing the initial consonant to be strengthened;
       (2) Five or six words cards, each beginning with the same initial consonant.
    b) The students:
       (1) Retell the story previously read;
       (2) Read each sentence silently to answer a question;
       (3) Read orally to prove the answer;
       (4) Read the sequence of sentences;
       (5) Recognize and match a word in a sentence-place; opposite the sentence in a pocket chart, such as the one illustrated in Figure D–10;
       (6) Cover the sentence strips;
       (7) Discover similarities and differences in the initial letter;
          Listen to other words that begin with the same letter;
          Substitute initial letters to form new words;

Sentence		Word
Sentence		Word
Sentence		Word
Sentence		Word
Sentence		Word

FIGURE D–10   Sample Pocket Chart.

(8) Uncover sentence strips and re-read;

(9) Evaluate.

An integral part of the lesson might be a follow-up activity in phonetic analysis. Figure D–11 illustrates a sample worksheet for such a lesson emphasizing initial consonants.

Name _____   Date _____

Directions:

Re-read the story. Add to each box the words or word that begins with the same letter as the other words in the box.

baby bear	neighbors new	went walked
_____	_____	_____
not no	they thought	mother more
_____	_____	_____

FIGURE D–11   Sample Worksheet for a Phonetic Analysis Lesson.

How to Use Preprimers

The teacher should:

1. Allow the students to examine the book.
2. Stimulate interest.
3. Continue to build readiness; have sentences from the story, with unfamiliar words underlined, written on the chalkboard or tagboard.
4. Check a vocabulary comprehension—have a student frame the sentence with his hands that answers a question.
5. Ask students to open books to the correct page (check) and ask them to study the picture, and then ask questions about it.
6. Enter the reading phase by having the students read one line silently to find the answer to a question. Tell students to point to words not known; give the students any needed words without delay.
7. Have a student answer the question and read the sentence aloud to prove he is right. The others follow along silently.
8. Have group interpretation of the story after reading several lines. "What do you think will happen next?"
9. Plan for rereading (optional). The teacher can start his own story (or the students their's), based on the picture and the book, or weave it into the book story, or end his story with the actual book story ending.
10. Plan a definite lesson in word attack skills.
11. Distribute followup material, workbooks or duplicated sheets; start students by getting a couple of answers first.
12. Remind the students of the assignment, then have them begin their independent work.

GRADE II AND FIRST HALF OF GRADE III

The teacher should:

1. Remember, students change in abilities and behavior at this period. Stimulate with a story, picture, object (not necessarily related to the story.)
2. Present the new vocabulary and write it on the chalkboard.
   a) Do not drill or spend much time on it.
   b) Ask a student to read the word and use it in a sentence.

3. Have the students turn to the correct page (write it on the board).
   a) Study the picture, then discuss it.
   b) Have a student read the title aloud.
4. Ask a stimulating question.
   a) Direct the students to read two or three lines silently to find the answer to the question.
   b) Watch to see who needs help. Be sure all are reading.
5. Call on a student to answer the question and then ask him to read orally to prove he is correct.
6. Repeat two or three lines at a time; this should give everyone a chance to read aloud.
7. Have some rereading to find a funny part, etc. (optional)
   a) This activity is especially good for third graders.
   b) Single purpose reading—extends interpretation, also.
8. Conduct a word attack skills lesson.
9. Present the follow-up assignment—workbooks or duplicated material that requires some rereading.
   a) Get two sample answers from students (matching endings, etc.).
   b) Give the students an opportunity to ask questions about the assignment.
   c) Let them skim the story to find words they need to know.

Suggested Independent Follow-up Activities for Primary Grades

1. *Best* independent activity: reading!
2. Research in story file (for a discussed need).
3. Research in informational books (for definite information).
4. Read easy books for information for social studies interest (*research*).
5. Hunt through magazines and discarded books for pictures for social studies interests. (Classify, arrange in sequence, put in browsing table booklet or mount for story file; for a bulletin board display; for a chart; or to take home or to share with another grade. Captions discussed and added later.)
6. Arrange books on shelves and browsing table per content (diary, pleasure, and so forth).
7. Rearrange on flannel board or table pictures of a story or social studies concept (e.g., "Milk from Pasture to You").

8. Look through picture file or story file.

9. Look through magazines to find pictures of grocery store insignias (i.e., Campbell's Tomato Soup) to be pasted on doweling for retail market. (Cut out and measure to decide on length doweling to saw at construction time.) Later paste on doweling and shellac, if desired.

10. Reread a story from directed reading lesson to find: the funniest part, the most important part, the part liked most, and so forth. (Report later to group on part selected, and why.)

11. Reread a story in preparation for reading of it to another group, class, to parents.

12. Reread a story or charts to a friend in your room but in another reading group or classroom.

13. Finish a story that the teacher or a friend reads to a certain point (should be a book two levels below present reading level).

14. Check dictionary box to be sure all words are filed correctly.

15. Alphabet and phonetic drill game (three students). Ask each other questions such as:
    a) Find a word that starts with the letter "T" or sound of "tu." (Other finds and reads it from dictionary box.)
    b) Find a word that starts with the letter directly after "C" or the letter before "E."
    c) Find a 5-letter word.
    d) Find a word that ends with "S."
    e) Find "E-A-T" (spelled out).
    f) Find something that lives on a farm. One student asks; two other students try to find it first. Keep score—one point for the one who finds it first. This activity must be practiced in directed lessons first. An "O" is recorded for the one who was not first to strengthen the concept of "O."

MIDDLE AND UPPER GRADES

The teacher should:

(Have the reading leader bring assignment chart, answer chart.)
1. Correct yesterday's follow up—answer chart ready. (1–2 min.)

2. Build readiness (2 min.)

   a) Stimulate/motivate: map of _____ , picture of _____ , other _____.

   b) Introduce new vocabulary: cards, read, chalkboard (if written, chalkboard is recommended), or 'verbalize' new vocabulary.

   c) Relate to _____ .

   d) Students discuss picture of_____. Read title. (One page for low group, more for top.)

3. Read pages_____and_____to answer . . . (ask a question). (Give any words students indicate they need individually.)

4. Read silently. Be sure to read to_____, even if you find the answer before you finish all of the assignment. If you need help with a word, point to it. Look up when you finish.

5. Call on student to answer the question. He gives page and paragraph where he found the answer. Students turn to that place. He reads orally to prove his answer is correct.

6. Repeat numbers 3 through 5 above for remaining pages of today's assignment. (It will probably prove helpful to list pages and questions on your plan.)

7. Word attack skills. In many situations the teacher may wish to spend an entire lesson on word attack skills, and to alternate this activity daily with the entire pattern.

   a) The teacher writes word on board e.g., "Driver."

   b) Students suggest similar words e.g., "Player," "Baker."

   c) Students cover all but root word.

   d) The teacher underlines the root word.

   e) Teacher: "How are the endings of these words alike? All alike—end in "er.""

   f) Students frame "er" ending.

   g) Teacher: "Let's see if we can find meaning."

   h) Teacher: "What is a driver?"
     Children: "A person who drives."

   i) Teacher: "Then "er" says, "a person who" (drives) (plays) (bakes) in *this* case."

   j) Teacher: "Write the word. Erase the final "e." Add "er." What are the vowels? Drop the final "e." Does that change the root sound?"

8. Give follow-up assignment (duplicate on chart or chalkboard).
   a) Introduce the assignment.
   b) Obtain two sample answers. Any questions?
9. Direct the students to skim for needed words and drill on needed words (see 2(b) above).
10. Remind the students about the follow-up assignment.

Notes on Follow-up Activities

MIDDLE AND UPPER GRADES

Follow-up activities usually require a rereading of the story.

1. Comprehension: questions, single purpose, steps in a process, write topic sentences, write summary paragraph, others.
2. Practice in using word attack skills: include words from story.
3. Vocabulary building: include building sight vocabulary.
4. Location skills
   [See Gertrude Hildreth, *Learning the 3 R's* (2nd ed; Minneapolis: Educational Publishers, Inc., 1947]
5. Organizing and classifying ideas
   a) Spanish house—stone
   b) Dutch house—logs

Steps in Teaching Library Research Skills: Book Reports and Reviews

1. Stimulation.
2. Standards for reading.
3. Teacher or pupil librarian notes which group (last names A–H, I–R, or S–Z) is to give oral book reviews.
4. Reports finished; skits or projects polished (15 minutes).
5. Reading only (15 minutes).
6. Oral reports and collection of written reports (25 minutes. Students are called on in alphabetical order. Those not giving oral reports turn in written reports.

7. Procedure in marking:

   a) Check ($\sqrt{}$) if not done. Students may say, "Not this week" without penalty *once* each ten weeks. If book is long, may be given a book slip good for two weeks.) Student turns in slip instead of report at end of first week.

   b) Blank ( ) if done.

   c) Plus sign (+) if extra credit such as a one-minute skit of "part I liked best," or a special project, or more material.

8. Standards are evaluated with the class.

9. Advertisements to be placed in the "We Recommend" file are selected.

10. Evaluation.

Steps in Teaching Social Studies and Science

Steps in Initiating a Social Studies or Science Teaching Unit

A. An arranged environment is one way to stimulate interest. (Other ways include: movies, a field trip, a short story.)

   1. Books, pictures, and other materials should be on display.

   2. Students circulate in small groups to see the displays (ask each group to report on one display).

B. The items they have seen and handled are discussed; questions and controversies should arise. The teacher should:

   1. Write the students' questions on the board. (The teacher may write the student's name after the question, but do not refer to it as "his.")

     a) Try to get a few questions of quality rather than a large quantity.

     b) Make a list of questions before the lesson, from the course of study.

     c) Evaluate and review the questions; add some of his own questions if needed, especially to be sure to cover the required information.

     d) Develop the purpose for going into step two.

   2. Organize the questions; write them on a chart before the lesson begins.

Outline for Developing a Social Studies Unit

The purpose of Social Studies is to learn and understand the ways people live and work, and how progress is affected by natural resources, geographical features, and human relationships. This purpose may be achieved by moving through a definite procedure, such as that which follows:

I. Teacher Preparation
    A. Selecting unit appropriate to grade level from the Course of Study
    B. Surveying and studying background materials
    C. Selecting and appraising reference materials
    D. Acquisitioning and organizing environmental materials
    E. Planning for possible uses of information to be gained

II. Motivation
    A. Identifying common group interest and needs
    B. Developing sufficient background to provide a basis for meaningful questions
    C. Establishing purposes for finding and using information

III. Raising Questions
    A. Using understandings and appreciations gained during the motivation
    B. Guiding the asking of questions
        1. Information needed to meet established goal
        2. Quality rather than quantity is stressed
        3. Avoiding questions which can be answered "yes" or "no"
    C. Recording questions in language meaningful to students

IV. Organizing Questions
    A. Recognizing categories reflected in the questions
    B. Organizing questions into categories

V. Obtaining Information
    A. Providing materials at appropriate reading levels
    B. Using information from several sources
    C. Employing learned skills to locate answers to questions

VI. Discussing, Summarizing, and Recording Information
    A. Contributing information from several sources

    B. Considering reliability and accuracy of information
    C. Recording pertinent ideas expressed
    D. Evaluating to determine if information gained has answered the question
  VII. Using Information
    A. Extending plans for use of information
    B. Application of learning to established purposes
       1. Dramatic representation
       2. Panel picture
       3. Construction
       4. Map-making
       5. Clay figures
       6. Illustrations
       7. Table models
       8. Written language
       9. Musical expression
      10. Rhythmic expression
      11. Field trip
      12. Others
    C. Culminating and evaluating the unit
 VIII. Teacher Evaluation
    A. Appraising outcomes in relation to pupil needs
    B. Noting successful techniques and methods for future experiences with the unit

How to Handle Committee Work in the Social Studies

1. Committees are not used as the main source of information, but as information to clarify material and for extra activities.
2. Students enjoy working on such activities making a time line and writing short stories.
3. Make a chart listing activities in addition to reading.

See Figure D–12 for a flowchart depicting the committee work cycle. Figure D–13 portrays two sample committee products.

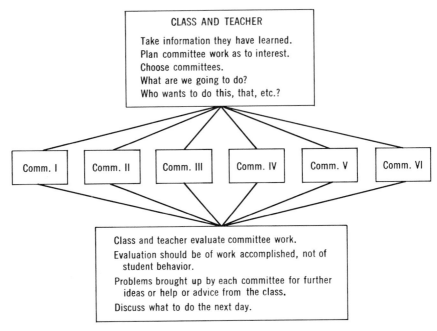

FIGURE D–12   Sample Committee Work Flow Chart.

FIGURE D–13   Salt and Flow Relief Map and a Student-Made Electric
Response Map.

Using Maps in Teaching the Social Studies

I. The Purpose
   A. To portray concepts learned
   B. To build understandings
II. Content
   A. Every map should be made for a specific purpose.
   B. Much class research, planning, and evaluation should precede all map making.
   C. Maps should be accurate in the facts presented.
   D. A map should be specific in content; it should tell one thing.
   E. Series of maps should be made to show a sequence of ideas.
   F. Maps may show, for example:
      1. Location of an industry or product
      2. Where and how products are transported to market
      3. Relative size of one country or region to another
      4. Rainfall
      5. Transportation—waterways, railways, airways
      6. Imports and exports to and from a region or country
      7. Mountains, plateaus, valleys, plains
      8. Territorial development of a country
      9. Places of interest in a region or country
      10. Historical trails
      11. Cities-industrial centers
      12. Population centers
      13. Sources of raw materials
      14. Regions
III. Materials

Suggested Background Material	Medium
1. Wrapping paper	Thick calcimine-chalk-crayola
2. Manila drawing paper	Water color-chalk-crayola
3. Newspaper	Calcimine-chalk
4. Oil cloth	Thick calcimine-chalk
5. Carton packing boxes	Thick calcimine
6. Unbleached muslin	Crayola-stitchery

Suggested Background Material	*Medium*
7. Burlap	Thick calcimine
8. Tag board	Ink-crayola-stitchery
9. Typewriting paper	Ink-pencil-crayola-water color
10. Cardboard	Flour and salt or clay

Crepe paper dye may be used to cover large areas without streaking.

IV. Making the Map*
   A. Use slides or overhead transparencies to project map. Freehand drawing is not accurate.
   B. Make individual or group maps.
   C. Make maps used for class discussion of a size visible to all.
   D. Indicate neighboring countries on map.
   E. Use complete map of country even when one region is emphasized.
   F. Make pictographs of size consistent with each other and map as a whole.
   G. Stencils may be used for repeated pictograph.
   H. Make explanatory key simple and concise.
   I. Lettering:
      1. Lettering is more effective when made to read horizontally.
      2. Letters can be varied in size and weight.
      3. Simple style of alphabet is best.
      4. A stencil or "window" of heavy paper or cardboard is helpful device to use in lettering.
      5. A box of stencils varying in size proves valuable.
      6. Importance of name or word determines the size of lettering.
      7. Lessons in making letters should precede the lettering of maps.
   J. Art principles to remember in cartography:
      1. Establish a dominant color.
      2. Use a definite color harmony to simplify the color problem such as:

---

*Note: Be alert to maps every day in newspapers, books, magazines, travel guides, and advertisements. Students should be taught to look for, to read, and to interpret a wide variety of maps intelligently.

a) Various values and intensities of one color.

b) Related colors.

3. When all colors are used, distribute black or white throughout the map to unify the composition.

4. Contrast land areas from water areas and pictographs from land and water through:

a) Variety in color

b) Variety in shade (dark and light)

c) Variety in pattern (if land is filled with design, keep ocean plain, and vice versa)

5. Outlining: vary width of line to show relative importance of areas.

6. Borders:

a) Lines may be used of heavier width than other lines on map and of same color as dominant color in map.

b) Pictures when used as borders should be of one color, but may be varied by using value or intensity of that color.

c) Tape edges of map for a finished durable effect.

Some Sample Steps in History, Geography, Civics, and Science: the Multitext Lesson

The supervisor should suggest the following steps:

1. Select one standard for emphasis.

2. Build readiness—stimulation (e.g., chart, physical features of _____ , picture, map story, others).

3. Relate to previous lessons; establish purpose.

4. Select students to read questions on chalkboard.

5. Outline on chalkboard *What We Think We Know*—two or three items.

6. Have students read Bibliography chart with page numbers.

7. Set standards for silent reading.

8. Guide students in selecting and obtaining books. (Teacher already suggested books in which to start for each reading-ability level. If duplicated reading material for low group, it should be distributed at this point.)

9. Have students read and take notes in outline form.
10. Suggest several methods teacher may help lowest ability group.
11. Conduct an open forum:
    a) Chairman selected
    b) Those to receive first chance to share chosen.
    c) Forum; teacher guides; answers are discussed.

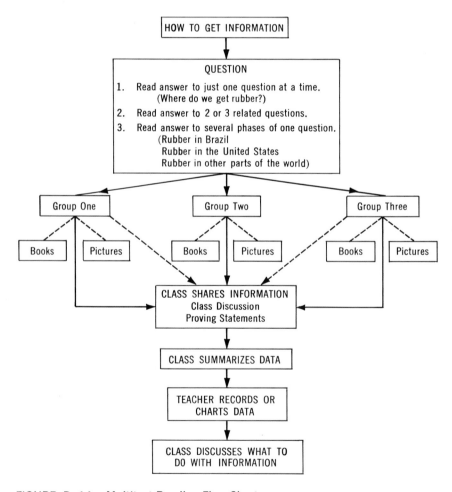

FIGURE D–14   Multitext Reading Flow Chart.

12. Summarize, writing on board "What We Know." Call on students; clarify ideas; check "What We Think." Evaluate those who shared, audience.

See Figure D–14 for a flowchart diagramming the multitext lesson. Figure D–15 illustrates question and answer charts.

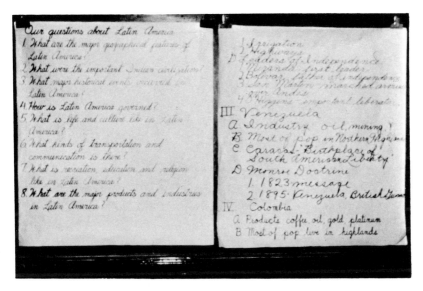

FIGURE D–15   History and Geography Question and Answer Charts in an Upper Elementary Grade.

Some Sample Steps in Science: Experimentation

The teacher should proceed through the following ten steps in conducting an experiment lesson:

1. Interest is stimulated;
2. The problem is posed, identified, delimited;
3. The problem is discussed;
4. Possible solutions, answers (hypotheses) are generated: "What We Think" is charted on the chalkboard;

5. The students read to find solutions, answers;
6. The experiment/demonstration is conducted;
7. Findings are discussed;
8. Findings are compared with "What We Think";
9. Conclusions; review: "What We Know About . . . ."
10. New science vocabulary words are charted.

For example, the teacher could:

1. Discuss the air around us. Of what is it composed? List on the chalkboard possible answers/solutions ("What We Think"; hypotheses). (Not always necessary to make a list first.)
2. Call on various students to read certain pages. Stop to explain and discuss various paragraphs.
3. Experiment (e.g., candle goes out when covered with a glass). (Several students could participate; they could help to conduct the experiment.)
4. Lead a discussion of the findings. Ecological implications?
5. List conclusions: *"We know* air is made of the following . . ."
6. Compare the two lists; erase erroneous material.
7. Summarize (review, clinch, and evaluate).
   Do not neglect to discuss hazards of alcohol, tobacco, narcotics.

Sample Lesson Plans, Social Studies, Secondary Grades

Sample Lesson Plan: Phase I

   I. *Objective:* To introduce unit on ancient China: town life and Confucius
  II. *Materials:* Pictures, agenda, map, globe, texts
 III. *Preliminary Details*
    A. Attendance accounting
    B. Necessary announcements
    C. Return marked papers
    D. Students study for short "quiz"
    E. Take and correct quiz; note scores on individual graphs
 IV. *Stimulation:* Relate saying of Confucius; show picture; use globe

V. *Procedure*

   A. After stimulation as in IV, teacher calls on students to read questions that have been written on board.

   B. Students are given an opportunity to ask questions about classwork.

   C. Directed reading: students respond to questions on board.

VI. *Evaluation and Review:* One student recalls stimulation at beginning of period, notes location of China on map.

VII. *Assignment:*

   A. Complete page _____ items _____.

   B. Extra credit work: _____.

VIII. *Directed Study:* Students begin assignment. Teacher provides individual assistance.

Sample Plan: Phase II

I. *Objective:* To review unit on ancient China: town life and Confucius

II. *Materials:* Colored chalk, map, globe, agenda, pictures, supplementary texts

III. *Preliminary Details*

   A. Attendance accounting, necessary announcements, return marked papers.

   B. Students study for short quiz; take same. Papers are exchanged; scores noted on graphs.

IV. *Stimulation:* Show picture; use globe.

V. *Procedure*

   A. After stimulation as above, class president selects four students to serve on panel.

   B. Panel and open forum.

   C. Informal lecture; question and answer.

VI. *Review and Evaluation:* Class members summarize most important points covered. Teacher outlines on board. Two people evaluate audience, panel, open forum.

VII. *Assignment*

VIII. *Directed Study:* Students complete outline from board.

Steps in Teaching Spelling

The teacher should:

1. Have students prepare one folded paper as per the diagram in Figure D–15, which is kept in a spelling folder, one page for each week.
2. Have students keep a graph of their scores from each week. This graph is on one-half inch graph paper and is also kept in the folder.
3. Each week, also have them prepare one sheet of lined paper folded so that it has four pages, numbered 1, 2, 3, 4.

Steps in Word Presentation and Study

THE PRESENTATION PHASE

1. The teacher says, "Pencils down, eyes front."
2. The teacher writes word on the board *while* students *watch* him write it.

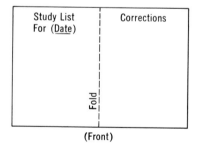

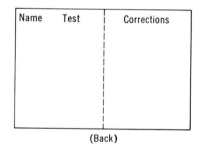

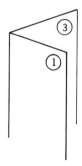

FIGURE D–15   Sample, Spelling Folder Sheet.

APPENDIX D

3. The teacher says the word.
4. The teacher says, "Use the word in a good sentence (*name*)."
5. The student replies.
6. The teacher says, "How many syllables are in this word?" and calls on a student.
7. "Say the word in syllables," and call on a student. (Teacher underlines the syllables with chalk. The supervisor should suggest that the teacher never use vertical lines or separate the word.)
8. The teacher says, "Say the word after I do." (Teacher says the word, and repeats with class.)
9. The students say the word with the teacher (teacher can underline word with hand as it is said.)

THE STUDY PHASE
1. The teacher says, "Close your eyes, imagine you see the word, open, check to see if you were right."
2. The teacher says "Write the word on page 1." Check to see that you are right."*
3. The teacher asks students what the hard part of the word is, or *other word attack skills.* (Structural analysis, how it ends, etc.)
4. The teacher says, "Say the word again after I do."
5. "Write the word on page 2 from memory."
6. Check.
7. The teacher writes word on board and students *watch* and check.
8. "If you made an error correct it. No erasing; cross it off and rewrite."

ADDITIONAL SUGGESTIONS
1. The teacher should repeat the presentation—study phase for the next words. He should not use this procedure for review words. The students should put them on their study lists the first day, in addition to the new words and personal words.
2. When the students with shorter lists reach their cut-off point, they stop listening to the presentation and begin to do their other spelling work (workbook, homework, etc.).
3. Homonyms should not be given together in the presentation phase.

*Stop here for the easier words. Continue steps 12–16 for harder words only.

Individualized Approach, Weekly Plan

A. *Monday*

The teacher should:

1. Have students take their spelling seats. Have them prepare pages 1–4 and study list.
2. Present and study six words as per directions for studying words. (Do not have a separate presentation.) See Figure D—16 for a chart used to aid individual word study.
3. Pre-test on page 4 of folded sheet.
   a) **Test** only on the six words he has presented that day, to see which ones the students need to study.
   b) *Say the word, use it in a sentence, say it again.*
   c) The pre-test is optional, because the entire class will not miss the same words.

STUDYING OUR WORDS

---

1) Look at the word. TAKE THE PICTURE. Say it to yourself. Spell it to yourself.
2) Close your eyes. Imagine what the word looks like. DEVELOP THE PICTURE.
3) Imagine you write the word. Spell it to yourself.
4) Open your eyes. Check. Were you right?
5) Write the word. PRINT THE PICTURE.
6) Check!
7) If you made a mistake write the word five times! Repeat (1–7).

FIGURE D—16   Chart Used to Aid Individual Studying of Spelling.

4. Before the students begin to write out their individual study lists, have them write the number of words they must take in the circle which is in the upper left-hand corner (individual matter). See the instructions for Friday for how to determine this figure.

5. Direct the students to add all the words to the *study list* in the spelling folder.
6. Have the students make their graph. (Give specific directions.)
7. Direct the students to underline syllables.
8. Have the students add their three personal words to the study list. Have them place a star by the personal words.
    a) If they have missed any words on Friday, these must be included.
    b) Other words (to complete the 3) are taken from language lessons, science, reading, and other subjects.
    c) If the student missed more than 3 words last week, he nevertheless adds no more than 3.

B. *Tuesday*

The teacher should:
1. Repeat Monday's steps 2, 3, 5, 7, with the seven new words which are presented on Tuesday.
2. Always present the words for each week in order of increasing difficulty.

C. *Wednesday:* Repeat Tuesday's steps.

D. *Thursday*

The teacher should:
1. Have a trial test on page 3 and directed study.
2. Assign homework, such as writing sentences which incorporate the spelling words.
    a) Students underline spelling words in the sentences they have written.
    b) If an assignment is not turned in on Friday it may be turned in on Monday, provided two sentences are written for each word.
    c) If not ready by Monday, a mark of "F" should be recorded and the counseling phase is suggested.
    d) Do not allow misspelled words on the homework. If any of the spelling words are misspelled, assign an automatic mark of "No credit" or "F."
3. Have study lists checked. Rubber stamps may save the teacher time; e.g., "Credit Memo" or "Approved." Corrections should be written in the "Correction" columns.

4. Those students whose lists are all right five times and have had 100 per cent correct five times on the final tests may spend spelling period working on some other related language arts activity. The exempted students, nevertheless, must take all tests and complete assigned tasks.
5. While most of the students are taking the trial test, the teacher can check the study lists and stamp them, as indicated above. Corrections should be written in the correction column, if any be necessary.

E. *Friday*
1. The final test is written on the back of the study list paper.
2. The teacher should write the score as the number correct over the number assigned (a fraction).
3. The students must memorize their three extra words and put them on the test with a star next to them. They could check the spelling of these words themselves.
4. The number of words each student studies next week is the number right on Friday's test plus three, if all the words are correct.
5. If any words are missed, it is the number right plus two.
6. If they only miss three or fewer of all the possible words, then they take all the possible words next week. Example

$$\frac{16}{16}: \quad 16 + 3 = 19 \text{ words next week}$$

$$\frac{15}{16}: \quad 15 + 2 = 17 \text{ words next week}$$

Presentation, Form II, for Use with Separate Groups. (Not Recommended!)

A. Method

The teacher should:
1. Have students take spelling seats.
2. Teach high group Monday and Tuesday.
3. Teach low group Monday, Tuesday, Wednesday, and, perhaps Thursday.

B. Procedure.

The teacher should:
1. Stimulate interest.

2. Write the word on the board.
3. Say the word.
4. Call on a student to say the word in a sentence.
5. Say the word in syllables, and say, "Say the word after I do." The teacher says the word.
6. Ask the students to say the word with him as he says it.
7. Erase the word. *Only one word should be on the board at a time.*

C. Implications of the two-group procedure:
1. The teacher must still have the study group as per single group procedure.
2. The mastery lists would be given to the second group.
3. There is significantly less time for study and individualized help.
4. A combination of the two-group method and the individualized method is not recommended.
5. The individualized method seems to be the better one. Usually there are only 4 or 5 students who do not take all the words in the individualized method; progress is much quicker.

Principles of Supervision

Questions

1. What have been your experiences and reactions to supervision? Can you account for your reactions? Were valid principles employed in the supervisory program?
2. How can the supervisor best gain the confidence and cooperation of teaching personnel? What principles are involved?
3. What are the advantages of democratic, cooperative supervision? The disadvantages?
4. How can desired changes best be effected by the supervisor?
5. The role of the supervisor is viewed differently by supervisors, teachers, administrators, and the school board. How can the supervisor best re-solve these differences of opinion?
6. What are some principles that a supervisor may use in order to gain rapport and cohesiveness within a group?
7. Can a school be known for its supervisory program, or is it restricted by the policies of the school system?
8. How much should a school be swayed by community pressures to which it is subjected?

Suggested Activities

1. List the various ways by which a supervisor can observe basic principles in aiding teachers.
2. List the basic principles of supervision violated by a group of teachers who have become tyrannical and unpleasant in their classes.
3. List some "do's" and "don't's" for the beginning supervisor. Refer to the list of basic principles.
4. List the qualifications of the ideal supervisor in training, experience, and personal qualities. What principles are involved?
5. List the differences in supervision which might be found between a small, rural district and a large, city school system.

6. List the changes which are currently taking place in education and their possible effects on supervision.
7. List the qualities of an ideal supervisor.

Special Problems: Role of the Intermediate Unit

Questions

1. What are the major activities of your local intermediate unit in the area of educational supervision?
2. How would you change the form of services rendered by your local intermediate unit?
3. What legal basis is there for the operation of the intermediate unit? What court decisions have been influential in this area?
4. How would you, as a junior high school supervisor, obtain the assistance of the consultants on the intermediate unit staff? What type of assistance would you expect from such specialists?
5. Do you believe that the intermediate unit can perform certain functions with more efficiency and/or economy than can the local school system? List such functions and indicate your reasons for including them in your list.
6. What services should the intermediate unit perform that it is now not providing? Indicate your reasons.
7. What training specifications would you recommend for the intermediate unit superintendent? The specialists?

Suggested Activities

1. Indicate your reasons for believing the intermediate unit board of trustees and superintendent should be elected or appointed.
2. List all of the services which should be performed by the local school system and compare these to the services of the intermediate unit and/ or the state.
3. Develop a chart showing the ratio or number of recommended intermediate unit specialists to the number of elementary, junior high school,

and senior high school teachers in the county or intermediate unit areas.
4. Analyze the relationship of the salaries of the administrators and specialist-consultants in the local school systems to those of the intermediate unit superintendent and his specialists.
5. Outline the organization of the intermediate unit nearest your home. Diagram line and staff functions.

Special Problems: Role of the State

Questions

1. How may your state constitution be amended?
2. Differentiate between the type of material included in your state constitution, your state education or school code, and the rules and regulations of your state board of education.
3. What part do the courts play in establishing educational practices for the entire state?
4. What qualifications do you believe the members of the state board of education should possess?
5. What qualifications do you believe the chief state school officer should possess?
6. Do you believe that your state should refuse to give supervisory assistance to a private or parochial school? Why?
7. Requirements for a high-school diploma are issued in written form by thirty-nine states. Should such requirements be listed for elementary school graduation as well? For a community college degree? Indicate the reasons for yours answers.

Suggested Activities

1. Outline the functions of the state in educational supervision.
2. Distinguish between the terms chief state school officer, state department of education, state board of education, and state legislature.
3. List general principles for the state's role in educational supervision.
4. Trace the historical development of the state departments of education.

5. Indicate the responsibilities of the chief state school officer. From the list of responsibilities, decide how the chief state school officer should be selected.

6. List the functions of the state department of education for your state. Prepare a chart indicating relationships between the various offices of the state department of education.

7. List the curriculum and supervision responsibilities of the state department of education for your state. Consider textbook selection; organization for curriculum development; organization for supervision; subject area consultive services and techniques used; workshops and work conferences; statewide, sectional, and local conferences; consultant services; grants of funds for special programs; curriculum materials, instructional technology (audio-visual aids) and programmed learning, research, and experimentation.

8. Analyze the role which your state department of education has played in submitting proposed legislation to the state legislature. Cite examples of laws which have been passed which were recommended by the state department.

9. Prepare a bibliography of material which has appeared in the periodical literature during the last year concerning the role of the state in supervision.

10. Differentiate between the terms approval and accreditation, and give concrete examples of each.

11. Study the form of the accreditation and approval program(s) employed by your state department of education. Show how they could be improved.

How to Organize for School Supervision

Questions

1. Can a "helper" relationship exist between the supervisory staff and the teacher if periodic written evaluations of the teacher's performance are required?

2. Who is responsible for the character and quality of the instructional program?

3. How can a school system organize for supervision with clear lines of authority and still be democratic?

4. What factors are responsible for the newer democratic approach to supervision?

5. What is the relationship of *line* officers to *staff* officers? Is it essentially democratic? Efficient?

6. What weaknesses are most apparent in the line and staff system of organization? Are the same weaknesses present in *linear responsibility charting?*[1]

7. What is the proper relationship between administration and supervision?

8. What is the supervising principal's role in the supervisory program? The superintendent's? The specialist-consultant's? The teacher's? The student's?

Suggested Activities

1. Chart the line of authority in supervisory practice from the board of education to the teacher in (a) an authoritarian type of organization, and (b) a democratic type of organization. Discuss the strengths and weaknesses of each type of organization.

2. List the apparent trends that are emerging in the organization of supervisory services.

3. Discuss the relationship of the supervisor to other staff and line officers and present a plan of coordination between these positions.

4. Compose a good job description for a supervisory position in your school system. Include duties, qualifications, and title of the position.

5. Describe from personal experience examples of organization that are operating effectively, whether authoritarian or democratic.

6. Describe the use of a standing committee to strengthen your supervisory program. Be sure to include the tasks and composition of the committee.

[1]See Chapter 4 and see David I. Cleland and William R. King, *Systems Analysis and Project Management* (New York: McGraw-Hill Book Company, 1968) Ch. 9.

E APPENDIX

How to Provide Instructional Leadership

Questions

1. What are the areas of instructional concern for the supervisor? In which areas is leadership most needed?
2. Whose responsibility is it to see that instructional leadership is provided in a school?
3. What recent changes and developments in the world have made leadership in curriculum construction and implementation more important?
4. What is the function of the local school superintendent in instructional leadership? Of the board of education? Of the specialist-consultant? The supervising principal? The teacher?
5. How do lay groups function in instructional leadership? How are leaders for lay groups procured?
6. How are community-school relations improved when mutual leadership is exercised between school and community?
7. How do you cope with pressure or interest groups that have intentions that would not be for the general good?

Suggested Activities

1. List representatives from professional and lay groups that you feel should comprise an instructional leadership council and discuss the roles of the professional and lay leaders of this council.
2. List some of the advantages for having cooperative leadership shared by the principal or supervisor and the certificated staff.
3. Discuss problems that may arise between the principal and teachers in relation to curriculum construction, revision, implementation, and evaluation.
4. Discuss the reactions of teachers when instructional leadership is initiated entirely by administration.
5. Outline methods of obtaining faculty participation in instructional improvement.
6. Devise a model for evaluating the effectiveness of instructional leadership.

7. List the areas of the curriculum which you feel are in need of revision as a result of technological, economic, social, and political trends.

The Supervisor and Professional Responsibilities

Questions

1. What do you consider as the main reason for education's not being considered as the leading profession in our country? Why is it so considered in some other nations?
2. How can a professional approach by supervisors and teachers develop morale?
3. Why should all educators be interested in a code of professional conduct and ethics?
4. What can teachers and supervisors do about colleagues whom they believe to be engaging in unethical or unprofessional conduct? (Recall, the term *unprofessional* has certain legal implications in some states; i.e., it may be a cause for dismissal and or credential revocation.)

Suggested Activities

1. Report on the effect professional organizations have had upon professional status and morale.
2. Determine what influence the medical and legal professions have had upon standards which determine who shall practice in those professions and indicate to what extent educators should follow their examples.
3. Investigate what has been done by the leading national organizations in education concerning professional standards and evaluate the influence of the organizations in upgrading professional relationships among educators.
4. Prepare an article suitable for publication concerning steps which should be followed by the supervising principal who hopes to make education a profession.
5. Prepare an oath for the supervising principal and for the teacher embodying ideals similar to those in the Hippocratic oath.

6. Prepare a bibliography of articles appearing in professional journals applicable to the subject of professional responsibilities. Delimit your study to articles published during the past twelve months.

7. Indicate reasons for exhibiting or not exhibiting the educator's framed credentials on the wall of the room within which he works.

8. List what you consider to be the ten most vital professional responsibilities of the educator. Indicate how the management of physical facilities could be related to the professional responsibilities of the educator.

9. Prepare a debate in which you and other members of the class argue the point of whether increased membership in a teacher's union could enhance education's status as a profession.

10. List the fringe benefits which you believe the educator should receive. Support your presentation with reference to practices and trends in industry, public administration, and education.

11. Prepare a skit in which you as the supervising principal speak out concerning procedure or policy which you believe requires immediate remediation. This policy, in the past, has had the wholehearted support of the superintendent and of the governing board.

How to Supervise the In-Service Education Program

Questions

1. What is the principal's role in organizing an in-service program?

2. What means can be found for identifying the great variety of needs and interests of teachers for setting up in-service programs?

3. What differences are there between the types of in-service programs found in school systems of 900 ADA and those in systems of 10,000 ADA or more?

4. What is the relationship between the principal and the curriculum coordinator in the in-service program? The consultants and the teachers?

5. What kind of in-service program should principals encourage beginning teachers to take? Highly experienced teachers?

6. What resources are available, either within or outside the school and/or school system to aid in the in-service program?

7. As a supervisor, what results of the in-service training program would you use to justify the appropriation of more funds?
8. What should be done at the local school system level and what should be the relationship of this program to the district or county program?

Suggested Activities

1. Select, describe, and make recommendations for the solution of a specific instructional problem in your school which lends itself to an on-going, in-service program.
2. Report to the class for analysis the in-service training practices in districts of 900 ADA and 10,000 ADA or more. Make recommendations outlining current trends.
3. Interview twenty-five or more teachers and report on the following: what they like and dislike most about in-service education; how in-service education practices, procedures, and interaction can be improved.
4. List the steps necessary for the reorganization of in-service training programs to meet teacher and administrator needs.
5. Discuss in-service programs and their implications for (a) the new teacher, (b) the transfer teacher, (c) the ineffective teacher, and (d) the "old-fashioned" teacher.
6. List several methods and develop criteria that could be used effectively to evaluate an in-service training program.

How to Improve Supervisory Visits and Follow-Up Conferences

Questions

1. What are some important objections to visiting the classroom only upon the teacher's invitation?
2. What techniques might be effectively employed for recording classroom activities? Could video recordings be helpful? How?
3. How can the supervisor insure that his presence is not threatening to the teacher or distracting to the students?

4. How does the role of the *line* supervisor differ from that of the *staff* supervisor in conducting supervisory visits and follow-up conferences?
5. How would the personality of the teacher determine the method of suggesting means to overcome weaknesses?
6. How can differences of opinion between the teacher and supervisor concerning content and teaching techniques be resolved?

Suggested Activities

1. List the most promising techniques for improving supervisory visits and conferences.
2. A principal has called regarding an antagonistic teacher who resents supervisors and supervision. Describe procedures for handling the situation.
3. Contrast supervisory visits in a small district with those in a large city school system.
4. Outline a plan for supervisory visits and follow-up conferences in a nineteen-teacher school.
5. Suggest ways in which a supervisor could help a group of teachers who have expressed awareness of a mutual problem.
6. Suggest techniques which a supervisor can use to get invitations from teachers for supervisory visits and conferences.
7. Outline a plan of public relations with teachers that may assist in obtaining better communications during supervisory visits and follow-up conferences.
8. Make a list of traits that a supervisor should possess if he is to work well with teachers.
9. List the points which should be considered in the write-up of the follow-up conference.

How to Improve Faculty, Committee, and Grade Level and Subject Area Meetings

Questions

1. What are the characteristics of a good faculty meeting?
2. How can faculty morale be improved or impaired through staff meetings?

3. What is meant by "restraint and acceptance" on the part of the supervisor during a staff meeting?
4. How would you solve the problem of: the talkative teacher, the poorly prepared teacher, the negative teacher?
5. As a supervisor you are challenged by a staff member during a meeting. How would you handle the situation?
6. What influence do teachers' vested interests, that is, their special interest in their subject or in a particular grade, have on group procedures in solving a particular problem?
7. As the supervisor you are supposed to be the leader, or chairman, of the group. How can you surrender this role to another member of the group? When, and how often, should you do this? Why?
8. Should the problem of the time for the lunch hour be settled by group discussion? The problem of the grouping of children for instruction? The problem of a new kind of report card?

Suggested Activities

1. Criticize a subject area or grade-level meeting which you have observed. Suggest how it could have been improved.
2. After observing a series of primary reading lessons, study your notes and plan for a series of meetings designed to help the teachers. Plan in detail the first of these meetings.
3. Outline the procedures to be followed in a series of six meetings planned to help the junior high school social studies teachers in improving their teaching of history, or some other social study. Explain the reasons for: (a) your choice of topics for each meeting, and (b) your proposed procedure for conducting each meeting.
4. After studying new methods for teaching mathematics, plan a series of school level meetings to be carried on throughout the year.
5. Plan a meeting with the teachers of Grade 6 to organize a program of instruction in global geography. Outline the steps to be taken.
6. Plan a social committee meeting to implement the social program for the year. Plan for such diverse functions as the orientation of new teachers and a Christmas party.

E

How to Help Teachers Understand and Guide Children

Questions

1. How can supervisors employ data processing to aid teachers in obtaining a better understanding of children?
2. How can supervisors encourage teachers to develop democratic group situations which encourages respect for the individual?
3. How may adequate cumulative records be kept to provide a continuous longitudinal record of the child's growth and development?
4. How may teachers be stimulated to participate in faculty meetings to further their understanding of children? What topics should be covered?
5. What assistance can supervisors give to teachers for classification and promotion of students?
6. How can the information from home, school, and community sources be coordinated by the supervisor to promote teacher understanding of student needs and problems?
7. What types of problems need psychological examinations and considerations? How may the supervisor establish satisfactory methods of referral?

Suggested Activities

1. Make a student survey of your school. Put the data on data cards and run correlations on attendance and dropouts, I.Q., and physical development, or reading speed and class marks.
2. Organize a Case Conference Committee within a school to study children.
3. Evaluate various cumulative record cards and make a list of acceptable comments that may be used.
4. Make a plan for a case study listing all types of data to be included and personnel involved.
5. Keep an anecdotal record of a student over a specific period of time.
6. Outline ways of helping teachers understand and meet individual needs in a democratic manner.
7. Make and interpret a sociogram of a class.

8. Plan a simulated parent conference to discuss a student's particular problem.
9. Make and interpret a personal interest sheet to gain further information about a child.

How to Help Teachers Improve and Adapt the Curriculum

1. What advantages or disadvantages are there in assigning teacher committees to revise the course of study?
2. How often should the curriculum be adapted or revised? By whom? How?
3. How can the range of workers on curriculum development be broadened to include everyone involved and to use appropriately the contributions of each?
4. What is the process wherein persons disinterested in schools become sufficiently concerned with the schools to learn about their objectives and programs and to do something to help improve them?
5. What contributions in curriculum committees should a teacher volunteer in addition to his regular teaching load?
6. How can the school determine that it is fulfilling the needs and desires of the local community?
7. What is the supervisor's role in curriculum development?

Suggested Activities

1. Acting in the capacity of supervisor, set up criteria for determining when curriculum revisions should occur.
2. Use a fact finding survey for ascertaining whether your school or district needs a revision of its curriculum objectives, activities, and materials. Use data processing techniques where possible.
3. Make a list of desirable ways to create direct communication with all concerned in curriculum planning.
4. Tell how curriculum revision can be incorporated into in-service training.

5. Make a collection of instructional guides that may be used by teachers in improving and adapting the curriculum of your school.
6. Outline the role of the specialist-consultant in curriculum revision.
7. Draw up a budget for curriculum improvement in your district.
8. Name the ways in which a rapidly changing world affects the course of study.

How to Help Teachers Improve Methods of Classroom Instruction

Questions

1. What knowledge of instructional procedures is essential to the success of the general supervisor in improvement of such procedures?
2. Who is involved in the supervisory function of aiding the teacher in improving his classroom methods?
3. How much time should the supervisor give to the "weaker-methods" teacher as compared to that of the resourceful teacher?
4. What techniques might be followed in converting traditional teachers to the use of modern methods?
5. What are some of the major obstacles to improvement of classroom methods of instruction?
6. Should the supervisor be responsible for preparing a formal rating of the teacher's method of instruction?
7. What methods would you recommend for the teaching of mathematics? science? languages?

Suggested Activities

1. Develop a general improvement program for the supervision of instructional methods in a school that has no such program.
2. List several techniques that you would employ to aid an inexperienced teacher in the methods he might use to organize his class at the beginning of the school year.
3. As a principal, draw up a plan that you would follow to aid a weak teacher in improving his methods of classroom instruction.

4. Outline a program for promoting experimentation in classroom methods by teachers.
5. Plan a staff meeting in which several teachers will discuss different methods of presenting the same lesson.
6. List several ways in which you, as a supervisor, would use superior teachers to help inexperienced and weak teachers improve their methods of classroom instruction.
7. Suggest several specific situations in which a supervisor can help teachers improve methodology without threatening teacher security.

How to Provide Improved Materials of Instructional Technology

Questions

1. How may the supervisor develop criteria and methods for procuring better materials of instruction?
2. To what extent can school and community facilities be integrated to bring about better instructional materials?
3. How can teachers be encouraged to prepare and share instructional materials?
4. How can the supervisor provide teachers with information on recent developments in instructional technology?
5. How can the supervisor insure that teachers are adequately trained in the use of special materials and equipment?
6. What procedures of check-out and accounting will insure the most efficient distribution of materials at the building level and from the educational materials laboratory?
7. Is the trend toward school provision of *all* materials used by students desirable?

Suggested Activities

1. Outline a plan of distribution for audio-visual materials and equipment for a twenty-teacher school.

2. Visit a nearby school district and investigate the program of procurement, storage, upkeep, distribution, use, and evaluation of instructional
materials.
3. Prepare an annotated list of commercial companies which have proved to
be reliable in the development of instructional supplies.
4. Examine several school budgets to find the amount per student spent on
materials of instruction.
5. List some techniques for the evaluation of teacher use of instructional
materials.
6. Discuss the feasibility of trying a teaching-machine pilot program in one
grade-level subject area.
7. Outline a plan for taking inventory of basic and supplementary texts,
for storing them during the summer months, and for their distribution
at the beginning of the school year.

How to Assist Classified Employees

Questions

1. What are the primary and secondary duties of the clerk and the
secretary?
2. How should office duties be allocated to the secretary and the clerk?
3. What are ways for making more effective use of the principal's office
time?
4. What time-saving equipment would you recommend for the school
offices?
5. What procedures should be adopted to handle petty cash funds for the
school?
6. What office procedures should be standardized?
7. To what extent should the clerk do typing and duplicating for the
teachers? Or, what clerical services provision should be made for the
teachers?
8. What provision should be made when the clerk goes to lunch or is away
from the office for any extended length of time?
9. What should a good office schedule include?

10. What are the ideal qualities and characteristics of the school secretary? How could you set up an in-service education procedure for your secretary?

11. What are the values and limitations of classified employee participation in supervision?

12. What should be the principal's role in providing for classified staff growth in job skills? The specialist-consultant's role? The supervisor's role?

13. What should be the principal's attitude toward employees who neglect needed growth?

14. How should a principal evaluate the effectiveness of a cafeteria worker? Of a clerk? Of a custodian? Of a bus driver?

15. What is the difference between the administration and supervision of classified employees?

16. How can the supervising principal create initiative and resourcefulness among classified employees?

17. How might the recruitment, selection, and assignment of classified employees be improved?

18. What is the difference between the authoritarian and inspirational concept of classified employee supervision.

Selected Activities

1. Prepare an assignment specification for the secretary of a school.

2. Prepare an assignment specification for the custodian of a school.

3. Prepare a list of topics that you believe should be included in orientation meetings for classified personnel. Be sure to indicate special topics that would be included in meetings for custodians, clerks, transportation employees, and cafeteria employees.

4. Indicate what you believe to be the responsibilities of the principal and the director of buildings and grounds in supervising the work of a custodian.

5. Prepare a list of in-service training activities that should be used in assisting the school secretary to improve her performance.

6. Prepare a sample table of contents for a handbook for school custodians.

7. Prepare a sample table of contents for a handbook for school bus drivers.

8. Prepare a list of equipment that you believe should be available to the school secretary and to the school custodian in order to facilitate job performance.

9. Prepare an annotated bibliography of the major works appearing in professional journals for the past year concerning the supervision of classified personnel.

10. Prepare a skit to be presented in class in which a principal introduces a new custodian to the school and its faculty.

How to Improve Auxiliary Services

Questions

Food
Services

1. What are some of the advantages gained when the school operates its own cafeteria?

2. What are some of the factors to be considered in planning the cafeteria facilities?

3. How can the cafeteria be related to the school's instructional program?

Health
Services

4. What are the functions and responsibilities of a school health program?

5. What is the role of the classroom teacher in the total school health program?

Special
Education

6. According to law, who are exceptional children?

7. What information is necessary before exceptional children can be accurately classified?

8. In general, should the severe physically handicapped student be placed in regular or special schools?

Library

9. What are some characteristics of good school library service?

Transportation

10. What are some of the advantages and disadvantages of providing student transportation through private contract?

Recreation

11. What agency should administer the community recreation program?
12. How should the community recreation program be financed?

Suggested Activities

1. List the topics which you would cover as the supervisor of student transportation in an in-service class for the employees of your section.
2. Indicate the items you would include in an in-service education class for health services personnel. Note how various members of the professional staff may participate.
3. Evaluate and compare three local school libraries. What items would you include in a listing of criteria for evaluating the school library? Select any level of education you desire.
4. Prepare a series of slides showing what you believe to be samples of outstanding organization in the school library.
5. Note how you would organize an in-service education program for food services personnel.
6. Evaluate the program for food services in your local school system. Indicate especially the adequacy of the money handling system employed.
7. Prepare an annotated bibliography of periodical references in the past two years concerned with auxiliary services. Do not include educational guidance or psychology.
8. Prepare a skit showing how members of the auxiliary services staffs play a part in the total instructional program of the school system.

How to Provide a Better Physical Environment for Teaching

Questions

1. What standards comprise an ideal number of lavatory units per 100 students? Number of square feet of classroom space per student? Amount of illumination in the classroom?
2. What is meant by mobility and flexibility of classroom equipment? Give examples.

3. What are some of the techniques necessary for studying community desires and needs in the way of a physical plant?
4. Why should the buildings and classrooms have aesthetic appeal?
5. What are the advantages and disadvantages of the bungalow type of construction over the multiroom type? What are permanent portables?
6. What factors dictate or justify new construction over rehabilitation of older facilities?
7. What is your evaluation of: windowless classrooms, air conditioning, underground construction, multiple story, and movable walls?

Suggested Activities

1. Give a report setting forth principles and precautions that may secure adequate protection from fire, earthquake, and other hazards to personal safety.
2. Prepare a list of suggestions that a principal may draw up for the consideration of his faculty in his effort to establish fine working relations between themselves and the custodial staff.
3. Review research to find the best physical facilities for the enrichment of learning at each grade level.
4. Draw up a list of instructional advantages and disadvantages that may be encountered in operating the cafeteria-auditorium combination room.
5. Give complete specifications for an average room at the sixth-grade level. Include the size and type of furniture, placement of seats, amount of closet and storage space.
6. List local and state standards for the selection of a school site.
7. List trends in the construction of physical facilities for schools.

How to Obtain Support for the Supervisory Program

Questions

1. What are the most important areas in your curriculum that are causing friction in the community? What, if anything, should be done about them?
2. What are the key activities in your school which have positive public relations value? How much time is being spent by personnel in your school on these functions?

3. What in-service functions have been planned in your school to acquaint school personnel with modern public relations techniques?
4. What are the most important attitudes, values, traditions, and customs in your school community? How do they manifest themselves?
5. Who are the official and unofficial opinion leaders in your community? In what ways do they exert their influence?
6. What is the attitude of your school personnel toward the school system? How are these attitudes projected to the community?
7. What are some of the common misunderstandings about supervisory programs? On the part of the teacher? Parents? Students?
8. Are public relations as important in education as they are in business or industrial enterprises, labor organizations, professional associations, and governmental agencies?

Suggested Activities

1. Prepare summaries of daily classroom activities that the child can take home to his parents.
2. Prepare a school letter, meaningful to parents, on an interesting new unit of study, materials, or techniques being developed in your classroom.
3. Write a newspaper release for the coverage of an unusual feature of your school program, such as dropout level, programmed learning, computer supported instruction, team teaching, or flexible scheduling.
4. Prepare a program to initiate or improve open house activities in your school system.
5. Review the report card system in your school from a public relations point of view and recommend ways this device may be used more effectively to communicate with parents.
6. Study the methods by which the telephone is answered in your school and recommend ways to improve telephone techniques.
7. Review the parents' association program for the year and recommend ways by which activities can be improved to gain maximum public relations value.
8. Study the extra class activities of your school and recommend ways to involve parents in problem-solving activities which will have optimum community relations value.

9. Prepare a plan for handling pressure groups that advocate cutting all appropriations for supervision from the budget.

How to Evaluate the Supervisory Program

Questions

1. How can the principal get group participation in evaluating supervision?
2. What statement of facts could be given to the governing board to get the board's support in a proposed evaluation program?
3. What outside evaluation help do you feel the school board should be willing to consider?
4. How much of a supervisor's annual allotment of time should be used in evaluating the supervisory program?
5. What steps would you take to assure the superintendent that you, as principal of the school, had given the board "the most supervision for its money"?
6. What are late trends in instruction and how would you evaluate their worth?

Suggested Activities

1. Interview a principal of a school to discuss the methods used in evaluating the supervisory program.
2. You are the assistant superintendent of instruction of a large school system. Prepare a list of criteria you would use in evaluating the work of specialist-consultants.
3. Prepare a plan for evaluating supervision in a school or school system of your choice.
4. The board asks for a specific evaluation of mathematics supervision. Prepare a report for the superintendent showing how you would go about evaluating mathematics supervision in your school that has an enrollment of 900.
5. Devise a check sheet that you could use to evaluate supervisory services in a junior high school.

6. Write an article suitable for publication in a professional periodical concerning the importance, purposes, and techniques of evaluation for supervisory programs at the junior high school level.
7. Evaluate your supervisory organization for the handling of innovations in curriculum, buildings, in-service education, and public relations.

INDEX